Practicing What We Know

Practicing What We Know

Informed Reading Instruction

Edited by
Constance Weaver
Western Michigan University

National Council of Teachers of English
1111 W. Kenyon Road, Urbana, Illinois 61801-1096

Staff Editor: Michael Greer

Production: City Desktop Productions, Inc.

Interior Design: Tom Kovacs for TGK Design

Cover Design: Carlton Bruett

NCTE Stock Number: 36753-3050

It is the policy of NCTE in its journals and other publications to provide a forum
for the open discussion of ideas concerning the content and the teaching of English and the language arts. Publicity accorded to any particular point of view
does not imply endorsement by the Executive Committee, the Board of Direc-
tors, or the membership at large, except in announcements of policy, where such
endorsement is clearly specified.

Library of Congress Cataloging-in-Publication Data

Practicing what we know : informed reading instruction / edited by Constance Weaver.
    p. cm.
   Collection of articles, some previously published.
   Includes bibliographical references and index.
   ISBN 0-8141-3675-3
   1. Reading (Elementary) 2. Reading—Phonetic method. 3. Miscue analysis. 4. Reading (Elementary)—Language experience approach. 5. Literature—Study and Teaching (Elementary) I. Weaver, Constance. II. National
Council of Teachers of English.
  LB1573.P67   1998
  372.41—dc21   98-10262
                                         CIP

Contents

Introduction: Literacy Education as a Political Act

Diane Stephens
University of Hawaii

In *Zen and the Art of Motorcycle Maintenance* (1974), the central character, Phaedrus, describes a motorcycle by dividing it into "component assemblies" (e.g., a power assembly and a running assembly) and into "functions." He divides each of these further and explains each part. He then comments on his description, pointing out aspects of it that are not, at first, obvious. He notes, for example, that "if you were to go to a motorcycle-parts department and ask them for a feedback assembly" (or any of these parts):

> they wouldn't know what . . . you were talking about. They don't split it up that way. No two manufacturers ever split it up quite the same way and every mechanic is familiar with the problem of the part you can't buy because the manufacturer considers it a part of something else (79).

What Phaedrus wants the reader to understand is that different people divide the world up differently. Different people have different ways of viewing the motorcycle, and, by extension, the world. In order to make sense of these multiple realities, Phaedrus believes that we need to take a step back from descriptions and perceptions to be able to see that what he calls a "knife" that is used to create categories and ways of seeing the world. He explains that this knife is

> an intellectual scalpel so swift and sharp you sometimes don't see it moving. You get the illusion that all these parts are just there and are being named as they exist. But they can be named quite differently and organized quite differently depending on how the knife moves. . . . It is important to see this knife for what it is and not to be fooled into thinking that motorcycles or anything else are the way they are just because the knife happened to cut it that way. It is important to concentrate on the knife itself . . . (79).

He also cautions us to remember that categories are inherent in any description and those descriptions, those categories, exist because someone, wielding a metaphorical knife, created them. He advises us not only to step back far enough to see the knife but also to see the knife holder.

I don't know enough about the author, Robert Pirsig, to explain why he wrote *Zen and the Art of Motorcycle Maintenance*. I suspect his motivation was personal and philosophical. I do know that my motivation, in choosing to tell this part of his story here, is political. I am worried about how decisions are being made in reading education, and by and for whom they are being made.

Since the early 1980s, various stakeholders have been debating what "should" be happening in classrooms in the name of reading instruction. Using Phaedrus' metaphor of the motorcycle parts, it is as if Person A walks into a store and tries to buy a part, as Phaedrus named it. The store owner, Person B, says he does not have that part. Person A argues that he should have. B says he should not. From B's point of view, the stock is organized in the best possible way. From A's point of view, A's way of organizing and categorizing is better. In reading research, the argument is similar. Researcher A asks for standardized test results from Researcher B as "proof" of his or her findings and Researcher B says "I don't have any and I don't believe I need them and besides I wasn't trying to prove but to understand" and Researcher A says, "Well, you should have them and you do need them and it is your job to prove" and Person B says, "No, I shouldn't and I don't and it isn't." So then A says and B says . . .

Just as Pirsig/Phaedrus wants us to step back from his description of the motorcycle, I believe that teachers need to step back from these debates. When we do so, we can see that each debater is a knife holder and each has divided up reading and reading instruction in different ways. This happens because each debater holds different beliefs about what reading is, how it can be understood, and how reading instruction can or should be improved. The debaters also divide up research and knowledge in different ways. They hold different beliefs about what kinds of questions are worth asking, what kind of data address those questions, and how to make sense of the data. When we are able to see the knives and the knife holders, we are able to juxtapose our beliefs with theirs and, in so doing, critically reflect on our own beliefs. We wield a knife and create a world that makes sense to us and to the children for whom we are responsible.

In the foreword to the companion volume, *Reconsidering a Balanced Approach to Reading*, I argued that teachers need to form their own beliefs and the argument I gave there and above makes it sound as if I think they should do so because I simply think it is a "good idea."

But it is more than a good idea. It is a political necessity. The stakes in the debate have escalated. The debate used to focus on what was known about reading instruction and what were the implications of that knowledge for classroom practice. In the last few years, however, the focus has shifted. The debate still includes conversation about what we know and what teachers should do, but it has broadened to include a new, and to my mind, dangerous, third topic: Who or what should decide and ensure that teachers do what they "should" be doing?

What is interesting about this question is that when you step back from it, it becomes clear that the only people who ask this question are those who believe that they know what teachers "should" be doing (that is, they believe there is one right answer—theirs); that something or someone needs to tell teachers what to do; and that someone or something needs to be in place to ensure that teachers will do as they are told. These question-askers have "fixated belief" about what teachers "should" be doing by reviewing research, and, sometimes, conducting their own. In their review of the literature, however, like most of us, they disregard that which they do not consider to be valid. Going back to the store analogy, it is as if Researcher A decided that Researcher B's work was not informative because it did not contain the parts that Researcher A wanted. In the example above, the work did not have standardized test scores. So Researcher A does not "count" the research of B when drawing conclusions about the findings from the literature review. Researcher B, again with the best of intentions, does the same thing: She or he does not include the findings from studies that she or he does not consider informative.

What makes this confusing is that each of these researchers then holds a press conference (or writes an article or book) and makes statements about what "the research" shows. Because each researcher has discarded some studies and included others, their statements conflict. What makes this scenario frightening is that some of the people listening to these announcements (or reading the texts) believe that the researcher they are hearing/reading is right and that the other researcher is wrong. Convinced of the right path to follow and believing that, without a mandate, teachers will not follow the right path, some of the question-askers join forces with legislators and businesspersons and attempt, and sometimes succeed, in getting their "right" answer made into a law to which all teachers are held accountable. In California, for example, it is not legal to use Goals 2000 funds for programs that encourage students to use context to figure out words instead of decoding words fluently. Meanwhile, the State Board of Education removed from the recommended texts list the materials published by the Wright Group and Rigby, both of whom publish extensive collections of predictable books for young readers.

Other people, similarly convinced that they know what is right for teachers, follow different paths. Some, for example, believe that literacy instruction could be improved if university professors came together and detailed what they thought good reading instruction should look like in the elementary classroom. Sometimes they do this by helping to construct national reading tests. David Pearson (1996), for example, seems to envision beliefs about reading education along a numbered continuum with everyone from 2 to 9 joined in a 15-year-long debate. During that time period, the radical left (the 1s) have been rallying for their cause and forming teacher support groups while the radical right (the 10s) have been collaborating with non-educators (businesspersons and legislators) to build a structure for reading education that can be legislatively mandated and that excludes everyone else on the continuum. Pearson believes that over these 15 or so years, the "center" has shifted, positively, to the left, but believes, because of the work done by the far right group, that the shift is about to swing in the other direction. He therefore suggests that educators like himself get together to detail a "balanced approach," a common ground "in the middle." In a recent article (1996), he describes what a "balanced" reading program should look like and calls for other educators to join him in the "Radical Middle."

The people who *are not* asking the question, Who or what should decide and ensure that teachers do what they "should" be doing?, are worried about the enormous pressure being put on teachers by those who *are* asking the question. They worry about the laws that are being passed, about the tests that are being written, and about the "middle ground" that is being proposed for teachers by others. Connie Weaver, like me, is one of those worriers. She believes that legislation and national examinations and prescribed "balanced" approaches serve to silence the voices and diminish the power of teachers. Her response is to make public a knowledge base so that teachers and other stakeholders can make informed decisions about their practices. *Practicing What We Know* and *Reconsidering a Balanced Approach to Reading* represent her attempt to do just that. In the first volume, she gathered together articles she felt would inform our understanding of the reading process, learning to read, and the teaching of reading and she particularly included those voices that currently are not being heard by legislators and others who think they should tell teachers how to teach reading. In this volume, she tries to show the readers what practice looks like when it is grounded in that understanding. In order to encourage teachers to broaden their conversations about literacy development and education, she has included some articles that differ somewhat from her own perspective.

David and Connie, however, like the rest of us, cannot stand outside their own reality. Despite his good intentions, David's solution, his "balanced approach," is not so much a response to the debate as a restatement of the position he has consistently held within it. The same can be said of these two volumes. Especially in her own articles, Connie offers a solution but it is not basically a new solution. Her solution, like David's, is a restatement and refinement of the position that she consistently has held. In their writing, David and Connie have made it clear how they have solved the tensions they have faced and how they believe others should or might solve theirs.

As teachers, then, we need to step back and see David and Connie and all other participants as knife holders who are constructing worlds. We need to see their texts as documents which describe the world they have constructed. Doing so gives us the freedom to act independently and prevents us from being held hostage by the debate and by the texts we read. If we cannot do so, if we cannot see knives and knife holders and see instead only "experts" with right answers, we become trapped in the illusion that ultimately there is one truth, one reality, one solution. It becomes too easy for others to prescribe for us what they want us to do in the world they are trying to construct around us.

If, on the other hand, we want teachers (and not legislators or businesspersons or presidents or testing companies or college professors) to be in charge of teaching, we can follow neither Connie nor David nor any of the others who urge us down a particular path. Nor can we sit quietly on the sidelines waiting for the debate to somehow be resolved. What we must do instead is leave the sidelines, accept that there are multiple realities, seize the knife, and construct our own reality. As in the first volume, it is my hope, and Connie's, that this text will help you do so.

Postscript: I have suggested that educators who read these volumes (or any other information about education), accept that there are multiple realities and try to see the knife and the knife holder. To that end, I'm adding this postscript so that I might more easily be seen. I've tried, throughout this introduction, to keep myself visible in the text. I used the phrase "I think" or "I believe" whenever possible even though I knew the editor might hate those phrases and want to delete all instances. I did so because I wanted to keep myself as visible as possible as a knife wielder. I want you to be able to see that, on David's continuum (the one I assumed he had), I am on the far left. I am not interested in joining the debate. I don't believe that the debate is resolvable because I believe that individuals cannot step outside their own realities. I have therefore done what I can to separate myself from it. I believe that teachers should do likewise. I believe that instead of either becoming participants or remaining on the sidelines, teachers should make their own informed decisions and stand firm enough in their knowledge base to weather the storm of the debate. I believe all of us as teachers should stand firm enough so that no one can make us fit into pre-established structures. I believe in strength in numbers and I believe we will hit a critical mass. At that point, teachers will simply have become too strong and it will be fruitless for legislators and senators and presidents and test makers to try to tell us what to do. Teaching will have become a profession and it will be the teachers themselves that have made it so. Along the way, like Connie and David, I seize opportunities to get my voice heard in the conversation and to help make room for the voices of others. Because this is my world view, my reality, I ended this introduction, and the earlier one, suggesting that others do the same. It is the only reality I know. From my perspective, it is the only chance we have.

Works cited

Pearson, P.D. (1996). Reclaiming the center. In M. Graves, P. van der Broek, & B. Taylor (Eds.), *The first R.* New York: Teachers College Press.
Pirsig, R. (1974). *Zen and the art of motorcycle maintenance.* New York: Morrow.

I Teaching Phonics and Word Skills

Teaching Phonics and
Word Skills

Educators, parents, and the public agree that children need to develop letter/sound knowledge to recognize words and to identify unknown print words. But how do they acquire such knowledge, and to what extent must this knowledge be conscious? How much phonics (including phonemic awareness) should be taught to *all* children? How much to only those who need *and* continue to benefit from more help? Is there an optimal time to teach phonics? What aspects of phonics should be taught? And how? Some research suggests one answer, while other bodies of research suggest other answers.

During the past decade or more, when some teachers began teaching less phonics, they did so because they saw that current practices in the teaching of phonics were producing some undesirable results, at least with some children:

- Many children were completing worksheets and drill exercises but the material "learned" wasn't necessarily very usable in actual reading. (In desperation, teachers would sometimes admit that the "rules" didn't work very well, or weren't very easy to apply, and would tell children "Just sound it out the best you can.") Children who had particular difficulty with phonics were sometimes given phonics-related instruction that was even more unusable than what most of the children received.

- Some children weren't tackling unknown print words in *chunks* of letters and their related sounds, as more successful readers do, while *also* trying to make sense of the text.

- Some children were tackling unknown print words by saying something that included some of the letters of the target word, but they would settle for non-words or words that weren't sensible in context and go blithely on.

- Children who did not succeed very well at isolated phonics work were typically given more phonics work—and less of the actual reading and writing that was enabling other children to become better readers and writers.

- Some children were given more and more phonics work, long after it should have been clear that they weren't benefitting.

Currently the alleged problem is that some children aren't learning to sound out words accurately. However, it is debatable whether or not this is more true than a few years ago. When we address this concern instructionally, we need to remember that sounding out words is often easier if we are also drawing upon context and everything we know, that it is difficult even for proficient adult readers to sound out a word "correctly" if the word isn't in their oral vocabulary, and that even pronouncing a word "right" isn't very helpful if we don't understand how it contributes to the meaning of the text.

Furthermore, we must be careful not to create, to an even greater extent, the problems that some teachers have been trying to alleviate. Most critical, perhaps, is this: the teaching of phonics, including phonemic awareness, must not be treated as a prerequisite to the reading and rereading of actual texts. We simply must not allow ourselves to assess children's evolving phonics skills, find some children wanting, and shunt them off to more and more skills work and less real reading and writing, as we have done in the past. The development of phonemic awareness and more broadly of phonics knowledge must not become a barrier that excludes some children from the world of books.

The articles in this section on teaching phonics and word skills were chosen to "talk" to teach other. That is, each one is somewhat different in the approach recommended. Nevertheless, most of the articles reflect the following widely accepted principles. They mostly reflect the view that effective teaching of phonics will

1. immerse children in significant reading every day, from which children can induce common letter/sound patterns (see also Visovatti, Chapter 10, and Chomsky-Higgins, Chapter 9).

2. include various kinds of assisted reading, in which children have the opportunity to match spoken words with written words: for example, reading environmental print together, Shared Book Experiences, and reading books while listening to them on tape.

3. include many writing experiences every day that promote and strengthen letter/sound knowledge: for example, the teacher writing in front of or collaboratively with the class and getting their help in deciding what letters are needed to represent certain of the sounds; children themselves writing, using "invented" spelling as needed, and receiving help as needed in hearing and writing the sounds they hear in words.

4. require children to think, not passively complete worksheets or engage in drill.

5. involve interaction and collaboration, with discussion with teachers and among children.

6. focus on patterns, not rules.

7. derive partly from alphabet books, nursery rhymes, other poetry with alliteration and/or rhyme, and tongue twisters.

8. relate to and derives from the reading and writing that the children are doing.

Some of the issues that separate the articles are these:

- the extent to which instruction derives from and is embedded within the reading and writing of actual texts;
- the extent to which the instruction is systematic and/or intensive;
- the order in which teachers are encouraged to deal with onsets and rimes, compared with phonemic awareness and correspondences between individual sounds and letters;
- the extent to which writing is emphasized as a vehicle for learning letter/sound relationships;
- the extensiveness of individual lessons and/or the extensiveness of the follow-up;
- and the extent of the emphasis on using letter/sound knowledge *along with* meaning, to get words.

In short, most of the differences are not clear-cut, a matter of either/or; they exist along various continuua of less-to-more, with respect to the principles above.

In reading the following articles and in deciding how they might want to teach phonics or change the teaching of phonics in their own classrooms, teachers may find it useful to consider these various factors and the research relating to them.

Editor's note: I considered inviting Linda Ayres to write an article describing her phonological awareness training program for young children (see her Chapter 8 in *Reconsidering a Balanced Approach to Reading* [Weaver 1998]). However, the program is now commercially available as The Phonological Zoo (1998). [. . .] It consists of three phases: Phase One, nursery rhymes and folk tales; Phase Two, rhyming; and Phase Three, alliteration, phonemic segmentation, and sound/letter correspondences.

Resources

Ayres, L. J. (1998). *The phonological zoo*. Dubuque, IA: Kendall Hunt.

Cunningham, P. (1995). *Phonics they use: Words for reading and writing*. New York: HarperCollins.

Goodman, K. S. (1993). *Phonics phacts*. Richmond Hill, Ontario: Scholastic; Portsmouth, NH: Heinemann.

Mills, H., O'Keefe, T., & Stephens, D. (1992). *Looking closely: Exploring the role of phonics in one whole language classroom*. Urbana IL: NCTE.

Powell, D. & Hornsby, D. (1993). *Learning phonics and spelling in a whole language classroom*. New York: Scholastic.

Wagstaff, J. (No date.) *Phonics that work! New strategies for the reading/writing classroom*. New York: Scholastic.

Weaver, C. (Ed.) (1998). *Reconsidering a balanced approach to reading*. Urbana, IL: NCTE.

1 Phonics and the Politics of Reading Instruction

Leah Brumer
Oakland, California

This article by freelance reporter Brumer has a dual purpose: to discuss the politics of reading education in California, with particular emphasis on the alleged (but erroneous) phonics/whole language dichotomy, and to clarify how effective whole language teachers teach phonics naturally, within day-to-day literacy activities, in contrast to phonics-intensive teaching. In pursuit of the former, Brumer discusses the claim that whole language has led to lower scores on the NAEP and documents the accusations of Marion Joseph (whose political influence is seen in California's recent "ABC" bills). Such accusations are countered by whole language teacher Sharon Zinke, who helps other teachers and schools understand how to implement a whole language philosophy successfully. She agrees that primary education suffered after California's 1987 adoption of an English/Language Arts Framework that promoted the use of literature in the classroom. However, Zinke claims that this framework didn't fail: it never had a chance to work, because teachers were not supported in making the shift to literature-based education. "In 1992," Brumer reports, "a University of Southern California study found just one-quarter of teachers surveyed used literature to teach skills." On the other hand, Zinke explains, schools will claim to be whole language schools, but "they're not": the teachers have little idea what whole language means or how to teach reading in a whole language classroom. Zinke too is concerned that there have been many classrooms where the teachers "didn't have a clue what they were doing," and especially had no idea how to teach phonics in a whole language context. However, whole language itself is not to blame.

Brumer discusses some of the NAEP data in explaining that "according to some researchers, evidence used to condemn the framework is hardly conclusive." This point is supported also by Zinke and her colleagues, who note that other factors may help explain why California children scored so low on the 1994 NAEP: factors like huge class sizes, the growing numbers of students who don't speak English at home, the fact that the state's per-pupil spending is among the lowest in the country, and the fact that school library holdings rank next to last in the country.

Interwoven with this discussion are examples of how Zinke tutors children in reading, emphasizing the making of meaning and focusing on individual words in the quest for meaning. Her methods are contrasted with the phonics-intensive teaching of kindergarten teacher Linda Rayford, who uses a program that "introduces letters and sounds in careful sequence, moving through initial consonants, final consonants, long vowels and short vowels." Phonics is taught prior to reading, and in isolation. In contrast is another vignette, from the teaching of Zinke's colleague Paul Cordero, who demonstrates how they teach the use of phonics in the service of making meaning. Still another vignette describes the teaching of bilingual teacher Jennifer Martinez, who demonstrates how she teaches spelling and phonics while she and the children write collaboratively. Zinke indicates that there is "really good research" to support the way they teach phonics and reading.

Editor's note: In *Looking Closely: Exploring the Role of Phonics in One Whole Language Classroom*, authors Heidi Mills, Tim O'Keefe, and Diane Stephens document in considerable detail how phonics is woven across the curriculum and through the entire school day, in Tim O'Keefe's transition classroom (post-kindergarten, pre-first grade). Like Zinke and her colleagues' teaching procedures, Tim's teaching reveals how phonics can be taught naturally in the service of making meaning.

A shorter version of this chapter originally appeared as "Whatever Happened to Dick and Jane? Exploring the Politics of Reading," *East Bay Express, 18*(26), April 9, 1996.

Damon, a slight fourth-grader, slips into a makeshift classroom at Hayward's Lorin Eden elementary school. Four days a week, he comes to this converted principal's office for extra reading help. Six children are already there; some working with an aide, some reading to themselves or each other.

Veteran reading teacher Sharon Zinke invites Damon to choose a story from shelves crammed with books. He selects "The Three Little Pigs" and begins reading aloud. Zinke pulls her chair close, bending her head to catch his soft voice.

Haltingly but willingly, Damon reads, ". . . to watch little pig replied . . . "

Zinke lets him finish the sentence. When he pauses, she says, "I'm going to stop you. Did that sound right? Did that make sense?"

Damon shakes his head and returns to the sentence, looking at the word again. This time he gets it right. ". . . To which little pig replied . . ."

He continues, but stumbles over one of the most famous lines in children's literature. "The wolf hu—, hu—. . . ?"

"Read past that word," Zinke suggests. "When you're stuck on a word, I want you to read past it and see if you can pick it up from what the story means."

He moves ahead, reading the next words, ". . . and puffed . . . " On his own, Damon rereads the whole phrase. "The wolf huffed and puffed . . ." "That's it," Zinke says.

Soon, they finish the story. "What are you reading in class?" she asks. "Is it easy enough? I'm going to give you something a little too easy. You can borrow books any time. Do you read every night? Do you know what happens if you read every night?"

"You get a free pizza?" he asks, referring to the familiar incentive schools offer for reading.

Zinke's rich contralto laugh rings out. "Yes," she says. "But you know what else? It keeps getting easier. Every time you read a book, you get better at all the other ones." She squeezes his shoulder as he leaves. Damon must feel sorry for the pigs because he chooses a modern retelling of the story: "The Three Little Wolves and the Big Bad Pig."

The flow of children into Zinke's room ends only when the 3 p.m. dismissal bell rings. Navigating between desks, chairs and bookcases, she moves easily in the cramped room. In one efficient tour, she scoops up books scattered on tables, returns them to shelves, grabs a pile of messages and heads for the phone in a nearby office.

One caller, an administrator in the district's special education program, needs help. "She said she's heard I can teach a dog to read," Zinke says.

Zinke, fifty, laughs again, but doesn't demur. In twenty-nine years of teaching elementary school (nearly half as a reading specialist), she's launched thousands of young readers. As a consultant hired by school districts across the state, she's shared her techniques with hundreds of teachers. She's studying for a third credential so she can work in special education. Despite skill and experience, Zinke still expresses an awe of reading. "I love the way words are made up," she says. Feathery brown hair frames her round face. "I love the reading process."

The Great Debate

For all her talent, Zinke's methods are probably unfamiliar to anyone who learned to read before 1987. Like teachers in some 20 percent of U.S. elementary schools, Zinke has replaced contrived Dick and Jane stories, known as basal texts, with real books. And she doesn't rely only on phonics and sounding out. Instead, when Damon reached an unfamiliar word, she asked him to look for clues in the story's meaning— "Does that make sense?"—and use what he knows about sentence structure—"Does that sound right?"

Zinke follows an educational philosophy known as whole language. Classroom traditionalists, who rely on phonics lessons, begin reading instruction with initial and ending consonants. Zinke's lessons teach even early readers that language expresses meaning. She provides tools, too, including phonics. But for Zinke, the reader's first charge is to find meaning by interpreting, questioning and reflecting. Children's literature best conveys the power and purpose of language.

Phonics-first advocates accuse teachers like Zinke, and California schools, of abandoning phonics and leaving children illiterate. Whole language proponents agree that far too few California children are learning to read and write well enough to meet society's demands for increased literacy. But sounding out won't solve this problem, they say.

While the debate has been over-simplified, what's at stake remains stark: the literacy of California's 8.5 million students. Even presidential candidates have joined the fray. Citing whole language as a culprit, Bob Dole recently found American schools—and California's in particular—guilty of faddishness and failure.

How children learn to read is unusual fodder for presidential campaigns. Why is this conflict so fierce? Some observers suggest anxiety about America's future fuels the reading debate. Phonics, with its back-to-basics appeal, conjures comforting images of a past when we all read from the same textbook and shared the American Dream. Today, job security is an anachronism. Illness can bring destitution. New neighbors speak unfamiliar languages. For many, the center no longer holds.

Seeking reassurance, we look to classrooms where our common future is forged. But whole language favors open-ended, not multiple-choice, questions. It encourages students to interpret meaning, not recite facts. It even challenges time-honored roles: teachers as dispensers of knowledge, children as receivers.

Zinke didn't expect the argument to become so heated, nor did she expect to take part. She fears attacks on whole language will bring a backlash, sending reading instruction back to the fifties when Dick and Jane reigned in classrooms. That fear propelled her into the politics of reading.

Those politics took a sharp turn in 1987, when the California Department of Education set the stage for today's controversy. That year, the department published an English/Language Arts Framework that turned reading instruction on its head.

The document described students and teachers bored and frustrated by endless drills and reams of worksheets. It proposed replacing makework with a literature-based program to "touch students' lives and stimulate their minds and hearts." Basic skills—phonics, spelling and grammar—would continue to be taught, but in the context of reading and writing. Even before they could read fluently and spell correctly, the youngest students would study classics of children's literature; meeting in book groups to critique stories and write their own tales.

Issued every seven years, frameworks present the state's view of the best educational practices and guide school districts in developing curriculum. Though frameworks are not edicts, district officials consider them powerful planning tools. Publishers use them as blueprints to develop textbooks they hope will win approval for use in California classrooms, the country's largest market.

This year, facing controversy and national attention, the Department will revise the document that inspired Zinke and other whole language advocates.

The 1987 framework is no dry government report. Rather, it issues a rousing summons to awaken students "to the magic of language if they are to learn." It reads like the catalog for a Great Books course. "We were famous all over the world for our framework," Zinke says. "Everybody was just in awe of it."

But the Great Debate moved into the headlines last spring, when results from the 1994 National Assessment of Education Progress (NAEP) showed 56 percent of California fourth graders reading at below basic comprehension levels. California students tied with Louisiana's, ranking above only Guam's among 39 participating states.

The Back-to-basics Backlash

News reports trumpeted students' low standing, wasting no time finding a solution. "It's back to basics for California schools," editorials proclaimed. Prominent critics—including the framework's architect, former Superintendent of Public Instruction Bill Honig—said the framework failed. De-emphasizing phonics, Honig has said, was "disastrous for huge numbers of kids."

Phonics-first advocates say they endorse literature in classrooms. But first things first. "Reading is an unnatural act," says Marion Joseph, who served as chief of staff to former State Superintendent Wilson Riles. Soon after the NAEP scores were released, current state schools chief Delaine Eastin appointed Joseph to a statewide reading task force charged with examining reading instruction and developing recommendations.

Joseph became a framework critic nearly ten years ago. Her then-first-grade grandson's school had just adopted the 1987 framework, and he had difficulty reading. "You can't read words if you can't decode them, take them apart," she says, adding that whole language is more a political cult than an educational philosophy.

Phonics instruction, on the other hand, seems straightforward. After all, most of us were taught to sound out words. Phonics-first supporters believe that before children can learn to read, they must crack the alphabetic code. Readers' eyes don't skim over texts, they say. They take in every letter of every word. Therefore, the first step in reading is decoding, a visual processing of letters. Readers can concentrate on text only when decoding becomes automatic.

Traditionalists teach decoding with daily lessons in phonics skills: recognizing letter-sound relationships, sounding out letters, and blending letter combinations into words.

If California children haven't been taught to decode, as framework critics claim, they can't read stories. So what do they do with books? Phonics-first advocates say whole language teaches children to guess at words. "The fundamental of whole language is that everything comes from guessing in context," Joseph says. "Well, I'm sorry, that is not reliable."

Zinke and other whole language advocates agree that primary education suffered after the framework's adoption. But the framework didn't fail. It never had a chance to work, they say. Teachers were not trained to make the monumental shift to literature-based instruction.

Even if teachers had abandoned systematic phonics instruction *en masse*, Zinke and her colleagues wonder how anyone could single that out as *the* cause of California's reading problems. Our classrooms bulge with students, they argue, huge numbers of whom don't speak English at home. Per-pupil spending is among the lowest in the country. School library holdings—key factors in determining academic and reading achievement—are among the nation's lowest. Since 1987, public library access has been slashed. Might such conditions help explain why children have problems learning to read?

Some teachers say the phonics debate is a simple-minded answer to a complex problem. It's also a smokescreen, diverting attention from politicians' failure to confront the legacy of Proposition 13 and education's real needs.

And according to some researchers, evidence used to condemn the framework is inconclusive. True evaluation requires scores from before and after 1987, when the framework was adopted. NAEP, the national standardized reading test, has been conducted for many years. But state-by-state results have been available only since 1992. Although California students performed miserably, national results offered little to celebrate, either. Are they all whole language states? Is California really a whole language state?

In their rush, framework critics ignored a critical piece of 1992 NAEP data. When teachers were asked to assess their fourth graders' reading proficiency, rankings were nearly identical—whether classrooms emphasized phonics or whole language.

Statewide reading test results from the California Assessment Program (CAP) offer a partial before-and-after view, but don't support framework critics or advocates. Recorded between 1984 and 1990, some CAP scores rose, while others fell.

Both sides seem to agree on major points: teach phonics, interest kids in books, and keep them reading. That's why Zinke shakes her head over critics' charges. She can't grasp how whole language advocates earned this anti-phonics label. "Everybody needs phonics," she wails, with the plaintive cry of someone tired of repeating herself. The question is: How should phonics be taught?

Whole Language in Practice

No one knows how—or whether—California teachers are practicing the framework's message of literature-based reading instruction. In 1992, a University of Southern California study found just one-quarter of teachers surveyed used literature to teach skills. Many, like Hayward kindergarten teacher Linda Rayford, remain convinced that without systematic phonics instruction, students will not learn to read. The program Rayford uses is one of dozens marketed to teachers. While lesson plans vary, they all introduce letters and sounds in careful sequence, moving through initial consonants, final consonants, long vowels and short vowels.

As her Ruus Elementary School kindergartners return from lunch, Rayford explains, "The children go to a place called 'Decode If You Can.' To learn to read here, you have to learn sounds. We've been reading sounds from pictures."

Rayford, a tall woman with short, dark brown hair and strong features, distributes slates and felt-tipped pens. "Please don't push," she says, as children jostle for a place at her feet. "What about that word 'push'? What do you hear besides the 'p'? 'P,' 'p', 'push'?"

"Good," she says, in response to a child who volunteers "h." "How would we write 'sh'?" No one answers, so she reaches for a stack of laminated sheets the size of large placemats. "Get a code sheet and see if you can find out."

The children lay the sheets next to their slates. Three rows of pictographs, forty-four in all, are printed across them. The first pictograph shows a growling bulldog. His face represents the sound made by the letter *r*, which is printed below the picture. But he also represents six more letter combinations—*er, ir, ur, or, ear,* and *wr.* Those appear on the sheet, listed under *r.*

A grandfather clock represents *t,* for tick-tock; a coiled snake, for the hissing *s;* and an airplane propeller, *n,* for the engine's hum. A startled face captures *oh.* A boy standing next to a mouse represents *ee.*

The children have memorized the pictographs and letters. They're ready to read and write, Rayford says. "I'm going to have you write words using letters we've learned," she proposes. "How would you write *ice*?"

"After *I* is *c.*"

"No," Rayford answers. "That's the *k* sound." Pointing to another slate, she says, "Yes, that's right. *Is.*"

One kindergartner, Marie, has trouble following the lesson. When Rayford asks them to write *see,* Marie's letters read *ic.* "What does your first letter say?" Rayford asks her, but gets no response. She tries again. "What do you hear?" Still nothing. Finally, Marie copies *se* from her neighbor's slate.

"Are you ready for some hard words?" she asks. "Are your eyes ready to work?" She pulls out a flashcard showing the clock, growling dog and child with mouse. The children respond quickly. "T-er-ee, tree!" This exercise, referred to as oral blending, helps them move beyond isolated sounds to blending words.

Next, the snake, clock, and growling dog. "S-t-er, stir!"

"You stir a birthday cake," Marie volunteers. "Yes, that's right," Rayford says, smiling, pulling out another card.

Brimming with stories and observations, the children bounce as they sound out each word. Rayford lets them speak for a moment, then moves on to the next flashcard.

Thirty minutes later, the lesson is over. As the children struggle into coats and wave to waiting parents, Rayford gathers the slates and code sheets.

Zinke knows many teachers think phonics programs are effective. She says she can prove otherwise. "The reading process is more complex than phonics." Readers, beginning and skilled, use phonics *and* the other cues she's teaching fourth-grade Damon. "You wouldn't want to just 'phonic' your way through the sentence," she says. "The English language isn't very phonetic. You'd get to the word *eight* and you'd be in trouble."

According to some reading experts, phonics rules—like the familiar, "When two vowels go out walking, the first one does the talking"— help readers sound out only half of all English words.

Phonics rules and gimmicks divert children, Zinke says. They make young students think reading is a difficult job when "it's just so simple. There are three critical things everyone needs to learn to read: to be read to, to read with someone, and to read independently."

Most importantly, drills and worksheets give the wrong lesson. Reading is *not* sounding out. But that's what many young students learn from isolated phonics, she says. They leave classrooms as skilled decoders, not readers. "They sound out pages and pages without knowing what it means," Zinke says. "They don't have to think."

As a roving specialist, Zinke visits Lorin Eden classrooms to demonstrate reading techniques to teachers and children. One day, she's arranged to bring several poems to a group of fourth graders. She enters the classroom as if striding onto a familiar stage.

Flipping on the overhead projector, she slides a transparency over the glass plate. Zinke and students begin by reading a poem aloud together. To emphasize syllables and rhythm, Zinke reads with an exaggerated cadence.

When they finish, she changes slides. "Here's a poem with something missing," she says. "It's called 'I Had a Little Turtle.' Read it to yourselves and see if you can figure out any of the missing words. Then we'll try it together."

> I had a _____ turtle,
> His _____ was Tiny Tim.
> I ____ him in the bathtub to see if he could _____.

Low voices murmur the verses displayed on the screen. When they reach a blank, the children make a game of substituting "humm" or "unh" or just a pause.

"Any ideas about what could go in that first line?" Zinke asks.

After offering "big," "small," and "tiny," they agree on "little."

"Try all four ways," Zinke suggests. "See which sounds best." She reads the sentence aloud, inserting each adjective. "We could put in any word that describes the turtle. But the poet thinks about what sounds right."

They fill in all the blanks. Now the poem reads:

> I had a little turtle,
> His name was Tiny Tim.
> I put him in the bathtub to see if he could swim.

Pointing to the last line, Zinke says, "It's interesting that you all gave me 'doing' words—verbs. Nobody said 'truck.' You know what doesn't go there."

In this lesson, Zinke encourages children to recognize syntax they've used unconsciously. She's trying to create a reading radar in each child that will flag errors. Even with fourth-graders she still asks, Does this make sense?

With that regular refrain, say Zinke and others, whole language encourages independent reasoning. But perhaps free thinking is the opposition's real target. Zinke says, "We're beginning to ask, Why do they care so much about the phonics?" Education's goal should be to teach students to question and analyze. "But [some opponents] don't want us to do that."

Phonics has long been the centerpiece of campaigns against what conservatives label left-wing influences in public schools. Bill Honig is no friend of fundamentalists, but his call to reinstate isolated phonics instruction pleases groups from Phyllis Schlafly's Eagle Forum to the Washington, D.C.-based National Right to Read Foundation. Waving the phonics banner, they hope to chip away at "secular humanist" forces entering schools under cover of literature.

Although literature is more prominent, even in phonics-first class-rooms, than 10 years ago, Zinke fears opponents could engineer a return to teaching methods she discarded years ago.

Often referred to as the "part-to-whole" method, children moved from sounds, to words, to short sentences, to paragraphs, to short sto-ries. Only when they learned phonics rules did students begin to read and write independently.

But phonics-first children graduated to stilted texts. Although Dick and Jane retired years ago, their names recall a stiff, sing-song rhythm. That rhythm still echoes in books written for today's phonics programs. Total Reading, another program popular among California teachers, offers the story of *Little Fox:* "This is a story about Little Fox. He was a boy. He was six years old. He lived a long time ago."

Stories include only words with letters that have been taught. New words appear in sequence. The language is uninspired, the stories boring. "That's not the way people talk," Zinke points out. "That's not natural language."

Warming her hands on a cup of tea in a Rockridge cafe near her Oak-land home, Zinke recalls the years of phonics programs and basals as the "drill and kill" era. "We had to keep track of every little skill," she says, cradling her head in her hands as if recalling headaches the task brought on. Teachers recorded students' mastery of vowels and con-sonants on long checklists and administered weekly skills tests.

A textbook publisher's representative once explained the level of detail in the teacher's manual. "He told us the system was supposed to be 'teacher-proof,'" Zinke says, rolling her eyes with an expression recalling teenage disgust.

Monitoring student achievement was intended to create classroom accountability. Instead, "accountability turned into accounting," she says. "For years, teachers have had this incredible conditioning. You've got to cover all these skills. We got away from asking, What does *this* child need?"

The lockstep approach ignored the varied pace of children's development. "You have kids who are adept at different things," Zinke says. "Kids who are really slow to mature, throwing, playing baseball. You don't bring their parents in and scare them to death, and say he's throwing below grade level. Yet we bring parents of first and second graders in and tell them their kid is reading below grade level. Then we wonder why these kids develop a problem."

If phonics-first was so successful, Zinke asks, why did so many students struggle? "I knew it wasn't working for one-third of the kids," she says. "Every classroom had what we called the low reading group. There's something the matter with that. That's not a natural law."

Zinke knew the curriculum frustrated children who entered school ready to read. "They had to read Dick and Jane. It held them back. They could've gotten somewhere if they'd been given *The Very Hungry Caterpillar*, looked at the word *stomachache* or *watermelon*—big, juicy words—and were able to make something of it. But all they ever saw was 'Nan can fan Dan.'"

The longer she taught, the more frustrated she became. "I would come to meetings, waving these texts around, saying 'We shouldn't be doing this to children.'"

In 1983, hoping to find answers, Zinke earned her master's degree and became a reading specialist in Hayward. She still didn't have an alternative to basal readers and reams of makework. She just knew she didn't like them. "Have you seen them?" she asks, her voice rising. "They're all about isolated skills. 'Let's practice the *s* sound on this whole page,' whether you need it or not. It's not how kids learn language."

But by the mid-1980s, ideas from New Zealand about early literacy began to circulate in the U.S. Theories based on these observations came to be known as whole language. Researchers estimated that young children begin school with thousands of vocabulary words and speech rules. Watching them scribble, early reading experts concluded that even preschoolers understand the use of written language.

Most importantly, they observed that young children search for patterns and generalizations that help them make sense of the world. They come to school with stores of knowledge acquired on their own.

Whole language pioneers concluded that learning is an active process. Zinke says this view contradicted earlier teaching approaches.

"We used to figure kids were empty slates and we would just tell them everything," she says. Drill and kill years reflected that attitude. "Now we realize learning doesn't take place like that."

Influenced by writer and teacher Sylvia Ashton-Warner, child psychologist Jean Piaget, and early twentieth-century progressive educator John Dewey, whole language advocates posit that we learn by negotiating with our surroundings. All of us—even children—bring knowledge to every encounter, test it, keep concepts that prove useful and discard others.

Whole language educators believe children learn by solving problems. In literate homes, they see adults writing shopping lists, paging through newspapers to find sports scores, and reading books. Children come to understand that reading allows them to find the ingredients in a favorite recipe and help make cookies. Writing allows them to correspond with far-away cousins. These activities have purpose and meaning. In the language of whole language, they are authentic.

Phonics rules, as well as spelling and punctuation conventions, make sense when children apply them to real activities: to finding or expressing meaning. Whole language teachers believe isolated letter-sound combinations, as taught in systematic phonics instruction, are too small and abstract to be meaningful.

"We are giving children literature from the very beginning," Zinke says. "We're teaching them phonics as they need it."

Zinke credits colleagues at Lorin Eden School with applying whole language ideas practically. The week before Christmas vacation, Paul Cordero's first- and second-grade class learned "'Twas the Night Before Christmas." Cordero, a pale young man, has taught for just three years, but shows no hesitation in front of his class.

Holding a pointer, Cordero stands before a blackboard nearly obscured by a large pocket chart. The children sit in a half-circle in front of him. Backed with bright blue fabric, the chart is a series of rectangular, clear plastic sleeves. Each sleeve holds lines of text. Each word is written on a separate card, so the text can be removed.

"Can someone find a synonym for 'evening'?" he asks.

Hands wave, and Cordero chooses an eager child. He nods as she answers. When she sits down, he covers the word 'night,' and asks, "How can I get a clue to that word if I can't read it?"

"You can look at the words that come before," one child offers.

"If I read past it, I'll get a better clue," Cordero says. "What do you think it could be? What might make sense when we read, 'Twas the _____ before Christmas'? Could it be morning? Night? Day?"

Someone offers light. "Does that make sense?" Cordero asks, scanning the group. "'Twas the light before Christmas'? If it's 'night,' what sound does it start with?"

"*N*," comes the answer.

"What does 'night' end with?"

"*T*," they respond firmly.

Cordero continues down the chart, covering words. Each time, he asks what word might make sense in the space. He offers phonetic clues, showing them how to weave everything they know about the poem's meaning with letter sounds to identify a word they might not recognize.

"There's a big interest in reading in my class," Cordero says. "We start with singing and finding rhyming words. They have little books and materials at their level . . . Sure, phonics is easier to teach because you go step by step. It does work for a lot of students, but today. . . ." He breaks off, shaking his head.

Few of Cordero's students are exposed to books and print before they come to class. He wants to create at school what's missing at home. "Phonics is not always the most interesting or fun," Cordero says. "Today, a lot of kids don't read at home. These kids need to be captured by reading, to fall in love with it. And I do a lot of phonics with the pocket charts. But we shouldn't be doing phonics in isolation in the classroom. Besides, phonics teaches only one strategy—to decode. Reading strategies have to assure that reading is meaningful. If it's not meaningful, what's the point?"

As children in whole language classrooms learn that we read for meaning, they also learn that we write to communicate. When children begin writing, whole language teachers welcome *tk* for *truck*, or *hs* for *house*. They consider these errors part of early writing.

Acceptance of children's unconventional spelling infuriates critics like Marion Joseph. Many phonics-first proponents believe that children should not be encouraged to write until they know letter-sound correspondences and can spell. "Spelling is a completely dirty word to people in whole language," she says. "Believe me, I don't understand that. Somehow, by some magic, they will all get it? No, they won't get it."

Whole language theory holds that children incorporate spelling rules when they need them to read and write. Whole language teachers want students to understand that ideas, not spelling, are the writer's first concern. They reinforce spelling rules through continued emphasis on reading. By leading children through the writing process from first draft to final copy, they also focus attention on spelling conventions.

Using these methods, primary-grade children write, critique, and edit each other's work. Many teachers hold publishing parties for young authors, inviting families to student readings.

Teachers who adopt whole language methods create classrooms where children read and write all day. They ask students to sign in each morning, even if some only scribble. The first letters of names offer natural headings for lists of words beginning with *D* for Daniel, or *S* for Suzanne. Reciting a poem about Brown Bear generates words that begin with *br* or rhyme with "bear."

When children recount weekend activities, they're asked for the first letter of "yesterday." Teachers read aloud several times a day, often repeating stories so children become familiar with sounds and language patterns. These activities incorporate phonics, Zinke points out.

The Education of a Reading Activist

All good teachers know children need lots of strategies to make sense of print. That's why whole language made so much sense to Zinke when she learned about it nearly ten years ago. She became a reading activist, trying to convince colleagues to give up phonics drills and controlled vocabulary basal readers.

As she ventured into new territory, so did the state Department of Education. Its 1987 language arts framework never mentioned whole language, but embraced some of its principles. One stood out for Zinke. "They were telling us to use real books," she says. "They were talking about putting actual literature in our classrooms."

The framework may have represented revolutionary thinking, but real change would come with books that reflected the literature-based approach. "To break out of [basal readers] was a bigger problem than to just write the framework," Zinke says.

Publishers scrambled to produce materials that would satisfy California's new literature-based guidelines. The state's textbook committee approved eleven sets of materials for language arts instruction.

Zinke served on Hayward's selection committee. She wanted to use textbook money to buy children's trade books and train teachers to use them in the classroom. She thought the state wanted that, too. She had just watched a department of education video showing children in classrooms. "They were reading real books," she says. "They were reading *Island of the Blue Dolphins*."

But she found committee choices limited. "Where are the books?" she asked.

Phonics-first advocates also found the materials flawed. For them, systematic phonics instruction was the missing link. Although the framework refers briefly to phonics programs in early grades, critics say that reference was ignored when textbooks were chosen.

Given the limited choices, Zinke favored an anthology, *Impressions*. "[The collected stories] were all real literature taken from all over the world," she says. But *Impressions* faced tough critics. Some educators felt the teacher's guide was inadequate. Phonics-first supporters tried to override committee decisions. Religious fundamentalists objected to a story about witches.

Though *Impressions* won, many teachers—long-accustomed to "teacher-proof" sequential phonics programs—were stranded. "They had their workbooks jerked," Zinke says. "[The state said to them] 'We're doing whole language now. Here are some journals. Immerse your students in literature and they will learn to read by reading.'"

Angry and confused, teachers received only stories in exchange for familiar manuals and curriculum management systems. Publishers provided training in newly adopted materials, but brief sessions, even combined with district-sponsored training, barely answered basic questions. Depending on commitment and money, training varied widely across the state's 1,000 school districts. Department of Education officials point to several successful literature-based districts, but acknowledge that those represent just a few pockets.

In the framework's early years, educators say no one understood how complicated it was to transform reading instruction. Even so, it might not have occurred to teachers to expect help.

Zinke looks blank at the suggestion that teachers should have asked for extensive training. "We're used to working in a deficit model," she says, after a pause. She speaks slowly, as if to make her point clear to a naive questioner. Pointing to a nearby supply closet, she says that Lorin Eden's speech teacher meets pupils there. Zinke's own classroom is a converted principal's office. "Education is used to not having support. When did we ever have it?"

In the years following the framework's publication, Zinke consulted with dozens of schools and found disarray. "Everybody was doing a million different things and everything in between. Some people were using the new books as basal readers. Some of us were reading the research and making our own evaluations of how it should be done."

Zinke and Hayward bilingual teacher Jennifer Martinez have been trading teaching techniques for years. Martinez, who favors whole language methods, works across the hall from Linda Rayford. Seated on a rug, with first graders in a half-circle facing her, Martinez tells them about the Nutcracker ballet she saw the day before. Using a large easel, she sketches a tree banked with Christmas presents and describes little Clara's dream.

"The orchestra sits in front of the stage," she explains in Spanish, "and suddenly the music grows very loud. And the tree becomes huge!" The children gasp as Martinez quickly draws a second, larger tree. "What should I write near the little tree?" she asks.

Hands wave. Children throw out words and phrases, and finally agree on the story's most important elements: *En el arbol chico, habian regalos chicos*. [By the little tree, there were little presents.]

Martinez repeats the sentence. "How many words are there?" They instruct her to draw seven lines, one for each word, under the sketch. Together, they spell them out.

"How do we write *arbol*?" she asks.

Voices offer *a*, then *r*. Martinez writes those down, leaving space for the letters to follow. "What else do you hear?"

Someone suggests *o-l*. She enters those, then points to the hole in the middle. "And here? *Ar_ _ol*?" The response bounces back, and she completes the word, adding the letter *b*.

The class works its way through the sentence. Martinez helps them distinguish sounds. She reminds them that the second *c* in *chico* makes a hard sound, like *caballo*. *Habian* provides a lesson in the silent *h*.

When they finish, she asks, "Since you weren't with me, I'd like to know what you did yesterday. Who has something to say?"

"I went to the park," one child volunteers. "I saw the movie about Winnie the Pooh," says another. And, "I saw *The Lion King*."

She sends them back to their tables, and works her way around the room. "Who went to the park with you?" she asks one child. "What did you like about the movie?" she asks another. "Can you write that down? What does lion start with?" She scribbles on yellow Post-Its, noting errors and progress. She'll add the memos to files she keeps on each child.

Martinez's first students showed her the power of literature. Early in her career, she was assigned a class she says should have been taught in Spanish. They had been using the same reader for three years. "They knew four words and filled out millions of worksheets," she says. "I said, 'I'm not doing that.' I got permission to use [humorous children's poet] Shel Silverstein. We came to a poem that read, 'I washed a behind that wasn't mine.' They were hooked on reading."

Martinez has taught for fifteen years. Like other whole language teachers, she says, "I don't want the state telling me I have to use a phonics kit. I do use phonics."

Call for "Balanced Reading Instruction"

Zinke says few classrooms resemble Martinez's or Cordero's. Many schools announce they've adopted literature-based reading programs, but she questions much of what is taking place in the name of whole language.

"I get phone calls from all over," she says. "They'll say, 'We're a whole language school'—which they're not—'but nobody can read. Will you come and talk?' I'll come in for half a day or a day to help them understand what they need to have in place for literacy. Then I leave and there's no follow up."

Zinke's especially worried about teachers who've abandoned familiar phonics methods and think children will "get it" if set loose in a garden of print. Theirs are probably the least effective classrooms. She'd rather see good teachers use methods they're comfortable with—even if it means retaining isolated phonics lessons—than floundering without proper training. Many teachers say they rely on canned lessons because they can't offer individual attention to thirty-some children.

Even so, Zinke is convinced lengthy phonics sessions aren't necessary. When she visits classrooms, she tries to chip away at what she considers outdated practices. "They [teachers] don't trust me at first," she says. "I tell them they don't need to do the letter of the day. They say, 'I know you're right, but I just have to keep doing it. I'll quit next year.' By Monday, they've dropped it. I just need to put a little germ of an idea in their heads, give them really good research to look at and they'll get it."

Her persistence has been rewarded at the district level. Hayward school officials now consider her a resource, not a troublemaker. When publishers preview reading materials at sales pitch meetings, administrators ask her to attend. She and Martinez helped draft Hayward's new language arts philosophy.

Even so, change has been slow and uneven. Zinke says she's hard-pressed to find more than a handful of classrooms she would define as whole language. So she was shocked to read last spring's news reports that whole language was to blame for California students' dismal performance on reading comprehension tests.

"I was horrified at the way the media was talking about whole language," she says, but the stories contained enough truth to be threatening. "There are a lot of people with a huge concern that phonics got left out all this time. Their concern is well-founded because there were a lot of classrooms where teachers didn't have a clue what they were doing. Nobody ever trained them. A lot of kids weren't learning to read.

I don't blame them for having that concern, but they think the answer is to go back to the fifties."

Zinke managed to track down an early draft of Superintendent Eastin's Reading Task Force report. She panicked, convinced the findings would require teachers to spend most of their language arts classroom time on isolated phonics. "They were going to fight for us to teach phonics as if it were more important than the rest of the reading process," she says. She called, faxed and wrote every state education official she could find.

No one told her about Task Force meetings, and she wrongly assumed they were closed. She thought she'd have to settle for submitting a statement. "I wanted to see if they really had the right information," she says. "I didn't know who they were hearing from, who was on the Task Force. I kept calling, and they kept saying, 'We'll make your letter available to the Task Force.'"

When she learned that textbook companies attended the sessions, Zinke knew she had to make the trip. Arriving for a July meeting at a Sacramento airport hotel, she was still unsure about the process. Even so, she worked the room. "I asked everybody I could, 'What can I do about this?'"

Returning home with a clearer picture of the state hierarchy and a heightened sense of urgency, she got back on the phone. "Time was running out. They were going to publish this thing [the report]. I was trying to convince somebody that Eastin should talk to other people besides the Task Force members. That would never happen because they have a system, but I thought, if anybody would listen. . . ." She never could deliver her message directly.

Zinke says the final report, calling for balanced reading instruction, is improved over the draft. Still, she's wary of how balance will be interpreted. She's heard that publishers are rushing to produce "stupid little books," as she calls them, in response to what they perceive as the pendulum swing back to phonics-first. Zinke fears a revival of "Nan can fan Dan."

For their part, phonics advocates are pleased, too. They say a key finding—that the 1987 framework gave insufficient attention to phonics instruction—sends the correct message. They're also reassured by a recent law requiring the state Board of Education to instruct publishers to include explicit phonics and spelling instruction in instructional materials.

By the time the report was issued last fall, Zinke realized it would not be the last word in California's Great Debate. She knew she'd arrived late on the political scene, unlike Marion Joseph and other phonics-first advocates. But Zinke was convinced the state would make grave mistakes if they didn't consult her. "They *need* me," she says, determination visible through her smile.

Her next chance to be heard came in January, when framework supporters and critics converged in the capitol to testify at a State Board of Education hearing. Zinke asked three teachers to make the trip with her. They couldn't take her car, though. She stores the overflow from her Hayward classroom in her late '70s Volvo station wagon.

Board members faced an audience of some eighty parents, teachers, administrators, professors, and staff. Zinke was among the first to speak and took the three-minute limitation seriously. "The framework was the most incredible thing to happen in my thirty years of teaching," she said. "Promote the framework, don't revise it."

Zinke returned to her seat, listening to opponents. Later, she complained, "They all went over their time—and the Board let them. Why did I stop at three minutes?" She studied faces, matching them with names she knew. As people began to drift out, she followed; cornering officials in hallways to press her points.

By the end of the day, Zinke was considering whether to apply for a seat on the committee to revise the language arts framework. If she were chosen, she'd have to come to Sacramento twice a month for meetings. She thinks her district would support her, but isn't sure she could make the commitment. She's also worried about being a lone voice.

Even so, thanks to the politics of reading, Zinke knows she'll soon be spending less time in the classroom. With invitations to run district-wide trainings on reading instruction and teach at a local college, she has found larger audiences for her views than she imagined just a year ago.

Speaking out has forced her to examine her deepest beliefs about education. "Doing the political stuff made me look at what I think is really important about teaching reading," Zinke says. "Is it about curriculum or is it about kids?"

2 Whole-to-Parts Phonics Instruction

Margaret Moustafa
California State University, Los Angeles

Moustafa begins by summarizing the research base for what she calls "whole-to-parts phonics instruction." This is followed by an explanation of how such instruction can be carried out during shared reading. Her suggested procedure draws upon Patricia Cunningham's concept of word walls (see Chapter 7) and Janile Wagstaff's ideas for combining whole language with phonics instruction that goes from whole to parts, yet Moustafa's procedure has unique characteristics, too. A useful table compares traditional phonics instruction with Moustafa's whole-to-parts phonics instruction, while two appendices help teachers further understand and prepare to do whole-to-parts phonics instruction with shared reading.

How can we best foster children's acquisition of the letter-sound system? In "Reconceptualizing Phonics Instruction" (*Reconsidering a Balanced Approach to Reading*, Chapter 5), I examined three important counter-intuitive research discoveries which have led to a new way of teaching letter-sound correspondences to emergent/early readers. I call this new method whole-to-parts phonics instruction. In this chapter I will briefly recount the research discoveries underlying whole-to-parts phonics instruction and describe such phonics instruction in more depth.

The Research Base for Whole-to-Parts Phonics Instruction

The discoveries underlying whole-to-parts phonics instruction are:

- *Early readers read print better in familiar context* than outside of such context (e.g., Goodman, 1965; Kucer, 1985; Nicholson, 1991; Rhodes, 1979; Stanovich, 1991). For example, early readers may see the print word *horse* in a list of words and say *house* but see the same word in a story about cowboys and say *horse*. Early readers also typically read stories with familiar language better than stories with unfamiliar language such as the language found in "decodable" text (e.g., *The fat cat sat on the mat*).

- *Young children are competent at analyzing spoken words into onsets and rimes but not into phonemes* when onsets or rimes consist of more than one phoneme (Calfee, 1977; Goswami & Bryant, 1990; Liberman, et al., 1974; Treiman, 1983, 1985). (Linguists call onsets and rimes the psychological units of a syllable; onsets are any consonants before a vowel in a syllable and rimes are the vowel and any consonants after it.) That is, young children can mentally analyze *smiles,* for example, into its onset, /sm/, and rime, /ilz/, without being taught to do so, but have difficulty analyzing it into its component phonemes, /s/, /m/, /i/, /l/, and /z/, even with instruction.

- *Young children who are beginning to read make analogies between familiar and unfamiliar print words to pronounce unfamiliar print words* and they make these analogies at the onset-rime level rather than at the phonemic level (Goswami, 1986, 1988). That is, by learning to recognize the print words *small* and *smile,* for example, children figure out that *sm-* is pronounced /sm/ and use that knowledge to pronounce *sm-* in other words with *sm-. The more print words children recognize, the better position they are in to make analogies between familiar and unfamiliar print words in order to pronounce unfamiliar print words* (Goswami, 1986, 1988; Moustafa, 1995).

How do these discoveries inform instruction in phonics? The last (and most recent) discovery informs us that if we help children learn to recognize many print words, they can make analogies between familiar and unfamiliar print words to pronounce unfamiliar print words. The first discovery informs us that the most effective way to help children learn to recognize many print words is to help them read stories with familiar language. This can be done through instructional techniques such as shared reading (Holdaway, 1979; Routman, 1991), the Language Experience Approach (Hall, 1976; Weaver, 1988), and free voluntary reading (Krashen, 1993). I will elaborate on the first of these.

Whole-to-Parts Phonics Instruction with Shared Reading

In shared reading, a teacher working with early readers may use a Big Book—an oversize book with oversize print—written in language familiar to children and illustrated with pictures which represent the language of the text. The teacher may introduce it to the children, read it *to* the children while pointing to the words in full view of the children, then read it *with* the children while continuing to point while reading, and finally, when the children are very familiar with the language of the story, invite the children to read it *by* themselves, alone or to student partners. *This both demonstrates the reading process to the children and establishes a basis for the phonics lessons to come, making the phonics lessons more memorable and hence, more effective. It also helps the children to see themselves as readers.*

Some early readers hypothesize that each print word in continuous text represents a syllable rather than a word. For these earliest of early readers, it is critical to help the children learn one-to-one matching of spoken and print words in the context of the story. This can be done by first demonstrating one-to-one matching through pointing to words while reading and then checking for understanding by asking each child to point to print words as he or she reads. If early readers point to two consecutive print words while saying a single multi-syllabic word, the teacher can guide their hands in one-to-one matching. Word hunts are a good next activity here. In word hunts the teacher asks the children to turn to a particular page and put their fingers under a particular word. Usually, the teacher needs to show the children how to track the words on the page, starting at the beginning of the first sentence, reciting the words on the page until they get to the word they are hunting for. In my experience, this type of guidance, given over several consecutive days, enables children to grasp the basic concept and move on.

Initially the children will have only their knowledge of the language represented in the text and the illustrations to help them remember text which has been read to them by an experienced reader. However, as they learn to recognize more and more whole, unanalyzed print words through such instruction, the letter-sound system will become more and more available to them. That is, as they acquire print words with similar parts, they will begin to see the parts in the wholes, and use that knowledge to pronounce more and more unfamiliar print words through analogy. As they encounter words which contain the same letters and letter strings but differ in their pronunciation, they will learn multiple possible pronunciations of given letters and letter strings. That is, they will learn -*eak* can be pronounced /ek/ as in *beak* or /ak/ as in *break*. Then as they encounter letters and letter strings with multiple possible pronunciations, they can use their knowledge of the language represented in the text to decide which of the possible pronunciations would be most appropriate for unfamiliar print words they encounter.

The research reviewed in "Reconceptualizing Phonics Instruction" (*Reconsidering a Balanced Approach to Reading,* Chapter 5) suggests that children do and will make analogies at the onset-rime level as they learn to recognize more and more print words. The question as to whether or not direct instruction in onset-rime analogy will facilitate or accelerate processes children naturally employ, given experience with text with familiar language, is a question for future research. However, in the meanwhile, just as no theory is ever abandoned until a new theory is provided (Kuhn, 1970), so too, many will not be able to let go of traditional parts-to-whole phonics instruction until another instructional practice which is easy to understand and implement is provided.

Wagstaff (1996) has developed one possible approach. In her book, *Phonics That Work!*, Wagstaff describes how she combines whole language reading instruction, instruction in onset-rime analogy, and Cunningham's (1995) word walls for second grade students. *After* Wagstaff reads a story *to* and *with* children, and the story has been read *by* the children, she or the children select words in the story to study. Wagstaff underlines the rimes—or, as she says to the children, "chunks"—to be studied in each word selected and then invites the children to suggest analogous words with the same chunks in them and lists the words on the board. When the children offer words with the same rime but different spelling, Wagstaff points out that the sound represented by the letter(s) in the word being studied is spelled two ways. When they sometimes offer words which contain the same letter(s) but different sounds, Wagstaff points out that the letter(s) can represent different sounds. At the end of the week Wagstaff puts the words studied on the wall, grouped with other rimes which begin with the same letter of the alphabet.

While Wagstaff's strategy of going from whole to parts—from whole text, to words, to parts of words—is supported by the research reviewed in "Reconceptualizing Phonics Instruction," the strategy of displaying a print word and inviting young readers to volunteer words with analogous rimes is not. I can, for example, think of at least eight ways to spell words which, in my Midwestern dialect, have the same rime as *blue*: -*ue* (as in *blue, true,* and *due*), -*ew* (as in *new, flew,* and *dew*), -*oo* (as in *too* and *moo*), -*o* as (as in *to* and *do*), -*oe* (as in *shoe*), -*u* (as in *flu*), -*wo* (as in *two*), and -*iew* (as in *view*). Surely, asking young readers to think of words which have the same rime as a given word when those rimes may or may not be represented by the same letter(s) would be confusing for emergent/early readers and unnecessary for children who are already proficient readers. Building on Wagstaff's contribution to instruction, I suggest the following.

I suggest that a teacher working with early/emergent readers ask the children for some of their favorite words in the story, write each word the children suggest on a separate piece of paper, highlight the letter(s) representing an onset or a rime to be studied, and tell the children while

pointing to the highlighted letter(s) "This/these letter(s) say (sound)."
Then, collaboratively, teacher and children can put the words on the
classroom wall, grouping them with other words with like letters or letter strings where the words come from previously studied stories. In
this way children can learn about letter(s) which represent given onsets
or rimes in given words without being confused by the arbitrariness of
our standardized spelling system. Figure 1 shows a possible movable
word wall in progress which a group of early readers may have collaboratively constructed with their teacher after learning to read "If
You're Happy and You Know It" and "The Eensy Weensy Spider."

Then, as words come up with like letters and letter strings which represent different onsets (e.g., *c-* in *cat* and *cents*) and rimes (e.g., *-ood* in
good and *food*), the teacher and children together can collaboratively
regroup the words into sub-sets of letter strings which represent different onsets or rimes and use different highlighter colors for each sub-
set (e.g., the *-ow* in *cow, how* and *now* might be highlighted yellow and
the *-ow* in *grow, know* and *throw* might be highlighted purple). In so
doing, children will learn that like letters and letter strings can represent different onsets and rimes. A system of displaying the words on
the wall which allows for their easy rearrangement, such as the one
described in Appendix 1, facilitates regrouping as more and more
words are studied and go up on the wall. These phonics lessons are
brief but build over time as more and more stories are read *to, with*,
and *by* children.

When print words are put on the wall they become removed from
the context of the story; they become decontextualized. A strategy that
would help emergent/early readers relate the words on the word wall
back to a known context is to have a small picture or logo from the story
the word came from next to each print word studied. As more and more
words go up on the wall, this would remind the children which story
each print word came from and enable them to return to the stories they
have studied to identify the words in context. One way to implement
this is described in Appendix 1.

Teachers working with very inexperienced readers may choose to
teach initial letters and letter-strings in the words the children have
picked. For example, if inexperienced readers who have just learned to
read *Row, Row Your Boat* pick the words *row, boat, down, dream*, and
stream to study, their teacher might choose to highlight and teach the *r*
in *row*, the *b* in *boat*, the *d* in *down*, the *dr* in *dream* and the *str* in *stream*.
As children have more and more experience with predictable stories
being read *to, by*, and *with* them, and more and more experience with
whole-to-parts phonics instruction, the teacher may choose to teach

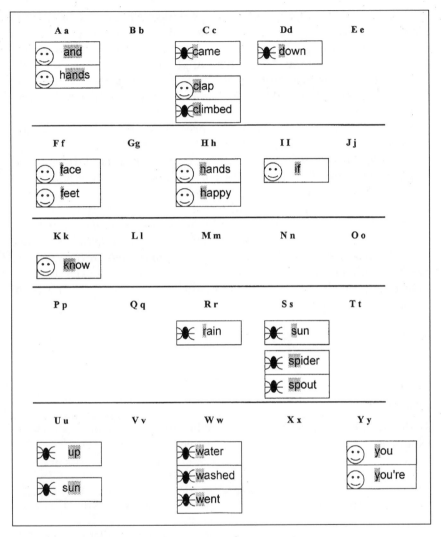

Figure 1. A moveable word wall in progress after two stories.

more complex letter-strings. For example, if more experienced early readers have just learned to read *Row, Row, Your Boat* and they, too, pick the words *row, boat, down, dream* and *stream* to study, the teacher may choose to highlight and teach the *-ow* in *row,* the *-oat* in *boat,* the *-own* in *down,* and the *-eam* in *dream* and *stream,* grouping *dream* and *stream* together on the word wall.

Teachers can also teach letter strings which represent salient syllables or compound words in a whole-to-parts phonics instructional
approach. For example, a teacher who has taught early readers to read
Row, Row, Your Boat may choose to highlight the *ly* in *gently* and *merrily*.
A teacher who has just taught children to read *Mary Had a Little Lamb*
may choose to highlight the word *every* or the word *where* in the compound word *everywhere*.

Some of the similarities and differences between whole-to-parts and
parts-to-whole phonics instruction are summarized in Table 1.

*Whole-to-parts phonics instruction proceeds from whole text, to whole
word, and lastly to parts of words.* It is like traditional parts-to-whole phonics instruction in that it is *explicit, systematic, and extensive.* However, it
has several advantages over traditional phonics instruction: *the words
being studied arise out of contexts which are meaningful to the children and
hence they are more memorable; the instruction is compatible with how we now
know children acquire a letter-sound system; and, the lessons are time-efficient,
inexpensive, and easy to implement.* In short, whole-to-parts phonics
instruction has far more to recommend it than traditional parts-to-
whole phonics instruction.

Table 1

Phonics Instruction

Traditional Phonics Instruction	Whole-to-Parts Phonics Instruction
explicit, systematic, extensive	explicit, systematic, extensive
based on assumptions dating back to Socrates	based on recent discoveries in linguistics and psychology
instruction goes from parts to whole (from letters to words)	instruction goes from whole to parts (from whole text, to words, to word parts)
instruction occurs before reading	instruction occurs after reading (e.g., after a predictable story is read *to, with,* and *by* children)
teaches letter-phoneme correspondences	teaches letter-onset and letter-rime correspondences
teaches unreliable rules	teaches multiple possibilities
abstract, difficult to remember	contextualized, memorable
logical, makes sense to literate adults	psychological, makes sense to children learning to read

Appendix 1

Preparing for Whole-to-parts Phonics Instruction with Shared Reading

The following tips on selecting stories, preparing paper with logos for the study words to be written on, preparing a word wall which allows flexible regrouping of study words, and identifying letters and letter strings which represent onsets and rimes or salient syllables may be useful to teachers preparing to teach whole-to-parts phonics.

Selecting stories for shared reading. The selection of appropriate stories is a critical first step in preparing to teach whole-to-parts phonics via shared reading. In addition to the usual criteria we use when choosing good stories for children (e.g., an engaging story line, an absence of stereotypes, etc.), two criteria which are important for whole-to-parts phonics instruction are that (1) the language represented in the text is language which is familiar to children and (2) the language and pictures are redundant. Language such as "out came the bee" is not as familiar to children as "the bee came out" and, hence, is more difficult to learn to read. In my experience, nonsense language is also generally more difficult for children to remember and hence to learn to read than language which is not nonsense, unless, of course, it is familiar nonsense (e.g., Fe Fi Fo Fum). If the language and pictures are redundant, the pictures will guide the children to use their knowledge of language and the story the teacher has read *to* and *with* them when they read it *by* themselves and with their classmates.

Preparing paper with logos for the study words. A quick and easy way to prepare paper with logos to write the study words on is to take an 11" × 8 1/2" piece of paper and section it into two sections, each 11" × 4 1/4" long by folding it in half lengthwise, creasing it, and unfolding it. Then, at the left end of each 11" × 4 1/4" section, tape identical pictures of a picture from the story representative of the story, e.g., a picture of the main character. Photocopy this paper to create as many copies as needed. Then cut the copies lengthwise on a paper cutter to make multiple pieces of 11" × 4 1/4" papers with logos on the left side.

Preparing a word wall which facilitates re-grouping. An inexpensive way to create a word wall where study words can be arranged and rearranged quickly and easily, is to mount plastic shower curtain liners, or similar sheets of plastic material available at material stores on the wall. Then, if scotch tape is used to attach the study words to the plastic, the study words can easily be arranged and rearranged since scotch tape can be ripped off and reattached to plastic multiple times.

Identifying letters and letter strings which represent onsets and rimes or salient syllables. Teachers not yet experienced in identifying letters which represent onsets and rimes may want to do the following exercise before teaching a whole-to-parts phonics lesson. Remember that onsets are any consonants before a vowel in a syllable and rimes are the vowel and any consonants after it in a syllable. When working with multi-syllabic words, be sure to mentally divide the words into syllables before identifying the letters which represent onsets and rimes. Now identify the letters and letter strings you might teach when children tell you their favorite words in the following passage:

> Row, row, row your boat.
> Gently down the stream.
> Merrily, merrily, merrily, merrily,
> life is but a dream.

Now turn to Appendix 2 and check your answers. How did you do? Like more practice? Study Appendix 2 and then, if you would like more practice, try the following passage:

> Mary had a little lamb
> whose fleece was white as snow
> and everywhere that Mary went
> the lamb was sure to go.

You can check your answers on this passage in Appendix 3.

Appendix 2

Row, Row, Row Your Boat

Print Word	Letters Onsets	Representing Rimes	Other Salient Letter Strings	Letters not Recommended for Highlighting
a:		[a]		
boat:	[b]	b[oat]		b[oa]t
but:	[b]ut	b[ut]		b[u]t
down:	[d]own	d[own]		d[ow]n
dream:	[dr]eam	dr[eam]		dr[ea]m
gently:	[g]ently	g[ent]ly	gent[ly]	g[en]tly
life:	[l]ife	l[ife]		l[i]f[e]
is:		[is]		[i]s
merrily:	[m]errily	m[er]rily	merri[ly]	m[e]rrily, merr[i]ly
row:	[r]ow	r[ow]		
stream:	[str]eam	str[eam]		[s]tream, str[ea]m
the:	[th]e	th[e]		
your:	[y]our			[you]r, you[r]

The header "Possible Letters to Highlight" spans the columns "Letters Onsets", "Representing Rimes", and "Other Salient Letter Strings".

Appendix 3

Mary Had a Little Lamb

Print Word	Possible Letters to Highlight			Letters not Recommended for Highlighting
	Letters Onsets	Representing Rimes	Other Salient Letter Strings	
a:		[a]		
and:		[and]		[a]nd, a[n]d, an[d]
as:		[as]		[a]s. a[s]
everywhere:			[every]where every[where]	
fleece:	[fl]eece	fl[eece]		fl[ee]s[e], flee[c]e
go:	[g]o	g[o]		
had:	[h]ad	h[ad]		h[a]d, ha[d]
his:	[h]is	h[is]		h[i]s
lamb:	[l]amb	l[amb]		l[a]mb, la[m]b
little:	[l]ittle	l[it]tle	lit[tle]	l[i]ttle
Mary:	[M]ary	M[ar]y Mar[y]	M[ary]	M[a]ry
snow:	[sn]ow	sn[ow]		
sure:	[s]ure	s[ure]		
that:	[th]at	th[at]		th[a]t
the:	[th]e	th[e]		
to:	[t]o	t[o]		
was:	[w]as	w[as]		w[a]s
went:	[w]ent	w[ent]		w[e]nt
white:	[wh]ite	wh[ite]		wh[i]t[e], whi[t]e
whose:	[wh]ose	wh[ose]		

References

Calfee, R. (1977). Assessment of individual reading skills: Basic research and practical applications. In A. S. Reber & D. L. Scarborough (Eds.), *Toward a psychology of reading* (pp. 289–323). New York: Erlbaum.

Cunningham, P. (1995). *Phonics they use: Words for reading and writing.* New York: Harper Collins.

Goodman, K. (1965). A linguistic study of cues and miscues in reading. *Elementary English, 42,* 639–643.

Goswami, U. (1986). Children's use of analogy in learning to read: A developmental study. *Journal of Experimental Child Psychology, 42,* 73–83.

Goswami, U. (1988). Orthographic analogies and reading development. *The Quarterly Journal of Experimental Psychology, 40A,* 239–268.

Goswami, U. & Bryant, P. (1990). *Phonological skills and learning to read.* Hillsdale, NJ: Erlbaum.

Hall, M. (1976). *Teaching reading as a language experience* (2nd ed). Columbus, OH: Charles E. Merrill.

Holdaway, D. (1972). *The foundations of literacy.* Sydney, Australia: Ashton-Scholastic.

Krashen, S. (1983). *The power of reading.* Englewood, CO: Libraries Unlimited.

Kucer, S. (1985). Predictability and readability: The same rose with different names? In M. Douglas (Ed.), *Claremont reading conference forty-ninth yearbook* (pp. 229–246). Claremont, CA: Claremont Graduate School.

Kuhn, T. (1970). *The structure of scientific revolutions.* Chicago, IL: University of Chicago Press.

Liberman, I., Shankweiler, D., Fischer, F., & Carter, B. (1974). Explicit syllable and phoneme segmentation in the young child. *Journal of Experimental Child Psychology*, 18, 201–212.

Moustafa, M. (1995). Children's productive phonological recoding. *Reading Research Quarterly*, 30, 3, 464–476.

Nicholson, T. (1991). Do children read words better in context or in lists? A classic study revisited. *Journal of Educational Psychology*, 83, 444–450.

Rhodes, L. K. (1979). Comprehension and predictability: An analysis of beginning reading materials. In J. Harste & R. Carey (Eds.), *New perspectives on comprehension* (pp. 100–130) Bloomington, IN: School of Education, Indiana University.

Routman, R. (1991). *Invitations: Changing as teachers and learners K–12.* Portsmouth, NH: Heinemann.

Stanovich, K. E. (1991). Word recognition: changing perspectives. In R. Barr, M. L. Kamil, P. Mosenthal, & P. D. Pearson (Eds.), *Handbook of reading research* (Vol. 2, pp. 418–452). Hillsdale, NJ: Erlbaum.

Treiman, R. (1983). The structure of spoken syllables: Evidence from novel word games. *Cognition*, 15, 49–74.

Treiman, R. (1985). Onsets and rimes as units of spoken syllables: Evidence from children. *Journal of Experimental Child Psychology*, 39, 161–181.

Wagstaff, J. (1996). *Phonics that work!: New strategies for the reading/writing classroom.* New York: Scholastic.

Weaver, C. (1988). *Reading process and practice: From sociopsycholinguistics to whole language.* Portsmouth, NH: Heinemann.

3 Learning about Phonics in a Whole Language Classroom

Penny A. Freppon
University of Cincinnati

Karin L. Dahl
The Ohio State University

In examining the summary of phonics information in Marilyn Adams' *Beginning to Read: Thinking and Learning About Print* (1990), the authors suggest additional bases of information "that need to be considered in deciding how to handle phonics effectively in beginning reading and writing instruction." One child in a whole language kindergarten class is then followed through some initial reading and writing experiences, documenting how the teacher helps children understand sound/symbol relations. The teacher, Kristin Schlosser, admits that there are a few children who have not yet grasped the alphabetic principle (the principle that letters represent sounds) by the end of their kindergarten year. However, Schlosser mentions the various other concepts about print and texts that they do typically learn and notes that there is often "great oral language growth," which transfers to certain literacy behaviors. Freppon and Dahl suggest that with such learners, focusing on what they do over time may be important (see Chapter 29). Then, in a useful summary section, the authors list and discuss eight principles underlying the phonics instruction in Scholsser's classroom —principles that underlie the teaching of phonics in other whole language classrooms as well.

Originally published in *Language Arts, 68*, (1991), 190–97. Copyright 1991 by the National Council of Teachers of English.

The "Great Debate" is under way again. This time there is new information, and there are some new players. In this article we take a whole language perspective and look briefly at one of the more prominent new summaries of phonics information, *Beginning to Read: Thinking and Learning about Print* (Adams, 1990). We suggest new bases of information that need to be considered in deciding how to handle phonics effectively in beginning reading and writing instruction, and we then present a description of phonics instruction in the classroom of a "new player," a teacher with a whole language kindergarten. It is our contention that the phonics controversy this time centers not only on instructional method but also on the extent to which educators utilize data about children as language learners. We think examples of instructional events that effectively support children's learning the code are important information for the current debate.

Theoretical Perspective

Our stance is based on sociopsycholinguistic theory, which holds that learning to read and write are language processes (Goodman, 1967; Smith, 1982), and on transactive theory (Rosenblatt, 1978; 1989), which grounds the learning of those language processes in each individual's interpretation of and transaction with the literacy events encountered in daily experience. We recognize that learners interpret and make sense of instruction and that their transactional stance (Purcell-Gates & Dahl, in press) influences what they learn. We believe that instruction in school-based settings is shaped by and includes the social and cultural contexts in which it takes place (Bloome & Green, 1982; Cook-Gumperz, 1986). Thus, to understand beginning reading and writing instruction and make judgments about learning the code, we necessarily must consider the language event, the learner's perspective, and also the social context of the classroom.

Reflections on the Phonics Summary

The new phonics summary (Adams, 1990) moves away from interest in a best or most effective way to teach phonics and instead integrates information from a variety of current sources including research-based information about sound-symbol relations, skilled reading, early reading, spelling development, and instructional interventions. Although many points of difference exist between the summary and a whole language perspective, we mention here three particular points.

First, the summary emphasizes that learning the code is *the key* in learning to read. We contend that one cueing system cannot be the single most important factor in reading. The child's orchestration of knowledge about written language includes crucial information from each of the cueing systems, as well as information about the function and form of print. We also contend that multiple factors, including context, sociolinguistic elements, and the learner's own purposes and motivations, influence learning to read (Bloome & Green, 1984; Cochran-Smith, 1984; Harste, Burke, & Woodward, 1983; Matthewson, 1976; Wigfield & Asher, 1984).

Second, in discussing the aspects of instruction to be presented to children, the report seems more curriculum centered than learner centered. We argue that reading and writing are language-based behaviors and that children learn them by engaging in meaning-centered exploration with written language. Therefore, sensitivity to and support for the explorations of children in beginning reading and writing are essential parts of school-based literacy instruction (Altwerger, Edelsky, & Flores, 1987; Dyson, 1982, 1984).

Finally, we suggest that not nearly enough is known about initial reading and writing development and school-based instruction from the perspective of the learner. It is in observations of children's literacy learning in varying contexts investigated through different theoretical perspectives that we find new insights and understandings about the complexities of learning written language (Dahl, Purcell-Gates, & McIntyre, 1989; Dyson, 1989; Harste, Burke, & Woodward, 1984; McIntyre, 1990).

Therefore, educators and researchers are challenged to present school-based descriptions of children in the act of learning to read and write. To decide the issue of how phonics is learned, we need to look closely at teachers and children in the process of working with sound-symbol relations, and we need to clarify how children in various instructional environments come to understand the written language code.

A Whole Language Classroom Example

This article presents a description of phonics instruction from a whole language perspective and serves as an account of learning within that instructional context. The kindergarten on which we focus is located in a midwest urban school serving approximately 400 children. This Victorian red brick school is surrounded by a cement play area with a high chain link fence. The school has been a neighborhood landmark for many generations. Most children entering the school are relatively inexperienced with written language.

In this example we show what one kindergarten teacher does to help children understand sound-symbol relations, and in the course of our description we follow one child, Jason, through some initial reading and writing experiences. We base this discussion on a year of close observation and analysis of urban children in a whole language kindergarten

(Dahl, Purcell-Gates, & McIntyre, 1989). We also draw on discussions with Jason's teacher, who is a leader among whole language advocates in her community and recognized for her success in providing instruction for children from low-income families.

Jason is typical of the learners in this classroom. Although shy, he seems interested in classroom activities and is attentive when his teacher reads aloud. Initial assessments of his written language knowledge at the beginning of kindergarten indicated that he did not grasp the intentionality of print, the alphabetic principle, or the nature of story structure. Kristin describes his learning at the beginning of the school year:

> When Jason came to school, I don't think he had ever paid attention to print or interacted with it very much. Basically, he didn't have experience with reading and writing; but he had a wonderful imagination, he was interested in stories, and he could pretend and talk really well when he played. This was a real strength, but he wasn't at all familiar with written language; and he had no idea of phonics.

Beginning Concepts about Written Language

At the beginning of the kindergarten year, the focus in the whole language program in Kristin's classroom is on the functionality of print as children explore the various ways print carries meaning. Kristin describes this early instruction: "I always work from whole to part. Children need time to gain an awareness of themselves as readers and writers, and from this they develop a need for phonics in order to communicate through written language."

Kristin continually demonstrates the functionality of print and provides children with rich and varied daily reading and writing experiences. Kristin includes repeated readings in a wide variety of children's literature. She chooses books recognized for their quality and illustrations, including big books. She reads three or four stories each morning, writes the agenda of the day, talks about words, and shows how words look and sound. She works with writing and reading the children's names in the context of songs and charts and uses written language for such purposes as writing notes on the message board.

In addition, children experience reading with the teacher in small heterogeneous groups of about five children once a week. During this reading time Kristin reads a small predictable book, encourages talk and predictions about story events, and has the children read to her. As one aspect of this activity, she helps children focus on words, word identification, and sound-symbol relations.

All of the children participate daily in journal time as they write about topics they select. Later, they discuss and share their writing. Class writing lessons focus on thinking and talking about the intended message, word awareness, and letter awareness. All of the centers in the classroom—the science center, writing center, book center, and dramatic play area—include invitations to interact with print. The dramatic play center changes frequently and features such themes as a restaurant, a flower shop, or a zoo baby animal center. Each version of the center contains opportunities for using written language in the course of dramatic play. For example, the center about zoo baby animals includes not only stuffed animals, a scale and a stethoscope, and a small table with a wooden telephone, but also some scrap paper for notations and a black bound calendar to sign up on a "waiting list."

During the beginning weeks of kindergarten, Jason spends a good deal of time watching his teacher and his twenty-six classmates. He wants to play; but when he interacts with the other boys, he and the rest of the group often become too boisterous. Play quickly becomes running, yelling, and wrestling; and his teacher spends a good deal of time helping the children get their behavior organized for the classroom.

By October, Jason learns to "do school" fairly well. In November, sporting a new burr cut and army camouflage fatigues, he approaches the telephone and writing table in the zoo baby animals' nursery. The center already contains the maximum number of children specified for the center, and Jason wants to sign up for a turn. He hesitates, picks up a pencil, and writes two short lines of scribble across one page. When asked to tell what he is doing, he holds his pencil in midair and responds tentatively, "Well, I guess I'm making an appointment." Later in the morning when asked to tell about his writing, he says, pointing to the two lines, "I want an appointment. "

The classroom environment supports many other initial experiences with print. Kristin requires children to write in journals, and she structures each activity of the day to include written language demonstrations and discussions. For example, she demonstrates the process of writing when she writes the agenda of the day by "thinking out loud" as she writes. Kristin comments:

> I provide lots of opportunities to write, and I believe journal writing, for some children, can build their confidence and ability as writers and so help them want to try writing in other contexts in the classroom. Just journal writing, just demonstrations by the teacher, just opportunities to write throughout the day in classroom centers does not do the trick. It all has to be there—integrated throughout the day.

Nudging Children toward Sound-Symbol Awareness

Once children understand the meaningfulness of print, the functions that print serves, and the nature of wordness and story, Kristin begins working toward sound-symbol awareness. She describes her approach, "I think children need a lot of time and examples and support. I do teach the code directly by sitting down with them individually when they write and also, in circle time with my demonstrations, by writing in front of them."

In individual sessions she helps children think about the words they choose. "The children generate the writing ideas first. Then I find ways to hook onto the child's ideas and work with that meaning. I might say to a learner, 'I can see this says *my* because it starts with m' or 'I can see this is *puppy* because it has *p* at the beginning and end.' I find the one thing that the child is trying to say and make the connection."

Kristin often says the child's intended word, slowly drawing out its sounds. Frequently, she also tells the child to say the words and asks, "What do you hear?" just after the child pronounces it. She often models listening for sounds and making connections to letters: "I want to write about dinosaurs, di-no-saurs, di-no, I hear a *D*, that starts *dinosaurs*." As she writes the letter *D* on her own paper, she adds as an aside, "Yes, *D* like in *dinosaurs* and *D* like in *David* in our class."

Jason proves to be particularly in need of these individual sessions. Kristin reports, "It was February before I saw signs of Jason beginning to understand letter-sound relations. In February I began to sit with him during journal time and nudge him along. I'd say, 'Jason, I can't read this; I don't see any sounds in your writing.' And I'd also say, 'What do you hear in that word?' and 'What else do you hear?'"

Weighing these questions, Jason begins consistently saying the words as he writes independently. He repeats the words as he writes, saying them slowly just as his teacher does when she helps him learn to listen for sounds.

In mid-February Kristin begins journal time in the usual way with a demonstration writing session during Circle Time. She tells about picking berries with her mom and sister when she was little, and after eliciting suggestions for her writing from the children, she demonstrates the writing process by writing several lines of print on chart paper and discussing the meaning, pronouncing each word, and naming the letter sounds.

When the children are dismissed to write, Jason gets his journal and goes to a nearby table. He opens his journal, looks at his letter card, and says, "Where's an *F* on here?" As he locates the *F* on his alphabet card, he begins to say the *F* sound, "Ffff," and write the letter. Another child interrupts with a request, "How do you spell 'Mom, in five days it's Valentine's Day?'" Jason thinks about it briefly, decides not to respond, and is quiet. In a few minutes he again picks up the pencil and says slowly and distinctly, "In my birthday." In the process he writes an *N* beside the *F* he had written earlier. He then announces, "I can't make an *M*." His neighbor Charlie leans over from across the table and says as he writes an *M* on Jason's paper, "You can't make an *M*?" Looking at the *M* Charlie produced, Jason continues, "In Mmmm, in my birthday," and quickly adds *BD*. He repeats, "In my Bbbb, birth, Dddd day. Then he says *E* but does not write the letter. Jason repeats "in my birthday" quickly and with conviction as his eyes track the letters just written. He looks up and says, "In my birthday someone gave me the, these shoes," and he holds up one foot, pointing to his shoe. "I just didn't want to wear them." Looking back at this writing, he repeats slowly and distinctly, "In my birthday, someone gave me these shoes. Some . . . Ssss Uuuu Mmmm . . . Ssss," and he writes the letter *C* backwards. "I'm listening to the sounds!" he announces, returning to his writing. "In, Nnnn, my birthday, Ssss, someone gave me, Thththth, Zzzz shoes."' He writes *Z* for *these* and then reads it to the researcher sitting nearby. "It says, 'In my birthday someone gave me these shoes.'" Seeing that he has not written shoes, he begins to write the letter *S*. "I'm going to share," he adds with the last letter completed and hurries off to show his teacher.

The instruction that undergirds this writing episode appears to shape the learner's experience. Jason uses the demonstrations his teacher has provided and copies her model of "listening for sounds." The context of the event also provides support. Jason is given information by other learners and is sustained in his effort by his own substantial interest and investment in the meaning he is trying to convey. He knows that others can read his message, and he wants to share. His responses indicate that he is gaining confidence and beginning to understand how to think about sound-symbol relations. We believe that reading instruction also contributed to his understanding; however, at this point in Jason's growth his knowledge of sound-symbol relations is most evident in his writing.

Other kinds of individual nudging in this classroom take the form of helping learners find a specific starting point for their writing. Kristin helps children segment their message into distinct words. She suggests, "You want to write 'It is raining today.' That is four words. Your first word is *it*. I'll be back after you write." Kristin explains that some of the starting points she provides focus on the sounds of the initial word in the intended message.

> Sometimes they will tell me a whole story so I say things like, 'Oh, you want to write about a castle? I remember you said it's about the dark castle. What does the word dark start with?'; and I help them hear the sounds in that word. I want them to learn to hold that idea or sentence in mind and realize that it is stable.

The other significant piece of the nudging toward sound-symbol understandings takes place in group settings. Kristin models writing as she interacts with children. She notes:

> It is not all right for me as teacher to write without talking. Children need to see me thinking through the process. I model my thinking, and I see them learning to think about letters and sounds. I didn't used to do writing demonstrations this way. I used to write a lot, but I didn't verbalize what it takes to write. Then my children didn't write, and I was very frustrated. I saw a big change in the children when I started this kind of modeling. I have learned that I can't expect my children to do what I don't do. I want to show that writers must think and make sense.

Building a Collaborative Community for Learners

As the year progresses, the children in this classroom increasingly work collaboratively. They spontaneously get books and read together on the floor each morning. Children also use some of their free choice time to experiment with written language collaboratively rather than engage in parallel play activities as they had been doing. At times the children's collaborative talk about words, sounding out words, and discussion of writing topics becomes a din; and it is difficult to distinguish one conversation from another. In the swell of these interactions, Jason continues his exploration of written language.

> On a morning in March Jason sits with several friends while his teacher distributes journals. He begins the writing session by trading pencils with other children.
>
> He then announces, "I am . . . I'm inviting you to my party . . . Devin." The name Devin is quickly copied from the front of Devin's journal.
>
> "Know what?" Jason says to Tara, "I'm inviting you and Rick. I'm inviting you and Rick to the party, you know."
>
> Turning to Toby, he says, "Will you write your name?" Toby reaches over as if to write, but instead Jason begins to write the letter *T*. "I know there is a *T* in your name."
>
> "*O*," says Toby simultaneously with Jason.
>
> Jason announces, "*Y*!!"
>
> Toby responds, "No, *B*."
>
> Jason retorts, "It ain't a *B*."
>
> Then, musing to himself, "How do you make a *Y*? Ah . . . I know how." "Now," says Jason confidently as his eyes track the print,

"Toby." Jason then shows the writing to Devin and comments, "I made that kind of *Y*."

"Yes, but you didn't; you forgot the *B*," says Devin.

"Well," Jason replies, "I made a big *O* here, so then I can make this *O* into a *B*. Toby. That's a list of who's going to my party. I don't have enough room for Charlie. Well, I could put it right here." Jason squeezes in Charlie's name as others spell it for him.

"Now you need Rick," says Tara.

"I don't know how to write Rick," says Jason.

Several children respond, "I do."

Tara, sitting the closest, writes the letters *R I C K* on his paper. As she proceeds, Jason says excitedly, "Rick, I'm inviting you to my party and Toby, too." His eyes rest on his paper as he runs over the list and thinks about the spelling of Rick's name. "*R I C K* . . . Rick, oh why didn't I think of that!"

This writing episode shows kindergarten children collaborating within a functional task. As learners pool their knowledge, they appear to be as interested in their neighbor's piece as they are in their own. Their learning is driven by the meanings and communicative purposes that they establish, and sound-symbol relations seem to be learned in tandem with other concepts about written language.

Learners Who Don't Grasp Sound-Symbol Relations

As supportive as this context is for exploring written language, a few of the children in this classroom still do not understand sound-symbol relations by the end of the year. The reasons for this are as complex and varied as the children themselves. One child, for example, spends a large portion of her kindergarten year trying to gain acceptance socially. She does not focus on literacy instruction until nearly the end of the year. Another appears to be distracted by a particularly chaotic set of circumstances at home, and still another seems to follow the classroom activities but is not able to integrate new information available in her instruction with her own existing knowledge about the function and form of written language. As we follow these learners into their whole language first-grade classrooms, we may see a change in their understanding. They may need more time, additional instruction, and additional experiences with print. It also is possible that instructional contexts other than whole language may be more productive for specific learners.

We asked Kristin about the children who had not yet grasped the alphabetic principle by the end of the year and she explained:

Well, a few of them don't get it. I have a few children every year that have difficulty, but I think they get something. They use print

in meaningful ways; they sign up on the waiting list to get into
favorite centers. And, they internalize story patterns and structure.
They learn directionality and words, and they know that meaning
is in the print and not the pictures. Often there is great oral language growth, and that transfers to such literacy learning and early
reading behaviors as choosing books and memory reading. But
some, in the kindergarten year, do not get the letter-sound relations
through the writing and reading we do in my classroom.

If we are to better understand learners who initially do not grasp
letter-sound relations, further investigations are crucial. Research that
provides examinations of learner stance, learner ways of organizing
information, and learner interpretations of instruction may provide
explanations for these differences. Further, focus on what these children
do successfully over time may provide additional explanations and
suggest other factors to investigate. Clearly, this issue requires additional information.

Principles for Phonics Instruction in Whole Language

In part, our focus in this article has been on the nature of the phonics
instruction in a whole language classroom. We turn now to a general
summary of the principles that guide this instruction in order to
describe what it consists of and how it is carried out.

- *Learner centered.* Phonics instruction in this whole language kindergarten is focused on learner needs. Rather than applying a predetermined sequence of phonics concepts, Kristin organizes and
  maintains a literate classroom and presents specific information
  as needs for instruction transpire. Thus, the instruction is developmentally appropriate for these urban learners.

- *Learned in context.* The whole language teacher's perspective holds
  that reading and writing are language processes and that they
  need to be learned in authentic language events. Phonics instruction, therefore, is contextualized in communicative acts such as
  writing notes or making lists.

- *Presented after foundation concepts are learned.* Phonics instruction
  begins when children exhibit knowledge of some foundation ideas
  about written language. The teacher believes that it is essential that
  children understand the functionality and intentionality of written language before being asked to respond to instruction about
  letter-sound relations. Children lacking these foundation concepts
  of meaningfulness cannot benefit from instruction about abstract
  sound-symbol relations.

- *Meaning-based*. Instruction rests on the meanings children are trying to communicate. The teacher uses children's intended meanings to provide occasions for discussing sound-symbol relations. Instruction arises from the communicative goals and purposes of the children.

- *Integrated with other written language concepts*. Learning about sound-symbol relations occurs in tandem with other concepts about the form and function of written language, rather than in isolation.

- *Learned through teacher demonstration*. The teacher shows learners how to think about letter-sound relations within the context of functional events such as constructing the agenda of the day or writing a letter. These demonstrations consist of the teacher's telling and showing her way of figuring out specific words.

- *Learned through active involvement*. The teacher invites children to become actively involved in trying to figure out how to write their intended messages. Kristin asks, "What do you hear in that word?" and encourages learners to "listen for the sounds."

- *Learned through multiple information sources*. Children learn from each other and from various print experiences. They pool their knowledge, look at print around the room, copy from each other, and ask the teacher.

Clearly, there are specifics to be taught ("What do you hear in that word?") and to be learned ("I know there is a *T* in your name . . . Toby"). And there is re-evaluation and adjustment by the teacher ("I have learned that I can't expect my children to do what I don't do"). The teaching and learning documented in this classroom example suggest that children learn about the code through direct involvement with written language, utilize the demonstrations and questioning provided by their teacher, and draw support from the social context of the classroom.

Final Perspectives and Future Directions

In this article we have looked at phonics learning and instruction through a whole language lens, describing some of the complexities that are evident. We have demonstrated the role of phonics in a whole language classroom and related a whole language perspective to the current phonics and beginning reading summary (Adams, 1990). We have shown a child learning about letter-sound relations while using written language to represent meaning, and we have seen a teacher learning from children's responses as she works to make instruction meaningful and accessible.

The future direction of the phonics controversy rests on the breadth of information that is taken into account. We agree with Dyson's contention that when we observe children's learning, the "windows" through which we look help determine what we see (Dyson, 1989). Thus, we need information from varying perspectives and information that looks at teaching and learning in all their complexities. Research that considers the influence of context, sociolinguistic elements, and the learner's responses to instruction will help clarify issues inherent in the phonics debate. First-hand classroom accounts from teachers about phonics teaching and learning will be helpful. Finally, studies investigating how the function, form, and code of written language are being taught and learned in a wide variety of classroom settings will provide information on children's orchestration of knowledge about reading and writing.

References

Adams, M. J. 1990. "Beginning to read: Thinking and learning about print." In *A Summary*, ed. S. Stahl, J. Osborn, and F. Lehr. Urbana, IL: Center for the Study of Reading/Reading Research and Education Center.

Altwerger, B., C. Edelsky, and B. Flores. 1987. "Whole language: What's new?" *The Reading Teacher* 41: 144–154.

Bloome, D., and J. Green. 1982. "Capturing social contexts of reading for urban junior high school students in home, school, and community settings." (Final Report of Grant No. 34-21-2915-02). Washington, D.C.: National Institute of Education.

———. 1984. "Directions in the sociolinguistic study of reading." In *Handbook of Reading Reasearch*, ed. P. D. Pearson, R. Barr, M. Kamil, and P. Mosenthal, 395–421. New York: Longman.

Cochran-Smith, M. 1984. *The making of a reader*. Norwood, NJ: Ablex.

Cook-Gumperz, J., ed. 1986. *The social construction of literacy*. Cambridge: Cambridge University Press.

Dahl, K., V. Purcell-Gates, and E. McIntyre. 1989. "An investigation of the ways low-SES learners make sense of instruction in reading and writing in the early grades." Final Report to the U.S. Department of Education, Office of Educational Research and Information (Grant No. G008720229). Cincinnati, OH: University of Cincinnati.

Dyson, A. H. 1982. "Reading, writing, and language: Young children solving the written language puzzle." *Language Arts* 59: 829–839.

———. 1984. "Learning to write/Learning to do school." *Research in the Teaching of English* 18: 233–266.

————. 1989. *Multiple worlds of child writers.* New York: Teachers College Press.

Goodman, K. S. 1967. "Reading: A psycholinguistic guessing game." *Journal of the Reading Specialist* 6: 126–135.

Harste, J., C. Burke, and V. Woodward. 1983. "The young child as writer-reader and informant." (Final Report of NIE-G-80-0121). Bloomington, IN: Language Education Department.

Harste, J., V. Woodward, and C. Burke, 1984. *Language stories and literacy lessons.* Portsmouth, NH: Heinemann.

Matthewson, G. C. 1976. "The function of attitude in the reading process." In *Theoretical models and processes of reading,* 2nd ed., ed. H. Singer, and R. B. Ruddell. Newark, DE: International Reading Association, 841–856.

McIntyre, E. 1990. "Young children's reading behaviors in various classroom contexts: Their relationship to instruction." Paper presented to the American Educational Research Association, Boston, Mass.

Purcell-Gates, V., and K. Dahl. 1991. "Low-SES children's success and failure at early literacy learning in skills-based classrooms." *Journal of Reading Behavior,* 23: 1–34.

Rosenblatt, L. 1978. *The reader, the text, and the poem.* Carbondale, IL: Southern Illinois University Press.

————. 1989. "Writing and reading: The transactional theory." In *Reading and writing connections,* ed. J. Mason. Needham Heights, MA: Allyn & Bacon, 153–176.

Smith, F. 1982. *Understanding reading,* 3rd ed. New York: Holt, Rinehart & Winston.

Wigfield, A., and S. R. Asher. 1984. Social and motivational influences on reading. In *Handbook of reading research,* ed. P. D. Pearson, R. Barr, M. Kamil, & P. Mosenthal. New York: Longman, 423–452.

4 Kindergarteners Talk about Print: Phonemic Awareness in Meaningful Contexts

Donald J. Richgels
Northern Illinois University

Karla J. Poremba
Wasco, Illinois

Lea M. McGee
Northern Illinois University

The authors note that while much of the research on the acquisition of phonemic awareness uses direct instruction focusing on isolated sounds and words, their experience leads them to conclude that phonemic awareness can be just as adequately developed in the context of "functional and holistic experiences with written language." First the authors discuss research on teaching reading and writing as meaning-making activities, using whole texts, and designing literacy experiences "that are fully functional in the sense of serving authentic purposes in children's everyday home and classroom lives." Then they discuss a *seemingly* incompatible body of research, which demonstrates the importance of phonemic awareness for independent reading. Of course several different instructional techniques have been proposed for developing children's awareness of phonemes (and some have been shown to be successful through research). The authors argue, however, that such "direct" instructional techniques are not necessary: "We believe that phonemic awareness can develop in the same holistic contexts as do other aspects of children's written language knowledge." This is especially true when children's meaningful and functional encounters with print involve guidance from more literate others—especially the teacher, but also their more literate peers.

The authors then explain the nature and results of a "What Can You Show Us?" activity, which kindergarten teacher Karla Poremba uses in conjunction with shared reading experiences. The heart of the activity is the student demonstrations. After conferring with one another about what they see, individual students take turns showing the class something they know about the text. The children may identify letters or words, or even try to read the text by themselves. But usually, "the focus of student demonstrations is on letter identification, word identification, sound-letter correspondences, punctuation, and text format features." The authors illustrate the "What Can You Show Us?" activity with examples from Poremba's classroom and point out how Poremba observed ("assessed") what the children knew and adjusted her responses accordingly.

Beginning reading instruction presents teachers with a challenge: Can they involve young children in meaningful and functional reading and writing while simultaneously teaching the special print skills and knowledge usually associated with phonemic awareness? This challenge is made especially difficult by the fact that much research about acquisition of phonemic awareness presents a model of direct instruction with isolated sounds and words (e.g., Ball & Blachman, 1991). In this article, we contend that teachers can meet this challenge without resorting to such direct instruction and that they can play an active role in guiding children's attention to print during functional and holistic experiences with written language.

We explain the importance of both contextualized reading and phonemic awareness, and we describe an instructional technique that embeds phonemic awareness in quality, contextualized reading and writing activities. We share how one of the authors, Karla Poremba, daily involves her kindergarten students in meaningful and useful reading and writing. Yet she also employs an especially powerful instructional activity that helps her children look carefully at print as they develop phonemic awareness. We call this activity the What Can You Show Us? activity. It is child centered and meets the needs of children who exhibit a variety of levels of print knowledge.

The Challenge

Beginning reading instruction has been significantly influenced by two seemingly incompatible bodies of research. The first of these highlights the contextualized nature of reading and writing. It includes Holdaway's (1979) work with the shared reading approach to beginning reading instruction and Clay's (1979) research on children's integrated use of semantic, syntactic, and graphophonic cues for learning to read.

Teachers who are influenced by this body of research include in their teaching a strong focus on meaning. They build on children's already significant spoken language abilities, design literacy activities that are fully functional in the sense of serving authentic purposes in children's everyday home and classroom lives, and use whole texts (Edelsky, Altwerger, & Flores, 1991; Goodman, Hood, & Goodman, 1991).

The second body of research indicates the importance of phonemic awareness and suggests that young children need special skills and knowledge about how print operates. Phonemic awareness is *conscious* attention to phonemes, which are the units of sound that speakers and listeners *unconsciously* combine and contrast to produce and perceive words in spoken language. For example, in English, the phonemes /d/, /ĭ/, and /p/ are combined to make the word *dip*, and the /d/ and /t/ phonemes are contrasted when distinguishing the words *dip* and *tip*. Children must go beyond such unconscious use of phonemes when they learn to read and write. Conscious attention to phonemes is involved when they isolate sounds in words during invented spelling or use the sounds associated with letters to identify words and recognize word families.

The current renewed attention to phonemic awareness can be traced to Adams' (1990) review of research related to beginning reading. She emphasized the importance of functional understanding of the alphabetic principle and concluded, "Faced with an alphabetic script, the child's level of phonemic awareness on entering school may be the single most powerful determinant of the success he or she will experience in learning to read" (p. 304). A large body of research has strengthened the notion that phonemic awareness, beginning reading, and beginning writing go together. Ehri (1989) and Scott and Ehri (1990), for example, demonstrated that alphabet knowledge facilitates the transition from visual-cue reading (being able to read *McDonald's* only in the context of the familiar logo for the restaurant) to phonetic-cue reading (being able to remember and read words because of knowing letter sounds). Even knowing the sounds of only a few letters plays a role in early word reading. Ball and Blachman (1991) found that phoneme awareness instruction contributed to invented spelling ability.

In the wake of this revival of interest in phonemic awareness, proposed instructional techniques have flourished (e.g., Griffith & Olson, 1992; Spector, 1995; Yopp, 1992). Typically, these involve direct instruction in analyzing words by sounds (e.g., separately pronouncing parts of words, such as onsets and rimes or beginning, middle, and ending phonemes), manipulating sounds in words (e.g., making rhyming words or adding or subtracting sounds from words), and associating letters with sounds (e.g., sorting words by beginning letter). Frequently these activities are with isolated words.

The Importance of Looking at Print

Learning to read and write is a long developmental process involving a great variety of accomplishments. Some of these have to do with understanding the meanings and functions of written language. Others involve looking at print in a special way, a way that includes the reader's phonemic awareness. All these understandings work together. Meaningful and functional use of written language is enhanced when readers attend to speech sounds at the level of the phoneme and use resulting discoveries about phonemes and letters of the alphabet to guide their writing and reading.

We present examples of six children's varied and changing understandings of written language. Early in the long developmental process of becoming literate, children may differentiate pictures from print in storybooks, recognize that alphabet letters are a special set of graphic symbols, read some very familiar words as logographs (responding to a whole word, such as *Coca-Cola* or *McDonald's*, as a picture-like symbol), write mock letters, know some letter names, write signatures, and pronounce rhyming words (Clay, 1975; Ehri, 1991; Ferreiro, 1986; Lass, 1982). For example, thirty-five-month-old Natalie asked her uncle to draw a baby. She began coloring his drawing, then stopped to make three zigzag, horizontal lines of scribble writing under the drawing. Kristen, thirty-two months old, read a Domino's pizza sign while riding in a car in an unfamiliar neighborhood; she pointed to the sign and said, "Pizza man." As a four-year-old played alone with blocks, he talked to himself and constructed rhymes from his name: "James, Fames, Wames" (McGee & Richgels, 1996).

Later, children discover that the English writing system is alphabetic. Words do not function as logographs, with an entire word acting as a single graphic symbol. Rather, they are built from combinations of alphabet letters, where the letter is the unit of symbolization, such that, ideally, each letter stands for a sound. Equipped with this knowledge, children may name and write nearly all alphabet letters, use sound-letter correspondences to invent spellings, finger-point to read familiar texts, and use phonetic or alphabetic cues to learn some sight words for reading (Ehri & Sweet, 1991; Morris, 1983, 1993; Read, 1971). For example, five-year-old Carrie drew a picture of herself on a diving board to write the story of her day at the swimming pool, but then labeled the spots on her legs by writing MSTOBTS (mosquito bites) (Richgels, 1989). Ian could read the name *Abraham Lincoln* in a poem his kindergarten teacher had copied onto a large sheet of chart paper. When asked how he knew those words, he explained that it was because of the A, h, and L. His classmate, Lauren, read the word *old* inside the words *told* and *gold* in another chart paper poem (McGee & Richgels, 1996).

All six children in these examples were attentive to print and demonstrated knowledge and abilities crucial to their development as readers and writers. Natalie and Carrie distinguished between drawing and writing; Kristen and Ian read important printed messages; James and Lauren knew about rhyming words. The reading and writing performances of Carrie, Ian, and Lauren, however, were influenced by print in a way that those of Natalie, Kristen, and James were not. They had learned to look at print in a new way.

A significant part of that new way is phonemic awareness. Carrie's invented spelling, Ian's alphabetic word reading, and Lauren's word analysis involved conscious attention to phonemes and the letters we systematically associate with them. Natalie's scribble writing, Kristen's logo reading, and James's oral language play did not.

How do teachers help children whose understandings about written language are more like those of Natalie, Kristen, and James develop an understanding of the alphabetic nature of print? The traditional answer has been provide isolated, "skill and drill" phonics instruction. The popular answer today is direct instruction in phonemic awareness. We suggest another way.

We believe that phonemic awareness can develop in the same holistic contexts as do other aspects of children's written language knowledge. The entire process of becoming literate can originate in children's meaningful and functional encounters with print, especially when such encounters include guidance from more literate others. Some children more frequently experience such encounters at home than do other children, but all children can benefit from regularly experiencing such encounters at school. The What Can You Show Us? activity is one way that teachers can ensure that this happens. It supports children's individual, long-term learning to look at print by giving them opportunities to experiment with what they know, share with one another, and respond to their classmates' varying abilities to link form and meaning.

The What Can You Show Us? Activity

The What Can You Show Us? activity takes place along with shared reading. Typically, shared reading involves the teacher's reading aloud a large-print text on a chart or in a big book, the teacher's and students' reading the selection together, and students' doing individual activities with the selection (Holdaway, 1979). There are four elements to the What Can You Show Us? activity: preparation, previewing, student demonstrations, and applications. The first three occur before shared reading; the fourth occurs during or after shared reading.

Preparation. Preparation includes selection and display of reading materials. As with any planned reading activity, it is important to choose or compose texts that are relevant to classroom events or units of study. These will include quality children's literature and teacher-written texts, such as a recipe for a class cooking activity. If the text is a big book, the teacher displays the book on an easel clipped open to a page that contains salient text, key words, and an intriguing illustration, but that does not reveal the ending of the story. For a copied text, the teacher may use different colors of ink to highlight features he or she wants students to notice, for example, capital letters, punctuation marks, or a repeated word. Finally, the teacher may draw small, simple pictures above some content words as clues for identifying them.

Previewing. Previewing a text may begin when students enter their classroom at the beginning of their day. The teacher casually alerts them to a newly displayed text: "You might want to visit the easel as you begin your day. There is a new poem there for you." Not all students will take advantage of this opportunity, but during a later whole-class time, previewing continues. The teacher directs students' attention to the text and gives them a short time to talk with one another about what they see. Then the teacher may turn to the cover of a displayed big book and point out the title or indicate the poet's name at the bottom of a chart paper poem.

Student demonstrations. The heart of the What Can You Show Us? activity is student demonstrations. Before the teacher reads the shared reading text, he or she invites volunteers individually to step before the class and show something they know about the displayed text. This gives children the opportunity to engage with the text based on their current interests and abilities. Children may identify letters or words, or even try to read the text on their own. The teacher learns about students' interests and abilities, and the children come to appreciate what their fellow students can teach them about the text. The teacher is observer, helper, and commentator. It is very important for him or her to hold back and let students do the teaching, and to make positive, affirming comments about whatever students demonstrate.

Applications. The usual three steps of shared reading (the teacher's reading, reading together, and student activities) offer opportunities for extending and applying what students discover in What Can You Show Us? Usually the focus of student demonstrations is on letter identification, word identification, sound-letter correspondences, punctuation, and text format features. With the teacher's shared reading, the focus broadens. As the teacher reads, he or she may stop to comment about characters or plot, to invite predictions, to remark about illustrations, and to accept and respond to students' comments and questions. Still, the teacher may occasionally point out a familiar word, note punctuation, or emphasize a sound-letter correspondence. The teacher is especially watchful for opportunities to remind students of what they learned during student demonstrations.

Often the reading-together step of shared reading is repeated over several days so that students can become competent with the text. Thus, opportunities for application are not limited to the initial What Can You Show Us? activity. Before later rereadings, the teacher can invite more student demonstrations. The difference between these and the initial demonstrations is that now children will demonstrate more and different readings than when the text was new. They will have memories of their classmates' and teacher's previous performances to help them.

In the following two sections, we share examples of What Can You Show Us? from Poremba's kindergarten classroom. These examples were audio and videotaped when one of the authors made daily visits to Poremba's classroom for a year.

Uncle Wally's Letter

A 10-minute, whole-class lesson on October 4 is a good example of a What Can You Show Us? activity from the beginning of the year in Poremba's kindergarten. Every few weeks, she shared a letter she had written to her class. They pretended it was from Uncle Wally or Aunt Edith, two large, floppy, stuffed dolls who resided in the reading center. On October 4, Uncle Wally and Aunt Edith each held an apple, and Uncle Wally held an envelope containing this letter:

Dear Kindergarteners,
    It is fall!
    Fall is apple time.
    We picked an apple
    on a tree.
        Yum! Yum!
           Love,
           Uncle Wally

Poremba (Mrs. P) had drawn an apple above the two places where the word *apple* appeared and a tree above the word tree. She removed the letter from its envelope and initiated previewing:

Mrs. P: I'm going to put their letter up on the board, but I'm not going to say anything right away. I want you to start doing your thinking, and if you need to turn and tell a friend things you notice in the letter, you may.

Children: Ooo! Apples in the tree. Dear Kindergarteners. Two apples in the tree.

Then Poremba invited student demonstrations:

Mrs. P: Would somebody like to tell us about the letter? If you need a turn to tell us all, be sure you raise your hand.

Eric C. was the first to tell what he knew about the letter:

Eric: Two apples in one tree.

Mrs. P: You noticed two apples in one tree. You want to come up and show us that, Eric?

Eric: And love.

Mrs. P: Come on up and show us those important parts.

(Eric goes to the easel and points to the apple and tree drawings.)

Mrs. P: And you said you noticed something else, Eric.

Eric: (pointing) Love.

Mrs. P: You noticed *love* also. Thank you, Eric.

Nathan raised his hand for the next demonstration.

Mrs. P: Nathan, would you like to come up and show us something you need us to see?

Nathan pointed to the *K* in *Kindergarteners* and the *K* in the *KP* written in the corner of his name collar to identify him as a member of Poremba's kindergarten. Her students had worn name collars since the beginning of the year—at first so that the art, music, and gym teachers would be able to call them by name, but now because they sometimes used the written models of their names and their classmates' names. Nathan said, "This is right here that's right there too." He did not know the name of the letter K, but he would learn it from the exchange that followed.

Mrs. P: Okay, turn around and show us what's on your collar. Okay, what did you notice, Nathan?

Nathan: That's right there and that's right there.

Mrs. P:	What do you think that is, Nathan? Do you know what that is?
Children:	*K*
Nathan:	*K*
Mrs. P:	A *K*.
Child:	*KP.*
Mrs. P:	And you noticed—
Nathan:	a *K* up there.
Mrs. P:	A *K* up there in the first part, the very first letter in that big, long word. Thank you, Nathan.

Several more student demonstrations followed. Erin called out "Kindergarteners" for "that big, long word" to which Poremba had just pointed. Ian came to the easel to point to and read "Dear Kindergarteners." Then, without pointing, he read the rest of the letter as "Uncle Wally and I picked two apples in a tree for the teacher."

Jason pointed to and read "Dear Kindergarteners. Then, looking at the first words of the text (*It is*), he said, "I have" but was unable to continue. Poremba said, "Ooo, he's thinking hard." She offered Jason more thinking time, and Erin stepped up and identified the *is* in *It is*. Alyssa showed where that same word occurred in the next line and Erin proceeded to identify *on* and *apple*. Then Jason said. "I know how to read it now." He again said, "I have," paused, correctly identified individual words (*is, apple, Love,* and *on*), and finally pointed to and read the last phrase of the letter. He said, "on (pointing to *on*) my (pointing to *a*) apple tree (pointing to *tree*)." Poremba praised him, "Good reading, Jason! Good job!"

Eric D. associated individual letters with classmates' names: "The *Y* for Freddy (pointing to the *Y* in *Yum*) . . . and he has an *F* (pointing to the *F* in *Fall*) . . . and an *I* for Ian (pointing to the *I* in It). . . . There's an *e* for me (pointing to the end of *tree*)." Elise told what she thought the letter was about, "They got in an apple tree." Zack pointed to and read, "Dear Kindergarteners." Finally, Kaitlynn returned the class's attention to the letter *K*, this time in the middle of *picked* and at the beginning of her name. Her classmates joined in her discovery: "*K* for Kaitlynn!"

Next Poremba proceeded with the usual steps of shared reading. She read Uncle Wally's letter, pointing as she read. Then she and the class read the letter together. Later, as a follow-up activity, the children made paper apples to hang on a tree in their classroom.

Throughout the student demonstrations on October 4, Poremba acknowledged and accepted her students' wide range of reading strategies, always holding back in order to let them make their own discoveries and share their knowledge with one another. These demonstrations were for the class, not for her. For example, she did not provide the name for the letter *K* during Nathan's demonstration.

She let it emerge from his and his classmates' discussion. At first, Nathan did not know the name for the letter *K*; after his classmates provided the name, Nathan used it himself. Similarly, Poremba did not supply *is* to get Jason through his difficulty with *It is fall*; Erin identified that word during the next demonstration.

Poremba was pleased with each of three nonverbatim, but very different readings of the text. Ian said what seemed appropriate given that the Aunt Edith and Uncle Wally dolls were holding apples. Jason used Erin's demonstration of the word *on*, the drawing clue for *tree*, and his awareness of word boundaries and written-to-spoken-word correspondence to read *on a tree* as "on my apple tree" (treating *apple tree* as one word). Instead of quoting Uncle Wally's letter, Elise told about it; she used the third person *They* rather than the letter writer's first person *We*.

Always Poremba provided supportive talk. Besides the comments already quoted, she thanked every student for his or her demonstration and said, "Ian was using his ideas to read what he thinks the letter might say, and he has some very good ideas there.... She (Erie) knows *on*! . . . Jason, I love the way you're thinking for us. That's great."

Chicken Soup with Rice

Poremba's What Can You Show Us? activity on January 4 includes a good example of the applications element. It shows how Poremba orients children to print while facilitating connections across everyday, functional literacy activities (in this case, calendar reading, poem reading, environmental print reading, and students' individual writing). As on October 4, the entire activity described here took only 10 minutes. Ahead of time, Poremba had copied the 10-line poem "January" from *Chicken Soup With Rice* (Sendak, 1991) and an author line ("by Maurice Sendak") on chart paper, using alternating colors of ink for alternate lines. She had glued an illustration of the poem in the upper right hand corner of the chart paper and placed the poem on the easel before the children arrived.

The poem is about outdoor winter play on the ice and eating chicken soup with rice. On a chair next to the easel, Poremba placed a large, institutional-size can of Campbell's™ chicken with rice soup. The writing on the front label of the soup can was:

Campbell's
FOOD SERVICE PACK
CONDENSED
Chicken
With Rice
SOUP

For this What Can You Show Us? activity, it is important to note that the children in Poremba's classroom sign in (write their names) as part of a daily attendance routine. Each child keeps his or her sign-in sheet on a clipboard during opening-of-the-day, whole-class activities. Poremba encourages children to write (by copying, spelling, or drawing) on the sign-in sheet at any time. For example, they might copy the name of a classmate who served as helper that day, or the date as demonstrated during calendar time, or a weather word displayed during the weather report (McGee & Richgels, 1996). On January 3, Poremba had changed the heading of the sign-in sheet from "Please Sign In" to "My Sign-In Sheet, by:_____"; so on January 4 the children were still becoming acquainted with this new sign-in sheet format (see Figure 1). They had their sign-in sheets on clipboards with them for the What Can You Show Us? activity we describe here.

Poremba invited previewing ("I want you to scoot on up and take a peak at the easel here because I have a new poem") and then demonstrations ("If you look at the poem up here—is there anything up there in the poem that you know about?"). Most of the demonstrations were word identifications. For example, Erin and Tara read the word *January*, which Poremba had introduced with the new calendar the previous day. Tara noted, "It says *January* in two places." Deborah read *in* and *to*. Then Kaitlynn used information from these demonstrations to read the title and the first two words of the poem as a phrase, with emphasis on the repetition of the word *January*: "January in *January*!" Poremba commented, "Did it help when Deborah told you that word was *in*, Kaitlynn?"

Jason helped the class to focus on the author line. His pointing to the word *by* in *by Maurice Sendak* led to the following exchange:

Mrs. P: Oh, Jason, you're pointing to an important word down there. What is that word down there?
Children: *by, by*

Jason wanted to move on to the next word (he read *Maurice* as "Me"), but the other children wanted to talk more about *by*. Poremba gave lots of time for children's thinking and responding, and then prompted a connection between the author line and the new sign-in sheet format.

Children:	*by, by, by, by, by*. It's called *by*.
Mrs. P:	Is it something you can find on your sign-in sheet, Jason?
Children:	Yes. Yes, right here. Right here, Jason. Jason, it's right here. Jason right here, in ink. B-Y, *by*.

Then when another student, Freddy, pointed to the word by during his demonstration, Poremba helped children to grasp its meaning.

Mrs. P:	What is that word, Freddy?
Freddy:	*by*
Mrs. P:	*by*! What do you think, what information do you think we get down here at the bottom of the poem?
Child:	Who wrote it.
Mrs. P:	Possibly who wrote it. Sure if it says *by*—
Child:	Read it!
Mrs. P.:	I'll read it to you. It says "by Maurice Sendak." Maurice Sendak is the person who wrote this poem. It was his idea. His words—are his ideas.

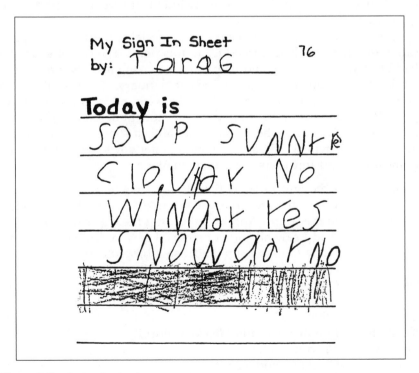

Figure 1. Tara's sign-in sheet.

As Poremba prepared the class for her reading of the poem, she told that it was one of her favorites. She invited predictions about the meaning of the poem, made a connection with yesterday's new calendar, and highlighted a sound-letter correspondence:

Mrs. P:	And I love doing it in January. I wonder why this poem is a good poem for January.
Child:	Because it's January.
Tara:	Because it's about January.
Mrs. P:	It sure is. If you look at the title of the poem, it tells us the name of our brand new month that we learned yesterday. It starts with a *J*—
Mrs. P.	and children: (together) January.

The children continued their predicting based on the poem's illustration. Then as she began reading the poem, Poremba again oriented the children to the print: "Let me read the poem to you. I just love this poem. 'January' (pointing to the title). Can you watch with your eyes as I touch the words? Are you ready?" After reading the poem, Poremba asked. "Did you like it?" Responses included, "I love it!" and "Are we going to make it?"

Then Poremba provided her students a special opportunity for application of what they had learned up to this point. The can of soup she had brought to school would be part of a cooking activity later in the week after additional shared readings of "January," but now it was to be the context for making connections between poem print and label print. Poremba held up the soup can. The student demonstrations that followed are typical of those that come after a shared reading; comments about letters, words, and sounds are interwoven with discussions of meanings and functions of written language.

Mrs. P:	I brought in something today I wanted to show you. I was at the grocery store last night . . . and I was looking in the soups. And I was reading the labels on the soups. And I saw all sorts of soups. I saw vegetable soup, and I saw tomato soup, and I saw broccoli soup, and I saw cheese soup—
Child:	Cheese soup?
Mrs. P:	—and I saw onion soup, and I saw this soup!
Child:	What is it?
Kaitlynn:	I know what it is. Chicken soup.
Mrs. P:	Do you think so?
Child:	Chicken noodle soup.
Child:	No.

Child:	Yeah! I can read it.
Child:	Chicken soup.
Child:	Chicken noodle soup.
Child:	*Chicken* starts with a *T*.
Child:	My favorite food is chicken noodle soup.
Erin:	My favorite one, my favorite soup is chicken noodle!
Mrs. P:	Is it your favorite kind?
Kaitlynn:	Me too. We're just like each other!
Mrs. P:	You agree with each other. . . . There are lots and lots of words on this soup, on this can of soup. Is there a word up here that you think you can read? On the can?
Children:	*Chicken. Chicken.*
Mrs. P:	Where do you think it says *chicken*?

Nicole pointed to the word *Campbell's*. Poremba said, "Ooo, good guess" and then explained that is the name of the company that makes the soup, Campbell's. This caused the children to laugh and joke with a classmate whose last name is Campbell ("I never knew you made soup"). Then Erin pointed to the word *Chicken* and Kaitlynn revealed that she was thinking along:

Mrs. P:	(to Erin) Now you pointed to this word right here. Why do you think that says *chicken*?
Kaitlynn:	Chi-Chi's, Chi-Chi (pronounced chee-cheez, chee-chee)
Mrs. P:	What do you think, Kait?
Kaitlynn:	Chuh.
Mrs. P:	You're thinking. You know, Erin, you're right. That is the word that says *chicken*. Right there. If you look at the chicken word right here in the poem. . . . See the *chicken* word right here in the poem? (Poremba points to and reads a line that includes the words *chicken soup with rice*.) There's the *chicken* word right there. Can you find the *soup* word?

Jason, Nicole, and Kaitlynn vied with one another to point out the word *SOUP*. Then a sound-letter correspondence discussion began:

Mrs. P:	It starts with an *S*. Well that makes a lot of sense.
Child:	I just wrote an *S*!
Tara:	I know how to spell *soup*!
Mrs. P:	If you'd like to write the word *soup* on your sign-in sheet today—
Tara:	I know how to spell *soup* without looking at the can!
Mrs. P:	Okay, how would you spell *soup*?

Tara:	S-O-U-P
Mrs. P:	Oh what a good word. Get your pencils ready for that one.
Kaitlynn:	S-O-U-P, *soup.*
Child:	(very fast) S-O-U-P!

This discussion of how to spell *soup* inspired other spelling practice. One child announced that he could spell *a*. Erin asked Jason how to spell their classmate Ian's name. Tara and Jason told her the correct spelling. Poremba continued about *soup*:

Mrs. P:	*Soup.* Do you hear the *S* in it?. . . You know what I noticed Deborah did? Some people looked at the word *soup* on the can to write *soup* (with emphasis on the /p/)-do you hear that *P* on the end, by the way? *Soup*—/p/.
Child:	*Super!*
Mrs. P:	Say the word *soup.*
Children:	(together) *soup*
Mrs. P:	*Soup.* (nodding) Do you hear the *P* on the end, Ian?
Child:	*Super*, like *super!*
Mrs. P:	Deborah looked up here at that *soup*, right there (pointing to the word *soup* in the poem).
Tara:	I don't need to look at a word. I'll spell it from, without looking at anything. I'll write it on my sign-in sheet. (See Figure 1)
Child:	I can do that too.
Child:	So can I.

Now Poremba was ready to conclude, with a promise and an invitation to do more with the "January" poem and their can of soup:

Mrs. P:	Great job! Tomorrow during our free choice time, at the snack table, we're going to have chicken soup with rice for you to taste tomorrow. We'll get to know the poem a little bit better, and I want to give you some time to look at this can and at the words that are on it. So this will be here on the blue chair today if you'd like to come up and look at it.

But the children were not ready to stop. Jason demonstrated that he too could spell *soup* without looking. Freddy showed Poremba where he had written his name on his sign-in sheet. And Ian showed where his phoneme awareness had taken him:

Ian:	Look what I spelled. I spelled *look.* (See Figure 2)

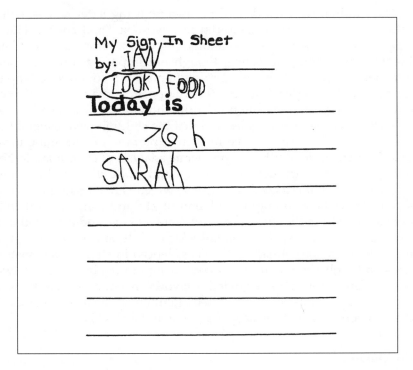

Figure 2. Ian's sign-in sheet.

Mrs. P:	You wrote *look*. That's good. That's a good word. This is a fun poem and we are going to do some more work with this poem this week, but how about if we get our [other group] work done now?
Ian:	I know what rhymes—*look* and *book*.
Mrs. P:	"*Look*" and "*book*" does rhyme.
Ian:	And they're almost spelled the same.

As on October 4, the What Can You Show Us? activity on January 4 prompted a great variety of reading performances. It also prompted writing experiences as children explored letter-sound correspondences and engaged in self-assigned practice using their sign-in sheets. In addition to Tara, six other children wrote the word *soup* on their sign-in sheets. Figure 2 shows that in addition to writing *look*, Ian copied the word *FOOD* from the soup label even though that word had never been part of a classmate's demonstration or the class discussion of the soup label.

The children read words and phrases by using letter names, letter sounds, co-occurrence of words in the two texts, and context clues. Again, they learned from one another as well as from their teacher. Poremba performed an active, though not imposing, role. She had intended to highlight the word *chicken* and the *S* sound-letter correspondence during her sharing a favorite poem and a related piece of environmental print, but the transcripts show that it was a child who first identified the word *chicken* and that the children went beyond the *S* sound-letter correspondence in their exploration of meaning-form links. For example, Kaitlynn's phonemic analysis of *chicken* led to her noting the similarity between *chicken* and *Chi-Chi's*; another child hypothesized that *chicken* starts with *T*, which is not a bad guess considering that the *ch* digraph is a blend of /t/ and /sh/; several children learned from Tara to spell *soup* without looking; and Ian noted that rhyming words are spelled similarly. Most of these ways of engaging the texts on January 4 had not been evidenced in student demonstrations on October 4. Poremba modeled using written language for two very different functions (enjoying a favorite poem and identifying a kind of soup), while she also focused attention on identity of words in the two very different formats of a poem and a food label.

Conclusion

What Can You Show Us? gives teachers an opportunity to facilitate children's emerging phonemic awareness in a meaningful manner that preserves children's initiative. One part of the teacher's active role is to observe what children know and adjust one's responses accordingly. Poremba did this when she first let word identification be the focus of Jason's and his classmates' work with the word *by*, and later, with that established, asked a meaning question ("What information do you think we get?") during Freddy's return to the same word in his demonstration. Preparation, previewing, and invitations to demonstrate ensure that students will not miss aspects of print that are important for developing phonemic awareness. The exchanges quoted in this article show that when children take the initiative, a large number of their demonstrations are print oriented. This may be due to the open nature of the invitation in What Can You Show Us? It is an invitation to students to show what they know rather than specifically to read.

What Can You Show Us? is a functional, contextualized, social literacy activity. It is about students' sharing with and learning from one another with texts that are chosen for their relevance to other classroom events and presented in their entirety.

References

Adams, M. 1990. *Beginning to read: Thinking and learning about print.* Cambridge, MA: MIT Press.

Ball, E. W., and B. A. Blachman. 1991. "Does phoneme segmentation training in kindergarten make a difference in early word recognition and developmental spelling?" *Reading Research Quarterly* 26: 49–66.

Clay, M. M. 1975. *What did I write?* Portsmouth, NH: Heinemann.

———. 1979. *Reading: The patterning of complex behavior,* 2nd ed. Portsmouth, NH: Heinemann.

Edelsky, C., B. Altwerger, and B. Flores. 1991. *Whole language: What's the difference?* Portsmouth, NH: Heinemann.

Ehri, L. C. 1989. "Movement into word reading and spelling: How spelling contributes to reading." *In Reading and writing connections,* ed. J. M. Mason, 6581. Boston: Allyn & Bacon.

———. 1991. "Development of the ability to read words." In *Handbook of reading research,* 2nd ed., ed. P. D. Pearson. New York: Longman, 395–419.

Ehri, L. C., and J. Sweet. 1991. "Finger point reading of memorized text: What enables beginners to process the print?" *Reading Research Quarterly* 26: 442–462.

Ferreiro, E. 1986. "The interplay between information and assimilation in beginning literacy." In *Emergent literacy: Writing and Reading,* ed. W. H. Teale & E. Sulzby. Norwood, NJ: Ablex, 15–49.

Goodman, Y. M., W. J. Hood, and K. S. Goodman, 1991. *Organizing for whole language.* Portsmouth, NH: Heinemann.

Griffith, P. L., and M. W. Olson. 1992. Phonemic awareness helps beginning readers break the code. *The Reading Teacher* 45: 516–523.

Holdaway, D. 1979. *The foundations of literacy.* New York: Ashton Scholastic.

Lass, B. 1982. Portrait of my son as an early reader. *The Reading Teacher* 36: 20–28.

McGee, L. M., and D. J. Richgels, 1996. *Literacy's beginnings: Supporting young readers and writers,* 2nd ed. Needham, MA: Allyn & Bacon.

Morris, D. 1983. "Concept of word and phoneme awareness in the beginning reader." *Research in the Teaching of English* 17: 359–373.

Morris, D. 1993. "The relationship between children's concept of word in text and phoneme awareness in learning to read: A longitudinal study." *Research in the Teaching of English* 27: 133–154.

Read, C. 1971. "Preschool children's knowledge of English phonology." *Harvard Educational Review* 41: 1–34.

Richgels, D. J. 1989. "Understanding and supporting children's invented spelling." *Illinois Reading Council Journal* 17: 32a–32d.

Scott, J. A., and L. C. Ehri, 1990. "Sight word reading in pre-readers: Use of logographic vs. alphabetic access routes." *Journal of Reading Behavior* 22: 149–166.

Sendak, M. 1991. *Chicken soup with rice: A book of months.* New York: HarperCollins.

Spector, J. E. 1995. "Phonemic awareness training: Application of principles of direct instruction." *Reading and Writing Quarterly: Overcoming Learning Difficulties* 11: 37–51.

Yopp, H. K. 1992. "Developing phonemic awareness in young children." *The Reading Teacher* 45: 696–703.

5 Why Talk about Phonics?

Regie Routman
Shaker Heights City Schools, Ohio

Andrea Butler
Chicago, Illinois

Routman and Butler begin by noting that the push for getting "back to basics" and for "direct instruction" as the core of a reading program currently overshadows "the goal of developing independent, thinking readers and writers," while it also ignores the literacy outcomes that were recommended in the 1992 National Assessment of Educational Progress (NAEP). However, they admit that educators have contributed to the problem by being remiss in informing parents and policymakers of current research and in explaining current practices. The major goal of this chapter, however, is not to focus on the research but to illustrate "practical suggestions for teaching phonics in the classroom without losing sight of the whole literacy context." Routman and Butler explain that good teachers have never abandoned phonics, clarify what they mean by phonics, and then describe five suggested ways to explore phonics while going from whole texts to parts, and back to the whole. The authors also discuss some of the things teachers look for in assessing their students' development of phonics knowledge. In a concluding statement, they remind us that "there is no reason to teach phonics unless our students are spending the majority of their time reading, writing, thinking, speaking, and responding to all kinds of meaningful texts."

Originally published in *School Talk, 1*(2), (1995). Copyright 1995 by the National Council of Teachers of English.

- "Bad Grades for New Age Education" (*Chicago Tribune*, May 1995)
- "Choral-Like Reading Plan Makes a Comeback" (*New York Times*, August 1995)
- "Ohio Lawmakers Must Read Phonics Bill Carefully?" (*Cleveland Plain Dealer*, July 1995)

All around the country—from New York to the Midwest to the West Coast—phonics and the teaching of reading are making headlines. In the frenzy to respond to falling test scores and the concerns of nervous parents, politicians and other "concerned groups" are lobbying hard to get "back to basics" and "direct instruction" as the core of the reading program. Unfortunately, this simplistic view overshadows the goal of developing independent, thinking readers and writers, and it also ignores the 1992 recommendations of the National Assessment of Education Progress (NAEP):

The Literacy Outcomes for the nineties should produce students who:

- construct meaning;
- elaborate and respond critically;
- exhibit effective strategic behaviors;
- know that they know how to read and write; and
- have positive habits, attitudes, and values.

Perhaps we educators share responsibility for the current political climate. We have often been remiss in informing parents and policymakers of current research and practice: without new information, parents and other members of the community hold on to old beliefs based on their own school experiences.

Our goal in this chapter is to clarify some of the dilemmas that we all are facing, and to give specific information and practical suggestions for teaching phonics in the classroom without losing sight of the whole literacy context.

Good Teachers Have Never Abandoned Phonics

We think that in the name of "whole language" and "literature-based instruction," some educators and publishers went too far. Thinking that *all* children would learn to read "naturally" if they were immersed in quality literature, many teachers abandoned formal instruction. In particular, the explicit teaching of phonics became suspect. But good teachers have never abandoned phonics. They always acknowledged that phonics had an important place in the reading and writing process, without being an end in itself. We believe the issue has never been whether or not phonics should be taught, but when, how, how much, and why.

Reading must always be viewed primarily as a meaning-making process; it is not just decoding. Emotional and political issues seem to have clouded the picture and made any discussion of phonics suspect. But phonics does need to be taught. It's all a matter of balance.

While phonics (or graphophonics) is integral to the reading process, it is subordinate to semantics (meaning, context, background knowledge) and syntactics (structure, grammar). Any one area cannot exist in isolation from the others if comprehension is to be maximized (see Figure 1).

Marie Clay explains it well in *Becoming Literate: The Construction of Inner Control:*

> Phonological information may be seen as a key variable but so are meaning, syntax, and visual information. Teaching one key variable can distort a complex process unless its learning becomes patterned with other key variables and opportunities are provided to work on the interplay between variables. (p. 314)

What Do We Mean by Phonics? What Don't We Mean?

So what are we really talking about? Let's review some common terms and clarify where phonics fits. *Phonics* generally is used to refer to the

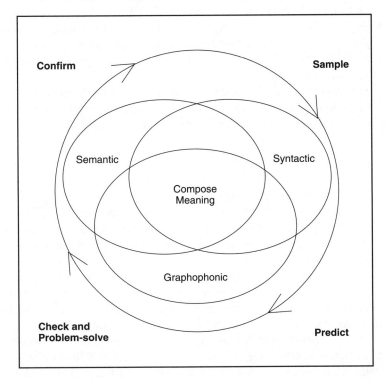

Figure 1. Place of phonics in the reading process.

sound-letter relationships used in reading and writing. Phonics begins with an understanding that each letter (or *grapheme*) of the English alphabet stands for one or more sounds (or *phonemes*). Knowledge of phonics is necessary for successful independent reading; however, young children can read predictable supportive texts without knowing all of their sounds and letters.

You also may have been hearing a lot about *phonemic awareness*. This term refers to the ability to hear and differentiate between the various words, sounds, and syllables in speech, and this ability is critical to success in beginning reading. Phonemic awareness develops through repeatedly hearing, saying, and singing traditional nursery rhymes, simple poems and songs, as well as through word-play:

> Children who have a rich knowledge of rhymes develop the ability to pay attention to sounds in words more easily. (Wells & Hart-Hewins, 1994, p. 25)

Additionally, using invented spelling in daily writing is one of the best ways for young children to develop phonemic awareness and sound-letter relationships (see Figure 2).

When we talk about phonics we do not mean worksheets and workbooks, nonsensical texts, "letter of the week," isolated scripts and drills, *Hooked on Phonics*, chanting with technical precision, and sophisticated linguistic labeling.

By contrast, by phonics we do mean teaching kids enough sound-letter knowledge to read and write continuous text in authentic literacy contexts. We'll spell that out in the rest of this chapter.

How Do We Teach Phonics?

We believe that phonics is best taught and learned when it is integrated into meaningful reading and writing across the curriculum. This does not mean that phonics teaching is left to chance. All children can benefit from whole-class, deliberate but incidental work with phonics during language arts time.

Here's what we are talking about. For some children, explicit teaching and mini-lessons are necessary. Such lessons, however, are never in isolation. The need for them grows out of what is developmentally appropriate and what is challenging children as they attempt to read and write independently. Always, most of classroom reading time must be spent reading, enjoying, and discussing wonderful literature. Phonics instruction, when it does occur, is short, specific, and related to the child's needs.

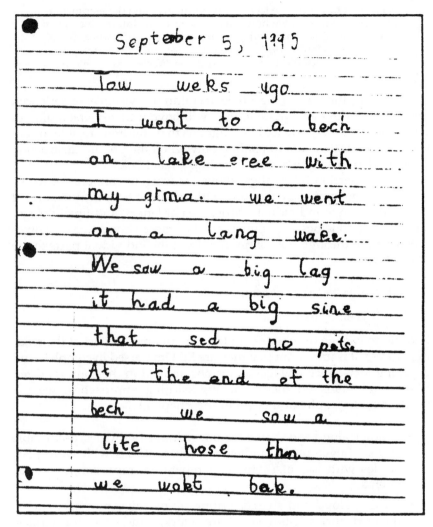

September 5, 1995

Tow weks ugo
I went to a bech
on lake eree with
my grma. we went
on a lang waee.
We saw a big lag.
it had a big sine
that sed no pats.
At the end of the
bech we saw a
lite hose then
we wokt bake.

Figure 2. Child's writing showing the use of invented spelling.

Going from Whole to Part to Whole

In all cases, we believe that children must see connections between the whole and its parts. According to recent brain research:

> The brain processes parts and wholes simultaneously. People have enormous difficulty in learning when either parts or wholes are overlooked. Good teaching necessarily builds understanding and

skills over time because learning is cumulative and developmental. However, parts and wholes are conceptually interactive. They derive meaning from and give meaning to each other. (R. N. Caine & G. Caine, 1991, *Making Connections: Teaching and the Human Brain*, Menlo Park, CA: Addison-Wesley; available from ASCD)

In reading, the book is the whole. If children have never experienced the joy of reading and writing, they will have little understanding of what phonics is. Experience has taught us that children are able to connect phonics instruction to reading only when the phonics instruction is embedded in or grows out of reading a real book.

The next section offers suggestions for ways to connect the whole to the part, beginning by working with an entire text, then looking at sentences, then at individual words, then at letters, and finally at syllables and phonemes. Of course, making these connections involves moving back through the continuum, from the individual parts to the whole text.

Suggested Ways to Explore Phonics

Start with Whole Texts

In order to engage the children in learning phonics as part of the reading process, it is important that they are first immersed in complete and engaging texts. Such engagement is encouraged in the contexts listed here. (For details on these teaching-learning approaches, see the resource bibliography at the end of this chapter.)

- Reading aloud and shared reading of: nursery rhymes, predictable stories, finger plays, riddles and jokes, stories with word-play, stories with lots of rhyme and repetition, raps, songs, chants, poems.
- Writing aloud and shared writing of: morning message, letters, dictated stories, lists, content-area work, signs, procedures, rules, language experience stories, innovations on stories, songs, and chants.
- Reading "just right" books.
- Journal entries and other free-choice writing.

Focus on Sentences

Starting with a meaningful text, sentences can be taken out of context, analyzed, cut apart, and then put back and read again in the context of the whole. These types of texts are useful starting points:

predictable stories

morning message

language experience stories

dictated stories

content-area work

letters

personal journal entries

stories with lots of rhyme and repetition

innovations on stories, songs, and chants

Focus on Words

It is appropriate to focus on words and word parts in isolation, but only as part of a larger literacy context such as writing in a content area, spelling words in a personal letter, or reading a book. Once again, we go from whole to part to whole. The best source of words are those that are familiar to the children, either through repeated readings or through stories they have authored. Activities that help focus on words include:

alliteration charts

word searches

personal dictionaries

cutting up sentences

milk carton dictionaries

masking (oral cloze) and framing

making and testing hypotheses

generating new sentences and text

writing generalizations

matching

word walls

word games

sequencing

word sorts

Focus on Letters

Young children do not necessarily understand the difference between a word and a letter, and this is an important concept for them to develop. Texts and activities that focus on letters include:

alphabet books

masking (cloze)

framing

magnetic letters

clusters and chunks

kids' names in your classroom

cutting up words into onsets and rimes plus endings

generating new words and sentences

Play with Syllables and Phonemes

Young children need to understand the alphabetic principle: Letters represent sounds, and these sounds or phonemes are represented by letters. Children need to be able to hear the sound sequences of words before they can read independently. See Marie Clay's *Becoming Literate* (p. 84) for one procedure; here are some others:

clapping

cutting

singing

working with onsets and rimes

We've mentioned onsets and rimes several times. The *onset* is the part of the syllable that comes before the vowel and is always a consonant or a consonant blend. The *rime* is the rest of the unit. Onsets and rimes are powerful for helping children to read and write because they are easier to learn than individual vowel sounds. The phonic patterns remain stable, and word families are easily constructed for reading and spelling.

For example, a child who can write and spell *meat* can be guided to read and spell *neat, eat, seat, beat*, and *heat*. In contrast, being able to read meat does not mean that the child can make the transfer to the word *meal*. It is harder for the child to isolate and apply the vowel sound than the rime.

What Phonics Generalizations Should Be Taught?

At best, phonics rules and generalizations hold up only some of the time for reading and spelling words. Generalizations are best learned by dis-

Table 1.

Starting chart to help create hypothesis about the long e sound in words.

weave	meet	Peter	key	happy	field	receive
heat	feel	meter	monkey	merry	piece	deceive
meal	see					
steal	tree					
feast	bee					
leaves	street					
reach	screen					
	steel					

covering patterns through making and testing hypotheses. For example, in a literacy context, we might have our students chart dozens of words containing the long *e* sound, (see Table 1) and then ask them which letter combinations usually represent the long *e*. Through this activity children may come up with the hypothesis, "Most of the time *ee* represents the long *e* sound." They then need to explore words in books and other print media to modify or confirm their hypothesis.

This sort of discovery method is in contrast to the teacher beginning the lesson by stating the rule and having the children search for examples of the rule. In the latter case, very little learning takes place.

Phonics in Perspective

Good teachers have always carefully observed their students to be sure the children are internalizing rules of language. Teachers notice such things as the following:

- Can the children identify all upper and lowercase letters of the alphabet?
- Can they apply phonics knowledge to reading and writing?
- Does their invented spelling reflect their growing understanding of phonics?
- Do their approximations in reading and writing make sense for their developmental level? Can they problem-solve and cross-check, demonstrating their ability to orchestrate their use of phonics in conjunction with semantics and syntax? Can they write

Marie Clay's dictation test from *An Observation Survey* (1993), demonstrating their knowledge of phonemes?

The bottom line for us is that there is no reason to teach phonics unless our students are spending the majority of their time reading, writing, thinking, speaking, and responding to all kinds of meaningful texts.

> Children's knowledge of letter names and of letter-sound relationships is not important in itself: but rather, it is a tool with which children develop principles to unlock the alphabetic nature of our writing system. Phonics is not a method for teaching reading or writing. It is only one cueing system for identifying and spelling words and should be taught as such. (British Columbia Ministry of Education, 1990, *Primary Program Foundation Document*)

Recommended Practical Texts That Support Integrated Phonics Teaching and Learning

Butler, Andrea, and Jan Turbill. 1984. *Towards a Reading–Writing Classroom*. Portsmouth, NH: Heinemann.

Clay, Marie M. 1991. *Becoming Literate: The Construction of Inner Control*. Portsmouth, NH: Heinemann.

———. 1993. *An Observation Survey of Early Literacy Achievement*. Portsmouth, NH: Heinemann.

———. 1993. *Reading Recovery: A Guidebook for Teachers in Training*. Portsmouth, NH: Heinemann.

Cunningham, Patricia M. 1995. *Phonics They Use: Words for Reading and Writing*, 2nd ed. New York: HarperCollins.

Holdaway, Don. 1979. *The Foundations of Literacy*. Portsmouth, NH: Heinemann.

———. 1990. *Independence in Reading*, 3rd ed. Portsmouth, NH: Heinemann.

Mills, Heidi, Timothy O'Keefe, and Diane Stephens. 1992. *Looking Closely: Exploring the Role of Phonics in One Whole Language Classroom*. Urbana. IL: NCTE.

Phenix, Jo. 1994. *Teaching the Skills*. Markham, Ontario: Pembroke (available from Bothell, WA: The Wright Group).

Powell, Debbie, and David Hornsby. 1993. *Learning Phonics and Spelling in a Whole Language Classroom*. New York: Scholastic.

Routman, Regie. 1994. *Invitations: Changing as Teachers and Learners K–12*, updated ed. Portsmouth, NH: Heinemann.

Weaver, Connie. 1994. *Reading Process and Practice: From SocioPsycholinguistics to Whole Language*, 2nd ed. Portsmouth, NH: Heinemann.

Wells, Jan, and Linda Hart-Hewins. 1994. *Phonics, Too! How to Teach Skills in a Balanced Language Program*. Markham, Ontario: Pembroke (available from Bothell, WA: The Wright Group).

Wilde, Sandra. 1992. *You Kan Red This! Spelling and Punctuation for Whole Language Classrooms, K–6*. Portsmouth, NH: Heinemann.

Books That Promote Phonemic Awareness

Chapman, Cheryl. *Pass the Fritters. Critters.*
Degen, Bruce. *Jamberry.*
Emberley, Barbara. *Drummer Hoff.*
Hopkins, Lee Bennett, ed. *Good Books, Good Times.*
Lester, Alison. *I'm Green and I'm Grumpy.*
Shaw, Nancy. *Sheep On a Ship.*

ABC Books

Base, Graeme. *Animalia.*
Bayer, Jane. *A My Name Is Alice.*
Brown, Margaret Wise. *Sleepy ABC.*
Cushman, Doug. *The ABC Mystery.*
Hausman, Gerald. *Turtle Island ABC: A Gathering of Native American Symbols.*
Viorst, Judith. *The Alphabet from Z to A: With Much Confusion on the Way.*
Weeks, Sarah. *Hurricane City.*
Zimmerman, Andrea G., and David Clemesha. *The Cow Buzzed.*

6 Learning Phonics while Sharing and Responding to Literature

Debbie Powell
University of Northern Colorado, Greeley

David Hornsby
Ringwood Heights Primary School
Melbourne, Australia

Drawing upon their experience with the ways phonics is taught in many "whole language" schools in Australia and New Zealand, the authors illustrate various kinds of activities that can derive from reading and discussing one particular book, *Possum Magic*, by Mem Fox (Harcourt Brace, 1983). Most of the examples were supplied by particular classroom teachers, from kindergarten through grade 2. Powell and Hornsby warn, however, that "there is no need to milk a book dry of skills and bore your students in the process." As they write here, "It is better to use the skills possibilities available in a variety of literature and other authentic texts."

Editor's note: In the literature chapter of Powell and Hornsby's *Learning Phonics and Spelling in a Whole Language Classroom*, a section on sharing and responding to literature includes other kinds of activities, too: singing the alphabet song and saying ABC rhymes, as well as making first-letter dictionaries, alphabet boxes, and alphabet books.

Originally published in Debbie Powell and David Hornsby, *Learning Phonics and Spelling in a Whole Language Classroom* (New York: Scholastic, 1993), pp. 44–52. Reprinted by permission of Sscholastic, Inc.

As you use literature and other texts, you also will be able to use many of the procedures we have included in this chapter to help your students learn graphophonic connections. The procedures employ inductive approaches that encourage risk-taking and promote discovery of language generalizations.

Sharing and Responding to Literature

During daily reading workshops, your students will be reading various texts, and the following example will show you how they can focus on reading for meaning while still learning phonics and spelling. In this illustration, second-grade teacher Helen Farthing used a shared text, *Possum Magic*, by Mem Fox (Harcourt Brace Jovanovich, 1983), a favorite piece of children's literature.

Making Connections with Literature

Because her students had enjoyed many of Mem Fox's other books, Helen was sure that this book would also be a favorite. Although many of her students were reading independently, there were still a few novice and emergent readers in the group. As a result, Helen decided that a shared book approach with the whole class would be appropriate. After introducing *Possum Magic*, Helen responded to the excited comments of the children who had already seen or heard the book, and then she quickly went on to read it with expression and enthusiasm. Although she stopped and responded to the children's comments and questions, she kept her pauses brief because she wanted to read the whole story before she actively encouraged oral responses and questions.

The students' subsequent discussion took some time because they talked about characters, their favorite parts, their own experiences with possums, and the illustrations—especially the way illustrator Julie Vivas used ghosted outlines for the invisible Hush. After several children added comments about other Mem Fox books, a few asked if they could read the book again. This time Helen invited them to read along with her. Afterwards, as the children identified the Australian animals, cities, and foods, she listed them on a piece of chart paper and hung it at eye level.

Later, during reading time, Helen made copies of the book available. Two children laid down on the floor with the big book, several pairs of children read from the library's two hardback copies, and several of the small versions (published as companions to the big book) were chosen by children who tucked themselves away in the reading corner for some quiet reading time. Three children spontaneously gathered in the art corner after reading the book to make stick puppets, an activity they had done as a class-response activity with a previous book. One made Hush, one made Grandma Poss, and one designed a ghostly figure of Hush. Afterwards, they went off to write a script for their puppet play.

Because Helen wanted to introduce one small group to story mapping, she prepared a map of Australia, which she traced from an overhead image projected onto a large sheet of paper. Then she distributed a set of atlases and asked the children if they could find any of the places named in *Possum Magic*. Together they used this information to mark on the map the places that Grandma Poss and Hush visited in their search for the right foods.

Over the next few days, Helen captured magic moments for skill development by conducting a series of lessons using *Possum Magic*. She planned instruction in the building of word families by beginning with rhyming words from the book and then brainstorming others. The children offered such words as *pink, shrink, think, stink, link, mink, rink, sink,* and *wink*. At one point, when Martin suggested the word *zinc*, the following exchange took place.

Helen:	Yes, *zinc* certainly rhymes with the words on our list. Let me write it here on the chalkboard so we can have a look. (She wrote *zink.)* Could that be right?
Children:	(There was general agreement that her spelling could be correct.)
Helen:	Listen to the sound at the end of our list of words. What other letter could we use for that sound?
Children:	It could be a *c*.
Helen:	Right! We actually spell *zinc* like this. (She wrote *zinc* on the board to the right of the *-ink* word list.)

Then Helen continued her instruction with the building of words that contained the *-ink* cluster by adding suffixes and prefixes to form words such as *stink, stinks, stinker, stinking; think, thinks, thinking,* and *unthinking*.

Two days later, she asked a small group of children with whom she was working to find and list all words containing the /o/ sound (traditionally referred to as the "short o" sound) in *Possum Magic*. They found the following words. As the children called them out, Helen wrote them on a chart.

upon	not	possums	Poss
wombats	of	crossed	from
what	on	body	stop
because*	squashed*	want*	was*

*NOTE: The examples used here were identified by Australian children living in Melbourne. Because the classifications were made according to their dialect, some will be different for children from other English-speaking countries. You may even have dialect differences within your classroom which would result in a single word being classified differently.

Helen and her students then classified the words above according to the spelling for the /ŏ/ sound as follows.

o	upon	not	possums
	Poss	wombats	of
	from	crossed	on
	body	stop	
a	squashed	what	was
au	because		

Helen then wrote the words on the following chart (Figure 1), which included words containing the /o/ sound that they had started some weeks earlier. (Similar charts can include words that have the same sound but different spellings for that sound.

Helen linked these activities to *Possum Magic* because these skills, which her students needed, were more meaningful when learned in context. Although she wants the children to be hooked on books, she also wants them to have the skills they will need to become lifelong readers and writers.

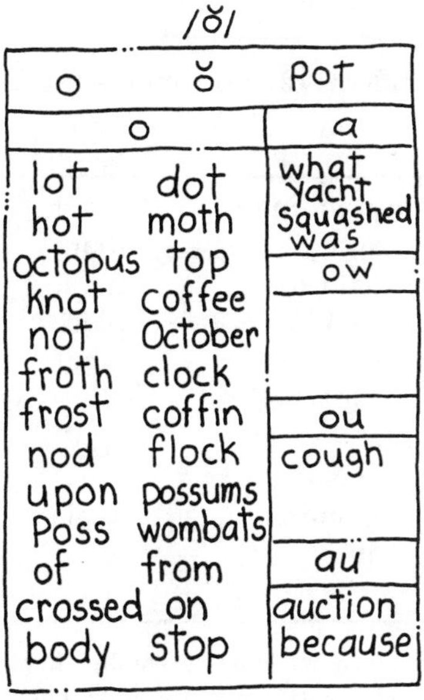

Figure 1. Helen's chart.

Possibilities: More Magic Moments

Since all text is language, all texts have numerous possibilities for highlighting different aspects of language. There is no need to milk a book dry of skills and bore your students in the process; it is better to use the skills possibilities available in a variety of literature and other authentic texts. However, to consider further possibilities for *Possum Magic,* we describe below alternative activities used by Marilyn Perry, another second-grade teacher. She chose different phonics and spelling patterns from *Possum Magic* because her children's needs were different.

Letter and Sound Search

One of the activities that Marilyn had her students do was to list words in *Possum Magic* that contain the letter *a*.

a	ago	names	grandma
made	all	and	magic
kookaburra	that	was	what
adventure	because	squashed	safe
had	wombats	snakes	koala

Then she and her students categorized the list according to the letter-sound relationships.

à	(æ)	grandma	magic	wombats
		and	that	
ä	(el)	names	made	safe
		snakes	place	day
ó	(o)	was*	what	because*
		squashed*		
ù	(/\)	a*	ago*	kookaburra*
		koala*		
ar	(a:)	grandma	koala	
or	(:)	all		

*NOTE: These classifications were made by the children in Marilyn's class. Dialect differences will determine how children classify the sounds. Linguistically, the vowel sound in *a, ago, kookabaurra,* and *koala* is actually the schwa sound.

As you do this activity in your classroom, keep in mind that your goal is to help your students learn about patterns of spelling. You shouldn't be overly concerned about differences in sound or correctness in the classification of the sound.

Other Skill Activities

Marilyn also decided to have her students focus on word endings, contractions, and opposites. The important point to consider when doing activities like these is that by helping your students learn about letters and the sounds they represent, they will become better spellers.

Word Endings:	squash<u>ed</u>	look<u>ed</u>	shout<u>ed</u>
	remain<u>ed</u>	cross<u>ed</u>	breath<u>ed</u>
	appear<u>ed</u>	wait<u>ed</u>	danc<u>ed</u>
	clos<u>ed</u>	work<u>ed</u>	nibbl<u>ed</u>
Contractions:	could<u>n't</u>	was<u>n't</u>	do<u>n't</u>
	ca<u>n't</u>	we<u>'ll</u>	they<u>'d</u>
	let<u>'s</u>		
Opposites:	visible/invisible	expected/unexpected	

Activities with Initial Letters for K–1

The previous activities are appropriate during the second half of grade 1 and higher, but there are different activities—still based on *Possum Magic*—you could use for kindergarten through the first half of grade 1.

K–1 Activities

Gayle Baker chose the following passage from *Possum Magic*.

> *Later, on a beach in Perth, they ate a piece of pavlova.*
> *Hush's legs appeared.*
> *So did her body.*
> *"You look wonderful you precious possum!" said Grandma Poss.*
> *"Next Stop—Tasmania." And over the sea they went.*

Then she wrote the following words from that passage on a chart.

Perth
piece of pavlova
precious possum

With these words, her students then composed the following tongue twister, which they all had fun trying to say quickly.

The precious possum had a piece of pavlova in Perth.

Gayle then began the following chart of words beginning with p, and during the next few days she added other *p* words. She included the *p* words from the story at the beginning of the chart—even though she didn't expect these words to become sight words for her early-primary level children.

Pp		
Perth	pavlova	precious
possum	Patrick	party
puppy	Paul	pink

Because poetry often contains alliteration, Gayle purposely selected poems that contain a high incidence of the letter p to read to her children, to further draw their attention to this letter. For example, after reading "Peter, Peter Pumpkin Eater" and the Southern American folk song "The Pawpaw Patch," her students added the following words to the class's chart of words starting with *p*.

Peter	pumpkin	pretty	pawpaw
picking	putting	pocket	patch

Eventually Gayle hung the letter chart on the wall—at the children's eye level—to encourage them to continue to add words on their own. The class made the following two charts.

Aa			Mm	
They ate Anzaac biscuits in Adelaide			Mornay and Minties in Melbourne	
Anzaac	ate	act	Mornay	Minties
Adelaide	Andy	acorn	Melbourne	munch
ape	add	animal	Monday	Morn

There are many other activities that will help your students learn the letters of the alphabet and initial letter-sound correspondence. Knowing the names of the letters is necessary metalinguistic knowledge if children are going to be able to talk about their language.

7 Looking for Patterns: Phonics Activities That Help Children Notice How Words Work

Patricia M. Cunningham
Wake Forest University

Cunningham's approach to teaching phonics, spelling, and vocabulary skills avoids teaching phonics first; focuses on onsets and rimes before individual phonemes (though some onsets *are* individual phonemes); involves teachers and children working interactively; engages children in thinking and working collaboratively; and teaches children how to apply what they are learning, though the learning is initially promoted out of context. The phonics is sometimes decontextualized and taught systematically and more thoroughly than in many whole language classrooms, but seems to share with whole language approaches an underlying constructivist theory of learning. For more details and examples, see Cunningham's *Phonics They Use* (Harper Collins, 1995).

Cunningham begins by describing some of the things we've learned about phonics, spelling, and word identification, through brain research and other psycholinguistic research. She points out that we read words by recognizing familiar letter patterns—in effect, reading by analogy (see Moustafa, Chapter 2). She also demonstrates how readers deal with big words in pronounceable "chunks," which again are familiar patterns. Noting that some children, "through lots of reading and writing, learn to read and spell many words and then figure out how to use the patterns found in these words to read and spell other words," Cunningham also notes that other children "read and write and learn some words but never quite figure out 'how it works.'" Thus, the various word activities that follow are designed to nudge children into this understanding. The first three activities—Rounding Up the Rhymes, Making Words, and What Looks Right?—are most appropriate in the primary grades. The final activities—Word Detectives, Prefixes and Suffixes, and Root Words—span the grade levels from grade three through high school. The article includes lists of common prefixes, suffixes, and Latin/Greek roots that occur in a lot of English words.

The issues of word recognition, and particularly of phonics, have seldom been associated with the concept of balanced reading instruction. Many educators believe that phonics is an all-or-nothing proposition. People are either for it or against it. It doesn't have to be that way, and more children would become fluent readers earlier if more schools approached word recognition and phonics in the way that teachers do in other countries. Phonics is part of the program—but it is not the program.

As they engage in reading and writing, children grow in their understanding of how our alphabetic language works. They learn that English is not a language in which one sound is always represented by one letter and that "spelling it the way it sounds" will often result in a word you can read but not the conventional spelling of that word. They also learn that "sounding out" an unknown word when reading is easier said than done. The letter-sound relationships in English are complex but they do exist. It is strange that r-i-g-h-t is the right way to spell *right* and -t-i-o-n spells the "shun" part of *vacation*. But there is "method to the madness." If you can read the word *right*, you can also read *tight*, *fight* and *blight*. The *-tion* at the end of *vacation* works the same way as it does at the end of *nation*, *action*, *election* and hundreds of other words that end in -t-i-o-n.

For a long time, the phonics debate centered on whether to teach using a synthetic or analytic approach. Synthetic approaches generally teach children to go letter by letter, assigning a pronunciation to each letter and then blending individual letters together. Analytic approaches teach rules. (The *e* on the end makes the vowel long.) Brain research, however, suggests that the brain is a pattern detector, not a rule applier, and that, while we look at single letters, we are not assigning them sounds; rather we are looking at clusters of letters and considering the letter patterns we know (Adams, 1990).

Although it is possible to read without any internal speech, we rarely do. Most of the time as we read, we think the words in our mind. This phonological information is then checked with the information we received visually by analyzing the word for familiar spelling patterns. Good readers use context to see if what they are reading makes sense. Context is also important for disambiguating the meaning of some words. (I had a *ball* throwing the *ball* at the *ball*.) Occasionally, readers use context to figure out words. Most of the time, however, words are identified based on their familiar spelling and the association of that spelling with a pronunciation.

When presented with unfamiliar but phonetically regular words such as *swoop* or *quest*, good readers immediately and seemingly effortlessly assign them a pronunciation. This happens so quickly that readers are often unaware that they have not seen the word before and that they had to "figure it out." Successful decoding occurs when the brain recognizes a familiar spelling pattern or, if the pattern itself is not familiar, searches through its store of words with similar patterns. *Swoop* and *quest* could be quickly decoded or spelled by using the similar known words, *loop, troop, best, west*. This process of using other words with similar patterns to figure out the unfamiliar word is commonly called decoding by analogy (Adams, 1990; Goswami & Bryant, 1990).

When the word to be identified is a big word, readers "chunk" or divide the word into manageable units. They do this based on the brain's incredible knowledge of which letters go together in words. A reader who did not immediately recognize the word *midnight* in print would divide between the *d* and the *n*. Seeing the word *Madrid* for the first time, the reader would divide after the *a*, leaving the *dr* together. Letters such as *dr* which are often seen together in the syllables of words (*drop, dry, Dracula*) "pull" together. Letters such as *dn* that are almost never seen following each other in the same syllable "pull" apart (Adams, 1990, Mewhort & Campbell, 1981). Big words are also decoded and spelled based on patterns from other words. The big word *morphophobia* is probably recognized as beginning like *morphology* and ending in *phobia*. For big words there is often a meaning link between words in addition to the sound-spelling links. Morphophobia, for example, is the condition some middle-school readers suffer from—fear of big words.

While the nature of the relationship is not completely clear, there is a strong relationship between reading level and morphological knowledge. Freyd and Baron (1982) investigated the extent to which readers' use of structural analysis is related to their reading ability. They found a strong relationship and concluded that skilled readers use structural analysis in three ways: to recognize known words more efficiently, to remember the meanings and spellings of partially learned words, and to figure out the meanings and pronunciations of new words.

To try to summarize what the brain does to identify words is to run the risk of oversimplification, but seems necessary if we want our instructional practices to be compatible with what we know about brain processes. As we read, we look very quickly at almost all letters of each word. For most words, this visual information is recognized as familiar patterns with which spoken words are identified and pronounced (aloud or through internal speech). Words we have read before are instantly recognized as we see them. Words we have not read before are almost instantly recognized based on spelling patterns the brain has seen in other words. Big words are "chunked" based on patterns that usually go together in other big words. Meanings are accessed through visual word recognition but the sounds of words support the visual information and help to hold words in memory.

Because patterns exist in words, they are there for children to find. Some children, through lots of reading and writing, learn to read and spell many words and then figure out how to use the patterns found in these words to read and spell other words. Other children read and write and learn some words but never quite figure out "how it works." All of the word activities described in the following section are designed to nudge children along in this understanding. The first three activities are most appropriate in the primary grades. The final activities span the grade levels from grade three through high school.

Rounding up the Rhymes

Rounding up the Rhymes is an activity to follow up the reading of a book, story, or poem that contains many rhyming words. Here is an example using that timeless book, *In a People House* (LeSieg, 1972).

The first (and often second) reading of anything should be focused on meaning and enjoyment. When reading *In A People House*, there is mcuh to think about and enjoy. As the mouse shows the bird what is in a people house, children encounter wonderful "Seussian" language and pictures. Mundane things such as bottles, brooms, and pillows come to life as the bird and the mouse juggle them, fly them and fight with them. Some words and pictures will require some explanation of "life in the old days" as today's children ponder the use of a cup and saucer, thread, and marbles.

Returning to the book for the second or third time, we draw the children's attention to the rhyming words. As we read each page or two, we encourage the children to chime in and try to "hear the rhymes they are saying." (We used to ask them to listen for the rhymes *we* were saying but have discovered that children with limited phonemic awareness are much more successful hearing rhymes when they say the words and hear—and feel—themselves making the rhyme.) As children tell us the rhyming words, we write them on index cards and put them in a pocket chart. Often children are confused about what rhyme means, and are particularly confused about the difference between "begins alike," "ends alike," and "rhymes." These children may offer words that begin alike when asked for rhyming words. We try to respond to their thinking in a way that encourages their continued participation and helps them clear up their confusion. If a child told us that *piano, peanuts, popcorn,* and *pails* rhymed, we would respond with something like:

> Let's all say *piano-peanuts-popcorn-pails.* That was very good thinking because *piano, peanuts, popcorn,* and *pails* do sound alike. But the sound is the beginning sound. Say them slowly and 'stretch out' the words. Do you hear the *p* at the beginning? *Piano, peanuts, popcorn,* and *pails* all begin with the same sound. But they don't rhyme. Say the words with me again and see if you can hear the rhyming words—*piano-peanuts-popcorn-pails-pencil-paper-hammer-nails.* Yes, *pails* and *nails* are the rhyming words.

I will write *pails* and *nails* on these index cards and stick them in the pocket chart.

We continue having children chime in with us as we read the pages until we have six or seven sets of rhyming words in the pocket chart. (If, as with *In a People House,* there are many more rhyming words, you could round up the remaining rhymes in a second rounding-up activity based on the same book. In order to avoid confusing and frustrating some children, however, you don't want more than seven sets of rhyming words for any one activity). Here are the rhyming words that would be in the pocket chart after reading the first half of the book:

mouse	chairs	brooms	thread	door	pails
house	stairs	rooms	bed	more	nails
				floor	

Because we limit lessons to fifteen to twenty minutes, the next part of the Rounding up the Rhymes activity usually occurs on the next day. We begin by having the children chime in on another rereading of *In a People House,* stopping after each page or two to identify the rhyming words we have rounded up in the pocket chart. We then say something like,"Now we know that all these words rhyme. Our job today is to look very closely and see which ones have the same spelling pattern."

We remind (or explain) that the spelling pattern in a short word includes all the letters beginning with the first vowel and going to the end of the word. After naming the vowels—*a; e; i; o; u*—we pick up the first set of rhyming words mouse and house, have the children tell us the spelling pattern in each—*o-u-s-e*— and underline the spelling pattern. We decide that h<u>ouse</u> and m<u>ouse</u> rhyme and have the same spelling pattern. We emphasize that we can *hear* the rhyme and *see* the spelling pattern. We put h<u>ouse</u> and m<u>ouse</u> with their underlined spelling pattern back in the pocket chart and pick up the next set of rhymes—*chairs* and *stairs.* Repeating the procedure, we get

-<u>airs</u> underlined in both, decide they have the same spelling pattern, and put them back. We do the same for br<u>ooms</u> and r<u>ooms</u>.

Next we pick up *thread* and *bed*. We say them together and hear once more that they do rhyme. We then underline the spelling patterns-<u>ead</u>; <u>ed</u>. They do rhyme, but they have a different spelling pattern. We remind the children that words that rhyme usually have the same spelling pattern but that sometimes they have different spelling patterns. Because we want to have in our pocket chart only words that rhyme and have the same spelling pattern, we toss *thread* and *bed* in the trash can. (Throwing these cards away is hard for some teachers to do, but doing so has a dramatic effect on the children. An alternative is to put these aside and then pull them out again on another day when you are doing a lesson on different spelling patterns for the same rhyme.) Next we take d<u>oor</u>, m<u>ore</u>, and fl<u>oor</u>, underline the spelling patterns and return *door* and *floor* to the pocket chart and throw away *more*. Finally, we underline the spelling patterns in p<u>ails</u> and n<u>ails</u>, decide they are the same and return them to the pocket chart.

We now have five sets of words that rhyme and have the same spelling pattern in our pocket chart:

| h<u>ouse</u> | ch<u>airs</u> | br<u>ooms</u> | d<u>oor</u> | p<u>ails</u> |
| m<u>ouse</u> | st<u>airs</u> | r<u>ooms</u> | fl<u>oor</u> | n<u>ails</u> |

The final part of this activity is to use these words to read and write some other words. This is the transfer step and is critical to the success of this activity for children who "only learn what we teach." So far, we have taught what rhyming words are and that many words that rhyme have the same spelling pattern. If we don't show them how to use this to decode and spell new words, they have not learned anything they can actually use. We begin the transfer part of this activity by telling children something like,

> You know that when you are reading books and writing stories, there are many words you have to figure out. One way many people figure out how to read and spell new words is to see if they already know any rhyming words or words that have the same spelling pattern. I am going to write some words and you can see which words with the same spelling pattern will help you read them. Then, we are going to try to spell some words by deciding if they rhyme with any of the words in our pocket chart.

Next we write two or three words which rhyme and have the same spelling pattern as the sets of words in our pocket chart. As we write each word, the children help us to decide which letters to underline for the spelling pattern and then a child puts that word in the pocket chart under the other words with the same spelling pattern. We then use the rhyme to decode the words.

Finally, we remind the children that thinking of rhyming words can help them spell words when they are writing. We say something like,

> What if you were writing and wanted to tell how your new bike zooms down the road. Let's see if we can find some words that rhyme with *zooms* and probably have the same spelling pattern.

We then lead the children to say the rhyming words and *zooms*— "*mouse, house, zooms; chairs, stairs, zooms; brooms, rooms, zooms.*" After deciding that *zooms* rhymes with *brooms* and *rooms*, they help the teacher to spell *zooms*. She writes *zooms* and puts it in the pocket chart under *brooms* and *rooms*.

Here are the words rounded up from *In a People House*, along with the new words read and spelled based on their rhymes and spelling patterns at the conclusion of this activity.

h<u>ouse</u>	ch<u>airs</u>	br<u>ooms</u>	d<u>oor</u>	p<u>ails</u>
m<u>ouse</u>	st<u>airs</u>	r<u>ooms</u>	fl<u>oor</u>	n<u>ails</u>
bl<u>ouse</u>	p<u>airs</u>	z<u>ooms</u>	p<u>oor</u>	sn<u>ails</u>

Rounding up the Rhymes is enormously popular with children. They all enjoy chiming in on the reading and rereading of the books. It is also a multilevel activity, an activity that has something for everyone. Struggling readers and writers whose phonemic awareness is limited learn what rhymes are and how to distinguish rhymes from beginning sounds. Other children whose phonemic awareness is more developed may learn spelling patterns and also that words that rhyme often share the same spelling pattern. Our most advanced readers and writers become proficient at the strategy of using words they know to decode and spell unknown words. This proficiency shows in their increased reading fluency and in the more sophisticated nature of the invented spellings in their writing.

Making Words

Making Words (Cunningham & Cunningham, 1992) is an activity in which children are given some letters and use these letters to make words. They make little words and then bigger words until the final word is made. The final word—the secret word—always indudes all the letters they have and children are eager to figure out what the word is. After making words, they put the letter cards away and the teacher leads them to sort the words into patterns and then use those patterns to decode and spell some new words. (The final step in Making Words is just like the final step in Rounding up the Rhymes.)

Here is a sample lesson. The children have the vowels *a* and *i* and the consonants *c*, *h*, *n*, *p*, and *s*. In the pocket chart at the front of the room, the teacher has large cards with the same letters. Her cards, like the small letter cards used by the children, have the uppercase letter on one side and lowercase letter on the other side. The consonants are written in black and the two vowels are in red.

The teacher begins by making sure that each child has all the letters needed. "What two vowels will we use to make words today?" she asks. The children hold up their red *i* and *a* and respond appropriately.

The teacher then writes a 3 on the board and says,

"Let's begin with some three-letter words. Take three letters and make *nap*. Everyone say *nap*. The children quickly spell *nap* in their holders and one child who has it made correctly is tapped to go and spell *nap* with the pocket chart letters. The teacher puts the index card with the word *nap* in the pocket chart.

Next, she says, "Just change your vowel and you can change *nap* to *nip*. Everyone say *nip*. A little dog will nip at your shoes." The children make *nip* and then make four more three-letter words—*sip*, *sap*, *pin*, and *pan*.

The teacher erases the 3 and writes a 4 on the board and tells them to add just one letter to *pan* and they can make the word *span*. Because this word is unfamiliar to some children, the teacher explains that the part of a bridge that goes over the river is called the span. "We say that the bridge spans the river. We also talk about how long an animal lives by calling it the life-*span*. The average life-*span* of a dog is about twelve years." If no connection can be made for this word, the teacher would just eliminate it from the lesson.

Next they change one letter to change *span* to *spin*. At this point, the teacher says, "Don't take any letters out and don't add any. Just change where the letters are and you can change *spin* into *snip*."

They then make two more four-letter words, *snap* and *pain*.

The teacher erases the 4 and writes a 5 and they use five of their letters to make the word *Spain*.

The teacher ends the word-making part of the lesson as she always does by asking, "Has anyone figured out the secret word—the word that can be made with all the letters? If you know, make that word in your holder and I will come and see what you have."

The teacher walks around and finds two children who have figured out the secret word. "This was a hard secret word today," she says as she sends both children to the pocket chart and jointly they manipulate all the letters to make the big word. As they get almost to the end, the other children realize what the word is.

"It's *spinach*!" they shout in amazement.

Several children make faces—presumably because spinach is not their favorite food and then they all make *spinach* in their holders.

After all the children have *spinach* made in their holders, the teacher has them close their holders and together they read all the words they have made which were lined up in the pocket chart:

nap nip sip sap pin pan span spin snip snap pain Spain spinach

The children know that after making words, they sort these words into patterns and then use these words to read and spell other words. The patterns they sort for include beginning letters, endings (*s, ed, ing, er, est*) and rhyming words. Today's lesson includes only words that begin with *s, p, n, sp,* or *sn*. The teacher has them sort the words according to the beginning letters, which the children know are all the letters up to the vowel. The words sorted for beginning letters look like this:

nap	*sip*	*pan*	*span*	*snap*
nip	*sap*	*pin*	*spin*	*snip*
		pain	*Spain*	
			spinach	

The teacher helps the children notice the beginning sounds and particularly the sound of *sp* and *sn* blended together at the beginning of words.

The next sort is for the rhyming words. The teacher asks "Who can come and find some rhyming words that will help us spell and read other words?" Several children come up, and the words sorted into rhymes look like this:

nap	*nip*	*pin*	*pan*	*pain*
sap	*sip*	*spin*	*span*	*Spain*
snap	*snip*			

When the rhymes are sorted out, the teacher writes on index cards a few new words such as *flip* and *twin* which can be decoded based on these rhymes. The children put the new words under the words with the same spelling pattern and use the pattern and the rhyme to figure out the words. Finally, the teacher reminds the children that thinking of rhymes can help them when they are writing too.

"What if you were writing and you wanted to write, *We set a trap to catch the mouse in our house*, how would you spell *trap*?"

The children decide that *trap* rhymes with *nap*, *sap*, and *snap* and will probably be spelled *t-r-a-p*. *Trap* is written on an index card and put with its rhyming counterparts. A similar procedure is used to decide that *brain* rhymes with *pain* and *Spain* and is probably spelled *b-r-a-i-n*.

Like Rounding up the Rhymes, Making Words activities help children look at words, sort those words into patterns, and use those patterns to read and spell some other words. Making Words is also a multilevel activity. Advanced readers are challenged to figure out the secret word and learn how thinking of rhymes and spelling patterns helps you read and spell lots of other words. Struggling readers are usually able to make some of the shorter words and change the vowels to make new words. They also develop phonemic awareness as they stretch out words while making them and sort the words made into beginning letter and rhyming patterns.

What Looks Right?

What Looks Right? is an activity through which children learn that good spelling requires visual memory and how to use their visual memory for words along with a dictionary to determine the correct spelling of a word. In English, words that have the same spelling pattern usually rhyme. If you are reading and you come to the unknown words *plight* and *trite* you can easily figure out their pronunciation by accessing the pronunciation associated with other *-ight* or *-ite* words you can read and spell. The fact that there are two common spelling patterns with the same pronunciation is not a problem when you are trying to read an unfamiliar-in-print word, but it is a problem when you are trying to spell it. If you were writing and trying to spell *trite* or *plight*, they could as easily be spelled *t-r-i-g-h-t* and *p-l-i-t-e*. The only way to know which is the correct spelling is to write it one way and see if it "looks right" or check your probable spelling in a dictionary. What Looks Right? is an activity to help children learn how to use these two important self-monitoring spelling strategies.

Here is a sample lesson for the *-ite/-ight* pattern. Using an overhead or the board, create two columns and head each column with a word, such as *bite* and *fight*, which most of your children can both read and spell. Have the children set up two columns on their paper to match your model. Have the children pronounce and spell the words and lead them to realize that the words rhyme but have a different spelling pattern. Tell them that there are many words that rhyme with *bite* and *fight* and that you can't tell by just saying the words which spelling patterns they will have. Next, say a word that rhymes with *bite* and *fight* and write it both ways, saying, "If *kite* is spelled like *bite* it will be *k-i-t-e*; if it is spelled like *fight* it will be *k-i-g-h-t*." Write these two possible spellings under the appropriate word.

Tell the children to decide which one "looks right" to them and to only write the one they think is correct. As soon as each child decides which one looks right and writes it in the correct column, have children work collaboratively to find that word in the dictionary. If they cannot find the one that looked right, then have them look up the other possible spelling. Compare what they have found, then erase or cross out the spelling you wrote that is not correct and continue with some more examples. For each word, say something like, "If it is spelled like *bite* it will be *f-l-i-t-e* but if it is spelled like *fight*, it will be *f- l-i-g-h-t*." Write the word both ways and have each child write it the way it looks right and then look in the dictionary to see if the word is spelled the way the child thought.

When you get to words such as *site/sight* and *mite/might* write them both ways and have children discover when they go to the dictionary that both spellings create words and that the dictionary—a most helpful book—will let them know which spelling has which meaning.

Here is what your columns of words would look like after several examples:

bite	*fight*
kite	~~*kight*~~
quite	~~*quight*~~
spite	~~*spight*~~
~~*tite*~~	*tight*
~~*mite*~~	*might*
~~*frite*~~	*fright*
site	*sight*
~~*flite*~~	*flight*

To make your lesson more multilevel, include some longer words such as *invite, delight, unite,* and *polite* in which the last syllable rhymes with *bite* and *fight*. Proceed just as before to write the word both ways and have children choose the one that looks right, write that word and look for it in the dictionary.

What Looks Right? is an active every-pupil response activity through which children can learn a variety of important concepts. Words that rhyme usually have the same spelling pattern, but sometimes there are two common spelling patterns and you have to write it and see if it looks right or use the dictionary to check your spelling. The dictionary can also help you decide which way to spell a word when there are two words that sound the same but have different spellings and meanings.

What Looks Right? is a versatile strategy and can be used to help children become better spellers of longer words. In addition to the common two-letter vowel patterns, we have done lessons in which the columns are headed with words like *motion* and *pension*. The words the teacher writes end in either *-sion* or *-tion* and the children use the same "write it where you think it goes then see if you can find it in the dictionary" procedure.

Word Detectives

There are two questions I would like to encourage every teacher of children from third grade through high school to get students to ask themselves. These two questions are: "Do I know any other words that look and sound like this word? Are any of these look-alike/sound-alike words related to each other?"

The answer to the first question should help students with pronouncing and spelling the word. The answer to the second question should help students discover what meaning relationships exist, if any, between this new word and others in their meaning vocabulary stores. This guideline and these two simple questions could be used by any teacher of any subject area. Imagine that students in a mathematics class are doing a unit on fractions. To help children remember how to spell and pronounce the word *fraction* and to help them learn to look for meaning links between words, the teacher could point to the word *fraction* and ask students if they know any other words that look and sound like these words. The children might name words such as:

<u>frac</u>ture, mo<u>tion</u>, vaca<u>tion</u>, multiplica<u>tion</u>, addi<u>tion</u>, subtrac<u>tion</u>

The teacher lists the words, underlining the parts that are the same and having students pronounce the words, emphasizing the part that is pronounced the same. The teacher then points out to the students that thinking of a word that looks and sounds the same as a new word will help you quickly remember how to pronounce the new word and will also help you spell the new word.

Next the teacher explains that words, like people, sometimes look and sound alike but are not related. If this is the first time this analogy is used, the teacher will want to spend some time talking with the students about people with red hair, green eyes, and so on who have some parts that look alike but are not related and others who are.

> Not all people who look alike are related but some are. This is how words work too. Words are related if there is something about their meaning that is the same. After we find look-alike/sound-alike words which will help us spell and pronounce new words, we try to think of any ways these words might be in the same meaning family.

With help from the teacher, the children may discover that a *fracture* is a break into two or more parts and that *fraction* also involves parts.

Imagine that the students whose attention was directed to fractions on Monday during math did some science experiments on Tuesday using *thermometers* and *barometers*. At the close of the lesson, the teacher pointed to these words and helped them notice that the *-meters* chunk was pronounced and spelled the same and asked the students if they thought these words were just look-alikes or were related to one another. The students would probably conclude that you use them both to measure things and the *-meters* chunk must be related to measuring, as in *meters* and *kilometers*. When asked to think of look-alike/sound-alike words for the first chunk, students thought of *baron* for *barometers* but decided these two words were probably not related. For *thermometer* they thought of *thermos* and *thermostat* and decided that all these words had to do with heat or temperature.

Throughout their school day, children from the intermediate grades up encounter many new words. Because English is such a morphologically related language, most new words can be connected to other words by their spelling and pronunciation and many new words have meaning-related words already known to the student. Some clever, word-sensitive children become word detectives on their own. They notice the patterns and use these to learn and retrieve words. Others, however, try to learn to pronounce, spell and associate meaning with each of these words as separate, distinct entities. This is a difficult task which becomes almost impossible as students move through the grades and the number of new words increases each year. Readers do not need to be taught every possible pattern because the brain is programmed to look for patterns. Some students, however, do not know what the important patterns in words are or that these patterns can help you with pronouncing, spelling and accessing/remembering meanings for words. The simple procedure of asking the two critical questions for key vocabulary introduced in any content area would add only a few minutes to the introduction of key vocabulary and would pay students back manifold for that time.

Prefixes and Suffixes

(Parts of the activities in this section are adapted from Cunningham, 1995.) The plan outlined in the previous section takes advantage of whatever words occur in the course of instruction. Many students could also profit from some explicit instruction with the most common prefixes and suffixes. White, Sowell, and Yanagihara (1989) analyzed the words in the Carroll, Davies, and Richman (1971) corpus and found that twenty prefixes accounted for 97 percent of the prefixed words. Four prefixes, *un-, re-, in-* (and *im-, ir-, il-,* meaning "not") and *dis-,* accounted for 58 percent of all prefixed words. The prefixes accounting for another 39 percent of the words were: *en-/em-, non-, in-/im-* (meaning "in"), *over-, mis-, sub-, pre-, inter-, fore-, de-, trans-, super-, semi-, anti-, mid-,* and *under-.* For suffixes, *-s/-es, -ed,* and *- ing* account for 65 percent of the suffixed words. Add *-ly, -er/- or, -ion/-tion, -ible/-able, -al, -y, -ness, -ity,* and *-ment* and you account for 87 percent of the words. The remaining suffixes, each occurring in less than one percent of the words were: *er/ -est* (comparative), *-ic, -ous, -en, -ive, -ful,* and *-less.*

When children are learning suffixes and prefixes, they should learn that these word chunks will usually help them pronounce and spell words and that sometimes, these word parts will give them meaning clues. Here is a sample lesson for the prefix *re-* which can be adapted to teach any of the prefixes.

Sample Lesson for re-

Write nine words that begin with *re-* on index cards. Include three words in which *re-* means "back," three words in which *re-* means "again," and three words in which the *re-* is just the first syllable and adds no apparent meaning. Use words for which your students are apt to have meanings such as:

rebound	*redo*	*record*
return	*replay*	*refuse*
replace	*rework*	*reveal*

Have students pronounce the words and notice that they all begin with *r-e-*. Next, arrange the words in three columns and tell the students to think about why you have put *rebound, return* and *replace* together, *redo, replay,* and *rework* together and *record, refuse,* and *reveal* together. If students need help, tell them that for one column of *re-* words, you can put the word *again* in place of the *re-* and have the meaning of the word. Explain that for another column, you can put the word *back* in place of *re-*. Once students have figured out in which column the *re-* means *back* and in which *re-* means *again*, label these columns, *back* and *again*. Help students to see that when you refuse something, you don't fuse it back or fuse it again. Do the same with *record* and *reveal*.

Have students set up their own papers in three columns, the first two headed by *back* and *again* and the last not headed, and write the words written on the board. Then say some *re-* words and have students write them in one of the columns.

reusable	*retire*	*retreat*	*rewind*
recall	*respond*	*remote*	*responsible*
recoil	*rewrite*	*refund*	*relief*

As each word is written, ask someone where they wrote it and how they spelled it. Write it in the appropriate column on the board. Conclude the activity by having all the *re-* words read and replacing the *re-* with *back* or *again* when appropriate. Help students summarize that sometimes *re-* means back, sometimes *re-* means again and sometimes, *re-* is just the first chunk of the word. Once this activity is completed, leave the chart with these *re-* words displayed and ask students to "hunt" for *re-* words in their reading for the next several days. When they find a word that begins with *re-* they should decide which category it fits and add it to the chart. At the end of several days, review the chart and help students summarize what they learned about *re-* as a pronunciation, spelling, and sometimes meaning chunk in words.

As you do lessons with other prefixes, your message to students should be the same. Prefixes are chunks at the front of words which have predictable pronunciations and spellings. Look for them and depend on them to help you spell and pronounce new words. Sometimes, they also give you meaning clues. If you are unsure about the meaning of a word, see if a common meaning for the prefix can help. Check the meaning you figure out to make sure it makes sense in the context in which you are reading. Here are the most common prefixes, along with their most common meanings and examples of words in which the prefix is a meaning help along with examples of words in which the prefix is only a help for spelling/pronunciation.

Prefix	Meaning	Meaning Chunk	Spelling/Pronunciation Chunk
re	back	replace	reward
re	again	repaint	refrigerator
un	opposite	unhappy	uncle
in (im, ir, il)	not	inactive	incident
		immature	imagine
		irregular	irritate

		illegal	illustrate
in (im)	in	inhale	instant
		import	immense
dis	opposite	disappear	distress
non	opposite	nonessential	——
en (em)	in	enclose	entire
		embrace	empire
mis	bad	misbehave	miscellaneous
	wrong	misdeal	mistletoe
pre	before	pretest	present
inter	between	international	interesting
de	down	depress	delight
sub	under	subway	subsist
fore	front/ahead	forecast	forest
trans	across	transcontinental	translate
super	more than	superman	superintendent
semi	half	semifinal	seminar
mid	middle	midcourt	midget
over	too much	overeat	——
	over	overhead	——
under	too little	underweight	——
	under	underground	——
anti	against	antifreeze	antique

Suffixes, like prefixes, are predictable indicators of pronunciation and sometimes signal a meaning relationship. The meaning signaled by suffixes is usually a change in how and in what position the word can be used in the sentence. *Compose* is what you do. The *composer* is the person doing it. A *composition* is what you have once you have composed. Students need to become aware of how words change when they are signalling different relationships. They also need to realize that there are slight pronunciation changes to root words when suffixes are added. Activities similar to those used with prefixes can be used to focus on the most frequently occurring suffixes.

Sample lesson for -tion/-sion.

-Tion is a common suffix which is always pronounced the same way and which sometimes signals a change from doing to the thing done. Students make this shift easily in their speech and need to recognize that the same shift occurs in reading and writing. On index cards, write some *-tion* words some of which have a related "doing" word and some of which don't. After students notice that the words all end in *tion-* and that the *tion-* chunk is pronounced the same, divide the words to form two columns on the board.

> *collection*   *nation*

election   *fraction*
attraction   *vacation*

Help students to see that when you collect coins, you have a coin *collection*, we elect leaders during an *election* and you have an *attraction* for someone you are attracted to. In *nation, fraction* and *vacation*, the *tion-* is pronounced and spelled the same but the meaning of the word is not obvious by looking at the root word. Have students set up their papers in the usual way and call out words for students to decide which group they fit with. Be sure to have students spell words as you write them on the board and talk about the meaning relationships where appropriate. Here are some starters:

traction	*subtraction*	*construction*	*rejection*
auction	*expedition*	*tradition*	*interruption*
mention	*action*	*pollution*	*correction*

Here are some *-sion* words you could use in a similar activity:

confusion	*invasion*	*vision*	*provision*
extension	*suspension*	*passion*	*expression*
collision	*mission*	*tension*	*explosion*

Here are the most common suffixes, along with their most common meanings and examples of words in which the suffix is a meaning help along with examples of words in which the suffix is only a help for spelling/pronunciation.

Meaning	Suffix	Meaning Chunk	Spelling/Pronunciation Chunk
plural change	s	pencils	—
es	parties	—	
verb endings	s	laughs	—
	es	carries	—
	ed	painted	—
	ing	crying	—
	en	forgotten	kitten
more/most	er/est	happier	character
		richest	interest
without	less	hopeless	unless
full of	ful	joyful	—
able or able to be	able	fashionable	miserable
	ible	digestible	dribble
thing or state	tion	reaction	station
	sion	confusion	passion
in that manner	ly	happily	family
person or thing	er	inspector	mirror
	or	generator	horror
state or act of	ance	ignorance	balance

related to	ence	obedience	silence
	ment	argument	document
	ness	laziness	witness
	y	honesty	pretty
	ant	ignorant	elephant
	ent	confident	moment
	al	comical	animal
	ive	creative	motive
	ous	nervous	delicious
	ic	heroic	public

Root Words

So far, we have talked about working from prefixes and suffixes back to the root word. Some children find it exciting to see how many different words they can read and understand from just one root word. Students need to learn that the pronunciation of a root word often changes slightly as prefixes and suffixes are added. They also need to learn that the root word sometimes helps them to come up with meanings. Here are some sample activities.

Sample Lessons with Simple Roots

Write the word *play* on the board. Tell students that a little word like *play* can become a big word when parts are added to the beginning and ending of the word. Write words that have *play* in them. Have the words pronounced and talk about how the meaning of the word changes. Have students suggest other words with play. Here are some starters:

plays	*played*	*playing*	*player*	*players*
playful	*playfully*	*playable*	*replay*	*playfulness*
misplay	*ballplayer*	*outplay*	*overplay*	*playground*
playhouse	*playoff*	*playpen*	*playwright*	*screenplay*

Other roots which have many words include *work*, *agree*, and *create*.

Sample Lessons with More Complex Roots

Sometimes, there are root words whose meaning must be taught so that students can see how words in that family are related in meaning. These are often Latin or Greek roots. Rather than teach the meaning of the root first, we begin with words that share that root and help children discover the meaning. We also use examples in which the root is a pronunciation chunk but there is no meaning relationship, or one so obscured by time that it is no longer helpful.

Here is an example for the word *port*. Write the words *reporter*, *portable*, and *export* on the board. Pronounce the words as you underline the <u>port</u> in each. Tell students that many words in English have the word *port* in them. Tell them to listen as you tell them some meaning for the three words on the board to see if they can hear a meaning all the words share.

> A reporter carries a story back to tell others.
> Something you can carry with you is portable.
> When you export something, you take or carry it out of the country.

Help students to understand that *port* often means "carry or take." Next write this list of words on the board one at a tune and help students to see how the meanings change but are still related to *port*. Label this list of words Carry/Take:

port	*import*
export	*importer*
exportable	*transport*
nonexportable	*transportation*

Begin another list with the words *portion* and *portrait*. Ask students what the words mean and whether *port* means "carry" or "take" in these words. Help students to see that not all words which have *port* in them have a meaning clearly related to *carry* or *take*. Tell students that when they see a word containing *port* whose meaning they do not know, they should try to figure out a meaning related to *take* or *carry* and see if that meaning makes sense in the sentence. Have students set up their paper in two columns like your board and call out some words, some of which have the meaning of carry or take and some of which don't. Here are some possibilities:

importer	*exporter*	*airport*	*deport*
unimportant	*porter*	*portray*	*passport*
misreport	*support*	*nonsupport*	*opportunity*
seaport	*important*	*portfolio*	*Portugal*

You could do a similar activity with the root, *press*. Write the words *depression*, *impress*, and *repress* on the board. Pronounce the words as you underline the *press* in each. Ask students what the words mean. Invite them to use the words in a sentence that shows their meaning. Next, ask them to listen to some sentences with these words to see if they can hear a meaning all the words share. "You make a depression when you push something down. You feel depression when you feel pushed down. When you repress a feeling, you push it out of your mind. You

impress people when you push your good image into their minds.
Help students to understand that *press* often means "push." Next write
these words on the board and help students to see how the meanings
change but are still related to press:

press	*oppress*
express	*oppressive*
expressible	*oppressiveness*
inexpressible	

Tell students that when they see a word containing *press* whose
meaning they do not know they should try to figure out a meaning
related to push and see if that meaning makes sense in the sentence they
are reading.

Begin another column with the word *cypress*. Have students notice
that *cypress* ends in *press* but there does not appear to be any "push"
meaning in *cypress*. Here are some words, only one of which does not
have any "push" meaning relationship.

expression	*expressway*	*inexpressible*	*antidepressant*
compression	*pressure*	*pressurize*	*suppress*
impressionable	*unimpressed*	*repressive*	*empress*

Similar lessons could be done with some of the other Latin/Greek
roots which have lots of English words. These include:

rupt	to break
script	to write
spect	to look
aud	to hear
cred	to believe
diet	to say
sta	to stand
trac	to drag or pull
derm	skin
photo	light
graph	writing
therm	heat
phon	sound

Lists of many more Latin/Greek roots and some excellent
games/activities for working with them can be found in *Words Their
Way* (Bear, Invernizzi, Templeton, and Johnson, 1996) and in *Teaching
Kids to Spell* (Gentry & Gillet, 1993).

English is not a one-letter equals one-sound language but it is a language in which there are links between letter patterns and sounds. For

short words, the major patterns are beginning letters (onsets) and spelling patterns which rhyme (rimes). For big words the patterns include various morphemes which help us spell and pronounce words and sometimes also give clues to word meanings. The patterns exist in the words and children can discover them on their own. However, not all children ask themselves the right questions as they encounter words in their reading to figure out that there are patterns to look for. Our job in helping children become fluent readers and writers is to provide them lots of time to read and write along with real purposes and enticing materials. It is also our job to "help them notice." Every pattern does not need to be taught but children's attention must be drawn to enough patterns and they must be shown how these patterns will help them read and write lots of other words so that they will begin to notice on their own and construct in their heads an organized store of words and a theory of how words work.

References

Adams, M. J. 1990. *Beginning to read: Thinking and learning about print.* Cambridge, MA: MIT Press.

Bear, D. B., Invernizzi M., Templeton, S. & Johnson, F. 1996. *Words their way: Word study for phonics, vocabulary, and spelling instruction.* Englewood Cliffs, NJ: Merrill.

Carroll, J. B., Davies, P., & Richman, B. 1971. *Word frequency book.* New York: American Heritage.

Cunningham. P. M. 1995. *Phonics they use: Words for reading and writing.* 2nd ea. N.Y: Harper Collins.

Cunningham, P. M. & Cunningham, J. W. 1992. Making words: Enhancing the invented spelling-decoding connection. *The Reading Teacher, 46,* 106–115.

Freyd, P., & Baron, J. 1982. Individual differences in acquisition of derivatianal morphology. *Journal of Verbal Learning and Verbal Behavior, 21,* 282–295.

Gentry, J. R. & Gillet, J. W. 1993. *Teaching kids to spell.* Portsmouth, NH: Heinemann.

Goswami, U. & Bryant, P. 1990. *Phonological skills and learning to read.* East Sussex, U.K.: Erlbaum Associates.

Le Sieg, Theodore. 1972. *In a people house.* New York: Random House.

Mewhort, D. J. K., & Campbell, A. J. 1981. Toward a model of skilled reading: An analysis of performance in tachistoscoptic tasks. In G. E. MacKinnon & T. G. Walker Eds., *Reading research: Advances in theory and practice, vol. 3.* pp. 39–118. NY: Academic Press.

White, T., Sowell, J., & Yanagihara, A. 1989 Teadling elementary students to use word-part clues. *The Reading Teacher, 42,* 302–308.

II Teaching Reading Strategies

Teaching Reading Strategies

The opening article by Goodman and Watson explains how critical insights into the nature of the reading process have been provided by analyzing proficient readers' miscues—i.e., departures from what the text itself would lead us to expect—in reading aloud. Goodman and Watson address some of the key reading strategies that readers use: sampling, inferring, predicting, and confirming (and sometimes disconfirming and reprocessing).

Some readers naturally adopt these strategies in their quest for meaning, whether or not they are aware of using such strategies. Typically, these readers are children who have been well read to and who have been encouraged to retell books as best they can, from the pictures and from memory. Some readers start with such strategies but become sidetracked when word identification and/or phonics are emphasized to the exclusion of meaning, as they read aloud. Other children have scarcely learned that reading is supposed to make sense, much less that it can be enjoyable or informational. These children, of course, are least likely to use effective reading strategies and most likely to need more help than other students in understanding and using the strategies of effective readers.

Readers of this and other sections will notice that authors other than Goodman and Watson characterize reading strategies somewhat differently. For example, Weaver typically focuses on predicting, monitoring comprehension, and confirming or correcting (that is, using fix-it strategies to correct or try to correct something that hasn't made sense or doesn't sound like normal grammar).

Another way of looking at strategies is in terms of the language cues they draw upon, in addition to the obvious—that is, in addition to the words on the page and the letter/sound patterns they represent. Proficient readers use grammar and meaning within the text plus their entire storehouse of knowledge and experience to think ahead, to predict (though usually we notice this only when they make miscues). Proficient readers use these same language cues and their own background to help them recognize when something they've said in reading aloud (or silently) isn't making sense or doesn't fit with the grammar of the sentence.

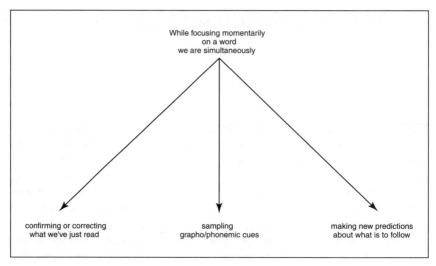

Figure 1. Simultaneous processes in reading.

Figure 1 (Weaver, 1994, p. 134) attempts to suggest the simultaneity of these strategies. At one and the same time, we are sampling new grapho/phonic cues, confirming or correcting what we've just read, and making new predictions about what is to follow. "Each [system or strategy] follows the others but at the same time precedes them, always moving toward constructing a text and making meaning" (Y. M. Goodman, Watson, & Burke, 1987, p. 33).

All of these ways of characterizing reading strategies reflect the same underlying conceptualization of the reading process. Differences among authors in this and subsequent sections do not mean that different authors conceptualize the reading process differently, but only that they have chosen to emphasize certain strategies in understanding and describing readers' strengths and trying to meet their needs.

References

Goodman, Y. M., Watson, D. J., & Burke, C. L. (1987). *Reading miscue inventory: Alternative procedures.* Katonah, NY: Richard C. Owen.

Weaver, C. (1994). *Reading process and practice: From socio-psycholinguistics to whole language* (2nd ed.). Portsmouth, NH: Heinemann.

8 A Sociopsycholinguistic Model of the Reading Process and Reading Strategy Instruction

Yetta Goodman
University of Arizona

Dorothy Watson
University of Missouri

Goodman and Watson begin by explaining reading as a meaning-making process, accompanied by a graphic model of reading. Next they explain key reading strategies: sampling, inferring, predicting, and confirming (and sometimes disconfirming and reprocessing). Readers' concern for constructing meaning (making sense of text) influences how readers use these reading strategies, while their purposes affect what they choose to remember. In using their reading strategies, readers necessarily use and combine the language cueing systems: graphophonemic, syntactic, semantic, and pragmatic. As the authors explain, "Sampling, inferring, predicting, and confirming strategies used by readers to transact with the language cueing systems occur so rapidly as to appear simultaneous."

After leading their readers to develop their own model of reading, Goodman and Watson explain how reading miscues are analyzed to give insight into readers' use of strategies—particularly their strengths in orchestrating language cues effectively to make meaning from texts. They point out that such analysis, or similar analysis, is the only way to know "whether students are profiting from different instructional procedures and whether those procedures actually encourage the development of successful reading strategies." Therefore, they briefly describe miscue analysis and list some of the questions that teachers can ask about miscues. The last major section deals with reading strategy lessons, which are "intended to strengthen the language cueing systems readers use, to justify the efficient strategies that readers have sometimes been taught to believe are inappropriate, and to develop readers' awareness of those strategies and cueing systems so they can be used more effectively and efficiently." Goodman and Watson discuss the construction of reading strategy lessons and illustrate with a lesson to help a child learn to use prior knowledge and context to support the use of graphophonic cues. After another specific example of a strategy lesson, they conclude by discussing strategy lessons to promote readers' self-evaluation and self-reflection (teaching and evaluation strategies called "Reader-selected Miscues" and "Retrospective Miscue Analysis), which is followed by a section emphasizing the importance of teaching strategy lessons at critical moments.

Adapted with permission from *Reading Strategies: Focus on Comprehension*, second ed., by Y. Goodman, D. Watson, and C. Burke. Katonah, NY: Richard C. Owen, 1996.

Reading is a problem-solving, meaning-making process. As readers, we consider the meaning the author is making while, at the same time, we build meaning for ourselves. We use our language, our thoughts, and our own view of the world to understand the author's meaning. The language, thoughts, and worldviews of both the author and the reader are influenced by personal and social histories. Our interpretations are structured and directed by what we know.

Because of the differences between the language, thoughts, and meanings of the author and those of a reader, reading can never be an exact process. Because the language and thought of the reader transact with the language and thought of the author represented in the published text, readers can never be certain that they have discovered the meaning the author intended. We use the term *transaction* to suggest the dynamic change that takes place in readers whenever they have decided to actively engage with a published text. The reader and the text are changed through the transaction (Rosenblatt, 1938, 1978). However, since readers are compelled to make sense, they interpret actively while reading in order to build meaning, thus achieving their ultimate goal. The reader is as active in constructing meaning as the writer is in producing written language. The author and the reader are also powerfully influenced by views of literacy held by their cultural groups. All these layers of complexity are necessary to understand the model of reading presented here.

Reading starts with an inquiry by the reader. To help solve the major problem confronting every reader—*What does what I'm reading mean?*—the reader uses a number of complex plans or reading strategies (K. Goodman, 1994). The significant strategies in reading involve *sampling, inferring, predicting, confirming,* and *integrating*. Simultaneously, the reader is integrating the new information, ideas, and feelings with the knowledge he or she already has (see Figure 1). These strategies are used by all readers with varying degrees of proficiency from the very earliest of reading experiences. In most cases, readers are not consciously

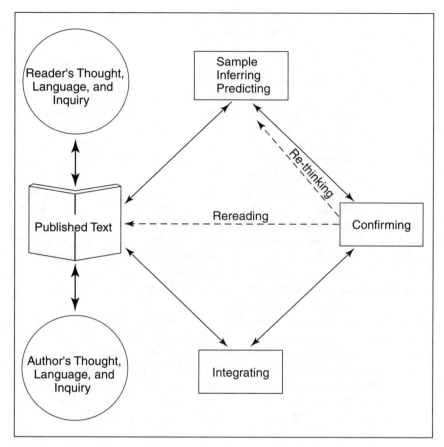

Figure 1. A graphic model of reading by Goodman, Watson, and Burke, 1996.

aware of the complexity of the reading process as they engage in comprehending what they read.

Sampling, Inferring, and Predicting Strategies

Readers use their purposes, language proficiency, and knowledge about the world to sample the printed material, to infer aspects of the text's meaning, to answer self-posed questions and simultaneously make tentative predictions about many of the text features. Some of the features include its genre (fiction, directions, exposition, recipes, poetry, etc.); the author's style (formal, informal, technical, etc.); the mood of writing (happy, sad, perplexing, exciting, etc.); meanings of words, phrases, idioms, and metaphors; the grammatical complexity and the orthography or the relationships between the written language and its oral forms.

When a teacher shows first graders a big book and asks, "What will this be about?" the readers might *hypothesize*, "It's going to be about a boy who is going to get into trouble." The children use their knowledge about stories, book handling, and print to *sample* format, illustrations, and print and to *infer* possibilities. Based on additional information they sample from the cover of the book and from what they hear from the discussions among other children and the teacher, readers infer and *predict* meanings and structures that seem appropriate at this particular moment. When mature readers sample from the sports page of a newspaper, they infer that they will read the language of sports, information about their local team, names of particular athletes, cities, and sports arenas, etc., and based on their knowledge of the sports world, they make predictions about what they expect to find in the text. The more a reader knows about the sport and is experienced in reading about it, the more likely it is that the predictions will be similar to the sports writer's language and content.

Such hypothesizing involves sampling, inferring, and predicting. As part of the cyclical nature of the reading process, more inferences and predictions are made based on what the reader samples. Sampling involves selecting information from the available print and illustrations on the basis of inferences and predictions. In sampling, the proficient reader selects the least amount of print information necessary to make inferences and predictions. Inferring is coming to understandings, based on informed predictions, and at the same time informed predictions are based on inferences. Inferring and predicting are not accidental phenomena. That is to say, a proficient reader approaches text expecting to make sense of it based on the cues gained within and surrounding the text and based on the reader's knowledge, understanding, and interest. Proficient readers do not expect to err; they confidently expect to construct something meaningful. However, proficient readers are not dismayed if their inferences and predictions are not on the mark. If their reading does not make sense or does not sound like language, they either immediately repredict or return to the actual text for more information. Sampling text, inferring, and predicting are integral and cyclical. These reading strategies usually occur without conscious awareness.

When we read, we infer, based on our schemas (the organized knowledge we have in our brains about the world), why certain text features have been written and what purposes they serve for the author and for us. Authors depend on the readers' schemas and therefore expect their readers to understand unstated assumptions and ideas. We do not make predictions on the basis of looking at every punctuation mark, letter, word, or sentence. Instead we sample the surface information, based on what we have learned over years of being readers (and writers) and what we consider to be the most significant aspects of the available language. We make predictions and inferences based on using the language of the text selectively and on what we bring from life experiences.

Young beginning readers also make appropriate predictions based on their print and life experiences as they interact with a variety of environmental settings, are read to, and see people write. They sample cues surrounding the print, such as pictures, nonalphabetic symbols, color, and graphic design, as well as information about the relevant contextual setting, in order to infer and predict something meaningful. For example, preschoolers predict on the basis of the stylized, multicolored letters, shape, and design of the carton, as well as the functional setting, and infer that the print is "Crest" or "toothpaste." On the other hand, they do not look at such a carton and say "McDonald's" unless perhaps someone had placed golden arches next to the toothpaste logo (Y. Goodman, Altwerger, & Marek, 1989). Although beginning readers sample a wide range of relevant cues for inference and prediction, they know that the print "says something," that it communicates. Young children's responses during the reading of patterned predictable books show their ability to infer and predict.

Confirming Strategies

As inferences and predictions are made, proficient readers test their hypotheses against their linguistic and conceptual knowledge to see if something meaningful is being constructed. Such hypothesis testing leads to the confirmation or disconfirmation of the semantics and of the syntax through which the meaning is being constructed.

Readers ask two questions to test their predictions: *Does this sound like language? Does this make sense to me?* If the answer to both questions is yes and if the material is worthwhile, reading continues. However, if the answer is no, optional confirming or disconfirming (often with self-correction) strategies are available to readers:

1. Regress and reread in order to sample additional meaning-making cues.

2. Stop, consider and rethink why what is being read doesn't make sense. Adjust the ongoing meaning making without rereading.

3. Continue reading in order to build additional context; in so doing, generate enough understanding to make sense of the text.

4. Stop reading, possibly because the material is too difficult or not relevant.

Readers bring their unique backgrounds and experiences to the material they read and consequently predict and confirm their predictions in unique ways. All readers, including beginning readers, test their hypotheses while they read, and they learn to self-correct only when it is appropriate to do so. The more knowledge readers have about the content and language of the written materials, the more appropriate their sampling, inferencing, predicting, and confirming will be. Illustrations and charts that accompany stories or articles are important sources of information that readers use in order to test their hypotheses about the content and structure of the story, as are their memories of other stories they've heard and read.

Constructing Meaning

The concern readers have for constructing meaning (making sense of what is being read) influences how readers use the reading strategies. Readers continuously make choices about which chunks of information to remember. They often take the following purposes for reading into consideration as they make choices:

- This is important for my purposes, so I will add the information I believe I've gained to things I already know.
- The information is not exactly what I expected; therefore, I will rethink my reasons for reading and perhaps set some new purposes.
- I'm not sure whether it's important for my purposes, so I'll remember what I'm reading for a while until I have enough information to make a better decision about its usefulness.
- This is not important for my purposes, so I'll ignore or forget it.

We build meaning for what we are reading by integrating the new information with our existing knowledge and schema. We make additional considerations as we read, depending on our purpose as well as our existing knowledge, schema, and beliefs about the world.

- This information is similar to what I know and fits my belief system, so I easily accommodate it to my view of the world.

- This information is new to me, but fits my belief system and what I know. I will think about it for a while: it will help me expand my view of the world.

- This information does not fit my belief system, but if the author makes a strong enough case, I might consider altering my belief system.

- This information does not fit my belief system. If the author does not make a strong enough case, I intuitively reject the information or distort it to fit my own view of the world.

Readers construct meaning as they transact with what they are reading, using their reading strategies along with the language cueing systems.

Language and Its Cueing Systems

Children come to school already in possession of a great deal of language knowledge. They are proficient users of the language of their home. They have begun to make use of written language and are aware that print can communicate such enticing messages as signs for McDonald's, labels for Coca-Cola, cartoon messages with speech balloons, notes on the refrigerator, and titles or captions on TV. Many children have the experience of being read to by parents, nursery-school teachers, or librarians and of paging through books by themselves, using pictures to tell or retell stories. Many young authors skillfully use pencils and magic markers to write and illustrate. They have a variety of experiences seeing adults in their world read and write for all kinds of purposes or functions. Children have a developing language knowledge to use as they transact with new printed materials. A clear relationship between the language and meaning of the text and the children's own experiences, language, and knowledge makes printed material predictable. The more this reading material reflects the meaningful language they use already, the more proficiently they apply their developing language knowledge and worldview to the construction of meaning. In the process of constructing meaning, readers make use of their developing language cueing systems: graphophonic, syntactic, semantic, and pragmatic.

Graphophonic System

In an alphabetic language, such as English, the *graphophonic system* refers to the symbol systems of oral and written language and the relationship between them. The sounds of the oral language are known as the *phonological system.* The written language system is known as the *orthographic system,* and the relationship between the two systems is known as *phonics.* The phonological system is not only the system of the specific sounds of the language but also includes the intonation system: the stress on syllables and words, the variations in pitch that help disambiguate meanings, and the juncture relating to breaths in the stream of speech.

The orthographic system is the way in which print is organized in the written language world. Differences in upper and lower case, punctuation, spacing, and the spelling system are all aspects to consider in understanding the orthography of written language. Phonics is not a simplistic relationship between single letters and single sounds. Phonics is not simply a program to teach reading. Phonics is what readers learn to understand as the relationship between how they talk and how language is organized in written texts. In other words, phonics refers to a set of complex relationships between the orthography of written language and the phonology of oral language (K. Goodman, 1994).

Contrary to a good deal of popular opinion, the English spelling system is relatively regular and not haphazard. However, there can never be a simple one-to-one correspondence between the orthography and the phonological system of any language. Some language features that exist in written language do not exist in oral language. *Once upon a time,* for example, is seldom used in oral language except in storytelling. Clauses such as *said Mother* or *John laughed* preceded or followed by quotations are common in written language, even in beginning reading material, yet are not commonly heard in oral language. There are many other influences that do not permit a simple one-to-one relationship between written and oral language: the complexity of intonation, the use of abbreviations, the personal relationship of speakers, the lack of familiarity between authors and readers, as well as dialect and other language variations.

Because of historically long and complex sociocultural, political, and linguistic influences, the English spelling system has more than one spelling pattern that relates to the same sounds, for example *ai* as in *bait* and *a-e* as in *hate.* Although the English spelling system is to a large extent consistent and dependable, there are different ways to pronounce the same written words. To some speakers of English, *Mary, merry,* and *marry* are homophones—pronounced exactly the same. For other speakers only two of those three are homophones, and for still others all three words are pronounced differently.

People who say *cuz, watchamacallit, jeet,* and *gonna* must learn to recognize their counterparts in written language as *because, what do you call it, did you eat,* and *going to.* The oral forms are not sloppy renditions of the written forms; rather they are different forms representing the same meanings. *Each reader must learn the set of relationships that exists between his or her oral language and its written counterparts: the phonics of language.* Because of differences in dialects, as well as individual differences, the relationships are not the same for all speakers. In addition, spelling has syntactic and semantic roots as well as sound/letter roots.

In recent years, research on young children's spelling patterns has provided us with evidence that, despite the complexities of the English spelling system, children's understanding of the relationship between the phonological and the orthographic systems of written language develops logically toward conventional spellings (Wilde, 1992). Beginning readers use their proficiency with the sound system of their language and their developing understanding of the systematic nature of print to build relationships between oral and written language. So spellings such as *grapa* for *grandpa, morosiacos* for *motorcycles,* or *frinstance* for *for instance* are not only understandable but help us see how readers build their phonics knowledge.

What's true for young children is true for proficient readers as well. Because the purpose of reading is comprehending—constructing meaning—readers use all the language cueing systems in an integrated way in order to build the relationship between the systems of oral and written language.

Syntactic System

The phrase *syntactic system* refers to the relationships of words, sentences, and paragraphs. These systematic relationships include word order, tense, number, and gender. *Grammar* is a more commonsense term for *syntax.* All children use the rules of their own grammar rather proficiently by the time they come to school. When English-speaking five-year-olds are asked to complete the sentence "A boy is sliding down the —," they will supply an acceptable noun or noun phrase at the end of the sentence. They will not be able to call the word they supply a *noun* or know the definition of the word *noun;* nevertheless, they know where nouns and other parts of speech go in English sentences. When we use the terms *syntax* or *grammar,* we refer not to the rules imposed on the language by grammar books but to the rules people know intuitively by virtue of being language users.

In some dialects of English, people say, "I'm going to university" while others say, "I'm going to the university." However, both groups of speakers could say "I'm going to college" or "I'm going to the college," depending on the meaning intended. How do we *know* whether or not to use *the* before *university* and *college*? Grammar books rarely provide rules about when we should or should not use the determiner *the* in such sentences because no clear-cut rule system has been discovered by linguistics concerning the syntactic phenomenon of the obligatory or optional determiner. The awareness you, as a speaker of your language, have that a sentence does or does not sound right is your intuitive knowledge of the syntactic system. Children also have a strong intuitive knowledge about the language they hear and speak.

Readers are better able to predict the language of written material and know whether a particular sentence is acceptable, when the syntax of the material is similar to the syntax most commonly experienced by the readers. But as stated earlier, there are forms of written language that are rarely part of oral language. It is through extensive experience with written language (being read to, for example) that readers become familiar with the syntax of written language. Even before their oral language is understood by adults, children exhibit understanding of grammatical knowledge; for example, two-year-olds have been overheard saying something that sounds like *The End* when they finish turning the last page of their favorite book.

In a list of isolated words with only graphophonic cues available, students may have difficulty remembering how *read* (present tense) and *read* (past tense) or *merry* and *marry* are different, and consequently they may be unable to provide a grammatical function or a meaning for the words. However, as soon as syntax is available, readers use their syntactic knowledge to support their predicting and confirming strategies, and they are then able to disambiguate any confusions between the words. The syntax of written material provides significant cues for readers. To answer the question *Does this sound like language?* readers use syntax to predict and then confirm the acceptability of their predictions.

But in order to comprehend, readers must also know how to use their knowledge of the *semantic* and *pragmatic* systems of language.

Semantic and Pragmatic Systems

The *semantic system* is at the heart of language because it involves the relationships between language and its meaning. The semantic system includes the meanings of words and phrases and how they change over time. It includes dictionary definitions but also definitions that change depending on their contexts. The *pragmatic system* involves the relationship of the semantic system with the social, cultural, and historical context of language in use. For example, a "Family Circus" cartoon showed Billy answering the telephone. The caller said, "Is your mother there?" Billy put down the phone and went into every room of the house, finally spotting his mother. He returned to the phone and said to the caller, "Yes." The cartoon suggests that children are sometimes more tuned into literal meanings than pragmatic meanings. Speakers of English learn to know that when a caller says, "Is your mother there?" this is not a yes/no question. In the context of a phone call, the sentence means, "If your mother is there, please ask her to come to the phone." Examining language, keeping in mind that the pragmatic system is strongly influenced by social and cultural conventions, helps us understand the many times in both oral and written language that people construct different meanings even though they are in the same language setting. Personal meanings are influenced by the society in which we live and interact, as well as by everything that the language user has been learning and thinking about the world.

People who live in apartments, trailers, or boxcars that are secure, warm, familiar places have established their various meanings of *house* and *home* through their own living experiences and their use of language in various real-life settings. Regardless of what kind of structure they live in, they say to others, "Come over to my house after school today" or "Take this home to your mother." They may, therefore, have difficulty with school lessons that try to explain an instructional meaning of *house* and *home* or may not understand why a poet would rhapsodize, "It takes a heap of living to make a house a home." Marlene, who travels from New York to Los Angeles in five hours to visit her grandmother and who speaks to her grandmother on the phone a number of times each year, may have difficulty understanding the total break of family ties and the trauma involved during the migrations of the Westward Movement. The closer the content of reading materials is to the life and experiences of students and the closer the concepts of reading materials are to what students already know, the easier it is for them to construct their personal meanings as well as to understand the meanings that the author may have constructed.

At the same time, a major goal of reading is to expand students' knowledge and views of the universe. If the material to be read has many known concepts along with some unknowns, readers can use what they know to build better understanding of the unknown content and concepts. When we comprehend, we connect new information to what we already know. In order to provide opportunities for expansion of experiences and broadening of concepts, teachers encourage students to read material that involves unique experiences or new ideas that are to some degree beyond the student's understandings. However, if too many of the experiences, ideas, or concepts are unfamiliar, the student will have difficulty making connections. You can explore this yourself.

Try to read something you know very little about. If you are a language person, try reading a physics or chemistry article. If you know most about biology, try to read an article by a linguist. When we explore reading experiences outside of our own expertise, we realize the important relationship between what we know, what we are reading, and the reading process. The important relationship between background knowledge of the reader and the content of the written material strongly suggests that teachers must carefully select reading materials for the purposes of instruction and evaluation.

The language cueing systems and the reading strategies must operate in an interrelated way in order for the reader to construct a meaningful text. We use our knowledge about the complex relationship between the letters and sounds of the language to predict and to confirm graphophonic units of language. (For example, we don't predict an *ng* as the beginning of an English word unless we have experience with the Vietnamese language and we are reading a text with Vietnamese names.) Our knowledge of the rules of grammar or syntax is brought to bear as we use appropriate linguistic cues to predict and confirm the syntactic system of language. (For example, we know when to expect dialogue or questions. We know when to expect male or female pronouns. If these features are not where we expect them to be, we disconfirm, select other cues, and self-correct.) Our understanding of the world around us helps us infer what the author means and helps us predict and confirm the language and meanings of the text as we use the semantic and pragmatic systems of language. (For example, we would hardly expect a robot to be in a chapter about George Washington unless we were reading a science fiction novel.)

Only when the semantic and pragmatic cueing systems are accessible to the reader and when these systems are in concert with the syntactic and graphophonic systems, are the necessary supports present for making the most proficient use for the development of the reading strategies. When all the systems of language are in place within a whole, authentic text, readers predict and confirm language using the semantic and pragmatic systems intelligently and at the same time are selective in their use of the graphophonic and syntactic information. Simultaneously, readers integrate what they are reading with what they know in order to comprehend and construct their own meanings. Proficient readers sample and infer the most significant graphophonic, syntactic, semantic, and pragmatic cues, and they predict what they believe subsequent graphophonic, syntactic, semantic structures are going to be. No reader uses all of the available cues. Reading would be too slow and inefficient if this were so. Nor are the cues sampled in any consistent order or sequence. The weight and significance readers give to individual cues varies with the experiences and language information they bring to their reading and depends on the predictions the readers make about the specific purpose and the nature and content of the text. Sampling, inferring, predicting, and confirming strategies used by readers to transact with the language cueing systems occur so rapidly as to appear simultaneous.

When readers are focusing on any one of the individual strategies or any one of the language systems, all the other strategies and systems are still operating. Although proficient readers balance their use of reading strategies and language cueing systems successfully, there are readers who need extra support in order to successfully use their reading strategies and their knowledge of language. Such readers may need to be directed away from over reliance on a single language cueing system and underutilization of one of the reading strategies. With experience with reading and writing and appropriate guidance by knowledgeable teachers and parents, beginning readers learn to integrate all the strategies and language cueing systems effectively and efficiently.

Developing a Model of Reading

Sampling, inferring, predicting, confirming, and integrating in response to the use of the language cueing systems—always resulting in a personal construction of meaning—are the key operations or natural strategies within the reading process. We have learned about these strategies and the knowledge readers have about language by using miscue analysis with readers of all ages and abilities. We encourage teachers or others interested in understanding reading to use miscue analysis with at least one reader in order to bring their own questions and understandings to this discussion. Participating in the following experience may help clarify some issues.

Read the following paragraph through once and only once. Then, without rereading, write down everything you've read.

> The king called the assembled to order. He stood regally waiting for silence. As the noise ceased, he spoke. "Tomorrow, I invite you all to the place. There we will make the decisions necessary to overcome the enemy."

Look back over your representation of the paragraph and compare it with the versions of other readers. Compare these versions with the original passage. Can you identify, through your observations, the various reading strategies and language cueing systems that you used?

Which cues did you sample as significant, and which did you discard? *Regally* is often omitted. Because readers assume that kings are regal, the word becomes redundant. Few people write both *waiting for silence* and *the noise ceased*. These, too, are redundant statements, and a reader needs only one, or some combination, of them to integrate that information into the meaning being constructed.

Can you provide evidence from your written statement that you were sampling, inferring, predicting, and confirming? When you read *assembled*, did you realize that you had actually anticipated people, courtiers or a meeting or assembly? Did you use a different syntactic structure expanding to an alternative noun phrase? Does your version contain *palace* instead of *place* because you sampled the graphophonic information in such a way that allowed you to confirm your prediction of *palace*?

At this and similar points in the published text, you might have felt the need to reread even though we asked you to read the paragraph only once. Some readers disregard the directions and reread. Other readers follow the directions but are frustrated by them. Both cases are instances of the use of confirming strategies. Readers often encounter unexpected cues in texts or they want clarification. Some people ignore directions because confidence in their reading strategies overrides the directions; comprehending takes priority. Others allow their need for clarification to frustrate them; they believe doing what a teacher or author says takes precedence over their personal needs to construct meaning.

Were the words and sentences of your version of the text more or less different from the versions of other readers and from the original text than were your *meanings*? There will always be variations in meaning attributable to personal reader experience and background. At the same time there are similarities in these versions because of similar literary experiences and common societal views about what we are reading.

Reading a short paragraph and then writing down what you remember is not like continuous silent reading, but examining miscues in other readers as well as your own responses provides insights into the reading strategies and language cueing systems that readers use. Reading begins when, based on some purpose, we decide to transact with an author through the medium of printed material. The reading process proceeds continuously, simultaneously, and transactively. This process results in reading comprehension, that is, the construction of meaning. As we read, we continuously add to, alter, or reorganize our meanings and, in doing so, add to or alter our existing knowledge.

Evaluating Reading Miscues

Reading is a discussion between reader and author. Both participants bring their language, their knowledge, and their thought processes to the discussion. As you read the paragraph in the previous section, it became obvious that there were points where you, as the reader, did not share common experiences, language, or knowledge with the author. Because readers are making use of the available cueing systems based on their personal knowledge and background, they may misinterpret the author's intentions. They produce unexpected responses or miscues because they are predicting alternative possibilities and constructing their own text. Because proficient readers are concerned with meaning, not surface accuracy, and because authors and readers never have exactly the same experiences, knowledge, schemas, or perspectives, miscues are natural to the reading process. All readers make miscues, and these miscues result from the same process readers use when they make no miscues. We evaluate readers' uses of strategies and knowledge of the cueing systems by examining their miscues. In a similar way that you evaluated your own miscues when you read the passage above, we can organize a setting to evaluate the miscues of readers with whom you work. Our purpose is not to eliminate miscues but to understand what readers know about reading strategies and language cueing systems that allow miscues to occur. Many miscues are high quality because they show that readers are using sophisticated knowledge.

Miscues are collected as readers read orally. Readers are given an unfamiliar but complete story or article to read and are informed that they will be totally dependent upon their own resources, that they must continue reading past any problems, and that after the reading they will be responsible for a retelling of the material. We do not interrupt or help the readers during this process because we want to see what they do on their own as they read through an entire text. If the readers hesitate for a long time or look to us for support, we simply smile and encourage them to continue reading on their own. We preserve the reading and retelling for evaluation by tape recording. It is rarely possible to gain a full profile of a student's reading without being able to relisten to the reading experience. Readers' miscues are then available for analysis by replaying the tape and comparing the reading with the printed text (Y. Goodman, Watson, & Burke, 1987). Only through careful analysis of a student's reading is it possible to know whether students are profiting from different instructional procedures and whether those procedures actually encourage the development of successful reading strategies.

In miscue analysis, significance is not attached to any one miscue or the quantity of miscues but to the general pattern of miscues made consecutively throughout a text. Proficient readers who are constructing meaning will produce a large percentage of sentences that remain syntactically and semantically acceptable regardless of the number of miscues in the sentence. (A syntactically acceptable sentence fits grammatically within the text. A semantically acceptable sentence makes sense within the text.) Although knowledge about miscue analysis is necessary to gain in-depth understanding of the reading proficiency of any reader, teachers can begin to learn about the reading process and their students' reading by thinking about the role that miscues play as a reader comprehends a text. In order to gain a thorough understanding of miscue analysis, its procedures, and what to do in response to the analysis, it is helpful to consult *Reading Miscue Inventory: Alternative Procedures* (Y. Goodman, Watson, & Burke, 1987). Teachers can consider the significance of miscue analysis by listening to an audiotape of a reader, noting the miscues on a copy of the original text, and asking the following questions:

Why did the reader make this miscue?

Does the miscue support the reader's construction of meaning?

Does the miscue result in a sentence or sentences that make sense in the text?

Does the miscue result in a sentence that sounds like language?

In what way does the miscue interfere with the reader's construction of meaning?

Are there other miscues or different responses later in the text that show that the reader has resolved earlier text difficulties, such as unusually difficult structures or semantic overload?

What does this reader have to know to make such a miscue?

As teachers develop a profile of their students from insights gathered from miscue analysis and from other careful observations of students as they read and write, they build a background for selecting appropriate reading strategy lessons for individuals and small groups of readers.

Reading Strategy Lessons

Our years of experience with research in miscue analysis, using miscue analysis to help teachers evaluate students' reading and working with teachers to plan reading instruction, have contributed to innovative reading strategy lessons embedded in a rich literacy curriculum. With Carolyn Burke, we have written reading strategy lessons that help readers focus on the reading strategies and language cueing systems we have documented in the above discussion on the reading process (Y. Goodman, D. Watson, & C. Burke, 1996). Reading strategy lessons are only helpful when a teacher organizes a classroom curriculum that includes functional, personal, and social reading experiences that involve students in learning to ask relevant questions and solve important problems. This kind of curriculum has become known as whole language. In developing whole language curricula, teachers relate daily reading and writing experiences in school to literacy events in the home and community so that children and their families know that reading the newspaper or comic books or writing a weekly shopping list is as important a part of reading development as is reading a math text or historical fiction at school. In school, students are involved in experiences that include reading and writing as a means of studying issues that affect them personally or that are significant to the communities in which they live. The classroom is organized to integrate the appropriate content areas in order to provide opportunities to support students' inquiry. It is within such a rich literate environment embedded in thought-provoking curricular experiences that reading strategy lessons are most successful.

Reading strategy lessons are intended to strengthen the language cueing systems readers use, to justify the efficient strategies that readers have sometimes been taught to believe are inappropriate, and to develop readers' awareness of those strategies and cueing systems so they can be used more effectively and efficiently. Reading lessons:

- highlight one or more of the language cueing systems within an authentic text;
- focus on the natural reading strategies;
- encourage talk about reading and the reading process; and
- support and focus the responsibilities of the reader.

The lessons involve the reader or a small group of readers, the author as represented by the published text, and the teacher who is knowledgeable about miscue analysis, reading strategy lessons, and the reading process. The teacher has important roles to play. First, the instructional experience is based on evaluative procedures such as miscue analysis that the teacher conducts and carries out through carefully selected and focused materials. A second role is that the teacher focuses on facilitating learning. When a teacher and a student or a small group share a learning experience and discuss it seriously, conscious awareness of the process is enhanced. Learners evoke insight in one another as they share both their attempts at processing information and their partially formulated ideas. The teacher acts as a sounding board against which ideas are played, and both the teacher and students ask immediately appropriate questions. Exploratory talk about reading strategies and language cueing systems within the community of students and teachers increases the likelihood that what is discussed during the instructional experience can be remembered and used by the reader during other literacy events.

Teachers encourage readers to ask questions such as the following:

- How important is this specific word or phrase or concept? (Is the missing information significant enough to the message to expend effort in finding out more or should I read on?)
- Which cues are available in the text, and where will I find them?
- What do I know from my past experiences with language and life that I should make use of in my reading?
- What is my best guess? (What tentative concept or meaning have I constructed?)

The questions teachers help students ask provide opportunities for them to discover what they know about their knowledge of the language cueing systems and the reading strategies they use. The questions enable readers to become secure in their quest for meaning. The specific strategy lessons grow out of our theoretical understandings about language, learning, and curriculum and what we have learned about the students' reading strategy use and language cueing system knowledge through miscue analysis.

Constructing Reading Strategy Lessons

Not only must readers become aware of alternate available cues, but they must develop flexibility in applying them. Reading strategy instruction supports both the conscious awareness of the cueing systems and the development of flexibility. When evaluation procedures indicate a need for specific strategies, reading material is written or carefully selected to highlight the use of that strategy.

The reading strategy lesson is constructed to help readers gain information from a language cueing system that they may not be using adequately or that they may believe they should not or can not use. The instruction makes readers aware of the reading process. The structure of the lesson focuses the readers' attention on the process of reading as well as on the content of the written text. The material must present the highlighted strategy in its most complete and unambiguous form. The strategy is considered within a language context complete with all the cueing systems, including those with which the readers are most successful. In such a setting, a reader is able to participate in the new learning supported by all the possible cueing systems. The structure of the material allows readers to discover the significance of the highlighted reading strategy and the language cues being used within the context of real reading.

The meaning carried by the selected material usually involves information and concepts familiar to readers, and must, as much as possible, support readers in making sense. When the written text is supportive, readers can afford to focus their attention on an aspect of the reading process without losing sight of the purposes of reading—communication and construction of meaning. Because the highlighted strategy is embedded in a context that has familiar meaning and language structure, readers' responsibilities are both focused and manageable.

Franklin, a third-grade reader, read a number of stories for us. His miscues revealed that he often substituted the preposition *from* for *for* (see Figure 2).

We wanted to focus his attention on how the two prepositions *for* and *at* differed, from his own perspective, when he was reading about something very familiar. So we wrote the following story about his birthday party in which it would be obvious which preposition would be appropriate (see Figure 3).

After he read this story, we talked with Franklin about the story itself, which he enjoyed and comprehended well. Then we talked about how he knew which preposition was *for* and which was *from* based on the

> from
> "This boy would like a flowered handbag for his mother,"
>
>
> said Aunt Betty. Then he thought, "I have looked at the toys
>
> from
> for a long time."

Figure 2. Sample miscue analysis from Goodman & Burke, 1972.

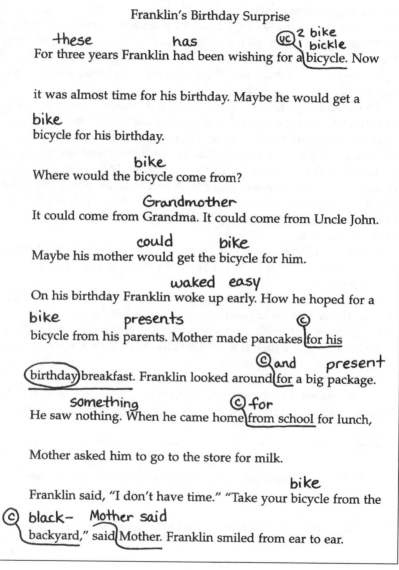

Figure 3. Sample miscue analysis from Goodman & Burke, 1972.

relationship between people and things that he knew within the context of the story.

The miscue markings show that Franklin substituted *bike* for *bicycle* throughout the story. Almost all of the other miscues were syntactically or semantically acceptable or he corrected them as noted by the *c* within the circle. But he only miscued on *from* or *for* once in the story (When he came home from school. . . .) He self-corrected immediately.

This one lesson was enough to help Franklin self-correct on subsequent miscues involving the two prepositions. In effect, talking with him about the meaning possibilities of the relationship between *for* and *from* helped him think about the relationships during his reading. His substitutions of one of the prepositions for the other almost disappeared.

Selected slotting strategy lessons encourage readers to make use of predictions involving all the cueing systems. These lessons help readers examine how confirmation of predictions takes place. To develop these lessons, we carefully select a content word that is important to the story or a grammatical slot that miscue analysis reveals the student has some difficulty with. We write the lesson replacing the specific word or phrase with an underlined blank. Sometimes we find a well-written short story in which the rest of the cues in the story support the reader's use of predicting and confirming strategies. Selected slotting lessons are appropriate for small groups, providing students with opportunities to discuss their different strategies. The purpose is for readers to predict a meaningful word or phrase for the slot that fits the context of the story or article, not to search for a correct answer or an exact replacement. We have used the following story for years with students. When teachers find stories such as this one that work well for reading strategy instruction, they often place them in a folder marked Reading Strategy Lesson Possibilities and keep the stories apart from other reading materials that students have access to. In this way, the reading material for the lesson is unfamiliar to all readers.

In the following short excerpt from *Miss Pickerell Goes Undersea*, the same base word is left out throughout, although it does have different suffixes in different slots (see Figure 4). Students discover that when they continue to read, even when they are not sure of a word or phrase, the subsequent language and content provide additional and supportive cues, thus reducing uncertainty (Smith, 1988) and giving them more confidence in their subsequent responses. Young readers often substitute a phrase such as *picture taking man* for some of the slots. We consider such substitutions acceptable and do not probe for the expected response although we always encourage acceptable and multiple alternatives.

Her next errand was at the Square Toe City _____ Studio
She crossed the sidewalk and opened the door of the _____ studio.

Inside, Miss Pickerell put the gilt picture frame on a desk in the
corner and closed the door behind her. A little bell attached to
the top of the door tinkled, but for a moment there was no other sound.

This was the _____'s office, a small room with a number
of pictures mounted on the wall. A curtained dorway separated the
office from the _____'s working quarters. Miss Pickerell could
smell the faint stinging smell of the chemicals the _____ used
in his darkroom.

With a sudden swish, the curtain across the dorway was pushed
aside, and the _____ appeared. He had gray hair and wore glasses.

"Good gracious!" he said, as he went around behind the desk. "It's
Miss Pickerell! Was there something wrong with the picture I took of your
cow last week?" the _____ asked.

"Not at all," Miss Pickerell said. "In fact--"

"Personally," said the _____ "I thought it was excellent.
Particularly the expression in her eyes." Most people are very well
pleased with my work," said the _____. "Most people think I'm
such a good _____ that they ask me to take more pictures. Instead
of coming back and complaining."/ It might be several weeks before I
could take her picture over again. Why don't you reconsider, Miss Pickerell?
It's really an excellent picture of your cow. It brings out her personality.
I'm even going to put it in my display window to show what a good _____
I am."

Miss Pickerell Goes Undersea
Ellen MacGregor

Figure 4. Excerpt from *Miss Pickerell Goes Undersea.*

Self-Evaluation and Self-Reflection Reading Strategy Lessons

It is appropriate to inform the reader that strategy lessons are often based on miscue analysis and to involve readers in considering the significance of their miscues. As students think about their own miscues, they often provide insights that help teachers understand not only the strategies the readers use but their knowledge of the language cueing systems as well.

The power of self-evaluation and self-reflection is that it brings readers to the forefront of their own learning, enabling them to take control of their goals and to understand their own development. As students understand the reading process and find ways to discuss their personal reading strengths, they are able to develop as proficient readers. The following instructional experiences, Reader-selected Miscues and Retrospective Miscue Analysis, involve students in discussions about their reading strengths and needs.

Reader-selected Miscues is both an instructional and an evaluation strategy that calls for participation of readers in the process (Watson, 1978; Watson & Hoge, 1996). Reader-selected Miscues provides the teacher and students with the opportunity to think and talk about reading without interrupting the reading process since it takes place initially while the students are reading silently. As students silently read a self-selected piece of material, they mark and later record any segment of the text that was troublesome. These miscues are then available for discussion and analysis by informally using some of the questions listed above. Reader-selected miscues are organized to occur during a segment of silent reading time. Students are asked to place a blank bookmark or self-stick note at the page where they realize that they have made miscues or been confused in some way. After they have read for a specific amount of time (ten to fifteen minutes), they write the sentence in which their miscue(s) was embedded onto the bookmark or self-stick note. After the students have read and recorded their miscues, they share them with each other. They discuss the category of miscues and the strategies readers use to solve the anomalies in their reading.

Retrospective Miscue Analysis (RMA) (Y. Goodman & Marek, 1996) also involves readers in reflecting on the role miscues play in their oral reading. In RMA, the reader, with the teacher present, tapes himself/herself reading a whole narrative or expository piece. The reader, with the teacher, then listens to the tape and stops at perceived miscues. The teacher helps the reader explore the miscues in order to determine how the miscues reflect the reading process and how they help or undermine the construction of meaning. Especially when working with a struggling, nonconfident reader, the teacher may preselect the reader's miscues to support the integration of reading strategies and focus the reader on the strategies that are most productive for meaning construction. By examining high-quality miscues first, it is easy for students to see their miscues as evidence of their developing proficient reading strategies. Such discussions about miscues demystify the reading process. Readers become aware that even proficient readers make miscues, that it is beneficial to self-correct only those miscues that disrupt meaning, and that miscues often enhance reading comprehension.

Writing self reflections in a journal and later sharing journal entries in a group discussion provides an opportunity for students to focus on their own strengths. These reflections on strategy lessons help students revalue themselves as readers. Readers' problems are addressed, but the best way to support reading development is first to help readers know what they do well so they can build on their strengths.

Strategy Lessons for Critical Moment Teaching

Some of the most powerful strategy lessons occur at times when a lesson has not been prepared in advance. These significant moments occur in many different contexts, especially in a whole language class: during a reading conference; over a student's shoulder as the teacher is moving around the class responding to children involved in a variety of learning experiences; or when a miscue is made by a confident child or by the teacher during daily oral reading. The examples we cite regarding critical moment teaching come from an article by Y. Goodman entitled "At the Critical Moment: RMA in Classrooms" (Y. Goodman & Marek, 1996).

Alan Flurkey, observing his students read, noticed that Maureen looked back at the beginning of the sentence and then read on. He interrupted Maureen when she finished reading the page to discuss her strategies:

Alan: I noticed that near the top of the page you stopped, backed up and then continued to read. . . . Why did you do that?

Maureen: You mean up here?

Alan: Yes.

Maureen: I thought it was going to say, like: he was scared: —was scared of what was there.

Alan: So then what did you do?

Maureen: It didn't say that so I just started over.

Alan:	. . . So what was it in the sentence that made you turn back?
Maureen:	Well, it wouldn't make sense to say, like: he was the lion: so I just went back.

Alan shared this discussion with the class to support Maureen's legitimate reading strategies and to help all his students consider the importance of talking and thinking about the reading process.

Wendy Hood's example of critical moment teaching occurred while she was reading with a small group of first graders. Although the children were all reading at their own pace silently, Wendy noticed that none of the students knew the word *mirror* when they came to it in the sentence *He looked into the mirror.* The word was on the bottom of the page toward the end of the story. Wendy, watching the children carefully, also noticed that when Eli came to the bottom of the page, he hesitated for a few minutes and then turned to the next page, which showed the main character's face centered within a frame. Eli looked back at the bottom of the previous page and said, "That says mirror."

Wendy:	How did you figure that out? What makes you think that's *mirror*?
Eli:	I sounded it out. Miiirrr-rrroar.
Wendy:	You don't call that *mir-roar* do you? Take another minute and think about what you did.
Eli:	I knew he was going to find them [glasses on his head]. I wondered where he could be looking that started with an *m*. I then looked at the next page and saw him looking in the mirror and then looked back at the word and I knew it was mirror.

Eli's response about sounding it out is typical of kids early in discussions about miscues, so Wendy asked him to reconsider his strategies once again. After discussion by all the kids in the group about Eli's and Wendy's interaction, Wendy summarized, "You did a lot of good things as you were reading. You knew that you wanted the story to make sense and knew he had to find his glasses. You knew that it would be in a place so you were looking for a place word—we call that a *noun*. You also used what you knew about the sounds . . . because you looked at the first letter of the word. You used the illustration to help you and decided the word was *mirror* and then you checked yourself by looking back at the word to see if all your thinking was right. You did a lot of hard work. You used a lot of good strategies and it worked for you."

Classroom teachers knowledgeable about the reading process engage their students in thinking about their own reading and in talking about the kinds of things that happen as they are reading. Such teachers are masters at making the most out of the critical moments that occur daily as they interact with their students, sometimes in the matter of a few minutes. Through these discussions, students reflect on their knowledge about reading and revalue themselves as readers. It is necessary to legitimatize and document critical moment teaching in order to share these rich experiences with other teachers.

Reading Strategy Lessons offer students opportunities to think about their own strengths as readers and to revalue who they are and what they can do as readers and writers. The strategies described here address readers' needs by starting with their strengths and experiences and then, by using the natural reading strategies of sampling, inferring, predicting, and integrating along with the language cueing systems, help students gain confidence and proficiency in reading.

References

Goodman, Kenneth S. 1964. "The Linguistics of Reading." *Elementary School Journal,* Volume 64, number 8, pp. 355–361.

Goodman, Kenneth S. 1994. "Reading, Writing, and Written Texts: A Transactional Sociopsycholinguistic View." In R. B. Ruddell, M. R. Ruddell, and H. Singer, eds., *Theoretical Models and Processes of Reading,* pp. 1093–1130. Newark, DE: International Reading Association.

Goodman, Yetta M., Altwerger, Bess and Marek, Ann. 1989. *Print Awareness in Preschool Children. Occasional Paper #4.* Tucson, AZ: University of Arizona, Program in Language and Literacy.

Goodman, Yetta M. and Burke, Carolyn L. 1972. *Reading Miscue Inventory, Manual For Diagnosis and Evaluation.* New York, NY: Macmillian Publishing Co.

Goodman, Yetta M. and Marek, Ann. 1996. *Retrospective Miscue Analysis: Revaluing Readers and Reading.* Katonah, NY: Richard C. Owen Publishers, Inc.

Goodman, Yetta M., Watson, Dorothy J., and Burke, Carolyn L. 1987. *Reading Miscue Inventory: Alternative Procedures.* Katonah, NY: Richard C. Owen Publishers, Inc..

Goodman, Yetta M., Watson, Dorothy J. and Burke, Carolyn L. 1996. *Reading Strategies: Focus on Comprehension, second edition.* Katonah, NY: Richard C. Owen Publishers, Inc.

MacGregor, Ellen. 1953. *Miss Pickerell Goes Undersea.* New York: McGraw-Hill Book Company, Inc..

Rosenblatt, Louise. 1938. *Literature as Exploration.* New York, NY: Appleton-Century Crofts.

Rosenblatt, Louise. 1978. *The Reader, the Text, and the Poem.* Carbondale, IL: Southern Illinois University Press.

Smith, Frank. 1988. *Understanding Reading: A Psycholinguistic Analysis of Reading and Learning to Read.* Hillsdale, NJ: L. Erlbaum Associates.

Watson, Dorothy J. 1978. "Getting More From Sustained Silent Reading: Reader Selected Miscues." *English Education,* Volume 10, number 2, pp. 75–85.

Watson, Dorothy J. and Hoge, Sharon. 1996. "Reader-Selected Miscues." In Y. Goodman and A. Marek, eds., *Retrospective Miscue Analysis: Revaluing Readers and Reading.* Katonah, NY: Richard C. Owen Publishers, Inc..

Wilde, Sandra. 1992. *You Kan Red This: Spelling and Punctuation for Whole Language Classrooms, K–6.* Portsmouth, NH: Heinemann.

9 Teaching Strategies and Skills during Readers' Workshop: Setting the Stage for Successful Readers and Writers

Pam Chomsky-Higgins
J.W. Killam Elementary School, Reading, MA

In Chomsky-Higgins's first-grade classroom, readers' workshop is a block of about seventy-five to ninety minutes in the school day when she and the children engage in a variety of reading activities. Each workshop has similar components: read-aloud, shared reading, guided reading, and independent reading. With concrete examples, the author explains and illustrates the commonalities and some of the variations within each component. She explains her criteria for choosing literature to read aloud and explains that they begin each afternoon by reading a chapter book, in addition to her reading aloud during readers' workshop. Following the morning read-aloud is SQUIRT time (Super Quiet Independent Reading Time). Chomsky-Higgins then explains procedures she uses in shared reading. Guided reading offers support and additional challenges for the children: "It is a time when children are encouraged to use the reading strategies that they have learned during shared reading and during independent conferences to read a book that is carefully chosen for them." Again, the author explains their procedures, including the fact that she usually chooses one child from each guided reading group to remain and read to her while she keeps a running record. In the section on independent reading, she explains how the books in the classroom are coded for difficulty level. Daily individual conferences (about five a day) are also an important part of readers' workshop, another time when she can assess the reader's strategies and skills, interests and accomplishments, strengths and needs. The conferences also give her the opportunity to teach strategies and skills that the child seems to need. Finally, Chomsky-Higgins focuses on family participation: how she informs parents about what they are doing in readers' workshop and what she would like the parents to do to support their children's reading.

In conclusion, this teacher notes that readers' workshop is the core of their first-grade curriculum, yet one "closely connected to all other parts of our day and our curriculum." Furthermore, assessment and direct teaching of strategies and skills are woven through various aspects of readers' workshop, making all its components together an ideal vehicle for learning to read.

There is a gentle but constant hum here in Room 13 with occasional voices rising above the rest in excitement or delight or discovery. Twenty-three children in our first-grade classroom are engaged in a number of activities during this time that we call readers' workshop. Glancing around the room you can see Mike and Shane sitting on pillows in the Quiet Zone reading *The Day Jimmy's Boa Ate the Wash*. This has been a favorite of Mike's, and he enjoys sharing it with Shane. Lindsey and Lauren are writing a letter to the principal asking him to repair a piece of playground equipment that is broken. Michelle, Janet, and Katie are reading the big book *The Three Billy Goats Gruff*. All three voices are reading aloud from this familiar text. Mike, Greg, and Billy are working with Mrs. Watt from the Learning Center on their research for a nonfiction book about sharks. Amanda and Jessie are copying a poem about flowers onto chart paper. When finished they will present it to the class as a shared reading. David, Adam, and Carl are writing the script for a play based on the books *Dogzilla* and *Kat Kong* (Pilkey). A great deal of discussion and negotiation is occurring during this collaboration. Kyle has a large pile of predictable texts at his desk, and he is reading each one in turn, transferring completed ones to a second pile. Eppie is sitting in a chair on the rug with three girls listening to her read aloud from one of the Amelia Bedelia books. Leslie is sharing with Nathan a piece of writing that she worked on earlier in the day. Janet's mom is reading aloud to a small group of children on the rug. I am sitting at the reading table with Rebecca as we begin her reading conference. Christine and Dan are looking over the books in their reading bags as they prepare for their conferences.

This is a snapshot of readers' workshop in our first-grade classroom in April. During the previous seven months, a great deal of discussion, modeling, explicit teaching, reading, and writing went into making this spring scene possible. In this chapter I will describe the different components of readers' workshop, how I teach skills and strategies that the children need in order to become strategic and competent readers, how I assess and evaluate what the children are doing, and how I manage all of this. When I use the term *readers' workshop* I mean a time block in our school day of about seventy-five to ninety minutes when the children and I engage in a variety of reading activities.

The Components of Readers' Workshop

Each readers' workshop has similar major components. These include read-aloud, shared reading, guided reading, and independent reading. Within each component are some variations. These components are closely related to each other and to many other activities which occur in the classroom, especially writers' workshop. I will describe these components of readers' workshop using examples from my own classroom.

Read-Aloud

I read aloud to begin readers' workshop for a number of reasons. I want the children to know and love a great number of authors and illustrators and their books. I want the children to hear the language that authors use. I want them to meet interesting characters; to be able to visualize different settings; to hear wonderful language; and more. In the beginning I read aloud with a minimum of comment. I often ask the children to offer their thoughts at the end of a book. They learn a great deal from each other during these conversations. One way of doing this is to have the children sit in a circle and pass the book from one child to the next. When a child is holding the book, she or he has the opportunity to make a comment about the book. Quite often a child notices something in a book that I missed entirely because I was focused on some other aspect of the story. One example of this was when I read aloud *Dear Annie* by Judith Casely. I was reading several books to the children at that time that had examples of different kinds of writing incorporated into the story. In *Dear Annie*, there are letters from a young girl to her grandfather and his replies. As the book was passed around the circle, several children mentioned the letters and commented on whom they wrote letters to. When the book came to David, he said, "I liked this book because the grandfather didn't die. We've read some other books about grandparents and they died in those books. I'm glad this grandfather didn't die." I was surprised by David's comment because I was thinking about the genre of letter writing. Many of the children who followed David in the circle made comments related to his. This changed the entire focus of our lesson. During that readers' workshop several children combed through our classroom library looking for books about grandparents. More discussions about grandparents followed. I knew that I could return to the genre of letter writing another time. As in this example, the children often lead me to real learning events.

Talk is a vital part of every readers' workshop. The children must be given many opportunities throughout the day to discuss their learning, to share their discoveries, and to question each other and to find answers for those questions.

It is incumbent upon me to choose the very best of children's literature for the children to experience. I don't censor what the children choose to read on their own. For example, there are usually some children reading *Goosebumps* books, but I choose not to read those books aloud in the classroom and I explain my reasons to the children.

I choose picture books based on topics that the children and I are studying as part of our social studies or science curriculum. I choose books written or illustrated by the person that we are exploring in our Author/Illustrator Study. I may choose a book because I just discovered it and can't wait to share it. Or one of the children may discover a new book and ask that I share it with the class.

Although it is not a part of readers' workshop, we begin each afternoon by reading a chapter book. It is a great way to come back together as a group. I often begin with *The Stories Julian Tells* (Cameron). *Fantastic Mr. Fox* or *James and the Giant Peach* (Dahl) are excellent choices, as is *Abel's Island* (Steig). *The Time Warp Trio* books by John Scieszka are favorites, including *The Knights of the Kitchen Table* and *The Not-So-Jolly Roger*. This is a great read-aloud time and a way to settle in after lunch.

After shared reading the children choose one or more books, find some place in the classroom, and read quietly. We call this time SQUIRT (Super Quiet Independent Reading Time). At the beginning of the year, we read for about five minutes. By June we usually read for twenty to twenty-five minutes. The children quickly become accustomed to this part of readers' workshop and have one or more books ready to read each day. After SQUIRT we move on to other choices. These choices are brainstormed by the children and me and are posted in the room. They include such options as read alone, read with a friend, read a big book, read the charts, go to listening center, go to first-grade reading wall (a place outside the four first-grade classrooms where we hang charts with enlarged texts of poems, chants, and songs for all of the first graders to read), read with a grown-up, have a conference, write, and do a special project. Early in the year, readers' workshop lasts for about thirty minutes and there are one or two choices. The length of workshop time and the number of choices grow as the year progresses. On most days a parent comes into the classroom to read with the children during this time. I find this particularly helpful when I begin scheduling reading conferences.

Shared Reading

Shared reading is an integral part of readers' workshop. It is during shared reading that a great deal of direct instruction occurs. By *shared reading* I mean a time when students and teachers join together to read aloud from an enlarged text. A smaller text could be used, but only with a small group of children. The important point is that all of the children have the opportunity to clearly see the illustrations and words. Shared reading can be accomplished using a big book or a chart on which a poem, chant, song, or paragraph is written in enlarged letters.

When doing shared reading, I (or a student who is familiar with the text) point to each word in the text, making sure that the pointer does not block the words. I want the children to focus on the words as I read. I am able to model a variety of reading behaviors during shared reading: reading left to right, word-by-word matching, return sweep, and more. The first time that I share a book or poem with the children, I simply read it for the enjoyment. I don't stop in the middle to discuss a strategy or skill. With a big book, I am sure to read the title, the author, the illustrator, the dedication, and the copyright date. These are all parts of a book with which I want the children to become familiar.

I usually use shared reading with the whole class because, particularly at the beginning of a school year, it helps to build the sense of community that is so important to everything that we do in the classroom. By sharing the experience of a story, we are creating a common background of book knowledge, story structure, book language, and literature appreciation. At the beginning of the year I am in the process of assessing what the children know about reading. During shared reading I am able to gather some of this information simply by watching how the children join in and respond. Throughout the year I choose to observe one or two children each day so that my observations are more focused. I take short, quick notes on a clipboard and then file these notes in the children's reading folders.

Shared reading gives children the opportunity to practice reading behaviors while being supported by their classmates. With everyone joining in there is no pressure for any one child to perform alone. Once the children have become familiar with a text, I try to have small copies of the book available for them to read during other parts of readers' workshop. If the text is a poem or song on a chart, I print out a small copy for each child to keep. The very strategies that I emphasize during shared reading are the ones that children will use during guided reading and independent reading. I look for evidence that these strategies are being used in order to give me information about our next shared reading session.

With the big book *The Enormous Watermelon*, I begin with an exploration of the cover. I read the title and then ask the children to predict what the story might be about. I take all predictions, asking children to explain their reasoning when I can't make the connection. I begin reading the book, which has a similar storyline to the folktale about the giant turnip that took an increasing number of characters in the story to pull up from the ground.

In *The Enormous Watermelon*, the characters who help to pull up the watermelon are from familiar nursery rhymes. There are many aspects of this book which support emergent readers. Each character is foreshadowed on a page with a visual clue, e.g., a wall for Humpty Dumpty, a pail for Jack and Jill. The text has a repeating pattern that is printed in a different color than the rest of the text. The word *enormous* is written in very large letters. The illustrations closely match the text. As I begin reading, the children usually join in the repeating text during the first reading. They also notice the visual clues and begin making predictions about the character on the next page without my asking. This book is a natural choice when prediction is one of the reading strategies that I want to explore with the children.

Once the children and I have read the book a few times, we can begin to explore other reading skills and strategies. We can look at letter-sound relationships, rhyming words, story sequence, and more. How do I choose what skills and strategies to focus on? In the beginning I present the early concepts about print in an explicit manner by asking the children such questions as *Where do I begin reading? Where do I go after I reach the end of a line?* I also ask open-ended questions that allow every child to be successful. One such question would be *Can you find a letter, a word, or some punctuation in this text that you can share with us?* This leaves the choice of what to share up to each child and ensures that each child will be successful.

A note of caution about big books: simply enlarging a book into big-book size does not make an appropriate choice for shared reading. Particularly with emergent readers, the book should have only one line of text on a page with ample space between each word. As the children become more competent readers, big books with more text can be shared, but there should still be only a few lines on each page and the text should be of an appropriate size.

With an enlarged text on a chart such as a poem or story that we have written together, I follow similar procedures. I read the poem through once or twice in order for the children to hear the rhythm of the language. Once the children have begun to join in, we can begin our exploration of the same skills and strategies as we do in a big book.

I am able to laminate the charts that I make so the children can write on them using a felt-tip marker. We can circle all of the words that rhyme or the words that begin with a particular sound. Once we have done several of these explorations together as a class, the children begin doing this as an independent activity during readers' workshop. I hear them say to each other, "Can you find a word that begins like *star*?" or "How many times is the word *with* in the poem?" I have also used colored transparent tape or wicky stix (waxy strips that stick temporarily to laminated charts) to highlight words. Having the children actively interact with the poem is very beneficial for most children.

Guided Reading

Guided reading is a very important part of readers' workshop. It is a time when children are encouraged to use the reading strategies that they have learned during shared reading and during independent conferences to read a book that is carefully chosen for them. Children are chosen for a guided reading group based on the strategies that they have established and the ones that they need to work on. For example, I may choose four or five children who read for meaning but who are not focusing on visual cues as they read. In other words, they are not using the phonics skills and strategies that they have learned as they read. Or I may choose a group of children who focus too heavily on visual cues, which causes them to simply word call and not to understand what they are reading.

When I have chosen a group of children, I then search for a book that will provide enough supports for the children to be successful as they read but which will, at the same time, offer some challenges for the children to meet. This matching of texts with children is a crucial part of guided reading and one that takes a good deal of knowledge on the part of the teacher about books and about the children in the class.

A typical guided reading session begins with the children and I sitting together around a small table or in a circle on the rug. I tell the children the title of the book, and we talk about what the book might be about. We go through the book together, looking at the illustrations to get the idea of the story. I do not read the book to the children, nor do I ask them to read aloud during our first look at the book. I may ask the children to point out known words in the text. After this supportive book introduction, the children read the book on their own. They read out loud, and I move among the children to listen to them read and to offer assistance if needed. After the children have read the book, we may have a brief discussion about what we read. I may also suggest an extension activity which is related to the book. I always ask the children to read the book alone or to a friend in the class. I also give the children a copy of the book to take home to read with someone that night.

I usually choose one child from each guided reading group to remain with me after the other children have gone to reread their books. I ask this child to read the book out loud to me so that I can do a running record. This is a method of collecting information about how a reader uses skills and strategies to meet the challenges presented by a text. On a blank sheet of paper I record exactly what a child reads, using check marks and a few symbols for miscues and self-corrections. Copies of each student's running records are collected in his or her reading folder. Instructionally, I use running records to note a child's progress, to plan guided reading groups, to determine what texts a child should be choosing to read independently, and to discover areas of strength and areas in which a child may need further support and instruction. With practice, running records are quite easy to do.

Independent Reading

During our early readers' workshops, I read aloud or give a brief book talk about the books that make up the core of our reading program. These books include predictable texts from several different publishers as well as a large number of trade books. The books are arranged in bins with a colored dot on the front cover of each book. I explain the kinds of books that are in each bin. It is important for the children to have a general understanding of the supports and challenges presented by the books. The dots indicate to the children the different levels of reading support that the texts offer to the reader. For example, yellow-dot books have a memorable, repetitive language pattern, illustrations that strongly support the text, consistent placement of text, and, a story line or topic that is familiar to children. These books are quite short, as are the sentences within them. Some books that the children would find in the yellow bin are *Growing Colors* (McMillan), *Count and See* (Hoban), *Rain* (Kalan); *All Fall Down* (Wildsmith); *Brown Bear, Brown Bear, What Do You See?* (Martin), and *Have You Seen My Cat?* (Carle).

Red-dot books have some memorable, repetitive patterns as part of the text but with more variation, illustrations that continue to support the text, and, generally familiar objects and actions. Some examples are *The Chick and the Duckling* (Ginsburg), *Mary Wore Her Red Dress* (Peek), *Where's Spot?* (Hill), and *Oh, A-Hunting We Will Go* (Langstaff).

Books with blue dots have longer sentences and varied sentence patterns. The illustrations provide some support, and written or book language is more evident as opposed to the oral language patterns of earlier books. Some books in this bin are *Rosie's Walk* (Hutchins), *Cookie's Week* (Ward), *Each Peach Pear Plum* (Ahlberg), and *The Carrot Seed* (Krauss).

Next the children find green-dot books that have a greater variety of words, longer sentences, and illustrations that provide some clues to the meaning but less support than in earlier levels. These books include *I Was Walking Down the Road* (Barchas), *Goodnight Moon* (Brown), *We're Going on a Bear Hunt* (Rosen), and *The Napping House* (Wood).

In the final bin (orange dots) are longer stories with rich and varied vocabulary and more evidence of literary language. Illustrations provide minimal support. Some of these books are *There's a Nightmare in My Closet* (Mayer), *Mouse Soup* (Lobel), *Where the Wild Things Are* (Sendak), and *A House Is a House for Me* (Hoberman).

I began the organization of these books in my classroom using the information from chapter 6 in *Bridges to Literacy* (DeFord, Lyons, & Pinnell, 1991). I now add books to the bins using the information from that chapter as well as conversations with my fellow teachers. Another excellent source for leveling books is the addendum in *Guided Reading: Good First Teaching for All Children* (Fountas & Pinnell, 1996). As I have become familiar with larger numbers of books, it has become easier for me to organize them.

Although the majority of students choose books from these bins at the beginning of the school year, they are not restricted to these bins. Books are stored in a number of different ways in our classroom. We have a large shelf with many bins on it which we call our library. All of the books here are organized by author and are facing forward. Although all of the children are responsible for replacing books appropriately, two children each week have the task of making sure that the books are where they should be in this library. Near the bins of leveled books the children can find wordless books, I Can Read books, chapter books, etc. In the listening center there are bags with tapes and multiple copies of the accompanying book. In the math area there is another bin of books related to this subject, such as *Anno's Counting Book* (Anno), *How Many Is a Million?* (Schwartz), and *Each Orange Has Eight Slices* (Giaganti). During the year one of the children may decide that a book in our library really belongs in our math area. She or he tells the class the reasons for moving the book to the math area. After some discussion a decision is made.

To continue around the classroom: in the science area are yet more bins with books about various areas of science. The majority of these books are nonfiction. During several readers' workshop sessions this year, the children took out all of the books in the science area and organized them by topic. Some of the topics they discovered were astronomy and space, animals, dinosaurs and fossils, and plant life. Near the library are three bins full of poetry books.

One area of the classroom is generally set aside for the science or social studies topic that we are focusing on. In this area are two bins for the books that pertain this topic: one for fiction and one for nonfiction. At the beginning of each unit of study, the children scour the room for all of the books we have that are related to this topic. Then they decide whether the books are fiction or nonfiction. This has been a topic of several previous discussions during readers' workshop. The conversations that accompany these choices and decisions are important and interesting.

Individual Conferences

Each child in the class meets with me at least once a week for an individual reading conference. During this time we discuss one of the books that he or she has read in the previous few days. Discussions focus on what was important to the reader. I may ask why the child chose the book, what it was that made the book interesting, what was hard about the book, what he or she liked best about the book. The child then reads the book aloud to me: the entire book if it is short or any part the child chooses if the book is quite long. During this oral reading I make notes on a reading conference sheet concerning the strategies the child is using as well as any miscues and self-corrections he or she makes. I also note any discussions we have about skills and strategies. I make additional comments as needed. In this way I have a great deal of information about each child and his or her reading progress. I record the title of book being read along with the level. These conferences usually last for five to six minutes, allowing me to meet with about five children each day.

These conferences give me the opportunity to focus closely on one child at a time. After the child has read aloud to me, I always point out the strategies that the child used successfully and the self-corrections that I noticed. I usually choose one teaching point from the book to discuss with the child. For example, if the child read the word *flower* as *tulip* in a sentence about a garden, I would return to that sentence. I would ask the child to read the sentence again. If the miscue occurred again, I would cover the word *flower* and ask the child to tell me what letter he or she would expect to see at the beginning of the word *tulip*. When he or she said *t*, I would uncover the first letter of the word and ask the child, "Could this be the word *tulip*? When he or she said that it could not be, I would ask what other word that begins with f or fl would make sense in the sentence

The same teaching strategy would have been modeled during a previous shared reading time using a big book with the entire class. This is another example of how the components of readers' workshop are closely connected and build on one another.

Usually during readers' workshop one or more projects are being planned and accomplished. The children brainstorm, write, and illustrate a number of class books throughout the year. I like to have enough class books completed by the end of the year so that each child can choose one to take home. The children may create an alphabet book based on a topic we are exploring in science or social studies or they may retell a story in their own words with accompanying illustrations. Small groups of children may practice the oral reading necessary in readers' theater and then put on a performance for the class. It is important to note that any project or activity that the children work on has been explained and modeled before they begin. Therefore the children have clear guidelines for working together and completing a project.

I have found that for the most part the children are able to appropriately choose and remain engaged in activities during readers' workshop for several reasons: We have discussed and planned the workshop time together as a class. The variety of choices meets the needs of all the children. We have spent a good deal of time at the beginning of the school year establishing a sense of community in our classroom. This affects everything we do. There is a real excitement about reading and writing among these six- and seven-year-olds. They have impromptu book discussions with each other. I hear conversations such as, "Have you read the new *Henry and Mudge* book that we just got?" "No. Is it funny like the first one we read?" "I just started looking at it. Want to read it with me?" Or I hear children initiate their own author study: "I liked *Thundercake* that Ms. C-H read to us. Will you help me find more books by that author?""O.K. Let's get the P bin." (Note: The author is Patricia Polacco.) These conversations and interactions let me know that the children are reading and thinking about books in much the same way that I talk about books with my friends.

Family Participation

As I have described, the children are given time to explore many books during readers' workshop each day. They then choose one or more books that they would like to read with someone at home. These books go into a plastic bookbag along with a letter to families explaining our reading program. These bookbags become a critical piece in the family-school work (homework) the students must do during the week. I ask families to read to their children and listen to their children read as often as possible. Included in the bookbag is a form for the adults at home to fill in with the book title, whether it was read to, with, or by the child, and comments or questions about the books or the reading their child did. This form becomes an excellent means for the families and me to communicate about what is happening with each child's reading progress. I am able to use it to make suggestions to adults at home about reading with their child. Everyone is able to see the progress being made throughout the year. The letter to families explains individual reading conferences, details schedules, explains the strategic process that is reading, and offers suggestions for ways that adults at home can support their child. This letter also explains that the children will be choosing their own reading material and will be learning to make appropriate choices. This make take a few tries for some children. I will support them in the classroom, but the final decision is theirs. I encourage daily reading from the books in the bookbag, but emphasize the fact that this reading should not take the place of the reading rituals already in place at home. The information in this letter is reinforced with weekly classroom newsletters that often explain or reiterate what we are doing in reading, as well as in all aspects of our school day.

I have found that the more information that I share with families, the more they understand what their children are doing in our classroom and the more supportive they become. Parents only want the best for their children but often aren't sure what this might look like in the classroom. In one letter I described how the children will begin to acquire sight vocabulary. Regie Routman calls these high-frequency words "bookwords" in her book *Transitions* (1988), and I have adopted this term in our classroom:

> **Bookwords** are the new thing in Room 13 this week. Bookwords are the words that the children see most often in books that they are reading. They are also called *sight words* or *high-frequency words*. The children copy the bookword into a small book that they have been given. Then they write a sentence using the bookword. They may use temporary spelling when writing the sentence. However, they must spell the bookword correctly. This activity gives the children the opportunity to practice the mechanics of writing. They will learn about spelling, capitalization, and punctuation rules. Each day the bookword will be posted on a wall in the classroom which becomes our wall dictionary. The children may refer to this wall when writing. I will let you know what the bookwords are each week in this newsletter. The children will learn these words most effectively by reading and by writing. It is not useful to the children

to make flashcards since it is much harder to read a word in isolation than in context. The bookwords for this week are *the, a,* and *and.* You may want to help your child notice these words in the books they are reading at home.

Another brief section in one of our newsletters described a discussion that the children and I had together and then a readers' minilesson:

> Before readers' workshop on Tuesday, the children brainstormed all the reading strategies that they can use to figure out a word they don't know. This is their list:
>
> - Sound out the word.
> - Skip that word and read the rest of the sentence and then go back.
> - Ask a friend.
> - Try different words to see what sounds right.
> - Look for the same word somewhere else.
> - Look at the illustrations.
>
> The children are learning when to use each strategy. Or to try each strategy until one works. This is what is known as becoming a strategic reader. I use all of these terms with the children so that we can talk about what they are doing when they read. It is important for the children to know what they are doing and why.
>
> Another example of a reading mini-lesson: In a big book, *Swimmy,* I covered some of the words in the text with self-stick notes before showing the book to the children. As we read it together, the children considered all the possibilities for each covered word. That meant they were using the context and maybe the illustrations to read the word. Then we looked at just the first letter of the word to narrow the possibilities. That meant we were using graphophonics to figure out the word. The children were surprised to find out that they could figure out a word without even seeing it. The first letter or letters confirmed the guess. The children could see that trying to read a word by sounding out each letter in the word is not the best way to read. I hope you will try this when you are reading with your children at home. With your child looking at the text, have him or her make some guesses about what a word might be based on the context and on the illustrations. Then use the first letter to confirm the guess. Any questions? I'll explain further at our upcoming conferences.

Summary

Readers' workshop is the core of our first-grade classroom; it is closely connected to all other parts of our day and of our curriculum. The children come to our classroom with a wide range of reading experiences and abilities. My goal is to help each child become a strategic reader and an avid reader. In other words, while I know that every child needs to learn the skills and strategies necessary to read competently, it is equally important that every child learns to love reading.

10 Developing Primary Voices

Kathleen Visovatti
Des Plaines Public Schools, Illinois

Visovatti first discusses how she began engaging her first graders in setting their goals for the year, which of course included learning to read and write. She decided to make immersion in reading "a major form of instruction," and to encourage the children to develop strategies for processing texts independently. They came to focus on a "Strategy of the Week," and the children were given bookmarks based on some of the their own suggestions for what you can do when you don't know all the words. Visovatti explains, too, how the weekly strategy lessons were organized. She emphasizes how the children learned to evaluate themselves as developing readers and writers. The article concludes with useful references and forms for portfolio assessment of reading and for assessing reading strategies.

Originally published in *Primary Voices K–6*, 2(2), (1994), 8–19. Copyright 1994 by the National Council of Teachers of English.

After thirteen years as a middle school language arts teacher, I asked to be moved to the primary grades so that I could teach more holistically than forty-five-minute departmentalized periods permitted. After five exciting years in second grade where student inquiry led to day-long reading and writing workshops, I asked to go to first grade as a team leader to share my vision of natural language learning with beginning readers/writers, their parents, and my colleagues.

Establishing the Circumstances for Inquiry

On the first day, I asked my first graders to brainstorm possibilities for study during our year together. I had written a letter to each of them in early August, inviting them to think about what they wanted to learn and ways they could share that learning with others (Crafton, 1991). The children became, as Jerome Harste suggests, the curricular informants (Harste, Woodward, & Burke, 1984). We were creating the curriculum rather than covering it, or, as Dorothy Watson said (1993), the children would begin to uncover the curriculum through invitations to inquire.

I must admit, I held my breath as I gave them the control. I felt an enormous sense of responsibility about their learning to read. I sincerely believed that the majority would teach themselves, but what about those that would need my help? I have another admission: In all my years of teaching, I have never spent a more exhausting and yet rewarding time as the two years in first grade. I felt pulled in twenty-four directions at all times: if children could do something on their own, they wanted to show me they could; if children couldn't operate independently, they wanted help from me. Being in first grade was like witnessing time lapse photography—their gradual independence and blossoming of self-confidence were glorious to behold.

I started first grade as an inquiry teacher, but not a particularly reflective one, so my second year in first grade, with Linda Crafton as a collaborator in the classroom, I set two new goals for myself: first, to help children become self-evaluators by reflecting on and becoming more aware of their literacy processes, and second, to explore portfolio development as an instructional opportunity as well as an assessment tool.

Meanwhile, the children had established their goals:

- To Read and Write
- To Tell Time
- To Subtract
- To Use a Calculator
- To Add 3 and 4 Digit Numbers
- To Spell More Words
- To Color
- To Train Pets
- To Find Out if Grown-ups Are Bigger than Cacti

Reflecting on Ourselves as Readers/Writers

On the first day of school nearly every child expressed a desire to learn to read and write. So, on an Environmental Print Walk around school that day, I commented, "I bet you already can read some things around you." This was met with a chorus of response: "I can read stop signs." "I can read restaurant and grocery store signs." "I can read boxes in stores." "I write stories." "I can read my favorite bedtime story." "I can write my name."

My expectation was that all the children were or soon would be readers and writers. They followed my lead, looking at all the things they could read already. If they realized today that they were readers of environmental print, tomorrow they would see themselves as readers of stories.

These kinds of investigations occurred often in the first few days of school and allowed all of us to establish a baseline profile that we could use to measure future growth and change. Baseline information through testing is something imposed on children to find out what they do not know. In contrast, our baseline data helped us to understand what we each knew and felt about our literacy environment.

The expectation that children would be immersed in reading as a major form of instruction was explained to parents in the initial issue of our weekly class newspaper which went home the first week of school. Parents were asked to incorporate reading, writing, and math activities into their child's daily routine. They were urged to let students choose their own read-aloud books, and to encourage questions and conversations about each page. Writing could take many forms, including a shopping list, a letter, or original prose. Parents were also reminded to allow their children to develop at their own pace, and to accept invented spellings as a normal step in literacy acquisition.

I asked the children how people learn to read and write. Some of the responses were: "From parents reading to me." "Older sisters and brothers playing school." "By sounding out words." I then introduced them to a text set on reading and writing which we added to all year and kept in a special place.

One student chose *I Can Read with My Eyes Shut* every day for Sustained Silent Reading (SSR) until he could! His mother sighed at the November conference, "He'll only read that one book and he isn't really reading it—he's memorized it."

At the January conference she said, "He's finally choosing a few other books, too. Do you know what he showed me? Some of the words in that first book are in the books he's looking at now. He recognized them. I am so proud. I think he's going to learn to read after all." I responded quietly, "I believe he already has."

During the April conference she confided, "I had misgivings when you said at the fall Open House that children learn to read by reading and being read to, and so both would go on throughout the school day and, hopefully, at home as well. But you were right. It worked. Look at him now." She pointed to Jay who was sorting through the reading section of his portfolio, looking at the photocopied covers of favorite books he had read (*I Can Read with My Eyes Shut* was on the top of the pile!), his response to literature journal, and his written thoughts about his reading. "Thank you," she said, "for giving him the time and the encouragement to teach himself to read."

Responding to children's avowed goal of learning to read and write in first grade led to a discussion of the routine we would follow every day. Thus the expectation was established right from the start that mornings and the first part of the afternoon would be devoted to reading and writing, reflecting, and sharing. Each child would have extended periods of time to read with others and to read alone. Support would always be available, but the reader would be encouraged to rely on her/himself by applying strategies. I made an observation at the first Sharing Time as the initial Reading Workshop came to an end, "I have been noticing how many books are being read in this classroom. You've brought favorites from home, know the ones from the text set about reading and writing, and have discovered others all over the room (e.g., books such as *The Art Lesson* and *Harold and the Purple Crayon* in the art corner, *As the Crow Flies* and *Folktales from Around the World* in the social studies corner *Amazing Animal Facts* and *The Magic School Bus* series in the science corner, *The Doorbell Rang* and *How Much Is a Million?* in the math corner, *Pyramid* in the block area, *You Be Me and I'll Be You* and assorted plays in the dress-up area, and Raffi books and tapes and taped books [recorded by older students and volunteer parents] about starting school in the listening area). Can you read all the words in these books?"

Most responded, "No." There were a few yeses. "Well, what do you do," I asked, "when you don't know all the words?"

"Give up. Pick another book."

"Look at the pictures."

"Skip them."

"Go on."

I introduced the word *strategies* as "ways to solve problems," and asked if they'd heard of the word in connection with coaches or athletes who try to figure out ways to win. Then I asked if Linda and I could make bookmarks out of some of their suggestions (see Figure 1).

The next day each child received a brightly colored, laminated bookmark. "Let's focus on the strategy of picture clues for the next two weeks." Thus began the "Strategy of the Week" instructional procedure, suggested by Linda who visited the classroom regularly. We practiced reading pictures by looking at bookcovers and predicting what they would be about, then looked at the illustrations to predict the content, guess the endings, and imagine the book to be funny or serious, fantasy or reality. I asked if they thought they'd like to read the words as

Figure 1. Bookmark sample.

well as the pictures, and if so, they could keep the book for a while. This seemed like the right time to take from their backpacks the following supplies requested from home:

- a pocket folder
- a box of sealable plastic bags—one was kept in the folder for taking books home
- an audio tape—to periodically record fluency and strategy awareness
- a spiral notebook—to keep a record of books read and to respond to literature.

I explained that I would meet with each of them once a week "so that you can talk about your reading and we can read together." There was much bustle as reading folders were begun that second day of school.

In the course of a week, I moved around the room during Independent Reading Time touching base with children, one on one. What had they learned about reading today? What would they do differently tomorrow? Would they like to read with or to me? What sort of entries had they made in their Writing about Reading Journal? These reflective questions set the tone for the whole year. The message was clear: You are in charge of your own learning. You can evaluate how it's going. You will always have choices and time. We will share responses as a group in order to support one another and to celebrate learning. I kept an alphabetical class list on a clipboard with me at all times so I could keep track of these conferences. I continued where I left off the next day. I kept anecdotal notes in a folder for each child. These proved an invaluable reference at future conferences. "I see in my notes that you've been reading the same book this week as last week. Would you like to take it home to finish it? Have you recorded anything about it in your journal this week? Last week you listed the title and author." This documentation was helpful at Parent-Teacher-Student conferences. I could support and extend what the child shared.

A Reflection Table was introduced where the Strategy of the Week was named. Children were invited to share their strategy applications in one of three ways: writing in an open journal (called the Strategy Log), ringing a bell to make an announcement, or speaking privately into a hand-held tape recorder about what they had learned and how they learned it. This encouraged students to become more aware of their literary processes.

The most popular reflective technique by far was Pictured Reflections, an idea shared by Carolyn Burke at the Whole Language Umbrella in 1991. Students asked a classmate to take an instant photo at a moment of meaningful inquiry. The caption under the photo explained the process underway.

Occasionally, the Strategy Log and, frequently, the photo album, dubbed "Catch Me Learning," were chosen as SSR selections by students. When the album sleeves were filled, the photos were put in students' portfolios and the album was returned to the Reflection Table to be used again. (The supply request list sent to parents in the summer included a double pack of instamatic film.) At the end of the year the photos went home.

As the months passed, one Strategy of the Week led to another. The strategy lesson was organized in the following way: demonstration, observation, conscious use, celebration, reflection, and action. The strategy sequence that evolved this particular year was:

- reading pictures
- making predictions
- confirming predictions
- rereading to make meaning
- substituting words that make sense
- using context clues
- using the first and last letter of a word to help sound it out
- scanning for important words
- looking it up

The order came about out of need (for example, scanning surfaced when children discovered the reference books in the room and began pouring through them, looking for key words) or what seemed logical to Linda or me (for example, following predictions with confirmation or rethinking). The growing list was posted above the Reflection Table.

At first it was hard for five- and six-year-olds to express how they had processed their reading. Many were eager to share *what* they had read, but few were able to verbalize *how* they had done it. As their abilities to talk about their strategies developed, the process sharing grew beyond a mere parroting of, "I used the strategy of . . ." to reflections like this:

> Yea, yea, I get it. Oops. What does that mean? I'll go back and reread this sentence, maybe I'll get it on the second try. Nope, it still doesn't make sense. Well, I'll just go on. Maybe I'll understand it later on, hopefully, it won't matter. Argh! It does matter and I don't get it. Now what'll I do? What's messing me up? That one word. Have I ever seen it before? Don't think so. What would make sense there? I'll put a word in I do know, and get on with my reading. What would fit? Let's see, I'll try to pronounce the unknown word. Hmmm. It starts with an "e" and this whole thing is about elephants. Is the word *elephant?* No. That doesn't make sense. Could it be *enormous?* Does huge fit here? Yes! I think I've got it!

Devoting as much time to process as to content during sharing times helped them become more reflective. The Reflection Table demonstrated abstract ideas concretely. The children decided to arrange books in crates on either side of the Reflection Table according to the strategies they highlighted. This organizational system grew as the year progressed.

Once again, the children asked their own questions and found their own answers. This practice was true in the realm of evaluation as well as in curriculum planning and class management.

Ending and Beginning with the Learner's Voice

During the first month of school, Linda and I introduced the idea of portfolio building as an instructional tool. We suggested building time into the Friday schedule for reflection on the week's learning by organizing desks. The first Friday, the children arrayed desk contents in front of them on the floor. There were five folders. The reading folder has already been described. Other folders held writing and math investigations. I asked, "What are you putting into your reading folder?" The responses included:

"Books," "My 'Writing about Reading Journal,'" "Plastic bags," "Bookmarks."

When one child answered, "Me reading," there was much laughter and discussion that resulted in "Photographs of me reading," "Photographs of projects about books," "Photocopies of covers of books I've read," "An audio tape of me reading," "A videotape of me acting out a favorite book."

Linda and I set a positive we-know-you'll-think-of-things tone and offered suggestions for possible ways to document reading progress, but the final list posted as a result of brainstorming belonged to the children. They decided to call it, "Proof I'm a Reader." Someone said, "Now let's make one for writing and one for math." More charts went up, "Proof I'm a Writer" and "Proof I'm a Mathematician." Every Friday students sorted through their work of the week, checking the charts, adding more evidence of themselves as readers, writers, and mathematicians. After a few weeks, several students complained that their folders were too full and the contents were getting damaged. At first, they wanted to take their work home, but I reminded them that it was important to keep this evidence of their learning progress—for themselves and for parents and visitors.

It was at this time that Linda showed the class her artist friend's portfolio and I shared one I was creating of myself as a reflective reader and writer for a graduate class I was teaching. Mine was made from two pieces of tagboard and I just happened to have a drawer of tagboard in the art area. The rest of the morning was devoted to portfolio building, literally.

Some spent time deciding what should go in them, but most of the energy went into decorating them, which told a lot about their interests and how they viewed themselves as learners. We tried out a variety of names to distinguish their work-in-progress folders from the folders storing finished work. We settled on "Working Folders" for the reading and writing in progress that would stay in their desks. Every

Friday desks were cleaned and completed pieces organized in the "Showcase Portfolios," which were kept in accessible cubbies. Children would often choose their portfolios as one reading choice during SSR, especially at Parent-Teacher-Student conference time. I observed them rehearsing what they would say when they presented their portfolios to their parents. This happened in the fall, winter, and spring.

Student-led conferences had been my practice for many years. This year, they were particularly effective because of the portfolios' concrete demonstration of growth. The child could say, "Look how my hand-writing has changed. I'm not writing so big anymore," and, "Here are the books I have read so far this year. See, I really like Dr. Seuss. Let me read one to you," or "I used to get confused about what was adding and subtracting. Now I know this is adding (showing a photo combining sets of manipulatives). There are fifteen here. And this is sub-tracting (pointing to a photo showing one set taken away). Now there are ten here."

That the portfolios were instructional opportunities as well as reflec-tive evaluation was demonstrated by comments to parents like these:

"Look at these journal entries. I have so many. Hmmm. Every page starts with I. That's kind of boring."

"I've read a lot of books. Most are real short. I might choose a chap-ter book someday."

"This photo shows my favorite manipulatives. These cubes are ones. This is a ten. That's the same as ten ones. Want to count tens with me?"

These moments of self-reflection were a pleasure to note and record, as were the smiles and winks of pride and appreciation the parents and I exchanged as children told us how they saw themselves as learn-ers. Even more rewarding were the follow-through discussions at later conferences. At the end-of-the-year conference, Jeff responded to the query, "What changes do you notice about yourself as a reader and writer this year?"

> I used to spend most of the Writing Workshop time drawing pic-tures. I got ideas from TV and computer games. I wanted to be an artist. Now I make up my own stories. I still draw pictures, but the words come first. It used to take me a long time to get an idea. Most of the Sustained Silent Writing (the first ten minutes of Writing Workshop) I'd doodle. Now I'm getting ideas all the time. I decide on the way in from recess what to write about.
>
> Now all of the Writing Workshop is SSW for me. I groan when we have to quit for Sharing Time, but I always want to be one of the ones to share because I get ideas for how to continue from the kids. If they laugh at a part, I make it longer and do it again. Some-times I work on the same story all week.

I used to be embarrassed when everyone was looking at me when I sat in the Sharing Chair (mini rocker on a rug). I'd mumble and everyone would say 'What? Speak Up!' Then I'd get even more embarrassed. Now I can hardly wait to share because I know they like my writing. Other kids get ideas from me. They'll come to my desk and ask me if they can write like me. That makes me feel good. I want to be a writer when I grow up.

One thing I've noticed. My stories are much longer than my journal entries. I write about myself in my journal. I've never written a story about me. I always write fantasies. Maybe I'll write about myself sometime, a chapter book, I think. I'll only write the good things, though.

At first, many students resisted analyzing why they had selected certain pieces. Jake, for instance, was unwilling to delve into the reasons for his choice.

"Why do I have to tell you why? I already know this is good. That's why it's in my portfolio" (see Figure 2).

"Why is it good?" I asked.

"Because."

"Because why?"

"Because I like it."

"Why do you like it?"

"Because it's good."

"What makes it good?"

"It's about my Mom."

As Donald Graves said (1993), children grow as evaluators of their work from naming it to comparing it.

"It's better."

"Better than what?"

Figure 2. Jake's drawing.

"What I used to write. The kids didn't use to laugh before and now they do."

During one student-led parent conference, a father listened to all his daughter had to say, acknowledged the contents of her portfolio, and then turned to me and said, "Yes, but what does she need to work on?"

I looked him in the eye and replied, "Let's ask Rhonda what she needs." At that moment of turning the reflection over to the child, I thought, this is what inquiry-based evaluation is all about—children owning the process from beginning to end as they ask their own questions, think about their own answers, and plan their own futures—children in charge of their own learning. As Rhonda began to speak, I leaned forward to listen. So did her father.

References

Burke, C. "Curriculum as inquiry." Presentation at the Whole Language Umbrella Conference, Phoenix, Ariz., August, 1991.

Crafton, L. 1991. *Whole language: Getting started . . . moving forward.* Katonah, NY: Richard C. Owen.

Graves, D. "Portfolio assessment." Workshop given at the Walloon Institute, Petosky, Mich., June, 1993.

Harste, J. C., V. A. Woodward, and C. L. Burke. 1984. *Language stories and literacy lessons.* Portsmouth, NH: Heinemann.

Watson, D., and J. Harste. "Moving into and moving with whole language." Presentation during the Whole Language Umbrella Teleconference. Oklahoma State University Extension, Stillwater, Okla., February, 1993.

11 The Teaching of Reading Strategies

Donna Maxim
Center for Teaching and Learning, Edgecomb, Maine

Cora Lee Five
Edgewood School, Scarsdale, New York

Maxim and Five begin by offering a definition of skills and strategies. As they clarify, "a skill becomes a *strategy* when the learner can use it independently, when he/she can reflect on it and understand how it works." After further elaborating the concept of strategies and how teachers can support learners in their development and use, Maxim and Five provide a wide range of sample strategies readers might use. These, in turn, are illustrated and amplified with powerful classroom vignettes written by Margaret Roberts and Kathy Short. The authors conclude that teachers should aim to help students acquire new reading strategies so that they have a variety of options to use as they encounter new reading experiences.

Originally published in *School Talk*, 3 (1997). Copyright 1997 by the National Council of Teachers of English.

How can we help our students become good readers? In this chapter, we will focus on the teaching of reading strategies and illustrate these with powerful classroom vignettes, written by guest authors Margaret Roberts and Kathy Short. We will show how strategies can be taught in meaningful contexts within whole-class settings, small-group instruction, and through individual conferences.

First, though, we want to share a useful explanation of skills and strategies: "*Skills* describes a set of helpful tools that students practice in order to improve reading. A skill becomes a *strategy* when the learner can use it independently, when he/she can reflect on and understand how it works and then apply it to new reading material" (Robb, 1996; emphasis added).

We believe in a developmental reading continuum, and we know that each child comes to us with individual reading strategies. As teachers, we continually demonstrate skills and strategies, modeling them through explicit, direct, and systematic teaching. Some of those reading skills and strategies include context clues, use of prior knowledge, and phonics. (We will not address the phonics vs. whole language matter in this issue, because we believe phonics is essential to any reading program. See chapter 5, "Why Talk about Phonics.")

As teachers, we need to be knowledgeable about the reading process. Our teaching of reading strategies is guided by three cueing systems (Goodman, Watson, & Burke, 1996):

Graphophonic—using relationships between the sounds and written forms of language. Does the word look right? Does the word match what we are saying?

Syntactic—using interrelationships between words, sentences, and paragraphs; structure and grammar. Does it sound right?

Semantic—using meaning, context, and background knowledge. Does it make sense? We want students to be aware of and be able to use all three cueing systems as strategies to make meaning, and not rely heavily on just one system.

Another integral part of becoming a proficient reader is the time students spend reading, writing, speaking, and listening, so we value students working with all kinds of texts across the curriculum. Connie Weaver (1994, p. 154) uses the reader's intention when approaching the text to categorize other reading strategies:

- reading with a purpose
- drawing upon prior knowledge
- predicting
- effectively sampling the visual display
- confirming and correcting
- monitoring comprehension
- reviewing and retaining desired information and concepts
- adjusting rate and approach depending upon purpose

Strategies:

- are general cognitive and social processes used by readers to construct meaning during reading and writing.
- focus on general processes of how to learn.
- support students in becoming independent learners/readers.
- help students develop a repertoire of options they can choose from when they encounter difficulty.

- have no particular sequence; students begin with whatever strategies they are currently using and add new strategies so they have a range of options.
- are developed as students actually engage in reading and writing.
- are a never-ending process of learning.

In a strategy approach, students do still learn pieces of information but their focus is not on isolated words and letters, but on broad strategies for reading and writing. Instead of focusing on learning the *M* sound, they learn that they can use the strategy of looking at the letters of a word, especially the first letter, to help them predict a word. They learn the sounds gradually as they read and write rather than being taught those sounds in isolation prior to reading. Phonics is an important aspect of reading but can be used easily only if the reader already has a rough idea of what the word might be through using context clues. Phonics becomes difficult to use if it is isolated from context (the meaning and structure of language and stories).

Examples of strategies readers might use:

- Predicting, using context and letter-sound relationships
- Reading on to see whether predictions make sense
- Self-correcting when something does not make sense
- Seeing whether the sentence sounds right (grammar)
- Thinking about what would make sense
- Thinking about what you already know about a topic
- Making a connection to other related stories
- Using the letters and sounds to make a prediction
- Breaking a word into parts
- Relating the word to a familiar word (*how–now*)
- Skipping the word and going on
- Reading on to get more information on what a word might be
- Looking up really important words in the dictionary
- Asking someone who knows the word
- Rereading a difficult passage, getting another running start
- Previewing a book: looking at title, headings, illustrations, summary (before reading)
- Reading faster for momentum and fluency

- Creating an image of the story, visualizing
- Creating a metaphor or analogy to understand the story
- Stopping at certain points to think and predict
- Asking yourself questions about what is happening
- Talking to someone else who has read the story
- Reading the first line of a paragraph and skimming the rest
- Reading what you don't understand slowly and what you do quickly
- Paying attention to what's new or contradictory

These examples of strategies come from what readers actually do when they read, rather than from instructional models of how we think readers should be taught.

Strategies are learned through:

- engaging in meaningful reading and writing.
- involving students in a wide range of types of reading and writing experiences (partner reading, literature circles, text sets, Say Something, Written Conversation, etc.)
- reading from easy, predictable materials for fluency as well as more difficult books for discussion.
- opportunities to reread books to gain fluency and integrate strategies.
- conversations with students after they read, to ask them what strategies they used on a difficult page and what other strategies they might have tried.
- teaching about language through guided reading, specific strategy lessons, or mini-lessons to individuals or groups.

Self-Monitoring

I teach self-monitoring, or checking on oneself, at the very early reading levels. For example, most of the children I work with don't read with a one-to-one match between voice and print; they will read, "I can see the bird" even if the page reads, I can see the big bird. I teach them to notice the correspondence between what they say and what's on the page.

One day, Cory has *Plop,* by June Meiser. He reads along, using his finger to match his voice with the text: "I can see the flower. I can see the fish. . . ." On page seven, however, the pattern breaks and the page reads, I can see the big bird. Regardless, Cory says, "I can see the bird," but he hesitates.

I say, "I'm glad you stopped. What did you notice?"

Cory replies, "Too many words."

"Yes, there are too many words. Take a good look at the size of the bird in the picture. Now, go back and try that again."

Cory reads, "I can see the big bird."

"Did that match? Does that make sense?"

Cory: "Yes."

He stopped because he knew there were too many words. He was checking on himself, and that's what I want my students to learn. Cory noticed when there wasn't a one-to-one match, but if a child doesn't pay attention to this, I say, "Make your finger match."

Some children find this concept hard, so I use little figurines I've collected from tea boxes to teach what matching means. I have students point to each one, and say what they are: cat, dog, lion. Then I have them just say the names of the figures, without using their fingers. Eventually, they learn what it means to match what they say to something else, and then to match to words.

To teach a child to match what is being said to printed words, I use a page of print which contains at least one word I know that the child knows, such as "the." I have the child frame that word with his or her fingers, and I say, "When you read, watch for this word. This will help you check yourself."

When the number of words on the page and the number of words the child utters don't match, I want the child to notice the discrepancy. This is one kind of situation where early readers can check themselves, and I help them to do so.

—*Margaret Roberts, Gilmanton School, Gilmanton Iron Works, New Hampshire*

Figuring Out Unknown Words

Kindergarten teacher Nancy Tindal helps students figure out unknown words by charting some strategies for them. This list is started in the fall and added onto all year. It includes strategies such as:

- look at the picture for clues
- look at the first letter(s) of the word

- think of a word that makes sense
- look for a rhyming pattern
- think if you have seen the word somewhere else
- look for a repetitive pattern
- ask yourself; Does it look right? Does it sound right? Does it make sense?
- look to see if there is a little word in a bigger word
- sound the word out slowly

Tindal has also set up reading partners between fourth graders and her kindergartners. She and the fourth graders meet briefly on Tuesday afternoons to review the reading strategies that she has highlighted with her kindergartners that particular week. Then the fourth graders and kindergartners meet Thursday mornings to read together and talk about strategies they used during their time together. The fourth graders finish by writing observations in their reading journals about their shared reading experience.

—Donna Maxim, Center for Teaching and Learning, Edgecomb, Maine

Reading-for-Meaning Strategies

As students become aware of how language functions, they take control of their own learning processes and grow as readers. We want students to learn about language, but we need to devote only a small part of their total reading time to this learning. One way to support students in learning a repertoire of reading strategies is through strategy lessons. Strategy lessons enable students to reflect on themselves as readers and focus on particular cognitive or social strategies that are used by proficient readers.

After reading and considering the meaning of a book, for instance, students might engage in a strategy lesson on the use of context clues or a particular story structure. A group of third graders laughed their way through Arnold Lobel's *Fables* and later figured out the story structure of the fable. As part of a unit on the ocean, I read aloud a book about ocean animals to a group of first graders. After talking about what they had learned, we discussed how they could use context clues to determine a particular animal before it was named in the text. Learning about language is thus embedded into meaningful uses of literature so that the readers have a purpose and context for exploring how language works.

Children can learn about written language through author studies, shared and guided reading, and strategy lessons. These engagements build from experiences where students read whole texts for real purposes. They are not isolated skill activities but responses to the needs of readers. They require a classroom where students read widely and where teachers and students are continually involved in evaluation to identify students' needs and strengths.

For example, I used Synonym Substitution (Goodman, Watson & Burke, 1996) with a group of third graders who were having difficulty reading unfamiliar terms and were overemphasizing letter-sound relationships to the exclusion of meaning and syntax clues. I gave students a version of the familiar story, "The Three Pigs," in which a number of words were underlined. Working in pairs, they created synonyms for the underlined words or phrases and then came together to share as a class or small group. I read the story aloud, stopping at underlined words and phrases, and students called out their substitutions. When I read the line, "Along came a big bad wolf," I stopped at the word "bad" and students called out synonyms, such as "awful, wrong, evil, not nice, young, naughty." We then went back and reflected on some of these synonyms, talking about why they did and did not work within the context of the story. The students also reflected on how and when they might use this strategy as readers.

In working with a group of fourth graders, I realized that they were having difficulty comprehending mystery stories because they did not understand how these books were organized and how authors provide clues for readers. As I read E. L. Konigsburg's *From the Mixed-Up Files of Mrs. Basil E. Frankweiler* aloud to students, we discussed the book and the kinds of connections and meanings children were finding. We also talked about how the book was organized and kept a chart of the clues in the book. After we finished the book, children met in literature circles to read and discuss their own choices of mystery stories. We met as a class several times a week to talk about their strategies for reading these books. At the end of the literature circles, we created a class chart we called "Strategies for Reading Mystery Books" which remained posted on the classroom wall.

Another time, some fifth graders who seemed proficient readers suddenly began experiencing difficulty when they were asked to read informational books. After talking with the students, I realized that many had only read narrative stories and weren't sure how to approach an expository text. To help them learn how to read informational books, I worked with their teachers to develop strategy discussions. As the students read historical informational books and biographies related to their inquiries on the Civil War, the teachers asked them to talk about the strategies they were using to understand these books. Students discussed how to make predictions, ask questions, and connect their own ideas and experiences as they read. They analyzed the organization and structure of these books, such as cause and effect or generalizations with supporting examples. They also learned how to preview a chapter or book by first skimming through the text, looking at headings and illustrations and reading the introduction and conclusion.

One of my favorite strategies is Say Something (Short & Harste, 1996). One student reads aloud a section of the story (several paragraphs) to a partner and stops. At that point, both students "say something" about the story: a connection, question, prediction, or comment. The second student then reads aloud the next section of the story and stops so that both can say something. After reading the story, the students gather as a class to talk about it. In this way, students become active readers who think about the story as they read. Many students do not realize that proficient readers "chunk" text into sections and constantly make predictions and connections and ask questions as they read. Instead, they focus on pronouncing the words correctly and lose sight of the meaning. Say Something allows them to experience the reading strategies of thoughtful readers. This engagement also helps them become comfortable with the process of talking and thinking about a book.

Many strategy lessons can occur as short, focused discussions at the beginning or end of the time period when students are reading. For instance, in reading with individual children or small groups, at the end of the story I find it helpful to ask them to find a place where they accomplished some good reading work or experienced difficulty. If they choose a page where they struggled with figuring out a word or phrase, I ask them what strategies they tried and what else they might have done. If appropriate, I then suggest an additional strategy that they might try. These brief but powerful interactions encourage children to think through their reading strategies and develop additional options.

—*Kathy Short, University of Arizona, Tuscon*

Conclusion

As teachers we take an active role in the teaching of specific reading skills and strategies. We know the importance of creating a language-rich environment that provides a variety of reading opportunities: lots of books in many different genres for our classrooms; read-alouds everyday; time to read independently and in small groups, and through shared and guided reading; time for response, discussion, and reflection as a whole class, in small groups, and by individuals. We know the importance of observing, recording, and assessing our students' progress as they develop as readers. We use this information to guide our teaching. Our goal is to help students acquire new reading strategies so that they have a variety of options to use as they encounter new reading experiences.

References

This list is provided to encourage further discussions about the teaching of reading; it also lists all the works cited in this chapter. Because numerous resources include both reading and classroom practices, most items in this bibliography deal exclusively with reading.

Clay, Marie M. 1991. *Becoming Literate: The Construction of Inner Control.* Portsmouth, NH: Heinemann.

———. 1993. *Reading Recovery: A Guidebook for Teachers in Training.* Portsmouth, NH: Heinemann.

Crafton, Linda K. 1996. *Standards in Practice, Grades K–2.* Urbana, IL: NCTE.

Fountas, Irene C., and Gay Su Pinnell. 1996. *Guided Reading: Good First Teaching for All Children.* Portsmouth, NH: Heinemann.

Glazer, Susan Mandel. 1992. *Reading Comprehension: Self-Monitoring Strategies to Develop Independent Readers.* New York: Scholastic.

Goodman, Ken. 1996. *On Reading.* Portsmouth, NH: Heinemann.

Goodman, Yetta M., and Ann M. Marek. 1996. *Retrospective Miscue Analysis: Revaluing Readers and Reading.* Katonah, NY: Richard C. Owen.

Goodman, Yetta M., Dorothy Watson, and Carolyn Burke. 1996. *Reading Strategies: Focus on Comprehension*, 2nd ed. Katonah, NY: Richard C. Owen.

Keene, Ellin Oliver, and Susan Zimmerman. 1997. *Mosaic of Thought: Teaching Comprehension in a Reader's Workshop.* Portsmouth, NH: Heinemann.

McIntyre, Ellen, and Michael Pressley. 1996. *Balanced Literacy Instruction: Strategies and Skills in Whole Language.* Norwood, MA: Christopher-Gordon.

Rasinski, Timothy, and Nancy Padak. 1996. *Holistic Reading Strategies: Teaching Children Who Find Reading Difficult.* Englewood Cliffs, NJ: Prentice Hall.

Reading Resource Book. 1994. First Steps Series. South Melbourne: Longman Australia PTY Limited (available through Heinemann).

Robb, Laura. 1996. *Reading Strategies That Work: Teaching Your Students to Become Better Readers.* New York: Scholastic.

Routman, Regie, and Andrea Butler, eds. "Why Talk about Phonics?" themed issue of *School Talk.* Vol. 1, No. 2. November 1995. Urbana, IL: NCTE. Reprinted as Chapter 5 in this volume.

———. "How Do I Actually *Teach* Reading Now That I Am Using Literature?" themed issue of *School Talk*. Vol. 1, No. 3. February 1996. Urbana, IL: NCTE. Reprinted as Chapter 12 in this volume.

Short, K., and Harste, J. 1996. *Creating Classrooms for Authors and Inquirers.* Portsmouth, NH: Heinemann.

Sierra-Perry, Martha. 1996. *Standards in Practice, Grades 3–5.* Urbana, IL: NCTE.

Smith, John W. A., and Warwick B. Wiley. 1995. *Learning to Read in New Zealand.* Katonah, NY: Richard C. Owen.

Taberski, Sharon. 1996. *A Close-Up Look at Teaching Reading: Focusing on Children and Our Goals.* Portsmouth, NH: Heinemann. Videocassette.

Weaver, Constance. 1994. *Reading Process and Practice: From Socio-Psycholinguistics to Whole Language,* 2nd ed. Portsmouth, NH: Heinemann.

Weaver, Constance, Lorraine Gillmeister-Krause, and Grace Vento-Zogby. 1996. *Creating Support for Effective Literacy Education.* Portsmouth, NH: Heinemann.

12 How Do I Actually *Teach* Reading Now That I Am Using Literature?

Regie Routman
Shaker Heights City Schools, Ohio

Andrea Butler
Chicago, Illinois

This chapter addresses the questions of many teachers—including teachers who claim to be whole language teachers but don't really understand how they can teach reading with and through literature. Explaining that they view literature not just as the basis for reading instruction but as part of a rich language-learning curriculum with several important components, Routman and Butler proceed to discuss the last two of these components: the development of skills and strategies, and the fostering of confidence and independence. In detail, the authors demonstrate how skills, strategies, confidence, and independence can be promoted through daily reading and writing aloud, shared reading and writing, guided reading and writing, and independent reading and writing. In other words, they show how important reading strategies like predicting, monitoring comprehension, and maintaining meaning are taught in the context of authentic literacy events. This is followed by a section on how assessment informs instruction—how, for instance, the authors assess which reading strategies the children are getting under control and which ones need further work. Then, they demonstrate how the teacher can help individual children develop and articulate a needed strategy.

Originally published in *School Talk*, *1*(3), (1996). Copyright 1996 by the National Council of Teachers of English.

Remember the good old days? When our hands were purple from all the dittos we ran? When the kids who couldn't "do" phonics got more phonics? When the "Buzzards" never saw a real book because they hadn't mastered their skills yet? And that's just for starters.

Sure we succeeded in teaching most kids to read, if you define reading as "reading the words." But many of those kids sure hated reading.

They never saw reading as connected to meaning or to their own lives. They never picked up a book for pleasure or information when they had free time. They certainly never saw reading as related to writing in any way.

And what about those kids who did *not* learn to read? What happened to their self-esteem, let alone their prospects of doing well at school in the future? They were doomed to failure. A disproportionate number of these were children of color.

No. We don't want to go back to "the good old days" with the hierarchy of skills, fixed-ability grouping, and the teacher as scripted technician. We've worked with children, as you have, from all cultures and all socioeconomic levels who *have* learned—and now love—to read and write successfully by using literature along with effective teaching.

While having lots of quality literature in the classroom is a good start, we know that literature alone won't do it. No one learns to read by simply "rolling around the floor with a book." As Charlotte Huck comments, "A literature-based program cannot operate where books are not available and teachers are not convinced or knowledgeable about the reading process or children's literature" (Huck, 1996, "Literature-Based Reading Programs: A Retrospective," *The New Advocate*, 9 [1]: 29).

We also know, from more than twenty years of research and practice from around the world, as well as from our own day-to-day teaching and reflecting, that all kids can learn to read and write by having rich language experiences in a safe, nurturing, social environment. That does not mean that no explicit teaching goes on. Just the opposite! The difference is that rather than following the script written for "all children" in some manual, the teacher is responsive to the actual children who are in the classroom. (As teachers, we focus on language learning in school—but we also recognize that in the home, much of this literacy learning occurs naturally. We need to build on the strong language foundations that all children come to school with, and involve parents by honoring the vital role they must play.)

Although in the rest of this chapter we will be talking about literature as it relates to reading, we view literature in a bigger context, as part of a rich language-learning curriculum which has several interwoven and interdependent dimensions:

- Experience with literacy and literature
- Ability to connect to and reflect upon all life experiences
- Knowledge and understandings of literacy
- Skills and strategies
- Confidence and independence

For this chapter, we have narrowed our focus to the last two dimensions: skills and strategies, confidence and independence. "Skills and strategies" are what you asked us for through the earlier "reader's feedback" survey. Because chapter 5 discusses phonics teaching in the context of reading, we will not address phonics specifically here. But before we take up our discussion of skills and strategies, let's focus on confidence and independence.

We have included "confidence and independence" here because without confidence and independence, we question whether we have truly taught someone to read or write. What do we mean by *independence?* To us, independent readers operate successfully by themselves. They treat reading as a problem-solving, meaning-making process. Among other things, independent readers can and do:

- Read a book with understanding.
- Use background knowledge of content and genre (types of text) to orient them to the selection.
- Use clues in the text to search, predict, and confirm meaning.
- Self-monitor.
- Choose appropriate self-correcting strategies in flexible and dynamic ways. (See Figure 1 for examples of how to do this at the word level).
- Maintain meaning through longer and more complex text structures, in various genres.

The kind of independence we are talking about does not just miraculously emerge at some end point. It needs to be fostered and modeled all along the way. At each and every stage of the learning process, we expect kids to do some part of the reading and the writing independently. It might be turning the pages of a book, or circling misspelled words in a first draft. Later on, independent behavior might mean rereading part of a book or draft for clarification. For sophisticated learners, it might be knowing how to research a computer database. There are always new genres to tackle, new challenges to overcome. No matter how old we are, as readers and writers, independence is always our goal.

Achieving that independence and confidence is easier when we have developed a set of skills and strategies to help us with our reading and writing activities. This is one of our central challenges as teachers:

> According to Vygotsky, the role of education is to provide experiences that are in the child's zone of proximal development—activities challenging for the child but achievable with sensitive adult guidance. (Laura E. Berk & Adam Winsler, 1995. *Scaffolding Children's*

Learning: Vygotsky and Early Childhood Education, Washington, D.C.: National Association for the Education of Young Children.)

The combination of daily teaching-learning approaches that we find most useful is:

- Reading and Writing Aloud
- Shared Reading and Writing
- Guided Reading and Writing
- Independent Reading and Writing

Let's look at each one of these approaches in turn.

Reading and Writing Aloud

Reading and writing aloud are wonderful ways of motivating children and for role-modeling for them what "expert" readers and writers look

---

Children ask themselves:

Does the picture help me?

What letter does the word begin with? End with?

Can I get more clues by reading on?

Can I pick up the threads by rereading?

Can I skip the hard word and still understand?

Can I put in another word that makes sense?

Can I sound the unknown word out?

Does it look like another word I know?

Have I seen that word someplace before?

Can I syllabify the word?

Do I need to ask for help?

Then children cross-check and confirm:

Does it make sense?

Does it sound right? Like English?

Does it look right? Match the letters?

Figure 1. Questions that promote self-correcting strategies for unknown words.

like. Our goal is to stretch the children, to immerse them in rich book language, and to introduce them to new authors, genres, and illustrators that might otherwise be inaccessible to them. During reading and writing aloud activities, we as teachers hold the book or the pen and read "on behalf of" the children, while they are actively involved in the thinking and meaning-making process while they enjoy the selection. Sometimes we encourage the kids to use the following sentence stems to help them shape thoughtful responses:

I noticed . . . to evoke personal observations.

I wonder . . . to elicit wonderings.

This reminds me of . . . because . . . to help make connections to the students' lives and literary experiences and to encourage them to back up their ideas with evidence from the text. (See Nancy L. Roser, et al., 1990, "Language, Literature, and At-Risk Children," *The Reading Teacher*, 43 (8): 554–59.)

We are careful not to require too much written response because it is not what we as adults do ourselves. This is not to say that there is no place for written response. We often find it a useful management strategy and excellent preparation for literature discussion groups.

Shared Reading and Writing

During shared reading and writing, we use texts that are closer to the children's instructional reading level. A big-book format is useful when teaching things like concepts of print, but it is not essential. What is more important is that the book or text can be used to demonstrate reading strategies in action. We do this by thinking aloud as we compose meaning, or by masking key words to demonstrate what we do when we get stuck. We often pose questions and practice answering them aloud to help children learn to flexibly use a range of strategies when reading independently.

It is important to note that shared reading is not just for younger readers. Andrea confesses she still employs shared reading with her lawyer when trying to understand legal documents! With older students, poems, songs, and nonfiction texts are ideal. Short selections lend themselves easily to repeated reading—a highly recommended reading activity, not just for enjoyment, but for developing fluency and confidence in struggling readers. (See John Pikulski, 1994, "Preventing Reading Failure: A Review of Five Effective Programs," *The Reading Teacher*, 48 [1]: 30–39.)

Guided Reading and Writing

During guided reading, we pull the kids together in small groups of four to six, based on student needs, and expect them to take the responsibility for the first reading of an unfamiliar text. The text must be at the children's instructional level, meaning that there are just a few challenges that require the use of strategies and teacher support. If the children don't need teacher support to read a particular text, they do not need to read it in a guided reading context. They can read it collaboratively, with a partner or alone.

Typically, we run a beginning guided reading session in three phases:

Phase 1: Teacher introduces and orients the children to the book.

Phase 2: Children attempt to read the text by themselves, with teacher support.

Phase 3: Children pair up and reread the book aloud to a peer.

During guided reading we expect the children to apply the strategies they have witnessed and practiced in the shared context. In order to set them up for success, we orient them to the book by reading the title with them and asking for predictions. With beginners, we then talk them through the illustrations and deliberately plant any challenging vocabulary "in their ears." As each child attempts to read the text alone, we are right there to help when needed—but the more we make them solve their own problems, the quicker they become self-reliant. Often the most effective teaching takes place during guided reading, because of the small group size and the possibility of responding to individual needs.

We should mention that although in this chapter we are focusing on strategies for teaching reading, we use "guided reading" to teach many aspects of literacy.

Independent Reading and Writing

In addition to meeting "texts-that-teach" in shared and guided situations, children need to read books and write at their independent levels every day for extended periods of time. This is when they practice their fluency and build up competence. It is essential that children choose the books they read and the topics they write for these independent activities.

With very young children, we often give them a "friendly box of books" from which they can select. With growing independence, readers learn how to choose books that present the appropriate level of challenge.

How Assessment Informs Instruction

No matter which of the above teaching approaches is used, we integrate assessment. We see teaching and assessment as inseparable.

When we teach reading as a problem-solving, meaning-making process, we constantly assess which strategies the children are getting under control and which ones they need further work on. One effective way to make this type of assessment is to organize regular one-on-one conferences with individuals, then take a modified running record and teach what the child needs to be taught, on the spot. If assessment does not lead to timely action, it is of little use.

In the assessment example we've included (see Figure 2), the classroom teacher was unsure whether or not the book chosen for guided reading was too hard for Michael. Michael seemed to be able to read the text, but was confused about what he read. So, Regie asked him to bring a "just right book" and read a favorite part. We have both found that it is often useful to ask a child to first read a familiar book before tackling an unfamiliar one. It helps build rapport and lets the teacher see if the student has chosen a book she or he can actually read. From this reading, Regie decided Michael was able to choose a book appropriate to his level, integrate the cueing systems, self-correct, and retell the story.

Next, Regie asked Michael to read the unfamiliar book—the one his teacher planned to use for guided reading. From this it was obvious he was able to read the text, except when he came to an unfamiliar word; he just read on, even when meaning was lost. He was not able to reread to clarify meaning and he needed particular help in using the strategy of "substituting a meaningful word for unfamiliar ones, and reading on." After Regie demonstrated the strategy again, she asked him to articulate what he could do in the future. He replied: "When I don't know a word, I need to put in another word that makes sense." Having students articulate strategies they are just learning helps them internalize and apply them in the future.

In this chapter, we have attempted to look at reading strategies—those "in-the-head plans"—that all of us as competent independent readers use. We want to reemphasize the need to embed all strategy

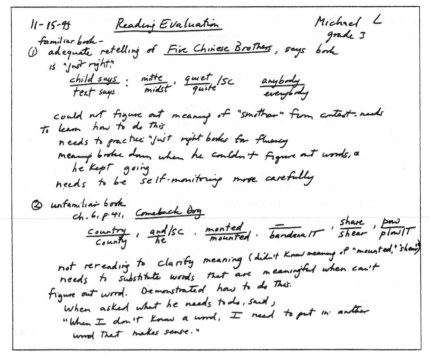

Figure 2. Regie's reading evaluation of Michael L., a third grader.

teaching in the context of enjoying wonderful literature. Whatever teaching points we make using literature, we must maintain the integrity and joy of the literary experience.

References

Avery, Carol. 1993. *. . . And with a Light Touch: Learning about Reading, Writing, and Teaching with First Graders.* Portsmouth, NH: Heinemann.

Butler, Andrea, and Jan Turbill. 1984. *Towards a Reading-Writing Classroom.* Portsmouth, NH: Heinemann.

Clay, Marie. 1991. *Becoming Literate: The Construction of Inner Control.* Portsmouth, NH: Heinemann.

———. 1993. *Reading Recovery: A Guidebook for Teachers in Training.* Portsmouth, NH: Heinemann.

DeFord, Diane E., Carol A. Lyons, and Gay Su Pinnell, eds. 1991. *Bridges to Literacy: Learning from Reading Recovery.* Portsmouth, NH: Heinemann.

Goodman, Yetta M., Dorothy Watson, and Carolyn Burke. 1996. *Reading Strategies: Focus on Comprehension,* 2nd ed. Katonah, NY: Richard C. Owen.

Harp, Bill, ed. 1993. *Bringing Children to Literacy: Classrooms at Work.* Norwood, MA: Christopher-Gordon.

Holdaway, Don. 1979. *The Foundations of Literacy.* Portsmouth. NH: Heinemann.

———. 1990. *Independence in Reading,* 3rd ed. Portsmouth, NH: Heinemann.

Mooney, Margaret E. 1990. *Reading To, With, and By Children.* Katonah, NY: Richard C. Owen.

New Zealand Department of Education. 1985. *Reading in Junior Classes.* Katonah, NY: Richard C. Owen.

Parents, Kids, and Books. Produced by KERA-TV, 3000 Harry Hines Blvd., Dallas, TX 75201. Videocassette.

Reading Developmental Continuum. 1994. First Steps series. South Melbourne: Longman Australia PTY Limited (available through Portsmouth, NH: Heinemann).

Reading Resource Book. 1994. First Steps series. South Melbourne: Longman Australia PTY Limited (available through Portsmouth, NH: Heinemann).

Ross, Elinor Parry. 1996. *The Workshop Approach: A Framework for Literacy.* Norwood, MA: Christopher-Gordon.

Routman, Regie. 1994. *Invitations: Changing as Teachers and Learners K-12,* updated ed. Portsmouth, NH: Heinemann.

Smith, John W., A. and Warwick B. Wiley. 1995. *Learning to Read in New Zealand.* Katonah, NY: Richard C. Owen.

Weaver, Constance. 1994. *Reading Process and Practice: From Sociolinguistics to Whole Language,* 2nd ed. Portsmouth, NH: Heinemann.

13 Authenticity as the Basis for Instruction

Stephen B. Kucer
California State University, San Marcos

In this chapter, Kucer expresses doubt as to whether many of the strategy lessons in whole language classrooms actually teach kids what we think we're teaching, even though the lessons may be cognitively and developmentally authentic. Why the concern? Because Kucer and third-grade teacher Cecilia Silva interviewed six representative children about the cloze activities done in her class. Despite Silva's repeated explanations of why they were doing a cloze activity, only 7 percent of the students' responses corresponded with Kucer and Silva's intentions—to help students learn to use context when encountering unknown words in reading, and to develop rereading and read-on strategies for dealing with problem words. Kucer concludes that classroom materials and instruction need to be socioculturally relevant: to "reflect real world (normative) literacy events and engage students in functional, purposeful, and organic activities." We need to find out how our students are perceiving our reading and writing strategy lessons. Otherwise, it appears, such lessons may be a waste of valuable class time.

Originally published in *Language Arts, 68*, (1991), 532–40. Copyright 1991 by the National Council of Teachers of English.

Until the fourth grade, I had "seasoned" teachers in the neighborhood elementary school that I attended. These women had been fed a diet of John Dewey and progressive education in their teacher education programs and were relatively unaffected by the "scientific" approach sweeping the nation's elementary school curriculum in the 1950s. While I certainly experienced a worksheet or two and some segmented instruction in the early grades, the focus of the reading curriculum was fairly story-centered. True, many of these stories came from basal readers; however, I don't recall the myriad workbook activities I suddenly confronted in Ms. Polinski's fourth-grade classroom.

Ms. Polinski was different from my previous teachers. She was young, newly graduated from college, and had a vivaciousness I had not experienced in a teacher. Ms. Polinski also was different in her approach toward reading and writing instruction. Having been trained in the latest methodology at the university, much of her literacy curriculum consisted of skill-and-drill sheets. The scope and sequence chart, which had emerged as an instructional mainstay within the elementary schools, governed our classroom activities.

The interesting thing about these fourth-grade instructional experiences is that I never understood why we did them. I can even remember puzzling over what "subject" these lessons represented but never being able to classify them. Although Ms. Polinski may have thought these skill sheets would help make me a better reader, I never applied them to reading—either inside or outside of the classroom setting—because I failed to understand the link between home and school literacy use.

The ability to link classroom-based literacy lessons with real-world, authentic reading and writing experiences is critical if our instruction is to promote literacy development in the children we teach. In fact, it would appear to be critical to the very functioning of the institution we call school. Most literacy activities are intended to help students learn a particular strategy or skill within a controlled environment—the classroom curriculum—so that it can then be used within authentic environments—the world. Students must understand the relations between what they do during reading and writing instruction and what they do when interacting with connected discourse outside of the school setting. Unfortunately, many of us involved in literacy education have simply assumed that children make this connection. However, as Frank Smith (1975) observed over a decade ago, there is a difference between teaching and learning, and we ought not confuse the two. Simply because children are learning to read and write does not necessarily mean that our instruction is the cause.

A strength of the whole language movement has been its attempt to link classroom and real world activities. Because meaning generation is the focus of literacy use in the world, advocates of whole language have rightfully insisted that classrooms should reflect this fact. Thus, rather than teaching isolated skills with segmented and frequently meaning-stripped pieces of language, whole language curricula have tended to focus on the development of literacy strategies through student interaction with meaningful pieces of connected discourse. In these "strategy lessons," particular cognitive processes for which the reader needs support are highlighted (see Atwell & Rhodes, 1984; Cochrane, Cochrane, Scalena, & Buchanan, 1984; Gilles, Bixby, Crowley, Crenshaw, Henrichs, Reynolds, & Pyle, 1988; Goodman & Burke, 1980; Harste & Short, 1988; Kucer & Harste, 1991; Newman, 1985; Watson, 1987).

As illustrated in Figure 1, the generation of meaning is always at the center of strategy lessons, with structure (syntactic as well as textual) and graphophonics serving to support the development of meaning. This concern for meaning and cognitive processes that strategy lessons attempt to reflect I have come to call "cognitive authenticity."

A second characteristic of a whole language curriculum has been its developmental nature. Drawing upon the work of such language developmentalists as Wells (1986) and learning theorists as Vygotsky (1978) and Wertsch (1985a, 1985b), advocates of whole language have argued that children actively construct the literacy system through interaction with, and mediation by, others. This construction is seen as largely inductive in nature and involves the young child in the scientific enterprise of data gathering, hypothesis formulation, testing, and modification. The passive, imitative, practice-and-master behavioristic paradigm is pointedly rejected.

Guiding the child in this constructive process are adults or more capable peers who demonstrate how reading and writing operate, both as cognitive as well as social enterprises (Smith, 1981). Initially, through collaborative, socially supported situations, the child develops literacy abilities that are interpsychological in nature.

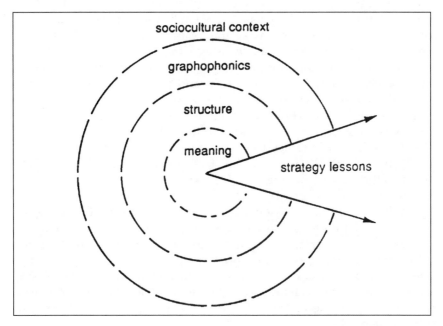

Figure 1. Whole language strategy lessons. Adapted from *Reading Miscue Inventory*.

That is, the child is able to read and write with the support of others. Eventually, through numerous meaningful experiences with literacy in these mediated contexts, literacy abilities become independent, or what Vygotsky termed as intrapsychological. In essence, whole language advocates view knowledge and knowing as first socially created, mediated, and shared before moving to an internal plane. Whole language classrooms attempt to create environments that support such development. This whole language characteristic I term "developmental authenticity."

Because of the emphasis on cognitive and developmental authenticity, it has been implicitly assumed that children will automatically connect their whole language lessons with literacy experiences outside of the classroom setting. Children within whole language classrooms need not puzzle over what "subject" is being taught because their lessons are authentic in nature. The issue of transfer which confronts children in the more traditional skills instructional paradigm becomes irrelevant because there is nothing to transfer; literacy inside the whole language classroom reflects literacy outside of the classroom.

During this past year, I have been involved with a third-grade teacher in a classroom-based, ethnographic research project which also assumed that students understood the link between school and home (Kucer, 1990). Because our literacy lessons were cognitively and developmentally authentic, the teacher, Cecilia Silva, and I simply assumed that the children would see the connection between school-based and world-based literacy activities. This assumption, however, was continually challenged throughout the year as we interviewed and talked with the children about the reading lessons they experienced and as we came to appreciate how and why the children understood their lessons as they did.

In this chapter, I present and discuss the findings from the classroom research that forced me to confront some basic beliefs which I had long held about whole language instruction. I suggest that some whole language lessons, including many of my own, suffer from some of the same problems as do traditional skill lessons because of a limited notion of authenticity. Finally, I propose that a gap has developed between whole language theory and some whole language practice, a gap between belief systems and how these beliefs are operationalized in the classroom. Through listening to the recipients of our instruction—the children—we can begin to understand this gap and more fully appreciate the effect our school literacy lessons are having on student reading and writing development.

The Literacy Curriculum

For one academic year Cecilia Silva and I developed and implemented a whole language curriculum within a third-grade classroom. The school was located in a large metropolitan area and served a diverse community. The children in our class were largely Latino, bilingual, and from working-class homes. Linguistically, most of the children entered kindergarten speaking predominantly Spanish and were in Spanish literacy programs until second grade. In second grade, because of the progress the students had made in their oral English, they were formally transitioned into English literacy.

There were 4 components to our curriculum: themes, teacher reading, free reading, and free writing. The themes engaged the children in literacy activities related to a particular topic under study, such as "Amphibians and Reptiles" or "Growing Plants and Seeds." Teacher reading involved Cecilia in reading aloud short stories, books, and articles related to the theme. Free reading and free writing were times during the day when the children determined what they would read or write about. Linked to free reading and writing were opportunities for the children to share what they had read or written. In the case of writing, the children also conferenced, revised, and published their favorite pieces.

Cecilia and I saw the thematic units as serving two purposes. First, the themes would develop the students' conceptual knowledge about certain topics and related concepts. All activities within the themes were to focus on the generation of meaning and the functional use of language. A second and related purpose of the themes was to help the students increase their proficiency with reading and writing. Because of their previous instruction, the students had a sound/symbol focus when reading and relied exclusively on "sounding out" and skipping strategies when they encountered unknown words. Our thematic curriculum, through the use of strategy lessons, was to help the students understand the recursive, contextual, and meaning-making nature of literacy.

The Use of the Modified Cloze Procedure

We used a variety of whole language strategy lessons during theme time to help the students develop a wider range of processing strategies. However, given the students' difficulty with contextual cues, one particular strategy, a modified cloze activity (Goodman & Burke, 1980,

p. 199; Goodman, Watson, & Burke, 1987, p. 164), was prominent within the curriculum. Students experienced this particular lesson thirteen times throughout the year. The purpose of the activity was to help students learn to use context, as well as to develop rereading and read-on strategies when encountering unknown words during their reading.

The cloze procedure was modified in three ways. First, in contrast to the deletion of every fifth word, words were deleted in the text where we felt there was adequate contextual information to support the generation of meaningful predictions on the part of the children. Second, rather than judging the acceptability of student responses based on exact or synonymous matches, student responses were evaluated in terms of whether or not they made sense within the context of the passage. Finally, we deleted groups of words as well as single words throughout the text.

I have noted that this particular activity was prominent within the curriculum. By this I mean that both Cecilia and I had great faith in the lesson. We believed that it was an effective way to help students develop the use of contextual cues and that it was one of the most authentic strategy lessons that existed. To us, encountering a blank in a text was similar to that of encountering an unknown word. We also felt that the strategy lesson kept the reading process intact in that there was no segmentation of language into bits and pieces. In addition, because the lesson can be used with theme-related material, it can easily be woven into the fabric of the curriculum rather than standing apart in both space and time.

Usually, the modified cloze lesson was taught to small groups of students. The pattern of instruction was as follows:

1. Students receive a copy of the text and read the entire piece chorally, generating responses for the blanks as they are encountered.

2. After the text is read, Cecilia returns to each blank and asks for all of the responses that were generated. These responses are listed on the chalkboard.

3. The student who provided each response identifies the textual information used to generate the response.

4. The other students in the group evaluate the meaningfulness of the response, though the teacher accepts all responses.

5. After all responses are discussed, the students chorally read the text a second time, putting in those responses that make the most sense.

6. In collaborative pairs, students receive copies of a second text to complete independently. Responses are directly written in the blanks on the copies. When complete, responses are shared and discussed with other members of the group.

How the Teacher and Students Understood the Modified Cloze Procedure

Four times throughout the year, and within twenty-four hours after the lesson had been taught, I interviewed the teacher and six case study students about the cloze activity. All interviews were audiotaped. The six students, three boys and three girls, were chosen because they were highly verbal in English, were comfortable interacting with me, and represented a range of literacy abilities within the classroom: two proficient, two moderately proficient, and two nonproficient. Degree of proficiency was determined through the *Reading Miscue Inventory* (Goodman, Watson, & Burke, 1987).

The interviews focused on how the teacher and the students understood the intention or purpose of the activity and the relationship between teacher and student understandings. The interview consisted of the following four questions, with the last three essentially being variations of the same question:

1. Teacher: What did the children have to do in this activity?
   Student: What did you have to do in this activity?

2. Teacher: Why did you have the children do this activity? What were you trying to teach the children?
   Student: Why did Ms. Silva have you do this activity? What was Ms. Silva trying to teach you?

3. Teacher: What did you want the children to learn from this activity? What did you learn from this activity?
   Student: What did you learn from this activity?

4. Teacher: What did you want the children to learn in this activity which would help make them better readers or writers?
   Student: Did you learn anything in this activity which will help you to be a better reader or writer? What?

After all the interviews were transcribed, a taxonomy was generated into which the responses could be classified. For ease of discussion, and because the answers were essentially the same across the last three questions, the responses to them have been collapsed. The taxonomy, shown in Table 1, contains three categories: match, mismatch, and unknown. In the match category, the teacher and the student understand the lesson in the same manner. In the mismatch category, the students understand the lesson differently from the teacher, and the sub-categories indicate the focus of their response (future, task, skill, content, opposite process, general). The unknown category represents those responses in which students indicate no understanding of the intent behind the lesson. Following each category in Table 1 are sample student responses. Responses to the first question (What did you have to do in this activity?) in the interview are not included in the taxonomy because all students fully understood and were able to articulate what was to be done in the modified cloze activity. At no time throughout the year was a single case study student unable to verbalize accurately the requirements of the lesson. In addition, these same students were highly effective at using context cues in these situations. An examination of eleven different texts containing a total of 202 blanks and 415 student responses indicated that 93 percent of all student responses were meaningful.

Table 1.

Taxonomy and Sample Responses

Match Definition:	The focus of the student matches the focus of the teacher.
Example:	Teacher: "To help students learn to use contextual cues for dealing with unknown words when reading so that they will have strategies beyond 'sounding out.'"
	Student: "If you don't know a word you can read back, skip it, or start all over again."
Mismatch Definition:	The focus of the student does not match the focus of the teacher.
Future Definition:	The focus is on doing the task so that it can be done with harder texts or in subsequent grades.
Example:	"We'll do it next year."
	"Teachers teach us this because we might have books with lines in them.
Task Definition:	The focus is on doing the task correctly.
Example:	"How to put words in the line."
	"Use words in sentences to fill in blanks."
Skill Definition:	The focus is on learning language parts, forms, or conventions.

continued on next page

Table 1 continued

Example:	"To make words rhyme."
	"Learning more words."
	"Learning to try to sound out hard words."
Content Definition:	The focus is on learning the thematic content expressed in the activity.
Example:	"Teaching about snakes, crocodiles, and alligators."
	"Snakes eat bugs. They can help around the farm."
	"Baby lizards are very small."
Opposite Process Definition:	The focus is on writing rather than reading.
Example:	"Learning how to write books."
	Learning "some words that I don't know how to spell very well."
General Definition	The focus is on giving general rather than a specific response.
Example:	"So we could learn to read better."
Unknown Definition:	The focus is on not having insights into the activity.
Example:	"I don't know."

Our field notes supported the notion that the students understood and were successful with these lessons. Throughout the year Cecilia and I recorded field notes related to the development, implementation, and modification of the cloze procedure. No entry indicates a perception on our part that the students were confused by the activity or that they produced patterns of responses that were not meaningful. All of these sources of information—students' work, student interviews, field notes—point to a clear student understanding of, and success in doing, the modified cloze task.

Given the success of the students in using context within this instructional context, Cecilia and I were surprised and challenged by what we learned from the interviews conducted with the children. As previously mentioned, the intent of these lessons was that students learn to use context when they read unaltered texts. Success in doing the instructional activity meant little if there was a lack of transfer to authentic discourse. However, as indicated in Table 2, there was very little shared understanding between the teacher and students as to the purpose of the modified cloze activity.

Only 7 percent of the time did students understand the activity as the teacher intended (match), and 10 percent of the time they had no idea why they were engaged in the task (unknown). This lack of under-

Table 2.

Student Response Summary

Category	Number of Responses	Percent of Total Responses
Match	5	7
Mismatch	57	83
Future	9	13
Task	12	17
Skill	9	13
Content	9	13
Opposite Process	8	12
General	10	14
Unknown	7	10

standing about the purpose of the lesson is particularly interesting since the teacher consistently and repeatedly discussed with the students why they were doing the activity. Cecilia helped the children make direct links to the library and trade books read during their thematic studies and during free reading. Students were told that coming to an unknown word was like coming to a blank and that context and the various strategies they used in the modified lesson could be applied to the unknown word. Additionally, during the month of December the teacher and students collaboratively created a reading chart that listed strategies for dealing with unknown words, strategies which had been learned and discussed with the modified cloze lesson. Included on this chart were such contextual strategies as read-on or reread. Finally, during theme time, students read trade books related to the topic under study. Following the reading, students were brought together in small book response groups. One issue discussed in these groups were words that the students did not understand and the application of various strategies for figuring them out. These experiences, however, had little, if any, effect on student understanding.

What is of interest, given this lack of understanding, is how the students actually did perceive the lesson. For the most part, the students clearly, and without hesitation, articulated their perceptions of the lesson during the interviews. Their understandings, as indicated in Table 2, are fairly evenly divided among six categories: future, task, skill, content, opposite process, and general.

Thirteen percent of the time, students thought the lesson focused on preparing them to do a similar task; with more difficult texts later that year or in the future grades (future). As one child stated, "We'll do the activity next year."

Another group of responses, the task category, indicated that 17 percent of the time students believed that the sole purpose of the lesson was to learn how to do the task in and of itself, i.e., to put words in blanks. As compared to the responses that focused on future activities, task responses are here-and-now-oriented and activity-centered.

The responses that fall within the skill category are both surprising and puzzling, given that the intent behind the lesson was to move the students beyond "sounding out" to the use of contextual cues. Thirteen percent of the responses indicate that the students thought Cecilia was teaching them such literacy skills as learning new words, making words rhyme, and even how to sound out.

Less surprising was the students' focus on the content of the material being read (content). Thirteen percent of students' responses discussed the idea that Cecilia had given them the piece to read so that they would learn more about the theme under study.

Though the modified cloze task was a reading activity, students thought the focus was on writing 12 percent of the time (opposite process). For the most part, students believed that they were being taught how to spell words. As one student put it, "We did the task so that I can learn to spell words that I don't know."

Finally, 14 percent of students' responses focused on reading, but lacked specificity (general). The students knew that the activity was intended to help them read better but were unable to articulate how. Follow-up questions failed to elicit additional information from the students.

Why the Mismatch?

Frequently, elementary school literacy tasks have little relevance or relationship to life outside of the classroom walls. It is only in the school environment that the child finds language that is segmented, stripped of meaning, and taken as an object of study. Although worksheets, flashcards, phonic charts, and lists of comprehension questions may be called reading in school, such tasks are unrelated to the literacy events students experience in noninstructional settings. In a sense, many school activities are "deviant" in that they fail to reflect normative use of, and behaviors with, print within the home or the wider culture.

This lack of correspondence between school and real world literacy events may ultimately force children to stop looking for school-world connections. Reading and writing activities come to be viewed as self-contained events, as "things we do in school," with little relevance to other experiences in the children's lives. The children in this study had experienced such reading instruction in kindergarten and first and second grade. It should therefore not come as a surprise that they used the schemata they had built for previous schooling activities as a base for interpreting our literacy instruction. This is the case even when the instruction, as ours attempted to do, contradicts previous instructional paradigms. Understanding is determined not only by the instructional event itself but also by what the student brings to the event.

The future, task, and skill responses of the children support such a conclusion. Thirteen percent of the responses focused on doing the task because it will be done again in the future; 17 percent related to doing the task just for the sake of doing it; and 13 percent focused on doing the activity to learn particular words level skills. In total, 43 percent of the responses related to a traditional schooling schema. Such a student view certainly reflects the "stuff' of many schooling experiences and appears to exert a powerful influence on student perception of school literacy events. The children in this study appeared unable to free themselves of past instructional influences.

The modified cloze procedure itself would also appear to have contributed to the students' inability to link school and real-world literacy events. In many respects, our lesson was an inauthentic task; and as deviant as many of the skill lessons the children had experienced in their previous years of schooling. Even with the use of whole texts, thematic content, and various contextual cues in the modified lessons, where else but in school would a child experience reading text peppered with blanks? Perhaps it should not be too surprising that the students were unable to discern the link between what they had done in these tasks and the reading of such material as library books. Library books contain connected discourse.

A Gap between Whole Language Theory and Practice?

As mentioned earlier, whole language theorists stress the cognitive and developmental characteristics of literacy learning and instruction. A third characteristic that they also highlight is what I term "sociocultural authenticity." Sociocultural authenticity reflects the pragmatic ways in which individuals within their society, culture, or discipline use literacy to mediate their interactions with the world. It represents the functional, or purposeful, dimension of language movement and continues to be highlighted by whole language proponents (Watson, 1989).

In order to be socioculturally authentic, classroom instruction and materials must reflect real world (normative) literacy events and engage students in functional, purposeful, and organic activities. Although the modified cloze activity reflects cognitive as well as developmental authenticity, the sociocultural dimension is missing. There is not a non-school environment of which I am aware in which readers encounter blank lines throughout a piece of otherwise connected discourse. In a real sense, or at least in a sociocultural sense, the activity violates established discourse norms. It should not be surprising that students had difficulty in perceiving the link between this activity and their reading of unaltered texts. And there is little reason to believe that in the future these students will suddenly discover and spontaneously apply to unaltered texts what they did in this particular strategy lesson.

Given the emphasis on the purposeful use of literacy by whole language advocates, it would appear that a gap has developed between whole language theory and some whole language practice. In the most obvious and crudest sense, this is reflected in skill-and-drill materials some basal publishers are now labeling "whole language." One publisher is even touting the fact that it has always been a whole language company in spite of the segmented instructional lessons that have characterized its basal series.

However, my concern is not with the basal publishers; their materials can easily be seen for what they are. My concern is with some strategy lessons that have moved beyond skill lessons in terms of their cognitive and developmental authenticity but still fail to reflect the purposeful use of literacy, i.e. sociocultural authenticity. For example, we have strategy lessons in which students reassemble stories which have been segmented into "chunks of meaning," lessons in which students insert text aids—titles, subtitles, pictures, graphs—into written discourse from which all such aids have been removed, and lessons in which students draw a picture summarizing what a particular story is about. Although such strategy lessons may have some merit, it is difficult to find literacy events outside of the classroom in which people engage in such activities.

True, the reassembling of story segments is intended to help students build coherent meanings when reading and writing, the inserting of text aids is intended to help students use text aids when reading and writing, and the drawing of pictures is to help students see the semiotic nature of all meaning making. My question is whether students actually understand these intentions and apply what has been learned from instructional experiences to functional literacy events. After a year spent struggling with my own belief system and what the interviews were telling me, my fear is that students do not.

Because of this concern, I have begun to evaluate school-based literacy activities in terms of the authenticity of the event. As illustrated in Figure 2, this involves examining the events in terms of their cognitive authenticity (Does the lesson engage students in those processes which we know proficient readers and writers use when interacting with written discourse?); developmental authenticity (Does the lesson allow the teacher to engage the students in collaborative, socially mediated situations before moving to independent situations?); and sociocultural authenticity (Does the lesson reflect the literacy norms of the society, culture, or discipline?). Asking these three questions, I believe, can help bridge the gap that exists between theory and some practice within the whole language paradigm.

Even more critical, however, in this bridge-building endeavor are the students. We need to begin to listen to our students as they participate in our reading and writing strategy lessons. Students have interpretations of lessons that may or may not match those of the teacher. These matches and mismatches need to be more clearly identified if we are to create effective programs that produce students who can read and write in authentic contexts.

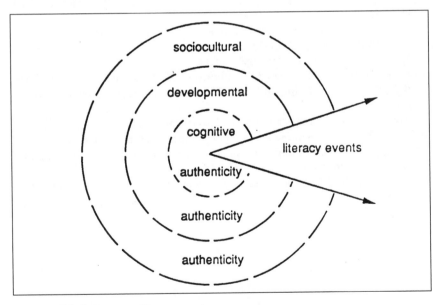

Figure 2. Whole language literacy events.

References

Atwell, M., and L. Rhodes, 1984. "Strategy lessons as alternatives to skills lessons in reading." *Journal of Reading,* 27, 700–705.

Cochrane, O., D. Cochrane, S. Scalena, and E. Buchanan. 1984. *Reading, writing, and caring.* Winnipeg, Canada: Whole Language Consultants, Ltd.

Gilles, C., M. Bixby, P. Crowley, S. Crenshaw, M. Henrichs, F. Reynolds, and D. Pyle, eds. 1988. *Whole language strategies for secondary students.* New York: Richard C. Owen.

Goodman, Y., and C. Burke. 1980. *Reading strategies: Focus on comprehension.* New York: Holt.

Goodman, Y., D. Watson, and C. Burke. 1987. *Reading miscue inventory.* New York: Richard C. Owen.

Harste, J., and K. Short 1988. *Creating classrooms for authors.* Portsmouth, NH: Heinemann.

Kucer, S. 1990. *"Investigating the development, implementation, and effects of an integrated literacy curriculum within a third grade classroom."* (Final Report to the National Council of Teachers of English Research Foundation). Los Angeles: University of Southern California, School of Education.

Kucer, S., and J. Harste. 1991. "The reading and writing connection: Counterpart strategy instruction." In *Effective strategies for teaching reading,* ed. B. Hayes. Boston, MA: Allyn and Bacon, 123–152.

Newman, J. ed. 1985. *Whole language: Theory in use.* Portsmouth, NH: Heinemann.

Smith, F. 1975. *Comprehension and learning.* New York: Richard C. Owen.

———. 1981. "Demonstrations, engagement, and sensitivity: A revised approach to language learning." *Language Arts* 60: 103–112.

Vygotsky, L. 1978. *Mind in society.* Cambridge. MA: Harvard University Press.

Watson, D. (1989). Defining and describing whole language. *Elementary School Journal* 90: 129–141.

Watson, D. ed. 1987. *Ideas and insights.* Urbana, IL: NCTE.

Wells, G. (1986). *The meaning makers.* Portsmouth, NH: Heinemann.

Wertsch, J. ed. 1985a. *Culture, communication, and cognition.* London, England: Cambridge University Press.

———. 1985b. *Vygotsky and the social formation of mind.* Cambridge, MA: Harvard University Press.

14 Teaching Reading Strategies in a "Remedial" Reading Class

Marie Dionisio
Klein Middle School, Harrison, NY

Dionisio treats the sixth graders in her "remedial" reading class like readers, not like non-readers. She does not begin with or focus on "skills" for unlocking words, except as these are part of the effective reading strategies she models and shares. In this chapter, she first explains several kinds of mini-lessons she offers to students: book talks on books she has read and other children have liked; a cloze passage through which she demonstrates to readers that they are language experts, capable of making sense of text; a demonstration of how reading too slowly can interfere with getting meaning; a demonstration of how skipping an unknown word can both increase speed and aid the construction of meaning; a discussion of several bad (nonproductive) reading habits; a discussion/ demonstration on the importance of reading for chunks of uninterrupted time; and mini-lessons focused on identifying with a character, thinking ahead (predicting), and visualizing. This section is followed by a discussion of Teri, one of the many children who have become competent and enthusiastic readers in Dionisio's class.

Teaching Reading Strategies in a "Remedial" Reading Class

The reading strategies that follow grew out of my study of the work of Frank Smith (*Understanding Reading* and *Reading Without Nonsense*) and Nancie Atwell, and out of my reflections on my own reading strategies. Nancie Atwell introduced me to Frank Smith in 1987, during a workshop on reading and writing at Northeastern University's Institute on Writing and Teaching. Her interpretation and application of Smith's work prodded my continued study of pyscholinguistic theory and language development. Atwell also encouraged me to share with my students my own process for making sense of text. Being a daily, visible model of an adult who values and enjoys reading and writing is the most important of my teaching strategies.

Reading Books Students Like

In order to be good readers, students must have positive and pleasurable experiences with books. This is especially important for students who associate reading with failure. Such readers must find books and characters they can enjoy before they can take the risk of trying new strategies. For this reason, it is essential that students choose their own books and be able to abandon books they do not like. To help my students, I do a great many "book talks," but only on books I have read. Many times the books were originally recommended to me by students from previous remedial reading classes; if that is the case, I always mention it. I give a brief description of the story, share my personal response to it, and read a short excerpt. I also provide opportunities for students to share with one another the books that they like.

Using Language Expertise

Poor readers do not trust themselves with written language. They have learned to think that they are not capable of making sense of text. To dispel this myth, I demonstrate to these children that they are language experts. The years of experience they have as language users has made them experts on how language works. On an overhead transparency I present a short expanded cloze technique, one in which only a few words are given. As a class, they guess the words in order, using only their knowledge of the way sentences are put together and the growing context of the text. We discuss how they made their guesses, why synonyms and correct parts of speech are good guesses, and where they found it easiest and most difficult to make a guess. We end our discussion with a reminder to trust our knowledge of language to help us make the same kinds of guesses when we read.

Reading Fast

Most remedial readers read too slowly to make sense of text. They focus on individual words or even syllables. I demonstrate how reading too slowly can interfere with meaning construction by slowing my speech down to an imitation of word-by-word reading and sounding out. Speaking this way of course makes my message hard to comprehend.

All students agree that my normal speech is much easier to understand. I draw a parallel with reading too slowly. To help them read faster I demonstrate the way peripheral vision aids readers. I discuss the idea of stopping one's eyes only on the words that carry the meaning and grouping other words around those words. We discuss the idea that increasing reading speed happens slowly.

Skipping Words Not Known

To break sixth graders of the habit of constantly sounding out words. I demonstrate how skipping an unknown word both increases speed and aids construction of meaning. I present short paragraphs that contain a word that the students do not know. I read the paragraph, skipping over the word. The students suggest meanings for the word as well as their reasons for suggesting it. We list possible meanings and identify synonyms in the list. We note how many of the suggested meanings are similar and why we think that happened. I end with a challenge for the day: in your reading today, skip over any word you do not know and see if you still understand what you read. Then, after reading time, we discuss our experiences.

Avoiding Bad Habits

Habits that slow readers down are the ones I want to eliminate. Such habits focus concentration at the word level instead of the meaning level. I discuss the following habits with students as well as the reason why they interfere with good reading:

- Moving your lips while you read slows you down.
- Pointing to the words or using a marker blocks your peripheral vision and slows you down.
- Constant rereading (which I demonstrate) confuses meaning and slows you down.
- Trying to remember all the details of what you read directs your focus from the global meaning of the text and from personal involvement in it.

Reading for Chunks of Uninterrupted Time

Comprehension hinges on exposure to chunks of text large enough to make meaning. Poor readers often take too many breaks while reading. These breaks seriously curtail meaning construction. I demonstrate how such breaks interfere with the ability to make sense of anything.

I use a video or I tell a story about watching a video and being interrupted four or five times. Then we discuss why I did not like the video. I ask students to suggest ways in which readers interrupt themselves, and I list them on the board. I challenge students to read without interruptions of any kind for the entire twenty-five minutes of class reading time. At the end of that time, we discuss our experiences.

Identifying with a Character

Involvement in reading begins with a reader's identification with a character. To promote this, I talk about how putting myself in a character's place has helped me as a reader. I use specific examples of book characters with whom I have identified, why I was able to do so, and how that helped me as a reader. I challenge students to try to put themselves in the character's place and to think about what they would do in the same situation. I share my discovery that I can identify with a character even if that character is not like me in every way.

Thinking Ahead, or Predicting

Prediction is at the core of good reading. To promote prediction among remedial readers, I suggest commonplace scenarios to the class and ask them to predict what will happen next. Sometimes I read a picture book and stop for predictions. In both cases. we discuss how we arrived at our prediction. As a follow-up on another day. I use examples of how prediction helped me while reading a particular book. I challenge students to predict as they are reading and end the class with a sharing of the predictions made that day and the reasons for them.

Visualizing

Movies and video games occupy a great deal of my students' time. I use that fact to suggest that they visualize what they are reading as a way of getting involved in a story. I tell them that I see a movie in my head when I read. I ask them to close their eyes, listen to me read, and try to see what they hear. I read a passage that is both easy to visualize and interesting to the age group. I ask students to share with the class what they saw in their minds. I challenge students to see a movie in their heads as they read.

Teri: A Sixth Grader in a "Remedial" Reading Class

Because of her second-grade standardized test scores, Teri had been labeled a remedial reader in third grade. Beginning in fifth grade, she also attended the resource room for assistance with her diagnosed learning disability. Now in sixth grade, she was still in the remedial reading class and still in the resource room. She hated reading and school. (Wouldn't you?) Four years of special reading class with another year ahead of her was proof to Teri that reading was something she would never be able to do. Furthermore, she saw absolutely no reason why she should want to read.

Remedial reading has traditionally been a sentence, like a jail term. Instruction has focused on a reader's weaknesses. Encounters with text are brief, and controlled by the teacher. The meaning of such text is minimal (if there is any meaning at all). Reading is reduced to an endless parade of skill-drill exercises. To paraphrase Frank Smith (1985), remedial reading instruction made nonsense out of what should be sense.

At the beginning of sixth grade, Teri's primary reading strategy was to sound out words. She was a word-by-word reader. To her, reading was the correct oral pronunciation of words. It had nothing to do with meaning. Even the questions at the end of everything she read were meaningless. She told me that she answered the questions by finding a word or phrase in the paragraph and copying that part as her answer. It was a matter of word matching, not meaning construction. Reading was truly meaningless for her.

Teri was like most of the remedial readers I had seen in the previous twenty years. I knew I had to change her view of reading to one of meaning construction. In order to do that, I would have to help her discover that reading could be enjoyable.

I started with allowing Teri to choose her own books. During the first ten weeks of school, mini-lessons focused on reading for meaning. I discussed the strategies that I thought would enable my students to abandon word-by-word reading and focus on meaning. During this time, Teri started ten books but finished only one: *When the Boys Ran the House* by Joan Carris. One of her classmates had read it and recommended it to her. The humor took hold of her. As a result, Teri had her first successful and enjoyable reading experience.

The concept of abandoning a book you do not like was new to Teri. Up to this point she had been told what to read. She had no choices and no ownership. Given her attitude toward reading and its lack of meaning for her, I expected her to abandon several books. I didn't expect her to abandon nine books, but it reminded me of how important it is to allow readers to abandon books they do not like. If I had interfered in Teri's decisions about books and made choices for her, she may never have come to that first enjoyable and meaning-centered reading experience.

After finishing *When the Boys Ran the House,* Teri wrote this letter to me in her reading dialogue journal:

> I liked *When the Boys Ran the House* because the author made me feel like I was a character and if it was a movie it would be a comedy movie so when I read the book it felt like a comedy to me.

This letter is evidence that Teri had adopted some new reading strategies. She was making sense out of text instead of reading purely as oral performance. She was beginning to imagine herself as the character and to visualize as she read. This novel was a clear turning point for Teri. Following it, she finished four more books and enjoyed them all. Each of them was recommended by Annie, the same classmate who had recommended *When the Boys Ran the House.* She also abandoned two books during this time.

During this same period, Teri and Annie began exchanging literary letters. In them they discussed the books both of them had read. After Teri finished the fourth of Annie's recommendations, she wrote in a journal letter, "Most of the time Annie and me compare our reactions to the same book. I like that." In their literary dialogue, Teri and Annie discussed characters, favorite scenes, and personal responses to the stories. They were discussing the very things I discussed with them, but they were doing it because they wanted to, because they saw value in it, because it was fun. Did Teri understand and enjoy what she was reading? Without a doubt!

During the third quarter, Teri began to choose books on her own and recommend them to Annie, to other classmates, and to me. After reading *Chocolate Fever* by Robert Kimmel Smith, Teri wrote to me, "I thought *Chocolate Fever* was good because I liked how the author put the characters into the story. It pulled me in." By this time Teri regularly verbalized her involvement in what she was reading. In this instance, she specified how the author had invited her into the story. I could see that she no longer saw reading as something she'd never be able to do.

During the third quarter I reviewed the reading strategies we had discussed earlier in the year by asking the class, "If a friend came to you said he or she was having trouble with reading, and asked you for help, what would you tell that friend to do?" The students generated a list of suggestions, most of which came from the mini-lessons I had done in the fall. I listed them on chart paper, pinned them to the wall, and invited the students to try one they hadn't tried before or one they would like to do better. I also asked them to write a letter and let me know how it worked out. Here's Teri's letter:

> Today I tried to read faster and it worked really good. I read about 25 pages today. I didn't talk or take any commercial breaks during reading time, and I didn't move my lips. It all worked because I read more and I remember everything and I like the story better too.

My response was deliberately short and simple: "You really took a risk trying three things today. Terrific. So, you are saying that you were able to understand more and enjoy reading because you read faster and didn't talk. That sounds logical to me." I was sure encouragement and reinforcement of the idea that she was continuing to improve as a reader were the most valuable teaching strategies I could use.

A week later Teri again wrote about her efforts to try new strategies as a reader. "I tried to put myself in the main character's place and it worked out pretty good. I just finished *Sudako and the Thousand Paper Cranes*. It was sad. I cried." Teri's willingness to take risks as a reader is obvious. She no longer saw such attempts as opportunities for failure. Rather, she saw these risks as voyages into unchartered areas that might yield new discoveries for her.

Toward the end of the third quarter, Teri's involvement in reading went even deeper. She wrote,

> I'm reading *Ace Hits the Big Time* by Murphy and Wolkoff. So far its good. I could actually hear and feel the action. It's got a lot of action. And it pulled me right in. I love it.

Clearly, Teri was no longer the passive and disinterested caller of words she had been in September. She had become an active reader, one who is involved with character and conflict, one who sees value in reading. Furthermore. she was reading a book that was considered appropriate for sixth graders!

During the fourth quarter, Teri took more risks as a reader, read more books than any of the previous ten-week periods, and continued to grow as a reader and learner. She began to spend time at home reading books, and she told her friends and me that she did. For a child like Teri to admit that she read at home was an enormous change. On one occasion she wrote, "I started reading a book at home. It's called *Just As Long As We're Together* by Judy Blume. The book is about friends." A month later she began her letter with, "Over the vacation I read *Jelly Belly* by Robert Kimmel Smith. It was a really good book. Funny and serious too." Reading had become part of Teri's life.

At the same time, she began to hone and vary her reading strategies. We had been discussing the strategy of putting yourself in the character's place as you read. Our share session raised a good question: could a reader put herself in the character's place with equal success in every book? We debated this issue and decided it was true. The next day, Teri wrote this letter:

> I just started *Blubber* by Judy Blume. Well I tried to put myself in the main character and it wasn't me. Because it's about this girl who's fat. But in *Class Clown* by Johanna Hurwitz I put myself in the main character's place and it was me sometimes.

Teri and I discussed the idea of pretending to be with the character instead of being the character. She thought that would work for her in books like *Blubber*.

By the end of the year, Teri had changed dramatically. She enjoyed reading, saw value in being a reader, spent time reading outside of school, owned a collection of books she loved, learned from the characters and conflicts in books and, best of all, recognized the ways in which she had changed. Since September she had read nineteen novels. This was quite an accomplishment and was indicative of the reader she had grown to be. Her final evaluation delineates the changes she saw in herself.

> I changed my reading a couple of ways this year. I don't move my lips anymore and that helps me read a lot faster. I focus on the book and don't take commercial breaks while I'm reading. I try to be the main character. I also like to read on my own now. I never knew how much fun reading can be. We got to pick our own books and if we didn't like the book, we could just drop the book and start a new one. I think if you want to be a good reader, you have to read books that you like, not books that other people like. We don't have to do any comprehension sheets or work in the workbooks. Instead we write in our journals to the other classmates or we write to Ms. Dionisio and tell her all about our book. I share my ideas with Ms. Dionisio and she shares hers with me. I really think I changed a lot this year and I'm glad I did.

Perhaps the most powerful statement in this letter is "I never knew how much fun reading can be." After all, if something is fun to do, we all tend to do it well. Certainly, Teri did not have another year of special reading class ahead of her. For the first time in her life, she saw herself as a reader.

15 Readers "Fresh" from the Middle

Linda R. Morrow
Oakland Junior High School, Columbia, Missouri

In the introduction to this chapter, Morrow explains the importance of miscue analysis in assessing her students' use of reading strategies. Observing and assessing these readers' strategies is an important starting point for instruction. In her fifty-minute class periods at a junior high school, Morrow has seven major goals, which include "demonstrate reading and writing strategies for my students." Morrow explains how the reading experiences provided for her students include encouraging the use of prior knowledge and the context or situation to make sense of texts; shared personal reading; book conferences; demonstrating and discussing reading strategies through examination of reader-selected miscues; making connnections with other content areas through literature study groups, writing, and other activities; the experience of listening to books read aloud by the teacher; and the use of newspapers as classroom texts.

Originally published in *Voices from the Middle*, 2(2), (1995), 13–20. Copyright 1995 by the National Council of Teachers of English.

Our students come to school with rich and varied experiences. Before we begin reading, my first question is, "What do you already know about this topic?" By asking them to share their expertise, I am not only validating them as learners, but I am also demonstrating how efficient readers use their prior knowledge to help make sense of new information.

I am alert to readers' strategies, such as rereading to correct what doesn't make sense, making meaningful miscues (for example, substituting an acceptable synonym for the word in the text), overrelying on graphophonic relationships (excessive "sounding out"), or skipping words they don't know. I make mental notes of their particular reading strategies and sometimes write my observations in my planbook or journal.

Goodman, Watson, and Burke (1987) remind us that an understanding of reading miscue analysis enables teachers to discover patterns of students' oral reading behaviors, thus providing more information about an individual reader than any other instrument available. Knowledge of the reading process gained through miscue analysis is essential for middle-school English/language arts teachers, allowing them to develop a greater understanding of students' reading strategies and, if needed, to help them develop more effective and efficient ones.

When students read plays aloud, I have the opportunity for an informal miscue analysis. My instructions to them as readers are to try to make sense as they read, and reread if necessary; I remind listeners to be patient and not to correct the reader. Being patient in this situation is difficult for some listeners, but it encourages readers to use their own strategies to construct meaning. This wait time also illustrates my confidence in student strategy use.

The overarching question for me and my students in any language context is, "Does this make sense?" I ask myself this question when considering the experiences I will offer my students in reading, writing, listening, and speaking. I want them to have authentic reasons for using the language arts; I also want them to make choices about those purposes. Throughout the school day and week, our program is organized around opportunities for varied language experiences; embedded in these experiences are opportunities for assessment of readers' strategy use, which provides me with information for instructional planning.

Organizing Our Program

I have the following goals in my seventh-grade language arts classroom:

1. read aloud to my students
2. give students choices in reading and writing
3. read a common text (students and teacher)
4. write every day (students and teacher)
5. share poetry with students
6. make connections with core subjects (science, math, and social studies) through literature
7. demonstrate reading and writing strategies for my students.

Right! you say. All of this in one fifty-minute class period.

Although our school is organized as a junior high, there is a very strong sense of middle-school philosophy among administrators and faculty, especially in seventh grade. Teachers are in close contact with parents regarding academic and behavioral issues. There is a strong sense of community in which the child feels safe, an atmosphere of collaboration where all are expected to be successful.

Our core classes (math, science, English, and social studies) are taught by interdisciplinary teams with flexible scheduling in order to emphasize the interconnectedness of concepts. Exploration is encouraged through electives, such as industrial technology, keyboarding, human environmental sciences, health, art, music, and foreign languages. This school-within-a-school is an attempt to provide a balance between teacher-subject specialization in the high school and the supportive interpersonal structure of the elementary school.

I teach English on a seventh-grade core team in a school containing grades seven, eight, and nine. Our core team from English, math, social studies, and science works with 100 heterogeneously grouped students. One of the goals of our team is to create an interdisciplinary experience for our students, where all subjects are closely integrated.

In order to conserve time in the fifty-minute period, we meet as a whole class for announcements, mini-lessons, reading strategy lesson instruction, and planning for the remainder of the period. Students then move to other areas of the classroom or into the hallways to pursue their day's plan. Dorothy Watson reminds us that we should never do for students what they can do for themselves. My students check the roll, put out the absentee slip, and record absences in the class attendance book. They also distribute and collect writing portfolios and other materials.

The reading experiences I offer my students are based on the understanding that reading is a meaning construction process that is embedded in the situational context; it requires readers to draw upon their prior experiences and their language strengths. These reading experiences include the following elements:

1. prior knowledge and context of situation
2. shared personal reading
3. book conferences
4. reader selected miscues
5. content connections
6. teacher read-alouds
7. newspapers as classroom texts.

Prior Knowledge and Context of Situation

I frequently use cartoons to demonstrate the importance of prior knowledge and how meaning is embedded within particular situational contexts. In order to "get the joke," we have to understand the cartoon's context and the author's reference to some idea in our commonly held experiences. At times, we have to work at making meaning from cartoons, but the sharing of ideas builds that meaning, becomes part of our knowledge base, provides an opportunity for identifying and labeling literary techniques, and sparks ideas for writing.

One of the first cartoons I use has no text, but features a police lineup of four little blonde-haired girls suspected of a crime. Accompanied by a police officer, the victims, the Three Bears, are viewing the lineup. I ask my students to study the cartoon, decide what makes it funny, and what we have to know in order to understand the cartoon.

Because this is a parody of a familiar story, most of the students are able to make the connections almost immediately. For example, as Frankie began to explain the story and our knowledge of the criminal justice system, I heard another "I got it!" from a student who struggles with reading and writing. Other responses ranged from, "You have to know the story of 'Goldilocks and the Three Bears'" to "The author was trying to make a new, funny twist on an old fairy tale."

It is valuable to do this activity first with a familiar text and always as a community of readers so that we can learn from each other in a nonthreatening situation. Because of our shared experience with "Goldilocks and the Three Bears," this strategy reaffirms the importance of using prior knowledge and emphasizes that we are all learners using similar meaning-making strategies although readers' abilities vary. The fact that a few students stated in their written responses that they didn't understand the cartoon at first underscores the need to demonstrate this strategy of drawing upon prior knowledge and making connections to other texts, and to encourage students to use this reading strategy in the future.

Shared Personal Reading

At Linda Rief's (1992) suggestion, I decided that the personal reading component of my curriculum would become homework. The standing homework assignment for my students is to read at least thirty minutes each evening from a book of their choosing. For the first two quarters of the school year, the students keep a log of dates and pages read in order to establish a reading habit.

In addition, we have sustained silent reading (SSR) each Friday for twenty to thirty minutes. Twice each quarter, students share their books through a conference with me, our librarian, another adult, or through a book review or a book talk. These book conferences give me information about readers that is available only in a one-to-one situation. In these conversations, students make theme statements, make comparisons with other books and movies, connect personal experiences, and describe personal reading strategies.

Book Conferences

In a recent conference, Christina and I were able to touch on several literary elements, and noticed how clues in the text affected our ability to make meaning. For example, we found we had differing opinions on the identity of the main character in *Daphney's Book* (Hahn, 1983) and we both had good arguments to support our views. As the discussion progressed, we focused on the setting, noting that it was raining in Maryland and that the protagonist kept hoping it would change to snow as the storm in New England grew. There was also a reference to another character's father's being killed in the Vietnam War, allowing me to point out that clues given by the author help to establish the historical time period.

Another student, Tri, speaks English at school and Vietnamese at home. He had read a collection of ghost stories, and I discovered that he couldn't retell much of his favorite story. We read the story aloud together to demonstrate the value of rereading in order to remember a good story.

Julie, Laura, and Stephanie recently read *A Taste of Blackberries* (Smith, 1973). Julie compared the character Jamie, who dies of an allergic reaction to a bee sting, to the boy who cried wolf and wasn't taken seriously when he was really in trouble. Laura connected the narrator's depression over his best friend's death with the study of depression in her health class. Stephanie, a new student, told me that she had difficulty remembering what happened from one chapter to the next.

Book conferences provide me with valuable information about my students' personal connections and difficulties with texts that I can't access in a whole-class setting. I learn a great deal about how readers are handling texts and this information helps me plan activities and reading strategies. I also benefit from the sheer enjoyment of discussing books with the kids.

Reader Selected Miscues

Reader Selected Miscues (RSM) (Watson, 1978) is a strategy lesson that gives me the opportunity to discuss my own reading strategies as well as those of my students. Hoge (1983) and Watson suggest giving students two-by-eight inch bookmarks to record three miscues (and their page numbers) that caused them to lose meaning or to be distracted from their reading. Reader selected miscues may include new or unusual words or confusing syntactic patterns. After sustained silent reading, these examples are shared in class. The miscues are discussed that day or are collected and used for a mini-lesson the following day. This enables me to demonstrate reading strategies for handling difficult text and to verbalize my thinking as I learn from text.

Following sustained silent reading, students share any unfamiliar, interesting, or confusing words or language patterns they have found and we talk about the strategies proficient readers use when they encounter such words or structures in text. For example, we ask: What information does the author give that explains the word or phrase? What do we already know about the topic?

Recently Jessica greeted me with "Hey, Mrs. Morrow, look what I found." She showed me a passage in her book which read, "Your salad days are over." "Salad days" was clearly an unusual term for this seventh grader. We read the passage together and Jessica decided that the rich young man in the novel was being forced to go to work. Jessica was using a reading strategy demonstrated in class, indicating her awareness of its usefulness.

I share my own reader selected miscues with my students. One example comes from an historical novel set in Germany during World War II. I showed my students the name of a political party discussed in the book: National Sozialistsche Deutsche Arbeiterpartei. Because I don't speak or read German, there was no way I could pronounce this term, but I knew from the other information the author provided that this was the name of the Nazi party. I told my students that, as I continued reading, I called it Nazi and did not worry about the pronunciation. In this naming strategy, the reader predicts that the word is a name; omits that name and substitutes another name, nickname, or initial; determines some characteristic of the name (person or place); and determines the importance of the name in the story (Hoge, 1983; Watson, 1978).

Joel provided an example of going back to the text for more information and using prior knowledge. He was reading a mystery and one of the clues was to be found on the moor. He read the piece of text aloud, and the rest of the class speculated on the meaning. From the context, we decided that it was a land form. Claire remembered reading about the moor in *The Secret Garden* (Burnett, 1987). At this point, Alan reminded us that moor can also mean to secure a boat or a native of Morocco. This exchange is a clear example of why it would be pointless to plan a vocabulary lesson prior to reading: I don't know what my students already know or what they might learn as they read. Reader Selected Miscues empowers students to use their background knowledge and to question the text for needed information.

Jackson was reading *Mississippi Bridge* (Taylor, 1990) and asked about *onliest*. He knew immediately what the word was after reading it aloud. This provided the perfect opportunity to discuss the author's use of dialect to create authentic characters. During this same discussion. Claire asked about the word *taffeta*. She read a description of a girl dressed for her senior prom. As we discussed the text, Claire explained that she knew about the situation, the fancy prom dress, and the fact that the fabric made a swishing noise as the girl walked. Claire knew that taffeta was a fabric, but she had not actually seen or worn it before. Claire needs to be aware that she has a clear understanding of the text, and knowing more specific information about such things as taffeta can satisfy her curiosity, but is not required to understand the story.

At the beginning of the year, I demonstrate the RSM strategy through shared reading of a short story. Our discussions have produced some clear examples of changes in word meanings over time, definitions determined by use or context, and etymologies.

Several students asked about the word *fresh* in Shirley Jackson's (1968) "Charles." When we discussed the term, I heard a ripple of giggles across the room because their first assumption was that it was a sexual innuendo. When I asked them to reinvestigate the text, they decided that the word, used by a kindergartner, was describing an example of backtalking or being a smart aleck. They came to this conclusion because they had already established the period as the 1950s and the character as being disrespectful to his parents. This led to a discussion of how the meanings of words change over time. A similar situation occurred when the students read "Practically Everyone Knows" (Blume, 1978). From the clues given by the author, they figured that a seventh-grade "mixer" was a party for seventh graders featuring a band because one of the characters was going to play drums.

In this same story by Blume, several students asked about the word *lectern*. We talked through the passage noting that it was something used in place of a desk when one was standing. Another clue in this particular story was that the lectern was in the auditorium. At this point, I heard a number of students say *podium*. This gave me one more opportunity to say, "See how much you already know." Switching the context from school to church, the students easily produced *pulpit*.

Content Connections

I encourage my students to continue the use of reader selected miscues as they respond in their reading journals. They often read non-English words or phrases in the novels and folktales we read as we follow their social studies class around the world. For instance, as some students' read *Waiting for the Rain* (Gordon, 1987), set in South Africa, they encountered Afrikaans words. This gave me the opportunity to become a learner with them. We used several strategies: What do I think it means based upon its use in the particular scene? What additional information does the author give me? Do we have any information from social studies materials? Is there a glossary? Can we use the glossaries in the other novel set in South Africa? For most of the Afrikaans words, one of the above strategies worked and we were able to confirm our predictions and construct meaning from the text. For those few where we just had to make our best guess, we were able to move on with the story rather than being overwhelmed and giving up. This is a very powerful demonstration for struggling readers because they can see that adults have to work at making meaning and that there are many strategies on which to rely.

Because my students do most of their individual reading as homework, I rarely give them additional outside assignments. Class time is used for writing and for reading texts that provide opportunities for making content connections with particular world cultures as the students explore them in the social studies segment of our interdisciplinary team. As Brozo and Tomlinson (1986), Du Bois and MacIntosh (1986), Levstik (1985), Sanacore (1990) and Spiegel (1987) remind us, the rationale for using literature in content areas includes broadening one's knowledge of the world, adding depth and meaning to concepts studied in a specific content area, encouraging comparisons of multiple texts, connecting prior knowledge with new information, generalization and application of concepts, affecting students' social attitudes, and presenting content in a dramatic and personalized manner.

The students exploration of India and Pakistan in social studies was complemented by reading a collection of folktales and nonfiction about this region. As we read *Shabanu: Daughter of the Wind* (Staples, 1989) together, my students were aghast that the protagonist was, at their age, betrothed to one of her cousins, enticed by the idea that she didn't have to go to school, and intrigued by the fact that she had the same worries as they did. Reading *Shabanu* enabled the students to acquire a feel for a young Muslim girl's way of life in present-day Pakistan. Because the book is written in familiar narrative style, they could easily add to their background information about this culture and relate to the concepts being presented in their social studies class. Students could not help but compare their own way of life with Shabanu's. They often asked questions and wondered why life-changing decisions were completely out of Shabanu's hands. As they wrestled with the fact that Shabanu was being forced into an arranged marriage, they began to think of possible alternatives, and realized that all adolescents must make tough decisions.

When my students studied Africa, the books *Journey to Jo'burg* and *Chain of Fire* (Naidoo,1986,1990) provided personal views of apartheid in South Africa, a policy that the students were exploring in social studies. Apartheid came to life as students made the more than 300-kilometer journey with thirteen-year-old Naledi and her nine-year-old brother Tiro from their village to Johannesburg to find their mother who was working for a wealthy white family. Through these novels, plus *Waiting for the Rain: A Novel of South Africa* (Gordon, 1987) and *In the Middle of Somewhere: A Story of South Africa* (Gordon, 1990), my seventh graders grappled with the realities of a political system that did not value its citizens as equals. Social attitudes were affected as my students expressed their anger over the inequities suffered by the black South Africans.

My goal is to provide literature study groups with enough titles for each culture that our students explore. Those involved in this search for sets of multicultural selections include my colleagues on the core team, our language arts department chair, our colleagues on the other seventh-grade team, our media specialist, and colleagues outside my school (such as local Teachers Applying Whole Language [TAWL] members). Margaret Mooney (1987) provides the following criteria for identifying high-quality literature:

1. Does the piece have charm, magic, impact, and appeal?
2. Does the piece say something worthwhile?
3. Is the shape and structure appropriate?
4. Is the language effective? Does the language suit the subject and the characters?
5. Is the piece authentic? Does it avoid the sham, the misleading, the prejudiced, the stereotyped, and the superficial?

I search for literature from the various world cultures that my students are exploring. We read fairy tales, folktales, poetry, novels, and nonfiction pieces. I use dialectical response journals, partner reading, and teacher read-aloud to support readers who are still word bound, overrelying on sounding out words, and those who would prefer walking on hot coals to reading. Students participate in literature study groups, reading novels set in various cultures of the world. As they read, they respond in dialectical journals, which become their agendas for group discussion. As students discuss the connections they have made, raise questions, and acknowledge strategies they have used for constructing meaning, they model effective strategies for students who are struggling with the reading process.

For example, Ryan, who was in a literature study group with three other boys and one girl, compared the friendship dilemma in *Waiting for the Rain* (Gordon, 1987) with the similar conflict between the animal characters in the movie *The Fox and the Hound*. As these group members shared their notebook entries, Ryan read, "The part where Frikkie has captured Tengo in an apartheid protest is like the movie *Fox and the Hound* when the animals realize that when they are grown up one will be chasing the other."

Other entries focus on new or unusual words such as *pannier* (camel saddle) in *Shabanu* and *veld* (open, rolling grassland) in *In the Middle of Somewhere*. In *Waiting for the Rain*, the main character, Frikkie, calls his little sister a domkop. Since there was no glossary of Afrikaans words, the students used their knowledge of syntax and their own experiences with siblings to surmise that the word meant dummy or stupid. In this same novel, the students discovered that often the writer will define unusual words such as *kraal* (a group of round mud huts with thatched roofs where the farmworkers lived, Gordon, 1987, p. 7) as a part of the text. These situations present opportunities for modeling independent reading strategies.

Students needing support in reading often engage in partner reading (reading aloud with another student) or, in the case of my class-within-a-class, another teacher reads aloud with small groups, using the hallway as an extension of the classroom.

Teacher Read-Alouds

I often introduce *Middle School Blues* (Kassem, 1986) at the beginning of the school year because the protagonist, like my students, is experiencing a new school setting: seven different teachers, classes with all new faces, lockers, hall passes, and choices in the cafeteria. I read this novel aloud because I want to demonstrate my own love of reading using a piece of literature that parallels my students' current experiences. While we enjoy a good story together, I also have the chance to demonstrate reading strategies such as prediction, using prior knowledge, using the context of situation in the story, graphophonic relationships, grammatical knowledge, and, most of all, meaning. As I read about Cindy's experiences in seventh grade, I ask my students to predict what will happen next or what they would do in the same situation based on their experiences and what has happened so far in the novel. I also ask them what specific events in the plot bring to mind. For example, at the beginning of the book, Cindy's grandmother passes away and the funeral is a fiasco. At this point, we talk about our own experiences at funerals. I often begin by relating a similar incident that involved my own children at their grandfather's funeral.

Newspapers as Classroom Texts

Current news provides another source for reading strategy lessons. I write a daily message on the chalkboard that deals with current events, often tying into the culture being explored in social studies. This gives the students a chance to use their knowledge from that discipline to make meaning of new information. Current events also give me a chance to think out loud or model how an adult deals with new and difficult information. For example, we followed the dismantling of apartheid and the elections in South Africa. As we read newspaper accounts, I struggled with the names of the tribal townships and the Afrikaans words, some of which we had not encountered in the novels we read or in the social studies textbook. I made the point that we knew what the words meant and quite possibly we would hear them pronounced by newscasters. Students need to know that at times we must look outside ourselves for more information.

Conclusions and Dilemmas

I want to provide two days of writing and two days of reading for my students each week. Friday is reserved for sustained silent reading and sharing personal reading. Unfortunately, this schedule is difficult to keep because we always seem to need more time for one or the other. I feel it is crucial to allow my students ample time for free writing in response to their reading. Their writing may take the form of jokes, poetry to share in class, or personal reflections on current events, family life, and extracurricular activities. These reading and writing processes spill over into each other. Most of this writing is done in class because I want to model the writing process as my students write, and I want them to avail themselves of help from their peers. The challenge is to make the time for these important activities.

Before starting any new reading activity, I ask myself the following questions:

1. What do my students already know about a particular topic?
2. Does this experience mirror life in the real world? Is it authentic?
3. How can I learn about my students' reading and learning strategies as they engage in this activity?

An understanding of the transactional, social, psychological, and linguistic aspects of the reading process (K. Goodman, 1979) is essential to us as English teachers in order to help students who are struggling readers. The expectation that in elementary school one learns to read and, consequently, will read to learn in middle and secondary schools is not always realistic, as middle-school teachers know. We need to present to our students the reading strategies that we use effortlessly and unconsciously, and help them become aware of and use the strengths they bring to their reading.

Knowledge of the reading process gained through reading miscue analysis enables us to examine a student's oral reading, thereby gaining specific information about his or her reading ability. This conscious knowledge of the reading process helps us plan reading experiences that will enhance that student's reading strengths rather than add to the struggle.

References

Brozo, W., and C. Tomlinson 1986. "Literature: The key to lively content courses." *The Reading Teacher* 40(3): 288–293.

Du Bois, B., and M. McIntosh. 1986. "Reading aloud to students in secondary, history classes." *The Social Studies* (September/October): 210–213.

Goodman, K. S. 1979. "The know-more and the know-nothing movements in reading: A personal response." *Language Arts*, 56: 657– 663.

Goodman, Y., D. Watson, and C. Burke. 1987. *Reading miscue inventory: Alternative procedures*. New York: Richard C. Owen.

Hoge, S. 1983. "A comprehension-centered reading program using reader selected miscues." *Journal of Reading* 27: 52–55.

Levstik, L. 1985. "Literary geography and mapping." *Social Education*, 1: 38–43.

Rief, L. 1992. *Seeking diversity: Language arts with adolescents.* Portsmouth, NH: Heinemann.

Sanacore, J. 1990. "Creating the lifetime reading habit in social studies." *Journal of Reading* 33(6): 414–418.

Spiegel, D. 1987. "Using adolescent literature in social studies and science." *Educational Horizons* (summer): 162–164.

Watson, D. J. 1978. "Reader selected miscues: Getting more from sustained silent reading." *English Education*, 10: 75–85.

Adolescent Literature Cited

Blume, J. 1978. "Practically everyone knows." In *To make a difference*, ed. T. Clymer and L. Ruth. Lexington, MA: Ginn. 56–62.

Burnett, F. H. 1987. *The secret garden.* New York: Henry Holt.

Gordon, S. 1987. *Waiting for the rain: A novel of South Africa.* New York: Bantam Books.

———. 1990. *In the middle of somewhere: A story of South Africa.* New York: Orchard Books.

Hahn, M. D. 1983. *Daphney's book.* New York: Clarion Books.

Jackson, S. 1968. "Charles." In *The best of both worlds: An anthology of stories for all ages.* Garden City, NY: Doubleday. 123–128.

Kassem, L. 1986. *Middle school blues.* New York: Avon Books.

Naidoo, B. 1986. *Journey to Jo'burg: A South African story.* New York: HarperCollins.

———. 1990. *Chain of fire.* Philadelphia: Lippincou Crowell.

Smith, D. B. 1973. *A taste of blackberries.* New York: Thomas Y. Crowell.

Staples, S. 1989. *Shabanu: Daughter of the wind.* New York: Alfred A. Knopf.

Taylor, M. 1990. *Mississippi bridge.* New York: Bantam Skylark.

III From Miscue Analysis to Revaluing and Assisting Readers

From Miscue Analysis to Revaluing and Assisting Readers

As explained in some of the articles in *Reconsidering a Balanced Approach to Reading* (Goodman and Goodman, Chapter 3, and Weaver, Chapter 1), a miscue is an unexpected oral response that occurs while someone is reading aloud. That is, a miscue is an oral response that differs from what the text would lead us to expect. Kenneth Goodman chose this term to get away from the idea that every departure from the text is necessarily an error, something to be viewed as wrong or at least undesirable. By analyzing how miscues fit within their semantic and syntactic context, we can infer the degree to which a reader is predicting, monitoring comprehension, and using fix-it strategies (or trying to), in order to make sensible meaning from the text. We have to be careful in drawing such inferences, since some readers make a lot of miscues that don't fit the context but still comprehend quite well; they may be correcting silently. On the other hand, some readers may read nearly word-perfect, yet understand little of what they have read. So miscue analysis is a valuable key to understanding a reader's strategies, but nevertheless there is not necessarily a strong correlation between the strength of a reader's strategies and the reader's comprehension of the selection.

Most basically, analyzing the miscues of proficient readers offers insight into the nature of the reading process itself. It appears that good readers just naturally think ahead, or "predict." This makes it easier to identify words but also leads to miscues: a reasonable prediction does not always fit, semantically and/or syntactically, with what follows. Other insight into the nature of the reading process is offered by miscues that reflect a person's native dialect or language, when that is not the dialect or language in which the person is reading. Consider, for instance, the passage in Figure 1.

In this example from Miramontes (1990), the reader was a sixth grader who spoke Spanish as her native language and who read in Spanish; she was now learning to read in English. Many of her miscues reflect her Spanish background: pronunciation miscues like "He"

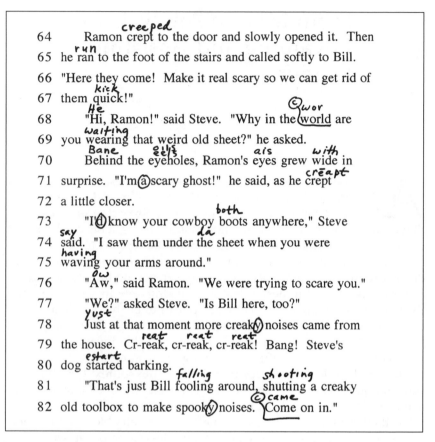

Figure 1. Miscue transcript.

for *Hi*, "ais" for *eyes*, "da" for *the*, and "estart" for *started*. The omission of various grammatical endings and markers is an "interlanguage" feature that commonly occurs as one is acquiring a non-native language. Examples are "creak" for *creaky*, "run" for *ran*, and "say" for *said*. To summarize, many of this reader's miscues simply reflect the fact that she is still in the process of acquiring English. They do not reflect a loss of meaning. In fact, such miscues demonstrate that in reading aloud, readers typically go from the visual display to meaning *before* saying the words aloud. Miscues that reflect one's native dialect or language, or the fact that one is still acquiring the language in which he or she is reading, provide powerful evidence that we do not decode to speech or silent speech *before* getting meaning, but typically afterwards.

More of what we can infer about the reading process itself is discussed in Goodman and Goodman (Chapter 3 in *Reconsidering a Balanced Approach to Reading*). Here, we see how miscue analysis can be used to understand readers' strategies, to revalue readers and help them revalue themselves as readers, and to assist them in becoming more confident and proficient readers.

References

Brown, J., Goodman, K. S., & Marek, A. (1996). *Studies in miscue analysis: An annotated bibliography*. Newark, DE: International Reading Association.

Miramontes, O. B. (1990). A comparative study of English oral reading skills in differently schooled groups of Hispanic students. *Journal of Reading Behavior, 22*, 373–394.

16 Miscue Analysis for Classroom Teachers: Some History and Some Procedures

Yetta M. Goodman
University of Arizona

As Goodman explains, she and Ken Goodman have been analyzing readers' miscues for about twenty-five years—readers of all ages and abilities, different languages and orthographies, and bilingual and ESL readers. She explains that "miscue" is "a good term because it reveals that miscues are unexpected responses cued by the readers' knowledge of their language and concepts of the world." From studying miscues, the Goodmans and other researchers have concluded that all readers make miscues; there is a single, underlying reading process; all readers use various strategies simultaneously and instantaneously as they strive to construct a meaningful and grammatical rendition of the text. Goodman explains such strategies in further detail, indicating that the construction of meaning involves use of all the language cueing systems. Next follows a discussion of miscue analysis procedures: basic procedures, plus the coding and analyzing of miscues. Goodman then illustrates readers' knowledge of the language cueing systems with examples from Gary, a thirteen-year-old sixth grader who spent most of his elementary school years in special reading classes. She concludes by saying that miscue analysis shows clearly that readers learn to read by reading, though this does not eliminate the role of the teacher.

Originally published in *Primary Voices, 3*(4), (1995), 2–9. Copyright 1995 by the National Council of Teachers of English.

Ken Goodman and I have been analyzing miscues for approximately twenty-five years. With our colleagues, we have studied miscues made by readers of all ages and abilities, by bilingual and ESL readers, and by people reading in many languages and orthographies. We've studied thousands of miscues made by hundreds of readers in order to understand the linguistic and conceptual insights that the study of miscues reveals.

Miscue is a good term because it reveals that miscues are unexpected responses cued by the readers' knowledge of their language and concepts of the world. Ken Goodman adopted the term *miscue* because of the negative connotation and history of the term *error* in first- and second-language research and language education. The term *unexpected response* suggests that a miscue is unexpected by an interested listener. It further suggests that when listening to someone's oral reading, listeners are also readers transacting with the text. In such a sociopsycholinguistic setting, both readers and listeners make miscues.

A major assumption of miscue research is that everything that happens during reading is caused by what the reader knows about language and the world. A reader's miscues or unexpected responses are produced in the same way as expected responses. Comparisons between expected and unexpected responses reveal readers' knowledge, experience, and intellectual processes, and the proficiency with which they use those processes. When expected and unexpected responses match, we get few insights into this process. When they do not match and a miscue results, teachers/researchers have a window on the reading process (K. S. Goodman, 1970).

Miscue analysis is based on oral reading and although there are differences between oral and silent reading, the use of the language cueing systems and reading strategies are essentially the same. The miscues we find in oral reading also occur in silent reading (Cambourne & Rousch, 1979; Gollasch, 1980; Chapman, 1981).

From the results of miscue research, we have concluded that

- All readers make miscues.
- There is a single underlying reading process.

Miscue analysis has resulted in fundamental insights about the reading process. All readers use strategies to construct meaning. Proficient readers use those strategies in efficient ways. Reading strategies include sampling the text once the reading has been initiated, making inferences, predicting, and confirming. Readers use reading strategies simultaneously and instantaneously as they continually ask themselves, "I wonder if this sounds like language in this context?" and "Is this making sense in this story or article?" During this problem-solving process, readers either *confirm* as they read and keep reading or *disconfirm* when their reading does not make sense or sound like language. If their reading does not make sense, they self-correct selectively to support their construction of a meaningful text.

Meaning construction involves active use of all the language cueing systems. The language cueing systems include the graphophonic system—the relationships between oral and written language (phonics); the syntactic system—the relationship among linguistic units such as prefixes, suffixes, words, phrases, and clauses (grammar); and the semantic system—the organization for the meaning system of language. Reading strategies and language cueing systems are also influenced by the pragmatic system—the knowledge readers have about the ways in which language is understood by others in their culture. Miscue analysis documents the reader's use of these elements.

Miscue Analysis Procedures

Miscue analysis requires that the written material have a beginning, middle, and end. Although the material should be new to the reader, the language and content should be familiar. The text needs to be long and challenging enough to produce sufficient numbers of miscues for patterns to appear. Single miscues do not provide evidence for any conclusions about a reader's proficiency; twenty-five miscues are the minimum to produce a pattern of miscue responses (Goodman, Watson, & Burke, 1987).

Prior to reading, readers are told the purposes of the miscue analysis and informed that, after they finish reading, they will be asked to retell what they have read. The purpose of the discussion prior to the reading is to establish rapport with the reader. The reader is informed that the teacher/researcher will *not* provide any help if the reader encounters problems: "Read as if you are by yourself and do what you would do if you were reading silently. If you come to something you don't know, guess at it or skip it but keep reading. After you finish reading, I'll ask you to tell me what you have read." Usually, we tape-record the reading so that afterwards, in a quiet place, the teacher/researcher can double-check all the miscues and any other phenomena that were observed. In addition to a tape recorder, necessary materials include a typescript and a pencil (with eraser). A typescript is a duplicate of the original text that has been retyped (maintaining original line breaks) in double- or triple-spacing to accommodate writing down miscues where they occur in the text (see examples).

As the reading commences, the teacher/researcher sits next to the reader and, with typescript in hand, begins to record the session. The reader reads from the original. The teacher/researcher notes the following by "marking" on the typescript

- miscues
- regressions (including self-corrections)

- oral asides
- any other behavior that will aid in understanding the reading (e.g., finger pointing or careful perusal of illustrations or graphs).

If readers hesitate (for at least 30 seconds), they are reminded to guess. If hesitation continues, they are told to keep reading even if it means skipping a word or phrase. After the reading, the student is asked to retell. Usually the retelling is oral, although there are times when a written retelling, sketches, time lines, or maps are considered appropriate (Goodman, Watson, & Burke, 1987).

In miscue analysis, it is not the number of miscues that a reader makes that is important but the *quality* of those miscues. Quality is determined by the degree to which a miscue disrupts or enhances the meaning of the text. High quality miscues do not interfere with the construction of a meaningful text and usually result in semantically and syntactically acceptable sentences; if they are unacceptable, the reader self-corrects. Semantic acceptability means that the miscue results in a sentence that makes sense in the whole story or article. Syntactic acceptability means that the language of the sentence in which miscues are embedded are grammatically acceptable.

A high-quality miscue that results in syntactic and semantic acceptability is shown in Example 1. (Example numbers refer to the order of examples within this article. Sentence numbers refer to the chronology of the sentence in the story.)

Example 1:

sentence 30 And this he did with such

might that soon the river

washed
rushed over its banks. . . .

Miscues that result in an unacceptable sentence but are corrected are seen in Example 2.

Example 2:

sentence 2 These he made into blocks

houses of
horses
horses
for building houses and roads.

Example 3:

sentence 45   There is nothing greater than

man and the work he is best

able to do.

Miscues that are not high quality include those that are syntactically and semantically unacceptable and the reader does not self-correct Such a miscue is shown in Example 3.

Coding and Analyzing Miscues

Teachers/researchers use a common marking and coding system for miscue analysis in order to establish a system that is read and understood in the same way. There are alternative coding systems described in *Reading Miscue Inventory: Alternative Procedures* (Goodman, Watson, & Burke, 1987) but, as shown in the Appendix (p. 234–35), the marking system is the same across procedures.

The Reader's Knowledge of the Language Cueing Systems

The miscue examples in this article come from Gary, a thirteen-year-old sixth grader who spent most of his elementary school years in special reading classes. He was reading a forty-six sentence story called "The Stonecutter" (1961; also appears in Goodman, Watson, & Burke, 1996), a folktale about a man unsatisfied with his position in life. With the help of a wizard, the stonecutter is transformed into different powerful forces of nature (a river, a boulder, a storm, the sun) and is eventually satisfied to be himself again.

Miscue analysis shows how readers monitor the semantic (meaning) cue system. Gary's miscues reveal his ability to sample the written text, to make appropriate inferences and, as a result, to predict semantically and syntactically acceptable possibilities. His selective use of self-correction is powerful evidence of his confirming strategies. Gary's miscues almost always make sense in the story and are explained through his predicting and confirming strategies.

His use of the graphophonic cueing systems shows his phonics knowledge. More than 80 percent of his substitution miscues show high graphic similarity to the expected responses. Only two out of his twenty-seven substitution miscues have no graphic similarity to the text. One is *of* for *and* (shown in Example 2) and is self-corrected. Another example (from sentence 41, not shown here) is the substitution of *a rock* for *the rock*, which is also self-corrected. This *a* for *the* substitution reflects his knowledge of the English determiner system.

In miscue analysis research, teachers/researchers also examine the syntactic nature of miscues. Our research has shown that readers' miscues often maintain the grammaticality of sentences even if the meaning is not maintained. The phenomenon of nonwords reveals this grammatical knowledge. Nonword miscues provide a grammatical structure that readers use to sustain their construction of a meaningful text. That is why knowledgeable teachers encourage readers to substitute appropriate alternatives when they come to unfamiliar language. In Example 4, Gary makes two unsuccessful attempts at the word *tassels* and settles for a nonword $*tessels* (rhymes with wrestles). The importance of nonwords as grammatical placeholders in reading is seen in his response to a question at the end of his retelling. I asked: "Can you remember one word that you had trouble with?" He responded immediately, "About little gold fringes on the sunshade." Maintaining syntactic acceptability of the text even without semantic acceptability allows readers to continue reading and maintain syntactic cohesion. This comprehending process allows meaning construction to continue throughout the reading.

By listening carefully, miscue coders can use readers' intonation to interpret the grammatical similarity between a nonword and the expected response and determine readers' control over syntax. Nonwords often retain similarities not only in number of syllables, word length, and spelling patterns, but also in bound morphemes such as "s" (see $*tessels* above) that show plurality or "ed" that marks tense. Miscues on the different forms of *to*, *two*, and *too* (as the initial part of the infinitive, as a preposition, as a number, and as an adverb) are easily disambiguated as teachers/researchers become adept at listening and relistening to intonation.

Whenever an author uses a pronoun to refer to a previously stated noun phrase, a reader may predict the original noun phrase. The reverse phenomenon also occurs. When the author chooses a noun phrase for

Example 4:

sentence 4   ... with golden｜tassels over him.

which the referent has been established earlier, the reader may use an appropriate pronoun.

Example 5:

sentence 9   Servants were holding
ⓒ   **him**
over his head the

turquoise sunshade.

Gary appropriately predicts *him* for *his head*. The author might have chosen this structure. Since Gary is reading the text closely and he sees an additional word, he self-corrects. More confident readers might not self-correct at this point, nor is self-correction necessary.

Most of Gary's substitution miscues retained the same grammatical function as the text word. Conclusions from miscue analysis research (K. Goodman and Burke, 1973) show that readers' word for word substitution miscues retain the identical grammatical function at least 60 percent of the time, with much higher percentages for noun and verb substitutions. This research documents the power of grammaticality on reading and readers' ability to use their syntactic knowledge.

It has confused teachers/researchers for a long time that a reader can know a word or phrase in one context but not seem to know it in another context. Such confusion comes from the belief that reading is simply word recognition so that once a word is known, it should remain in long-term memory. On the contrary, words that look the same but occur in different syntactic and semantic contexts are often different entities for readers.

This issue is addressed by examining how Gary responds to the word *contented* that occurs three times in "The Stonecutter." In the first occurrence (sentence 3), the expected response is "the stonecutter was contented," and in the next two (sentences 38 & 46), "he was contented." After a number of attempts to sound out *contented* in sentence 3, Gary finally reads the expected response. However, it is obvious when he makes a number of attempts to correct *contented* on the two subsequent occurrences ($con-ten-; $conted; $con-nen-ted; continent) that he does not know this word in this story context. These attempts across the text make it clear that Gary knows he does not know and he applies various strategies to solve his reading problem. He probably has not seen this word in its predicate adjective position. However, his retelling reveals his developing understanding of the concept of contented. When we asked him what he thought the story was trying to say, he responded, "Well, you can't be anything else without trying to be whatever you want to be."

The Interrelationships of Cueing Systems and Reading Strategies

The pattern of miscues throughout a reading, including the retelling, provides a fairly complete profile of a reader's abilities. Through thoughtful and interpretive observation and evaluation, miscue analysis provides evidence of the ways in which the published text teaches the reader (Meek, 1988). Through continuous transaction with the text, Gary continuously problem solves, explores concepts, and is able to provide a thorough and appropriate retelling. The published text representing the author is itself like a teacher or a mediator (Vygotsky, 1978). Gary is in a continuing zone of proximal development, working and transacting with the author to construct a meaningful text. Because the text is a complete one and within his language and conceptual understanding, it mediates Gary's development in reading and helps to expand conceptualizations, such as speculating on what $tessels might be or deducing that *contented* has something to do with people being satisfied with who they are. Through these understandings as revealed by miscue analysis, it becomes clear that readers learn to read by reading. This does not eliminate the role for a teacher. It simply indicates the importance of readers being in control of and taking responsibility for their reading process.

References

Brown, J., A. Marek, and K. Goodman. 1994. *Annotated bibliography of miscue analysis.* (Occasional Paper No. 16). Tucson: University of Arizona, Program in Language and Literacy.

Buck, P. S. 1986. *The big wave.* New York: HarperCollins.

Cambourne, B., and P. Rousch. 1979. *A psycholinguistic model of the reading process as it relates to proficient, average and low ability readers.* Wagga Wagga, NSW, Australia: Rivenna College of Advanced Education, Sturt University.

Chapman, J. 1981. "The reader and the text." In *The reader and the text,* ed. J. Chapman. London: Heinemann, 1–15.

Cowley, J. 1983. "Rain, rain." In *Ready to read series.* Auckland, New Zealand: Ministry of Education.

———. 1987. *Los animales de Don Vicencio. II.* I. Lowe. Trans. P. Alrnada. Auckland, New Zealand: Shortland.

———. 1989. "My bike." In *Ready to read series.* Auckland, New Zealand: Learning Media (distributed by Richard C. Owen, Katonah, NY).

Crews, D. 1978. *Freight train.* New York: Scholastic.

Substitutions

Substitutions are shown by writing the miscue directly above the word or phrase.

He was sitting comfortably in the carriage.

Omissions

Omissions are marked by circling the omitted language structures.

"I can do all that," replied the husband.

Insertions

Insertions are shown by marking a proofreader's caret at the point of insertion and writing the inserted word or phrase where it occurs in the text.

"Now I've got more work to do," said the man.

Regressing and Abandoning a Correct Form

Abandonments are marked by drawing a line from right to left to the point at which the reader went back to repeat but abandoned the expected text. An inscribed (AC) is used to indicate this type of regression. In this example, the reader first reads *head against the wall*, then rejects this possibility and produces the more sensible *hand against the wall*.

"How many times did I hit my head against the wall?" she asked.

Regressions or Repetitions

Linguistic structures that are reread are underlined to explicitly show how much the reader chose to reread. Regressions are marked by drawing a line from right to left to the point at which the reader went back to repeat. A circle inscribed with an (R) designates simple repetitions. Multiple repetitions, words or phrases that are repeated more than once, are underlined each time they occur.

Why don't you do my work some day?

All at once I was covered with red paint.

Regressing and Correcting the Miscue (Self-corrections)

Self-corrections are marked by drawing a line from right to left to the point at which the reader went back to repeat in order to correct the miscue. A circle inscribed with a (C) indicates a correction. (The (UC) is described on p.9.)

The markings in this example show that Gary predicted *horses* (which he repeated twice), followed by a correction to *houses*, followed by the substitution *of* for *and*, followed by the correction to *houses and roads*. His multiple attempts are written and numbered in the order of occurrence above the sentence.

These he made into blocks for building houses and roads.

Substitutions Often Called Reversals

An editor's transposition symbol shows which words have been reversed.

I sat looking down at Andrew.

Was something wrong with Papa?

Appendix: Markings for Miscue Analysis.

Gilles, C., M. Bixby, P. Crowley, S. Crenshaw, M. Henrichs, F. Reynolds, and D. Pyle, eds. 1988. *Whole language strategies for secondary students*. Katonah, NY: Richard C. Owen.

Gollasch, F. 1980. "Readers' perception in detecting and processing embedded errors in meaningful context." Doctoral diss., University of Arizona–Tucson.

Goodman, K. 1970. "Behind the eye: What happens in reading." In *Reading Process and Program*, ed. K. Goodman, and O. Niles. Urbana, IL: National Council of Teachers of English, 3–38.

Goodman, K. 1982. "Revaluing readers and reading." *Topics in Learning and Learning Disabilities* 1: 87–93.

Regressing and Unsuccessfully Attempting to Correct

Unsuccessful attempts to correct are marked by drawing a line from right to left to the point at which the reader began to repeat in an attempt to correct. An inscribed *UC* is used to designate this type of regression.

In this example, Gary repeats *river washed* twice and this is marked as *UC*, an unsuccessful attempt at correction.

And this he did with such might that soon the *washed* river rushed over its banks, ...

Partial Miscues

Partial miscues are marked by putting a dash after a partial word when a reader attempts but does not produce a complete word. Intonation is used to determine partials.

Often readers start to say a word and self-correct or attempt a correction before a word is completed. Here, Gary predicts *ability*. He only starts the word and immediately self-corrects to *able*. Partial attempts that are corrected are marked on the typescript, with a dash following the partial, but are not transferred to the coding sheet.

There is nothing greater than man and the work *in his abil-* he is best able to do.

Dialect and Other Language Variations

Miscues that involve a sound, vocabulary item, or grammatical variation that is perceived as a dialect difference between the author and reader are marked by a balloon with an inscribed *d*.

headlights d I switched off the headlamps of the car. . . . *like d* . . . just about everybody likes babies.

Nonword Substitutions

A dollar sign ($) indicates that a reader has produced a miscue that is not recognizable as a word in the reader's language. Retain as much of the original spelling of the text word as possible.

$shrickled Judy shrieked and jumped up in her chair.

Intonation Shift

An accent mark indicates intonation shifts within a word. Intonation shifts are marked only if there is a change in meaning or grammatical structure of the original text.

He will récord her voice.

We want the project to succeed.

Pauses

A *P* marks noticeable pauses in reading. It is useful to mark the length of unusually long pauses.

12 sec. *when   always.* "What do you do all day while I am away

cutting wood?"

Repeated Miscues

Repeated miscues are marked with an encircled *RM* to indicate the same miscue for the same text item.

can off came our boots *can RM* off came our socks

Appendix: Markings for Miscue Analysis *(continued)*.

Goodman, K. S. 1986. *What's whole in whole language?* Portsmouth, NH: Heinemann.

———. 1994. "Reading, writing and written texts: A transactional, sociopsycholinguistic view." In *Theoretical models and processes of reading,* ed. R. B. Ruddell, M. R. Ruddell, and H. Singer. Newark, DE: International Reading Association, 1093–1130.

Goodman, K., L. Bird, and Y. Goodman, eds. 1991. *The whole language catalogue.* Santa Rosa, CA: American School Publishers.

———. 1992. *The whole language catalogue: Supplement on authentic assessment.* Santa Rosa, CA: American School Publishers.

Goodman, K., and C. Burke. 1973. "Theoretically based studies of patterns of miscues in oral reading performance." (Final Report, Project No. 9-035, OEG. 0-9-3230754269). Washington, D.C.: U.S. Department of Health, Education, and Welfare.

Goodman, K., & S. Gespass. 1983. "Text features as they relate to miscues: Pronouns." (Occasional Paper No. 7). Tucson: University of Arizona, Program in Language and Literacy.

Goodman, Y. 1985. "Kidwatching: Observing children in the classroom." In *Observing the language learner,* ed. A. Jaggar, & M. T. Smith-Burke. Newark, NJ: International Reading Association; Urbana, IL: National Council of Teachers of English, 9–18.

Goodman, Y., B. Altwerger, and A. Marek. 1989. "Print awareness in preschool children." (Occasional Paper No. 4). Tucson: University of Arizona, Program in Language Literacy.

Goodman, Y., and C. Burke. 1972. *Reading miscue inventory: Readings for taping.* New York: MacMillan.

———. 1980. *Reading strategies: Focus on comprehension.* New York: Richard C. Owen.

Goodman, Y., and A. Marek. *Retrospective miscue analysis: Readers revaluing themselves and reading.* Katonah, NY: Richard C. Owen, in press.

Goodman, Y., D. Watson, and C. Burke. 1987. *Reading miscue inventory: Alternative procedures.* Katonah, NY: Richard C. Owen.

———. 1996. *Reading strategies: Focus on comprehension.* Katonah, NY: Richard C. Owen.

Krauss, R. 1945. *The carrot seed.* New York: Scholastic.

Martin, B., Jr. 1983. *Brown bear, brown bear.* New York: Henry, Holt.

Meek, M. 1988. *How texts teach. What readers learn.* Stoud, Great Britain, Thimble Press.

Mooney, M. 1994. *Developing life-long readers.* Katonah, NY: Richard C. Owen.

Petrie, C. 1982. *Joshua James likes trucks.* Danbury, CT: Children's Press.

Pfeffer, S. 1987. "Kid power." In *Connections, grade 5.* New York: MacMillan.

Potter, R., and C. Hannemann. 1985. *Just dues: Experiences in reading comprehension, gr. 2–4.* Mountain View, CA: Creative Publications.

Steig, W. 1982. *Dr. De Soto.* New York: Farrar, Straus, and Giroux.

"The Stonecutter." 1961. In *Roads to everywhere.* New York: Russell, Gates, McCullough, Ginn, & Co.

Swim, R. C. 1964. *Paulossie, an Eskimo boy.* New York: Holt, Rinehart, and Winston.

Tapp, K. 1987. "The code in the mailbox." In *Connections, grade 3,* vol. 1. New York: MacMillan.

Tolstoy, A. 1987. "El nabo grande." In *Fiestas,* ed. R. B. Barrera, and A. N. Crawford. Boston, MA: Houghton Mifflin, 49–57.

Vygotsky, L. 1978. *Mind in society.* Cambridge, MA: Harvard University Press.

Weaver, C. 1994. *Reading process and practice: From socio-psycholinguistics to whole language.* Portsmouth, NH: Heinemann.

17 Revaluing Readers while Readers Revalue Themselves: Retrospective Miscue Analysis

Yetta M. Goodman
University of Arizona

In this chapter Goodman discusses a reading instructional strategy called Retrospective Miscue Analysis, which draws upon miscue analysis and reflects her observation that "readers' beliefs about themselves as readers often influence their literacy development." She recounts an incident in which she and her then-seven-year-old daughter Wendy discussed a miscue Wendy had made—an incident from which Goodman learned that she could discuss reading and the reading process with young children. She explains that both miscue analysis itself and the instructional procedure Retrospective Miscue Analysis stem from the conviction "that everything readers do is caused by their knowledge—their knowledge of the world, their knowledge of language, and what they believe about reading and the reading process." RMA basically involves revisiting a reader's miscues. Typically the reader is tape-recorded for later playback. In planned retrospective miscue analysis, the teacher pre-selects the miscues to discuss; the initial sessions (even with graduate students) are focused on helping readers realize that they are using strategies for constructing meaning. Once this is accomplished, the teacher may select miscues that show disruption in meaning construction. The teacher helps the reader explore the reasons for the miscues and how his or her knowledge of language and reading strategies can help resolve problems encountered in reading a text. Alternatively, students may select their own miscues for discussion. This is especially valuable when students are grouped to support each other in understanding and developing their reading strategies: readers take turns letting others listen to their audiotaped reading and retelling, and then the group discusses what they have heard. In group RMA, any listener can stop the tape recorder for discussion whenever he or she hears something unexpected. Goodman's last major section focuses on four opportunities for "critical moment" teaching: when teachers themselves make miscues; during reading conferences; during reading instructional episodes; and over the back of a chair. The procedures, insights, and instructional benefits are illustrated with rich examples.

Originally published in *The Reading Teacher, 49*(8), (1996), 600–09. Copyright 1996 by the International Reading Association. Reprinted with permission.

For the last 10 years I have been researching a reading instructional strategy called Retrospective Miscue Analysis (RMA). As I have been writing articles and monographs about RMA (Y. Goodman & Marek, 1989, 1996), I have begun to realize how my interest in exploring RMA is built on and grew out of my earlier work in miscue analysis and kid-watching. My involvement in miscue analysis resulted from my interest in understanding how young people learn to read. As part of miscue analysis, I realized that readers' beliefs about themselves as readers often influence their literacy development. As I realized the importance of such observations of students' reading, I coined the term *kid-watching* (Y. Goodman, 1978, 1985).

Although the concept of informed observations of students' learning experiences is not new, I wanted to legitimatize the importance of knowledgeable teachers' ongoing evaluations of their students' learning experiences. Learning from careful observation is basic to all scientific endeavors; learning from our students as we watch them learn is important not only for the planning of curriculum and instruction but also for constantly expanding our knowledge about teaching and learning. Kidwatching is equally necessary for researchers and teacher educators.

One experience during a longitudinal miscue study of my daughter Wendy's reading when she was 7 years old exemplifies the experiences that eventually led me to retrospective miscue analysis. (Wendy is now an experienced teacher in the Tucson Unified School District.) She was reading a realistic fiction account of a group of children visiting a *live animal museum* called *Let's Go to the Museum*. Wendy read *maximum* for *museum* each of the six times it occurred throughout the text, intoning it as a noun. In her retelling, after the reading, she kept telling me about the live animal maximum that the children had visited as she thoroughly discussed the events and characters in the story. I asked her what she thought a live animal maximum was. She responded quite confidently that she thought the word might be *museum* and "animals live in museums except, most of the times, when they live in museums, they're dead and stuffed." So she decided the word couldn't be *museum* and tried *maximum* instead. It was obvious that she knew that the word wasn't *maximum* so we talked about how sometimes words are used in unusual ways and that readers have to decide, like she did, whether to use the word they think it is even if it doesn't make sense or to try something else. I remember thinking how confusing it was that the author would write about a live animal museum; I didn't have a schema for it either. Ironically, both Wendy and I have spent almost 20 years in a city with the famous Arizona Sonoran Desert Museum that includes live animals in its displays.

When I revisit my early experiences with miscue analysis research, I realize that Wendy and I both learned more about the reading process during our discussion than we had known previously. We became aware of the importance of the reader's background and experience. We realized that readers make decisions and problem solve as they read. I learned that I could discuss reading and the reading process with a young child. And I gained additional support for the results from miscue analysis research (Allen & Watson, 1977) about the importance of substitutions, even unusual ones, because substitutions act as syntactic or grammatical placeholders that provide support for readers to continue to make sense as they read.

In all kidwatching, including miscue analysis, the observer's beliefs influence what he or she understands from the observation. As Piaget is often quoted as saying, we see what we know, we do not just know what we see. Our perceptions are influenced by our conceptions: our beliefs and our knowledge about the world. So kidwatching is more than merely looking, and miscue analysis and RMA are more than listening to kids read. Both involve seeing based on knowledge and understanding about development and language. Therefore, if teachers and researchers are to fully examine students' miscues and their unique retellings, they need to be aware of the understandings about the reading process that emanate from miscue analysis research and theory (Y. Goodman, Watson, & Burke, 1987). At the same time, examining miscues and asking "what knowledge do these readers have about language and the reading process that causes them to make these miscues" provide information about readers and the reading process that informs the planning of reading instruction and the development of curriculum (Y. Goodman & Burke, 1980; K. Goodman, Bird, & Y. Goodman, 1990, 1992).

Retrospective Miscue Analysis

From the beginnings of my wondering about how kids such as Wendy read, I have observed readers with the belief that everything readers do is caused by their knowledge—their knowledge of the world, their knowledge of language, and what they believe about reading and the reading process.

Miscue analysis, first developed by Kenneth Goodman (1969) helped me construct my views about reading. I have spent years researching miscue analysis with teachers and learning from them how their knowledge about miscue analysis influences their developing understandings about the reading process and their teaching of reading. Teachers often say that once they have participated in doing a complete miscue analysis of one of their own students, they never listen to a kid read in the same way. They become aware that miscues reveal the strategies kids use when they read and the knowledge kids have about language. Miscues show the degree to which readers use the graphophonic (including phonics), syntactic, and semantic/pragmatic language systems. Teachers come to realize that most readers self-correct only those miscues that are disruptive to reading and do not usually self-correct predictions that make sense as the reader is constructing a meaningful text. Miscue analysis provides teachers with a lens through which to observe the reading process. Over time they learn to discover patterns of miscues that reveal readers' linguistic and cognitive strengths as well as those that need support from the teacher. Because of teachers' interest in miscue analysis and discussing their insights with their students, I have become interested in involving students themselves in the miscue analysis process. I call readers' reflection on their own reading process retrospective miscue analysis (RMA).

Over the last decade, with teachers and graduate students, I have been researching strategies that involve readers in evaluating their own reading process (Y. Goodman & Marek, 1996). Research into the use of RMA procedures develops understandings about how readers make shifts in their views about the reading process and in themselves as readers as a result of examining the power of their own miscues. Revaluing themselves as readers often leads to greater reading proficiency. We have learned about these processes by engaging in conversations with readers as they examine their miscues and talk about the reading strategies and the language they use.

Many readers, even in graduate classes, have built negative views about themselves as readers. Such readers believe that it is cheating to skip words, that slow reading is evidence of poor reading, and that good readers (something they can never call themselves) know every word and remember everything that they read. Through RMA, readers "demythify" the reading process as they discover that reading isn't a mysterious process about which they "haven't a clue." They come to value themselves as learners with knowledge. They begin to realize that they can question authors and not believe everything that is in print. They become critical of what they are reading and confident to make judgments about the way a published text is written and the quality of the work.

At the same time, they demystify the process as they discover that they already use reading strategies and language cues in ways that can help them become even more proficient as readers, especially as they acknowledge what they can do. They build a more realistic view of how readers read than they held before and become aware that reading is more than calling words accurately and reading fluency. They realize that a mythical perfection and recall of every item in a text is not the goal of reading. They come to understand that reading is a meaning-making, constructive process influenced by their own investment in and control over that process. They learn that all readers miscue and transform the published text as they read, constructing a text parallel to that of the author (K. Goodman, 1994). They are often amazed to discover that proficient readers also skip words, phrases, sentences, paragraphs, and sometimes even pages, not necessarily reading from the first page of a work to the last, and that it is not cheating to do so.

The RMA process helps readers become aware that they are better readers than they think they are. Ken Goodman (1996) has termed this process revaluing. Readers who revalue themselves become confident and willing to take risks.

At the same time that we conduct research on RMA, we are involved in the use of RMA as an instructional strategy since many of the researchers with whom we work are classroom teachers. In this article, I focus on ways to involve readers, especially readers who are considered to be or consider themselves to be troubled readers, to participate in retrospective miscue analysis in classroom settings.

Planned Retrospective Miscue Analysis: An Instructional Tool

I used and researched a number of different instructional settings for retrospective miscue analysis. In this article, I discuss two such settings. In the first, RMA is a planned experience during which students ask questions about their miscues by listening to their own audiotaped readings as they follow a typescript of what they have read. This is done in a face-to-face conference between teacher and student or in small groups usually with the teacher as one member of the group. The second setting is in the classroom when there are specific moments in a school day during a variety of curricular experiences during which

RMA is an incidental reading instructional strategy. During these critical teaching or learning moments either the students or the teacher decide to engage in talk about miscues and the reading process.

In order to organize for observational analysis of miscues, a traditional reading miscue inventory (RMI) (Y. Goodman et al., 1987) is collected. In this procedure, a reader reads a whole text orally without any help from others and retells the story or article after the reading. The RMI is tape-recorded. After the RMI has been collected, the teacher/researcher can take two different roads to planned retrospective miscue analysis. If a reader lacks confidence or has a teacher who believes the reader is not successful, the teacher/researcher may decide to preselect the miscues. For readers who generally are considered to be average or better readers, the teacher may involve the reader or readers in an examination of the whole reading from the beginning of the text during the RMA session. The decision about which procedure to follow depends on the teacher's purpose, taking into consideration the age and confidence level of the students. I discuss each of these possibilities separately.

Teacher selection of miscues. To preselect miscues, teachers first mark the miscues on a typescript of the material. They then analyze the quality of the miscues, searching for patterns that highlight each reader's abilities in using reading strategies and that reveal the reader's knowledge of the language cueing systems.

The teacher sets up a series of RMA sessions with the student after selecting five to seven miscues for a 40-minute session and planning the sequence of miscue presentation. The student reads a new selection for RMI purposes after each RMA session in order to demonstrate changes in reading strategies over time and to have new miscues for discussion purposes. At these sessions, it is helpful to have two tape recorders. One is used to listen to the recording of the original reading, and the second one is used to record the RMA session in order to keep track of the student's changes in attitudes and beliefs.

The teacher selects miscues initially to demonstrate that the reader is making very good or smart miscues. The initial sessions are planned to help readers realize that they are using strategies that support their meaning construction as they read. For example, teachers initially select high-quality substitution miscues that result in syntactically and semantically acceptable sentences and make little change in the meaning of the text. (The reader in the following examples is Armando, who will be introduced later.)

Text: All I have to do is move this stick up and down so the
             cream will turn into butter.

Reader: All I have to do is move this stick up and down. Soon the cream will turn into butter.

Or the teacher selects word or phrase omission miscues where the reader has retained the syntactic and semantic acceptability of the sentence.

Text: What do you do all day while I am away cutting wood. . .
Reader: What do you do all day while I'm cutting wood . . .

Or the teacher selects miscues that show good predictions followed by self-correction strategies only when necessary.

Text: The big pig ran around and around the room.
Reader: The big pig ran out. . . . (self-corrects to) around and around the room.

During subsequent RMA sessions, the teacher selects more complex miscue patterns that may show disruption to meaning construction. Examples include miscues that the reader unsuccessfully attempts to self-correct at first, but eventually reads as expected. The teacher and student examine each instance and discuss the cues the reader uses and what strategies eventually led to the expected response. During the discussions about the miscues, the teacher helps the reader to explore the reasons for the miscues and to see how knowledge of language and reading strategies can help resolve any problems encountered in the text.

The following questions help guide the discussion with the reader:

Does the miscue make sense? Or sound like language?
Did you correct? Should it have been corrected?
Does the word in the text look like the word substituted? Does it
    sound like it?
Why did you make the miscue?
Did it affect your understanding of the story/article?
Why do you think so? How do you know?

The following conversations between a teacher and Armando, a seventh-grade student whose miscues were used for the above examples, provide examples of these discussions.

Teacher: Did what you did make sense?
Armando: Yes.
Teacher: Should you have corrected it?
Armando: Yes.
Teacher: Why?
Armando: Because it didn't make sense with around and around.

Teacher: Why do you think you read *ran out* before you corrected
              it?
Armando: Because I thought he ran out of the house, like the wood-
              man scared him out of the house.

Of all the readers with whom we worked in a research study of seventh graders (Y. Goodman & Flurkey, 1996), Armando was most reluctant to talk about his strengths and abilities, yet at the same time he
was able to discuss issues of language and the reading process with his
teacher.

Text: Then he climbed down from the roof.
Armando: Then the . . . (self-corrects) Then he climbed down from
              the roof.
Teacher: Did your miscue make sense?
Armando: No.
Teacher: Why not?
Armando: Because it wouldn't say he or she climbed down.
Teacher: Why did you miscue?
Armando: I probably thought something else was going to happen.

The teacher's discussions with Armando provide evidence that many
readers believe in the efficacy of the text. Through RMA discussions
readers have the opportunity to demystify the power of the author and
to consider their own roles as active readers. After a number of RMA
sessions, Tomás, another seventh grader, begins to understand that he
has the right to construct meaning.

Text: I'm sure somebody left it here because it's boring.
Tomás: I'm sure somebody let it to be because it's so boring.
Tomás: It's so boring (commenting on what he heard).
Teacher: OK. Let's talk about that one.
Tomás: . . . It's so boring . . . there's more expression with so
              boring. 'Cause if you put, it's boring, you don't know
              what's boring really. . . . But if you say so, then he must
              be really bored, so it sounds better.
Teacher: Did that miscue change the meaning of the sentence?
Tomás: No, it made it better, I think.
Teacher: Now let's listen to something else that happened in the
              sentence (rewinds the tape and listens again).
Tomás: Left it to be . . . I guess I was reading, predicting the words
              [that] are going to come up. Left it to be (laughs). It's
              like . . . I think it makes sense. Left it to be . . . because to be
              means like let be . . . like some older talk, like let the snake be
              or like let the animal be.

Teacher:	Is that what you were thinking?
Tomás:	Yeah, like let it be. If it was there, don't touch it.
Teacher:	Someone let it be because it was so boring.
Tomás:	Yeah. . . . And I guess I have a lot of stuff in here in my brain and I guess sometimes some words get mixed up, . . . and then sometimes it sounds OK in a way.

Students select their own miscues for discussion. If students are involved in the total process, including selecting the miscues to be discussed, the teacher doesn't have much preparation prior to the RMA session. This procedure is especially supportive of students revaluing themselves when two or more readers participate (Costello, 1992, 1996; Worsnop, 1996). In this case, one student volunteers to let the others listen to his or her audiotaped reading and retelling. Students work on their own in groups of up to four for about 30 minutes. After the students become experienced with the procedures, the teacher is involved only during the last few minutes to answer questions or to raise issues that push students to consider aspects of their reading they may not have attended to. Sarah Costello (1992, 1996) calls this procedure Collaborative Retrospective Miscue Analysis (CRMA).

Any listener can stop the recorder when he or she hears something that is unexpected. Using the term *unexpected response* is in keeping with the notion that miscues are not mistakes but unexpected responses that occur for a variety of linguistic and cognitive reasons. When the tape recorder stops, students determine whether a miscue has occurred and then talk about the nature of the miscue. Students ask the reader questions similar to the ones asked in the previous procedures: Why did you make the miscue? Did you correct it? Should you have corrected it? Does the miscue make sense and sound like language? If it is a substitution miscue, does it look like the word or phrase for which it is substituted? Sometimes, these questions are on a form the students use. However, if the students participate in the procedure over a period of time, it is important to not allow the form to become formulaic and followed without thoughtful discussion.

If the teacher is not continuously part of the collaborative RMA group, he or she often presents strategy lessons to the whole class during which the students discuss the nature of the reading process (Y. Goodman & Burke, 1980). Through examples of miscue patterns, the teacher helps readers understand that not all miscues need to be corrected. The teacher helps the readers know that there are high quality miscues that retain the syntactic and semantic acceptability of the text that indicate sophisticated reading. Through analysis and discussion of miscue patterns, the teacher highlights how readers predict and confirm and points out how the miscues reveal the reader's knowledge about the language cueing systems and reading strategies. The teacher engages the class in additional strategy lessons (Y. Goodman, Watson, & Burke, 1996) about the reading process. For example, it is easy to show readers that they are predicting when a strategy lesson is planned by choosing a cohesive section of a text that is an important repeated noun or verb omitted throughout. By using such selected slotting strategy lessons, the teacher explores with students how they use their knowledge about the world and about language as they read.

The following is a transcript of a group of seventh graders as they focus on one miscue during a collaborative RMA session (Costello, 1992):

Text:	He stood in the hall gasping for breath.
Carolyn:	He stood in the hall gasping for his breath.
Carolyn:	Gasping for his breath instead of air.
Jose:	No, you said gasping for his breath.
Carolyn:	But it's air.
Kirb:	Where?
Jose:	You didn't say air.
Carolyn:	Oh.
Kirb:	Where is air? It's supposed to be breath.
Carolyn:	OK. Who wants to tell me the answers. This is my miscue.
Terry:	Does it make sense?
Jose:	It does make sense!
Kirb:	It doesn't make sense there. I mean do you gasp for breath?
Carolyn:	Gasping for HIS breath! Does the miscue make sense? Yes, it does. I just added his.
Kirb:	It means the same thing.
Carolyn:	No, I shouldn't have changed it.
Kirb:	It would have been a waste of time.
Carolyn:	What I said makes more sense. Why do I think I made this miscue? Because I was predicting.

Carolyn made an additional miscue in listening to herself read. She thinks the text reads "gasping for air" and that she said "gasping for his breath." The group discusses this and then focuses on the acceptability of the miscue in the context of the story.

Involving students in planned sessions during which they become expert at talking about miscues and the reading process works successfully with students in upper elementary grades, middle schools, and secondary schools and with adults who do not value themselves as readers. For all ages, however, it is helpful to recognize the power of discussing miscues and how students read incidentally throughout the school day during appropriate moments.

Retrospective Miscue Analysis and Critical Moment Teaching

The teachers with whom I work in using retrospective miscue analysis are masters at making the most out of the critical moments that emerge whenever students ask serious questions about their reading. Students begin to talk seriously about the process of reading when their responses are treated with respect during discussions. An Australian fifth grader in a classroom where exploring the reading process is a common daily practice discussed his reading with me, showing me how he uses different language cues in order to understand what he is reading. At one point, he said in a confident and serious manner, "If you don't know what it is—you have a go at it."

The RMA critical moment teaching often takes place in a matter of a few minutes as the teacher supports the reader's move toward new understandings. The learner experiences an intuitive leap (Bruner, 1977)—the insightful "aha" moment. Critical learning/teaching moments can happen whenever teachers or students read aloud in the class, whenever the students ask questions about what they are reading or why the author has chosen to write in a certain way as they are struggling with new concepts or challenging language.

I credit teachers, as my colleagues in research and curriculum planning, for having taught me much about involving students in self-reflection of their miscues. I want the role of these teachers/researchers explicit because they have continuously influenced my own professional development and theoretical understandings of the reading process (Y. Goodman & Marek, in press). The most important learnings in classrooms are often the result of a critical teaching moment recognized and supported by a knowledge-able and successful classroom teacher. Teacher educators and researchers in universities and colleges need to help teachers and administrators value the importance of these moments and to document their occurrences.

When teachers make miscues. Don Howard has taught primary grades for many years in southern Arizona and in the Chicago area. Don discovered early in his teaching that it wasn't necessary to pretend to make miscues in order to talk about them with his students. His students noticed most of the miscues he made spontaneously during his daily oral reading to them. As Don realized the teaching potential of the moments in which he made miscues, he began to exploit his miscues whenever they occurred. He talked with his students about how his miscues showed that he was a good reader and that they were his way of always trying to understand what he is reading.

Don believes that kids feel very comfortable when they see adults making mistakes. In an environment where the authority in the class makes mistakes, students can make mistakes as well. Students are willing to take risks because they become aware that mistake making is simply a natural part of learning. Don makes this last statement explicit during appropriate moments in the classroom and encourages his students through open-ended discussions to believe and talk this way themselves.

Don and his students explore the reasons learners make miscues. They decide together that some miscues are good ones and some are not depending on whether the miscues make sense. The good miscues are celebrated and accepted as helpful to the students' learning. The other miscues need to be fixed, especially if they are important to the reader's comprehension. The reader decides which need to be corrected and which are unimportant. In the latter case, the reader usually decides not to worry because the miscues don't disrupt the meaning construction of the story or article.

Many teachers produce tape recordings for listening centers to accompany books they want kids to read or that are the students' favorites. I know teachers who spend hours rereading to make the tapes completely accurate. I suggest to them that high-quality miscues be left on the tape and if a student notices, the teacher has another critical moment to explore the significance of a miscue and to reflect on its meaning.

Using critical moments during reading conferences. Don Howard also uses regularly scheduled reading conferences to help his students reflect on their effective reading strategies. Students bring a book that they are reading and start reading orally where they left off in their silent reading, or they choose from a carefully selected range of books, usually not accessible to the students, that Don sets aside for reading conferences. Don makes notes about their miscues and their reading strategies. When they finish their reading and complete a retelling, Don asks the students to discuss anything they noticed about their reading that they would like to talk about. By focusing on the reasons for their miscues and the range of strategies they use, the students come to appreciate the flexibility they have in selecting appropriate reading strategies. Don says that he and the kids talk about strategies and the role of making miscues daily.

Reading instructional episodes. Wendy Hood, a primary teacher in Tucson, Arizona, uses critical moment teaching when she leads a reading strategy group of second graders. She noticed one day, as the group was reading a story silently together, that none of the students knew the word mirror when they came to the sentence *He looked into the mirror* at the bottom of the page toward the end of *Nick's Glasses*. The story is a take-off on a folk tale of a wise man looking for his glasses and using logical elimination to find them—on his forehead. Nick is involved in a similar search in this story. Wendy noticed that when Eli came to the bottom of the page, he hesitated for a few seconds and then turned to the next page, which showed the main character's face centered within a frame. Eli looked back at the word on the previous page and said aloud, "That says mirror."

"How did you figure that out?" Wendy asked. Wendy queries kids' responses regardless of whether the responses are the expected ones or not. That way students don't conclude that she only questions them when their responses are wrong and they consider all of their answers thoughtfully.

Eli said, "I sounded it out. See . . . mmm-iiii-rrroooaaarrr." Wendy responded by saying, "You don't call that mirroar, do you? Take another minute and think about what you did."

Then Eli reported: "I knew he was going to find them. I wondered where he could be looking that started with an *m*. I then looked at the next page and saw him looking in the mirror and then looked back at the word and I knew it was *mirror*."

After the other kids discussed whether they agreed or disagreed with Eli's explanation and why, Wendy summarized the literacy lesson they all shared: "You did a lot of good things as you were reading. You knew that you wanted the story to make sense and knew he had to find his glasses. You knew that it would be in a place so you were looking for a place word; we call that a noun. You also used what you know about the sounds of the language because you looked at the first letter of the word. You used the illustration to help you and decided the word was *mirror*, and then you checked yourself by looking back at the word to see if all your thinking about it was right. You did a lot of hard work on that; you used a lot of good strategies and it worked for you."

When Wendy teaches kindergarten, she often discovers that a few children read conventionally but aren't aware of their own abilities. She helps such children think of themselves as readers by involving them in talking about their reading. In order to plan for such an experience, Wendy carefully selects the written text to suit the purpose of her interactions with the student. In order to work with Robin, for example, she selected a predictable book that had high correlation between text and illustration but that had an ending that shifted in a different way than the more common predictable books do.

Wendy chose "Eek, A Monster," a story from an out-of-print basal reader, in which boys and girls are chased by a monster. The language of the text builds on and repeats common phrases such as: *Boys. Boys run. Boys run up. Boys run down.* Towards the end there is a page where the pattern changes, eliminating the noun: *Jump up.* While reading, Robin demonstrates a number of things that he knows about reading. He knows how to handle a book in terms of directionality and moving continuously through the text page by page. He makes good use of the illustrations. But he also knows that the printed language that he reads as *Boys run* is different than what he says when he looks at the picture: "the boys are running." In other words, he knows that what he sees in the illustration and the written language do not match in any simplistic way.

Retrospective miscue analysis helps Robin discover his power over print. When Robin got to the page that says *Jump up*, he read: "Boys jump up." He looked closer at the print and read: "Boys." With his index finger, he touched the word *jump*, and again read: "boys"; he touched the word *up* and read: "jump." He picked up his finger, moved his head closer to the print, sat up triumphantly, and read: "jumped up."

Wendy used this critical moment to get this five-year-old to reflect on his reading. "Tell me about what you just did."

Robin replied, "It was supposed to say *Boys* but there weren't enough words and that word is jump (pointing again to *jump* in the text). It has the *j*."

And Wendy said, probing a bit, "How did you know that wasn't *boys*?"

And he said, "It's *jump* like on the other page," and he turned back to a previous point in the text where the word *jump* was first introduced.

Wendy said, "That's a good thing to do when you read. You thought about what it would be and when it didn't match what you saw, you thought about it again."

And Robin responded, "I could read" and proceeded to finish reading the story.

Over the back of a chair. When Alan Flurkey moved to teaching first grade, he was surprised that first graders could talk about the reading process. He had used RMA with uppergrade special education students and knew that they could engage in retrospective miscue analysis, but he didn't expect first graders to discuss reading with such sophistication. Alan often walked around the room when the students were reading independently, stopped at a child's desk, and asked him or her to keep reading but to read aloud so he could hear. One day, early in the school year, he stopped at Maureen's table, peering over her shoulder. Maureen produced a miscue, regressed to the beginning of the sentence, self-corrected, and read on:

Text: As he turned the corner he saw the lion.

Maureen: As he turned the corner he was . . . (regresses to beginning of sentence and rereads) As he turned the corner he saw the lion.

Alan wanted to help Maureen see the importance of the predicting and confirming strategy she was using. He waited until she came to the end of the page where there was a shift in the plot, and the following conversation took place.

Alan: I noticed that near the top of the page you stopped, backed up and then continued to read, and I'm just wondering what you were thinking about. Why did you do that?

Maureen: (pointing) You mean up here?

Alan: Yes.

Maureen: Well, when I got to the middle of the sentence, it didn't make sense so l just started over.

Alan: What didn't make sense?

Maureen: Well, I thought it was going to say, like, ". . . he was scared . . .," was scared of what was there . . .

Alan: So then what did you do?

Maureen: It didn't say that so I just started over.

Alan summarized for Maureen that she was employing predicting, confirming, and self-correcting strategies; that she was clearly aware of how and when she was using these strategies; and that she was able to discuss her reading strategies with confidence.

Critical moment teaching provides powerful learning experiences for teachers and kids and needs to be legitimatized in planning for reading instruction. Critical teaching moments not only document what knowledge students use as they read but also reveal the knowledge and capabilities of teachers. These important moments show what teachers know about the reading process, about language, and about learning. They show what teachers know about their students reading and how to select materials to meet their students' needs.

Students who engage in retrospective miscue analysis become articulate about the reading process and their abilities as readers. In order to use language with confidence, students need to feel comfortable to make mistakes, to ask "silly" questions, to experiment in ways that are not always considered conventional. Readers who are confident, who develop a curiosity about how reading works, and who are willing to take risks in employing "keep going" strategies are most likely to become avid readers. They are willing to risk struggling with a text at times because they are confident that eventually their meaning construction will be successful. In addition, I have discovered that RMA provides an environment in which students become capable of talking and thinking about the reading process. When they are in environments where what they have to say about their reading and the reading of others is taken seriously, the language that is necessary to discuss the issues emerges. Through kidwatching using miscue analysis and RMA such insights into readers' abilities are readily available to every teacher/researcher.

Retrospective miscue analysis is not necessarily an easy strategy to put into practice because the procedure often means shifts in both teachers' and students' views about readers and the reading process. It means revaluing and learning to trust the learning process and to respect the learner. But I know of no experience that provides teachers/researchers with greater insights into the reader and the reading process. There is much left to learn about how readers of a range of ages talk and think about the reading process. I know that planned RMA sessions work well with middle school and older readers. I believe that, for the most part, younger readers are best served through more spontaneous conversations as reflected in critical moment teaching. All readers, including teachers, benefit from critical moment teaching, which most often turns into critical moment learning. There is no doubt in my mind that the teacher is the essential element in organizing classrooms that invite readers to think seriously and talk openly about reading and the reading process.

In closing I must make it clear that retrospective miscue analysis is a small part of a reading program. The procedures that I have described take place no longer than forty minutes a few times a week for middle school children and older and much less than that for younger children. The heart of a reading program is using reading as a tool to enrich literacy experiences. As students read and write to get in touch with their world, to discover worlds beyond theirs, to solve important problems, and to inquire into significant questions, RMA and related reading strategy instruction used selectively by knowledgeable teachers can support the development of lifelong readers.

Author Notes

The concepts of *demythify* and *demystify* are from Barbara Flores in personal conversation and presentations at conferences.

I use teacher/researcher to recognize the growing involvement of teachers in classroom research as well as to denote that either teachers or researchers may be engaged in RMA.

References

Allen, P., and D. Watson, eds. 1977. *Findings of research in miscue analysis: Classroom implications*. Urbana, IL: ERIC and National Council of Teachers of English.

Bruner, J. 1977. *The process of education*. Cambridge, MA: Cambridge University Press.

Costello, S. 1992. "Collaborative retrospective miscue analysis with middle grade students." Doctoral Diss., University of Arizona–Tucson.

Costello, S. 1996. "The emergence of an RMA teacher/researcher in retrospective miscue analysis." In *Retrospective miscue analysis: Revaluing readers and reading*, ed. Y. Goodman and A. Marek. Katonah, NY: Richard C. Owen, in press.

Goodman, K. 1969. "Analysis of oral reading miscues: Applied psycholinguistics." *International Reading Association* v: 9–29.

———. 1994. "Reading, writing and written texts: A transactional sociopsycholinguistic view." In *Theoretical models and processes of reading*, 4th ed., ed. R. Ruddell, M. Ruddell, and H. Singer. Newark, DE: Intentional Reading Association, 1093–1130.

———. "Revaluing." 1996. In *Retrospective miscue analysis: Revaluing readers and reading*, ed. Y. Goodman, and A. Marek. Katonah, NY: Richard C. Owen.

Goodman, K., L. Bird, and Y. Goodman. 1990. *The whole language catalog*. Santa Rosa, CA: American School Publishers.

———. 1992. *The assessment supplement to the whole language catalog*. Santa Rosa, CA: American School Publishers.

Goodman, Y. 1978. "Kidwatching: An alternative to testing." *National Elementary Principal* 57(4): 41–45

———. 1985. "Kidwatching: Observing children in the classroom." In *Observing the language learner*, ed. A. Jagger and M. Trika Smith-Burke. Newark, DE: International Reading Association, 9–18

Goodman, Y., and C. Burke. 1980. *Reading strategies: Focus on comprehension*. Katonah, NY: Richard C. Owen.

Goodman, Y., and A. Flurkey. 1996. "Adapting retrospective miscue analysis for middle school readers." In *Retrospective miscue analysis: Revaluing readers and reading*, ed. Y. Goodman and A. Marek. Katonah, NY: Richard C. Owen.

Goodman, Y., and A. Marek. 1989. "Retrospective miscue analysis: Two papers." (Occasional Paper #19). Tucson, AZ: University of Arizona, Program in Languages and Literacy.

Goodman, Y., & A. Marek, eds. 1996. *Retrospective miscue analysis: Revaluing readers and reading.* Katonah, NY: Richard C. Owen.

Goodman, Y., D. Watson, and C. Burke. 1987. *Reading miscue inventory: Alternative procedures.* Katonah, NY: Richard C. Owen.

―――. 1996. *Reading strategies: Focus on comprehension,* 2nd ed. Katonah, NY: Richard C. Owen.

Worsnop, C. 1996. "Using miscue analysis as a teaching tool: The beginnings to Retrospective Miscue Analysis." In *Retrospective miscue analysis: Revaluing readers and reading,* ed. Y. Goodman and A. Marek. Katonah, NY: Richard C. Owen.

18 I Do Teach and the Kids Do Learn

Wendy J. Hood
Warren Elementary School, Tucson, Arizona

In her work in kindergarten through grade three, Hood first gets to know her students as readers. She looks for evidence that they construct their own meaning from print and for evidence of their confidence as readers. She looks at the strategies these young readers use, drawing upon miscue analysis, print awareness tasks, and bookhandling analysis as assessment instruments. From this documentation, she builds her instructional program. Hood explains and illustrates how she makes observational notes about children's reading and writing. With the older readers, she preselects three texts to use in miscue analysis: one as a starting point, one that is simpler, and one that is more challenging. She uses short texts so that she can complete the reading and retelling with more than thirty children in a week. Based upon this data, she plans, for her youngest readers, whole class activities that support all of her students' emergent abilities. She models reading strategies like prediction and confirmation, interweaves strategy development into reading and writing experiences, and uses special centers—what we might think of as play areas—that encourage reading and writing. Hood comments that every child benefits from participation in such centers, and she is the only one who knows that certain children are targeted by certain activities.

Hood also uses flexible Reading Strategy Groups, based upon the students' strengths. She explains and illustrates how she prepares for and conducts such strategy group sessions, which may last anywhere from ten minutes to an hour. The text is chosen to challenge but also support the readers, and the students support one another as they read and discuss the text and also their reading strategies, as needed. In concluding, Hood explains that the children come to expect print to carry meaning, and will settle for nothing less. "They begin to use the language of the reading process to talk about reading. I do teach and the kids do learn. The children constantly show me that it works."

Originally published in *Primary Voices*, 3(4), (1995), 16–22. Copyright 1995 by the National Council of Teachers of English.

I have worked with readers from kindergarten through grade three. I provide a classroom environment in which my students engage in a myriad of literacy experiences. I believe my role in the classroom is to mediate the literacy process, to maximize learning opportunities, and to help my students find themselves as readers. I do teach and the kids do learn. Let me tell you how it works.

First, I get to know my kids as readers: individuals who construct their own meaning from print. I look for evidence of confidence as a reader. I look at the strategies that my young readers use. I use miscue analysis, print awareness tasks, and bookhandling analysis (Goodman, Altwerger, & Marek, 1989). From this documentation, I build my instructional program. The time I take to evaluate informs all my instructional decisions.

Observing Beginning Readers

With the youngest readers, I first observe the kids interacting independently with books, noting the choices they make and looking for bookhandling knowledge. (See Observation Notes on Jorge and Kelly.) I follow the observations with a one-on-one interview. I begin the interviews by asking children to write their names and anything else they can write. If I've seen evidence of invented spelling in their journal writing, I will ask those children to write a sentence like "I like school." Then I do a miscue analysis. I have a book and a copy of the text for marking miscues. The book is short and simple. Some years I've used *A Carrot Seed* (Krauss, 1945). This year I selected *Joshua James Likes Trucks* (Petrie, 1982).

Observation Notes: Jorge

Jorge immediately found *Brown Bear, Brown Bear* (Martin, 1983), opened to the first page, and began to chant the text. In our conference, Jorge had written his first name. He read willingly. He took the book, turned it right side up, flipped pages until he came to the first page of the story and, running his finger left to right under the text, constructed a story that went with the pictures. The number of words on the printed page had little relation to the number in his story. [Jorge's reading of *Joshua James Likes Trucks* for miscue analysis follows.]

Text:	Jorge:
Joshua James likes trucks.	*The boy was playing with his remote control truck.*

BIG TRUCKS . . .   *He took it outside and talked to the man.*

little trucks . . .   *He played inside.*

l-o-n-g- trucks . . .   *He said, "Mom, look at that truck." He was happy.*

short trucks.   *He made the truck stop at the stop man.*

Joshua James   *He saw a fire truck.*

just likes trucks!

Red trucks . . .   *And the garbage man. He had a truck to ride in.*

green trucks . . .   *He was friendly.*

yellow trucks . . .   *He waved out the window. His mom said to get back inside.*

blue trucks.   *The men had a dump truck.*

Joshua James

just likes trucks.

Trucks that go up . . .   *He looked out the window.*

trucks that go down . . .

and trucks that   *He saw a cement truck.*

go round and round.

Joshua James   *He went to bed and dreamed about trucks.*

just likes trucks.

About the author   *The End.*

Observation Notes: Kelly

Kelly browsed the shelf for a bit, opening first one book, then another. She looked at the title page and the first page of each book before returning it. Finally she selected *Freight Train* by Donald Crews (1978). Then she moved to a private spot, sat, opened the book to the first page, and silently ran her finger under the text on each page, taking more time on some pages than on others.

In my conference with Kelly, she said, "I can read this." And she did. I marked her miscues on the typescript as she read from *Joshua James Likes Trucks* (see Figure 1). Kelly's early writing had not led me to view her as a strong reader. Her invented spelling was not easy for me to read; she often used *L* and *H* to represent vowels. Interestingly, as the school year progressed, I noticed that while most of my students used graphophonics as a primary spelling strategy, Kelly's invented spelling was visually close to conventional. It became very clear that Kelly's early reading was a primary influence on her early writing.

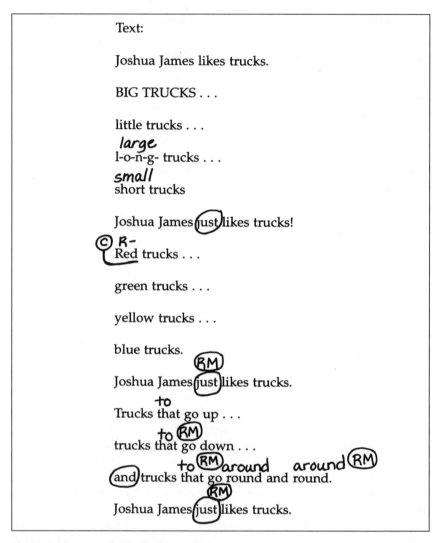

Figure 1. Miscue analysis—Kelly.

Using Miscue Analysis with Older Readers

With older readers I preselect a trio of texts to use for miscue analysis. I use one as a starting point; another is simpler, more predictable. The third is more challenging than the first piece. For most purposes, longer texts yield more complete information. However, with thirty-two kids in one class, I make some compromises in text length. I choose a short, complete text so I can read with all the kids within one week. I make several typescripts ahead of time so I'm always ready to mark miscues. Following each reading, I look for understanding by asking the children to tell me about the story. After school, I examine the patterns of miscues and strategies used by each child (see Figures 2 and 3).

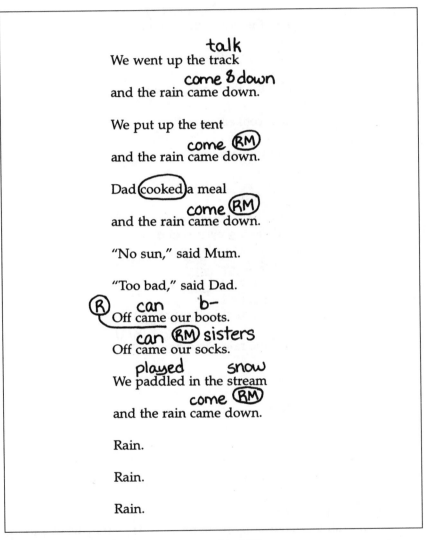

Figure 2. Miscue analysis—"Rain, Rain" read by Nicky.

Nicky's Retelling:

They went camping and it rained. Rain, Rain. It was raining. They had a tent. They played in the rain.

Figure 3. Miscue analysis—"Rain, Rain" read by Geraldo.

Geraldo's Retelling:

They were stupid to go camping in the rain. Then they went into the puddle. That's stupid, too. It could get flooded.

When I look at strengths and strategies, it becomes clear that while my students use the same reading process, they emphasize different strategies to varying degrees.

Nicky's miscues indicate that while she can focus on meaning, she shows an overdependence on the use of the graphophonic system when dealing with unknown words. One strength for her is what my students call the "going-on" strategy. She does not allow herself to get bogged down in miscues or misunderstandings; she keeps on reading. In this sample, Nicky has not self-corrected at all. Her retelling indicates some understanding.

Geraldo has already become a critical reader. He reports that the story and the characters are stupid. He shows no evidence of self-correction; when he makes significant miscues in this story, which he has decided is stupid, he no longer cares about the meaning. After the retelling, I give him another text to read. Within that text, meaning construction is evident, as is self-correction when meaning was lost.

Instructional Implications

Gathering information about bookhandling knowledge or the miscues of emergent readers is only a beginning. Initial evaluation leads to further evaluation, and in all cases, I use the information I gather to design my instruction.

For my youngest readers, I plan whole class activities that support all my students' emergent abilities. Using quality big books as well as small picture books, I model reading strategies such as prediction and confirmation. I keep strategy discussions brief, minimizing the interruptions of the story. We sing from song charts, using a pointer to follow the print as we sing. Initially I lead the chart reading but soon Geraldo and others take turns leading. I make certain that children are treated to lap reading with me, older students, and adult volunteers. For students who have begun to read independently, an eager audience supports their developing strengths.

I interweave reading and writing strategy development. Reading and writing materials are provided in all play areas. At times, special centers are developed that encourage reading and writing—perhaps a classroom store complete with newspaper ads, empty food cartons, coupons, and play money; or a classroom post office that has stationary, envelopes, a list of classmates' names and photos, mailboxes, and stamp-designing equipment. We've had restaurants, pagodas, pet shops, airplanes, airports, and so on. The centers are often related to ongoing inquiry themes. Every child benefits from participation in these centers. I am the only one who knows that certain kids are targeted by certain activities. As the children grow, the reading process is no different. What is different is the sophistication and effectiveness of the strategies they use.

Reading Strategy Groups

When I evaluate the reading strategies of all my students through miscue analysis, I summarize each students' strengths and then group the students with similar strengths together. (Homogeneous groups in my classroom are rare. Most groups are heterogeneous—research groups, literature study groups, math problem-solving groups.) During language arts, I hold reading conferences with the students and work with Reading Strategy Groups. The children in these groups only come together a few times a week. They grow at different rates, enabling me to reevaluate and rearrange the groups on a regular basis. I make it a point to regroup the children at least every six weeks.

A typical Reading Strategy Group session lasts from ten minutes to an hour. I preselect at least one text to read with the kids. I base my selection on what I know of the children and how I believe the text will support them as readers. I choose texts to read with them that will challenge them slightly, but which they can handle within the social context of a group setting (Mooney, 1994). I try to have one copy for each member of the group, including me.

At one point, Nicky's group was focused on meaning making. Sometimes, though, students made substitutions that had little relationship to the meaning of the text. As I took a closer look at their substitutions, I realized that they were strongly keyed in to the initial and final consonants and that they often substituted similar words or nonwords. I selected the book *My Bike* (Cowley, 1989). It is a cumulative story, like *The House that Jack Built*. It begins, "On Monday, I rode my bike around the tree. On Tuesday, I rode my bike around the tree and under the branch." The text continues building, each day illustrated by a clear photograph until the final day, "On Sunday, I crashed!"

The kids read the title from their own copies. I asked who had bikes, where they liked to ride, and if any kids ever had problems with their bikes. This discussion got the kids thinking. It built background as they got ready to read. We turned to the first page and each child read independently. At this age, children usually read out loud so it is easy for a teacher to eavesdrop on their "silent" reading! We have established a pattern where we wait until everyone is ready before discussion or going on to the next page. I provide support, not answers, as the kids take the lead:

Nicky:	One Monday, I ride my bike. [She turns to Kim next to her] What's that word? [pointing to *around*]
Kim:	I don't know. Arrild?
Mario:	After
Nicky:	One Monday, I ride my bike after the tree.
Teacher	Does that make sense?
Mario:	Sort of.
Teacher	Let's read the next page and see if we get more information. [The children turn the page and read. They are stumped again by *around* when it appears again.]
Kim:	After doesn't make sense. I rode my bike under the branch and after the tree.
Teacher:	Let's take a closer look. Turn back to the first page. Let's look at the picture. Where else could the kid ride, under . . .
Nicky:	Above [the kids laugh]
Mario:	Along
Kim:	Over
Teacher:	When I am reading, and I get stuck, I have to decide, is this word important to the story? Do you want to keep reading and come back to it later?
Trio:	NO!
Teacher:	OK. I can see that you're all looking at the beginning of the word. What else can you see there that might help you?
Mario:	The end?
Teacher:	How?
Mario:	/nd/
Teacher:	How will that help?
Mario:	Arrnd [giggles abound in the little group]
Teacher:	Don't laugh, it sounds weird but he's trying to figure it out.
Nicky:	Around!
Teacher:	What makes you think that?
Nicky:	Around starts like that and ends like that.
Kim:	And it makes sense, around the tree.
	[Abruptly the kids turn to the second page and proceed reading with no teacher direction but I'm there observing, taking notes, and ready to support as necessary.]

With more proficient readers in Reading Strategy Groups, we do what I call "parallel reading." Once again, I preselect a text based upon student strengths, strategies, and interests. I usually introduce the text, and then we each read the first page to ourselves, checking individual understandings. Following a brief discussion of page one, we all proceed to read at our own pace. If any group member has problems, I encourage that child to ask a groupmate. Because the groups are homogeneous, it frequently happens that all the kids get stuck at the same point. Then we'll have a strategy discussion similar to the ones in the other groups. The role I take at this time is minimal. Here is a sample from *Paulossie, an Eskimo Boy*.

Text:	Through the binoculars Paulossie watched two walruses sleeping on the ice. Suddenly he saw a great polar bear swimming toward the two sleeping walruses. The polar bear swam closer to the ice. He climbed onto the ice and with his mouth grabbed the nearest walrus by the nose and mouth, so that the walrus could not use its sharp tusks. The walrus cried out,
Estevan:	"The walrus cried out." Walrus don't talk. I thought this was a real story.
Jenny:	Read it again.
Estevan:	"The walrus cried out"
Jenny:	Let me see. [She takes his book, looks closely at the words for a moment and reads from his. Estevan picks up her book.]
Jenny:	"The walrus cried out" [She turns back to the previous page and reads orally. Then trades books back with him!]
Text:	But he was caught. The other walrus woke up, and slipped quickly into the water. There was nothing he could do to help his friend. It was too late. The polar bear was going to have his dinner.
Estevan:	The walrus gets eaten. It still seems like a true story.
Jenny:	Yeah. Maybe walrus make a noise like crying when they're caught.
Estevan:	Maybe. Or maybe he (the author) meant it made a warning noise like some animals do.

[They return to their reading.]

As time progresses, the interactions we have in instructional settings become evident on a daily basis. The kids expect print to carry meaning and to make sense; they accept nothing less. They begin to use the language of the reading process to talk about reading. I do teach and the kids do learn. The children constantly show me that it works.

References

Brown, J., A. Marek, and K. Goodman. 1994. "Annotated bibliography of miscue analysis." (Occasional Paper No. 16). Tucson: University of Arizona, Program in Language and Literacy.

Buck, P. S. 1986. *The big wave.* New York: HarperCollins.

Cambourne, B., and P. Rousch. 1979. *A psycholinguistic model of the reading process as it relates to proficient, average and low ability readers.* Wagga Wagga, NSW, Australia: Riverina College of Advanced Education, Sturt University.

Chapman, J. 1981. "The reader and the text." In *The reader and the text,* ed. J. Chapman. London: Heinemann, 1–15.

Cowley, J. 1983. "Rain, rain." In *Ready to read series.* Auckland, New Zealand: Ministry of Education.

Cowley, J. 1987. Los animales de Don Vicencio. II. I. Lowe. Trans. P. Almada, Auckland, New Zealand: Shortland.

Cowley, J. 1989. "My bike." In *Ready to read series.* Auckland, New Zealand: Learning Media (distributed by Richard C. Owen, Katonah, NY).

Crews, D. 1978. *Freight train.* New York: Scholastic.

Gilles, C., M. Bixby, P. Crowley, S. Crenshaw, M. Henrichs, F. Reynolds, and D. Pyle, eds. 1988. *Whole language strategies for secondary students.* Katonah, NY: Richard C. Owen.

Gollasch, F. 1980. "Readers' perception in detecting and processing embedded errors in meaningful context." Doctoral diss. University of Arizona–Tucson.

Goodman, K. 1970. "Behind the eye: What happens in reading." In *Reading: Process and program,* ed. K. Goodman, and O. Niles. Urbana, IL: National Council of Teachers of English, 3–38.

Goodman, K. 1982. "Revaluing readers and reading." *Topics in Learning and Learning Disabilities.* 1: 87–93.

Goodman, K. S. 1986. *What's whole in whole language?* Portsmouth, NH: Heinemann.

Goodman, K. S. 1994. "Reading, writing and written texts: A transactional, sociopsycholinguistic view." In *Theoretical models and processes of reading,* ed. R. B. Ruddell, M. R. Ruddell, and H. Singer. Newark, DE: International Reading Association, 1093–1130.

Goodman, K., L. Bird, and Y. Goodman, eds. 1991. *The whole language catalogue.* Santa Rosa, CA: American School Publishers.

———. 1992. *The whole language catalogue: Supplement on authentic assessment.* Santa Rosa, CA: American School Publishers.

Goodman, K., and C. Burke. 1973. "Theoretically based studies of patterns of miscues in oral reading performance." (Final Report, Project No. 9-035, OEG. 0-9-323075-4269). Washington, D.C.: U.S. Department of Health, Education, and Welfare.

Goodman, K., and S. Gespass. 1983. "Text features as they relate to miscues: Pronouns." (Occasional Paper No. 7). Tucson: University of Arizona, Program in Language and Literacy.

Goodman, Y. 1985. "Kidwatching: Observing children in the classroom." In *Observing the language learner*, ed. A. Jaggar, and M. T. Smith-Burke. Newark, NJ: International Reading Association; Urbana, IL: National Council of Teachers of English, 9–18.

Goodman, Y., B. Altwerger, and A. Marek. 1989. "Print awareness in preschool children." (Occasional Paper No. 4). Tucson: University of Arizona, Program in Language and Literacy.

Goodman, Y., and C. Burke. 1972. *Reading miscue inventory: Readings for taping.* New York: MacMillan.

———. 1980. *Reading strategies: Focus on comprehension.* New York: Richard C. Owen.

Goodman, Y., and A. Marek. 1996. *Retrospective miscue analysis: Readers revaluing themselves and reading.* Katonah, NY: Richard C. Owen, in press.

Goodman, Y., D. Watson, and C. Burke. 1987. *Reading miscue inventory: Alternative procedures.* Katonah, NY: Richard C. Owen.

———. *Reading strategies: Focus on comprehension.* Katonah, NY: Richard C. Owen, in press.

Krauss, R. 1945. *The carrot seed.* New York: Scholastic.

Martin, B., Jr. 1983. *Brown bear, brown bear.* New York: Henry, Holt.

Meek, M. 1988. *How texts teach. What readers learn.* Stoud, Great Britain: Thimble Press.

Mooney, M. 1994. *Developing life-long readers.* Katonah, NY: Richard C. Owen.

Petrie, C. 1982. *Joshua James likes trucks.* Danbury, CT: Children's Press.

Pfeffer, S. 1987. "Kid power." In *Connections, grade 5.* New York: MacMillan.

Potter, R., and C. Hannemann. 1985. *Just dues: Experiences in reading comprehension, gr. 2–4.* Mountain View, CA: Creative Publications.

Steig, W. 1982. *Dr. De Soto.* New York: Farrar, Straus, and Giroux.

"The Stonecutter." 1961. In *Roads to everywhere.* New York: Russell, Gates, McCullough, Ginn, & Co.

Swim, R. C. 1964. *Paulossie, an Eskimo boy.* New York: Holt, Rinehart, and Winston.

Tapp, K. 1987. "The code in the mailbox." In *Connections, grade 3,* vol. 1. New York: MacMillan.

Tolstoy, A. 1987. "El nabo grande." In *Fiestas,* ed. R. B. Barrera, and A. N. Crawford. Boston, MA: Houghton Mifflin, 49–57.

Vygotsky, L. 1978. *Mind in society.* Cambridge, MA: Harvard University Press.

Weaver, C. 1994. *Reading process and practice: From socio-psycholinguistics to whole language.* Portsmouth, NH: Heinemann.

19 Taking Another Look at (Listen to) Shari

Alan D. Flurkey
Hofstra University

This is a chapter about revaluing readers. Considering nine-year-old Shari's reading through the lens of miscue analysis led Flurkey to an understanding of the reading process itself and to a revaluation of Shari as a reader who uses effective reading strategies. Miscue analysis enabled him "to see that Shari wasn't doing something 'wrong' when she produced substitutions, omissions, regressions, and insertions"; indeed, these were high-quality miscues that reflected Shari's quest for meaning. (Her retelling confirmed that she had understood what she had read.) Having come to view reading differently through miscue analysis, Flurkey began to seriously doubt that there was something essentially "different" about children assigned to learning disabilities programs. He came to the conclusion that such readers weren't severely disabled because they made miscues. Rather, they were hampered as readers by their uncertainty: about how reading works, about the goal of reading, and about what a teacher or fellow students considered acceptable in a performance. Flurkey concludes with several provocative questions about the construct of "learning disabilities" and related issues—questions that invite teachers to look again at all of their readers, and to listen.

Originally published in *Primary Voices*, 3(4), (1995), 10–15. Copyright 1995 by the National Council of Teachers of English.

Nineteen ninety-five has been a year marked by historical milestone—fifty years since the end of World War II; twenty-five years since the beginning of human exploration of the moon. For teachers another milestone must be considered, though it will not be celebrated in the national media. Thirty years ago, miscue analysis was fueling a "Copernican revolution" (K. Goodman, 1994) for the field of reading—a way of thinking about the process of reading that was as different from the models of reading-as-word-identification that preceded it as Copernicus's sun-centered model of the solar system was different from Ptolemy's geocentric model. Just as Copernicus's discovery changed the

267

way astronomers constructed mental models of the universe, teachers who have learned miscue analysis say that it forever changes the way they think about readers and reading.

Detailed memories of the exact times and places where we experience important events have a way of staying with us; I remember what I was doing when Neil Armstrong stepped onto the moon's surface, for example. This is also true of my experiences of rethinking reading through miscue analysis.

Shari was typical of the students who find their way into Learning Disabilities resource "pull-out" programs. A nine-year-old, she had been receiving reading and writing instruction in the resource room since she was in first grade, three years before I met her. As a Learning Disabilities resource teacher, I was coming to know what struggling readers sounded like and Shari was "typical" of that group. I knew about the hesitations, the multiple errors, the labored, plodding pace, and the frustrated attempts to get a sentence or a paragraph "right." "Right," of course, meant reading the text exactly as written, without errors. As I tried to help Shari and other readers cope with their classroom assignments—social studies readings, spelling tests, and basal reader stories—I shared their frustration, not sure how to help them, not even sure what it was they were doing wrong or why reading was so difficult for them.

To help meet the needs of my students, I was provided with the latest materials that state-of-the-art learning disabilities teaching technology had to offer high interest/low vocabulary readers; story starter boxes; reading inventories; tests constructed by basal reader publishers; and a profusion of "programmed learning" kits composed of reading and spelling textbooks, workbooks, tests, and teacher manuals of seemingly every make and level. Dry and tedious, none of these worked as advertised. And while they provided measures of progress in an artificial, programmed curriculum, their use only seemed to intensify the frustration felt by my students and me. This kind of reading was neither fun nor interesting (two criteria that I personally applied) and every "learning experience" seemed to inadvertently communicate failure even though they were designed to ensure success.

Several months after I began to work with Shari, I attended a daylong miscue analysis workshop given by Yetta Goodman. Colleagues who had spoken excitedly about miscue analysis shared how "it changes the way you think about reading." Even though my colleagues were describing a perspective that seemed to contradict my training in special education methods courses, they were persistent enough and I was intrigued enough to give it a try.

The workshop portrayed reading as a process of meaning construction where making personal sense of the text was the goal, and everything a reader did served that goal. This seemed like a reasonable premise to me. With the exception of activities that require an oral performance, like delivering proclamations or newscasts, why else read if not to understand written text? That part made sense. But it also raised questions that flew in the face of conventional thinking about reading: If "everything a reader did" included making mistakes, as my readers did, how could that be of any help to a reader? Wasn't it the making of mistakes that made poor readers in the first place?

In its interpretation of reading as a language process, miscue analysis shows that "mistakes" aren't really mistakes; they are merely phenomena that occur in most any act of reading. Indeed, thirty years of miscue research has demonstrated that every reader, regardless of how effectively or efficiently they read, makes miscues. Of course, there are different levels of miscues: high-quality miscues preserve a reader's meaning construction, and low-quality miscues result in disruption of meaning (Goodman, Watson, & Burke, 1987). This seemed a much more reasonable explanation of what happens during reading. Reading-as-meaning construction, high- and low-quality miscues—that was what I took back to my classroom the morning after that first miscue workshop, and when I did, everything changed.

I clearly remember the odd, trapezoid-shaped room with no windows, the small chairs at low rectangular tables. I can see Shari's head slightly bent with her straight, shoulder-length brownish-blonde hair getting in her way as she read aloud. But most of all, I remember that Shari was making sense as she read. I was jolted by the difference in what I was able to "hear" from the previous time I listened to Shari read. The personal meaning that Shari was constructing was evident in her retelling as well as in the oral text she produced as she was reading; Shari's story retelling was complete, demonstrating that she understood the plot, characters, and events, and nearly all of her miscues reflected grammatical and semantic strengths.

Miscue analysis enabled me to see that Shari wasn't doing something "wrong" when she produced substitutions, omissions, regressions, and insertions; she was using her own language to do what was sensible for her. And she seemed very "able" in doing it. Shari and my other students helped me to see that reading was not about "getting words right"—the errorless reproduction of a printed text; reading was about making sense for oneself, regardless of how unpolished it might sound.

After Shari read aloud *Doctor De Soto* (Steig, 1982), she produced a story retelling that confirmed that she had understood what she read.

The excerpt of Shari's reading (see Figure 1) provides a clear demonstration of how readers construct meaning for themselves as they read, and how their concern for meaning construction is reflected in the quality of miscues that they produce.

For example, in the first sentence (lines 111 & 112), Shari produces a regression by repeating the words *and bravely entered* one time. She then omits the word *the* and continues to the end of the sentence. In analyzing the acceptability of the sentence as Shari finally left it, note that the regression does not result in meaning loss since the wording of the sentence is unchanged. The omission of *the* has the effect of changing the noun modifier *fox's* to a reference that functions as a proper name (Fox's mouth). The net result is the production of a sentence with no disruption of meaning. Further, it can be argued that the textual change of *the fox's mouth* to *Fox's mouth* represents a shift in wording that is consistent with language used in similar fantasies of this genre. As such, the omission can be thought of as a window into the "personalization" of Shari's construction of meaning, i.e., she transformed the published text to a personal text that contained language with which she was familiar.

Indeed, Shari's reading is filled with high-quality miscues. Consider the following substitutions: *answered* for *announced*, *whispered* for *whimpered*, *the* for *some*, *shiver* for *quiver*, and *said* for *yelled*. Some of these miscues bear a high degree of graphic similarity to the text while others bear little or no similarity, but none result in the production of a structure that disrupts meaning. In addition, Shari demonstrates that when she produces a structure that does not make sense, such as the clause on line 113 which reads "and unusually bad breath," she is able to regress to the beginning of the clause and self-correct to produce an acceptable structure.

Shari does produce some miscues that result in meaning loss, such as *biscuit* for *bicuspid* in line 112. But note that the miscue occurs in a structure that makes sense up to that point (The fox had a rotten biscuit . . .), and her inferencing results in a prediction that turns out to be unfulfilled in the published text that follows. Shari is also using graphic information as well: *biscuit* and *bicuspid* have a high degree of graphic similarity, or perhaps she is over-relying on graphic information given the partial acceptability of this miscue. Then again, *bicuspid*, a particular type of tooth, is a term that probably is not expected in stories of this genre (Steig's books make a notable exception), and the substitution of *biscuit* might represent the admirable use of a "place holder" strategy for dealing with an unknown.

The published text:

Doctor De Soto climbed up the ladder and bravely entered the fox's mouth. "Ooo-wow!" he gasped. The fox had a rotten bicuspid and unusually bad breath.

"This tooth will have to come out," Doctor De Soto announced. "But we can make you a new one."

[page break]

"Just stop the pain," whimpered the fox, wiping some tears away.

Despite his misery, he realized he had a tasty little morsel in his mouth and his jaw began to quiver. "Keep open!" yelled Doctor De Soto. "Wide open!" yelled his wife.

Marked typescript of Shari's reading*:

111   Doctor De Soto climbed up the ladder and bravely entered   ⓡ 5 sec.

112   (the) fox's mouth. "Ooo-wow!" he gasped. The fox had a rotten bicuspid

113   (and unusually bad breath.

114   "This tooth will have to come out" Doctor De Soto answered announced.

115   "But we can make you a new one."

ⓤⓒ 2. whispered
1. wh-
[page break]

121   "Just stop the pain," whimpered the fox, wiping some tears away.

122   Despite his misery, he realized he had a tasty little morsel in his   mouse

123   mouth and his jaw began to quiver. "Keep open!" yelled Doctor De   note storytelling intonation

124   Soto. "Wide open!" yelled his wife.   said

*In these line designations, the first two digits refer to page numbers, while the third digit refers to line numbers on that page.

The oral text that Shari produced:

Doctor De Soto climbed up the ladder and bravely entered—and bravely entered Fox's mouth "Ooo-wow!" he gasped. The fox had a rotten (5 sec pause) biscuit and usually bad breath—and unusually bad breath.

"This tooth will have to come out," Doctor De Soto answered. "But I can make a new one—But we can make a new one."

"Just stop the pain," whi—whispered the fox, wiping the tears away.

Despite his mice-ery—Despite his mice-ery, he realized he had a tasty little mouse—he had a tasty little mouse—he had a tasty little mouse in his mouth and his jaw began to shi-shiver. "Keep open!" yelled Doctor De Soto. "Wide open!" said his wife.

Figure 1. Shari's reading sample of *Doctor De Soto*.

It is this puzzling through the reading process that makes miscue analysis so fascinating—a fascination that we can share with our students. Acceptable omissions, substitutions, and self-corrections such as those cited here are examples of what we've come to refer to with students as their "smart miscues"—miscues that do not disrupt meaning but rather enable readers to proceed through a text. For students such as Shari who are struggling to understand what reading is all about, discussions involving miscue analysis and terminology like "smart miscues" help convey that personal construction of meaning is the goal of reading, and the production of miscues is simply a part of that process.

A Changing Perspective

Through careful kidwatching (Y. Goodman, 1985), I realized that all of my students were making sense—some more efficiently than others, but making sense of text nonetheless. This was an insight that caused me to have profound doubts about the assumption that there was something essentially "different" about students who found their way into an LD program, that they were LD because of some inferred neurological dysfunction. It became clear that these "severe" readers weren't severely disabled after all, and poor readers weren't "poor" because they made mistakes. Rather, the readers I worked with were hampered by their uncertainty: uncertainty about how reading works, uncertainty about the goal of reading, uncertainty about what a teacher or fellow students considered acceptable in a performance. This uncertainty contributed to a lack of confidence in using the reading process or to the belief that the goal of reading is the faithful reproduction of the published text.

For my colleagues and me, these insights about the nature of reading lead us to consider a set of more provocative questions, questions we continue to consider. For example, if these readers are effectively constructing meaning when they read, what are the implications for the construct of "learning disabilities"; what does that term mean? And the related questions: What is it that makes a teacher refer a reader for LD placement and services? How do beliefs about what curriculum should look like from the point of view of the students, parents, teachers, psychologists, and administrators shape our conceptions of what it means to be a learning disabled reader? What is curriculum and why is it organized in its current form? Who does it serve?

These last questions are not ones that teachers are normally invited to ask. In fact, in some settings, they are interpreted as threatening and insubordinate. But when we look closely at what our students do when they read real texts for their own purposes, and when we engage in an open discussion of the socio- and psycholinguistic nature of the reading process, we cannot help but pose questions that challenge traditional conceptions of the nature of learning and schooling. As informed by miscue analysis, these questions about readers, the reading process, and curriculum invite us to look again at all of our readers. And listen.

Miscue Analysis as Foundation for Further Inquiry

Miscue analysis isn't just a means for evaluating reading proficiency. The knowledge that miscue analysis reveals about the nature of learning and language processes allows us to raise questions that challenge nearly all of the assumptions that underlie traditional beliefs about teaching and learning (K. Goodman, 1986). Because of what I learned through miscue, I liberated my resource students from skill-oriented reading and writing workbook exercises and instead involved them in the study of literature and the pursuit of personal inquiry-oriented projects. When we focus on the meaning that readers and writers are constructing and look past the surface features of a performance (the spelling, punctuation, penmanship, or expectation of error-free reading), we are able to get a more inclusive sense of underlying competence. And our students will follow in kind. For example, when Shari is free to write about her impressions of Pearl S. Buck's *The Big Wave* (1986) without worry about maintaining the conventions of written expression (and yet knowing that it is through her meaningful writing that she will come to control those conventions), we can begin to appreciate Shari as a thinker. And Shari can finally begin to appreciate herself as a thinker.

Draft of book review from Shari's journal (with conventional presentation):

> I liked *The Big Wave* because it related to reality. It is saying things that can happen and has. I liked it because it did not take a long time to introduce the characters. The author expressed the story good. And it was easy to understand. I felt like I was in the book. The only thing I did not like was he or she said the word *replied* too much. I thought it was a very good book!

References

Brown, J., A. Marek, and K. Goodman, 1994. "Annotated bibliography of miscue analysis." (Occasional Paper No. 16). Tucson: University of Arizona, Program in Language and Literacy.

Buck, P. S. 1986. *The big wave*. New York: HarperCollins.

Cambourne, B., and P. Rousch, 1979. *A psycholinguistic model of the reading process as it relates to proficient, average and low ability readers*. Wagga Wagga, NSW,
Australia: Riverina College of Advanced Education, Sturt University.

Chapman, J. 1981. The reader and the text. In *"The reader and the text,"* ed. J.
Chapman. London: Heinemann. 1–15.

Cowley, J. 1983. "Rain, rain." In *Ready to read series*. Auckland, New Zealand
Ministry of Education.

Cowley, J. 1987. Los animales de Don Vicencio. II. I. Lowe. (P. Almada, Trans.).
Auckland, New Zealand: Shortland.

Cowley, J. 1989. My bike. In *Ready to read series*. Auckland, New Zealand: Learning Media (distributed by Richard C. Owen, Katonah, NY).

Crews, D. 1978. *Freight train*. New York: Scholastic.

Gilles, C., M. Bixby, P. Crowley, S. Crenshaw, M. Henrichs, F. Reynolds, and D.
Pyle, eds. 1988. *Whole language strategies for secondary students*. Katonah, NY:
Richard C. Owen.

Gollasch, F. 1980. "Readers' perception in detecting and processing embedded
errors in meaningful context." Doctoral diss. University of Arizona–Tucson.

Goodman, K. 1970. "Behind the eye: What happens in reading." In *Reading: Process and program*, ed. K. Goodman, and O. Niles. Urbana, IL: National Council of Teachers of English, 3–38.

Goodman, K. 1982. "Revaluing readers and reading." *Topics in Learning and
Learning Disabilities*. 1: 87–93.

Goodman, K. S. 1986. *What's whole in whole language?* Portsmouth, NH:
Heinemann.

Goodman, K. S. 1994. "Reading, writing and written texts: A transactional,
sociopsycholinguistic view." In *Theoretical models and processes of reading*, ed.
R. B. Ruddell, M. R. Ruddell, and H. Singer. Newark, DE: International
Reading Association, 1093–1130.

Goodman, K., L. Bird, and Y. Goodman, eds. 1991. *The whole language catalogue*.
Santa Rosa, CA: American School Publishers.

———. 1992. *The whole language catalogue: Supplement on authentic assessment*.
Santa Rosa, CA: American School Publishers.

Goodman, K., and C. Burke. 1973. "Theoretically based studies of patterns of
miscues in oral reading performance." (Final Report, Project No. 9-035,
OEG. 0-9-323075-4269). Washington, D.C.: U.S. Department of Health, Education, and Welfare.

Goodman, K., and S. Gespass. 1983. "Text features as they relate to miscues:
Pronouns." (Occasional Paper No. 7). Tucson: University of Arizona, Program in Language and Literacy.

Goodman, Y. 1985. "Kidwatching: Observing children in the classroom." In *Observing the language learner*, ed. A. Jaggar, and M. T. Smith-Burke. Newark, NJ: International Reading Association; Urbana, IL: National Council of Teachers of English, 9–18.

Goodman, Y., B. Altwerger, and A. Marek. 1989. "Print awareness in preschool children." (Occasional Paper No. 4). Tucson: University of Arizona, Program in Language and Literacy.

Goodman, Y., and C. Burke. 1972. *Reading miscue inventory: Readings for taping.* New York: MacMillan.

————. 1980. *Reading strategies: Focus on comprehension.* New York: Richard C. Owen.

Goodman, Y., and A. Marek. *Retrospective miscue analysis: Readers revaluing themselves and reading.* Katonah, NY: Richard C. Owen, in press.

Goodman, Y., D. Watson, and C. Burke. 1987. *Reading miscue inventory: Alternative procedures.* Katonah, NY: Richard C. Owen.

————. *Reading strategies: Focus on comprehension.* Katonah, NY: Richard C. Owen, in press.

Krauss, R. 1945. *The carrot seed.* New York: Scholastic.

Martin, B., Jr. 1983. *Brown bear, brown bear.* New York: Henry, Holt.

Meek, M. 1988. *How texts teach. What readers learn.* Stoud, Great Britain: Thimble Press.

Mooney, M. 1994. *Developing life-long readers.* Katonah, NY: Richard C. Owen.

Petrie, C. 1982. *Joshua James likes trucks.* Danbury, CT: Children's Press.

Pfeffer, S. 1987. "Kid power." In *Connections, grade 5.* New York: MacMillan.

Potter, R., and C. Hannemann. 1985. *Just dues: Experiences in reading comprehension, gr. 2–4.* Mountain View, CA: Creative Publications.

Steig, W. 1982. *Dr. De Soto.* New York: Farrar, Straus, and Giroux.

"The Stonecutter." 1961. In *Roads to everywhere.* New York: Russell, Gates, McCullough, Ginn, & Co.

Swim, R. C. 1964. *Paulossie, an Eskimo boy.* New York: Holt, Rinehart, and Winston.

Tapp, K. 1987. "The code in the mailbox." In *Connections, grade 3,* vol. 1. New York: MacMillan.

Tolstoy, A. 1987. "El nabo grande." In *Fiestas,* ed. R. B. Barrera, and A. N. Crawford. Boston, MA: Houghton Mifflin, 49–57.

Vygotsky, L. 1978. *Mind in society.* Cambridge, MA: Harvard University Press.

Weaver, C. 1994. *Reading process and practice: From socio-psycholinguistics to whole language.* Portsmouth, NH: Heinemann.

20 Listening to What Readers Tell Us

Paul Crowley
Sonoma State University

Crowley indicates the importance of understanding the reading process ourselves, and then helping readers reconsider the reading process and revalue themselves as readers. In discussing the miscues made by Gregg, a severely labeled reader in his seventh-grade class, Crowley shows how miscue analysis uncovers readers' strengths in using reading strategies and in comprehending, in contrast to traditional assessment, which notes only errors and dysfluency. Because Gregg had adopted this view of himself as a failed reader, Crowley concluded that the first step in creating a reading program for him was to help him appreciate his strengths as a reader, and to "unlearn the view that he is a poor reader because he messes up on words." Then, Crowley explains, Gregg's reading program must help him move more efficiently through a text, so that he will read more willingly and thereby grow as a reader. Crowley's program for Gregg included taping and discussing selected miscues that Gregg had made (through individual conferences, Retrospective Miscue Analysis, and class discussion of reader-selected miscues); reading aloud to the students; giving Gregg time and opportunity to do extensive uninterrupted silent reading; helping Gregg read intensively (which included support for participating in literature study groups). In addition, Crowley helped Gregg develop valuable strategies for reading: a "keep going" strategy to keep him from getting bogged down at the word level; a strategy for dealing with unfamiliar names he couldn't pronounce; and a strategy for dealing with other unfamiliar words. Crowley concludes that middle school is not too late to help readers in trouble, that informed teacher observation can replace formal miscue analysis for most students, and that students who understand the reading process can support one another's effective reading strategies.

Originally published in *Voices from the Middle*, 2(2), (1995). Copyright 1995 by the National Council of Teachers of English.

The other day, I received a call from the mother of a first grader who expressed concern that her son wasn't progressing well in reading.

Her fear was that he would reach sixth grade and be lagging behind his classmates. She said she was desperate and would do anything possible to "catch him up."

I urged her to return the commercial reading kit she had purchased; I wanted her to know that the only thing first graders need to be "hooked on" is books, as Daniel Fader told us in 1966. We talked about how naturally he learned to talk; and how we expect children to develop oral language at different rates; parents don't ponder sending their infants to "remedial talking" classes if they haven't begun speaking by a certain date. Children learn to talk because they are social beings and language serves both personal and interpersonal functions. Talking always takes place in a sensible, meaningful context. I wanted her to understand that in a literate society, learning written language is just as natural as learning to talk.

We agreed on the importance of taking the pressure off this young reader, supporting his efforts with meaningful and familiar print, identifying for ourselves how much he knows about written language (even though he could not, as yet, read unfamiliar print), and helping him appreciate all he knows.

The rules don't change for middle-school readers. We cannot expect all thirteen-year-old readers to look the same, any more than we can expect it of six-year-olds or sixteen-year-olds. However, as readers approach the middle grades and are struggling with reading, concern mounts on the part of the parents, teachers, and students.

We don't hide our heads in the sand. There are students in middle school (and beyond) who are struggling with the reading demands of school. Ken Goodman uses the term "readers in trouble" (1996, 1982a) to describe these students. The value of this term is that it doesn't place blame on students, teachers, or parents. What really matters is that these students become readers who can meet the reading demands in the curriculum and come to enjoy books. Teachers of English/ language arts, though, can do much to help readers in trouble by changing their views of themselves as readers and their notions about reading process. Goodman (1996) points out that, in order to help readers in trouble, we must

> help them revalue themselves as language users and learners, and revalue the reading process as a transactive, constructive language process. They must set aside the pathological views of themselves, cast off the labels, and operate to construct meaning through written language using the strengths they have built and used in making sense of oral language or sign. To do that they need support and help.

Helping readers revalue the reading process and themselves as readers requires us to have an understanding of this process. As we assist readers in developing reading strategies for handling different texts and for responding to literature, readers must engage with texts. We learn to read by reading.

Gregg

Books were enemies to Gregg, a severely labeled reader in my seventh-grade class several years ago. He had been in special education classes since early in his elementary school career, and he now found himself in my classroom for students designated "learning disabled." The ill-defined label given to Gregg did not do justice to his strengths as a reader. I interviewed Gregg about his views of reading and had him read aloud for me so that I could analyze his miscue behaviors to determine the reading strategies he used.

Goodman (1982b) defines a miscue as "an actual observed response in oral reading which does not match the expected response" (p. 94). Reading is not an exact process; readers do not replicate the text. Readers sample from the text and make predictions as we construct meaning. As we formulate a personal text, we make miscues including substitutions, insertions, omissions, and regressions to correct.

Goodman favors the use of the term "miscue" in order to avoid the negative connotations of "error." All miscues are neutral until they are analyzed linguistically and pragmatically. Goodman, Watson, and Burke (1987) point out that the most important aspect of miscue analysis is that it assists teacher researchers in developing a personal model of the reading process. They offer a list of questions teacher researchers ask in order to determine miscue quality.

- Does the miscue make sense? (semantic acceptability)
- Does it sound like language? (syntactic acceptability)
- Does it change the meaning of the text?
- Was it corrected?
- Does it look like the text item? (graphic similarity)

As we listen to our students read, we begin to internalize these questions, allowing us to become informed observers of readers, which, in turn, provides us with insight into the reading process. Gathering information about Gregg's control of the reading process through miscue analysis was the starting point for developing a curricular plan.

Before beginning, I asked Gregg what he did when he came to something unfamiliar in his reading. Gregg reported that he "sounded out" words or asked for help. He said that he would suggest the same strategies to someone else who was having difficulty reading. As I listened to Gregg's reading, I kept these reported strategies in mind to compare with his actual reading behaviors.

Using standard miscue analysis procedures, I chose a text of substantial length that would be unfamiliar to Gregg; this gave him the opportunity to get into the text in some depth, while enabling me to determine how he handled new information. I audiotaped his reading so that later I could compare the tape with a copy of the story, and mark and analyze his miscues.

My instructions to Gregg were, "I want you to read this aloud and if you come to something that gives you trouble, just do whatever you would do if you were by yourself. Be sure to read to remember because after you read, I'm going to ask you to tell me about what you read."

Gregg read a story about an elephant named Sudana who lived in the zoo and was suffering from a fever. The zoo doctor and his helper tried to give Sudana a dose of sulfa in her water, which she spit out at them. The same happened when they put the sulfa in ice cream. Then they gave Sudana an injection of penicillin and all was well. (The story doesn't have to be compelling to be suitable for miscue analysis!)

At the beginning of the story, a number of Gregg's miscues were of low quality syntactically and semantically unacceptable). For example:

TEXT

> The big African elephant was leaning against the steel bars of her cage in the Elephant House.

GREGG

> A big African elephant was leaning against still bars for her change in the Elephant House.

Menosky's (1971) research shows that readers' miscues are often of lower quality at the beginning of the text because the reader has not built up enough background from the text. As the reading progresses, though, the text becomes more predictable because the reader is constructing meaning.

After reading only one paragraph, Gregg produced the following miscues:

TEXT

He reached through the bars to lay a hand on the elephant's trunk.

GREGG

He reached through the bars and laid his hand on the elephant's tusk.

In altering the verb in the phrase "to lay a hand," so that it read "and laid his hand," Gregg shifted the verb from the infinitive to the past tense, thereby maintaining tense agreement with the rest of the story. Also, tusk is highly predictable when the topic is elephants. Gregg drew upon all of the cueing systems of language—graphophonic, syntactic, and semantic information—as he constructed his text. This was a pattern in his miscue behaviors throughout the story.

However, when Gregg encountered difficulty with individual words, he reverted to the most abstract cueing system, graphophonics. He did what he said he would do when he came to something that gave him trouble: He "sounded it out."

TEXT

Maybe if she's thirsty enough, she'll take some sulfa in her drinking water.

GREGG

Maybe if she's thirty, thirty en-thirty enough, she'll take some s-. sss, shovel in, in her water dish.

Gregg hammers away at *thirty* because he knows it doesn't make sense. Although this indicates that he was monitoring his comprehension, it was clear that Gregg was frustrated and uncomfortable with his attempts. He was probably unaware of his substitution of "water dish" for "drinking water," a high quality miscue (syntactically and semantically acceptable; no loss of meaning). Gregg could not have made this miscue unless he was in control of the process, making predictions and confirming them as he made meaning.

We make predictions based on the meaning we have built up in our particular world, our knowledge of language, and the social context in which the language occurs. This explains why a friend's Jewish mother looked at the sign in the store window that said "Boxes and Labels" and read "Lox and Bagels." Our brains tell our eyes what to see.

Gregg overused graphophonic cues in a number of places throughout the text, as evidenced by his multiple attempts at individual words.

For example, when he got to the word *patient*, he read *pat* (fourteen-second pause); *pat* (nine-second pause); he regressed to the prior word, *heavy*, paused for eleven seconds, and then read *patnight*, and mumbled "or something." Clearly, Gregg had little confidence in his attempt. His editorial comment indicated that he knew the word wasn't *patnight*.

TEXT

> As he stepped back over the guardrail, the doctor spoke to Bob, her keeper. "Did you give her anything to drink today?"

GREGG

> As, as he stepped down over the guardrail, guardrail, the doctor spoke to Bob. Her, Her keeper didn't (five-second pause) Her keeper didn't (five-second pause) Her keeper did you give her anything to drink today.

Gregg substituted a period for the comma after Bob. (It is clear through intonation.) This caused him to change the dialogue to a declarative sentence with "Her keeper" being the subject. Gregg substituted didn't for did, but when the structure of the sentence broke down, he was unable to work it out for himself, even after multiple attempts. Although Gregg's miscues rendered the sentence syntactically and, therefore, semantically unacceptable, his multiple attempts and grammatical transformations indicate his facility with the structure of the language. As Gregg read further into the text, though, his regressions to correct were successful more often than not. As he constructed a meaningful text, it became more predictable and Gregg's miscues were fewer in number and higher in quality.

The word *sulfa* gave Gregg problems throughout most of the reading. He made multiple attempts to "sound it out" (s-/sss/shovel [perhaps looking for the /sh/ as in sure]; suchful/shmmm; shiffa; shome; snufn), and grew visibly frustrated. At one point, he growled at the book as he held it up and shook it when he came to the ubiquitous *sulfa* yet one more time. Gregg finally pronounced the word /surum/ (the first *u* as in *surf*) and stuck with it. I can't help but think he was trying to say *serum*. Interestingly, toward the end of the story, Gregg read "injection of penicillin" without hesitation.

No miscue analysis is over until the reader retells what was read. Frequently readers are able to retell a great deal more than we may expect from the observed miscue behaviors because they have silently self-corrected as they read, rather than regressing to correct. Gregg was able to retell the main points of the entire story and many details.

He talked about the elephant without referring to her name and described the way the doctor and his helper tried to get the medicine into the elephant. Gregg knew that *sulfa* was a medicine because the text taught him. His frustration with the word throughout the reading was unnecessary; his "sounding out" strategy got him nowhere.

Gregg was an effective reader; he understood the text. However, he was also an inefficient reader because of the high degree of effort he put forth to get through the reading. At one point, Gregg tapped the table vigorously and grunted in frustration as he attempted to force his reading to make sense.

Gregg's tenacity with the story was context-specific. That is, in his first week of seventh grade at a new school, he found himself across from an attentive adult, clipboard and pencil in hand, who was audio-taping his reading. Gregg was willing to stick with the task because he was a captive audience. Otherwise, he would use his most common reading strategy—abandoning the text (which, by the way, is a strategy proficient readers use as appropriate).

There is much to value in Gregg's reading. His greatest strength is that he understood what he read; he was able to retell all the main points of the story. To the untrained ear, Gregg's reading can be almost painful to listen to. He made many partial attempts, regressions, and pauses up to seventeen seconds. However, an analysis of his miscues indicates that many of his miscues fit the structure of the text and made sense. He made sensible predictions (e.g., "her water dish" for "her drinking water") and his regressions were made in an attempt to correct. As the reading progressed, Gregg's miscues decreased in number and were of a higher quality. He developed strategies to handle the words that gave him problems early in the text. For example, after making multiple attempts at the elephant's name, *Sudana* (e.g., S/Sha/Shado-Shadan/Shadan; Sh-/Shu- /Sh/Shuden), he said *Shana* and used it, almost exclusively, from then on without making multiple attempts at sounding it out; similarly, *sulfa* became *surum*.

Gregg saw himself as a failed reader. The first step in creating a reading program for him was to help him revalue his reading strengths, and to gain an accurate view of reading so that he could gradually unlearn the strategies that were tripping him up.

From Miscue Analysis to Reading Instruction:
A Program for Gregg

The reading strategies Gregg employed at the beginning of seventh grade, while successful in helping him gain meaning, frustrated him to the point of seeing books as enemies. Gregg's miscues show us that he isn't just making haphazard random errors, but that he, based on the cues available to him, is predicting, confirming, disconfirming, and repredicting when necessary, and constructing meaning. This information is essential for building a reading program for him.

Gregg also needs to know his strengths as a reader, and to unlearn the view that he is a poor reader because he messes up on words. Gregg's reading program must provide him with strategies that will assist him in moving more efficiently through the text. It isn't enough that Gregg has these strategies; he must also *use* them. He must be willing to put in the effort to engage with texts in order to grow as a reader—to learn to read by reading.

Revaluing Gregg's Reading

Following the reading and the retelling of a miscue analysis story, I ask readers how they feel about their reading. Gregg, like many readers both successful and less successful, was critical of his reading. He talked about "messing up" a lot. I used this opportunity to give my side of the story, to tell Gregg that he was already successful in the most important aspect of reading—making meaning. I also pointed out places in the text where he regressed and corrected.

Over the next few weeks, I would sit next to Gregg and ask him to read aloud from whatever he was reading at the time (or *should* be reading, such as his science book). We would stop once in a while to reflect on what he was doing; we talked about the miscues he made and evaluated their quality. I wanted Gregg to know that he is responsible for getting his reading to make sense and, if it doesn't sound like language, it can't make sense. The revaluing process requires readers to realize that *they* are in control of the process of meaning making.

Retrospective Miscue Analysis

A number of teachers and researchers have investigated the power of teaching students miscue analysis (Goodman & Marek, 1996). A set of procedures called "Retrospective Miscue Analysis" has been developed in which readers, as young as elementary age, tape their reading, listen for miscues, and ask themselves: Did the miscue make sense? Did it sound like language? Did it look like the text. Did you correct?/Should you have? Readers' examinations of their own and their classmates' miscues provide them with specific data for discussions of the reading process. Knowledge of the reading process provides students with an explanation for their reading behaviors, and helps to establish what they are doing well and what they need to change.

Reader-Selected Miscues

As they read independently, readers are invited to jot down those places in the text that give them problems. Readers' selected miscues (Watson & Hoge, in press) also help them move through the text because they know that following the reading, they will have the opportunity to discuss these problems. Readers often find that when they finish the selection, they have figured out the miscues they selected earlier. They may also and that the difficulties they experienced did not interfere with their understanding.

I shared my confusion about Wilson Rawls's reference to the "coon hounds barking treed" in *Where the Red Fern Grows* (1961). When I reported this to the class, Randy (who took two weeks off each year during deer-hunting season) was incredulous. Hooking his thumbs into his jeans and crossing his cowboy boots, he told me, "the dogs barked treed." (Maybe I hadn't been listening the first time.) "What does that mean?" "You know, they barked TREED." (Maybe he's hard of hearing.) "I still don't get it." (Who's on first?) Rusty finally explained that coon dogs bark as they're chasing a coon, but that their bark changes when they get the coon trapped in a tree.

It is important that students see their teachers as readers and know that, as readers, we employ the same strategies we encourage them to use. We can share how we handle tax forms (I phone my accountant), requests for grant proposals (I study the proposal to learn the language of the funding organization so that I can use it in the writing of my proposal; then they can know how smart I am and how worthy of their money), and James Joyce novels (I don't worry about understanding everything; when I'm confused, I just enjoy the language). These open discussions demonstrate how proficient readers' strategies always focus on meaning, the social demands of the situation, and the purpose for reading.

Reading Aloud

Hearing good literature read aloud gave Gregg access to books that he would have avoided because he found them too difficult or, as most middle school teachers have heard many times, too boring. This pressure-free activity allows readers to hear the flow of written language, as well as their own teachers making miscues. Reading aloud demonstrates to students that written language does not sound like oral language. This is why the stories of six-year-olds often start with "once upon a time." They are learning the conventions of written language that will make independent reading more predictable. Similarly, hearing books read aloud helps older readers gain a tacit understanding of their structure and conventions, which will assist them as independent readers. Reading aloud to Gregg also helped him know that there are compelling books out there about kids like him and the people he knows.

Reading Extensively

Gregg was given numerous opportunities for uninterrupted silent reading time. He was invited to read texts that offered the potential for engaging him, that is, books about things that interested him and that spoke to his experiences. He was *able* to read a great deal more than he was *willing* to read, but he avoided many appropriate books because of the pressure he put on himself to "get all the words right." Therefore, the challenge was to maintain a ready supply of materials that would be interesting and effortless enough for Gregg to buy into. He read magazines about fishing (one of his passions), paged through *Rolling Stone* and *National Geographic* magazines (looking at the pictures and reading captions, as I usually do), and read poetry by Shel Silverstein, Nikki Giovanni, and Eloise Greenfield.

As Gregg felt more comfortable with reading and himself as a reader, I wanted to engage him with texts that were challenging for him. I had picked up Robert Cormier's *I Am the Cheese* (1977) a year before and, after reading a few pages, put it on my guilt shelf (the place where unread and unfinished books stay and haunt me to the grave . . . or until they're read). I had recently resurrected the book and read it with a vengeance in an afternoon. I knew the book was for Gregg. It was strange and troubling (highly appealing qualities to many middle school kids, including Gregg; Robert Cormier knows his stuff). I told Gregg that I had put this book down for a long time because of its strange beginning; it hadn't hooked me at all. When I finally read it, though, I loved it and thought of Gregg a number of times during the reading. I said it was a "weird book" (I knew this would carry weight) and I thought he would like it. Gregg picked up the book and began reading, only looking up to say, "This really is weird! He finished it in a week. Gregg learned that not all books are immediately accessible, but that if you give them a chance, they might be worth the effort.

Reading Intensively

All of the readers in our classes—successful readers and readers in trouble—deserve access to the ideas that come from books. Gregg joined in intensive reading with a community of readers in literature study groups. If students have difficulty reading the literature study book, we can support them in a number of ways. If they are having trouble keeping up with the other readers, we can invite them to read as much as they can with understanding and then fill them in on the rest. We can read the book to them or put it on tape. The important thing is that they are members of the community of readers and have the opportunity to share their perspectives and to hear those of others.

Readers negotiate meanings in literature study groups, but then can also discuss *how* they make meaning. The students or teacher might ask: How did you handle that part of the story? What did you do when you came to that word? Why does the author use this kind of language? As we explore answers to questions like these, we add to our repertoire of reading strategies.

Reading beyond Words

Gregg thought reading was about words. In response to the question on the Reading Interview (Goodman, Watson & Burke, 1987), "When you are reading and you come to something you don't know, what do you do?" he said he would "sound it out" or ask someone to tell him the word. I wanted Gregg to learn that individual words are rarely problems for proficient readers.

Glossaries, dictionaries, and asking someone for help—going outside ourselves—are *confirming* strategies, and, even then, rarely does a single word make much difference in a text. I've had graduate students who swear they always stop reading when they come to a word they don't know and look it up in the dictionary. If they really do that, I tell them, they must not read very much. And if they do, they must not be reading many challenging books.

As teachers, we need to define for ourselves what we mean when we say a reader "doesn't know a word." Do we mean: The reader is unfamiliar with the concept? The reader is unfamiliar with the label? The reader can't pronounce the word? The reader is unfamiliar with the label in English, but understands the concept and knows the label in a primary language?

In order to engage with larger units of text, Gregg needed to "keep going" in his reading and not become hung up on individual words and confusing syntax. If he understands the story, he should keep reading.

Naming Strategy

As Gregg progressed through the miscue analysis text, he developed a successful strategy for dealing with *sulfa* and *Sudana*. Although Gregg didn't believe he was successful with these words, he eventually began using a "naming strategy" that helped him move through the text. At the beginning of the story, Gregg made multiple attempts at a number of words, including the name of the elephant, the medicine, *patient*, and *thirsty*.

It was important for Gregg to understand that his naming strategy was good, he just needed to use it earlier in his reading and with more consistency. Once you know that *Sudana* (however you pronounce it) refers to the elephant's name, call her Shana (or *Sinbad* or *Sherry*) and move on, sticking with that name throughout the story. Removing this self-imposed pressure makes reading much easier.

The next time I scooted my chair up to Gregg and listened to him read, he began again to sound out words. I told him to skip them or say "blank" and go on. This simple suggestion met with incredulity; Gregg's view of successful reading was reading all the words correctly, and here he was being told skip words. As Gregg began to abandon the misguided notion that reading is an exact, word-by-word process, though, he was much more apt to spend time reading. A burden had been lifted. He stopped asking himself to attempt an impossible task.

Selected Deletions

At times, no matter how we cajole them not to get stopped by individual words, some readers continue to make multiple and futile attempts at reading every word. "Selected Deletions" (Watson & Crowley, 1987) is a strategy lesson to help these readers keep going.

Selected Deletions involves removing potentially troublesome words from the text. The first two or three sentences of the text are left intact to help the reader get a handle on the story, and then only highly predictable words are removed. If readers have difficulty putting in a word that makes sense, the purpose is defeated; coming up with a sensible word must be effortless in order to demonstrate to readers that they bring something to the reading process and that the text helps them to make meaning.

A single unfamiliar word that occurs repeatedly in the text can also be deleted. It would be interesting if Gregg had read this story with the word *sulfa* deleted. It probably wouldn't have taken him long to begin putting the word *medicine* in the blank.

Writing to Support Reading

Although this discussion highlights Gregg as a reader, he was also engaged in oral language and writing activities each day. Nothing is more predictable than our own language, and Gregg, as the first reader of his own writing, regularly connected with texts he could handle well. Through writing, Gregg had many opportunities to engage with his own texts as well as with his classmates' and mine.

It was important that Gregg be involved in varied writing experiences with real audiences, including written conversation (legal note passing), dialogue journals (if I neglected to write back, I was quickly told), pen pals with Education majors at a local university, story writing, book publishing for elementary school partners, and literature response logs. Gregg learned that writing, like reading, serves multiple functions.

Reading and Writing with Younger Students

Gregg and his classmates met regularly with primary-age students at a nearby elementary school to read and write with them. I used this opportunity to discuss the reading process with my middle-school students. We talked about how young readers have varied interests and facility with oral language. They are involved with written language every day on cereal boxes, T-shirts, books, TV. They need to use the language cues that they have the most control over, syntax (grammar) and meaning, in order to gain command of the abstract (symbolic) cueing system, graphophonics. Providing young readers with good stories that have supportive structures helps them to use these strengths and enjoy the reading experience.

In preparation for writing their own predictable books, our class read (aloud and silently) many predictable books for young readers. Approaching these books with an eye to studying technique and elements of story prevented these readers from being insulted by their easy reading level. Each student then began to write a book—one line of text and one illustration per page. Figure 1 is the text of Gregg's book.

Gregg was funny and smart and contributed a lot to our class. He was also surly, distracting, and moody in that unique teenage way. So one morning, when I received a call from the teacher in the first-grade classroom where Gregg had been reading and writing with a little boy, a multitude of potential horrors flashed through my mind. What had he done? The teacher, however, was delighted. "He was listening to Ty reading and when Ty asked Gregg, 'What is this word?' Gregg told him not to worry about it—to put in something that makes sense or go on.

No Excuses

by Gregg

One day my teacher asked where my homework was. I told her
my dog ate it!

The next day my teacher asked me where my homework was. I
told her a bird used it to wallpaper his nest.

The next day my teacher asked me where my homework was. I
told her a giant fly took it!

The next day my teacher asked me here my homework was. I told
her it got caught in a big spider web.

The next day my teacher asked me where my homework was. I
told her a flying saucer stole it!

Then all of a sudden a dog, a bird, a fly, a Martian, and a big spider said, "Sorry" then gave her the papers and left.

Figure 1. Gregg's book.

He said it's more important to get the meaning of the story and to enjoy
it. When Ty asked Gregg to spell a word for him while writing in his
journal, Gregg told him that his ideas were more important than
spelling and besides, it only interrupts your ideas when you stop to get
help." She was pleased to see this first grader gaining confidence using
Gregg's advice.

Gregg had recommended strategies that he was not yet using consistently, but this was a good start. He was able to articulate what we
had talked about and must have thought it had some validity. In the
context of working with a younger reader, he had had a chance to look
at the reading and writing processes from a teacher's perspective.

Organizing Our Classrooms for Reading Instruction

It is unnecessary for teachers to conduct a formal miscue analysis with
each student. The teachers in this issue describe ways in which they
gather the information about their students, and how they use this
information—in concert with their knowledge of the reading process,
readers, and learning—to build curriculum with their students.

Linda Morrow describes how natural curricular contexts enable
her to listen to her students read aloud. She then incorporates the

information she has gleaned into her instructional planning. Judith Wright paints a portrait of her students' varied experiences with literature, and explains how, in this context, she brings the reading process to a conscious level with her students and their parents in order to help them appreciate readers' strengths. Carol Evans Treu uses her understandings to "lure readers from hiding" by demonstrating to them how much they know and can do with reading. These teachers know that middle-school students are still growing as readers, and that teachers can make a difference in helping them see themselves as readers in control of their reading process.

Middle school is not too late to help readers in trouble. Students come to us with a wealth of language, experiences, and curiosity that form a solid basis for a meaning-centered reading program. The challenge for us is to strip away the sense of failure, to overcome the defensive attitude, and to involve them as members of a community of readers. This is not an easy task, but helping readers revalue themselves and what they know about reading is the starting point.

A powerful aspect of involving all of our students, including successful readers, in discussions and analysis of the reading process and their own reading is that they can begin to see the reading strengths of their classmates. With an understanding of the reading process, our students no longer hear only mistakes when they listen to their colleagues read. They hear readers.

Ken and Yetta Goodman (1994) remind us:

> Everything people do, they do imperfectly. This is not a flaw but an asset. If we always performed perfectly, we could not maintain the tentativeness and flexibility that characterize human learning and the ways we interact with our environment and with one another. This model of imperfection causes us as researchers not to worry about why people fall short of perfection; rather, we are concerned with why people do what they do and with what we can learn about language processes from observing such phenomenon. (p. 104)

Middle-school kids are trying to figure out who they are and who they want to be. They need to feel comfortable with their successes and their errors, to know what they know and use it. They need to know that taking risks is essential to learning, including learning language, both written and oral. It's liberating for students to acknowledge that errors are natural and can demonstrate complex problem-solving. These are things I tried to teach Gregg and his classmates.

Gregg is still teaching me.

References

Cormier, R. 1977. *I am the cheese.* New York: Dell.

Fader, D. N., and M. H. Shaevitz. 1966. *Hooked on books.* New York: Berkley.

Giovanni, N. 1973. *Ego-tripping.* New York: Lawrence Hill.

Goodman, K. S. 1982a. "Revaluing readers and reading." *Topics in Learning & Learning Disabilities,* 1(4): 87–93.

———. 1982b. "Miscues: Windows on the reading process." In *Language and literacy: The selected writings of Kenneth S. Coodman: vol. 1. Process, theory, research,* ed. F. V. Gollasch. Boston: Routledge & Kegan Paul.

Goodman, K. S. 1996. "Principles of revaluing." In *Revaluing readers and reading: Retrospective miscue analysis,* ed. Y. M. Goodman, and A. M. Marek. Katonah, NY: Richard C. Owen.

Goodman, Y. M., and K. S. Goodman. 1994. "To err is human: Learning about language processes by analyzing miscues." In *Theoretical models and processes of reading,* 4th ed., ed. R. B. Ruddell, M. R. Ruddell, and H. Singer. Newark, DE: International Reading Association, 104–123.

Goodman, Y. M., and A. M. Marek. 1996. *Revaluing readers and reading: Retrospective miscue analysis.* Katonah, NY: Richard C. Owen.

Goodman, Y. M., D. J. Watson, and C. L. Burke. 1987. *Reading miscue inventory: Alternative procedures.* Katonah, NY: Richard G. Owen.

Greenfield, E. 1972. *Honey, I love and other love poems.* New York: Thomas Y. Crowell.

21 Reconceptualizing Reading and Dyslexia

Constance Weaver
Western Michigan University

Weaver begins by observing that, among reading professionals, a basic controversy exists between those who conceptualize proficient reading as first and foremost a matter of identifying words automatically and fluently and those who conceptualize proficient reading as first and foremost a matter of orchestrating various reading strategies to construct meaning. The view of reading that underlies conventional concepts of dyslexia is the word-identification view; indeed, this concept of reading underlies both the deviance and the delay hypothesis, which are described. Briefly cited is some of the evidence from which researchers have concluded that difficulty in reading coherent and connected text may often be instructionally induced, through an overemphasis on skills for identifying words in isolation. This chapter further explains and challenges the word-identification view of reading and the resultant assumption that anyone who has difficulty reading words is dyslexic. Two decades of miscue analysis demonstrate unequivocally that even though many proficient readers identify most of the words correctly, they focus more upon constructing meaning than identifying words; that constructing meaning involves using prior knowledge and context along with letter-sound knowledge; and that readers who make many miscues (either on isolated words, connected text, or both) may nevertheless construct meaning effectively from conceptually appropriate and naturally written texts. That is, this research demonstrates that accuracy in word identification is less important in proficient reading than being able to coordinate various language cues and metacognitive strategies to construct meaning.

Reconsidering the nature of proficient reading leads us to discover the reading strengths of readers who have difficulty with word identification but who nevertheless control the needed strategies to construct meaning from appropriate texts. This leads to a reconceptualization of dyslexia as the ineffective use and/or coordination of strategies for constructing meaning. The argument is illustrated by a case study of Erica, diagnosed as dyslexic in the first grade, and who indeed has difficulty identifying words when reading aloud, but who nevertheless has developed effective strategies for constructing meaning and for dealing with words in context by using all the available language and meaning cues and not just her letter-sound knowledge.

Since this article was originally published, dyslexia has been redefined as "a specific language-based disorder of constitutional origin characterized by difficulties in single word decoding, usually reflecting insufficient phonological processing abilities" ("Operational Definition of Dyslexia," Orton Dyslexia Society Research Committee, 1994, in C. Scruggs, Ed., *Perspectives, 20*, v, p. 4). This redefinition serves to further accentuate the differences between a traditional definition of dyslexia and that proposed in this article.

Originally published in *Journal of Childhood Communication Disorders, 16*(1), (1994), 23–35. Copyright 1994 by The Division for Children with Communication Disorders. Reprinted with permission.

As speech-language pathologists and reading specialists increasingly come to work together and/or to take on each other's traditionally defined roles, it is imperative that we share our knowledge and expertise with one another. Within each group of professionals, however, there are contrasting and often conflicting viewpoints. Among reading professionals, a basic controversy exists between those who conceptualize proficient reading as first and foremost a matter of identifying words automatically and fluently (e.g. Adams, 1990; Stanovich, 1991) and those who conceptualize proficient reading as first and foremost a matter of orchestrating various reading strategies to construct meaning (K. Goodman, 1965, 1973, 1982; Smith, 1988; Weaver, 1988, 1994). The view of reading that underlies conventional concepts of dyslexia is the word-identification view, which has led researchers and clinicians to diagnose readers as dyslexic on the basis of their relative inability to identify words in isolation, or their relatively ineffective strategies for identifying words.

Those who have researched dyslexia from this perspective have typically considered dyslexia to stem from either a neurological deficiency (deviance) or a neurological delay in coming to read words easily and effectively. After briefly describing some of the research that leads to the deviance or the delay hypothesis, this discussion will focus on an alternative conception of reading, derived from analyzing the miscues ("errors") of proficient readers. Conceptualizing reading as the construction of meaning leads to reconceptualizing dyslexia as the ineffective use and/or coordination of reading strategies to construct meaning. Consideration of a girl named Erica demonstrates that a reader seen as dyslexic from conventional perspectives will often be viewed as much more proficient through the lenses of miscue analysis

and the understandings derived from miscue analysis research. Historically, this research has led to a whole language approach to helping readers develop and coordinate strategies for constructing meaning,
while reading and discussing natural, coherent, and interesting texts.

Dyslexia As Difficulty in the Reading of Words

Since before the time of Samuel Orton and his original 1937 hypothesis that dyslexia might result from poorly established hemispheric dom-
inance in the brain, dyslexia has typically been conceptualized as a
neurological problem of some sort. This is not surprising, since the original observations of severe reading difficulty came from the medical
community and stemmed from investigations into the reading of individuals who had suffered brain injury or brain-affecting diseases (Monaghan, 1980, offers an interesting history of dyslexia as a medical
concept). The notion that is still common today is articulated in a 1970
definition from the World Federation of Neurology. Their official definition of dyslexia—also known as a "specific reading disability" and
as "specific developmental dyslexia" (to distinguish it from dyslexia
caused later in life by brain injury or disease)—is as follows:

> A disorder manifested by difficulty in learning to read despite con-
> ventional instruction, adequate intelligence, and socio-cultural
> opportunity. It is dependent upon fundamental cognitive disabili-
> ties which are frequently of constitutional origin. (Critchley, 1970)

Dyslexia is commonly diagnosed when readers are two or more
years behind "grade level" on standardized reading tests (e.g., as indicated in Boder, 1973); when there is a significant discrepancy between
I.Q. scores and reading achievement scores on standardized tests (e.g.,
Shaywitz et al., 1992); and/or when there is a significant discrepancy
between certain subtest scores within an intelligence test.

Usually only after readers have been diagnosed as dyslexic on the
basis of such discrepancies have researchers looked for possible evidence of neurological functioning that might account for the discrepancies. Such research has typically investigated the reading strategies
of readers labeled as dyslexic by considering (exclusively, in most studies) how they read words in isolation—*not* how they read connected,
coherent, and authentic texts.

Even from this limited and limiting perspective, the research is far
from conclusive. Some of the research seems to support the hypothesis of neurological deviance, while other research—especially some of
the more recent research—seems to support the hypothesis that dyslexia

merely reflects a developmental delay in acquiring and/or effectively orchestrating strategies for reading words.

Evidence for the Deviance Hypothesis: A Sampling

In a widely cited article Boder (1973) presented what has been considered groundbreaking research on subtypes of dyslexia, using strategies for reading isolated words and strategies for word decoding as her measures. Of the 107 dyslexic students in her study, approximately 9 percent had a poor memory for visual patterns and tended to read analytically, "'by ear', through a process of phonetic analysis and synthesis, sounding out familiar as well as unfamiliar combinations of letters, rather than by whole-word visual gestalts" (Boder 1973, p. 670). They read "laboriously, as if . . . seeing each word for the first time" (p. 670). They also tended to spell phonetically, with the result that even the simplest "sight words" were often misspelled, yet the children's spellings of unfamiliar words were usually readable because they were phonetic. Not surprisingly, these readers typically had a much lower sight vocabulary than those in the major group, whose sight vocabulary itself was characterized as limited."

The largest group was comprised of children who read words globally as instantaneous visual gestalts, rather than analytically. Lacking word-analysis skills, they were unable to sound out and blend the letters and syllables of a word. Such readers made substitutions based primarily on visual resemblance and apparently grammar ("horse" for *house*, "monkey" for *money*, "stop" for *step*). However, their most striking substitutions were words closely related conceptually but not phonetically to the original word. Examples are "funny" for *laugh*, "chicken" or "quack" for *duck*, "answer" for *ask*, "stairs" for *step*, "airplane" for *train*, "person" for *human*, "planet" for *moon*, and "Los Angeles" for *city* (Boder 1973, p. 670). Such semantically-based substitutions occurred even though the words were presented in isolation. This group's spelling strategies also resembled their reading patterns. That is, they could spell familiar words that they recognized on sight, even irregular and long ones, but they had difficulty spelling even the simplest regular words if the words were not already familiar. Typically they did not produce good phonetic spellings. Boder indicates that the largest percentage of dyslexics in her study, approximately two-thirds, exhibited the latter reading and spelling patterns.

Overall, 9 percent of the dyslexics in Boder's study read words analytically rather than globally, while the rest (22 percent) exhibited both patterns (Boder 1973, p. 676). According to Boder, these proportions seem to be typical of other studies as well. In particular, the major

proportion of readers diagnosed as dyslexic seem to have difficulty with
analytical letter-by-letter processing—or with letter-by-letter phonological processing, as many researchers would put it. For example, in
an excellent review article on the cognitive and neuropsychological
foundations of word identification in poor and normally developing
readers, the reviewers conclude that "Research in this area of inquiry
is consistent with our suggestion that reading disability, in otherwise
normal children, is due, in most cases, to constitutionally and/or expe-
rientially derived deficiencies in language that lead to ineptitude in
acquiring either meaning-based or code-oriented strategies for word
identification, although the largest proportion appears to be deficient
in the use of code-oriented strategies" (Vellutino & Denckla, 1991, p.
604). From their own research and that of many others, Goswami and
Bryant similarly conclude that "Children who make slow progress in
reading and spelling often have phonological problems, even in comparison to children who have reached the same absolute level in reading and spelling" (1990, p. 94). Another researcher who has recently
found evidence to support a similar conclusion is Elbro (1990).

Evidence for the Delay Hypothesis: A Sampling

Even when considering just word identification, however, such research
conclusions as those above do not necessarily mean that the neurological functioning of readers labeled dyslexic is necessarily *deviant* from
the range of what is considered normal. For example, Elbro compared
twenty-six developmental dyslexic adolescents attending a school for
those who have been unresponsive to remediation in regular schools
with twenty-six normal readers of the same I.Q. and "reading age," the
latter as measured by a standard silent reading test with sentences. The
dyslexic adolescents ranged from thirteen years seven months to seventeen years three months, while the normal readers were in the second or third grade, ages eight years four months to ten years eleven
months. When Elbro measured their responses on seven measures
designed to determine their acquisition of the phonemic principle and
their tendency to use a letter-level recoding strategy, he obtained results
that pointed toward a specific phonemic deficit in the dyslexic adolescents. Also, half the dyslexic readers displayed a more whole-word oriented reading strategy than did any of the normal subjects. However,
when Elbro compared the distribution of normal readers' and dyslexics' strategies for reading words, he did not find distinct groups among
the dyslexics, based on their use or non-use of a letter-level reading strategy (Ebro, 1991b, 1990). Reading skills and strategies were distributed
over a continuum in both the normal and the dyslexic group.

Another interesting set of studies is reported by Goswami and Bryant (1990, pp. 134–136). They describe a study by Temple and Marshall (1983) in which these investigators described a seventeen year old girl (HM) with a reading level of ten years, who seemed to rely almost exclusively on a whole-word strategy: she found it almost impossible to read nonsense words and long regular words, and other errors suggested she was relying heavily on the visual appearance of words in order to read them. In contrast is another seventeen year old girl (CD), likewise with a reading level of ten years. According to the report of M. Coltheart, Masterson, Byng, Prior & Riddoch (1983), the symptoms shown by this girl were almost the mirror image of those made by HM: she could read regular words much more easily than irregular ones, and she made other errors typical of dyslexics who rely heavily on a letter-by-letter strategy (my terminology, based on the descriptions). But in a later study that compared HM's and CD's patterns of reading words with a group of "normal" readers having a mean reading age of ten years one month, the investigators found that all but one of the "symptoms" of dyslexia found in one or the other of these young women was found in the reading of the normal readers at essentially the same reading age (Bryant & Impey, 1986; for a summary, see Goswami & Bryant, 1990, p. 135). There were differences among the normal readers, too: some were more like HM, some more like CD. As Goswami & Bryant put it, "This suggests striking qualitative differences between normal readers, and underlines the point that these differences cannot be used to explain the difficulties of the dyslexic children" (1990, p. 136). Or in other words, it's not differences in strategies for reading words that accounts for readers being labeled dyslexic in the first place, nor do the word-reading strategies of alleged dyslexics often differ from the range of differences found among younger unlabeled readers.

Related conclusions about the range of differences being similar among allegedly dyslexic readers and unlabeled readers were drawn from a recent longitudinal study involving more than 400 children. Defining "dyslexia" as a significant discrepancy between intelligence and observed achievement level in reading (as measured by the revised Wecshler Intelligence Scale for Children and the Woodcock-Johnson Psychoeducational Battery, respectively), the investigators found no *qualitative* differences between "dyslexic" children and children showing no significant discrepancy between these scores. More technically, the children identified as dyslexic simply fell at the lower end of a normal curve. Moreover, only seven of the twenty-five children classified as dyslexic in grade one met the same criteria for dyslexia in grade three (Shaywitz et al., 1992).

The recognition that "dyslexics" employ roughly the same range of strategies and have the same range of difficulties in reading words as younger unlabeled readers has prompted the developmental hypothesis: that those labeled dyslexic are simply delayed in reading development. This has led to various stage theories of dyslexia (e.g. Frith, 1985,1986) and to other kinds of developmental hypotheses (e.g. Goswami & Bryant, 1990, pp. 141–150), including the hypothesis that strategies for processing words develop along more than one continuum (e.g. Elbro, 1990). In short, the word-reading strategies and underlying neurological functioning of those labeled dyslexic may reflect not a deviant neurological development, but simply a lag in neurological development. Given the way dyslexia is commonly diagnosed, it should not be surprising that readers labeled as dyslexic exhibit reading patterns found among younger readers.

Assumptions Commonly Underlying Research on Dyslexia

Whether supporting a deviance or a delay hypothesis, the conventional research on dyslexia usually reflects such assumptions as the following:

1. Reading is first and foremost a matter of identifying words.
2. Readers must be able to demonstrate word-reading skills in isolation from actual reading in order to make effective use of them during actual reading.
3. Scores on standardized reading tests are appropriate measures of how a student reads.

The first two assumptions seem to be bolstered by the research that demonstrates a strong correlation among fluent word identification and comprehension, especially among good readers (e.g. Stanovich, 1980, 1981, 1984; for summaries of this and other research, see Stanovich, 1991, and Adams 1990). However, this correlation should be no surprise when reading comprehension is measured by timed tests that necessarily put a premium upon rapid word identification, and that measure comprehension via multiple choice questions about relatively short texts that offer little redundancy or opportunity for concepts to be developed in print, much less understood by the reader.

The correlation between fluent word identification and comprehension is not nearly so strong when reading is assessed by the set of procedures collectively known as miscue analysis, which involves— at a minimum—eliciting the reader's understanding of the text read and analyzing the reading strategies reflected by the miscues (conventionally called errors) that the reader has made in reading longer, natural, and conceptually appropriate texts (for such procedures, see

Y. Goodman, Watson, & Burke, 1987; a related alternative is offered in Weaver, 1988, 1994).

Miscues and Miscue Analysis: An Alternative Perspective of Reading and Dyslexia

From more than two decades of miscue analysis and hundreds of studies of readers' miscues and their correlation with the comprehension of text, researchers have drawn such generalizations as the following, with regard to the nature of proficient reading, reading strategies and their use, and appropriate assessment of reading strategies and abilities (Goodman, 1973; Brown, Goodman, & Marek, 1996; also described in Weaver, 1988, 1994):

1. Proficient readers focus more upon meaning than upon words.

2. The construction of meaning involves such strategies as using prior knowledge and context to predict, sampling the visual display, monitoring comprehension, employing "fix-it" strategies when meaning has gone awry, and so forth; and this repertoire includes the productive strategy of occasionally skipping problem words and not even returning to them, if they seem not to affect meaning significantly. Such strategies are used simultaneously and cyclically more than linearly.

3. Readers who make many miscues—either on isolated words, connected text, or both—may nevertheless construct meaning effectively from appropriate texts. Consequently, testing readers on isolated words, or even assessing their reading by considering the strategies reflected by their miscues, may often underestimate the ability of seemingly less proficient readers to construct meaning from connected, coherent, and authentic text.

From such conclusions as these, educators grounded in miscue research reflect a significantly different set of assumptions in their teaching and assessment of readers:

1. Reading should not be considered first or foremost a matter of identifying words, but rather a matter of constructing meaning from connected, coherent, and authentic text.

2. Readers do not have to be able to demonstrate word-reading skills in isolation from actual reading in order to make effective use of those skills (or strategies) during actual reading. Furthermore, the most important strategies they need to develop are strategies

for constructing meaning from text, even when words are not or cannot be identified.

3. Scores on standardized tests are not nearly as appropriate for understanding or assessing students' reading as the process of recording and analyzing their miscues and comparing this information with notes from their retelling and discussion of the selection.

In part, what this perspective means is that readers diagnosed as dyslexic by means of standardized test scores and/or by means of the number or nature of their errors in identifying words may not be seen as dyslexic at all, when assessed though miscue analysis.

This revaluing of readers reflects the research-derived conclusion that reading means not identifying words per se, but constructing meaning from text (see, too, other lines of research and theory, such as that found in Rosenblatt, 1978, and in the subsequent reader-response theory of literature). Most educators steeped in miscue analysis would prefer not to think of *readers* themselves as dyslexic at all. Rather, we might define dyslexia as the ineffective use or coordination of strategies to construct meaning from conceptually appropriate and aurally comprehensible texts. Locating dyslexia within the strategies and their coordinated use, not within the reader, this reconceptualization emphasizes the possibility that the ineffectiveness of the strategies may result partly or mostly from teachers' or parents' conceptualizing reading as first and foremost a matter of identifying words, and providing instruction that reflects this view (Weaver, 1994, Ch. 11).

Miscue analysis does not automatically offer any means of deciding between the deficiency hypothesis and the delay hypothesis, insofar as the less-than-fully-effective reading strategies might actually result from some neurological factor. In fact, though, what we often have reason to suspect is that the neurological function may be more instructionally induced than genetically programmed. In other words, instruction overly focused on word identification may have promoted a delay in learning to coordinate needed reading strategies effectively.

Dyslexia as Instructionally Induced

Because of the pervasive concept of reading as first and foremost a matter of identifying words, readers who have word-identification difficulties have traditionally been given instruction that places even more emphasis on word identification and promotes a limited range of strategies for identifying words. This discourages them from developing the strategies needed to construct meaning effectively.

That is, students considered to be poorer readers are especially likely to spend most of their reading time in oral reading, done round robin—in trying to say the words correctly while the teacher listens and corrects (Allington, 1983, 1989b). When readers in higher groups make a miscue, teachers typically ignore the miscue or suggest how the context may clarify meaning; that is, they recommend a strategy that is crucial in constructing meaning from texts. But when readers in lower reading groups make a miscue, teachers typically stop them and often call attention to the letter/sound cues exclusively or correct the miscues immediately, thus giving the students in lower groups much less impetus or opportunity to discover a lack of continuity in meaning and to correct themselves. Overall, teachers have traditionally had students in lower reading groups spend most of their time doing skill and drill work on isolated words and in reading orally as if each and every word had to be decoded, and decoded without any reference to the context (see summaries in McGill-Franzen & Allington, 1991; Allington & McGill-Franzen, 1989a; Shannon, 1985; Hillerich, 1985; Cazden, 1985). Inadvertently but systematically, such teaching must convey to less proficient readers the impression that they can't read independently because they can't identify all the words without help. Furthermore, by failing to encourage the development and coordination of effective strategies for constructing meaning, such instruction also inadvertently promotes "dyslexia," as I have defined it.

It should not be surprising, then, that the students most likely to be dosed with such skills-oriented instruction are those taught in Title 1 programs and those labeled learning disabled or dyslexic—in other words, the students who have suffered the most from such instruction in the first place. Nor should it be surprising that such dyslexia-inducing instruction serves to perpetuate their status as labeled readers (McGill-Franzen & Allington, 1991; Allington & McGill-Franzen, 1987), or that students once assigned to traditional kinds of remedial or compensatory programs typically remain in such classes ear after year (Anderson & Pellicer, 1990). At least one reason may be that they are genuinely not becoming proficient at using and coordinating the strategies that miscue research shows to be characteristic of good readers.

Learning about Proficient Reading from the Miscues of Good Readers

Before presenting a particular case study of an allegedly dyslexic reader, it is important to clarify the concept of miscues, how miscues are conventionally marked, and what has been learned from good readers about the strategies most important in constructing meaning.

Kenneth Goodman adopted the term "miscue" in the 1960s to describe any departure the reader makes from the actual words of the text (e.g., K. Goodman, 1965). For example, if a reader substitutes one word for another, omits or adds a word, or reorganizes a sequence of words, he or she has made a miscue. Goodman's purpose in using this term "miscue" was two-fold. First, he wanted to avoid the notion that every departure from the words of the text is necessarily bad, something to be considered an error. Second, he wanted to emphasize how such departures from the text indicate which language cue systems the reader is using and not using, at least at that particular moment—the moment of the missed cue(s). The pattern of miscues is then examined for insight into the use of reading strategies.

There are three major cue systems within the language of a text:

SYNTACTIC CUES:	that is, grammatical cues like word order, function words, and word endings
SEMANTIC CUES:	that is, meaning cues from each sentence and from the evolving whole, as the reader progresses through the entire text
GRAPHO/PHONEMIC CUES:	that is, letter/sound cues, the correspondences between letters (graphemes) and sounds (phonemes) and the larger letter/sound patterns

Rarely does a miscue show attention to only one of these language cue systems. The following are some extraordinarily "pure" examples, and even in most of these cases, the reader has paid attention to more than one kind of language cue (Weaver, 1988, 1994, Ch. 1) (see Figure 1).

Figure 2 (Y. Goodman, Watson, & Burke, 1987) indicates how to interpret the major markings in the transcript from Jay's reading, and in the later examples from Erica's reading. (One or more letters followed by a hyphen indicate that the reader uttered what he or she apparently considered only part of a word, judging by the reader's intonation.)

An example of Jay's reading (Figure 3) further shows how good readers typically construct meaning as they read, and sometimes even reconstruct the grammar of texts in doing so. Once you can read the passage fluently, with Jay's miscues intact, it should be instructive to ask someone who is prevented from seeing the transcript to keep track of the miscues noticed as you read the passage aloud. Experience suggests that most listeners notice few if any miscues, an observation that helps those new to miscue analysis appreciate why Jay was considered an excellent reader: the most proficient reader in his sixth grade

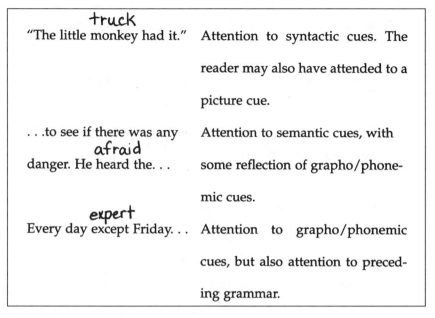

Figure 1. Miscue example.

class. The passage is from an O. Henry story, "Jimmy Hayes and Muriel" (O'Henry, 1936, p. 670).

Almost all of Jay's miscues fit the context: the preceding syntactic and semantic context, and the following syntactic and semantic context. In fact, when Jay made a miscue that would disrupt the structure of the text, he then made other miscues to restore grammatical structure. He drew upon prior knowledge, changing *frog*(s) to "toad(s)," and he even added to the dialect O. Henry was trying to portray by reading *blame* as "blamed." In short, Jay effectively coordinated prior knowledge with preceding context to predict; as he read, he monitored how the text sounded (i.e., "Does it sound like language?") and what it meant ("Does this make sense?"); and he employed fix-it strategies to maintain both syntactic appropriateness and a coherent, meaning-preserving rendition of the text. As one would reasonably predict, Jay's retelling of the text was excellent. Analysis of the miscues and concomitant comprehension of thousands of readers suggests that these are hallmarks of proficient and efficient readers (e.g. K. Goodman, 1973).

In short, when good readers read connected and natural text rather than lists of words, observers find themselves concluding that proficient and efficient reading is not miscueless, nor in many cases even close to miscueless. Though many good readers do make fewer miscues than

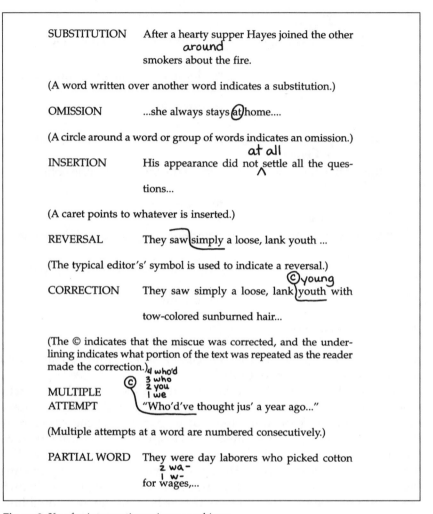

Figure 2. Key for interpreting miscue markings.

substantially poorer readers, the *critical* difference is the quality of the miscues, and/or the readers' ability to construct meaning from appropriate texts. Or in other words, a good reader could make as many miscues as a less effective reader, but the use of language cues and reading strategies would ordinarily be different. Typically this difference is reflected in their differing use of context—the degree to which they use context along with prior knowledge to predict and then to confirm or correct as they read.

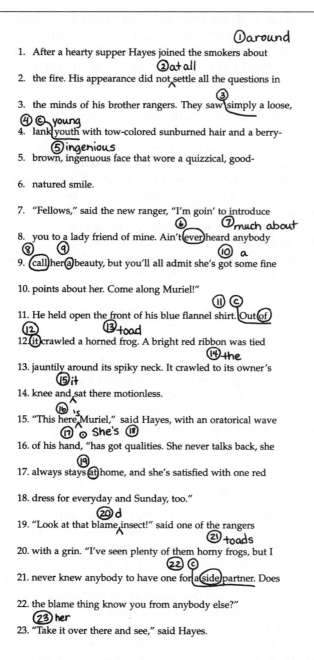

①around
1. After a hearty supper Hayes joined the smokers about
②at all
2. the fire. His appearance did not settle all the questions in
③
3. the minds of his brother rangers. They saw simply a loose,
④ ⓒ young
4. lank youth with tow-colored sunburned hair and a berry-
⑤ingenious
5. brown, ingenuous face that wore a quizzical, good-

6. natured smile.

7. "Fellows," said the new ranger, "I'm goin' to introduce
⑥ ⑦much about
8. you to a lady friend of mine. Ain't ever heard anybody
⑧ ⑨ ⑩ a
9. call her a beauty, but you'll all admit she's got some fine

10. points about her. Come along Muriel!"
⑪ ⓒ
11. He held open the front of his blue flannel shirt. Out of
⑫ ⑬toad
12. it crawled a horned frog. A bright red ribbon was tied
⑭the
13. jauntily around its spiky neck. It crawled to its owner's
⑮it
14. knee and sat there motionless.
⑯ 's
15. "This here Muriel," said Hayes, with an oratorical wave
⑰ o She's ⑱
16. of his hand, "has got qualities. She never talks back, she
⑲
17. always stays at home, and she's satisfied with one red

18. dress for everyday and Sunday, too."
⑳d
19. "Look at that blame insect!" said one of the rangers
㉑ toads
20. with a grin. "I've seen plenty of them horny frogs, but I
㉒ ⓒ
21. never knew anybody to have one for a side partner. Does

22. the blame thing know you from anybody else?"
㉓ her
23. "Take it over there and see," said Hayes.

Figure 3. Jay's reading.

Thus miscue analysis indicates that reading is more a strategic process of constructing meaning than a matter of identifying words per se. Word identification is after all a means to an end, and that end is commonly achieved with substantially less than perfect identification of words, even among readers who are both effective and efficient at constructing meaning.

Given this example of Jay and the subsequent discussion, it should be obvious that from the perspective of miscue analysis, the major problem with a traditional characterization of dyslexia is the underlying notion that reading means identifying words correctly. In addition, the consequent and exclusive use of word identification tests and timed comprehension tests to diagnose dyslexia is viewed as equally damaging, because it results in identifying as dyslexic many readers who are reasonably proficient at constructing meaning, given enough world knowledge and time.

In the next section we shall consider the reading of just such a reader: a girl named Erica.

Dyslexia Reconsidered: The Case of Erica

Erica's reading has been analyzed at different times and in different ways. In the primary grades, she was judged dyslexic by traditional criteria. Her fifth grade teacher and I concluded that she was not dyslexic, based upon the alternative definition I have developed and the evidence from Erica's miscues. Two years later, I conducted some further assessment with Erica and concluded that she might nevertheless have a word-finding difficulty that her parents and teachers should consider how to circumvent.

Erica in the Primary Grades

Erica's kindergarten teacher noted that she had difficulty attending to tasks except in a one-on-one setting. With regard to "reading readiness," the teacher noted that Erica only confused a couple of letters (*u* and *v*) by the third marking period, and she could give most consonant sounds. Erica spent a second year in kindergarten, though, because she was deemed not ready for the demands of first grade. Near the end of first grade, Erica scored in the middle range in reading on the Stanford Achievement test, but her reading scores were considerably less strong than those for listening. Her first grade teacher noted that she needed improvement in sight vocabulary, word attack skills, and phonics skills, indicating that she had difficulty with short vowel sounds and with reversed letters in writing; the teacher noted that "visual and auditory discrimination difficulties limit her output." Like her kindergarten teachers, her first grade teacher indicated that Erica was very interested in learning and tried hard, though she had difficulty concentrating except when working individually with the teacher.

During March of her first grade year, Erica was referred for a learning disability evaluation by a psychologist, who noted that "Erica's academic problems began in kindergarten when she demonstrated visual perceptual problems." Administering a battery of psychological tests, the psychologist indicated that she tested in the average range on the verbal scale and in the above average range on the performance scale of the WISC-R, with great variation among various subtests. His conclusion: "This variability and the pattern of scores is suggestive of Specific Developmental Dyslexia." Furthermore, he indicated that when reading single words, Erica's most frequent errors were reversals and word calling errors, such as "when" for *then*. She obtained a score of 1.0 on the IOTA word list. When reading paragraphs aloud, she scored at the 1.3 grade level on the Gray Oral Reading Test. "She demonstrated good comprehension when she was able to read a significant number of the words." However, the discrepancy between her intellectual development and her grade level scores on these tests ("she should have the academic skills of a late second grader") led the psychologist to conclude that her "highly significant deficits in reading and spelling" and the types of errors were "highly suggestive of Specific Developmental Dyslexia."

Further noted were Erica's word finding difficulties and word choice errors ("bath them"), apparently in speech. Perceptual tests indicated that Erica had difficulty discriminating between visual stimuli, which "appeared to be due to the reversal and transposition of sequential information," such as choosing "dady" for "baby." Finally, the psychologist noted that such deficits in visual processing, which have often been referred to as "visual dyslexia," meant that Erica might have difficulty developing a sight vocabulary for reading and spelling. The recommendation: individual tutoring with a structured multisensory phonetic approach, the Orton Gillingham method being the treatment of choice. Erica was also diagnosed as having an attention deficit disorder.

For the next six school years, Erica continued to have resource room tutoring. For four of those six years, she was tutored by a teacher with training in the Orton-Gillingham approach, though the teaching went beyond strict O-G methodology. The final third grade report from her resource room teacher was, however, focused entirely on isolated skills, such as the identification of single consonants, short vowels, syllable patterns, syllable divisions, spelling rules and generalizations, and a few other areas. The teacher noted that Erica still made frequent errors with syllable patterns.

Fortunately, Erica's work on language skills in isolation never deterred her interest in reading literature, which was fostered in the regular classroom settings and noted by virtually all of her teachers.

Erica in the Fifth Grade

When I met her, Erica was clearly a bright fifth grader who enjoyed discussing literature and who offered insightful comments into the characters' feelings and motivations. However, both her writing and her reading were rather slow and painful—much less fluent than one would have predicted from her intelligence and liveliness. Each week she attended reading classes with two different special reading teachers.

Her classroom teacher and I decided to see what we could learn from analyzing Erica's miscues. The class was reading and discussing *Roll of Thunder, Hear My Cry,* by Mildred Taylor, with me reading and discussing the book with the least proficient readers, including Erica. Below are excerpts from a passage she read while her teacher, Ruth Perino, listened and tape recorded the session. The story revolves around a black girl, Cassie, and her family in the rural South in the 1930s. At this point in the story, Cassie has just been ignored by a storekeeper as soon as white customers enter the store, then scolded and told to leave the store when she protested this treatment. Shortly after she and her older brother Stacey part from each other outside the store, she has another painful awakening: she accidentally bumps into a white classmate on the sidewalk, Lillian Jean, and is humiliated by being forced to apologize and then to walk in the street.

Subsequent retelling and discussion of the reading demonstrated that Erica's understanding of the text was excellent.

In analyzing Erica's use of language cues and reading strategies through her miscues, the following questions were considered. In every instance, her miscues warranted a response of "almost always." The examples should clarify this strong affirmative (see Examples 1–4). Each example shows Erica making an appropriate prediction from context. Her prior knowledge of the story is especially evident in Example 1 in the miscue "wearily" for *wryly,* and even more in "proudly" for *properly:* Cassie was indeed a proud young girl.

For Example 2, in each instance, Erica corrected the miscue when it did not sound like language or make sense with what followed in the sentence.

> 1. *Does the reader use prior knowledge and context to predict effectively?*
> Yes, almost always:
>
> 2 when the-
> I when you
> "You bumped into me. Now you apologize."
>
> glanced
> I stopped and gazed over my shoulder...
>
> wearily
> Stacey laughed wryly.
>
> © 2 proudly
> I proudl-
> "I ain't nasty," I said properly holding my temper in check.

Example 1.

Example 3 shows Erica making good use of grapho/phonemic cues along with prior knowledge and context. When the actual word was not something that made sense to her in context (*flush*, in the first example, and *apologize*, the first time it occurred), she was unable to get the word using grapho/phonemic cues alone. But when context supported her sounding-out strategy, she was able to get the word. Indeed, she didn't need to sound out *apologize* the second time she encountered it: the word made sense to her in this context. Thus Erica was quite effective in using grapho/phonemic cues *along* with semantic and syntactic cues.

Considering Erica's excellent understanding of the passage and her highly effective use of reading strategies, researchers and educators

> 2. *Does the reader monitor comprehension and correct, or try to correct, miscues that don't make sense in context?* Yes, almost always:
>
> © Don't ca- © to
> "You can't watch where you going, get in the road.
>
> © 's © discount
> Maybe that way you won't be bumping into decent
>
> white folks with your little nasty self."

Example 2.

3. *Does the reader use grapho/phonemic cues effectively, along with prior knowledge and context?* Yes, almost always:

3 gruffily
2 flusk   2 gruf-
1 flu   © 1 gruf-
Stacey swallowed to flush his anger, then said|gruf-

2 sul-
© 1 silen-
fly,... He crossed the street|sullenly.

a-a-ah-ā-ā-āpō-apolə-gĭz- āpolah'gĭz
"Well, apologize," she ordered.

"What?"

2 when the-
1 when you
You bumped into me. Now you apologize."

Example 3.

4. *Do the sentences, as the reader left them, make sense in the context of the story? (Or, do the sentences preserve meanings essential to the story?)* Yes, as almost all of the previous examples would suggest. Indeed, though Erica did not regress and overtly correct her first prolonged attempt at sounding out *apologize*, it was obvious from her reading as well as later discussion that she realized the word had been *apologize*.

In short, Erica makes highly effective use of reading strategies.

Example 4.

whose thinking reflects the assumptions derived from decades of miscue analysis would certainly not consider her dyslexic. It is also relevant that she enjoyed reading, as indicated in Example 5, where she reflected upon her reading tastes and habits. Thus as a fifth grader Erica seemed neither dyslexic nor alliterate. Her classroom teacher and I further concluded that *if* Erica had ever needed and/or benefited from tutoring on isolated elements of phonics (which we questioned), there

Example 5. Erica's description of herself as a reader.

was certainly no indication that further work on phonics in isolation would benefit Erica as a reader. Her original need for an effective sounding-out strategy was even more critical than that of readers who can easily read most words they encounter on sight, but like proficient adult readers, Erica was already proficient at sounding out words when meaning could come to her aid.

What I did use with Erica, however, is an instructional procedure called Retrospective Miscue Analysis, or RMA (Marek, 1989; Y. Goodman & Marek, 1989, 1996). The reader is tape recorded, the teacher usually selects the miscues for discussion, and the reader and the teacher consider the miscues together—either by looking at the miscues marked on a copy of the selection, or by listening to the tape, or both. That is, they consider in retrospect the reader's miscues and the reading strategies they reflect. This provides the context for promoting more effective use of reading strategies, as needed. See Table 1 for suggestions as to when RMA might be appropriate and what the teacher and student might concentrate on, in each instance.

Retrospective Miscue Analysis

Below are some reader characteristics, with suggestions for the kinds of miscues a teacher, tutor, or clinician might choose for discussion

Table 1

Occasions for doing Retrospective Miscue Analysis

Reader characteristics	Kinds of miscues that could be examined
Lacks self-confidence	Select miscues that fit the context appropriately.
Thinks reading means getting all the words	Select miscues that fit the context appropriately; might also consider the completely acceptable miscues of someone who is clearly a good reader—perhaps the teacher.
Seldom corrects miscues that don't go with the following context	Compare miscues that didn't go with following context but were corrected with similar miscues that weren't corrected.
Makes miscues that don't go with the preceding context	Compare miscues that do go with the preceding context with those that don't.
Makes non-word substitutions that suggest underuse of syntactic and semantic cues and overuse of grapho/phonemic cues	Select miscues wherein all three kinds of cues were used effectively: contrast with miscues that reflect a sounding out strategy with insufficient regard for meaning and/or grammatical cues.
Makes non-word substitutions for words in reader's oral vocabulary	Select miscues where persistence resulted in real words that fit the context; contrast these with the nonword substitutions.
Makes miscues that suggest difficulty in sounding out long words that are in their speaking vocabulary	Select miscues where sounding out has been successfully used in conjunction with prior knowledge and context; contrast with miscues where the reader seems not to have used an effective sounding-out strategy for multi-syllabic words, or not to have used this strategy along with prior knowledge and context cues.
Consistently corrects high quality miscues that fit the context	Select fully acceptable miscues where correction is unnecessary.

in each case. These are a combination of Ann Mark's practices (Marek, 1992) and my own (Weaver, 1994). Marek's purpose in contrasting miscues that do exemplify a desirable strategy with those that don't is to demonstrate to the reader that he or she is capable of using the strategy and just needs to use it more consistently.

> When listening to miscues that don't fit the context, teachers can ask "Does that make sense?" and/or "Does that sound like language?" Often, readers will quickly internalize these questions and comment spontaneously that "that doesn't sound right."

After having Erica recapitulate the reading strategies her literature discussion group had brainstormed, I told Erica that while we replayed the tape recording of her reading, I would like her to stop the tape recorder whenever she heard herself making a good miscue; that is, a miscue that reflected a good reading strategy. Of course she was then to explain why it was a good miscue—what good reading strategies she was using as she tried to construct meaning from text. Erica was absolutely thrilled to hear herself making good miscues and to be able to explain why they were good. She still thought of herself as dyslexic because others thought of her that way, but she also came to realize that she used reading strategies effectively to construct meaning.

Erica in the Seventh Grade

More recently, toward the end of Erica's seventh-grade year, Erica agreed to work with me to try to give us further insight into her reading strengths and difficulties. In the intervening two years, for some of her reading and language arts instruction she had continued to go to a resource room, where she received tutoring with a heavy emphasis on phonics. When we first met again, Erica indicated that yes, she was still considered to be dyslexic and still considered to have an attention deficit disorder, though the latter no longer seemed to cause her problems in school.

Using mostly questions from Carolyn Burke's reading interview (included in Y. Goodman, Watson, & Burke, 1987; and adapted in Weaver, 1988, 1994), I asked about the reading strategies Erica was aware of using in dealing with problem words. Here was her first response:

> Sometimes I just sit and stare at the word. 'Cause I know what it is and I just can't say it. But at times I sound it, but it's not my first choice. Or I'll read the word before it and after it and I'll probably know what the word is in the middle. Or I'll just leave the word out of the sentence.

During our second meeting, Erica described her strategies similarly:

> I go over words I don't know and try to decode it. Or I'll try to read the rest of the sentence and I'll probably know what the word is. Or if I just know the meaning I'll try and see if it fits with the sentence. And if it makes sense I'll read on. And if it doesn't, I'll try and make the sentence make sense.

I asked if the latter was a strategy someone had taught her or one that she learned on her own. "I learned it on my own," was her response.

She later indicated that she sometimes gets a word by spelling it out, a strategy that I observed while listening to her read. Our conversation also gave me insight into her sounding out strategy. I asked whether she tended to lose meaning when she spent a lot of time sounding out a word (a leading question, to say the least!). Erica's response was:

> Sometimes I just lose it because sometimes when I decode words
> I take the first, two [letters], then the next two. If that doesn't work,
> I'll try the first three, until I get it.

This, too, was a strategy she had developed on her own. Interestingly, she did not seem to have made much use of her years of phonics skills training in developing a workable sounding-out strategy.

We again did Retrospective Miscue Analysis, with both of us listening to a tape recording of her reading and Erica listening for good reading strategies to describe. This time, what she mostly commented upon was how she had sounded out words successfully. Together, we noted how she used context to help: how, for instance, the phrase *trickled down my arm* had helped her in sounding out the preceding word, *perspiration*.

What Erica had chosen to read for me was not a more difficult text than she had read for miscue analysis in the fifth grade, but a sequel containing the same characters and essentially the same kind of language: *Let the Circle Be Unbroken*, by Mildred Taylor. Therefore, I was surprised and disappointed to notice that more often than previously, Erica didn't even try to correct some of the miscues that didn't sound grammatical or didn't make sense. When we talked, I suggested that though she was doing an excellent job with problem words, she might not be doing as good a job as two years ago in trying to say words that would make sense in context: "You might be concentrating so much on saying the exact word on the page, that you're losing sense more. Am I right?" (Another leading question, unfortunately.) Erica's response was, "Yeah. I can spend two minutes on just one word. I have to go back."

Given the previously demonstrated effectiveness of Erica's reading strategies, I was not convinced that this trade-off was necessarily an improvement in Erica's reading. What seemed to be happening was that the effort to sound out some words until she finally got them right was sapping her energy so much that she would let other words go, even though what she had said didn't sound like language and/or didn't make sense in context. (For example: The sentence *Mama had some milk and preserves and stuff she wanted 'em to have* was read as "Ma had just milked a per-serv-es and stuffed she wanted 'em to have.") Erica seemed convinced, however, that it was important for her to sound out every word she couldn't immediately recognize. The six years of phonics work had perhaps been taken too strongly to heart, as her reading seemed even slower and more labored than before, though there was no noticeable difference in her construction of meaning.

What triggered some of my latest insights into Erica's reading, though, was a contrasting perspective offered by Diane German of the National College of Education, an expert on word-finding disorders (German, 1983, 1992; see also *Word Finding Problems*, 1992), who heard me give a presentation that focused on Erica's miscues. Asking me if Erica could read words better silently than orally, Diane suggested that I take words that Erica had difficulty reading out loud and see if she could select them from, in each case, a list of four words. When I did so, the results were amazing: Erica could identify the "problem" words quickly and accurately, even when the other words in the set were visually similar.

This data from the second of our recent sessions correlated with other data that I was beginning to accumulate from the interviews/ discussions with Erica, and from her additional reading. When we were discussing Erica's concept of reading and her reading strategies, she commented that

> What happens to me is I can read real good inside my head, fast, but when I read out loud, it . . . I don't know. . . . When I read big words in my head, I know them like that. But when I read out loud, it's like "What?" But when I know it in my head, I can't really say it. . . . I read better without talking out loud.

Furthermore, in reading lists of words for me, Erica several times muttered under her breath "I know that word" before trying, in frustration, to sound out longer words (short words were relatively easy for her). As Diane German had thought, Erica's problem with oral reading seems to lie not in understanding frequently encountered words, but simply in translating them as wholes from their visual representation into a phonological representation. Another researcher, Elbro, has suggested that so-called visual dyslexics may not necessarily have trouble with visual processing per se, but with rendering the visual representation orally. As he noted in one of his research studies comparing adolescents labeled as dyslexic with unlabeled readers of the same reading age, "The most striking finding was that dyslexic adolescents traditionally termed 'visually' impaired or 'dyseidetic' [Boder's term] because of relatively poor whole-word reading seemed to be impaired by slow lexical access to whole-word phonology"

(Elbro, 1991a, p. 238). Perhaps this is a problem with coordinating the functioning of the two cerebral hemispheres. In any case, a consideration of Erica's reading of words suggests that this kind of problem may account for her dysfluency in reading aloud.

Unfortunately, Erica now seems to think that reading well means reading out loud. Perhaps related to this perception is the fact that Erica no longer likes reading so much, especially in school, where they read round-robin with about ten people taking turns reading only a paragraph or two.

Conclusions and Recommendations

The more recent analysis of Erica's miscues, using reading material that is virtually the same as before, leads me to conclude that she is now closer to being dyslexic than she was two years ago, if we define dyslexia not in terms of identifying words but in terms of using and coordinating strategies for constructing meaning. To some extent, instruction may have induced a tendency toward dyslexia, so defined. However, the reading interviews suggest that Erica still knows that reading is supposed to be meaningful, and that she reads much more for meaning than for mere word identification when reading silently. Analysis of the miscues still shows good use of strategies for constructing meaning, even though the pattern is not quite as consistent as before.

Combining insights from the recent miscue analysis with insights from the word-identification assessment suggested by Diane German, I would again conclude that Erica has only a slight tendency toward dyslexia as I have defined it, but that she may indeed have difficulty translating written words into spoken words—especially when the written words are presented in isolation, without surrounding context to provide clues. According to Erica's account, the problem is much less severe, perhaps non-existent, when Erica can go directly from the printed text to meaning, as she does when reading silently.

Together, these conclusions give rise to the following recommendations:

1. That Erica spend her time reading silently in school rather than in reading aloud.
2. That she be encouraged to read books that she chooses; to keep a dialogue journal or literature log; to discuss books with other classmates and the teacher; and within the context of literature discussions, to discuss various strategies for coping with text and with problem words.

3. That she be helped to understand that good readers do skip words when the meaning doesn't seem to be endangered, and that this might be a strategy she should consider adopting.

4. That in reading more challenging texts, she receive tutorial help as needed, to focus her attention more on constructing meaning than on identifying every word.

5. That as she progresses in school, her parents and her teacher consider the appropriateness of having her textbooks recorded on tape, if this would significantly lessen the time required to understand the material. Such a support strategy may be important in high school and especially college, when the volume of required reading may otherwise become too great.

These suggested strategies capitalize upon Erica's reading strengths while minimizing or circumventing her difficulties as a reader.

Figure 4 provides a brief annotated bibliography of resources for understanding some of the insights from miscue research, learning how to analyze readers' miscues, and using insights from miscue research and from the analysis of individual readers' miscues to help them become more proficient as readers.

Conclusion

Miscue analysis research suggests, then, that if teachers and clinicians want to help children become genuine readers, it is crucial first of all to conceptualize reading as a matter of constructing meaning from text, not as a matter of identifying every word. One of the major benefits of such a reconceptualization is that it leads us to view as proficient many readers who otherwise would be perceived merely as nonproficient at word identification. That is, it helps us realize that what from a conventional perspective would be perceived as a weakness in identifying words may better be considered as a strength in constructing meaning, as we have seen through Jay's miscues. In consequence, this reconceptualization of reading leads us to emphasize readers' strengths in constructing meaning and to downplay possible weaknesses in identifying words, as I have done with Erica.

More than that, however, the miscue research (e.g., K. Goodman, 1973; Brown, Goodman, & Marek, 1996) encourages us to help readers develop strategies for becoming genuinely effective readers, not mere word-callers who read so ineffectively that they may be permanently consigned to remedial instruction that perpetuates their difficulties.

Goodman, Y. M., D. J. Watson, and C. L. Burke 1987. *Reading miscue inventory: Alternative procedures.* Katonah, NY: Richard C. Owen. For beginners and experienced analyzers alike, this book describes insights from miscue research, explains step-by-step how to do miscue analysis, and offers four different forms for miscue analysis.

Goodman, Y. M., D. J. Watson, and C. L. Burke. 1996. *Reading Strategies: Focus on comprehension.* (2nd ed.). Katonah, NY: Richard C. Owen. Includes strategy lessons for various needs and levels.

Goodman, Y. M., and A. M. Marek, eds. 1996. *Retrospective miscue analysis; Revaluing readers and reading.* Katonah, NY: Richard C. Owen. Offers important insights into the reading process and how one can work with readers.

Goodman, Y. M., and A. M. Marek. 1989. *Retrospective miscue analysis: Two papers.* Occasional Papers No. 19. Tucson, AZ: Program in Language and Literacy, University of Arizona. Explains RMA and its benefits.

Marek, A. M. 1989. Using evaluation as an instructional strategy for adult readers. In *The whole language evaluation book,* eds. K. S. Goodman, Y. M. Goodman, and W. J. Hood. Portsmouth, NH: Heinemann. Demonstrates how Retrospective Miscue Analysis can help readers gain confidence in their reading. 157–164.

Norris, J., and P. Hoffman. 1993. *Whole languge intervention for schoolage children.* San Diego: Singular Publishing Group. Describes Communicative Reading Strategies, a procedure whereby tutors and clinicians can help individuals process written language more effectively.

Rhodes, L. K., and C. Dudley-Marling. 1996. *Readers and writers with a difference: A holistic approach to teaching struggling readers and writers* (2nd ed.). Portsmouth, NH: Heinemann. Gives sample miscue analyses of poor readers, describes ways of helping readers develop more effective reading strategies, and much more.

Routman, R. 1991. *Invitations: Changing as teachers and learners K–12.* Portsmouth, NH: Heinemann. Chapter 14 describes ways of helping learning disabled readers develop more effective reading strategies. Excellent for those new to whole language teaching.

Weaver, Constance. 1994. *Reading process and practice: From sociopsycholinguistics to whole language.* (2nd ed.) Portsmouth, NH: Heinemann. Discusses the reading process as illuminated by miscue analysis research; provides step-by-step directions for conducting a miscue analysis; discusses ways of fostering effective reading strategies, including Retrospective Miscue Analysis; offers a systems-theory model of dyslexia and learning disabilities; demonstrates the effectiveness of whole language teaching with labeled students: and more.

Figure 4. Resources on miscue insights, miscue analysis, and teaching reading strategies.

Over time, readers need to develop a variety of strategies for constructing meaning from text, revising those meanings as necessary, and dealing with words in the construction of meaning. These include the strategies of (1) drawing upon prior knowledge to make sense of text and to identify words; (2) predicting from context as well as prior knowledge; (3) coordinating all the language cue systems in the quest for meaning; and (4) confirming and correcting words and understanding as one reads. These strategies can be effectively taught—and their actual use most effectively developed (Kucer, 1992)—within the context of authentic reading experiences Below are some of these procedures and contexts.

1. Reading aloud. After reading a book aloud to students, the teacher may comment on his/her reading strategies, such as the strategies used when encountering a difficult word.

2. Mini-lessons. The teacher may conduct brief mini-lessons on a reading strategy, for a student or group who seem to need it, or occasionally for the whole class. A key aspect of such mini-lessons in whole language classrooms is that the teacher does not immediately ask the student(s) to do independent practice using such a strategy, nor does the teacher test the students on their understanding of the strategy (Atwell, 1987; Calkins, 1986; Weaver, 1994, Ch. 9). Rather, the teacher observes children's progress in adopting the strategy in typical reading situations, such as individual conferences, and re-teaches the strategy as needed.

3. Discussion of reading strategies in the context of a shared reading experience (Holdaway, 1979: described in Weaver, 1994).

4. Discussions in literature groups. The teacher can invite students to make note of troublesome words or passages in their reading journals (see below) and make sure that the subsequent discussions in literature groups include consideration of reading problems and strategies for dealing with them.

5. Class discussions, drawing from their shared experiences with literature, notes in their literature logs, and so forth. For example, teacher and students can compile a list of reading strategies for dealing with problem words—a list that can be displayed in the classroom and called to students' attention as needed. A fairly complete list might look something like this, worded in adult language:

   A. THINK what would make sense here; then, more or less simultaneously

continued on next page

Figure 5. Demonstration and discussion of reading strategies.

Figure 5 continued

    B. Try to sound it out, and/or

    C. Look at meaningful parts.

    D. Regress and read.

    E. Substitute a word that seems to make sense, or a placeholder word like "something," and go on.

    F. Continue—see if following context clarifies:

      If YES, continue reading.

      If NO, decide if the word is important.

        If NO, continue reading.

        If YES, regress and reread and/or ask someone and/or look it up in a dictionary or reference book.

6. Tape recording and discussion of a reader's miscues: what has come to be known as Retrospective Miscue Analysis (Marek, 1989; Y. Goodman and Mark, 1989; see Table 1.)

Figure 5. Demonstration and discussion of reading strategies.

The miscue research also provides us with the understanding and the impetus to help readers develop strategies for constructing meaning. Ironically, one of the easiest ways to do this is to broaden the repertoire of strategies we help children develop for identifying or otherwise dealing with individual words. Figure 5 includes a list of word-handling strategies I brainstormed with a college class. Developing a similar list with children can be an excellent starting point for encouraging them to focus on constructing meaning and to use meaning as a cue for dealing with problem words, simultaneous with other cues such as letter/sound patterns and meaningful word parts.

In short, reconceptualizing reading as constructing meaning and reconceptualizing dyslexia as the ineffective use and/or coordination of strategies for constructing meaning leads to many benefits for the individual reader. So does the idea of circumventing weaknesses rather than dwelling on them, particularly if these weaknesses seem particularly resistant to instructional alleviation. This instructional strategy will be especially important if the reader's strategies do in fact stem from some neurological limitation (deficiency) instead of merely resulting from a maturational or instruction-induced delay. Helping readers develop and orchestrate strategies for constructing meaning while reading interesting and conceptually appropriate text is one of the basics of whole language teaching. In this context, Retrospective Miscue Analysis (Marek, 1989; Y. Goodman & Marek, 1989, 1996) and other kinds of scaffolding (e.g., Norris & Hoffman, 1993) are among the best strategies that teachers, tutors, and clinicians can use with individual children. Discussing reading strategies in the context of discussing a work of literature is also one of the best strategies for preventing dyslexia in the first place (e.g., Weaver, 1994, especially Ch. 9).

Acknowledgments

I want to thank Erica for allowing me to work with her, and to thank both Erica and her mother for allowing me to use the data from this informal case study. Never would I have met Erica if it weren't for Ruth Perino, who graciously invited me into her classroom; I thank both Ruth and the director of her school, Bonnie Regelman. 1 am also especially grateful to my colleague Nickola Nelson in the Department of Speech Pathology and Audiology for inviting me to be a speaker in their Van Riper lecture series and thereby introducing me to Diane German and other leading thinkers and researchers in the field of speech and language pathology. Most of the material in this chapter is derived from various chapters of the second edition of my *Reading Process and Practice* (Heinemann, 1994).

References

Adams, M. J. 1990. *Beginning to read: Thinking and learning about print.* Cambridge: Harvard University Press.

Allington, R. L. 1983. "The reading instruction provided readers of differing reading abilities." *The Elementary School Journal* 83: 548–xx9.

———. 1987. "Shattered hopes: Why two federal reading programs have failed to correct reading failure." *Learning* 87: 61–64.

Allington, R. L., and A. McGill-Franzen. 1989a. "Different programs, indifferent instruction." In *Beyond separate education: Quality education for all*, ed. D. Lipsky, and A. Gartner. Baltimore: Paul Brookes, 75–98.

———. 1989b. "School response to reading failure: Instruction for Chapter 1 and special education students in grades two, four, and eight." *The Elementary School Journal* 89: 530–542.

Anderson, L. W., and L. O. Pellicer. 1990. "Synthesis of research on compensatory and remedial education." *Educational Leadership* 48: 1016.

Atwell, N. 1987. *In the middle: Writing, reading, and learning with adolescents.* Portsmouth, NH: Heinemann.

Boder, E. 1973. "Developmental dyslexia: A diagnostic approach based on three atypical reading-spelling patterns." *Developmental Medicine and Child Neurology.* 15: 663–687.

Brown, J., K. S. Goodman, & A. M. Marek. 1996. *Studies in miscue analysis: An annotated bibliography.* Newark, DE: International Reading Association.

Bryant, P. E., and L. Impey. 1986. "The similarities between normal children and dyslexic adults and children." *Cognition* 24: 121–137.

Calkins, L. M. 1986. *The art of teaching writing.* Portsmouth, NH: Heinemann.

Cazden, C. B. 1985. "Social context of learning to read." In *Theoretical models and processes of reading,* 3rd ed., ed. H. Singer & R. B. Ruddell. Newark, DE: International Reading Association, 595–610.

Coltheart, M., J. Masterson, S. Byng, M. Prior, and 1. Riddoch. 1983. "Surface dyslexia." *Quarterly Journal of Experimental Psychology* 32: 469–595.

Coltheart, M., K. Panerson, and J. C. Marshall, eds. 1980. *Deep dyslexia.* Boston: Routledge & Kegan Paul.

Critchley, M. 1970. *The dyslexic child,* 2nd ed. Springfield, IL: Charles C. Thomas.

Elbro, C. 1990. *Differences in dyslexia: A study of reading strategies and deficits in a linguistic perspective.* Copenhagen: Munksgaard International Publishers.

———. 1991a. "Differences in reading strategies reflect differences in linguistic abilities." *International Journal of Applied Linguistics* 1(2): 228–245.

———. 1991b. "Dyslexics and normal beginning readers read by different strategies: A comparison of strategy distributions in dyslexic and normal readers." *International Journal of Applied Linguistics* 1(1): 19–37.

Frith, U. 1985. "Beneath the surface of developmental dyslexia." In *Surface dyslexia,* ed. K. Patterson, J. Marshall, and M. Coltheart. London: Erlbaum.

———. 1986. "A developmental framework for developmental dyslexia." *Annals of Dyslexia,* 36: 69–81.

Fulwiler, T., and A. Young. 1982. *Language connections: Writing and reading across the curriculum.* Urbana, IL: National Council of Teachers of English.

German, D. 1983, 1992. *Word finding referral checklist.* Riverwoods, IL: Word Finding Materials Inc. (distributed by Academic Therapy Publications and Speech Bin).

Goodman, K. 1965. A linguistic study of cues and miscues in reading. *Elementary English,* **42,** 639–643.

———. 1973. "Theoretically based studies of patterns of miscues in oral reading performance." Detroit: Wayne State University. ERIC document no.: ED 079 708.

———. 1982. *Language and literacy: The selected writings of Kenneth S. Goodman.* Ed. Frederick V. Gollash. 2 vols. Boston: Routledge & Kegan Paul.

Goodman, Y., and A. Marek. 1989. *"Retrospective miscue analysis: Two papers."* (Occasional Papers No. 19). Tucson, AZ: University of Arizona, Program in Language and Literacy.

Goodman, Y. M., and A. M. Marek. (Eds.) 1996. *Retrospective miscue analysis: Revaluing readers and reading.* Katonah, NY: Richard C. Owen.

Goodman, Y. M., D. Watson, and C. Burke. 1987. *Reading miscue inventory: Alternative procedures.* Katonah, NY: Richard C. Owen.

Goodman, Y. M., D. J. Watson, and C. L. Burke. 1996. *Reading strategies: Focus on Comprehension.* Katonah, NY: Richard C. Owen.

Goswami, U., and P. Bryant. 1990. *Phonological skills and learning to read.* Hove, East Sussex: Lawrence Erlbaum.

Hillerich, R. L. 1985. "Let's pretend." *Michigan Journal of Reading* 18: (summer): 15, 18. 20.

Holdaway, D. 1979. *The foundations of literacy.* Sydney: Ashton-Scholastic. Available in the United States from Heinemann.

Kucer, S. B. 1992. "Six bilingual Mexican-American students, and their teachers' interpretations of cloze literacy lessons." *The Elementary School Journal.* 92: 550–570.

Marek, A. M. 1989. "Using evaluation as an instructional strategy for adult readers." In *The whole language evaluation book,* ed. K. S. Goodman. Y. M. Goodman. and W. J. Hood. Portsmouth, NH: Heinemann, 157–164.

Marek, A. M. 1992. "Retrospective miscue analysis lesson plan." Distributed at a session on miscue analysis at the International Reading Association annual convention, Orlando, Fla., May, 1992.

McGill-Franzen, A., and R. Allington. 1991. "The gridlock of low reading achievement: Perspectives on practice and policy." *Remedial and Special Education* 12: 20–30.

Monaghan, E. 1980. "A history of the syndrome of dyslexia with implications for its treatment." In *Inchworm, inchworm: Persistent problems in reading education,* ed. C. McCullough. Newark, DE: International Reading Association, 87–101.

Norris, J., and P. Hoffman. 1993. *Whole language intervention for school-age children.* San Diego: Singular Publishing.

O. Henry [William S. Porter]. 1936. *The complete works of O. Henry.* Garden City, NY: Doubleday, Doran.

Phinney, M. Y. 1988. *Reading with the troubled reader.* Richmond Hill, Ontario: Scholastic. Available in the United States from Heinemann.

Rhodes, L. K., and C. Dudley-Marling. 1988. *Readers and writers with a difference: A holistic approach to teaching learning disabled and remedial students.* Portsmouth, NH: Heinemann.

Rosenblatt, L. 1978. *The reader, the text, the poem: The transactional theory of the literary work.* Carbondale, IL: Southern Illinois University Press.

Routman, R. 1991. *Invitations: Changing as teachers and learners K–12.* Portsmouth, NH: Heinemann.

Shannon, P. 1985. "Reading instruction and social class." *Language Arts* 62: 604–613.

Shaywitz, S. E., M. D. Escobar, B. A. Shaywitz, J. M. Fletcher, and R. Makuch. 1992. "Evidence that dyslexia may represent the lower tail of a normal distribution of reading ability." *The New England Journal of Medicine,* 326(3): 145–150.

Smith, F. 1988. *Understanding reading,* 4th ed. Hillsdale, NJ: Erlbaum.

Stanovich, K. E. 1980. "Toward an interactive-compensatory model of individual differences in the development of reading fluency." *Reading Research Quarterly* 16: 32–71.

Stanovich, K. E. 1981. "Attention and automatic context effects in reading." In *Interactive processes in reading*, ed. A. M. Lesgold and C. A. Perfetti. Hillsdale, NJ: Erlbaum, 241–267.

———. 1984. "The interactive-compensatory model of reading: A confluence of developmental, experimental, and educational psychology." *Remedial and Special* Education 5: 11–19.

———. 1991. "Word recognition: Changing perspectives." In *Handbook of reading research*, Vol. 2, ed. R. Barr, M. L. Kamil, P. B. Mosenthal, and P. D. Pearson. New York: Longman, 418–452.

Taylor, M. 1976. *Roll of thunder hear my cry*. New York: Bantam.

———. 1981. *Let the circle be unbroken*. New York: Puffin.

Temple, C., and J. C. Marshall. 1983. "A case study of developmental phonological dyslexia." *British Journal of Psychology* 74: 517–533.

Vellutino, F. R., and M. B. Denckla. 1991. "Cognitive and neuropsychological foundations of word identification in poor and normally developing readers." In *Handbook of reading research*, vol. 2, ed. R. Barr, M. L. Kamil, P. B. Mosenthal, and P. D. Pearson. New York: Longman, 571–608.

Weaver, C. 1994. *Reading process and practice: From socio-psycholinguistics to whole language*, 2nd ed. Portsmouth, NH: Heinemann.

"Word finding problems in children and adolescents: Intervention issues." 1992. Themed issue of *Topics in Language Disorders* 13(1).

IV Teaching Literacy through Literature

Teaching Literacy
through Literature

Literacy includes much more than merely being *able* to read and
write. A literate person not only *can* read and write but actually
does so, voluntarily, for a variety of his or her own reasons and
purposes, such as to experience and express, to enjoy and appreciate,
to create for the enjoyment and appreciation of others, to obtain information and inform, to research and record, to persuade and be persuaded, to inspire and be inspired (Weaver, 1997).

As children become literate, they also become increasingly well
informed about themselves and others, and about their world. That is,
they learn about people, history, various cultures and lands, science and
technology, and the arts. They *use* literacy to become more and more
literate. Thus literacy is not merely a goal, but a means; not merely a
product, but a lifelong process of learning. This is the kind of literacy
promoted by literature study groups.

More particularly, there are many benefits of students discussing literature in groups, with or without the teacher as a participant. As various teacher/researchers have demonstrated (Raphael et al., 1995;
Gilles, 1993; Eeds & Wells, 1989), students typically

- clarify points of uncertainty or confusion
- come to a deeper, richer understanding of the text
- discover similarities and differences between characters, books
  on the same theme, authors, and so forth
- make various kinds of connections: with other books, authors,
  their own lives
- develop critical thinking skills, such as analyzing, synthesiz-
  ing, drawing inferences, making hypotheses, interpreting, and
  evaluating
- develop a greater understanding of literary elements and the
  writer's craft
- become more conscious of reading strategies they can use
- develop discussion skills

When children make decisions about books to read and then discuss them with peers, they get excited about reading books. Many children read more and enjoy reading more when they can make choices about what to read and who to talk with, and when they are not evaluated on their recall of small details but rather on their ability to discuss the work thoughtfully and insightfully. Less proficient readers gain especially from hearing others discuss their reading strategies. And all readers gain enjoyment and enlightenment from the books they read and discuss.

Egawa's article demonstrates that literature discussions can be held with first graders; the teacher simply needs to take a more central role. Smith describes how she leads up to, initiates, and conducts literature study groups with fifth and sixth graders. Raphael and McMahon describe a "book club" initiated with fourth and fifth graders and explain how it related to other literacy events and to instruction. And all three articles demonstrate, through concrete examples, several of the elements and benefits described above. We see that the children in these classrooms are well on their way to becoming fully literate adults.

References

Eeds, M., & Wells, D. (1989). Grand conversations: An exploration of meaning construction in literature study groups. *Research in the Teaching of English, 23*, 4–29.

Gilles, C. (1993). We make an idea: Cycles of meaning in literature discussion groups. In K. M. Pierce & C. J. Gilles (Eds.), *Cycles of meaning: Exploring the potential of talk in learning communities*. Portsmouth, NH: Heinemann. 199–217.

Raphael, T. E., McMahon, S. I., Goatley, V. J., Bentley, J. L., Boyd, F. B., Pardo, L. S., & Woodman, D. A. (1995). Research directions: Literature and discussion in the reading program. *Language Arts, 69*, 54–61.

Weaver, C. (1997). *A balanced approach to reading and literacy*. Video. Plano, TX: Skyhooks.

22 Harnessing the Power of Language: First Graders' Literature Engagement with *Owl Moon*

Kathy Egawa
Madrona Elementary School
Seattle, Washington

Egawa explains why she chose to use quality literature at the center of the curriculum in her first-grade classroom, along with predictable books and basals. Next she offers step-by-step guidelines for implementing literature study in a primary classroom. We see this process in action as Egawa discusses how the study of Jane Yolen's *Owl Moon* evolved over several group meetings. We also see how the richness of this book stimulated children to write, through samples of their letters and an original story inspired by *Owl Moon*. Based on her experience with literature study among first graders, Egawa argues that "our challenge as teachers is not to purchase books of literature activities or think them up, not to direct children's responses, but to trust the connection between readers and powerful stories."

Originally published in *Language Arts*, 67, (1990), 582–88. Copyright 1990 by the National Council of Teachers of English.

"This is one of my friends from first grade . . . one of my friends that's a book."

The words above came from Brie Schmidt, hugging the book *Owl Moon* to her chest. First grade had ended the Friday before. I had invited Brie and six other students to speak to a class of teachers that I was teaching with a colleague. I felt it was important that these teachers see and talk with children who had been involved in literature study. I had hoped they might get a glimpse of the rigor and enthusiasm that had directed these students' energies as they had read and discussed books and authors, but I couldn't have predicted this comment from Brie. She shared it casually, yet it says a great deal about her interaction with books.

Clearly one of the motivations in my own decision to use literature in a first grade classroom was my value of rich, descriptive language. I didn't find it in the district-adopted text. When students returned to the books that I read during storytime, they had no problem reading or understanding vocabulary that was not controlled. In fact, I noticed very early in my teaching that wonderful language captured children's attention and interest. There were always favorite story lines they would repeat many times. Another motivation was my trust in the connection between a reader and an author with a significant story to tell. It seemed that the very essence of what children loved most was missing from the beginning texts that predominated in classrooms.

I saw the choice as simple. I could use the vocabulary-controlled readers and provide children with an artificial notion of language and story; I could use predictable stories that would support their beginning reading efforts; or I could choose from the wealth of children's literature. A classroom where the use of literature received priority would look noticeably different.

Many might argue that basals and predictable stories have a place in a primary classroom. As a first grade teacher I have too. I cannot imagine my classroom without a generous supply of predictable texts. They are essential in supporting students' growth toward independent reading in the first months of school. Class members checked them out nightly for homework reading. Yet the stories offered little to discuss. The language was predictable, but inconsequential. The powerful experience of a beautifully written story offers no comparison. The classroom shelves provided choices among all these books. The basal texts had to be covered for end-of-the-year testing. But the literature engagements that resulted tell a further story.

Placing literature at the center of the curriculum also established my belief and trust in these young students as literate human beings, based on their abilities to discuss stories rather than merely to decode print. Transactional theory (Rosenblatt 1978) suggests that the meaning of text is created in the space between the actual reading and the reader's own background, memories, and feelings. Supporting students as they began to articulate and share those connections with other readers was the foundation upon which the reading program was built.

How I Organize Literature Study in a Primary Classroom

The following guidelines are offered as suggestions There are many ways to use literature in a classroom. Most important is to retain the essence of story—to demonstrate for young readers how you might yourself connect with books. (For thorough and rich elaboration of this perspective, see R. Peterson and M. Eeds's [1990] *Grand Conversations*.)

Choosing the Books

The importance of this step cannot be overemphasized. Meaningful connections with books will only occur with meaningful stories.

Is there something significant to talk about?
Do the illustrations enhance or tell a further story?

Traditional readability guidelines are seldom considered.

Introducing the Books

Briefly read a section of each book or share your genuine enjoyment of a particular aspect. Provide sign-up sheets with five or six invitations per book. Let children peruse the books. Invite children to choose.

I generally choose five books for each study, allowing five to eight days to read and meet. Five groups meeting concurrently during those days' s necessitates a minimum of two adults available to help guide and demonstrate discussion. I am also careful to ensure multiple support opportunities (stories on tape, reading with friends, books available for homework reading with families). The ability to decode is not a prerequisite to participate.

Meeting 1: Read the book to the children as an aesthetic whole, avoiding teacher talk. When finished, leave the children with multiple copies of the text.

As students become more capable readers, they will often have read the book alone or among themselves prior to the first meeting. A first meeting with older readers may result in an agreement to independently read part of the book prior to the next meeting.

Meeting 2: Read the book again. This time, pause when the children are eager and anxious to comment. Let them talk and explore and discover language for their responses and ideas. Feel free to join in—but not with a "teacher" question. Inquire and nudge when they seem perplexed or need support. Leave plenty of time for their discussion. Remember each child needs the opportunity to contribute. Encourage response in a notebook or log if that is a meaningful activity.

Meetings 3-4: Continue the discussion. Read the entire book or parts of the book the students identify. Ask questions like:

What is this book really about?
Does this story matter to you?
What's on your mind after reading this book?

What are you interested in after this reading?
Who will share from their log?

Be a part of the conversation. Explore ideas together. Trust that most of these questions will be generated from the students themselves if this kind of discussion has been demonstrated in response to reading. Highlight and name the elements of story as they naturally emerge through group conversation.

Meetings 4-5: Talk of a way to share the experience, to remember the experience of the book. Rather than provide students with prearranged activities, I encouraged their discussions to lead them toward some way of sharing the book. With adult support, these sharings took many forms: a walk-through museum, word cards in various theme shapes from the story, plays (I encouraged improvised drama rather than scripted plays), stick puppets and a backdrop scene, discussions, questionnaires, small take-home books and a big book with a variation of the story, posters, dramatic readings, music, and dance.

The preparation and engagement with these activities replace what might normally be seatwork in a traditional primary classroom. There were also other multiple reading and writing activities in which children were engaged as the adults moved among the literature study groups sharing in continued discussion, securing materials, or supporting completion of projects.

Sharing

Meet to share the interpretations, questions, and enjoyment that the study session's books raised. Talk about what you might want to know or study next.

Students eagerly awaited a chance to share as well as hear from their fellow classmates. As one group shared, others in the room informally assumed the role of audience. We generally gathered in one area of the room. Each presentation was always followed by a discussion or questions. I initially demonstrated questions if the students had none: Why was it that that particular aspect of the story caught your attention? What was it about the story that led you to share it with us through drama? What do you want to study next? Why is this story important enough to share?

How the Study of One Book Evolved

Brie identified *Owl Moon* as a particular favorite, so I'd like to share my students' experience with that book. Recognized for the quiet, poetic story and rich illustrations and the recipient of the 1988 Caldecott award, this book was a gift to my students from a university methods class with which we had shared a penpal experience. Once I had secured multiple copies, *Owl Moon* became another piece of literature that I offered as a study choice. It was one of five books I briefly introduced for study during one of these periods.

First Meeting: I spent our first meeting reading the book through without interruption. Their responses reflected the hushed and solemn mood of the story as revealed in the stillness of the snow, the night, awaiting the owl that might or might not appear as the father and child waited. How perfectly John Schoenherr had illustrated this story that was very real to his life. The children's attention was drawn to the rich illustrations. I left the children with five copies of the text and moved on to meet with another group.

Second Meeting: Again I read the book, this time pausing for the children's comments. After some conjecture about the child's age and gender and how many years he or she had been waiting to go owling, the talk moved to a discussion of the language. Everyone quickly identified favorite phrases. Those who shared favorites were inspired to seek another. "The snow below it was whiter than the milk in a cereal bowl" was a unanimous choice. Erin, who had chosen the words "If you go owling, you have to be quiet and make your own heat," repeatedly murmured how beautiful the words were. Eric loved the picture of the father shining the flashlight up into the tree when Pa's hoot-echoing finally drew the owl. A couple of the students had already taken the book home to read. Several more checked it out for that night. I reminded them of the audiotape that was available if they couldn't read the entire text. I left them in pairs, talking and reading for twenty or thirty more minutes. After seven months of discussing books, these children needed little direction. They carefully looked at illustrations; they ran to find other books by the same author; they gathered both fiction and nonfiction to extend their reading or illustrating. They were engaged in normal, everyday literate activity!

Third Meeting: After leading the first couple meetings with a deliberate rate reading of the text, I opened this one up to their discussion. What were they thinking about? There was a lot of speculating as to whether Jane Yolen had based this story on one of her life experiences. Where had she lived? How long had the child in the story waited to go owling; why couldn't he or she go as a younger child? It was established tentatively that the child was a girl. Why didn't she talk even after her father had told her it was okay? These were some of their questions that directed the conversation, for which they shared thoughts and opinions. I read an interview of the illustrator, John Schoenherr, in a *Scholastic Book Club* flyer. He shared that he had painted his own house, woods, a neighbor's barn, and a friend's owl. The students commented on their parents' delight with the book during homework reading. One child had already purchased the book. I asked the children to listen together to the audio tape as I moved to another group.

Fourth Meeting: After reading their favorite phrases again, someone suggested we make a large poster using Eric's favorite illustration and adding their chosen words. It was soon decided that the poster would have to be a general collection of the illustrations that portrayed their chosen words. I supplied a large piece of dark blue paper (36" × 48") to fit with the night scene This entailed discussions about how to draw the father, child, and owl so they would show up against the background. We used white paper for these characters as well as for the words. I helped sketch in the shape and wrote my own favorite words on a piece of paper: "When their words faded away, it was as quiet as a dream." Boualian, a Cambodian ESL student and beginning reader, was supported by friends in his search for favorite words and where to start and stop copying. Initially, he could not find his words on the page, yet he knew exactly what they were. A couple of children practiced with him so he could read these words unaided in front of the class. These children worked and read and drew for over an hour on their own. A Caldecott medal was carefully copied for the corner of the poster "Drawing by:" with a list of their names was crossed out and replaced with "Poster by:."

Fifth Meeting: The following day we met again to trace over the words with black felt pens. Brie decided to cut her paper with the words about the dangers lurking behind the trees into the shape of her imagined dangerous animal. This inspired the same from the other children. A few had to rewrite the words on another paper to enable the shape cutting. The poster was looking great. The discussion continued to center on the beauty of the words and illustrations: "I just *love* these words about searching the stars!"; "How long do you think they *really* stared at each other? I know how it could seem like a hundred minutes!" As I left the group that day, I suggested that readers who particularly loved a book often wrote to share their pleasure and ask any questions of the author or illustrator. Two of the students continued working on the poster. Brie talked Boualian into finishing her coloring, then joined Eric and Erin to respond in these ways:

> Dear Jane Yolen   March 6
>   I am in Mrs. Egawa's class. I love *Owl Moon* bekus the whaye
> it flose like a thin brees. Have you rittn any uther books? Wut were

threr names? Tell me ubaout ritting chrildrins books. I wont to rite chidrin's books too. I need some ideeus. I'm infrst grade. Has John Schoenherr illustrated for your books? Did thea win Caldecott medals?   from Gabrielle

Dear John Schoenherr,   March 6
    My name is Eric. I love Owl Moon. I LOVE your pichers. You are a grat artist!! I thek you shude dro whith the illustrater of the Polar Expressbecas you and him are grat artists. Do you kno Chris Van Allsburg? You and Chris VanAllsburg shod dro sum books. I LOVE that pichier where the man shins the flashligt in the owls fas.

Lov Eric
P.S. Im in frst grad

Dear Jane Yolen,   March 8
    My name is Erin. I love the book Owl Moon. I love the werds in it. I dont know why but I get a weerd filling inside becuse the werd's are so pritty. I get the filling evrytime I read the book. I think that Owl Moon shud come in frst and it did! I'm so happy! My favorite werd's are ["] as if searching the stars, as if reading a map up then The moon made his face into a silver masc.["] (Tern over) Well that's all I have to say.

Love Erin
P.S. I'm in frst grade

These letters were written in the students' spiral notebooks—no different than the notebooks we as educators carry with us to conferences and meetings to record our thoughts. A couple of letters were copied onto stationery; another was torn from the notebook. Writing letters was an activity we had done many times in the class. Erin, accustomed to quick letter exchanges through various penpal projects throughout the year, was anxious to mail off her thoughts. I had told her I would ask the librarian for an address. I found this note in my classroom mailbox the next day.

Dear Mrs. E.,   March 8
    Do you have the address?

       to Jane?

Love, Erin

Sharing: Several days later the book and poster were shared with the class as part of that session's sharings. But the love of this book didn't stop there. As these students became more capable oral readers over the course of the year, they asked to read favorite homework books to the class. Eric was the first to tackle the entire *Owl Moon* text as a read-aloud sharing. Replete with starts and stops, Eric read the story, occasionally assisted by more capable but no less enthused readers. The class was amazed. "How long did it take you to practice that book?" "Oh, I'd say a week." In the following weeks the five or six copies were seldom on the shelf. Another two or three children chose to read the book again to the class.

In May a third grade teacher in my school asked about the how-to's of literature study. What books did I use? How did I use them? Did I use one book with the entire class? I suggested that I ask my first graders which books they thought third graders might enjoy. They drafted letters, and again *Owl Moon* surfaced:

> Dear Third Graders,   May 25
>
> You should study Owl Moon because it has the most butufle pichre's and you will love the wrde's in it. Here is some of the wrde'sl loved a lot. ["] For one minute, three minute's, maybe even a hundred minute's, we stared at one another.["]
>
> love, Catie

During a recess break, as I was wandering around to children's desks to read their latest writings, I found the piece depicted in Figure 1 on Reid's desk. Through the scrawl of his letters I made out:

> Sawlumender Sun
> by Reid
>
> It was lat one spring afternoon a long time after lunch when ma tact me sawlumendering There was no wind only a brise. The tree's shivered in the brise as mooving stajyou's in the sky and the sun was so brit. A car horn blue long and low like a ~~low~~ sad sad song
> ~~It was late in the~~
> ~~It~~ I could hear it froo the woo wood I pould over my   . A dog joynd the car and then a second dog joynd in.

Owl Moon was nearby on the desk top. When Reid returned from recess, I asked what he was writing. "A story about salamandering." "Are you getting some ideas from *Owl Moon*?" He glanced at it. "Well yeah, kinda. Really I'm just getting the rhythm of the story." Later he came up to tell me how crazy he had been to name this story "Salamander Sun," laughing that salamanders couldn't be in the sun—that amphibians lived in damp places, and he'd changed the title to Salamander Dusk." Reid had initiated this writing on his own. As Yetta Goodman (1988) describes, the author was a teacher in Reid's exploring the power of language and his ability to harness that power for himself.

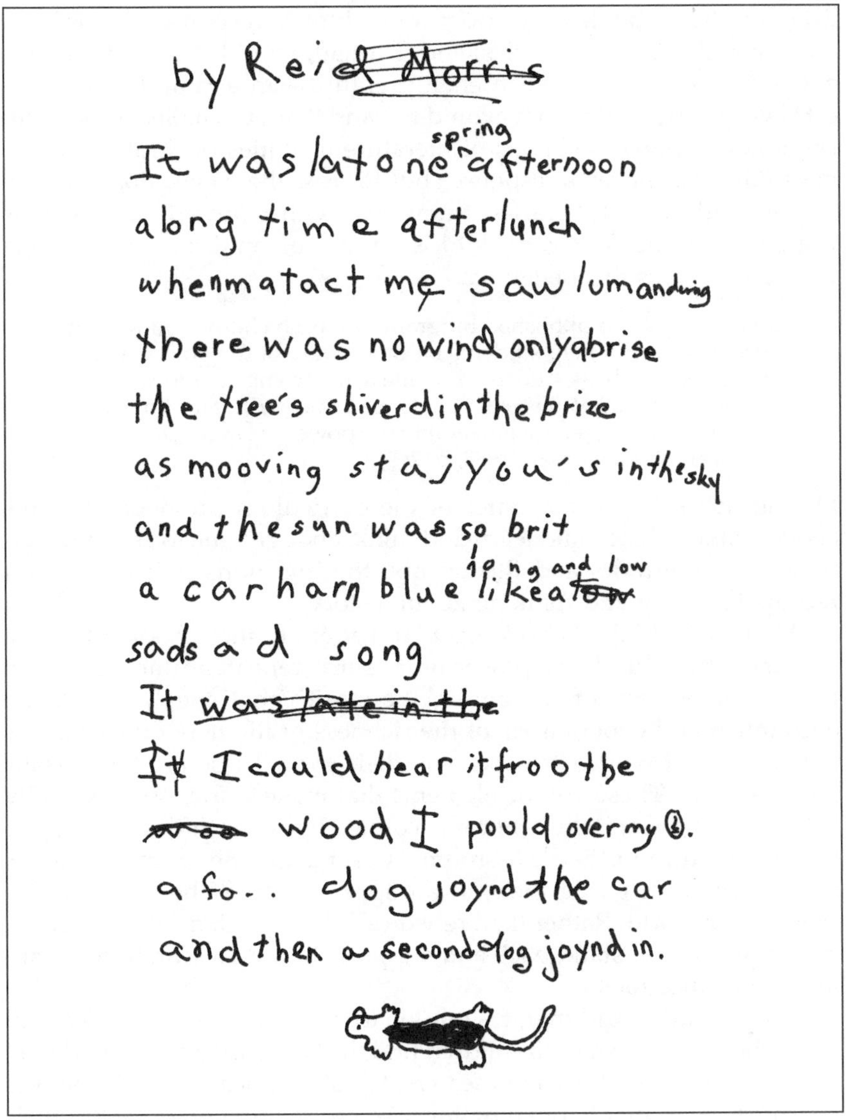

Figure 1. Reid's writing.

New Ways of Thinking

Where would these "skills" fit into a program scope and sequence? Are these first-grade skills? Could they be found in workbooks? Would a

list of teacher-provided directions for children's responses to this book
have included these activities; and if it had, would the children have
entered into them with such energy, enthusiasm and authentic interest? I would argue that they would not and that our challenge as teachers is not to purchase books of literature activities or think them up,
not to direct children's responses but to trust the connection between
readers and powerful stories. Know that with repeated engagements
responding to books, every child is capable of similar response. Yetta
Goodman shares this belief:

> I believe that no published program can teach children to read or
> write, nor can it help students become aware of the power of lan-
> guage. It is only as students become actively engaged in wonder-
> ing why and what reasons people read and write and how such
> processes affect their own lives that the power of language will tale
> on meaning (Goodman, 1988, p. 263).

Placing literature at the center of the curriculum provided students
enough time to listen and learn and think, enough time to ask the questions of the authors and illustrators, the questions that come with
repeated reading and thinking about a story.

What leads students back again and again to these books? It is the
language, the sound and power of it as it is repeated time after time;
it is the substance of the books, the stories that speak of real life
encounters and experiences, of the richness of life here on earth. It is
the creation of worlds that become their own. These are the reasons
authors write. These are the elements that make stories so powerfully
engaging. Six years old is not too young. Teachers can find a way to
honor literature in their classrooms, to set aside the teacher's guides
and let children guide them in an appreciation of how they make
sense of the world. Rather than rely on adult-generated response activities, teachers can stand back and support children's search for meaning and connections.

I have heard it said that it is our job to introduce kids to books until
the authors take over, until children find the books they can't put down,
until each book sends them in search of another. Clearly Jane Yolen was
instrumental in that happening for many of my first graders. But their
enthusiasm was not limited to Jane Yolen. I could continue to share stories that would include many other books and talented authors. I am
amazed by my students' ability to discuss these loved "friends." And
I ask myself, given the reality of teacher's guides and scope and
sequences and test scores, how often we give time and importance to
real engagement with literature and its potential for impact in our lives.

Yolen (1989) notes that when the *New York Times* reviewed *Owl Moon*, its reviewer noted the potential for this:

> The very best books for the not-quite-reading children must be written to charm and astonish the adults who will read them aloud; thrill that reader, who will communicate those prickles at the nape of the neck, and you'll have created a desire in the young listener to learn how to read books alone. *Owl Moon* does this better than any new children's book I have seen in a long time (cited in Yolen, 1989, p. 206).

Predictable books, readers, and children's literature still fill my classroom shelves. Visitors do see that reading and writing look different in this room. One of the reasons is the connection with authors, a connection that inspires cheerful referral on a first-name basis. We sent Jane the letters through the publisher. Her responses arrived the day before Brie acknowledged *Owl Moon* as a best friend.

Dear Brie,

> Thank you for your letter about my book *Owl Moon*. I have written *100* other books, many of them just right for a 1st grader.

Love,
Jane Yolen 1989

The potential for fresh and distinctive engagements with literature is limitless. I continue to search for books that share the anomalies of life, the books which provide rich opportunities for discussion and contain language worth repeating. Engagement with literature opens up a new way of constructing the world.

References

Goodman, Y. M. 1988. "Exploring the power of written language through literature for children and adolescents." *The New Advocate* 1: 254–265.

Peterson. R., and M. Eeds. 1990. *Grand conversations*. New York: Scholastic.

Rosenblatt, L. M. 1978. *The reader, the text, the poem: The transactional theory of the literary work*. Carbondale, IL: Southern Illinois University Press.

Yolen, J. 1989. "On silent wings: The making of 'Owl Moon.'" *The New Advocate* 2: 199–211.

———. 1987. *Owl Moon*. New York: Philomel.

23 Bringing Children and Literature Together in the Elementary Classroom

Karen Smith
National Council of Teachers of English

A former fifth/sixth-grade teacher, Karen Smith is a pioneer in leading students to explore literature through literature study groups. However, she did not usually begin such groups until November, after paving the way. Smith explains how first she helps students learn to work independently in her classroom and how to respond appropriately in various situations. She introduces them to various modes of responding to literature, such as art, drama, and music, and helps them establish routines for accomplishing their goals. Smith describes how she and the students establish the classroom environment for reading self-chosen books, how she deals with individual problems and distractions, and how she promotes recognition for reading. By reading aloud to the students and discussing the literature with them, she establishes a way of talking about the literature. Basic story elements, such as character, place, point of view, time, mood, and extended metaphor, emerge naturally in the conversations, and Smith may supply a literary term if needed. She then explains in detail how she handles the literature study groups that begin around the beginning of November. From this chapter, one can see why "Literature study is contagious."

Originally published in *Primary Voices K-6, 3*,(2), (1995), 22–32. Copyright 1995 by the National Council of Teachers of English.

It's November 15th, and all thirty-two fifth and sixth graders are busily engaged in meaningful work. Seven students are in the reading corner. This is their day to be "rug readers," a title affectionately bestowed on them by a group of students who developed a plan allowing everyone a weekly time to spread out on the rug and read. Tomas and Martin laugh their way through a beat-up copy of *Mad*. Juan has *Sports Illustrated for Kids* in his lap, apparently planning to turn to it as soon as he finishes reading his superhero comic book. Sabrina and Martha snuggle together in the beanbag chair, reading books by Cynthia Voigt, their favorite author. And Mary, whose head is resting on a pillow in Sabrina's lap, is lost in the world of Terabithia.

In another corner, four pairs of students practice reading aloud to one another from picture books written in Spanish. They're preparing oral readings for their second-grade partners. They know that to read well orally they have to rehearse, so they're both listening to and evaluating one another for fluency, expression, and clarity. Yolanda, Robert, Jorge, Sergio, Marcela, and Danny are creating a mural that will represent their rendering of *Shadow of a Bull* (Wojciechowska, 1964). They discuss the size of the mural and what medium they will use to create it. A fourth group is gathered around a table reading and discussing *Let the Circle Be Unbroken* (Taylor, 1981). The previous week I had been a part of this group and we had read *Roll of Thunder, Hear My Cry* (Taylor, 1975). Now they're reading its sequel, independent of me. The remaining six students make their way to the round table with books and contracts in hand. We are about to meet for a literature study session.

Promoting Independence

These students are confident and serious because they know how to work independently and how to respond appropriately in each situation. I help them learn these things during September and October, when we spend time each day engaging in literary events and then talking about specific behaviors that contributed to the success or failure of each situation. We discuss what went well, and why. We also talk about what didn't go well and come up with ways we can improve next time. I introduce them to a range of response modes (art, music, drama, etc.); usually, I begin with art. Students select a picture book and respond to it using some art form. To give students an idea of the variety of projects possible and the quality of work expected, I share projects completed by former students. The first two days, the students immerse themselves in picture books. The third day, they (alone or in pairs) pick one picture book to respond to. They organize their time on a form that asks them to list whom they will work with, what they plan to create (a diorama, a mural, an abstract rendition of the story, etc.), what materials they will need, where they will get the materials, and where they will work. The form also has a section that asks students to note what worked well and one thing they could have done to make things better. They decide how much time they will need, and spend the next two to five days completing the project. At this point, students turn in their organizational forms, which are evaluated along with the project itself.

We spend about ten minutes at the end of each session discussing what they did and how they proceeded. For example, clean up is almost always an issue with art projects, so we think through several ways to handle it. If students are working in pairs, they may choose to assign specific tasks for each to do: one student cleans the paint jars and brushes and the other cleans the area. Sharing solutions is important because it presents a range of possibilities for students to consider as they listen to what worked for others. If students have trouble working independently, I meet with them individually, and we talk through why they are having a problem and what goals they will set to take care of it. My objective is not to punish students but to find strategies that will help them be successful. I always follow up the next day to see if their behavior matches their goals. If not, we keep brainstorming and developing new strategies until we find something that works. After everyone has finished an art project, I move to a different form of response, usually drama and music, following basically the same procedures.

Every day after lunch, we have silent reading time that we call "just reading." During this time block, we just read and share. Students choose their own books; the only requirement is that it must be a literature book (fiction or nonfiction). There is no quiz over what is read, nor are students required to respond in any way except to talk briefly to a classmate. I encourage them to share with different partners each day. Students spend 35 minutes reading and 10 minutes sharing. This sharing time is important: It makes students think about what they read, it entices other students to read the same book, and it creates a place for us to come together and think and talk as a community of readers.

"Rug reading" begins during this block of time in September and October. Decisions about who gets to read on the rug and when have to be resolved anew each year. Usually a group is assigned to set some guidelines, and then these guidelines are implemented and evaluated for a week or two until the group comes up with a set that works. After several revisions, one group resolved the reading corner problem by creating a chart that listed the students in groups of six next to the day of the week they could read on the rug. Next to the chart was a set of rules: 1) You can read on the rug only on your designated day. [If you don't want to read in the reading area, that's okay, but you can't let someone else take your place.] 2) You are free to read any text in the classroom library (i.e., magazines, joke books, comic books, etc.) or anything that has been approved by the teacher. [This is unlike the rules for other students, who are required to read books.] 3) You cannot disrupt other students on the rug. [If you do, you must leave and read silently at your desk.] 4) You must straighten up the area before you leave. [Otherwise, you lose your rug privilege the following week.]

I play two important roles during this time block: I read with the students and discuss my reading with a partner, thus establishing myself as a member of this reading community. (I always have at least four novels on my desk and often talk with the students about other books I am reading at home.) I also observe students as they read silently, noting patterns of behaviors that seem to keep them from enjoying silent reading.

Dealing with Problems and Distractions

Students who already enjoy reading are left alone. They select a novel from a large array of books; find a comfortable place where they can read without interruption; and at the end of the period, they record the title of their book and the pages read on a reading record form and talk to a classmate about what they read. Less interested or less able readers often have trouble seeing themselves as readers. These are the students who distract other students; start a new book every day; read the same pages over and over again; or watch the clock, counting minutes until silent reading time is over. One by one, I meet with them and ask them to talk to me about what they are experiencing during this time. I make inquiries into their history as readers, asking why they think they have trouble reading, why they think it is important to read, if they ever read a book they liked, and so on. They usually tell me their frustration with little probing. Tomas, for example, described how he looked at every word on a page and turned every page in a book, yet he didn't know a thing he'd read. Other students admit they have never read an entire book. Again, I work with these students individually to find strategies that help them overcome these obstacles. We become co-investigators in solving the problem.

If a student is not reading as effectively or efficiently as I think he or she should be, I use the short version of the miscue analysis inventory (Goodman, Watson, and Burke, 1987) to gather information. Together we consider the types and level of miscues being made and what they tell us about the student's reading strategies. If a student is a proficient reader but doesn't like to read, l use other means of support. For example, children who have a hard time keeping their mind

on what they read often benefit from sketching interesting or important ideas as they read. I recommend folding a piece of newsprint in
quarters for sketch paper. Students then read a short section and sketch
a part they find interesting. I do the same and then we compare and
talk about why we picked what we did. There are times when we are
amazed that one of us has drawn something that the other person
didn't remember happening in the story; at other times, we find that
both of us picked the same event or character to sketch. Some students
need to do this for only a book or two. Others rely on this process for
several weeks. They seem to know when they no longer need it and do
away with it on their own.

Still other students have problems finding a book they want to read.
I encourage these students to read with a classmate. After the two have
agreed on a book, they read and share together until they finish it. If
possible, I read the same book so I can support them by sharing
insights, providing previews of things to come, or helping to sort out
parts they find confusing. I talk with students often to see how things
are working out and how they are doing. I acknowledge all progress
(no matter how small) by calling parents or reporting to former teachers (who always manage to seek out these students and congratulate
them on their success).

I want students to understand that being a reader counts. It carries
status. Reading three books at once or going to the public library on
your own are acts that are important and get noted. Reading three chapters ahead of assigned pages makes you worthy of public acknowl-
edgment by classmates and the teacher alike (Smith, 1993). Because I
value reading, students learn to value each other as readers and receive
recognition for their reading acts. When other teachers visit our classroom, students often introduce each other by pointing out reading
behaviors. Sara is the student who always reads the last chapter first.
Efrin is our historical fiction buff. John finally moved away from sports
and into fantasy books. Discussing the merits of reading even showed
up in a personal note written by a classmate to our Student of the Week
(see Figure 1).

By the middle of October, students are usually able to act independently: they know how to prepare and participate in buddy reading;
they can respond to books using art, music, and drama; and they have
settled into silent reading. This independence frees me to work intensively with small groups of students, shifting my focus from creating
routines that promote independence to developing students' abilities
to respond to literature in deeper and more meaningful ways.

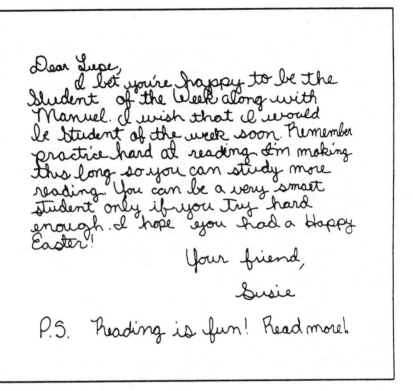

Figure 1. Susie's note to the Student of the Week.

Supporting More Complex Responses

I want students to appreciate literature as aesthetic experience and grow in their ability to respond to it in more sophisticated ways. I also want them to value literature for the roles it can play in their lives. I believe that literature entertains, that it is a wonderful way to spend time; it provides a context for exploring the human condition, helping us to understand who we are and why we exist; and it helps us recognize that there are many worldviews and that no single one constitutes the standard against which others can or should be judged (Smith, 1995). These beliefs impact the response stance I want students to take. I want them to bring to bear on each reading their worldviews, experiences, and concerns. In addition, I want them to learn to move beyond their

own rendering of a text and consider alternative and opposing interpretations of the same text.

By mid-October, most of the students value literature as entertainment. They enjoy reading and freely choose to read during and out of
class. They have experienced the emotional and imaginative pull of a
good story, and recognized the pleasure of being carried to other places
and involved in the lives of other people. Also by mid-October, they
have been introduced to a particular way of thinking and talking about
story. During read-aloud time, when I finish reading a chapter, short
story, or picture book, I ask students to sit up straight and get ready to
share the thoughts and feelings they experienced while I was reading.
Often these responses are about people or events the students either
liked or disliked. I accept all responses as important. Some students hesitate to share thoughts and feelings, so when they risk a response, I
always acknowledge their contribution. Other students, who are more
confident responders, are sometimes asked to substantiate their
responses. This often results in personal stories that they call on to make
connections to what an author is saying.

I usually make sure some time is spent attending specifically to the
story world. Story worlds provide a context for sorting out our
thoughts and feelings about a particular aspect of life. I rely on the
basic concept and elements of story to help shape our conversation.
Leland Jacobs's (1980) notion of story—characters coping in terms of
quest—sets the stage for this talk. This framework focuses our attention on the characters we meet in stories and on the tensions they are
coping with. I ask students to attend to book characters with the same
recognition and concern they give (or should give) new acquaintances
in their daily lives. Basic story elements—character, place, point of
view, time, mood, and extended metaphor (Peterson & Eeds, 1990)—
fall into place as students work to make sense of the characters they
meet. I never directly teach elements of literature; they emerge naturally as children begin talking about story. What I do, however, is
build on students' responses using the elements if I think it will enrich
their current understandings. For example, when the class was talking about the tensions that exist between M.C. Higgins and his father
in the story *M.C. Higgins, the Great* (Hamilton, 1974), I responded by
talking about how much of the tension was related to place. I wanted
the students to see that the more insight we gained into Sarah's Mountain (a place named after M.C.'s great-grandmother and deeply cher-
ished by his father), the more we would understand the relationship
between M.C. and his dad. Some students saw the connections, others
did not. I never worry about whether they "get it." The students who

do make the connection often start considering the significance of place in other stories. The students who don't make the connection will have plenty of other opportunities during the year to see the interactions between characters and place.

Besides demonstrating response to literature using a particular literary element, I also name the element or literary device when a student grounds his or her response in it, but doesn't know the word for it. When one of the students voiced amazement that the story of M.C. Higgins took place in a very short time period (two days, to be exact), another student, Alonso, pointed out that we really understood more because the author "told stories about M.C.'s grandmother from 100 years ago." I validated Alonso's insight by noting that what the author had done was use a literary device called flashback and corroborated his response by pointing out specific ways the flashbacks enriched our understanding of the father's tie to the mountain and his deeply felt commitment to his grandmother, Sarah.

In addition to helping students frame their discussions in a basic concept of story (such as the one provided by Leland Jacobs), and giving students language to use when talking about story, I also try to help students understand that each story is told and interpreted from a particular perspective. They need to recognize that the author provides one lens on the world, and their reading provides another. The more students know about the world, and the more perspectives they consider, the broader their interpretive lens will become. To accomplish this, I provide additional information about what is being read. For example, as we read stories that came out of World War II, I provided maps which the students and I studied and compared, helping them to see that even mapmaking is a political act. I invited WW II veterans and Holocaust survivors to speak to the class from their experiences. I found and read letters written by soldiers from both sides of the war. I didn't always relate these events to a particular book, but time and time again they were used as a heuristic device by students as they struggled to make sense of the books they were reading and the characters they were meeting and trying to understand.

I intentionally select books to read aloud that are written by authors who I think portray, in accurate and authentic ways (Sims Bishop, 1993), the diverse peoples who represent multiple perspectives on the world. This deliberate effort helps students learn that an important goal in our classroom is not to homogenize the human experience, but to entertain multiple ways of understanding and being in the world. I also offer students articles by critics who disapprove of particular books because of their doubtful cultural accuracy and authenticity and ask students for their thoughts on the critic's perspective.

Literature Study Groups

About the first week in November, I usually invite five or six students to join me in a discussion of a particular book. We call these discussions Literature Study. All students are expected to join at least one literature study group each month for the rest of the school year. These studies provide a context for an intensive exploration of a particular book. Over a period of three or four days, we come together to think and talk about how and why particular characters in particular settings think, feel, and behave as they do. These studies offer me an important opportunity to see how well students are using talk to learn; how they are progressing in their abilities to listen to and consider views that differ from their own; or, conversely, how well they are hanging onto and defending views they believe to be true and fair and just. It is also a time when I can stretch students' imaginations, asking them to reconsider their initial reading from other vantage points.

I wait until November to begin literature study groups because, by then, many of the necessary elements for having a successful small-group discussion are in place: 1) students not in the study know how to work independently, so full attention can be given to the small-group; 2) students in the group have had practice and feel comfortable talking to others about books; 3) students have begun to develop a particular way of thinking and talking about story; and 4) students have learned to listen and consider alternate interpretations.

Students need access to books that support deep reading—books that have characters who deal with life and its complexities in believable ways. Therefore, I set aside particular books from among which they can choose. Once the group has agreed on a book, students are given a week to read the book, and they are expected to come to the study group well prepared: They must have read the entire book and thought deeply about the characters they met, the relationships that formed among the characters, and the events that unfolded in the story. When we meet, we sit in a circle, either at a round table or on the floor, where we can speak and hear without strain or interruption. A circle symbolizes equal participation—all voices count. And, even though this may not be a reality, the circle constantly reminds me that issues of voice and access are at the heart of all we do; it is what we are striving for and what we consciously need to work towards.

My role in these groups is much like my role described above during read aloud time. I validate and corroborate students' responses; and, when appropriate, I challenge students to reconsider their interpretations from new or different perspectives. I also take notes on what students say. This note-taking strategy serves two purposes: It moves me out of the discussion so that the responsibility for carrying on the conversation falls on the students, and it gives me an opportunity to find the topics that are significant to the particular group of students discussing the book. Usually I note responses that suggest a particular feeling about a character or event in the story. At the end of each session, I recap what has been discussed and ask students what they would like to explore for the following day. For example, while reading *Sounder* (Armstrong 1969), one group kept using the word *prejudice*, but gave little evidence of what they meant by that word. The homework assignment that evening was to find and mark story events that show prejudiced behavior, which we discussed the next day. The discussion was, of course, embedded with the students' own experiences with prejudice. This led to a discussion about prejudiced behavior in different age groups, so that evening the students interviewed their parents or caregivers about acts of prejudice they had experienced, and those were the focus of the next day's discussion. The last day of the study, I talked to the class about some critiques of the book *Sounder* that had been made in an article written by Ann Trousdale. I asked the students to think about and discuss these arguments. (In Trousdale's article, "A Submission Theology for Black Americans: Religion and Social Action in Prize-Winning Children's Books about the Black Experience in America" [1990], she argues that the black characters in *Sounder* are presented as "docile, submissive towards whites, and accepting of injustice and oppression" [p. 137].) The students had a hard time comprehending this perspective because they had been pulled along by the emotional impact of the story. However, when I compared it to stereotypes made about their culture (mostly Hispanic/ Latino), they could understand why Trousdale's comments were important ones to consider. A few weeks later, I shared with the whole class a critique of *The Indian in the Cupboard* (Banks, 1980) that accuses its author, Lynn Banks, of similar stereotyping of Indians. The students who had been in the literature study group on *Sounder* seemed more prepared to deal with this critique (whether or not they accepted it) than did the other students. This confirmed for me, once again, that the more practice and experience we have with particular strategies, the more competent we become in using them.

Literature study is contagious. Many students participate in literature discussion groups whether I am there or not. The sessions without me are less formal and are often sessions where students get together after reading a predetermined number of pages or chapters and talk their way through the book. Students often follow up these discussions with an art, music, or drama project that they later present to the whole class. These presentations are excellent ways of introducing books. Usually, they result in lively discussions over who gets to read the book next. I sometimes ask students to tape-record these sessions. When I listen, I hear students validating, probing, and challenging each other. I hear them using the language of story to bring order to their reading experience: They attend to characters and their situations in the story world. I hear them telling their personal stories in an effort to clarify or make sense of a certain aspect of life. And, I hear them comparing the book they are reading to other texts they have read or viewed (i.e. other books, movies, TV shows, etc.). These tapes are excellent tools to evaluate if students are, in fact, buying into the goals set up for them.

Teachers who want to make effective use of literature in the elementary classroom, who truly want literature for all, face challenges that are both organizational and academic. We need to attend to both; otherwise, the likelihood of success is slim. However, when the challenges are successfully met, and the students tap in to the various potentials literature has to offer, they learn and they grow. They discover that by reading widely and deeply, they not only have a wonderful way to spend time, they may even develop a better understanding of people whose cultures and experiences differ from their own. And in they end, they may come to a better understanding of themselves as well.

References

Armstrong, W. 1969. *Sounder*. New York: Harper & Row.

Banks, L. (1980). *The Indian in the cupboard*. Garden City, NY: Doubleday.

Goodman, Y., D. Watson, and C. Burke. 1987. *The reading miscue inventory: Alternative procedures*. Katonah, NY: Richard C. Owens.

Hamilton, V. 1974. *M. C. Higgins, the great*. New York: Macmillan.

Jacobs, L. 1980. "On reading story." *Reading Instructional Journal* 23: 100–103.

Peterson, R., and M. Eeds. 1990. *Grand conversations: Literature groups in action*. Richmond Hill, Ontario: Scholastic-TAB.

Sims, Bishop, R. 1993. "Multicultural literature for children: Making informed choices." In *Teaching Multicultural literature in grades K–8*, ed. V. Harris. Norwood, MA: Christopher-Gordon Publishers, 37–53.

Smith, K. 1993. "A descriptive analysis of the responses of six students and their teacher in literature study sessions." Doctoral diss., Arizona State University, Tempe, Ariz.

Smith, K. 1995. "Children, literature, and passion: Bringing it all together." In *All that matters: What is it we value in school and beyond?*, ed. L. Rief, and M. Barbieri. Portsmouth, NH: Heinemann.

Taylor, M. 1975. *Roll of thunder, hear my cry*. New York: Dial.

———. 1981. *Let the circle be unbroken*. New York: Dial.

Trousdale, A. 1990. "A submission theology for black Americans: Religion and social action in prize-winning children's books about the black experience in America." *Research in the Teaching of English* 24: 117–140.

Wojciechowska, M. 1964. *Shadow of a bull*. New York: Atheneum.

24 Book Club: An Alternative Framework for Reading Instruction

Taffy E. Raphael
Michigan State University

Susan I. McMahon
University of Wisconsin–Madison

Placing their Book Club within a theoretical framework, Raphael and McMahon next describe the initial experiences with the Book Club—experiences from which they learned, among other things, the need for guiding children in moving away from the kinds of question-answering and turn-taking that characterize basal reading programs in use. In the fourth- and fifth-grade classes that then adopted a book-club format, there were four original components that soon began to blend together: instruction, reading, writing, and community share (whole class sharing), revolving around chosen themes. Each of these components is explained. Reading instruction concerned "fluency, reading vocabulary, comprehension strategies, genres, and aesthetic and personal response." Fluency was addressed through extensive reading, and the authors incorporated into Book Club selected strategies mandated by the state assessment program and included within the district-adopted reading program. Raphael and McMahon give numerous examples of activities and how these changed as the students became more and more immersed in reading and writing. We see how the children's initial non-discussions give way over time to genuine conversations about literature. As Raphael, McMahon, and their co-authors explain in a related article (*Language Arts*, January 1992), the classroom talk about texts particularly involved the sharing of written responses from reading logs, clarifying points of confusion, discussing the main theme of the story or other text, relating the text under discussion to other texts, critiquing the author's success, identifying the author's purposes, discussing the process of response itself, relating ideas from the text to personal experiences and feelings, and relating to prior knowledge.

In this chapter, Raphael and McMahon note that the students in the Book Club classrooms had standardized test scores "as high as those of students in a more traditional reading program where tested skills were directly taught." Furthermore, the next fall, when the students were interviewed, Book Club students remembered and could talk about at least 9 of the 16 books they had read. Students who had previously been in the commercial textbook program could not recall titles, authors, or stories from that year's instruction.

Originally published in *The Reading Teacher, 48*(2), (1994), 102–116. Copyright 1994 by the International Reading Association. Reprinted with permission.

From teachers' lounges to principals' meetings, from individual schools to districts, from local to national professional meetings, talk has turned to literature as the basis for reading instruction and to how reader response fits into current instructional models. This chapter explores the Book Club program, one model for literature-based reading instruction. We begin with the context in which our work was done, then examine students' early book clubs. We then describe Book Club as it developed in two classrooms and look at students' discussions after their participation for one and two years.

Background to the Book Club Program

The growing interest in literature and reading instruction reflects major changes in our fundamental beliefs about how literacy is developed, goals for reading instruction, and the nature of curriculum materials.

Theories about literacy development. For years, reading instruction involved breaking the reading process into smaller, more manageable units. Instruction focused on helping students master individual skills until they could orchestrate their use when reading. This approach was influenced by behavioral learning theories, which described how observable behaviors were acquired. In reading, this often meant a focus on oral fluency and the ability to answer literal comprehension questions.

Basing instruction on behavioral themes was called into question in the 1970s and 80s, when we became concerned with how little time students spent reading and the view of reading as merely an accumulation of skills (Anderson, Hiebert, Scott, & Wilkinson, 1985; Durkin, 1978–1979, 1981). Research indicated the value of building instructional models around authentic literacy experiences, especially the value of using real literature.

Current views of reading instruction are based in social constructivist theory (Gavelek, 1986; Tharp & Gallimore, 1988; Wertsch, 1985), which emphasizes learning as a social process. Reading and writing develop through interactions with both adults and peers; students should not sit in isolation, working on individual worksheets to practice skills outside the social and cultural contexts of normal use. Instead, students should interact using oral and written language to construct meaning about what they have read.

Beliefs about the goals of reading instruction. Early beliefs about reading instruction were based on defining reading as a process of getting meaning from the printed page. Not surprisingly, instruction emphasized decoding the print, assuming that decoded print would automatically be understood. By the late 1970s, we had learned much more about comprehension, particularly that it did not necessarily follow successful decoding (Anderson & Pearson, 1984). We began to emphasize teaching comprehension strategies (Brown, Armbruster, & Baker, 1986; Duffy, 1993).

More recently we have begun to recognize that instruction in decoding and comprehension may be important, but it is not sufficient for bringing students into the community of readers. It is also important to provide opportunity for personal response, to encourage students to construct meaning with their peers, and to question whether meaning is inherent in text (Harker, 1987; Rosenblatt, 1978).

Beliefs about curriculum materials and literature. The move to literature-based reading instruction reflects a change in our beliefs about curriculum materials. Traditional reading programs emphasized the use of a teachers' guide to determine when and how particular strategies and skills should be taught. The movement underlying the use to literature for reading instruction views curriculum materials as tools used by professional teachers who know their students' needs and interests. Thus, it assumes that teachers are better able to shape instruction than are the developers of generic curricula.

It is within this context that the Book Club program evolved as a collaborative study among university- and school-based researchers (McMahon, 1992; Raphael et al., 1992). The program involves four components that support the student-led discussion groups, or book clubs: reading, writing, whole-class discussion (i.e., community share), and instruction (see Figure 1). These four components evolved as the research team examined students' reading logs, observed and analyzed their conversations about books, and discussed the nature of instruction for each of the components. The book clubs were groups of three to five students, mixed on several traits (e.g., gender, ethnicity, reading ability), who discussed ideas related to the books they had read. Students' initial book club interactions influenced how we developed these components to provide the support they needed.

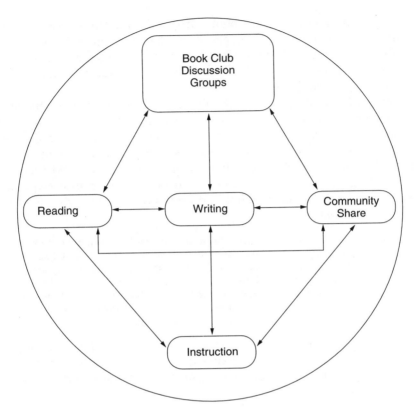

Figure 1. Book Club components.

Students' Early Book Club Experiences

Drawing on others who have written about literature-based instruction, we: (1) Identified good literature around an identifiable theme, (2) talked with students about the differences between conversations about books and answering questions, (3) introduced reading logs instead of workbooks, and (4) discussed characteristics of good speakers and listeners in small groups. We selected books using criteria that included quality, relevance to the theme, text difficulty, potential interest to students, and variety of texts per unit. For example, in our first unit we focused on Japan during World War II and used three books with the whole class: *Sadako and the Thousand Paper Cranes* (Coerr, 1977), a chapter book about a young girl who developed leukemia in the years following the Hiroshima bombing; *Faithful Elephants* (Tsuchiya, 1988), a picture book about dilemmas faced by zookeepers in cities where bombs were being dropped; and *Hiroshima, No Pika* (Maruki, 1982), a picture book about the day the bomb fell. Other relevant books were in the classroom library and selected by students to read on their own. We used this unit to explore students' abilities to participate in book clubs.

Two early conversations highlight some of the challenges the students faced in moving away from interpreting Book Club in light of their previous experiences in school reading. In the first, a diverse group of fourth-grade students discussed the first half of the book about Sadako after Ms. Woodman, their teacher, had asked them to think about important ideas that could be displayed in a sequence chart. Ken began book club, holding up his reading log with its illustrations and text:

> Chapter 1. When Sadako sees the spider she said it was a good luck sign. Chapter 2. When her and her friend went to the circus. Chapter 3. When Sadako ran she got dizzy . . . she was thinking, er, she told somebody she could not run anymore. Chapter 4. I think that she told someone to tell her mother because she could not tell herself. Chapter 5. Her friend gave her one paper crane and told her to make more. She told her to make a thousand.

Ken's peers listened politely, looking at him or his log. They knew from earlier instruction that asking questions was important. However, Eva's question and Ken's response reveal the superficial nature of this understanding:

| Eva: | A thousand what? |
| Ken: | A thousand more. |

If Eva's question had been authentic, Ken's response would have been unacceptable—it revealed no new information. However, all the students seemed satisfied, since they moved to the next student, Mei, who paralleled Ken's turn. She shared her log, followed by a single question from Ken asking which chapter she was currently reading, and then Ken turned to Joshua.

Ken:	Your turn Joshua.
Joshua:	I don't got nothing to read.
Ken:	You gotta tell about, go, you gotta tell about your picture. Talk!
Eva:	You copycat [referring to his log entry].
Ken:	Talk!
Mei:	Tell us about your picture

This exchange illustrates two norms of classroom literacy that may hinder authentic conversations about books: turn taking and the emphasis on individual work. In school reading settings, turn taking emphasizes each student's obligation to contribute to the discussion. In contrast, in authentic conversations, participants usually contribute when they feel they have something to say. The exchange above underscores how Joshua's peers valued the school-like rules of turn taking over those of authentic conversation.

School norms emphasize doing one's own work with the expectation that each student will be judged on his or her individual accomplishments. When Eva saw the similarity between Joshua's reading log and her own, she called him a copycat despite the fact that they were responding to the same assigned prompt. Eva and her peers did not realize that the activity had been designed to help them explore ideas central to the story and apply their own background knowledge, experiences, and strategies as they constructed their understanding of the story. One of our goals was to help students learn the difference between their preconceptions about book discussion and authentic discussion that arises when readers are engaged with their texts.

However, even when students engaged in more authentic conversations, we could not assume that the conversations reflected understanding of the literary selections. The need to help students consider the deeper meanings in the texts they read was obvious when we analyzed a discussion of fifth-grade students from Mrs. Pardo's classroom in late September. The discussion centered around a picture that Bart had drawn (from McMahon, 1992; see Figure 2).

In an early chapter in the book, Sadako and her mother discuss the Peace Day Carnival, a memorial event to honor those who had died from the bomb. Bart's picture reflected an American boy's conceptions of a carnival including a roller coaster and Ferris wheel. He meshed that with the notion of war by illustrating several falling bombs. The short segment below illustrates how Bart's and his peers' conceptions of war were shaped more by movies and television than by reality:

Bart: I drew, um, that um, airplane dropping a bomb on that fair. And there's dead people laying on the ground [he laughs] and um, it, it exploded, and gas is killing them, they're all falling on the ground, and their eyes are popped out. An' they're dead. And they fell off the roller coaster, splattered [laughter from the rest of the group throughout].

Chris: I drew, I drew, I drew a story of the bomb falling on the fair [laughter from the group and from Chris]. Boom!

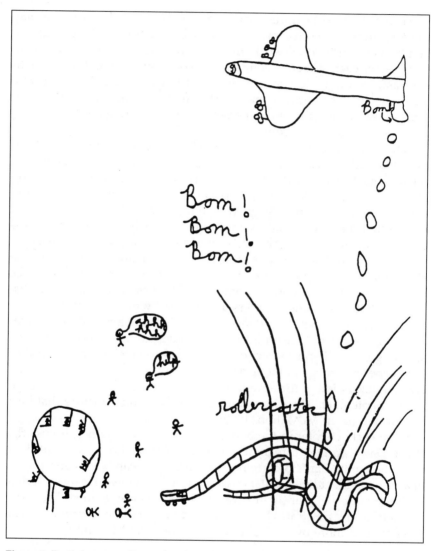

Figure 2. Bart's log entry, September 28, 1990.

	Boom! And people said "Heeelp! Heeelp!" [laughter from group and Bart interrupts]
Bart:	I'm dying! The gas is getting to [inaudible; drowned out by group's laughter]
Chris:	And they trying to run to their houses saying "Help! Help! Let me in!" And their brains poppin' out their heads.

Although this may be authentic conversation, students seemed distant from the ideas in the text, not relating to the main character and her problems. This suggests that focusing on themes and issues in a mature way may not occur without support. We developed the Book Club components with these challenges in mind.

Adjusting the Multiple Literacy Components to Support Students' Book Clubs

Our original components (i.e., instruction, reading, writing, and community share) served to guide initial planning, but the distinction among the components blurred as we implemented the program. For example, during reading time, we often observed students writing in their logs as they recorded thoughts for later discussion. Even though these components merged during implementation, for the convenience of the reader we describe the individual components that supported book clubs.

Reading. Reading instruction concerned fluency, reading vocabulary, comprehension strategies, genres, and aesthetic and personal response. Teachers addressed fluency indirectly by providing time and assigning daily reading of the selected stories and related trade books. Students often read ahead due to high interest in the stories but were asked to reread the section that would be discussed during that day's activities.

To help increase vocabulary, teachers used different strategies to build upon the current reading. For example, when students read a relatively challenging book, such as *Island of the Blue Dolphins* (O'Dell, 1960), they kept think sheets such as Mei's (see Figure 3) in their reading logs. These helped draw students' attention to interesting or unknown words; to locate the words in the text; and to determine meaning from context clues, reference materials, or other sources.

Students referred to one another and used dictionaries and other reference materials to determine word meanings. Books containing more challenging vocabulary led to discussions about the relationship of the words to the plot, theme, or other literary aspects of the story. For example, Mei had listed *olivella* on her vocabulary think sheet as a word she did not understand. Her questioning about the meaning during community share led to an extended conversation about Karana's making jewelry from things found in nature and her use of what she had made to demonstrate friendship to an Aleut visitor.

Experience in using strategies for enhancing reading comprehension was important to the book club program, since it was the only reading program in both classrooms. Reading strategy use and instruction were

Name Mei Dec. 1991 Story/Article Island of the Blue Dolphins

Moving Through: Vocabulary

Date	Word	Page	Meaning
12-6-91	gnapan	108	a thick leaved plant.
12-6-91	dwilfish	105	like an octupus beak, large eyes
12-6-91	reefs	107	small ridge of sand.
12-9-91	lupines	112	plant with long spikes colorful flower
12-16-91	glittering	128	glowing sparkling
12-12-91	wintcha	138	wich mean pretty.
12-12-91	Tutok	142	
12-12-91	Wonapalei	143	means The girl with the long black hair
12-12-91	divellia	149	very small shell
12-13-91	smelts	150	a fish.

Figure 3. Mei's vocabulary think sheet, December 1991.

embedded within the context of reading and writing about the literature. Selected strategies mandated by the state assessment program and included within the district-adopted reading program were incorporated into Book Club. For example, students learned to develop sequence charts to enhance their understanding of the important events in the story as well as to discuss and debate these events. They learned to generate a range of questions to elicit discussion from their peers as well as to ask for clarification for confusions they faced. Through book and chapter critiques they learned to analyze literary elements, such as clarity of plot and depth of character development.

Reading literature of different genres stimulated discussions about the different types of books students read over the year, such as historical fiction, folk tales, and biography. The teachers encouraged students to read for similarities within a genre—for example, features of folk tales or characteristics of biographies. These were integrated with writing when students created their own folk tales or wrote their autobiographies.

Writing. The writing component focused students' attention on issues for discussion about texts, encouraged students to adopt relevant stances toward literary understanding (Langer, 1990), and underscored ways to link ideas from different sections within a text and across the different books they were reading in their themed units. Students consulted a reading log map (see Figure 4) for ideas about writing responses in their reading logs. Categories such as "wonderful words" and "character map" helped them with comprehension and clarification of ideas and encouraged them to bring their own background knowledge and experiences to bear to make sense of the text. Categories such as "me & the book" or "book/chapter critique" enabled students to be analytical about the story and their responses.

Teachers and students used the map as a guide early in the project. As students became more comfortable with their logs and open to writing personal response, we felt they were ready for a broader vision of the reading log. Researchers (e.g., Hartman, 1991) have shown how mature readers draw connections to ideas within a single text but also make intertextual links across different texts they read. We identified different strategies and log activities to encourage students to synthesize ideas within a text as well as across the texts they read on a particular theme, within a genre, or by a particular author.

For within-text synthesis, the distinct curriculum guides and scope and sequence charts from the district's reading source were a useful source for ideas, including summarizing, predicting, questioning, sequencing, and identifying theme. Activities such as comparing and contrasting different texts (e.g., characters, settings, plot structures, illustrations), reflecting on what was learned from the different books within a unit, and identifying issues reflected across different books encouraged across-text synthesis. Think sheets such as the one Randy used to consider what he had learned from the three books in the Japan during World War II unit, supported these activities (see Figure 5).

As the program evolved, students and teachers increased the range of options. For example, in the second year of the program, Mrs. Pardo and her fifth graders brainstormed a reading log idea list that became a permanent bulletin board on display. As individual students created new possibilities, they taught them to their peers, revealing their own sense of ownership and voice (Pardo, 1992). They used various combinations of the ideas in a single log entry. Eva's entry toward the end of her second year in the program (see Figure 6) illustrates how some students had gained control over their logs, choosing their own path to prepare for discussions. Students' broad range of log entries showed how they prepared for discussion groups and their sense of engagement in book club discussions.

Community Share. The community share component of book club provided a context for teachers to meet with their students as a whole

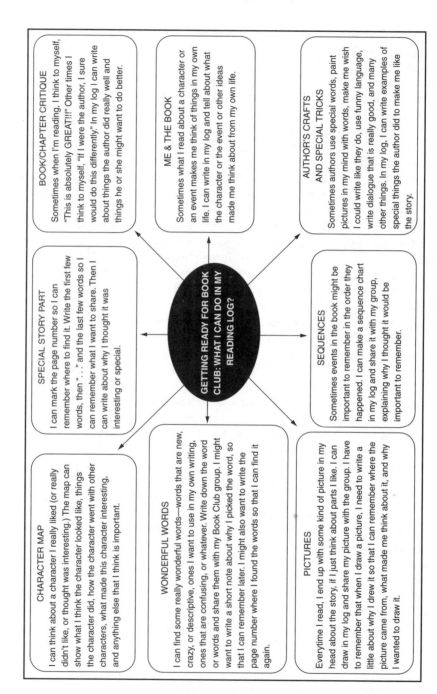

CHARACTER MAP

I can think about a character I really liked (or really didn't like, or thought was interesting.) The map can show what I think the character looked like, things the character did, how the character went with other characters, what made this character interesting, and anything else that I think is important.

SPECIAL STORY PART

I can mark the page number so I can remember where to find it. Write the first few words, then " . . . " and the last few words so I can remember what I want to share. Then I can write about why I thought it was interesting or special.

BOOK/CHAPTER CRITIQUE

Sometimes when I'm reading, I think to myself, "This is absolutely GREAT!!!" Other times I think to myself, "If I were the author, I sure would do this differently." In my log I can write about things the author did really well and things he or she might want to do better.

WONDERFUL WORDS

I can find some really wonderful words—words that are new, crazy, or descriptive, ones I want to use in my own writing, ones that are confusing, or whatever. Write down the word or words and share them with my Book Club group. I might want to write a short note about why I picked the word, so that I can remember later. I might also want to write the page number where I found the words so that I can find it again.

GETTING READY FOR BOOK CLUB: WHAT I CAN DO IN MY READING LOG?

ME & THE BOOK

Sometimes what I read about a character or an event makes me think of things in my own life. I can write in my log and tell about what the character or the event or other ideas made me think about from my own life.

PICTURES

Everytime I read, I end up with some kind of picture in my head about the story, if I just think about parts I like. I can draw in my log and share my picture with the group. I have to remember that when I draw a picture, I need to write a little about why I drew it so that I can remember where the picture came from, what made me think about it, and why I wanted to draw it.

SEQUENCES

Sometimes events in the book might be important to remember in the order they happened. I can make a sequence chart in my log and share it with my group, explaining why I thought it would be important to remember.

AUTHOR'S CRAFTS AND SPECIAL TRICKS

Sometimes authors use special words, paint pictures in my mind with words, make me wish I could write like they do, use funny language, write dialogue that is really good, and many other things. In my log, I can write examples of special things the author did to make me like the story.

Figure 4. Reading log entry possibilities, Fall 1990.

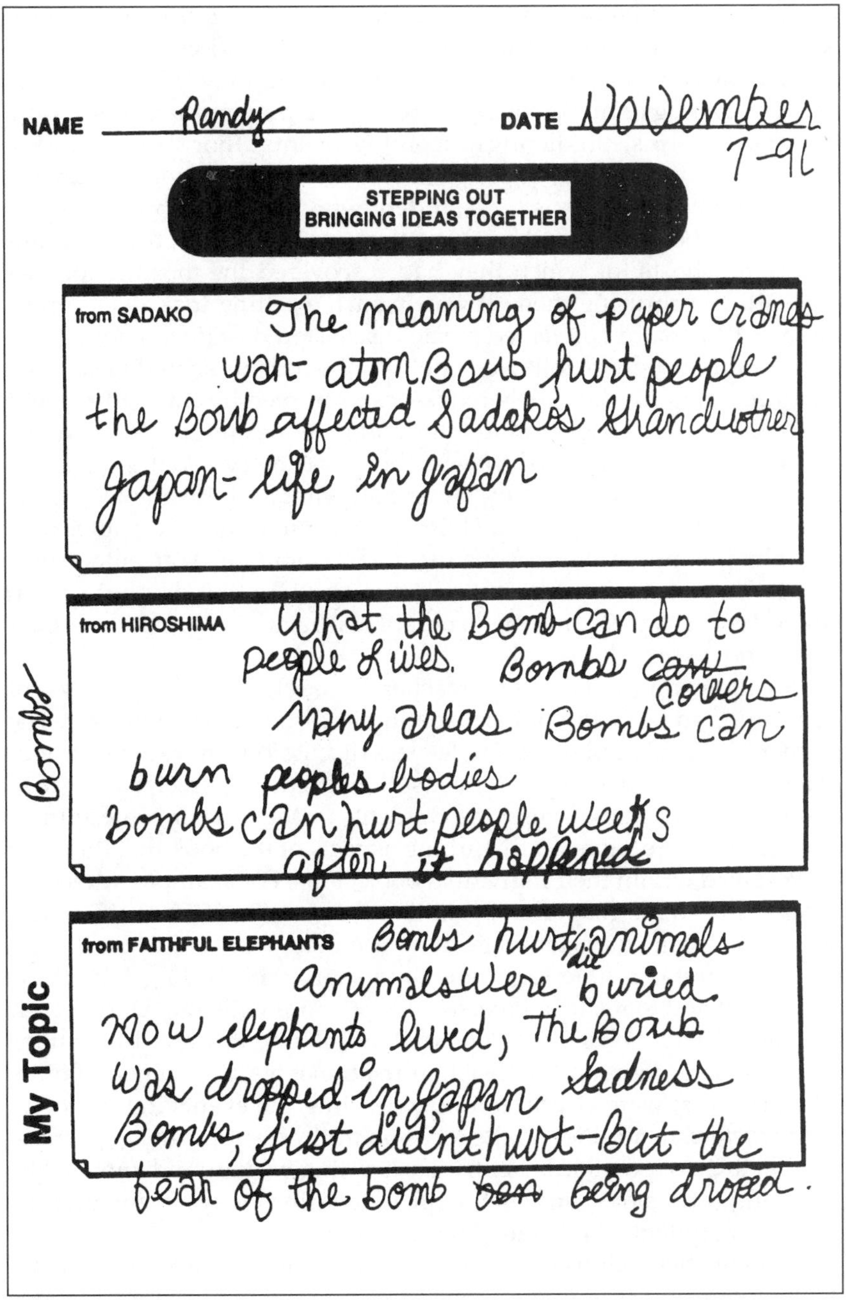

NAME Randy DATE November 7-91

STEPPING OUT
BRINGING IDEAS TOGETHER

from SADAKO The meaning of paper cranes
war- atom Bomb hurt people
the Bomb affected Sadako's Grandmother
Japan- life in Japan

Bombs

from HIROSHIMA What the Bomb can do to
people Lives. Bombs ~~can~~ covers
many areas Bombs can
burn peoples bodies
bombs can hurt people weeks
after it happened

My Topic

from FAITHFUL ELEPHANTS Bombs hurt animals die
animals were buried.
How elephants lived, the Bomb
was dropped in Japan Sadness
Bombs, just didn't hurt-But the
fear of the bomb ~~ben~~ being droped.

Figure 5. Randy's "What I learned" think sheet, November 1990.

group. This setting served different purposes depending on when it occurred in relation to the students' book club discussions. Prior to book clubs, community share was a time for teachers to help students prepare for reading or book clubs (e.g., reviewing previous text, discussing interesting terms, predicting upcoming events). For example, Mrs. Pardo began community share prior to book club by inviting students to review important ideas for a student who had been absent the previous day. She also invited students to share terms from their vocabulary think sheets for which they had discovered the meaning or that may still be confusing them. It was in such a setting that Mei's contribution of the word *olivella* led to the discussion described above.

If community share followed book clubs, students shared ideas from the different book clubs, debated issues prompted by the reading, and discussed relevant background information. For example, during a discussion in January, 1991, of *Number the Stars* (Lowry, 1989), students in one book club wondered why Hitler had wanted to invade Denmark. One of the students explained Hitler's actions in terms of disputes over oil rights, mapping the reasons for the Persian Gulf War onto World War II. The discussions during community share that day focused on Hitler, World War II, and the geographical relationship between Germany and Denmark.

During community share teachers modeled different ways of responding to texts and of participating in discussions about text. The teachers generally led these whole-class discussions in response to students' specific questions or needs the teachers perceived as they observed Book Club discussions. Students or the teacher could initiate discussion of confusing or disturbing aspects of the book that they had not resolved within their individual book clubs. For example, when students had read the chapter in Paterson's *Bridge to Terabithia* (1977) where one of the main characters dies in an accident, Mrs. Pardo used community share as a time for students to share their feelings about the story event and to relate it to personal experience with loss. During their reading of Paterson's *Park's Quest* (1988), students raised questions about divorce, step- and half-sibling relationships, and general family structures that were critical to understanding the events in the story.

Instruction. In addition to the focus on indirect support (e.g., increasing the range of possible log entries, extending background knowledge, clarifying confusions), instruction included direct ways to enhance the quality of students' book club conversations.

Students' book clubs were regularly audiotaped. Teachers used students' interest in listening to their tapes as a way to elicit evaluations of their meetings. For example, selected book clubs were transcribed

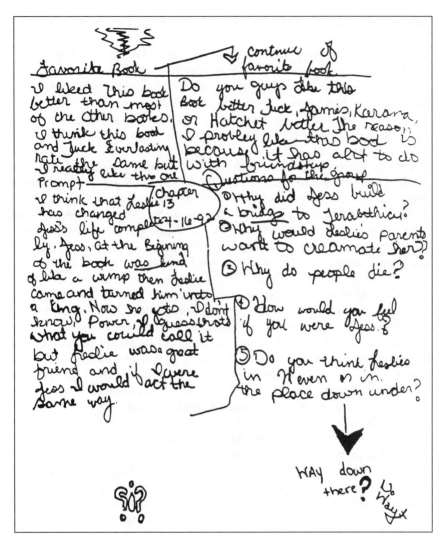

Figure 6. Eva's reading log, April 1992.

using pseudonyms. Students then read and analyzed the transcripts to identify what seemed to be going well and ways in which they could improve. A related activity involved playing short segments of book club conversations and asking students to evaluate what a group did particularly well and what they could improve. For both activities, the teachers always began with the positive (e.g., more than one person talked; they seemed interested in what each other said) before moving into improvements.

A third whole-class activity involved role playing. Teachers circulated transcripts of book clubs for students to perform as plays. After a dramatization, the class discussed how they might feel if they never had the floor, were bossy, asked silly questions, or started a good discussion. This activity gave students a chance to assume alternate personae during book club discussions and test them in low-risk environments.

Finally, students observed each other. For example, one group of fifth graders demonstrated book club discussion for a special education class that was beginning to use the program (Goatley & Raphael, 1992). In another situation, Mrs. Pardo asked a student experiencing trouble interacting with her peers to watch a group and write field notes about what she saw. Then Mrs. Pardo used the notes for a teacher/student conference about how the student could change her behavior and attitude toward book club (Parch, 1992). Together, these teacher-led activities allowed students to examine their own discussions, identify what they were doing well, and make suggestions about how to improve.

As the above examples illustrate, the instruction component was integrated into the other three. Further, students' input and needs helped the collaborative research team make decisions about subsequent instructional foci. Thus, instruction for the reading component focused on fluency, vocabulary development, knowledge of genre, the implementation of various strategies, and personal response. Instruction for the writing component focused on ways in which ideas could be recorded, added to, changed over time, and synthesized across entries and texts. Instruction for the community share component highlighted both the content and process of interacting, as well as the development of background knowledge. Instruction for book club discussions highlighted the balance between the multiple guidelines for active participation and engagement in meaningful talk.

Students' Development through Literature-based Reading Instruction

The Book Club project was designed to enhance students' ability to talk about books, based on our assumption that students' interest in reading and ownership of ideas developed through reading would increase. Over time, we found that students developed their ability to synthesize information (Goatley, Brock, & Raphael, 1993), weave conversations around important themes (McMahon, 1992), use a range of ways to represent their ideas in writing (Pardo, 1992), and take different perspectives (McMahon, 1994). The following conversation occurred in mid-February during the first year of the Book Club project and illustrates changes in students' conversations about books.

Students had read a chapter in Lowry's *Number the Stars* (1989). Set in Denmark during World War II, the story uses the relationship of two close friends to depict how the Danes helped the Jews escape to Sweden. In this chapter the three main characters were stopped by German soldiers. After banning the girls from running, one soldier ruffled the blond curls of the younger sister, saying that she reminded him of his little girl.

The following conversation reflects multiple purposes—clarifying confusing elements, evaluating characters' behavior and motivation, and placing themselves in the situation in the story—and conversational strategies ranging from asking questions to challenging each other's ideas. Students began by sharing their responses to the book so far. Richard's comment about the soldier's "messing with" the younger sister's hair led to extended discussion.

Richard: Well, I think it was really interesting. I like it. The only thing I didn't really like about the book so far is why the soldier um, was messing with what her head, I forgot her name.
Helena: The girl's hair? I agree with Richard.
Randy: Yeah I do too, Annemarie, Annamarie and all.
Helena: Cause he touched Kirsti's hair, and her curls.
Randy: Oh yeah, the little, the little girl?
Helena: Yeah, I didn't think it was fair at all because that was not his daughter. OK, she looked like his, but that's not his daughter.

Richard, Helena, and Randy established one topic of concern, sharing their personal response to this event in the story. The discussion shifted briefly to another topic, but Crystal returned to Richard's point, asking Helena to place herself in a similar, though not identical, circumstance. Helena accepted this change in premise and the discussion continued.

Crystal: Um, Helena, how would you feel if um, the soldier came up and hit you? What would you feel as Kirsti?
Helena: Um, I would be scared because um she's Kirsti is 5 years old and the story says she was 5 years old, so if I was 5 years old I would be really scared. What would I do, I don't know cause I was so small and don't understand anything, so l don't know what I would do.

Crystal: Um, Randy, if you were one of the people in the story,
              how would you feel? Not the soldier but one of the peo-
              ple, like, how about the mother? If you were the father of
              the kid, what would you feel?
Randy: I would feel kind of angry and tell the soldier to not to
              be doing, go in my daughter's hair like that because she
              didn't like it. She didn't.

Not only did students ask authentic probing questions, they continually modified them to clarify their ideas. Students used questions to
bring peers who had not participated into the discussion—questions
in remarkable contrast to early superficial ones, or to students' use of
commands, such as "Talk!" or "You gotta share. . . ."

As their conversation continued, Crystal elicited Richard's participation by asking him how he felt about the story, and Helena drew him
into the debate.

Helena: But what if the soldier killed you for it? What would you
              do? If he was to shoot you for it, what kind of pain would
              you think you would feel? You'd feel more pain about
              what he did to your daughter or more pain about the gun?
Randy: More pain, both, I think both because he shouldn't have
              um his hands on my daughter anyway or he shouldn't
              have his hands on me. I just told him, just told him a
              thing or two, 'cause if he did it again, I would probably
              shoot him.
Crystal: Richard, what do you think about this story?
Richard: Well, I think it was pretty interesting so far.
Helena: OK, how would you feel if someone was come up to your
              head and start stroking and saying, you think you would
              be, what kind of reaction would you give?
Richard: I would probably move and tell him to stop touching my
              hair. Why, what would you do? What would you do,
              Helena?

Students took turns debating what they would do if they were Kirsti.
Then Crystal shifted the debate slightly, asking her peers to imagine
being in Annemarie's place. They accepted the shift from the more
innocent term of rubbing Kirsti's head to the more ominous term in
today's society, touching. Further, they added a hypothesis that the soldiers had a gun.

Crystal: If you were in Annemarie's place, um what would you
              feel if someone was touching your sister?

Ken: I'd tell them to leave her alone.
Helena: But they were scared. You see, they had a gun to your back, what would you do? It was probably real steel or something.
Ken: I'd say "leave her alone" and then I'd go hit him. I'd sock 'em all!
Richard: What happens if they shot you with the gun?
Ken: If they shot me?
Richard: Yeah.
Randy: But they had a gun. You shouldn't do that, you should just stand there—
Ken: I'd risk my life for my sister, yeah.
Crystal: I would.
Helena: I would.
Richard: It depends which sister I am talking about here.

This book club conversation contrasts with our early examples. It reflects a real conversation—an interest in each other's ideas and opinions, a discussion based on the themes within the text (e.g., characters' motivations and beliefs) rather than more surface features, and above all, engagement in ideas introduced in the literature. Despite some of our initial concerns that instruction focused on the tools for successful reading, writing, and discussion might impede students' personal response, this conversation illustrates that such tools helped students to discuss the content of the book as well as their personal responses to the story.

Literature-based Instruction through Book Club

We began the Book Club project to understand the complexities involved in moving to an alternative model of reading instruction. We learned the importance of integrating reading within the language arts since both discussion and writing promoted students' reading and interpretation of texts. We learned the importance of time, of not giving up when students and the adult collaborative team felt initial uncertainties. We learned that alternative models of instruction are not only possible, but they benefit our students' literacy development. We were pleased that students in the Book Club classrooms had standardized test scores as high as those of students in a more traditional reading program where tested skills were directly taught. Further, when Book Club students were interviewed in the fall following their first year in the program, students remembered and could talk about at least nine of the sixteen books they had read the previous year. In contrast, students who had been in the commercial textbook program could not recall titles, authors, or stones from their previous year's instruction (McMahon, Raphael, & Goatley, 1994).

During Book Club conversations students held coherent thematic discussions and encouraged all book club members to make meaningful contributions to the discussion (McMahon & Hauschildt, 1993). We analyzed one group's interactions throughout their reading of *Park's Quest* (Paterson, 1988) and saw that diverse youngsters (e.g., second language, Chapter 1, special education) participated actively and assumed leadership in discussions regardless of the challenges presented by the text (Goatley et al., 1993). We analyzed students' reading logs for content, format, and range of ideas and found that writing became more sophisticated over time (Raphael, Boyd, & Rittenhouse, 1993).

Not surprisingly, our Book Club work has raised many questions that members of the collaborative team continue to pursue. What is the optimal way of grouping students? We have had students select their groups, assigned students to groups, and used combinations but see advantages and disadvantages within each approach. What is the best way to assess students' progress? Portfolio assessment seems to be most consistent with our approach to instruction, but determining means for evaluating students' reading, writing, and oral language abilities and for conveying the range of response in all areas is not clear, nor is the relationship between current standardized assessment measures and alternative approaches. How can thematic units best be developed? We have begun to examine issues such as selection of meaningful themes, related texts, and the relationship of book club to the other content areas, but much work remains. As each question begins to be addressed, we find that new questions emerge and that we, along with our students, continue to learn from our participation in Book Club.

References

Anderson, R. C., E. H. Hiebert, J. A. Scott, and I. A. G. Wilkinson. 1985. *Becoming a nation of readers: The report of the commission on reading*. Washington, D.C.: U.S. Department of Education.

Anderson, R. C., and P. D. Pearson. 1984. A schema-theoretic view of basic process in reading comprehension. In *Handbook of reading research*, ed. P.D. Pearson. New York: Longman, 255–291.

Brown, A. L., B. B. Armbruster, and L. Baker. 1986. The role of metacognition in reading and studying. In *Reading comprehension: From research to practice*, ed. J. Orasanu. Hillsdale, NJ: Erlbaum, 49–75.

Duffy, G. G. 1993. "Rethinking strategy instruction: Four teachers' development and their low achievers' understanding." *The Elementary School Journal* 93: 231–248.

Durkin, D. 1978–1979. "What classroom observations reveal about reading comprehension instruction." *Reading Research Quarterly 15:* 481–533.

Durkin, D. 1981. Reading comprehension instruction in five basal reader series. *Reading Research Quarterly 16:* 515–544.

Gavelek, J. R. 1986. "The social context of literacy and schooling: A developmental perspective."In *The contexts of school-based literacy,* ed. T. E. Raphael. New York: Random House, 3–26.

Goatley, V. J., C. H. Brock, and T. E. Raphael. "Diverse learners participating in regular education 'Book Clubs.'" Paper presented at the University of Pennsylvania Ethnography Forum, Philadelphia, Penn., February, 1993.

Goatley, V. J., and T. E. Raphael. 1992. "Nontraditional learners' written and dialogic response to literature." In *Literacy research, theory and practice: Views from many perspectives,* 41st Yearbook of the National Reading Conference, ed. C. K. Kinzer, and D. J. Leu. Chicago: National Reading Conference, 312–322.

Harker, W. J. 1987. "Literary theory and the reading process: A meeting of perspectives." *Written Communication 9:* 235–252.

Hartman, D. K. 1991. "The intertextual links of readers using multiple passages: A postmodern/semiotic/cognitive view of meaning making." In *Learner factors/teacher factors: issues in literacy research and instruction,* 40th Yearbook of the National Reading Conference, ed. J. Zutell and S. McCormick. Chicago: National Reading Conference, 49–66.

Langer, J. A. 1990. "Understanding literature." *Language Arts 67:* 812–816.

McMahon, S. I. 1992. "A group of five students as they participate in their student-led book club." Unpublished Doctoral diss., Michigan State University, East Lansing.

———. 1994. "Traversing the river of interpretation." *The New Advocate 7:* 109–125.

McMahon, S. I., and P. Hauschildt. "What do we do now? Student struggles with talking about books." Paper presented at the annual meeting of the American Educational Research Association, Atlanta, Georgia, April, 1993.

McMahon, S. I., T. E. Raphael, and V. J. Goatley. 1994. "Changing the context for classroom reading instruction: The Book Club Project." In *Advances in research on teaching,* (vol. 5), ed. J. Brophy. Greenwich, CT: JAI Press.

Pardo, L. S. *"Accommodating diversity in the elementary classroom: A look at literaturebased instruction in an inner city school."* Paper presented at the meeting of the National Reading Conference, San Antonio, Tex., December, 1992.

Raphael, T. E., F. B. Boyd, and P. S. Rittenhouse. *"Reading logs in the book club program: Using writing to support understanding and interpretation of text."* Paper presented at the meeting of the American Educational Research Association, Atlanta, Georgia, April, 1993.

Raphael, T. E., S. I. McMahon, V. J. Goatley, J. L. Bentley, F. B. Boyd, L. S. Pardo, and D. A. Woodman. 1992. "Research directions: Literature and discussion in the reading program." *Language Arts 69:* 55–61.

Rosenblatt, L. M. 1978. *The reader, the text and the poem: The transactional theory of the literary work*. Carbondale, IL: Southern Illinois University Press.

Tharp, R.G. and R. Gallimore. 1988. *Rousing minds to life: Teaching, reaming, and schooling in social context*. Cambridge, England: Cambridge University Press.

Wertsch, J.V. 1985. *Vygotsky and the social formation of mind*. Cambridge, MA: Harvard University Press.

Children's Books Cited

Coerr, E. 1977. *Sadako and the thousand paper cranes*. South Holland, IL: Yearling.

Lowry, L. 1989. *Number the stars* . South Holland, IL: Yearling.

Maruki, T. 1982. *Hiroshima, no pika*. New York: Lothrop, Lee & Shepard.

O'Dell, S. 1960. *Island of the blue dolphins*. New York: Dell.

Paterson, K. 1977. *Bridge to Terabithia*. New York: Harper Trophy.

———. 1988. *Park's quest*. New York: Puffin.

Tsuchiya, Y. 1988. *Faithful elephants*. Boston: Houghton Mifflin.

V Working with Special Populations

Working with Special Populations

As Allington explains in Chapter 33, children who are "different" have often been shortchanged by our educational system. Children have often been shortchanged whenever they are viewed as different from the norm—or, more accurately, the apparent ideal: whether their difference is one of socioeconomic status, ethnicity, native language, learning style or speed, or alleged learning disability. How have they been shortchanged? Typically through assessment that labels them as unready or unable, followed by instruction focused in isolated skill work that does little to promote genuine literacy—in contrast to the reading and writing of whole texts, which is much more effective.

As Linda Erdmann puts it (1994),

> The instructional programs in our schools have created educational disabilities by:
>
> - Teaching children in ways they can't learn.
> - Marching them through prescribed sets of curriculum objectives as though the sequence were sacred.
> - Putting kids into ability groups, forcing those in low groups to see themselves as nonreaders and nonwriters.
> - Denying kids access to real books until they can "read."
> - Putting six-year-old children into a position to fail.
> - Expecting kids to learn language from sitting all day without talking.
> - Asking questions that call for only one right answer.
> - Reprimanding children for wrong answers so that they don't dare to respond again.
>
> And then by:
>
> - Referring children to resource rooms.
> - Subjecting them to testing that would further convince them they know little.
> - Stigmatizing them with a pathological diagnosis.

Whether children perceived as different experience all of these treatments or not, many of them have been less than successful in school at least partly because they've been given more skills-oriented, less literacy-oriented kinds of instruction. We have systematically, if unknowingly, given them an inferior education.

The articles in this section were chosen to dispel the myth that such limiting education is the kind that such children need. Routman focuses on teaching skills and strategies to students labeled as learning disabled, demonstrating that needed skills and strategies can indeed be taught in the context of authentic reading and writing. Strickland challenges the myth fueled by Lisa Delpit's 1986 article, that African American children, particularly those from lower socioeconomic homes, need to be taught skills directly and out of context. Freeman and Freeman demonstrate that the particular needs of students for whom English is not the native language can be met within a whole literacy context. To generalize, it appears that children with various kinds of differences can engage in genuine literacy experiences while learning the skills and strategies they need, given adequate support.

References

Bertrand, J. E., & Stice, C. F. (Eds.) (1995). *Empowering children at risk of school failure: A better way*. Norwood, MA: Christopher-Gordon.

Chew, C. R. (Ed.). 1991. *Whole language in urban classrooms: Encounters with literacy*. Roslyn, NY: Berrent.

Delpit, L. 1987. Skills and other dilemmas of a progressive black educator. *Harvard Educational Review, 3*, 9–14.

Erdmann, L. (1994). Teaching "learners with a difference" in a whole language classroom. In C. Weaver, *Reading process and practice: From sociopsycholinguistics to whole language* (2nd ed). Portsmouth, NH: Heinemann.

Five, C. L. (1992). *Special voices: Teaching children with special needs in the regular classroom*. Portsmouth, NH: Heinemann.

Rhodes, L. K., & Dudley-Marling, C. (1996). *Readers and writers with a difference: A holistic approach to teaching struggling readers and writers* (2nd ed.). Portsmouth, NH: Heinemann.

Stires, S. (Ed.). *With promise: Redefining reading and writing needs for special students*. Portsmouth, NH: Heinemann.

25 Selected Reading-Writing Strategies for L. D. and Other At-Risk Students

Regie Routman
Shaker Heights City Schools, Ohio

Routman explains that these are strategies that she and other teachers have used successfully with students labeled "learning disabled," and with other at-risk students. These strategies are used with, and helpful to, all children, but are especially important for at-risk children, whose instruction has often not led them to experience the reading of whole, meaningful, enjoyable texts. Such students can often complete phonics or language workbook exercises, Routman points out, but are still unable to apply these skills in a meaningful context. Needed skills and strategies are therefore best taught in the context of actual reading and writing. Illustrating many of the teaching strategies in detail from examples with real children, Routman discusses ways of teaching reading skills and strategies within the following kinds of literacy events: creating predictable text from the child's language; using predictable, well-written literature; creating predictable text from literature; reading aloud to the student and by the student; shared reading; repeated reading; paired reading, sustained silent reading of self-selected text; emphasizing silent reading as part of instructional time; self-selected writing; valuing oral responses; writing aloud; shared writing; sustained silent writing for teachers and students; and conferencing with peers.

Originally published in *Invitations: Changing as Teachers and Learners K-12* (Heinemann, 1991, pp. 390–402). Reprinted with permission.

This chapter encompasses selected strategies I and other teachers have used successfully with L.D. and remedial students to teach reading and writing. However, these strategies are not just for the L.D. or special education teacher. The classroom teacher also has the responsibility to teach the L.D. student—usually the major responsibility. As such, the classroom teacher must be knowledgeable and flexible enough to set up a learning environment in which every student becomes literate.

I believe all of us learn language most easily when the language is whole, and when the experiences, contexts, and texts are meaningful and relevant to the learners' lives. Therefore, the strategies for teaching L.D. students and other at-risk learners should be similar to the meaning-based, holistic strategies recommended for teaching all students.

Fragmented instruction is particularly difficult for at-risk learners. While efficient language learners figure out what makes sense regardless of the instruction and ignore what doesn't fit, the at-risk population becomes further handicapped by splintered instruction. These are the students who do not learn language efficiently. They are often unable to filter out what doesn't make sense.

For example, at-risk students may be able to complete phonics or language workbook exercises but still be unable to apply those skills in a meaningful context. When instruction has focused on disconnected parts and isolated skills, students often find the bits and pieces insufficient to enable them to make sense of language and texts. These students need better instruction, more of it, and lots of opportunities to practice and apply meaning-based strategies.

Paul's mother told me,

> If the teacher or I take the time to give Paul an overall sense of what the story is about, or to discuss what the main concepts or questions to be answered are in a social studies or science text, he can pretty much figure things out for himself—even if the reading level is hard for him. But if he is just given an assignment without any background information, he is at a loss to make sense of it.

While the strategies discussed in this section may be used successfully with all students, they are especially helpful for the at-risk children. When applicable, I have used specific examples from working with Paul, Chris, and Onajé, as well as from a group of L.D. students, to demonstrate how a strategy has been used. Although the strategies that follow are presented one at a time, in the actual teaching-learning situation, they are often integrated and used interactively.

Creating Predictable Text from the Child's Language

This is a sure-fire technique that has never failed me. The child's own language becomes his beginning reading material. The approach has worked successfully for first-graders as well as for high school students, and I believe it can also work well for illiterate adults. By encouraging the student to talk and write about what is important to him, and by writing for and with the student, by hand or on the word processor, the student engages in the material. The "skills" are taught as they come up, in the context of reading and writing together.

Although the specific examples cited come from working with one student, predictable text can easily come from a group of students. A common experience, a series of books by an author, or a favorite book can all be used as a springboard for a shared writing. The story can then be reproduced so each child has a personal copy for reading and illustrating.

The following techniques have been successfully utilized with a child's natural language, predictable text:

Cutting Apart a Sentence from the Child's Story

A sentence from the child's story is written with a marker on a vertical strip. The words, and in some cases the word parts, are cut apart. The student attempts to put the sentence in proper sequence. If necessary, the student goes back to the text to check or correct herself.

With Chris, L.D. teacher Margie Glaros or I would choose a sentence that had one or more basic sight words that we knew Chris would encounter often in other contexts. We would write the sentence from his illustrated story on a sentence strip that had been cut lengthwise from the photocopy paper. Next, we would cut the sentence apart, word by word. (Later some words might also be cut apart to emphasize a teaching point, such as a consonant digraph or blend, for example, *wh en, th ird, gr ade.*) Although Chris saw words in isolation, they always went back into the context. Chris was expected to put the sentence back together in sequence and read it aloud as he did so. He would then check himself against the written text. If he had made a mistake, he was expected to self-correct using his book's written model.

Chris kept all sentences from each book (cut apart and held with a paper clip in a large envelope labeled with the book title) so he might practice often on his own.

Referring to Other Texts the Child Can Read

When a student gets stuck reading or writing a word that has been known in another context, he is guided to go back to a familiar source, read the particular word in context, and then apply it to the new situation. Students get very proficient at locating the unknown word, reading it in the familiar context, and applying it to the new context.

When beginning to write *About the Gerbils*, I asked Chris, "Where have you seen 'About' before?" He was able to find his previously written book, *About My Friend Brian,* and read and write "About" for himself in the new title.

Making a "Words I Can Write" Booklet

When it appeared that Chris was reading a high-frequency word without any help, I would ask him to try writing it. If he wrote it correctly, he was able to add it to his "Words I Can Write" booklet. He could eventually read all these words in isolation. If he got stuck, he referred to one of his books for help. He was very proud of his growing list of words and seemed eager to add new words to his booklet (see Figure 1).

Teaching Some Short Vowels, or Other Phonics Generalizations, through the Child's Name or Other Well-Known Words

Many children like Chris have a difficult time applying short vowels, particularly "e" and "i," to reading and writing words. When Chris was unsure of what letter to put in the middle of words such as "with" and "get," which came from his stories, he referred back to his name, "Chris Jenesin." With guidance, he could make the correct connection. Eventually, he would do this on his own.

Sharing the Scribing Process

For some L.D. students, writing has been so difficult that the teacher needs to sit right next to the child to provide emotional and physical support. An environment in which the child feels valued and safe enough to take a risk must already exist. Even students who have been reluctant to write can usually be persuaded to give it a try if the teacher takes over when the child falters. If a word processor is available, the child is even more willing to get started.

Once Chris knew he could read and write some words, he was willing to risk writing for himself with some support. In his third book, *About the Gerbils,* he was encouraged to write as much of each word as he was able and to use all of the above strategies. For his sentence "Sometimes I get to pick them up," he was able to write all of the letters that are underlined.

<u>Some</u><u>t</u><u>imes</u> I <u>get</u> <u>to</u> <u>p</u>ick <u>them</u> <u>up</u>.

On a subsequent page, "Sometimes I get to go down to the boy's bathroom to fill up the bottle," he referred back to the above page and was able to write "Sometimes," "get," and "up" in their entirety.

He decided "sometimes" was a word he wanted to have in his "Words I Can Write" booklet. In spite of its length, he mastered the

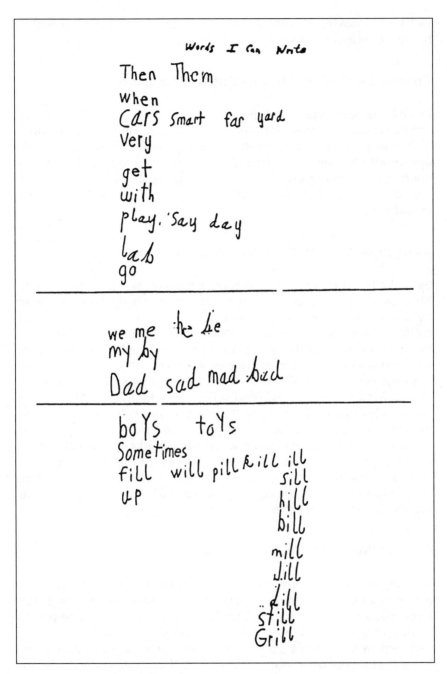

Figure 1. Chris's "Words I Can Write" list.

word after looking at it many times, writing it, and referring back to his stories when he got stuck.

Creating Predictable Text from Patterned Language

Little books that repeat a pattern such as "I can. . . ." or "This is. . . ." can be used as a springboard for writing and reading original stories. Using simple patterned text with matching pictures, Mary Leo's developmentally handicapped students in grades two to four did the first reading and writing they had ever done using an "I Can . . ." text as a model. Prior to that time, all skills and sight words had been taught in isolation.

Using Predictable, Well-written Literature

Special education teachers who formerly used basal texts report a big difference in interest level and motivation, not only by the students but by the teachers themselves, when quality literature is used to teach reading. Both teachers and students were bored with dull materials. At the secondary level, this also means supplementing the literature of the 1970s with more relevant and interesting texts.

Onajé became a reader only when the emphasis of his instruction shifted from structured texts and skills sheets to predictable texts and books at his interest level. Then the pleasure of reading could be combined with skills instruction arising from his on-site needs.

Allowing the student to self-select reading books is especially important. A high school teacher reported her first success with a student who had a keen interest in all aspects of building. She brought in everything she could find on the subject, and all the student's reading and writing emanated from those books.

Creating Predictable Text from Literature

Working in a small group, students can create their own text to use as reading material. Because the language is their own, students are highly motivated to read it. After students have heard or read several poems, stories, or books by an author, they can be encouraged to create their own text in that author's style. The teacher acts as guide and scribe. Because students are already familiar with the characters, settings, and plots in a series, they feel confident developing a sequel or related chapter or story. A group of second-graders enjoyed writing their own *Nate the Great* text, based on the series by Marjorie Sharmat (Putnam, 1977), while a group of sixth-graders created an epilogue to *The Great Gilly Hopkins* by Katherine Paterson. The text can be written on overhead transparencies or large chart paper for group reading or photocopied so each student has a copy to read. Students' original texts may take the form of a conversation between two characters, a scene in a play, a chapter, or a complete story.

Using Wordless Picture Books

Wordless picture books work wonderfully well with elementary and secondary students as a springboard for developing oral language and for creating original stories to read. 0Students begin by orally retelling the story through the pictures. The original text can then be written by the teacher or another student. Older students can create text for younger readers. Students can also work in pairs to create original wordless books, with one student creating the pictures and the other writing the text.

Besides wordless books, familiar picture books can also be used, and the existing text can be covered up. The new text becomes a retelling or new version in students' own language. Even in schools where the basal text is the mainstay of the reading program, students can cover up the text of a dull story, rewrite it, and practice reading the new, improved version.

Reading Aloud to the Student and by the Student

Reading aloud *to* the child—for vocabulary development, literature appreciation, exposure to literary-level language and authors' styles, and comprehension—continues to be of utmost importance for attitude, motivation, and just sheer enjoyment.

Reading aloud by the teacher is important even at the secondary level where lack of vocabulary and word meanings interfere with comprehension. Reading aloud helps build needed vocabulary and lets the student hear what fluent reading sounds like. In addition, it is recommended in a test-taking situation where the student is unable to read the test.

Reading aloud *by* the child, in a one-on-one or small-group setting where the child feels safe enough to take a risk, provides the teacher with information on the strategies the child is using or not using. The teacher can then guide the child to employ various strategies that good readers use. At times, the child's reading aloud can be documented with a running record or tape recording.

Relating the Known to the Unknown

Whenever possible, it is advisable to use what the child already knows and apply that knowledge to a new situation. When Chris could not read "them," we went back to "then" in one of his stories. When he could not write "by," we used "my," which he already knew. After he was able to read and write "play," we wrote and read "say," "day," "may," and other words that fit the pattern.

Shared Reading

Shared reading is an excellent technique for getting the student engaged in reading. I find using a transparency on the overhead projector invaluable for maintaining attention, focusing eyes on the print, and immersing the student in reading without singling her out. Students get to hear and feel the appropriate phrasing and fluency for poems, songs, raps, or excerpts from a book. The reading is always invitational; students are expected to follow the text with their eyes and join in orally if they choose to do so. While the emphasis is always on enjoyment in a social setting, one or two teaching points—such as calling attention to conventions of print—may be made on subsequent rereadings.

Repeated Reading

Reading a selection over and over again increases fluency and improves word-attack skills, building confidence and enabling the student to focus on comprehension. Working alone, with a partner, or with the aid of a tape recorder, the student chooses a paragraph or excerpt and practices it until he can read it fluently. Students can tape record themselves, evaluate where they need to improve, and then rerecord themselves.

Paired Reading

Paired reading occurs when one reader supports another in the reading of the text. The student has a personal copy of the text and follows along visually as he:

Hears the text on tape
Listens to a peer read the text
Has the support of a peer when needed in reading the text for himself
Follows the voice of the teacher or reader

Once the student is familiar with the text he can try it again on his own. More important, he can be included in group discussion of the text. Paired reading assumes that a reader will be able to understand the text even if he is unable to read it all independently.

Having Books Available on Tape

Many L.D. students who have difficulty reading do quite well understanding text and contributing to oral discussion if they can hear the text and follow along with a tape. Students can then "read" literature that is at their listening comprehension level, even though the text is above their instructional and independent levels. Literature and content area tapes are made by the teacher or parent volunteer or are available free from the local public library through the federally funded "Talking Book" program.

Paul's mother reported that her son experienced success when his L.D. teacher sent home tapes from chapters in his science and social studies texts. When the key vocabulary and focus of the chapter were discussed prior to reading-listening, Paul was able to answer orally questions about the chapter without difficulty.

Sustained Silent Reading of Self-Selected Text

Sustained silent reading, where the student engages in uninterrupted reading of a book of his choice, is one of the most important strategies for increasing fluency, vocabulary, and overall reading ability. Students need to do lots of reading of easy books for pleasure to become fluent, confident readers. Before students willingly and successfully engage in this activity, they must be able to help themselves—beyond "sounding out"—when encountering an unknown word. They must be integrating all cueing systems—using semantics and syntax along with graphophonics.

Promoting Independent Silent Reading and Self-monitoring

Using a line marker, verbalizing the strategies used when in difficulty, jotting down important vocabulary that interfered with understanding the text, and connecting the known to the unknown all helped Onajé read more independently.

In reading *My Robot Buddy* by Alfred Slote, Onajé had difficulty with the sentence "I couldn't really believe they'd hear me, but suddenly the air cruiser started its descent onto the road" (p. 58). He could not read and did not know the exact meanings of "cruiser" and "descent." Thinking while reading, he was able to substitute "vehicle" for "cruiser" and "landing" for "descent." Because he had jotted down both those words, we worked on them graphophonically and for meaning. For "cruiser" I wrote the word "bruise," which was in his vocabulary, and related it to "cruise." We talked about what kind of vehicle an air cruiser could be. For "descent" he could read "de," but could not apply "sc." I wrote down "<u>sc</u>ience," "<u>sc</u>ene," and "<u>sc</u>ent," which he could read, and had him apply what he already knew to "descent." We used "ascend" and "descend" together, and I graphically demonstrated the opposite meanings by moving my body and my arms.

Providing books at Onajé's interest and reading level helped him begin to read on his own. Setting realistic expectations with him and his mother contributed to his success.

Promoting Reading Comprehension

Some L.D. and classroom teachers note that many at-risk learners have difficulty grasping the major points of a story once they move into longer books where most of the reading is done independently. These children need to understand why we read. They also need to be carefully monitored and held accountable for what they have read. I have found that assigning only a few pages of silent reading at a time works well. In severe cases, silently reading and monitoring one paragraph at a time may be necessary until the student begins to self-monitor and think about what he is reading.

I was recently asked to work with Robert, a third-grader, who could read the words in a grade-level book but could not say what he had read beyond giving some unrelated details. When I asked him, "Why do we read?" he replied, "to know the words." Because he viewed reading only as reading the words, he did not stop when something didn't make sense, and he never went back to reread or refocus.

I asked Robert to read a passage orally (pp. 15–16) from *Mr. Popper's Penguins* by Richard and Florence Atwater (Little, Brown, 1938), a book he had never seen before. Before he began reading, I gave him some general background information about what he was about to read, and then I took a running record of his reading. Although he read with 92 percent accuracy, indicating the book was at his instructional level, when I asked him to tell me what he had just read (what Mr. Popper wanted to do and why), he gave me misinformation. I sent him back to the text to reread. When he again gave me inaccurate information, I sent him back to the specific paragraph and asked, "Where does it say that? Find the line that says that, and read it to me." He finally replied, "It doesn't say that anywhere." I asked him, "What does it say? Now put that into your own words." With prodding, and my insisting he reread, think about his reading, and stop every time something didn't make sense or sound right, Robert could eventually come up with an intelligent response.

By continuing to ask Robert very specific questions that focused on main ideas, by verbally modeling thinking processes aloud, and by guiding him to reread a small chunk of text silently and do a retelling, Robert gradually improved in overall comprehension. Although he had been expected to be reading a chapter book as part of his independent, nightly reading, he had never received guided instruction in understanding what he was reading silently. He was now asked to slow down and read only several pages a night. He knew his teacher would be asking him to do a retelling, and that if he could not do it, he would be asked to reread. He was also asked to verify his oral responses. He would be asked, "How do you know that? Where in the text does it say that?" By being held accountable on a daily basis, by talking through specific passages with his teacher, and by being shown where he needed to reread, Robert gradually improved his comprehension abilities.

Emphasizing Silent Reading as Part of Instructional Time

Typically, most of the reading instruction time for remedial students is spent in oral reading and practice exercises. Even when L.D. and remedial learners use real literature, the tendency is to have students read aloud. Since most of the reading students will do in school is silent reading—and since silent reading is how reading is used in the world outside school—students need to be guided in the transition from oral to silent reading. As teachers, we tend to feel slightly uncomfortable allowing silent reading during "teaching" time, but it is necessary if students are to become successful, independent readers. When students find that they can begin to monitor their own reading and work out trouble spots on their own, their reading confidence, along with the amount of time they spend reading silently, increases.

I was asked to work with a group of third grade L.D. students reading *The Mouse and the Motorcycle* by Beverly Cleary (Morrow, 1965). Up
to this time, their reading in the L.D. class had been done mostly round-
robin style, with each child taking a turn reading orally. At the same time
that I asked them to read several pages silently, I asked them to "write
down any words you can't read or don't know the meaning of." Then
we took the words they had trouble with and worked them through
together. Mostly, they worked them through after I asked them, "What
could you try that might help you?" As they worked through their difficult words, I kept asking, "What can you do?" and then, "What did
you do to work that out? What could that word mean? Reread that paragraph, and see if you can figure it out." Margie Glaros, the L.D. teacher,
and I had already spent a lot of time putting the responsibility for learning on them and emphasizing meaningful language strategies.

Donald had written down the word "automatically" from the sentence "He did not even have to think what to do—he automatically
grabbed for the motorcycle and held on with all his strength" (pp.
82–83). When he went back to work it out, he skipped it and got the
meaning through the context by predicting what the word could mean.
He substituted "quickly." Because what he put in made sense, it was
not significant that he could not read the exact word.

Below is the chart that came out of several short sessions and stayed
posted in the L. D. classroom for referral. It is shown exactly as the students wrote it.

What to Do When You Can't Read a Word

1. Look at that word again—ending, middle, beginning.
2. Read on, and then come back to the hard word and try again.
3. Stretch out the letters; take the word apart.
4. Think about what would make sense.
5. Think about what would sound right.
6. Substitute a word that makes sense.
7. See if it looks like a word you've seen before.
8. Put word parts together (relief).
9. Skip the word and go on.

It is very valuable to take the time to get students to verbalize what
works for them. The list you and your students come up with will be
worded differently but will be even more valid because it will come

from your students. If the strategies they come up with are limited, the teacher needs to guide them and demonstrate meaningful alternatives.

When, after several silent reading sessions of short passages, it became clear these students were reading for meaning and using the above strategies, I asked them to read an entire chapter in *The Mouse and the Motorcycle* silently (pp. 79–85). Before they started reading, I explained that we would begin to use a reading log. The students were asked to answer the following question: "What's the most important thing that happened in this chapter?" They were told they needed to write only one sentence. To help focus their attention, I sat with them and read the chapter silently at the same time. Damon wrote, "Ralph got caught in a vacuum cleaner but he chewed himself out." It was clear from each of their individual responses that they had gleaned the main ideas of the chapter.

After the students had moved almost totally into silent reading during their instructional reading time in the L.D. class, I asked them, "How do you feel about reading silently versus reading out loud?" These were their responses:

"You can go faster."

"I like reading in my mind."

"You don't have to express yourself, or change the tone of your voice."

"I like it 'cause if I don't know a word, I can ask someone who is also reading silently."

"If I don't know a word, I can figure it out myself without anyone helping me."

Self-Selected Writing

For many L.D. children, their own writing—in language that is predictable and familiar to them—leads to their first successful reading. Teaching needs become apparent from a close look at the child's self-selected, frequent writing. Journal writing is a powerful vehicle for evaluating the child's phonics, spelling, use of syntax, and ideas. Writing as a response to reading also indicates the thought processing and connections the child is making.

Using Post-its or a Copy of an Original Piece of Writing

Students are sensitive to "marks" made by the teacher on their writing. Leaving the original writing intact sends a message of respect and value to the student. I find students more receptive to working out problem areas when the "marks" are made on a copy. Instead of a reproduced copy of the original, some teachers write on Post-its and place them strategically on the original writing to draw attention to particular strengths and concerns.

Using Self-selected Writing to Teach Spelling

Onajé's L.D. tutor, Ellen Potter, used, his personal writing to teach phonics and spelling. For example, she took "thair" and "stithes" as an opportunity to teach "ch." They kept a chart of "ch" words as they came across them, and several weeks later we noted the correct usage of "ch" in Onajé's journal writing.

Many L.D. students are able to find their own misspelled words from journal entries or other writing and use the Have-a-Go sheet effectively. Ellen often used a Have-a-Go sheet to help Onajé work out his misspellings. First he would find and circle those words that "looked" wrong. Then he would work them out with help from his tutor, a spelling dictionary, and other resources available.

Typing or Word-processing the Student's Writing

Students are more willing to make revisions and corrections when the text is clean and easily readable and spaces are left between lines. In addition, a typed copy sends a message to the student that the writing is appreciated.

Valuing Oral Responses

When Paul had to respond to a test by writing, he stated, "I know the information but it doesn't come out right."

Some L.D. students can really shine when they are encouraged to contribute their thoughts orally. Students need to know that verbal responses are just as valid and valued as written responses. A student who is unable to read and write sufficiently well to complete a test should be given the test orally. When the spelling and handwriting are poor, the student should be allowed to dictate to the teacher or volunteer. In addition, some students find when they can tape their original story or responses and go back to the tape at their leisure, they can write adequate responses.

Using a Tape Recorder in the Content Areas

Older students who cannot copy well from the board or take notes quickly or in an organized fashion benefit from taping the discussion in the content areas. On their own, or with assistance, they can work at their own pace to write down necessary information.

Using a Tape Recorder for a Final Copy

Some teachers allow students to put their final copy of a story on tape, so that writing and editing are not required.

Writing Aloud

Writing aloud is an excellent, nonthreatening way for students to observe frequently the conventions of writing. Seeing words formed, spaced, spelled, and used in context with correct capitalization and punctuation eventually imprints on the students. The teacher can incorporate and highlight conventions and words that students need or are struggling to learn.

Shared Writing

Shared writing is appropriate and desirable even at the high school level. The teacher, in collaboration with the students, guides the students in the composition of a common interest and demonstrates the process of writing. While the chalkboard may be used, Magic Marker on large chart paper or a transparency on the overhead projector is even more attention getting.

Sustained Silent Writing for Teachers and Students

Typically, because writing is an area of difficulty for L.D. students, much encouragement is needed. Margie Glaros and I have found students will make a much greater effort and maintain attention longer when teacher and students write simultaneously in a shared setting.

Valuing Time for Talk and Sharing Before Writing

Margie and I asked a group of five third grade L.D. students to write about their relationship with a sibling or other family member. Our purpose was to get these students, who normally wrote very little and who stopped writing after just a few minutes, to write for a sustained period. We began by sitting around a table with the students. Margie and I each spoke in detail about our relationship with one of our siblings. We then encouraged the students to verbalize their thoughts about a sister, brother, or family member—what they liked about them, what drove them crazy, special interests shared. If they got stuck talking, we asked questions to help stimulate thinking. We allowed about fifteen to twenty minutes just for talking. The students later told us that talking over what they might write about made the writing "easy." Not only did their talking to the group help clarify what they already knew and could write about but listening to their peers triggered memories and generated fresh ideas for their own writing. Later, they were also eager to share orally their completed stories with each other.

Writing While Students are Writing

When Margie and I wrote with the students, we found that they were less distracted and more willing to invest in their writing. They saw each of us look up as we stopped to think and put out heads down and be seriously quiet as we engaged in the writing. When a student looked up as though she was finished, even though everyone else was still writing, we reminded the student—based on her oral sharing—that she probably had more she could write. Eventually, the student went back to adding to her piece. The students later acknowledged feeling pleased with and surprised by the quantity of their writing. We teachers were surprised that each student was able to stay with the writing for about twenty minutes.

Demonstrating

Once the students were convinced they could write a substantial amount on a topic they knew about, we moved into refining the writing. We asked them to choose one small part of their sibling story and try to develop it in some depth. First Margie and I talked about what parts of our stories we would pick. I told them I was going to expand on one line in my story: "When my sister Adrienne and I were little, we used to fight all the time except when we built cities together in our bedroom." Then I went on to explain in detail how we moved our furniture, spread blankets and bedspreads across desks and beds, fortified our "city" with comic books, games, and snacks, and played happily secluded "under wraps" until our parents insisted we clean up. Margie told about an incident in a restaurant as an example of how her brothers always teased her. Then each of the students, with guidance when necessary, talked about a part that could be expanded into its own story. We then wrote quietly together for about thirty minutes. Again, seeing teachers writing was a powerful inducement for students to write.

Conferencing with Peers

We have found students are more willing to make revisions if feedback is given in a group setting. Working with a group of L.D. students in the middle grades, Margie and I noted that when we demonstrated positive comments and questions to each other about our writing, students were eager to participate and were very willing and able to provide appropriate feedback to each other.

In one situation, we gave the students a choice. Did they want to put the piece away, revise it, or edit it? We were surprised that even though they didn't want to do revisions, they opted to edit their pieces so they could be published. Because the choice was theirs, they were willing to make the required effort.

Since we wanted most of the responsibility to rest with the students, we first spent time making a chart of what to look for while editing. We wrote the chart using their responses in their own language. To our surprise, the students knew what needed to be done in the editing process. After going over their chart, they began by circling all misspelled words, and with guidance and encouragement, they went on to self-edit their pieces with a greater effort and involvement than usual.

26 Educating African American Learners at Risk: Finding a Better Way

Dorothy S. Strickland
Rutgers University

Strickland begins by noting that even before they start school, at least a third of our nation's children are at risk of school failure—simply because they are poor. Among the children living in poverty are a large proportion of African American children. Herself an African American educator, Strickland focuses on these children in particular, but her observations and recommendations are generally relevant for all poor and/or minority children. She first discusses several of the new trends in literacy education: increased attention to writing and its relationship to reading; greater use of trade books or library books rather than textbooks; greater student choice in what they read and write; greater integration of oral language and literacy across all subjects in the curriculum. Next, she discusses the arguments of other educators, especially African American educator Lisa Delpit, who expresses concern "about the lack of a display of power and authority in process-oriented classrooms." Delpit thinks teachers must be much more authoritative and directive when working with lower socioeconomic status African American children. Others, too, have questioned the value of holistic approaches with at-risk learners: for example, phonics advocate Jeanne Chall thinks that whole language is "particularly harmful for below-average children or children at risk of failure because of poverty or learning problems." Mindful of these concerns, Strickland nevertheless raises concerns of her own about the traditional heavy emphasis on basic skills for at-risk children. She notes that supplementary skills teaching, highly structured and in isolation, has indeed served to improve student performance on standardized tests. However, children in such programs do not typically achieve the kind of literacy demanded by today's society. "Teaching to low-level, basic skills apparently places an unintended ceiling on learning." Students subjected to heavy skills instruction "may conscientiously take in the information dispensed to them, and they may spout it back on cue. But they are frequently left not knowing how to use that information, how to learn on their own, to think for themselves, solve problems, and critique their own work and the work of others." The last half of this chapter focuses on key points for "A Better Way" of teaching—a way of teaching not just unlabeled learners, not just African American children, not just minority children living in poverty, but all learners.

Originally published in *Language Arts, 71,* (1994), 328-336. Copyright 1994 by the National Council of Teachers of English.

Even before they enter school, at least one-third of the nation's children are at risk for school failure. The deck is stacked against them, not because of anything they have done or failed to do. Most of these youngsters live in poverty, and they are members of a minority group. A large proportion of them are African American. The fact that they are poor is the key reason they are at risk for failure. Indeed, children from middle-class black families academically outperform poor children, regardless of ethnicity (Hodgkinson, 1991). Although education cannot solve all the societal problems that poor, African American children face, it remains an important and powerful weapon against poverty and crime. It is becoming increasingly obvious that whether or not these children become literate has a profound effect on all our lives. For these children, the successful application of what is known about the teaching and learning of literacy is of critical importance. In this article, I bring that knowledge together with my very deep concern for a group of children who are in desperate need of our help.

New Trends in Literacy Instruction

Throughout the United States, teachers and administrators are thoughtfully reexamining the assumptions underlying their literacy programs. Dramatic changes have taken place in many individual classrooms and schools. In some cases massive reforms have been initiated across entire school districts. The changes appear under the heading of various holistic and process-oriented terms such as literature-based curriculum, integrated language arts. Language across the curriculum, whole language, and emergent literacy (Allen & Mason, 1989; Cazden, 1992; Edelsky, Altwerger, & Flores, 1991; Hiebert, 1991). Among the changes in evidence are:

- *Increased attention to writing and its relationship to reading.* Students in these classrooms write every day. The writing does not stem from a series of teacher-based assignments to be collected, corrected, and returned. Rather, it is grounded in the ongoing activities of the classroom and the interests of individual students. Students are helped to see their writing through the entire process of prewriting, drafting, revising, editing, and publishing (Fornan, Lapp, & Flood, 1992; Jensen, 1993; Shanahan, 1990).

- *Greater use of trade books or library books rather than the more traditional reliance on textbooks.* Children in these classrooms read and are read to every day. Sharing and responding to literature are fundamental to all aspects of the curriculum. The reading aloud continues long after children are fluent, independent readers. Textbooks remain important as one of many resources for learning literacy and learning through literacy. Response to literature takes many forms: personal reflection, group discussions, writing, art, and drama may act as a means of reformulating children's understanding and interpretations of texts. Poems, stories, and informational texts are discussed in terms of their content, their literary qualities, and the art of writing. Students are encouraged to apply what they learn about the author's craft to their own writing (Cullinan, 1992; Huck, 1992; Norton, 1992).

- *Greater student choice in what they read and write in the classroom.* Teachers encourage children to share in the decision making regarding choice of topics to write about and materials to read. Making thoughtful selections and decisions is considered to be a valuable part of students' literacy development (Calkins, 1986; Cambourne, 1987; Wells, 1986).

- *Greater integration of oral language and literacy across all subjects in the curriculum.* Literacy learning is viewed as a key element of every aspect of the curriculum. Reading, writing, speaking, listening, and reasoning are integral to every subject throughout the day (Lipson, Valencia, Wixson, & Peters, 1993; Pappas, Ouler, Barry, & Rassel, 1993).

Dissenting Voices

These ideas and their applications are continually gaining acceptance and applicability where mainstream, "typical" learners predominate. There is disagreement, however, about how these principles and practices might relate to more diverse populations. Some educators have expressed their concern about the effect of holistic practices on the reading and writing achievement of learners considered to be at risk for school failure, particularly when those learners are black.

Lisa Delpit (1988), a prominent African American educator, has complained about the lack of a display of power and authority in process-oriented classrooms: "The teacher has denied them access to herself as the source of knowledge necessary to learn the forms they need to succeed" (p. 288). She stresses the need for teachers to be explicit, "both with what you're trying to communicate and why that information is important to the task at hand" (Teale, 1991, p. 541), particularly when they are teaching across cultures, as is often the case in schools where African American children are prevalent.

Others have questioned the value of holistic approaches to any learners considered to be at risk for failure in school. When questioned by the *Washington Post* regarding practices associated with young children's emergent literacy and the whole language approach, Jeanne Chall of Harvard University responded: ". . . the new approach is particularly harmful for below-average children or children at risk of failure because of poverty or learning problems" (1991, p. A16). More recently, Chall expressed similar concerns, directing them specifically at what she perceives to be a lack of appropriate phonics instruction in programs that engage in holistic approaches. Once again, she is concerned for "especially those who are at risk" (Willis, 1993, p. 8).

Still others express concern about the change process itself. Walter MacGinitie (1991) warns that advocates of holistic approaches are doomed to repeat the failures of the past if they are not more specific in their descriptions of what they propose. "Those who seriously wish to improve education must do more than describe a classroom atmosphere; they must describe how that atmosphere can be achieved and maintained and how people function within it" (p. 57).

Each of these individuals is a highly respected scholar whose words require serious consideration. Perhaps even more importantly, their concerns are shared by many well-intentioned, caring parents and teachers of African American children. Unfortunately, when these views are expressed by those less well informed or less well intentioned, two very fundamental but faulty assumptions often underly them. One is rooted in learning; the other, in teaching.

First, there is widespread belief, whether tacit or explicit, that African American children are inherently less capable than most other learners. Indeed, many black children are at risk for failure. But, the risk is neither inevitable nor inherent (Heath, 1983; Shepard, 1991). Second, the traditional view of "teacher as source of knowledge and power" remains highly prevalent, not only among the general public, but among many educators as well. Effective teachers are far more than repositories and dispensers of information. Their primary goal is to help children become independent learners. They share power in order to empower. Even Delpit (1988) concedes that, "The teacher cannot be the only expert in the classroom. To deny students their own expert knowledge is to disempower them" (p. 288).

Effective teachers also regard the direct instruction of strategies (with their attendant underlying skills) as fundamental to the "new" approaches outlined above. At the same time, however, they reject instruction that relies heavily on merely transmitting, "explicitly," a body of information from a single viewpoint or relaying only one way to solve a problem or address an issue. While such instruction may be explicit and clear, it risks denying the strengths that diverse views and cultural frameworks bring to the classroom. Moreover, effective teachers take care not to reduce explicit teaching merely to "telling." They know that modeling and demonstrating are key to being explicit (Duffy, Roehler, & Rackliffe, 1986).

Still, it behooves those of us who espouse new approaches to heed MacGinitie's admonition to be clear about what we advocate and to relate new practice to the many traditional practices that should be presented. Indeed, Chall's concerns may be well founded in classrooms where basic principles of holistic education are not well understood and only in evidence at a superficial level. Fortunately, there is a growing body of literature written not only by university theorists and researchers but also by classroom teachers and teacher-researchers, in which classroom environments and practices are explicitly described and related to theory (see Atwell, 1987; Chew, 1991; Feeley, Strickland, & Wepner, 1991; Routman, 1991, among others).

It is not surprising that some are skeptical about the new approaches to helping children learn literacy. For many educators, shifting to a new paradigm or to a new way of thinking is difficult under any circumstances. It may be virtually impossible when old ideas are tenaciously held, regardless of new evidence. For others, the reservations are guided by a healthy and informed skepticism. Their expressions of concern should be welcomed and reflected upon by all those working to help African American children become literate. They serve as a reminder of the constant need to reexamine our changing beliefs and practice.

Basic Skills: Pros and Cons

In the past, the educational problems of at-risk African American children have received a great deal of attention. The Johnson era brought about widespread attempts at school reform. Most of the resulting efforts were characterized by highly structured, isolated skills instruction in reading, with little or no attention given at all to instruction in writing. In schools where low student achievement was persistent, the emphasis was placed on increasing test scores in reading and math; and, for the most part, that focus remains today (Strickland & Ascher, 1992).

Oddly enough, the initiation of these "basic skills" reforms had a positive side. Applied skillfully, the conventional ways of responding to the educationally disadvantaged did improve student performance on standardized tests. This was especially true in the elementary grades. It demonstrated that when schools rallied around a common purpose, were goal oriented, and were given explicit help to achieve those goals, students would learn what was taught. For some, it may have been the first real evidence that these students were capable of learning. This proved to be a morale builder for students and teachers alike. When administrators and teachers saw their efforts pay off, they felt good about themselves and their clients—the students they served. And, the community also felt a sense of pride (Knapp & Turbull, 1990).

There was also an ominous and negative side to this, however. As the definition of what it means to be literate in our society becomes more demanding and more complex, the constraints of this type of teaching become increasingly evident. Teaching to low-level, basic skills apparently places an unintended ceiling on learning. Those rising test scores, the pride of a school district, begin to level off, and children actually appear to stop learning. In an effort to increase test scores at any cost, many schools may spend excessive amounts of time and effort aligning curriculum to test and valuable instructional time teaching directly to the test. Focusing so much attention on tests and so little on true instructional reform tends to yield benefits that are both limited and temporary (Darling-Hammond, 1993b; Shepard, 1991).

The really important message in all this, however, lies well beyond what the test scores reveal. When students are repeatedly served a diet of low-level, impoverished basics, they accumulate a kind of knowledge that is neither empowering nor self-improving. Students may conscientiously take in the information dispensed to them, and they may spout it back on cue. But, they are frequently left not knowing how to use that information, how to learn on their own, to think for themselves, solve problems, and critique their own work and the work of others.

A Better Way

Fortunately, some promising instructional alternatives exist. Building on the work of previous researchers' contemporary investigators have broken fresh ground to create new paradigms for the way we view children's literacy development and the way adults can best help them learn. Much of what has been learned applies to all children regardless of race or socioeconomic level. Several major principles seem to stand out regardless of the learner variables present. Whether the learners be high achieving or at risk, inner city poor or affluent suburban, second language or native speakers, certain learner characteristics are maintained:

Literacy Learning Starts Early and Continues throughout Life

African American children deserve early literacy programs that are framed from an emergent literacy perspective. Such programs would capitalize on the fact that, like all other children, African American children enter school eager to learn and to please the responsive adults around them. They are aware of the print in their environment: their names, the names of siblings, the logos and slogans from fast food restaurants, and various other signs representing environmental print. (Goodman & Goodman, 1979; Harste, Woodward, & Burke, 1984; Teale & Sulzby, 1986).

Recommendations

1. Avoid readiness tests that screen children out. Implement instructional strategies and systematic observational techniques that allow children to demonstrate what they do know. Use what is learned to build their linguistic awareness and expand their knowledge about the world.

2. Create learning environments that give children confidence that they can learn and let them know by your actions that you believe they can learn.

3. Initiate family literacy programs in which adults and children approach literacy learning as a cooperative social experience. At the very least, such programs would make books and other materials available to parents for reading to and with their children.

4. Seek out information from parents about their perceptions of their children as learners and their educational goals and concerns as a family. Let parents know you value whatever literacy experiences they give to their children. View home and school as making different but interdependent contributions to the child's total education.

5. Start coordinated school and social service intervention programs early and make them ongoing. The purpose should be to prevent failure and promote accelerated achievement rather than merely to remediate problems.

6. Treat instruction in phonics as an important part of beginning reading and writing, but not a precursor to it. View phonics for what it is—one of several enablers (including word meanings and sentence structures) to success in literacy. Nothing more! Nothing less! Allow neither students nor their parents to think they are receiving instruction in reading when they are merely receiving instruction in phonics. Emphasize sound/symbol relationships during the reading of interesting, predictable texts and during writing through children's own attempts at spelling.

Literacy Learning Is Used to Make Meanings out of Our World

African American children deserve literacy programs that stress the construction of meaning right from the start. As with every other aspect of their learning, these young children are attempting to make sense of the world around them. Print is simply one of the many curiosities in the world about which they are eager to learn. (Donaldson, 1978; Smith, 1982; Wells, 1986).

Recommendations

1. Take care to see to it that the tasks students are given make sense to them. Keep in mind that low-level, rote tasks tend to make less sense than tasks that require reasoning and reflective thought (Resnick, 1987).

2. Select instructional materials that employ whole texts, including a wide variety of fiction and nonfiction. Avoid meaningless drills on isolated skills delivered in the form of workbooks and worksheets.

3. Integrate instruction in the language arts so that students connect learning how to spell with proofreading a composition, expanding their vocabularies with comprehending stories and informational books, authoring and responding with what they do as writers and readers, and so on.

4. Foster inquiry-based curricula, in which individuals and groups of children pose questions and seek to answer them. Allow the teaching of literacy to be largely driven by needs arising from the content and questions that children are curious about—for example, learning how to conduct a good interview during the study of personal health in order to learn what nurses do. Even when content foci are preset by a fixed curriculum, independence and motivation can be fostered by allowing children to pose their own questions within the sphere of the content they are required to study.

Literacy Learning Takes Place through Active Involvement and Use

African American children deserve literacy programs that recognize that knowledge is not merely an accumulation of assorted facts absorbed like a sponge. Knowledge is constructed by active minds and grounded in life experience. (Lindfors, 1987; Wells, 1986).

Recommendations

1. Plan instructional activities that involve children in a high degree of critical thinking and problem solving. For example, postreading activities based on student- generated questions and observations related to key ideas in a text are more likely to stimulate active response and involvement than those that simply require students to answer a preset list of teacher generated questions.

2. Help students use talk as a means of mediating what they are attempting to understand. Engage students in literature study groups, collaborative group discussions, partner activities, and research groups. Rather than attempting to keep students quiet, plan activities where talk is channeled and used along with reading and writing as a tool for learning.

3. Employ collaborative group learning strategies and peer teaching methods to promote active learners. Approaches that emphasize the fact that everyone in the classroom is both a teacher and a learner help increase student involvement and tend to promote active learning.

4. Keep instruction as close to the point of use as possible. Expand the definition of direct instruction to go beyond conveying information to an entire group of students in a pre-ordered way. Include the demonstration of strategies for individuals and groups of students that they actually need to complete a given task. Both the how and the why of a strategy are made explicit when the need is clearly understood.

Literacy Learning Is Influenced by One's Language and Cultural Background

African American children deserve literacy programs that build on and expand their language and culture with a view toward helping them understand and value their heritage and respect the heritage of others They deserve teachers and administrators who value diversity and recognize its presence in every child (Au, 1993).

Recommendations

1. Never use a child's dialect, language, or culture as a basis for making judgments regarding intellect or capability. Competence is not tied to a particular language, dialect, or culture.

2. Learn as much as you can about students' language and cultural backgrounds. Avoid making sweeping generalizations based on skin color or surnames. There is a high degree of variability within every cultural group. Learn as much as you can; then keep an open mind.

3. Give students literature that reflects a wide diversity of cultures. Take special care to see to it that African American children are familiar with literature by and about African Americans as well as with the writers and illustrators themselves.

4. Encourage Standard English through exposure to a variety of oral and written texts and oral language activities. Keep in mind that while competence in Standard English is a worthy goal for all children, it must not mean a rejection or replacement of one language and culture with another. Rather, it should be viewed as language expansion and enrichment of the students' home language to include Standard English, giving them the opportunity and the *choice* to communicate with a broader speech community (Galda, Cullinan, & Strickland, 1993).

Literacy Learning Is Influenced by Social Context

African American children deserve opportunities to learn in contexts that reflect what is known about the social nature of literacy and literacy learning. This requires administrators and teachers who know how to establish supportive and responsive contexts for learning. According to Darling-Hammond (1993a), "the problems of equity are constrained by the availability of talented teachers, by the knowledge and capacities those teachers possess, and by the school conditions that define how that knowledge can be used" (p. 754). (Cazden, 1992; Moll, 1990; Scribner & Cole, 1981).

Recommendations

1. Foster a sense of community and interconnectedness within each classroom and throughout each school. Keep schools and classes small enough, or divide them into manageable units, so that individual students feel known and recognized as participants in

community, and closer student-teacher relationships are more likely to develop.

2. Avoid long-term ability grouping and tracking. These deny equitable access to learning opportunities (Epstein, 1985; Oakes, 1985). Seek alternatives such as flexible grouping practices, which may include some short-term ability grouping and cooperative learning instructional methods that treat diversity as a valued resource.

3. Create large, uninterrupted blocks of time for language arts instruction, during which no children leave the classroom for special activities. Short time periods lead to a one-size-fits-all instruction, in which every student is assigned precisely the same tasks and given the same amount of instructional support and time to complete them. Large time frames foster integrated learning and allow for differentiated instruction, thus fostering true educational equity.

4. Give incentives to attract the very best teachers available and provide ongoing professional development focused on empowering teachers to make instructional decisions. Emphasize classroom observation—how to assess what students are learning and use it to plan accordingly.

5. Encourage ongoing professional development such as teacher networks that operate as voluntary support groups. Professional networks allow teachers to organize their own staff development efforts so that ideas close to the classroom may be discussed in a risk-free atmosphere of mutual support. Avoid placing all resources in one-shot staff development days, and be wary of intensive "training" programs on narrowly construed, highly prescriptive models of instruction.

Conclusion

For most educators, the ideas offered here are neither new nor revolutionary. In fact, some would argue that these suggestions are appropriate for any child, regardless of ethnicity, socioeconomic status, or intellect. And that is precisely the point. We now know enough about the learning and teaching of language and literacy to offer some basic principles to guide instructional decision making for the education of every child. Perhaps the greatest value of these principles and recommendations is that they are learner centered and thus adapt to and support all learners, no matter who they are.

Teachers who work with large numbers of African American children in situations where failure is chronic may wonder how these ideas will help them deal with diversity. Having placed so much emphasis on how their students are different from others, they may be confused by the suggestion that there are "universal" principles of learning and teaching from which all children may benefit. They want advice specific to the needs of the children they teach. This is highly understandable. Yet, these teachers should know that the ideas offered here are not meant to suggest a one-size-fits-all curriculum. They in no way negate the fact that there are great differences among the children we teach. Respecting and building on these differences is an important part of what good teachers do. The differences we face in schools, however, go far beyond those distinctions commonly made *between* various ethnic groups. There are important differences among children *within* ethnic groups and linguistic communities, even among those who live at the poverty level. These include children's interests, experiential backgrounds, abilities, and motivation. These differences may be overlooked by teachers who come to the teaching situation with preconceived ideas about how certain children learn and behave. Moreover, when the curriculum fails to value each learner's unique background, there is a risk that important individual characteristics may never be revealed as potential building blocks for instruction.

Dawn Harris Martine, a second-grade teacher in Harlem, once told me that she could trace at least a dozen different national origins among her group of twenty-six children. More than half her students had very recent roots in several countries in Africa, the Caribbean, and Central America, as well as various parts of the United States. Yet, she said, to most people they simply look like any other group of African American kids. To Dawn, the differences were very important and helped shape the curriculum and the ways in which she interacted with each child.

What then should teachers know that is specific to these youngsters? Teachers who work with these children should enter the classroom informed as much as possible about the broader population from which these children come—both from reading the relevant literature and from first-hand experiences with others who belong to that population. They should also learn as much as they can about the immediate community and the families of these children. They should use what they learn as a framework for understanding who and where their learners are. At the same time, they should use the principles described here to develop a literacy curriculum that is both rigorous and learner centered. Most importantly, they should avoid assigning preconceived characteristics and attributes to any child, bearing in mind the need to suspend judgment and respect each as an individual.

Irving Harris (1993), a philanthropist and child advocate, recounts a parable about some people picnicking beside a river. Suddenly, they see an enormous number of babies being carried down the river by the current. Their first impulse is to jump in and pull out as many of the babies as possible. But they keep coming, and the rescuers can't save them all. Finally, someone is smart enough to run up the river to see who is pushing them in (p. 30).

As teachers of the language arts, we sometimes feel like those rescuers—attempting to "save the children" despite overwhelming forces beyond our control. Indeed, the responsibility for helping African American students, or any other students who are at risk for educational failure, is not ours alone. The problems are serious and demand the attention of everyone—the home, the school, and the community.

Nevertheless, there is a great deal that we can do. We can work as individuals and within professional and civic organizations to effect social policy change; and we can work with students and their parents to achieve better mutual support between home and school. Most importantly, we can take advantage of a growing body of research that suggests better educational policy and more comprehensive and meaningful approaches to raising the academic achievement of African American students. The knowledge is available. It is time we demonstrated the commitment to seek a better way.

References

Allen, J. B., & Mason, J. M. eds. 1989. *Risk makers, risk takers, risk breakers.* Portsmouth, NH: Heinemann.

Atwell, N. 1987. *In the middle.* Portsmouth, NH: Heinemann.

Au, K. 1993. *Literacy instruction in multicultural settings.* Orlando, FL: Harcourt Brace.

Calkins, L. 1986. *The art of teaching writing.* Portsmouth, NH: Heinemann.

Cambourne, B. 1987. *The whole story.* Sydney, Australia: Primary English Teaching Association.

Cazden, C. 1992. *Whole language plus.* New York: Teachers College Press.

Chall, J. May 13, 1991. As quoted in "Armed with pen and lots to say." *Washington Post*, p. A 16.

Chew, C. R. ed. 1991. *Whole language in urban classrooms.* Roslyn, NY: Berrent Publications.

Cullinan, B. ed. 1992. *Invitation to read: More children's literature in the reading program.* Newark, DE: International Reading Association.

Darling-Hammond, L. 1993a. *Federal policy options for Chapter 1: An equity agenda for school restructuring.* New York: National Center for Restructuring Education.

Darling-Hammond, L. 1993b. "Reframing the school reform agenda." *Phi Delta Kappan,* 74, 753-761.

Delpit, L. 1988. "The silenced dialogue: Power and pedagogy in educating other people's children." *Harvard Educational Review,* 56, 280–298.

Donaldson, M. 1978. *Children's minds.* Glasgow: William Collins Sons.

Dufty, G. O., L. Roehler, and G. Rackliffe. 1986. "How teachers' instructional talk influences students' understanding of lesson content." *The Elementary School Journal,* 87, 4–16.

Edelsky, C., B. Altwerger, and B. Flores. 1991. *Whole language: What's the difference?* Portsmouth, NH: Heinemann.

Epstein, J. L. 1985. "After the bus arrives: Resegregation in desegregated schools." *Journal of Social Issues,* 41, 23–43.

Feeley, J., D. S. Strickland, and S. Wepner, eds. 1991. *Process reading and writing: A literature-based approach.* New York: Teachers College Press.

Fornan, N., D. Lapp, and J. Flood. 1992. Changing perspectives in writing instruction. *The Reading Teacher,* 35, 550–556.

Galda, L., B. Cullinan and D. Strickland. 1993. "Language, literacy and the child." Orlando, FL: Harcourt Brace.

Goodman, K. S., and Y. A. Goodman. 1979. "Learning to read is natural." In L. B. Resnick & R. A. Weaver, eds. *Theory and practice of early reading, vol. 1* (pp. 137154). Hillsdale, NJ: Erlbaum.

Harris, I. B. 1993, Spring. "Education: Does it make a difference when you start?" *Aspen Institute Quarterly,* 5, 30–52.

Harste, J. C., V. A. Woodward, and C. V. Burke. 1984. *Language stories and literacy lessons.* Portsmouth, NH: Heinemann.

Heath, S. B. 1983. *Ways with words. Language, life and work in communities and classrooms.* Cambridge, England: Cambridge University Press.

Hiebert, E. H., ed. 1991. *Literacy for a diverse society.* New York: Teachers College Press.

Hodgkinson, H. 1991. "Reform versus reality." *Phi Delta Kappan,* 73, 9–16.

Huck, C. 1992. "Literature and literacy." *Language Arts,* 69, 520–526.

Jensen, J. M. 1993. "What we know about the writing of elementary school children." *Language Arts,* 70, 290294.

Knapp, M. S., and B. J. Turnbull, 1990. *Better schooling for the children of poverty: Alternatives to conventional wisdom.* Washington, DC: U.S. Department of Education.

Lindfors, J. 1987. *Children's language and lecturing.* Englewood Cliffs, NJ: Prentice Hall.

Lipson, M. Y., S. W. Valencia, K. K. Wixson, and C. W. Peters. 1993. Integration and thematic teaching: Integration to improve teaching and learning. *Language Arts,* 70, 252–263.

MacGinitie, W. H. 1991. Reading instruction: Plus ça change. . . . *Educational Leadership,* 48, 55–58.

Moll, L., ed. 1990. *Vygotsky and education.* New York: Cambridge University Press.

Oakes, J. 1985. *Keeping track: How schools structure inequality.* New Haven, CT: Yale University Press.

Norton, D. E. 1992. "The impact of literature–based reading." New York: Macmillan.

Pappas, C., C. Ouler, A. Barry, and M. Rassel. 1993. "Focus on research: Collaborating with teachers developing integrated language arts programs in urban schools." *Language Arts,* 70, 297–303.

Resnick, L. 1987. "Learning in school and out." *Educational Researcher,* 16, 13–20.

Routman, R. 1991. *Transitions.* Portsmouth, NH: Heinemann.

Scribner, S., and M. Cole. 1981. *The psychology of literacy.* Cambridge, MA: Harvard University Press.

Shanahan, T., ed. 1990. *Reading and writing together: New perspectives for the classroom.* Norwood, MA: Christopher-Gordon.

Shepard, L. 1991. "Negative policies for dealing with diversity: When does assessment and diagnosis turn into sorting and segregation?" In *Literacy for a diverse society,* ed. E.H. Hieben. New York: Teachers College Press, 279–298.

Smith, F. 1982. *Understanding reading.* New York: Holt.

Strickland, D. S., and C. Ascher. 1992. Low income African American children and public schooling. In *Handbook of research on curriculum* , ed. P.W. Jackson. New York: Macmillan, 609–625.

Teale, W. H. 1991. "A conversation with Lisa Delpit." *Language Arts 68*: 541–547.

Teale, W. H. and E. Sulzby. 1986. *Emergent literacy: Writing and reading.* Norwood, NJ: Ablex.

Wells, G. 1986. *The meaning makers: Children learning language and using language to learn.* Portsmouth, NH: Heinemann.

Willis, S. 1993, November. Whole language in the 90's. Update, pp. 1, 5, 6, 8. Alexandria, VA: Association for Supervision and Curriculum Development.

27 Effective Literacy Practices for English Learners

Yvonne S. Freeman
David E. Freeman
Fresno Pacific College

The authors begin by observing that more and more students come to school speaking little or no English. Noting that teachers who understand the needs of English language learners can plan effective literacy instruction for them, they devote the first section of their article to recent theory and research concerning successful approaches to working with English learners. They point out that learning a second language well enough to compete academically with native speakers takes a long time. It helps substantially if students who are speakers of other languages continue learning through the primary language while they acquire English. "During the two years students in English-only classrooms take to become proficient enough to carry on conversations and to understand what the teacher is saying, they aren't learning as much of the school subjects as their English speaking peers. . . . On the other hand, students who are taught in their first language while they are learning English can continue their academic development." The authors mention other reasons, too, that children should continue to receive instruction in their first language: one is that concepts that are learned in one language transfer to another, and this includes the concept of what reading is and what it requires. Freeman and Freeman then discuss second-language acquisition theory, emphasizing particularly the work of Stephen Krashen and his concept of learners acquiring language through "comprehensible input." They conclude this section with three points important to keep in mind when working with English learners. In a subsequent section, they offer a checklist of eight effective literacy practices for English language learners: questions teachers can use to determine whether they are providing the maximal support that English learners need in order to become literate in English and to succeed in school. The sections that follow describe lesson activities from two classrooms, one an inner-city fourth grade classroom and the other a rural second-third grade combination with a bilingual teacher. The details from these two classrooms richly illustrate the kinds of teaching that Freeman and Freeman recommend, based on their experience and research.

Introduction

Teachers today face the challenge of providing effective language arts instruction to an increasingly diverse student population. More and more students come to school speaking little or no English. Teachers who are knowledgeable about the needs of second-language learners can plan effective literacy instruction for their English language learners. In the first section of this chapter we discuss recent theory and research concerning successful approaches for working with English learners. In the second half of the chapter, we present a checklist of effective practices to help teachers support their students' literacy development in their first and second languages. Through specific classroom examples, we show how teachers working with students acquiring English have implemented this checklist, creating a balanced approach to reading and writing for English learners.

Challenges for English Learners

Whether second-language students have always lived in the United States, have arrived recently as refugees, or have immigrated, if they are of school age, they are faced with both the task of learning English and the task of learning the academic content of school subjects. Learning a second language well enough to compete academically with native speakers takes a long time. While students are acquiring English and becoming accustomed to a new school in a new country, their native English-speaking classmates are continuing to learn and advance. In trying to catch up, students acquiring English are shooting at a moving target.

In many cases, second-language students students will acquire conversational proficiency in English fairly rapidly, often in about two years. After two years bilingual learners may still have a slight accent, but they understand the English spoken to them, and they can express their ideas in oral English quite well. Although their conversational proficiency may be on a par with that of their classmates, their academic language proficiency, especially their ability to read and write in English may lag behind.

Bilingual students who have already learned to read and write and "do school" in their first language can transfer those skills into English and achieve academically in English more quickly. However, even students with strong academic backgrounds in their native languages take at least five years to reach the fiftieth percentile on most standardized tests. Those who come to school with no previous schooling can take between seven to ten years to reach grade-level norms. (Collier 1989; Cummins 1989).

The Role of Students' Primary Languages

The research that shows how long it takes students to acquire English also emphasizes the importance of continuing to develop students' primary languages. During the two years students in English-only classrooms take to become proficient enough to carry on conversations and to understand what the teacher is saying, they are not learning as much of the school subjects as their English-speaking peers, and this gap in their academic development causes real problems. Once students fall that far behind, it is hard for them to catch up. On the other hand, students who are taught in their first language while they are learning English can continue their academic development. That is one important reason for students to receive instruction in their first language. There are other reasons.

English-speaking students who enter our schools have not yet developed their English to a full degree. That is why we teach language arts. In fact, we require English right up through college. In the same way, students who enter our schools speaking Spanish or Chinese have not fully developed that language resource either, and one of the goals of school should be to develop a student's first language as well as English. Unfortunately, many students who enter our schools as monolingual Spanish or Chinese speakers leave as monolingual English speakers, and our society loses a valuable resource in the process. Effective programs would produce competent bilingual and biliterate individuals.

Another reason that it is important to teach students in their primary languages is that concepts learned in one language transfer to another. This idea of a common proficiency that underlies languages comes from Cummins (1981), who showed that it does not matter what language a concept is learned in. For example, a student who knows his or her colors, has the concept of color. Then, when students learn a new language, they do not need to learn the idea of "color" all over again. They just need to learn how to express that idea in their new language. In the same way, if students can read and write in their first language, they learn to read and write in English much more quickly. They do not have to learn how to read all over again. They already have acquired the process.

A final reason for teaching students in their primary languages is that parents can provide greater support. Teachers depend on parents to help students complete homework assignments. When the homework is in a language the parents do not speak well or a language they have trouble reading and writing, the assistance parents can provide is limited. On the other hand, parents can help a great deal when assignments are in their native language. Primary language instruction also promotes better home-school connections. When parents can understand the schoolwork and talk with the teachers, they are more apt to get involved in school activities and may volunteer to come into the classroom to work with children there.

Second-Language Acquisition Theory

The actual process of language acquisition is not clearly understood. Debates continue over the role of the direct teaching of grammar in the process, but it is fairly well agreed that for younger students, language is acquired, not learned through direct instruction. One theory of second-language acquisition developed by Krashen (1982) has been the basis for much of the second-language instruction in schools across the country. Krashen believes that second languages are acquired in natural settings when learners receive lots of comprehensible, understandable, input. He points out that the best comprehensible input is input in the first language. Comprehensible input in English can be oral or written. In fact, a key recommendation of Krashen's for second-language learners is to read lots of understandable texts in the target language (Krashen, 1993, 1985).

Krashen's theory of language acquisition helps teachers understand what to do in class. We have drawn on his theory and our own work to develop three points that are important to keep in mind in working with English learners.

1. Acquisition takes time. Students should not be forced to produce too soon. At the same time, they need input that is comprehensible to build their receptive vocabulary. Students should be involved in literacy from the start. Written language is fixed. It does not speed past the way oral language does. So when teachers read big books, students acquiring English can follow along and start to make connections between the print and the new language they are acquiring. Students should be encouraged to read lots of predictable texts and to talk or write about them with their peers and their teachers. They also benefit from following along as they listen to taped versions of a story at a listening center.

2. Students need opportunities in class to develop academic language. They have many chances outside class (on the playground

or at home) to develop conversational language. Research shows that students can learn both language and academic content at the same time. In fact, when students focus on the content, they learn the language more naturally and quickly. So students acquiring English should be involved in as many activities as possible with other students. They may need extra support to help them understand the activity, and they may need to be allowed to use various means (gestures, drawings, primary language, etc.) to show they have understood. As long as students are engaged in meaningful activities, they will be developing both English and the kind of language they need to succeed in school.

3. Students will continue to acquire English as long as they can understand and participate in classroom activities. Teachers can make lessons understandable for English learners by employing specific techniques. Themes limit the range of vocabulary presented and ensure that the same concepts and vocabulary occur frequently. In addition to using visuals, realia, and gestures, teachers can help students understand important concepts through graphic organizers and semantic webs. Paraphrasing and frequent comprehension checks are also helpful. If possible, teachers should provide students with a preview in their first language before presenting content in English. As often as possible teachers should have students work together in English to find key ideas. When teachers discover creative ways to make the language accessible to their students, they receive enthusiastic responses from their second-language learners.

When teachers support students' first languages and make lessons understandable by using an approach that includes the techniques described above, they improve the chances for school success for students acquiring English. However, second-language acquisition and school success involves factors beyond language.

The Complexity of Language Acquisition

Collier (1995) has developed a model of language acquisition for school that shows the complexity of the process. In this model Collier proposes that language acquisition includes three elements: language development, cognitive development, and academic development. It is important for teachers to understand that their students must grow linguistically, cognitively, and academically if they are to to achieve English-language proficiency.

In addition, development in all three of these areas is influenced by social and cultural processes. These sociocultural factors are at the heart of Collier's model. They include individual variables such as anxiety and self-esteem as well as larger social factors, like discrimination, overt or covert. For that reason, even if the school provides opportunities for positive language, cognitive, and academic development, social and cultural influences must also be examined because they have such strong positive or negative influences on students' language acquisition and academic performance.

Checklist for Effective Practice

Drawing on this research and theory for first-language support and second-language acquisition, we have developed a checklist of effective literacy practices for English-language learners. The checklist consists of a series of questions. If teachers can answer "yes" to these questions, they are probably taking into consideration key factors that will improve the chance of school success for all their students. We will first list the questions and comment on each. Following that, we will give two extended classroom examples of effective practice.

Is Curriculum Organized around "Big" Questions?

Cognitive development results from solving problems. In classes organized around themes or interesting and significant questions, students develop higher levels of cognition as they explore their own questions. In this process, students read both fiction and nonfiction texts. For second-language learners, predictable whole stories, novels, plays, and poems, as well as complete pieces of nonfiction are more comprehensible than simplified texts or excerpts because the context is richer. Authentic literature promotes literacy as well as language development.

Are Students Involved in Authentic Reading and Writing Experiences?

As students explore important questions, they naturally turn to both fiction and nonfiction texts as sources for information. For example, a book such as *Who Belongs Here?* (Knight, 1993) provides students with both a fiction story of an immigrant boy who feels unwanted and the fascinating history of many immigrants groups who have come to the United States. Second-language learners would relate to the story and the content information in exploring the "big" question in the book's title.

For English learners, predictable whole stories, novels, plays, and poems as well as complete pieces of nonfiction are more comprehensible than simplified texts or excerpts because the context is richer. Once students have researched their question, they write to present their understandings to classmates or to a wider audience. Engagement with authentic literacy activities of these kinds promotes literacy as well as cognitive, academic, and language development.

Is There an Attempt to Draw on Student Background Knowledge and Interests? Are Students Given Choices?

Smith (1983) has explained that we do not learn if we are confused or bored. On the other hand, when we receive comprehensible input and are interested, we learn. Students are more likely to be interested when the academic content is linked to their lives and when they have choices in what they read and what they study. It is critical to build on knowledge and concepts students bring to school. For English learners, use of the first language allows students to access their background knowledge as they learn in their second.

Is the Content Meaningful? Does It Serve a Purpose for the Learners?

Too often, instruction is organized around skills that would have students learn rules and practice language until it is automatic. These activities do not involve learners in real problem solving nor are these activities pleasurable. Skill building does not build literacy or promote cognitive development. Such instruction is not meaningful to second-language students, nor does it serve their immediate purposes.

Do Students Have Opportunities to Work Collaboratively?

Holt (1993) has shown clearly the benefits of collaboration for language-minority students. Smith (1983) points out that language acquisition is a social activity. Students help each other make sense of content and concepts. In the process of collaborating while reading and discussing authentic literature, writing responses and authoring their own books, and investigating interesting questions and reporting their findings, students develop their language or languages as they expand their knowledge of academic content areas.

Do Students Read and Write, as well as Speak and Listen, during Their Learning Experiences?

Second-language learners acquire language through all four modes. They should be encouraged to read and write as well as speak and listen from the beginning of their experiences with English. Research has shown that many second-language learners may read or write before they speak and that comprehension is often enriched by literacy experiences (Freeman & Freeman, 1992; Hudelson, 1984; Rigg & Hudelson, 1986). Development of literacy is crucial for academic success, and teachers should not delay reading and writing for second-language students.

Are Students' Primary Languages and Cultures Valued, Supported, and Developed?

Students who fully develop their primary language acquire a second language more quickly. In addition, both academic concepts and knowledge of literacy are most easily learned in the primary language. Cummins (1981) has shown that a common proficiency underlies languages. Because of this common underlying proficiency, knowledge developed in the primary language transfers to a second language. Further, bilingualism enriches the individual and the community. Even when teachers are not able to provide instruction in all their students' primary languages, they can find ways to support those languages and can also involve students in activities to explore the cultures of all the students in the classroom (Freeman & Freeman, 1993; 1994).

Are Students Involved in Activities that Build Their Self-esteem and Provide Them with Opportunities to Succeed?

When teachers have faith in their students and the students themselves believe they can learn, these high expectations lead to academic success (Collier, 1995; Freeman & Freeman, 1992).

_____

In the following sections we describe lesson activities from two classrooms. When we evaluate these activities using the checklist, we can answer an emphatic "yes" to each question.

Elaine

Elaine, an inner city fourth-grade teacher has Hispanic, Hmong, Cambodian, Laotian, African American, and Anglo students. The students were, for the most part, born in this country and many have little understanding of or appreciation for their own roots or those of their classmates. The different groups of students in Elaine's classroom do not always appreciate each other or value each others' cultures, and many of their older brothers and sisters are members of rival ethnic gangs. Elaine wants to help her students value their own and each others' cultures. To achieve this she and her students begin the year answering the question, "Who am I and what are my roots?"

Elaine believes that building a strong classroom community is critical for her students, and they can only do this if they have a strong sense of themselves and respect for each other. Early in the year Elaine uses several different strategies to build community. During the first week of school, students are asked to do a heritage investigation. They interview family members to find out about their own birthplaces and those of their ancestors. Then the students find their birthplace and that of their ancestors on a map. They put a card with their name on the map and connect their name to their birthplace with one color of yarn and to their ancestors' with another color yarn. When the entire class has finished, they have created a colorful representation of the multiethnic make-up of their class (see Figure 1). Elaine believes this activity validates each child's cultural heritage, provides opportunities for parents to communicate with their children about their family's history, ignites students' curiosity about their own cultural heritage and that of their classmates, and visibly shows students that together they have a rich cultural heritage.

Another strategy Elaine has developed to encourage students to think about who they are is a culture share. For this activity students bring from home some object that represents their culture. It could be an object, a picture, a piece of clothing, a recipe, or a piece of writing. Before and after students choose their own item to share, Elaine reads stories which tell of objects like those the students might bring or talk about. She reads books like *The Whispering Cloth* (Shea, 1995) the story of a young Hmong girl learning to make a Hmong story cloth, *Angel Child, Dragon Child* (Surat, 1983), which tells of a Vietnamese child who keeps her mother's picture in a matchbox so as not to forget her, or *Saturday Sancocho* (Torres, 1995), the tale of a girl and her grandmother bargaining to get the ingredients for a delicious chicken soup, sancocho. Reading these books helps students think about the importance of cultural objects in their own lives. Students share the objects they bring to school in small groups and, if they are willing, with the whole class. Elaine has found that this activity validates students' cultures, communicates the teacher's acceptance and celebration of multiculturalism to parents and students, and provides a casual environment that encourages oral language development.

These early activities lead students to reading many pieces of literature that feature immigrants and celebrate cultural diversity. Some of Elaine's favorites include, *Talking Walls* (Knight, 1992), *Who Belongs Here?* (Knight, 1993), *Grandfather's Journey* (Say, 1993), *Amelia's Road*

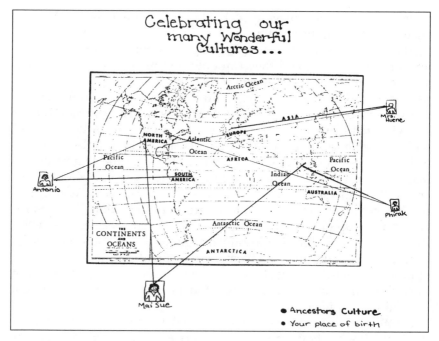

Figure 1. Elaine's Heritage Map activity.

(Altman, 1993a), and *My Name is María Isabel* (Ada, 1993). Because students have already seen the importance of appreciating the diversity in their classroom, they welcome these stories and eagerly discuss them and write about them, relating them to their own experiences.

Elaine also encourages the students to study their own cultures. One activity that supports this particularly well is the making of class alphabet-culture books. Students get together in same-culture groups with a primary language and culture specialist and brainstorm what object or concept each letter of the English alphabet could represent from their culture. Then each letter and what it stands for is illustrated and explained on a separate page. When the whole alphabet is finished, the pages are bound and the book is put in the class library. These alphabet-culture books are very popular. Students constantly check them out. Figure 2 shows the cover and several pages of the "H is for Hmong" book. Figure 3 shows the cover and some pages for the "C is for Cambodian" book, and Figure 4 shows the cover of the "A is for African American" book.

Besides supporting the cultures of her students, Elaine has found a way to develop literacy in their first languages even when few resources are available. First, Elaine reads with her students predictable books in English, with fairly limited text. She chooses books that were students' favorites when they were younger, stories such as *The Very Hungry Caterpillar* (Carl, 1969) or *Ten, Nine, Eight* (Bang, 1993). Next, primary language tutors translate the texts of these stories into Khmer, Hmong, and Spanish and write or type the text for each page on blank sheets of paper. Then, after a discussion of how text and illustrations should match, students work in cross-cultural teams to illustrate the books. Students often have to go back to the familiar English stories to be sure they understand the text for each page. Even the native speakers of each language may have trouble reading texts in those languages, and one of Elaine's goals is to move them toward primary language literacy. Once the books are illustrated, they are laminated, bound, and put into the classroom library. Figure 5 shows pages from *Ten, Nine, Eight* in Hmong, and Figure 6 shows pages of *The Very Hungry Caterpillar* in Khmer.

One other activity that Elaine organizes for her class is what she calls a "Cultural Pot Luck." These pot lucks are designed to help students appreciate each others' cultures through food. Twice a year, students make invitations for their families for this event. The families are asked to bring some food that is representative of their culture to the school. The day before the pot luck, primary language tutors call home to remind the family about the pot luck and to answer any questions.

Figure 2-1. Student artwork for "H is for Hmong" book cover.

Figure 2-2. Student artwork for "H is for Hmong" book page.

Figure 2-3. Student artwork for "H is for Hmong" book page.

Figure 2-4. Student artwork for "H is for Hmong" book page.

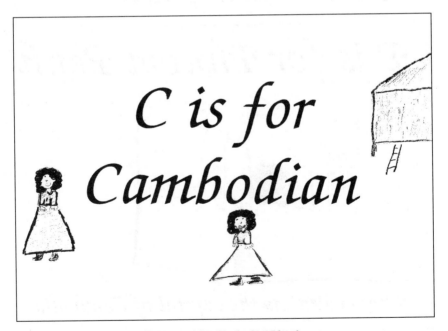

Figure 3-1. Student artwork for "C is for Cambodian" book cover.

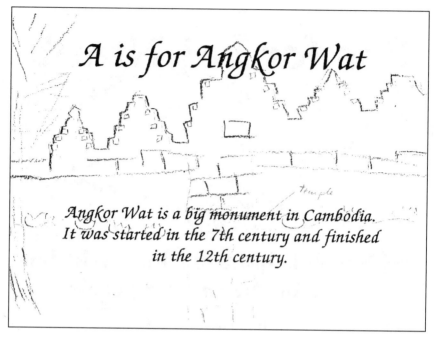

Figure 3-2. Student artwork for "C is for Cambodian" book page.

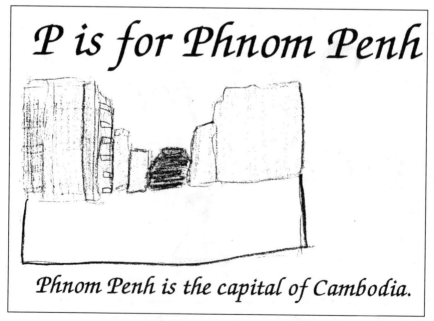

Figure 3-3. Student artwork for "C is for Cambodian" book page.

Figure 4. Student artwork for "A is for African American" book cover.

Figure 5-1. Student artwork for *Ten, Nine, Eight* in Hmong book cover.

Meanwhile, students discuss what is polite to do if you do not like something from another culture. Elaine explains that she will bring soup and pickled okra, something that not everyone will probably like. Everyone is encouraged to at least try a little of everything. If they do not like something, they should just leave the rest on their plates without saying anything.

The day of the pot luck, parents bring food to the classroom around lunch time. The cafeteria provides drinks, plates, silverware, and napkins. Parents and children organize the food on tables according to culture and make signs that name each dish. Students describe the food their parents bring and the ingredients. Much discussion of similarities always takes place. After the meal, students perform cultural dances and sing. Elaine has found that these student performances, which celebrate yet another aspect of the cultures represented in her classroom, help ensure that parents will not just bring in their food and leave quickly.

Elaine always uses experiences like these to promote student writing. The following day, the students write their response to the potluck. Figure 7 and 8 are two writing samples. The first writer recounts the day's events clearly. The second writer raises an interesting question,

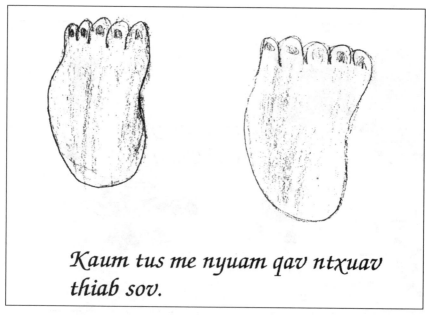

Kaum tus me nyuam qav ntxuav thiab sov.

Figure 5-2. Student artwork for *Ten, Nine, Eight* in Hmong book page.

"I wonder why do Hmong people food are almost the same as Cambodia culture." Later, Elaine can discuss with the whole class how foods are similar or different across cultures. This student also comments that she wishes "that I know how to make it to eat everyday when I grow up." She is starting to be aware of the importance of retaining some of her heritage, one goal of an activity like this.

If Elaine evaluated these lessons using the "Checklist of Effective Practice," she could answer "yes" to all eight questions. She organized activities around an important question, "Who am I and what are my roots?" In the process of answering that question students read and discussed a rich variety of literature and wrote responding to both the literature and meaningful activities. Every activity drew upon the students' backgrounds, and they were given choices in what they shared. As students worked together on different projects, it was clear that the content was very meaningful for them. They did lots of reading and writing as well as oral sharing. The primary language books helped them value and develop their first languages. Perhaps most important, however, is that students felt good about themselves and could see the results of projects completed successfully.

Figure 5-3. Student artwork for *Ten, Nine, Eight* in Hmong book page.

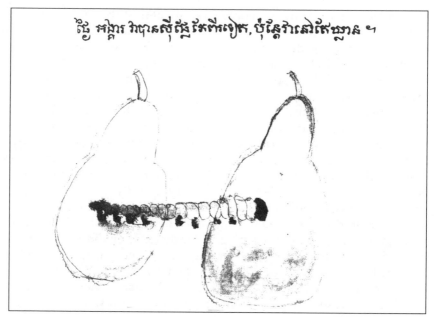

Figure 6-1. Student artwork for *The Very Hungry Caterpillar* in Khmer book page.

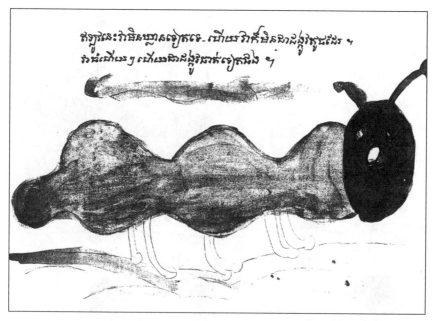

Figure 6-2. Student artwork for *The Very Hungry Caterpillar* in Khmer book page.

Figure 6-3. Student artwork for *The Very Hungry Caterpillar* in Khmer book page.

Silvio

Silvio is a new second-third combination bilingual teacher in a rural school. Most of his students' families are associated in some way with agriculture, either as laborers in the fields or as supervisors. Silvio understands his students and their families well because he was a migrant child himself. When he was young, a teacher encouraged him, and that encouragement helped him to struggle to get through college and become a teacher so that he, in turn, could inspire children.

One of his key concerns as a teacher is that some of his colleagues at the school do not seem to expect much of the students who come to school speaking Spanish. The curriculum that most of these students get in both English and Spanish is simplified, fragmented, and unrelated to their interests or to the reality of their daily lives. Silvio's class consists of students with different backgrounds. Some have been in this school or434 nearby schools since kindergarten. Most of them speak Spanish and some English but have little interest in reading and writing in either language. Several other students are new arrivals from Mexico and El Salvador and speak only Spanish. He also has two students

Figure 7. Student response to Cultural Pot Luck.

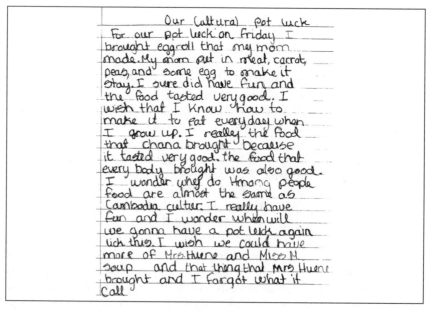

Figure 8. Student response to Cultural Pot Luck.

from Oaxaca, Mexico who speak Mixteco and a little Spanish but very little English.

One of Silvio's first decisions is to get his students reading and writing in both Spanish and English, beginning with texts that are not too long or overwhelming. Since a local poetry festival is coming up, he chooses to start a unit on poetry. He pulls together a series of poetry resources in Spanish to begin with and then reads some different pieces of poetry to his students asking them to *pensar en cómo son iguales y diferentes los poemas* (think about how the poems are the same and different). He reads some rather sophisticated poetry from Fernando del Paso (Del Paso, 1990) and Pablo Neruda (Neruda, 1987), some very short poems from alphabet poetry books (Broeck, 1983; Sempere, 1987), and some traditional playful poetry by Alma Flor Ada (1992a).

After reading each poem, Silvio asks his students what their impressions are and lists their ideas on chart paper. Since the poems are in Spanish, the ensuing discussion occurs naturally in Spanish as well. By the time Silvio has finished reading some ten different poems, the chart contains many different thoughts and questions about the poetry:

Students' comments	English translation
tiene rima	it rhymes
me hace sentir confundido	it makes me feel confused
me gusta porque es alegre	I like it because it is happy
algunos poemas no tienen rima	some poems don't rhyme
¿una canción puede ser un poema también?	Can a song be a poem too?

Silvio and the students look at their chart and talk about their observations and questions. Silvio then describes the upcoming local poetry festival to his students. This leads to a discussion on what they might do to prepare for it. Together they decide how they should study poetry together as a class. First, they should read many poems in Spanish. Then each student should memorize some poems and practice them in small groups to present to the class and maybe present at the festival.

In addition to reading the poetry of published authors, the students wonder if they can write some poetry of their own during their writing time each day. They decide that after they have read lots of poetry, they will be ready to think about writing their own. In addition, they talk about writing bilingual poems in both Spanish and English and also writing poetry only in English.

Silvio's students begin the year with poetry and revisit poetry throughout the year. As the year progresses Silvio draws on resources such as *Días y días de poesía* (*Days and Days of Poetry*) (Ada, 1991) for seasonal poetry ideas. He also reads different poems from the Mexican series *Reloj de Versos* (*Rhyming Clocks*) (Bartolomé, 1991; Cabrera; Cross, 1992; Forcada, 1992; Sabines, 1990). For English and bilingual literature he draws on resources such as *A Chorus of Cultures: Developing Literacy through Multicultural Poetry* (Ada, Harris, & Hopkins, 1993), as well as on local poets and his school library media specialist. Poetry is an excellent way for Silvio's students to develop literacy in both Spanish and English (Bartolomé, 1991; Cross, 1992; Forcada, 1992; Sabines, 1990).

Silvio sees the excitement of his students as they work with both familiar pieces and new poetry, but he wants to extend their reading and writing into other content areas, too. Some of his students are not yet proficient readers and writers in Spanish or English. Others read and write quite well. Silvio needs to provide literacy experiences that will interest and involve students with very different academic backgrounds and different language-proficiency levels. He realizes that an excellent way for his students to develop academic competence and become truly biliterate is by teaching content through a theme that draws on student background and experiences and encourages collaboration.

The small community where he lives and teaches depends heavily on agriculture. Many of Silvio's students are presently from migrant families or were at one time migrant children, moving from town to town with the crops. Certainly, all the students in his class understand the importance of the land and of growing crops, including those whose parents are foremen or landowners. Silvio wants all his students to realize the importance of the work that so many of their parents are involved in. He decides to have his students explore the question, *¿Por qué es importante la agriculture?* (Why is agriculture important?) He knows that his students' background experiences will help them as they read both literature and content texts on this topic.

Because the students began the year with poetry, it seems natural to Silvio to move into the agriculture theme through poetry. He begins the unit by reading a stanza from the poem *"Son del pueblo trabajador"* ("Sound of the Working People"):

Cuando sale el sol	When the sun rises
las tierras de mi tierra	the earth of my land
cultivo yo,	I cultivate
cuando sale el sol,	when the sun comes out

| que soy el campesino trabajador, cuando sale el sol. | I am the field laborer when the sun rises. |

(Ada, 1991, p. 41)

Silvio asks the students to jot down the thoughts or memories this poem brings to mind. They share their ideas in pairs and then make a class list.

Silvio passes out a copy of the stanza for students to take home and read to their parents. He encourages the students to discuss the poem with their family to find out what ideas it raises for them. He suggests that they write down their parents' impressions and come prepared to share their results in class the next day. Silvio uses this information to create a second list. Then the class compares the two sets of responses to the poem and discusses some of the reasons for similarities and differences. In some cases, the parents have a stronger response because their work experience is more immediate while the children's impressions have come secondhand as they hear their parents talk about their days in the fields. In other cases, the responses are similar because the children have worked alongside their parents.

In November, during harvest time, Silvio chooses songs and poetry about the harvest of corn, the historic staple for the people of Mexico and Central America. From *Días y días de poesía* (Ada, 1991) the whole class memorizes *"El maíz"* ("Corn"), (p. 64), a traditional poem that describes mature corn on the stalk and *"Día de gracias"* ("Thanksgiving Day"), (p. 70) and *"Día feliz"* ("Happy Day") (p. 71), poems that describe traditional celebration meals in Spanish-speaking homes. They also sing together *"Pizcamos mazorcas"* ("Picking Ears of Corn") (Ada, 1991).

During English language arts time, the students enjoy learning "Opening Corn," (Ada, Harris, & Hopkins, 1993, p. 95) a poem about an ear of corn. The poem draws on the senses with lines like "sounds like pulling down a zipper," "smells like onions," "feels like the road has bumps" and "looks like a witch's yellow white hair." The students brainstorm other comparisons that would describe corn. Then they try making up similar poems about pumpkins and onions.

From poetry Silvio turns the students to riddles beginning with the following one for corn:

| Allá en el llano está uno sin sombrero. Tiene barbas, tiene dientes y no es un caballero. | There in the plain is one without a hat. He has a beard, he has teeth and he is not a horseman. |

(Gallego et al., 1993, p. 29)

After reading and guessing several different riddles, the students write their own riddles in pairs and read them aloud for the class to guess. This activity also spills over into English language arts time, and the students often use the same topics in English that they first wrote and talked about in their native language. These similarities offer Silvio the opportunity to encourage his students to compare and contrast the stories. In addition, since the animals in the stories use mainly their sounds to try to get the pests out of the crops, poetry and stories using other animal sounds such as *Sonidos y ritmos* ("Sounds and Rhythms"), (Dubin, 1984), *Pepín y el abuelo* (*Pepín and the grandfather*), (Perera, 1993), *Alborada* ("Dawn") (1993, p. 51), *El coquí* (El Coquí—a Puerto Rican tree frog"), (Ada, 1992a, p. 12), and *Concierto* ("Concert") (Ada, 1992b, p. 11) offer the students further play with the sounds of language as well as additional opportunities for reading and writing.

Next, Silvio reads the big book, *Granjas* (*Farms*), (Madrigal, 1992), to the class. The students are fascinated by the description of *la granja de hortalizas* (vegetable farm), *la granja lechera* (dairy), *la granja triguera* (wheat farm), and *la granja de naranjas* (orange farm). The students excitedly share their own and their parents' experiences on the different types of farms and one proudly tells how his own father often tells him what the book said, *La agricultura es la actividad más importante del mundo* (p. 6) (Agriculture is the most important activity in the world).

After this discussion, Silvio explains that the class is going to do different inquiry projects on the topic of *La agricultura y su importancia* (Agriculture and Its Importance), and he asks the students *¿Qué más quieren saber ustedes sobre la agricultura?* (What else would you like to know about agriculture?). The students write questions in groups and then share their questions as Silvio writes them on a large piece of butcher paper. Some students want to know about what kinds of things make the plants on a farm grow better. Some want to know why pineapples and mangos from their countries will not grow in this area. Others want to know why farm laborers earn so little money and how much it costs to run a farm. Others want to know more about irrigation, and still others want to know what is necessary to raise farm animals properly. The class decides to form groups to investigate these topics. Each group will write a report to share with the class, and the reports will be combined to create a class book on agriculture.

To get the information that they need to explore their questions, the students decide to use different resources. They plan to interview people in their families and the community, to call or write the local farm bureau for speakers and information, and to look at resource books they have in their classroom including reference books such as *La vida de las plantas* (*The Life of Plants*) (Costa-Pau, 1993), *Plantas* (*Plants*) and *Animales* (*Animals*) (Sealey, 1979a; Sealey, 1979b), *Experimenta con las plantas* (*Experiment with Plants*) (Watts & Parsons, 1993), *Quiero conocer la vida de las plantas* (*I Want to Know about the Life of Plants*) (Marcus, 1987a) and *Quiero conocer la vida de los animates* (*I Want to Know about the Life of Animals*) (Marcus, 1987b).

Two of Silvio's students who came to his class directly from Mexico had very little previous schooling. The limited texts of the poetry, riddles, and the two stories about animals (Kratky, 1989; Seale & Tafolla, 1993) are accessible to these older emergent readers especially when the class reads them together or when they have opportunities to read with a buddy. However, Silvio also wants these students to do other reading so he provides them with books about farms and agriculture that have more limited text to use as they explore their questions. These include books such as *El rancho*, (*The Ranch*) (Armada, 1994), *Chiles*, (Kratky, 1995), *El campo*, (*The Country*) (Rius & Parramón, 1987), *Mi primera visita a la granja*, (*My First Visit to the Farm*) (Parramón & Sales, 1990), *Las plantas* (*Plants*) (Walker, 1995), *De la semilla a la fruta* (*From the Seed to the Fruit*) (Zenzes, 1987).

As the inquiry continues, different topics lead to different readings. Since cotton is an important crop locally, one group of students decides to study how cotton is changed into cloth. To help all the students understand this process, Silvio reads *Las cosas cambian* (Bourne, 1992a), the story of how cotton is converted into jeans. Since this book is also available in English, *Things Change* (Bourne, 1992b), it is also an excellent book for reading during English language arts.

A literature book that Silvio reads to his students during English language arts that connects with the topic of growing cotton especially catches his students' attention. *Working Cotton* (Williams, 1992). This book tells of an African American family picking cotton in the central valley of California where Silvio teaches. After the children listen to the story, they begin to talk about how hard it is to work in the hot fields. Some of the children who have to move with the crops also talk about how they do not like to move.

Another book that evokes student discussion in English language arts is *A Handful of Seeds* (Hughes, 1993). This book describes how an orphaned Mexican girl teaches other street children lessons she learned from her grandmother about growing vegetables from seeds so that they would not starve.

These discussions encourages Silvio to bring out two books in Spanish about children of migrant families who move with the crops: *El camino de Amelia* (*Amelia's Road*) (Altman, 1993b) and *Tomates California*

(Seale & Ramirez, 1993). The students discuss the children in these stories. This leads to the topic of rights for farm workers and the hero of
the farm workers, César Chávez. One of the students runs to the book
corner and pulls out, *César Chávez: Líder laboral* (*César Chávez. Labor
Leader*) (Morris, 1994). Silvio tells them that they should read the book
in small groups if they have not already read it, and that they will watch
a video about César Chávez in class.

During English language arts the next day, Silvio reads the English
version of *El camino de Amelia* (*Amelia's Road*) (Altman, 1993b), and the
students talk in English about how Amelia felt. The class then looks at
the book, *Earth Angels* (Buirski, 1994), a powerful book of photographs
and short quotes from field workers about the difficulty of their lives,
including the problems of child labor and pesticides. This book gives
the students background for viewing a video about the life of César
Chávez. After some discussion of the video, Silvio reads the students
two other books that deal with farm workers and their children: *A
Migrant Family* (Brimner, 1992), *Lights on the River* (Thomas, 1994). Both
of these stories evoke strong emotions in the children because of the
difficult life the migrant children lead.

The weeks that follow in Silvio's room are full of activity. Students
read, share, and write about what they are learning. They decide that
what they have learned about plants, animals, and agriculture, in
general is important to share with others in their school, and they plan
a day when other classes will come into their room so that they can
read the stories and reports they have written and explain what they
have learned.

Silvio has accomplished his goal. His students are reading and writing. However, he has accomplished some other things that may be
even more important. Through a curriculum that is relevant to the
lives of his students, he has helped them appreciate what they and their
families contribute to society. His students are becoming biliterate by
reading both quality literature and content texts in Spanish and English,
by discussing what they read with their peers, and by engaging in
meaningful writing. The writing allows students to show not only what
they have learned but also how they have been touched by this empowering curriculum.

Clearly, Silvio's teaching would also be evaluated positively with the
checklist. He focused on a big question and brought in a great deal of
authentic literature. The topics he chose built on students' backgrounds
and interests. Members of his class collaborated frequently as they
engaged with this meaningful curriculum, and they had many opportunities to read, write, speak, and listen in both English and Spanish.

Since Silvio's is a bilingual class, he could more fully bring the students' primary languages and cultures into every activity. Silvio was also careful to provide activities that all his students, from those very proficient in both Spanish and English to those who were older emergent readers in their primary language, could complete successfully, and in this way he built their self confidence and their self esteem. Silvio provided all his students with a strong start on the road to full linguistic and academic proficiency.

Conclusion

Teachers of multilingual students naturally do many of the kinds of things that are helpful to second-language students. They use pictures, gestures, and hands-on activities to make lessons understandable. They start where students are and build the background students need so they can link prior knowledge to new reading and writing activities. They organize curriculum around themes so students can make a rich web of connections.

When teachers understand the process of second-language acquisition and realize the importance of finding ways to incorporate students' primary languages and cultures into the curriculum, they can enrich their teaching in ways that increases the chances for success of students acquiring English. They can find as many ways as possible to engage these students in the reading and writing activities the students need to develop English proficiency.

However, teachers working in multilingual classrooms must not simply teach their students to read and write in English. They must also help them maintain their first languages and cultures and teach them to think and to want a better world. Biliterate people are going to be leaders in the next century, and only if we help them understand how to make the world a better place can we say that our teaching has really been successful.

Professional References

Collier, V. P. (1989). How long? A synthesis of research on academic achievement in a second language. *TESOL Quarterly 23* (3):509–32.

Collier, V. P. (1995). Acquiring a second language for school. *Directions in Language and Education 1* (4).

Cummins, J. (1981). The role of primary language development in promoting educational success for language minority students. In *Schooling and language minority students: A theoretical framework.* Los Angeles: Evaluation, Dissemination and Assessment Center California State University, Los Angeles.

Cummins, J. (1989). *Empowering minority students.* Sacramento: CABE.

Freeman, D. E., & Freeman, Y. S. (1993). Strategies for promoting the primary languages of all students. *The Reading Teacher 46* (7):552–58.

Freeman, D. E., & Freeman, Y. S. (1994). *Between worlds: Access to second language acquisition.* Portsmouth, NH: Heinemann.

Freeman, Y. S., & Freeman, D. E. (1992). *Whole language for second language learners.* Portsmouth, NH: Heinemann.

Holt, D. (Ed.). (1993). *Cooperative learning: A response to linguistic and cultural diversity.* Washington, DC.: Center for Applied Linguistics.

Hudelson, S. (1984). Kan yu ret an rayt en ingles: Children become literate in English as a second language. *TESOL Quarterly 18* (2):221–37.

Krashen, S. (1982). *Principles and practice in second language acquisition.* New York: Pergamon Press.

Krashen, S. (1985). *Inquiries and insights.* Haywood, CA: Alemany Press.

Krashen, S. (1993). *The power of reading: Insights from the research.* Englewood, Colorado: Libraries Unlimited.

Rigg, P., & Hudelson, S. (1986). One child doesn't speak English. *Australian Journal of Reading 9* (3):116–25.

Smith, F. (1983). *Essays into literacy: Selected papers and some afterthoughts.* Portsmouth, NH: Heinemann.

Literature References

Alborada. (1993). In R. Barrera (Ed.), *Yo Soy Yo.* Boston: Houghton Mifflin.

Ada, A. F. (1991). *Días y días de poesía.* Carmel: Hampton-Brown Books.

Ada, A. F. (1992a). *Caballito Blanco y otras poesías favoritas, Días y días de poesía.* Carmel: Hampton-Brown Books.

Ada, A. F. (1992b). *Cinco pollitos y otras poesías favorites, Días y días de poesía.* Carmel: Hampton-Brown Books.

Ada, A. F. (1993). *My name is María Isabel.* New York: Atheneum Books.

Ada, A. F., Harris, V. J., & Hopkins, L. B. (1993). *A chorus of cultures: Developing literacy through multicultural poetry.* Carmel: Hampton-Brown Books.

Almada, P. (1994). *El rancho, literatura 2000.* Crystal Lake, IL: Rigby.

Altman, L. J. (1993a). *Amelia's Road.* New York: Lee & Low Books Inc.

Altman, L. J. (1993b). *El camino de Amelia.* (D. Santacruz, Trans.). New York: Lee & Low Books.

Bang, M. (1993). *Ten, nine, eight.* New York: Mulberry Books.

Bartolomé, E. (1991). *Mínima animalia, reloj de verses.* Mexico, DO.: CODICIL.

Bourne, P. M. (1992a). *Las cosas cambian.* Carmel: Hampton-Brown Books.

Bourne, P. M. (1992b). *Things change.* Carmel. Hampton-Brown Books.

Brimner, L.D. (1992). *A migrant family*. Minneapolis: Lerner Publications Company.

Broeck, F. V. (1983). *ABC animales, colección piñata*. México, D.F.: Editorial Patria.

Buirski, N. (1994). *Earth angels*. San Francisco: Pomegranate Artbooks.

Cabrera, M. *Chiquilín*. Caracas, Venezuela: Conceptos.

Carl, E. (1969). *The very hungry caterpillar*. Cleveland: The World Publishing Company.

Costa-Pau, R. (1993). *La vida de las plantas, mundo invisible*. Bogotá: Editorial Norma.

Cross, E. (1992). *El himno de las ranas, reloj de versos*. México, D.F.: CIDCLI.

Del Paso, F. (1990). *De la A a la Z por un poeta*. México, D.F.: Grupo Editorial Diana.

Dubin, S. D. (1984). *Sonidos y ritmos*. Boston: Houghton Mifflin Company.

Forcada, A. (1992). *Despertar, Reloj de versos*. México, D.F.: CIDCLI.

Gallego, M., Hinojosa-Smith, R., Kohen, C., Medrano, H., Solis,J., & Thonis, E. (1993). *Cultivos alternados, HBJ Estrellas de la literatura*. Orlando: Harcourt Brace Jovanovich.

Hughes, M. (1993). *A handful of seeds*. New York: Orchard Books.

Knight, M. (1992). *Talking walls*. Gardner, ME: Tilbury House.

Knight, M. (1993). *Who belongs here? An american story*. Gardiner, Maine: Tilbury House.

Kratky, L. J.(1989). *El chivo en la huerta*. Carmel, CA: Hampton- Brown.

Kratky, L. J. (1995). *Chiles, pan y canela*. Carmel: HamptonBrown Books.

Madrigal, S. (1992). *Granjas*. Carmel, CA.: Hampton-Brown Books.

Marcus, E. (1987a). *Quiero conocer la vida de las plantas, Quiero conocer*. México, D.F.: Sistemas Técnicos de Edición.

Marcus, E. (1987b). *Quiero conocer la vida de los animales, Quiero conocer*. México, D.F.: SITESA.

Morris, C. Sanchez de. (1994). *César Chávez: Líder laboral*. Cleveland: Modern Curriculm Press.

Neruda, P. (1987). *El libro de las preguntas*. Editorial Andres Bello. Santiago de Chile.

Parramón, J. M., & Sales, G . (1990). *Mi primera visita a la granja, Mi primera visita*. Woodbury, NY: Barron's.

Perera, H. (1993). *Pepín y el abuelo*. Boston: Houghton Mifflin Company.

Rius, M., & Parramon, J. M. (1987). *El campo, Un día en*. Woodbury, NY: Barron's.

Sabines, J. (1990). *La luna, Reloj de versos*. México, D.F.: CIDCLI.

Say, A. (1993). *Grandfather's journey*. Boston: Houghton Mifflin.

Seale, J., & Tafolla, C. (1993). La marrana dormida. In R. Barrera (Ed.), *Yo Soy Yo*. Boston: Houghton Mifflin.

Seale, J. E., and Ramirez, A. (1993). *Tomates, California*. Boston: Houghton Mifilin Company.

Sealey, L. (1979a). *Animales, colección nuestro mundo*. Barcelona: Editorial Juventud.

Sealey, L. (1979b). *Plantas*. In L. Sealey (Ed.), *Colección nuestro mundo*. Barcelona: Editorial Juventud.

Sempere, V. (1987). *ABC*. Caracas, Venezuela: Ediciones EkareBanco del Libro.

Shea, P. (1995). *The whispering cloth: a refugee's story*. Honesdale, PA: Boyds Mills Press.

Surat, M. M. (1983). *Angel child, dragon child*. New York: Scholastic, Inc.

Thomas, J. R. (1994). *Lights on the river*. New York: Hyperion Books for Children.

Torres, L. (1995). *Saturday Sancocho*. New York: Farrar Straus Giroux.

Walker, C. (1995). *Las plantas, concept science en español*. Cleveland: Modern Curriculum Press.

Watts, C., & Parsons, A. (1993). *Experimenta con las plantas*.(B. Rodriguez, Trans.).

Ginzo, C. In W. Baker & A. Haslam (Eds.), *Make it work!* Madrid: Ediciones SM.

Williams, S. (1992). *Working cotton*. Orlando: Harcourt Brace Jovanovich.

Zenzes, G. (1987). *De la sernilla a la fruta*. México, D.F.: Fernandez Editores.

VI Providing Extra Help: In the Classroom and Beyond

Providing Extra Help: In the Classroom and Beyond

Of course this is a somewhat arbitrary section, as some of the articles could just as readily be included in another section (so too, some of the articles in other sections could be included here). What the articles in this section all have in common, though, is an emphasis on providing the extra support, guidance, and time that some readers need.

Recently, public concern has arisen with regard to children who do not use letter/sound knowledge effectively in dealing with words—children who appear, at least, not to have had enough phonics, or not to have had the right kind of phonics teaching (including training in phonemic awareness). However and whatever they've been taught, they are not able to *use* their phonics knowledge very effectively in dealing with unknown print words.

In the frenzy over phonics, however, there are other problems we must try to prevent (see the introduction to Section I) and, meanwhile, other children we also need to help: children who have difficulty making sense of texts that should be appropriate for their age and background knowledge, and children who don't even seem to realize that reading should make sense.

Some of these children may have, or appear to have, particular problems with certain features of language—for example, with realizing what noun a pronoun refers to. More generally, they may have problems connecting ideas across sentences and paragraphs and drawing inferences. *Such problems will not be noticed if teachers only listen to children read aloud and do not discuss the reading selection with them.* This is one of the values of the miscue analysis procedures discussed in Section III.

Sarah, for instance, was a child who apparently had little difficulty saying the words in a text, but did have difficulty in relating ideas in one sentence to those in another. Ten years and nine months old at the time of this assessment, Sara read the following from a book about a pioneer girl, *Felicity*. Her decoding skills were fine, and she read this passage aloud without any miscues:

> "Oh, father! You know I don't fancy this old hat at all," giggled Felicity. "I wear it only because Mother insists." She pushed the straw hat off her head so that it hung down her back.
>
> "Aye," agreed her father. "It's supposed to shade your face, so that the sun does not make your nose red."
>
> Felicity rubbed her nose. It *was* rather pink. "I do forget to wear my hat sometimes," she said. (p. 2)

Sarah's clinician at Western Michigan University, Nicole McDonnell, wrote the following in her journal about what happened next:

> An interesting discussion was held about things that are implied. Sarah read the sentences "Felicity rubbed her nose. It *was* rather pink" [with no miscues]. When I asked Sarah why Felicity's nose was pink, she attributed it to the rubbing. She neglected the fact that the previous sentence talked about Felicity's dad lecturing her on how "It's supposed to shade your face so the sun doesn't make your nose red."
>
> The *it's* referred to the previous sentence, which talked about Felicity's straw hat.
>
> Sarah had difficulty taking all of this information and processing it to come up with the implication that Felicity hadn't been wearing her hat and let her nose get sunburned. She found this a difficult concept to understand. (From Nickola Nelson, "Implementing a Language-Based Homework Lab: A Plan for Conducting Curriculum-Based Language Intervention," a videotape published by Singular Publishing, 1997).

Apparently this kind of difficulty with inferencing was not uncommon for Sarah. Therefore, her goals included reading comprehension for stories and expository texts.

All of the articles in this section include ways of helping children who need additional help with phonics skills, reading strategies, and/or understanding what they are reading. However, Norris in particular explains how the same kind of tutorial intervention can assist readers with any or all of these needs, and others.

In the spirit of articles "talking" to one another, though, we surely can speculate: Would these individual needs be met just as well by literature discussions of the sort described in Section IV? By some combination of silent reading, literature discussions, and teacher conferencing? It's interesting to speculate, and might be valuable to research. Meanwhile, it's clear that, as Allington explains, we need to consider and implement various ways of providing children with the extra support they need, including the extra time they need to read, read, and read some more.

28 Reading Express: Supporting Literacy in First-grade Classrooms

Kathryn Kinnucan-Welsch
University of Dayton

Dodie Magill and Barbara Schmich
Partee Elementary School, Lithonia, Georgia

Marie H. Dean
Mountain Park Elementary School, Lilburn, Georgia

In this chapter the authors, a university collaborator, two elementary teachers, and an assistant principal, describe the development, implementation, and initial experiences of the Reading Express Program at Mountain Park Elementary School in Liburn, Georgia. This program began when the first-grade teachers began to see positive effects for the students who were receiving Reading Recovery tutoring. Conversations among the faculty and administration led to the development of Reading Express, a collaborative effort between the first-grade teachers and the Reading Recovery teachers. Their goal: for all children to be readers by the end of first grade.

In the first year of this project, the Reading Recovery teachers spent one hour per day in each of the first-grade classrooms, engaging in both whole class and small-group instruction. The purpose of integrating Reading Recovery teaching into the classrooms was twofold: (1) to provide instruction for all first-grade students in the use of specific reading and writing strategies; and (2) to provide additional in-class support for children identified as being placed most at risk for failure in reading. An additional result of this project was the change experienced among the first-grade teachers in their teaching practices as they collaborated with the Reading Recovery teachers. Initial data from this first year demonstrate that the program was highly successful.

In this chapter, the authors describe how the Reading Express project came about and what the teachers' goals were; what reading strategies were emphasized; initial assessments that formed the basis for instruction; how the program was first implemented and the reading strategies taught, and then how and why the program was restructured later in the school year; initial data on the success of the program; reflections on how the first year went; and thoughts about changes as they looked forward to implementing the program for a second year. One of the best outcomes has been the increased learning by and collaboration among the teachers, and the trust in each other that has begun to develop.

This is the story of how teachers, with support from building administrators, addressed a concern about the literacy development of all first-grade children at Mountain Park Elementary School, Lilburn, Georgia. Our story describes the Reading Express Program, and we tell this story chronologically, beginning with the initial conversations in which the seeds for the idea began to germinate. We then describe the Reading Express Model as it was implemented during the first year, followed by some of the changes in the model that were made in that first year as the need arose. Next we present some of the initial data we collected during the first year of Reading Express to see if what we are doing is making a difference for our children. Finally, we make public our thoughts on how we—a group of teachers, an administrator, and a university collaborator—worked together throughout the year. We are telling this story as a collection of our perspectives: Marie Dean, a first-grade teacher, Dodie Magill, a Reading Recovery teacher, Barbara Schmich, the assistant principal, and Katie Kinnucan-Welsch, a university collaborator. When speaking collectively, we will use first person; when referring to a single person's perspective, we will use our first names to avoid any confusion for the reader.

The Origins of Reading Express: Conversations Across Time and Places

In sharing the evolution of Reading Express, we hope to emphasize how important it is for all educators to create opportunities for conversations that lead to collaboration in improved practice among teachers and enhanced learning for students. The detail that is provided here hopefully will encourage all members in communities of learning to let their untried thoughts become part of the rich texture of ideas that are woven through conversations among teachers, administrators, and university collaborators.

In the fall of 1994, Dr. Robert Clark, principal of Mountain Park Elementary School, hired two Reading Recovery teachers. Reading Recovery is a one-to-one early intervention instructional program that supports the literacy development of children who have been placed most at risk for failure in reading. During that year, Dodie Magill, the Reading Recovery teacher, and her colleague taught first-grade children in a one-to-one pull out situation for thirty minutes each, using knowledge and expertise developed in their year-long Reading Recovery training (for descriptions of Reading Recovery, see Clay, 1979, 1985; Pinnell, Lyons, DeFord, Bryk, & Seltzer, 1994; Shanahan & Barr, 1995).

During the 1994–1995 school year, the first-grade teachers began to see the results of Reading Recovery with those first graders who had been in the program. Marie Dean recalls watching in amazement as Callie (a pseudonym), one of the children experiencing difficulty in reading in her class, began to use the reading strategies that she had learned in her Reading Recovery sessions. Marie recalls thinking to herself that she wanted to know more about the reading strategies the children were learning as well as wanting to learn more about her students as readers. She also wanted to be able to more effectively communicate with parents about their child's reading performance.

As Marie was toying with these thoughts, conversations were taking place with the first-grade teachers as a team. At Mountain Park, teachers on each grade level meet regularly to discuss a variety of issues, including curriculum. During these grade level meetings as well as those informal conversations in the hall, the teachers began to realize the potential in teaching all first graders to become problem-solving, sense-making, independent readers through instruction and support in reading strategies. Out of these conversations, which soon moved out of the first- grade hallway and into the offices of the principal and assistant principal, the first-grade teachers began to clearly articulate a goal that would guide the development of Reading Express: All children will be readers by the end of first grade.

Barbara Schmich, the assistant principal, and Dodie remember a conversation during the spring of 1995 in which they explored the "what if" scenario. What if we want all children to be readers by the end of first grade? What if we want all children to experience the same benefits as those who are in the Reading Recovery Program? What if the Reading Recovery teachers went into the first-grade classrooms to teach all children the same strategies the children in Reading Recovery are learning?

Barbara pursued the conversation with Dr. Clark, the principal. This conversation explored the possibility of having the Reading Recovery teachers work in the classroom with the first-grade teachers for part of the day. This would provide the teachers with an opportunity to learn through observation and modeling from peers with special expertise. It would also capitalize on the interest generated by the first-grade teachers. They were ready to bring these strategies to all of the first-grade students; they just were not sure how as yet. Dr. Clark and Barbara discussed the issue of personnel allotment. In order to keep two Reading Recovery teachers full time, some other personnel would have to be given up.

The personnel issue was approached with the first grade teachers. They decided they would be willing to give up the paraprofessional assigned to their grade level to bring Reading Recovery teachers into their classrooms. This only provided for one-half of the needed full-time allocation. At an all-grade chair meeting, Barbara described the possibility of enhancing reading instruction for all first-grade students. The teachers recognized the positive effects that would be seen in the upper elementary over time. The upper elementary teachers also agreed to give up part of their paraprofessional support. Through collaboration across grade levels, the personnel issue was resolved.

In conjunction with her conversations with Barbara, Dodie and the first-grade teachers explored the possibility of what it might look like if Dodie spent time in their classrooms. By the time the 1994–1995 school year had ended, Dodie had worked with individual and small groups of children in two of the five first-grade rooms. Marie was now even more convinced that bringing Reading Recovery strategies to both the children and to the teachers would benefit everyone.

At a School Improvement Team meeting at the end of the year, Marie, who was a member of that team, emphasized to Dr. Clark, the principal, "We want every one of our first graders to be readers by the end of the first grade. Period." Dr. Clark's response was "Tell us what you need in order to have that happen." And so, after one year of conversations, observations, and reflections, the first-grade teachers and the Reading Recovery teachers began to put together what is now known as Reading Express. The teachers met during preplanning during mid-August 1995 and drew up a schedule for the Reading Recovery teachers to spend time each day in the first-grade classrooms. This schedule is outlined in the next section of this chapter.

Katie Kinnucan-Welsch joined the conversations as a university collaborator when she came to Mountain Park in September 1995 as a post-doctoral researcher from the League of Professional Schools, University of Georgia. Katie's role during the 1995–1996 school year was to study and support the action research efforts at Mountain Park. Since one of Katie's main interests was early literacy, her involvement in the Reading Express program was a natural. Katie's initial awareness of the Reading Express program came at a meeting in early September with Bob Clark, Barbara, and the teachers who were leaders of the five task forces—school improvement groups based on action research. Although Reading Express was not identified as one of the goals of the Local School Plan for Improvement task force, the nature of the teacher-driven inquiry embedded in the Reading Express model lended itself to thinking of this venture as action research driven by teacher concern.

One of the focused conversations that helped lead to a more clear definition of exactly what we were trying to accomplish with Reading Express took place at Dodie's house on October 13, 1995. Dr. Clark had requested a written plan for what was up to this point called the "First Grade Collaborative Model." The structure for that plan included a goal statement, what we intended to do, what results we anticipated, and how we would assess our results. We also needed to come up with a name that was more descriptive than the First Grade Collaborative Model. This half-day meeting was the first of three half-days for planning that Barbara provided to the Reading Express team. By the end of the morning, as the teachers and Katie returned to Mountain Park, what had been a somewhat loosely conceived idea forged through the multiple conversations now had clearly articulated goals, intended results, and a plan for data collection. The texts of the conversations across time and space had come together in a written text that we were to return to many times during the 1995–1996 school year as the conversations about Reading Express continued.

The Description of Reading Express

As with the recounting of the origins of Reading Express, our description of the program itself is a blend of our perspectives and voices. Some of the narrative here is contained in the description of the model written by the teachers in October. Pieces of the narrative are from a description that Dodie and Marie have offered to various audiences during multiple presentations about the program that began in Spring 1996. All of the teachers' perspectives are represented in the transcriptions of the audiotaped Reading Express meetings and in field notes that Katie wrote during her weekly visits to Mountain Park during the 1995–1996 school year. Artifacts such as a newspaper article from the Atlanta Journal Constitution also contribute to the multiple perspectives.

The document that we prepared during the fall of 1996 articulated the Reading Express model as it was conceived at that time. Although the schedule and instruction were to shift later in that first year, the goal and basic format of the program remained true to the original conceptualization. Following is the description of Reading Express as contained in the original plan.

"Reading Express" is a model first-grade language arts program, developed cooperatively by the first grade and Reading Recovery teachers at Mountain Park Elementary School. The name "Reading Express" depicts the close relationship between reading and writing as important means of expression. It also indicates our goal of accelerating the reading and writing progress for all first-grade students by taking the "express" route this program offers. Children are instructed in whole groups and individually, as well as in small groups in which students work homogeneously in literacy "stations."

The goals providing initial direction for planning included:

- To provide more instructional time with each student in his/her own level

- To provide a more individualized program for every student in reading and writing

- To enable every student to experience success and a level of competence in reading and writing

- To enable the classroom teachers to utilize Reading Recovery strategies in their own classrooms

The program looks like this. The first-grade classes have been divided in two teams. Each team works with one Reading Recovery teacher. The Reading Recovery teacher goes to each of her team's first-grade classes for one hour every day during the language arts block of time. Monday is devoted to whole-group instruction. On Tuesday through Thursday, the children participate in small-group instruction, and Fridays are flexible, depending on the prioritized needs of the children.

The whole-group instruction on Mondays is directed by the Reading Recovery teacher. The content of these lessons focuses on some literacy strategy or skill based on Reading Recovery methodology and terminology. The Reading Recovery teacher models the strategy for the children and the classroom teacher supports the Reading Recovery teacher by providing assistance and monitoring student understanding and application of the strategy. During our first year of Reading Express, the first-grade teachers were learning about strategic reading instruction as part of this process.

The core of instruction at the beginning of the year consists of five strategies that the children can use when they come to a "tricky word." These five strategies were introduced and reinforced during the whole-group instruction over the first four months of the 1995–1996 school year. The "Five Things Good Readers Do" when they meet a "tricky word" are as follows:

- Think about the story
- Check the picture
- Go back and reread, and get your mouth ready
- Look for "chunks"
- Ask yourself, "Does that make sense?"

As each of these strategies was introduced and modeled by the Reading Recovery teacher to the whole class, the first-grade teacher was also learning how to support the development of that strategy among the children. Graphic representations of the strategies were displayed in the classrooms to remind the children what they could do when they "met a tricky word," and parents received newsletters describing the strategies. An excerpt of one of the newsletters is displayed below in Figure 1.

Read All About It!
Reading News
from Mrs. Magill

All of us - even Moms and Dads - meet words that are difficult to read. Knowing what to do when we come upon "tricky" words can make us better, and more confident, readers. We learned this week that there are FIVE SECRET WEAPONS that good readers use when they meet "tricky" words. . . and we have now learned how to use <u>two</u> of them!

Think about the story.

One thing we can do is to "**think about the story.**" By thinking what the whole story is about, we may be able to figure out what the "tricky" word is. For example, if our story is about <u>Bears</u>, and the sentence reads, "He likes to eat h_____", we could guess that the word might be "honey" since we know bears like to eat honey.

√ Check the picture.

Another strategy, or "Secret Weapon" we can use is "**check the picture.**" Illustrations in children's books may make the story look more appealing, but they are actually included for another reason: to assist the child as he reads. Often checking the picture will help a child when he is "stuck" on a word. All readers should be encouraged to use the pictures.

Figure 1. Excerpt from newsletter.

The whole-group instruction of reading strategies is only one aspect of Reading Express. From Tuesday through Thursday, we utilize small group instruction. Children work for one hour each day in literacy stations, which are designed to extend the instruction of the introduced skill and other language arts goals established for a two-week period. A total of six literacy stations are operating at one time. Children at two stations work with either the first-grade teacher or the Reading Recovery teacher; the other children work independently. The children rotate from one station to the next after thirty minutes. Children are grouped homogeneously for this small-group instruction, but these groups are flexible. The children move in and out of the groups as their needs change. The groups are small, two to four per group.

Friday is flexible in that the instruction may be delivered to the whole group, to small groups, or to individuals. Children who are not enrolled in Reading Recovery but who may need additional one-on-one instruction are targeted during this time.

Instructional decisions are based on data. We do not make instructional decisions because they "seem" right. In the beginning of the school year, we tested every first-grade child using the Observation Record (Clay, 1993), a collection of six informal assessment activities that are given to Reading Recovery students. These observations measure each child's ability to:

- Identify letters of the alphabet
- Read a list of words in isolation
- Understand basic concepts about print
- Write and spell words from the child's own language repertoire
- Hear sounds in words by writing a dictated sentence
- Implement reading strategies during a continuous text reading

The original grouping and choices for strategy instruction were based on the results of these observations.

Throughout the year, we continually assess our students' progress. We use Running Records, a recording of oral reading text, to assess the appropriate text level for each student. In addition, the Running Records reveal not only the child's accuracy in reading, they also supply us with the information needed to determine why errors were made and what strategic instruction was needed at that point in time. The classroom teacher and the Reading Recovery teacher also keep anecdotal records during small group instruction. These individual records note shifts in reading performance as well as areas of difficulty in reading or writing.

A picture of what the Reading Express program looks like can also be constructed from field notes that Katie wrote during her visits to the first-grade classrooms. Although Katie's role as action research facilitator at Mountain Park did not entail exclusive focus on the first-grade literacy effort, she began to take a special interest in that project very early in the year.

Excerpts from field notes throughout the year are shared below to give a flavor of what the Reading Express model looked like through Katie's eyes. An "OC" notation is an indication that Katie departed from recording to what she is observing in order to note a thought, question, or area to pursue with the teachers.

Field Notes

10-6-95

> I spent two and one-half hours in first-grade classrooms with Dodie Magill. She was part of the station rotation in Garner's class and in Rice's class. The stations were organized so that the class was divided into about six or seven small groups and they moved to a different spot after thirty minutes. Dodie and the first-grade teachers then worked with two groups for the hour that Dodie was in there. The rotation took place on Tues-Thurs (OC: I think—I'll have to confirm that) and the Monday and Friday schedule when Dodie is in there was somewhat different.

> The first classroom I went in, Garner's, was a room that exploded with print. That is the best description I can think of. There was not an open space in the entire room and there were also pieces of chart paper hanging from the ceiling that had words on them beginning with the various letters of the alphabet. If the letter of the alphabet on that page was "c," the words that began with c were listed and the "c" was circled. Everything was labeled, the children's work was on every wall, there was a calendar corner, the desks were organized in groups of four or five.

> [Becky] then called the students to the carpet and she sat in a rocking chair while the students told stories about how the storm [Hurricane Opal] affected them. She said they would talk for a while until Ms Magill came in. She organized the lunch count and attendance and had the two designated helpers for the day take them to the cafeteria and the office.

> Dodie came in and I sat at the center while she worked with two groups of students, each for thirty minutes. Dodie started the station activity with introducing a new book. Each child had their own copy of the book and they went through the book together page

by page talking about the story using the pictures for support. Dodie also had the children point to words as they talked about each page. After the introduction, the children read the book together. I recognized several prompts I had seen in Reading Recovery lessons elsewhere. Next, Dodie had a set of tagboard letters and pocket folders for each student. The activity was to have the children take one vowel, "u," to make words. She had given them six letters and a pocket folder. They progressed from two through six letter words. She reviewed the lesson she had done with the whole group earlier in the week. A lot of support for children to hear sounds and use what they know—to recognize familiar chunks, and generally play with letters.

This routine was repeated in Rice's room.

———————

OC: I need to ask Dodie how she determines what she is going to do with the kids. One of the pieces of information that I think is important here is the comment that Marie Dean made. [She said] Dodie is ready to move into having children recognize chunks of words in the other first grades; the children in Marie's room are just beginning to hear the sounds. They aren't ready for chunking. This is a piece of anecdotal evidence that the teachers are targeting the individual needs of students in the collaborative model. It is also evidence that the teachers are beginning to use the language of Reading Recovery strategies.

Field Notes

10/26/95 [Dodie in Becky Garner's room, small group time at literacy stations]

Once we got back into the room [after a fire drill], the children resumed their work. Dodie introduced a new book by talking about each picture and asking the children to respond to what was happening on each page. She also talked the pattern through. Then the children had to find two words from the story: "laughing" and "stop." They talked about the chunks the kids knew in those words. Then they moved to reading the new book. . . . Becky signaled the station change with a xylophone. The children hadn't quite finished reading the new book; she told them to take the copies and read it during their free reading time. Dodie then asked when they had free reading; she said she would come in then.

The second group came to the table and Dodie followed a similar lesson but with a different set of books. She asked them what books they had read, an indication that she was individualizing for each group-at least on book selection if not on focus for the lesson.

Field Notes

3/11/96 [Dodie in Marie Dean's room]

I went into Marie's room—Dodie was doing a whole group as is standard for Monday. She was using a puppet, a dog named Jasper. I later found out that the children are familiar with Jasper. Dodie told me Jasper has been with her for several years. She was using a big book, Jasper was reading, and one of the first-grade students was running his finger along the text. Certain words were underlined with yellow tape. The book was "This is the Place for Me" by Joanna Cole.

Dodie started the lesson by going through the book introducing the concepts and letting the children hear words that might cause them trouble.

After that, "Jasper" began to read the book. As Dodie came to each word she pretended to struggle with, maybe one per page, she said (through Jasper's voice): "What can I do to help me?"

Individual children responded by suggesting one of the strategies they had learned this year. "Look for chunks" was a common one. "Check the picture" was another common one. Dodie then modeled how she would find a chunk or think aloud about the picture.

After Dodie did the whole group lesson, she had the students write a new ending for the story and draw a picture.

End of notes.

The above excerpt illustrates the learning opportunities available to the first graders as part of the Reading Express instruction. Every child could identify with "Jasper" when he came to a word he did not know. What was different for many children, however, is that over the course of the year they had learned strategies, "secret weapons," they could employ when they came to a "tricky word." As they read this book together, it was evident they were using the strategies Dodie had modeled and supported during both whole group and small group instruction. For some students, modeling the thought process of employing the strategy was a necessary scaffold for them as they had not yet fully integrated the strategies during reading of connected text.

Although these excerpts from field notes offer to the reader a detailed slice of the Reading Express program, the complexity and breadth is somehow lost in our narrative. As the children were beginning to use the language and incorporate the strategies into their reading of text, so, too, were the first-grade teachers. Katie noticed numerous times when the first-grade teachers referred the children to one of the strategies during times when the Reading Recovery teacher was not in the room. For example, Marie suggested that the children listen for chunks as they tried their best invented spelling during writing time. It is important to note that whole-group instruction incorporated more than instruction on the five strategies. By the middle of the year, writing strategies were taught to the children as well. The mainstay of instruction, however, continued to be the "good things readers do when they come to a tricky word."

Reading Express, as any evolving program designed by teachers to meet the needs of all students, had its share of challenges. Some of the dilemmas we encountered the initial year and how we approached those dilemmas will be the next topic in our story.

Changes over the Year

We had an awareness based on our initial conversations that each of the participating teachers brought different philosophies and unique experiences to Reading Express. Christine was committed to making sure the children had a strong foundation in decoding through phonics. Sonja had experienced success in having her children grouped so that she could hear them read every day round-robin style. Becky saw the value in incorporating children's choice in learning through a center structure that incorporated curriculum content and language arts. Marie saw the need to know these children as readers in order to support their literacy growth throughout the year. Caroline brought a rich set of experiences from kindergarten and a strong commitment to developmentally appropriate practice.

Although Reading Express had a standard structure and common set of goals for first grade, the differing perspectives of each teacher and the unique character of each classroom made for distinct experiences. Some of these experiences were positive for the teachers; some of them were a source of frustration as the first-grade teachers realized some of their classroom goals and expectations were not being met within the Reading Express structure. By February of 1996, we realized that some changes needed to be made in how the instruction was organized. The teachers requested a meeting, and Barbara arranged for a block of time. The meeting of February 12 served to be a pivotal point in the evolution of Reading Express, both in terms of how the program was organized as well as how we were collaborating as a group.

Up to this point, the children were still rotating as small groups through literacy stations. The Reading Recovery teachers planned station activities that incorporated instruction typical of a Reading Recovery lesson and the first-grade teachers were planning activities that incorporated broad language arts goals. The original intent was that this planning be accomplished by all seven teachers involved, but as the year progressed, less of the station planning was done collaboratively. As a result, the station work was meeting neither the expectations of the first-grade teachers nor the needs of the children. Although the station work in each of the classrooms mirrored how that teacher might organize reading and writing instruction, the teachers felt the stations were disconnected from their curriculum. It seemed as if the teachers had separated what was planned for stations and what had been planned in years past for a two-hour block of language arts. The teachers were concerned that they had not incorporated their social studies and math curriculum into their morning block as they had been accustomed to doing in the past.

A second concern that was voiced during this meeting involved those children who had made significant progress in their literacy development, those kids who were "getting it." Station instruction seemed to target those strategies and knowledge of our language that early and emergent readers still require rather than strategies needed for the children who had made progress. The individual needs of the children had changed dramatically since the beginning of the year, and we felt that perhaps a change in the structure was warranted.

A third concern related directly to discipline during station time, but more indirectly related to the relationship between the Reading Recovery teacher and the classroom teacher. The question arose related to who was responsible for disciplining the students during station time. Dodie remarked that she and her team members had worked it out that the teacher in closest proximity to a group of children at a station where a disturbance was occurring would be the one to address the problem. Dodie remarked during this conversation that when two teachers are working together in a room, their different styles and tolerances become apparent. This particular issue reflected a much broader reality that teachers often face: educators are typically not accustomed to more than one teacher in a classroom. Katie noted in her field notes for this meeting that the structure of Reading Express challenged some of the historical norms of education by bringing two teachers into the classroom at the same time, if only for an hour a day.

The conversation during the February meeting led to major changes in how Reading Express was organized. The rotation of stations on a thirty-minute schedule was abandoned. The classroom teachers decided to go to a center structure wherein each first-grade teacher would plan centers that incorporated the content of the curriculum and allowed for some choice among the children. The Reading Recovery teachers would still go into the classroom, but on Tuesdays through Thursdays they would work only with those children who were experiencing some difficulty in reading and writing. The other children in the class would go to centers on a flexible basis. Thus Dodie might work with a group for fifteen minutes or for twenty-five minutes, depending on the needs of the children of that day. Dodie also would see the same children every day while the classroom teachers organized reading and writing time for all the children some time during the morning. Monday would continue to be whole-group instruction with the Reading Recovery teacher; Fridays would be flexible, depending on the needs of the children.

Katie noted to the group during the February meeting that the teachers had obviously conceptualized the "stations" of Reading Express as being very different from the "centers" they had incorporated into their routines in years past. One of the dilemmas the teachers had faced was they missed the center time; somehow it was replaced by stations in the Reading Express model. Coming back to center time was an important revision in Reading Express.

The decision to adapt the structure to meet the needs of the children at that point in time was constant with the goals we had established at the beginning of the year: to individualize instruction. We also decided that the focus of instruction on the five strategies at the beginning of the year was important, but as some students became proficient in employing the strategies the focus for whole group should change.

We met again as a group on April 17 for a "taking stock" meeting. The changes we had agreed upon in February were examined. We all agreed that the revised structure was working well. The students who were most in need of the expertise offered by the Reading Recovery teachers were receiving it. The first-grade teachers felt more freedom to incorporate curriculum into the centers that were more fluid than the stations that had preceded them. Discipline problems had abated because fewer children were at centers (there were more than six centers in each room). All in all, the decisions that had been made seemed to be working well.

A Look at How the First Year Went

The data we collected the first year are just preliminary. These include pre- and post-test scores on the Observation Record, periodic running records for each first-grade child throughout the year, anecdotal records, videotape clips of text reading, and writing samples. We have some ideas about what we want to do next year to give us a better picture of how Reading Express helps our children become better readers and writers and us become better teachers. But we are also encouraged about what we have learned from our results.

We have seen student achieve the following:

1. Acquire a broader range of reading and writing strategies and are able to apply those strategies as they read and write.
2. Make gains in reading and writing.
3. Exhibit enthusiasm and confidence in reading and writing.

We know from observation and videotape footage that the children are using the strategies in their text reading. We also have test scores that indicate we have met our goal of gains in reading. During the 1994–1995 school year prior to implementation of Reading Express, the median student from all first-grade classes completed first-grade reading at Reading Recovery Text Level 14, which is equivalent to the beginning first-grade reader. During the 1995–1996 school year, the median student from all first-grade classes completed the year at Reading Recovery Text Level 24, which is equivalent to the end of third grade reader.

Text Level	Grade Level
34	8
32	7
30	6
28	5
26	4
22-24	3.1/3.2
18-20	2.1/2.2
14-16	1
9-12	Primer
7-8	PP3
5-6	PP2
3-4	PP1
A-2	Readiness

Figure 2. Text level to grade-level conversion.

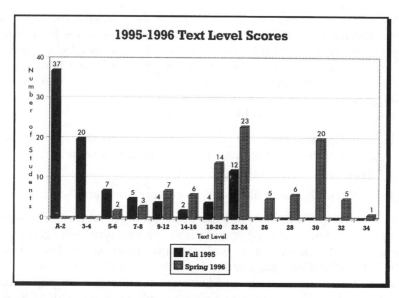

Table 1. Fall 1995/Spring 1996 reading text levels.

We also have a picture of how children progressed from the beginning to the end of the 1995–1996 school year. We are looking at these text level scores with caution, however. All pretest scores are based on the text-level reading using the Reading Recovery text-leveled passages. At the end of the year, Katie and the first-grade teachers assisted the Reading Recovery teachers in collecting data with some children using graded passages from Informal Reading Inventories. We converted the instructional reading grade-level scores for those children to the comparable text level according to Reading Recovery text levels. See Figure 2 for the approximate grade level for each Reading Recovery text level.

Results from all first-grade children are represented in the following table, including those who received one-to-one instruction in the Reading Recovery program. Table 1 displays reading text-level data for first-grade students in fall 1995 and spring 1996 respectively.

As this table indicates, as a group our children made dramatic gains from the beginning of the year to the end of the year. Only five children were not yet reading from a primer text comfortably, and seven were reading at a primer level. We had met our goal for our first-grade children; they were all reading. Hopefully, next year every child will be reading comfortably, at the very least, in a first-grade text.

We also feel we have a more organized, systematic approach to teaching reading. We feel we are stronger as teachers because we are able to accomplish the following:

1. Use Reading Recovery strategies in classroom instruction
2. Provide a more individualized program for every student in reading and writing
3. Have a more accurate understanding of students' strengths and weaknesses
4. Communicate more effectively with parents

Because parents play an important role in literacy development, we are also aware of the impact Reading Express has had with the parents of our students. We communicated regularly with parents through a newsletter where we described the five things a good reader does when he/she comes to a tricky word, and we provided practical suggestions for the parents to help their children at home. We found that the parents played a more active role in their children's reading, and they expressed satisfaction in their increased ability to help their children at home.

One of the most powerful and poignant statements of the success of this program comes from one of the first-grade children who was part of our initial year of Reading Express. The following words were written at the end of the year. The words speak not only to the impact of the program, but to the writing ability of the child as well.

> When I came into the classroom this year, I didn't know how to read. I felt left out of reading. I could read some, but not that much. I thought I would never get over it. It felt hopeless. It felt like you're not there. It was not a good feeling to not be able to read. I was sad. My friends could read better so they were happy. But I was not happy. I didn't feel good like them. But now I can read just like they can. Now we can all be happy.

What about Next Year?

We are convinced that Reading Express has made a difference in the lives of many of us at Mountain Park. We realize, though, that we have just begun the hard work of implementing a new program. What are some of our challenges for next year?

First, we realize that we need to secure the planning time that is so essential in any collaborative venture. We all bring unique expertise to this venture, and we can only benefit from that if we have time to share and reflect on what we are learning from our experience.

Second, we will be extending Reading Express into other grades. The Reading Recovery teachers will be going into second grade classrooms three times per week during the first weeks of school to provide ongoing support for our students who have just come through Reading Express. We will also provide some modeling and support for the second grade teachers in the use of strategies in reading. In addition, we will be working with our kindergarten teachers to help them identify children who may need early intervention through developmentally appropriate instruction.

Third, we will be incorporating additional research into the program. We will be using the Reading Recovery text-level passages for all post-test readings. We have also developed an observation sheet where each teacher can note when and with what assistance a child uses the strategies during text reading. We will be looking for a shift from reliance on one or two strategies to a balanced approach as the year progresses. Not only will this sheet provide additional data about each child, it will help us enhance our understanding of the relationship between learning the strategies and successful reading of text.

Fourth, we have learned some important things about collaboration. Reading Express has been a venture based on the collaboration of seven teachers and a university collaborator. Collaboration is a complex process that is as much about relationships as it is about the content of the collaboration. We found that the necessary time for planning together was very difficult to capture in a day already filled with personal and professional responsibilities. Barbara was a strong advocate for securing the time for planning together, but meetings every few months did not prove to provide sufficient time. We found that much of our grade level planning time, time in which we had in the past planned first-grade curriculum, was consumed with ironing out details and addressing issues related to a project that challenged many of our current practices. Finding that time in the second year of Reading Express will be a priority.

We are also aware, however, that we have established a common language in this first year. We have a better sense of what each of us brings to the table when we begin these conversations anew. The context will be different in that we will have only four first grades instead of five, and a new Reading Recovery teacher has joined the staff. Barbara decided to leave administration for a time, and Dr. Clark has accepted a principalship in another building. Katie completed her year with us, but is still in close contact.

All of these changes will bring a different context to the one in which we collaborated this year. We do have a year of experience, however, from which to build. As in any collaborative effort, those concerns such as those that may have been difficult to voice during that meeting in February will be easier to raise as the trust among us continues to grow.

We have had a demanding but exhilarating year. We are looking forward to new challenges as we learn more about ourselves as teachers and researchers through learning more about our children.

References

Clay, M. M. (1979, 1985). *The early detection of reading difficulties* (2nd & 3rd eds.) Auckland: Heinemann.

Clay, M. M. (1993). *An observation survey of early literacy achievement.* Portsmouth, NH: Heinemann.

Pinnell, G. S., Lyons, C. A., DeFord, D. E., Bryk, A. S., & Seltzer, M. (1994). Comparing instructional models for the literacy education of high-risk first graders. *Reading Research Quarterly, 29*(1), 8–39.

Shanahan, T., & Barr, R. (1995). Reading Recovery: An independent evaluation of the effects of an early instructional intervention for at-risk learners. *Reading Research Quarterly 30*(4), pp. 958–996.

Acknowledgment

We would like to acknowledge the other participants in the Reading Express project: first-grade teachers Christine Hanning, Caroline Ryan, Sonja Rice, and Reading Recovery teacher Ritsuko Adams.

29 Becoming Readers and Writers over Time

Jean W. Fennacy
Fresno Pacific College

In this article, Fennacy documents how three boys—Brad, Paul, and Andrew—became readers and writers in Debbie Manning's first-grade classroom. She explains that they were very different from one another when they entered first grade, each with his own particular background of literacy experiences and strengths as a literacy learner. Nevertheless, "What they shared in common was that they were among the least proficient readers and writers in the classroom." Brad and Paul entered first grade with a traditional kindergarten background; they had been exposed to a systematic introduction to letters and sounds and had filled out numerous worksheets, but they were not able to use that information in either their reading or their writing. Andrew had not had any kindergarten experience at all, he stuttered severely, and he had been told he was stupid; his foster mother's first priority was that he develop a healthy sense of well-being.

Fennacy documents the abilities and strengths of these three children as, each in his own way, they all three made progress in or toward literacy in the first grade. She describes, too, the classroom context ("Thirty-eight children . . . from a variety of socioeconomic and ethnic backgrounds") and the philosophy of the teacher, who chooses to view each of her students as readers and writers regardless of whether or not they are "conventional in their performance and production." Mrs. Manning moved with her students to second grade and then to third grade, so Brad, Paul, and Andrew continued in the supportive environment of her classroom. Fennacy again documents the children's idiosyncratic progress. It becomes clear in her account that the boys are learning to read by reading books they enjoy: by reading predictable books (Brad), Dr. Seuss books (Paul), and books by Robert Munsch (Andrew). In each case, rereading familiar texts not only made reading easier, but enabled the boys to become more proficient as readers.

At the end of their third-grade year together, Mrs. Manning requested a multi-age classroom, grades one through three. Concerned about the least proficient students, among them these three boys, Manning also began to realize it would be helpful to have in the class some older students who knew how the classroom operated. Therefore, she asked the parents about keeping the boys in her new multi-age classroom. Fennacy documents their growth in the fourth grade, including how it helped them to be the responsible "olders" in the class. Brad blossomed as a writer and reader. Andrew became a stronger reader, at last able to tackle the science and other nonfiction books that interested him; his writing showed some progress as well. While Paul's reading was not as advanced as that of the other two boys, his writing was strong. Woven throughout this account, of course, are details of what the children read, wrote, and studied in this classroom; what kinds of activities they engaged in; and how Manning put her whole language philosophy of learning and teaching into practice. The boys' transition to and success in fifth grade is then described. Fennacy includes four "lessons to be learned" from the boys' development in Manning's classroom. She notes that "The public has every right to hold schools and teachers accountable for their work. However, that accountability cannot be measured reasonably by comparing one child to another. Instead, teachers need to be accountable for providing rich, meaningful literacy experiences for each and every child." Clearly, this is what Debbie Manning does.

One morning toward the end of the school year, I slipped into Room 4 during quiet reading time. Because I am a frequent visitor in this multi-age classroom and because everyone was so engrossed in what they were doing, no one paid attention to me. I knew this reading time had been preceded by a predictable daily routine. The students had each signed in as they entered the room, read a message to them written by the teacher on a chart near the sign-in table, chosen their books for quiet reading time, and collected other materials needed for the day. They had gathered on the rug for sharing time and had listened to the teacher read to them. And they had engaged in a class discussion in response to that book. Finally they had moved off toward comfortable places in the room to read their books.

Now Mrs. Manning, their teacher, was chorally reading with a group of six students at the back table. Across the room the student teacher was sitting next to one youngster, listening to him read and at times reading along with him, helping him navigate the text. Two girls were on the rug reading Scieszka's *The Stinky Cheese Man and Other Fairly Stupid Tales* together. The rest of the twenty-eight students were spread throughout the room, engaged in reading various trade books and magazines.

I sat down next to Andrew, who was so engrossed in a *Zoo Book* magazine that he did not even acknowledge my presence. As he read the article, I heard him exclaim to himself, "I didn't know that!," obviously caught up in the information he was discovering. At another table Paul had been reading a chapter book by Mary Pope Osborne and now was engaged in reading the picture book *Amazing Grace* by Mary Hoffman. In another part of the room I spotted Brad lost in Betsy Byars's *Summer of the Swans.* I thought back to when these boys had been in Mrs. Manning's first-grade classroom. Over a four-year period, I had watched them become readers and writers. They began first grade clearly as novices. The vast majority of their classmates had been far more proficient than they. Now, however, as fourth graders, they had become avid and eager readers and writers. In the following pages I briefly describe the growth in their literacy as well as the context in which it occurred. Although I have changed the boys' names for purposes of privacy, the teacher's name is her own.

In the Beginning

At the beginning of first grade, the three boys varied in age, size, background, and experience. What they shared in common was that they were among the least proficient readers and writers in the classroom. In fact, many teachers would have labeled them as nonreaders. However, their teacher viewed each of her students as readers and writers whether they were conventional in their performance and production or not. She assumed that all students enter school with their own particular background of literacy experiences and believed her responsibility was to take into account what they already did know (Y. Goodman, 1996). She did not believe that children first learn to read so they can later read to learn. She held strongly to Smith's (1985) belief that the only way to learn to read and write is by reading and writing. As a result, she immersed her class in all kinds of meaningful reading and writing experiences from the beginning, and trusted that with time and help each of her students would grow into a competent reader and writer. Like Krashen and McQuillan (1996), she believed there is no "critical period" for learning to read, but she was active in providing help for her students when she saw they needed it. She based her instruction on the children's needs and interests, not on prescribed programs or materials.

Brad

Six-year-old Brad entered first grade having spent a year in a typical kindergarten classroom. He had been exposed to a systematic introduction of letters and sounds and had filled out numerous worksheets on them. He had been directed in how to make art projects just like everyone else's, and how to make little books that followed the teacher's text and allowed him to perhaps fill in a word of his own to a limited degree. At home, Brad had been exposed to books and numerous literacy events. He was a well-behaved child who did not cause problems in kindergarten, but he also did not leave kindergarten viewing himself as a reader and writer.

Brad began first grade reluctant to take risks. He would thumb through familiar simple, predictable books like *Brown Bear, Brown Bear, What Do You See?* by Bill Martin Jr. but he depended on pictures and memory to sustain his efforts; he drew little if any information from the print itself. He was reluctant to write and would do as little as possible. His writing consisted of what appeared to be random letters, and he needed to interpret his text for his teacher. He preferred to draw, and when he did write he made huge letters. Toward the middle of the year, he became increasingly aware of children in the room who were moving ahead of him in reading and writing. One of his friends, Michael, entered school reading. Michael's writing was already conventional, and he was reading chapter books by the time he was six. This disturbed Brad, and he went through a period when he was reluctant to come to school, saying, "I can't read." Yet, when he came to school, he appeared happy and engaged in activities.

He loved to be read to by both his parents and the teacher, although his oral responses to books read to him were minimal. Even in this aspect of literacy behavior, many of the students in the class were far more proficient than he. As such, they provided numerous demonstrations of how people can respond to literature. The teacher continued to support Brad's efforts, engaging him in extensive shared reading, giving him time to read each day, and celebrating his writing. She read with him in small groups and individually. Generally, Mrs. Manning and the students simply choral read in unison. She insisted that the students track with their fingers and helped them if they lost their place. She also found volunteers to come into the classroom to read with students one-on-one, and Brad had many opportunities to do this.

In addition, Mrs. Manning spent time with Brad as he wrote, encouraging and nudging him. He often began by drawing a picture. She would ask him to tell her about it. Then she would suggest he write what he had said. She would repeat his words, almost dictating his own verbal text back to him one word at a time. She would emphasize sounds in words, helping him "hold" a sound long enough to determine what letter he wanted to use to represent it. By so doing, she was helping him develop phonemic awareness as it served his needs and purposes. Toward the end of the year, Mrs. Manning assured Brad's worried parents that Brad would become a conventional reader and writer. She urged them to continue to read to him and have faith that he would blossom in his own time.

Paul

Paul was a few months older than Brad and also entered first grade from a traditional kindergarten setting. He too had received systematic instruction in phonics, and, like Brad, he was not able to use that information in either his reading or writing. He liked to draw and would generally draw during writing time, produce a few letters when encouraged to do so, then return to drawing. At home he had encountered few school-like literacy experiences, but he was certainly aware of print in the environment. Unlike Brad, Paul was a risk taker. He seemed oblivious to the progress others were making in reading and writing. He was a "wiggler" and was not used to listening to stories. When the children gathered on the rug for reading, Mrs. Manning had Paul sit close to her so that he could see the text easily and so that she could keep her eye on him and encourage him to keep engaged.

As the year progressed, so did Paul's writing. In time, if the teacher knew the subject of his text, she could pretty well figure out his inventive spelling. He used salient consonants, and if she thought about how Paul articulated his words (*dat* for *that*, *dem* for *them*) she was more apt to make sense of his writing. He read from highly predictable texts and had several favorite ones which he read again and again. These included *Brown Bear, Brown Bear, What Do You See?*, Dr. Seuss's *Hop on Pop*, and *Bears in the Night* by the Berenstains. He still relied primarily on familiar syntax and semantics to read, drawing little information from the print. However, his invented spelling gave proof he was developing phonemic awareness.

Andrew

The third child, Andrew, was the only child who did not begin first grade with a prior kindergarten experience. He had had a traumatic life prior to school age, he stuttered severely, and he had been told that he was stupid. His foster mother had learned of Mrs. Manning's classroom and insisted he be placed there. Her first priority was that he develop a healthy sense of well-being. He was seven when he began first grade.

What Andrew excelled at was conversation and humor. He could keep a dialogue going with anyone, especially adults. From the very beginning of the year he took delight in talking about books that were read to the class. He knew about all sorts of things, from space to spiders. One of his best friends was Michael, who was an exceedingly proficient reader, writer, and conversationalist. The students and any visitor to the class were readily aware of the contributions these boys made to class discussions, and it was easy to conclude that Andrew was one of the most outstanding students in the class.

When it came to reading and writing, however, it was a different matter. Andrew's writing showed no apparent correspondence between oral and written language. There were certain letters he used extensively, some of which came from his name, but unless the teacher got to him while he was writing or just afterward, neither of them could read it. The letters he did write were often reversed. He was aware that he could not write the way his classmate Michael did and, as a result, would often write with his arms surrounding his text as much as possible to prevent others from seeing it. For him to say out loud the words he wanted to write and listen to what he heard himself say was tedious, for he continued to stutter throughout first grade, and it is not clear what aspect of his own articulation he could concentrate on.

He enjoyed listening to stories and soon had a fairly large repertoire of highly supportive predictable books he could read by relying on familiarity and pictures. *Brown Bear, Brown Bear, What Do You See?* and *It Looked Like Spilt Milk* by Charles Shaw were among those he depended on. However, his interests far exceeded what he could read. He was fascinated with topics in science and very adept at gleaning information from nonfiction books. By studying the pictures, he could share all kinds of information and sound like quite the literate authority.

The Classroom Context

The three boys joined a first-grade class that in many ways reflected the crowded conditions and diversity in California classrooms. The thirty-eight children came from a variety of socioeconomic and ethnic backgrounds. Some children were big and some were little. They ranged in age from just under six to nearly eight. A few of their parents were professionals, some were receiving public assistance, and most were working class. Several spoke English as a second language.

Unlike the vast majority of teachers in California, their teacher taught from a whole language perspective. Although newspaper articles would have readers believe that most schools in California "went whole language" after the publication of California's 1987 *English Language Arts Framework*, in reality most schools adopted and used basal readers along with a few pieces of core literature per grade level. While some of those classrooms might be referred to as playing "whole language dress-up" (Church, 1996), the boys' teacher knowingly embraced a sociopsycholinguistic perspective on reading (Weaver, 1994) and set out to immerse the students in authentic literacy events (Edelsky & Smith, 1984). She placed great value in the power of literature to provide students with demonstrations (Smith, 1981) of rich language. She read to the class several times a day and engaged them in shared reading on a regular basis (Manning & Fennacy, 1993). She filled the room with hundreds of books for the children's use and made sure there was time each day for them to read books of their own choosing. Like Krashen (1993) she recognized that access to books is critical to literacy development, so she made sure her students had many, many books available to them. She also arranged to have a low-power radio station in her classroom, run by the students. Each afternoon students could sign up to read books "live on the air." This provided tremendous incentive for children to practice books so they were ready to go public and read on the radio.

Songs also played an important role in this classroom. Singing together served as a way to bind the class into a community. Students enjoyed gathering together on the rug as Mrs. Manning played her guitar and shared numerous silly songs with them. Sometimes Mrs. Manning used singing as a way to settle the class down, and occasionally she used songs as a means to dismiss students at the end of the day. But singing also served as a way to help children grow as readers and writers. Often everyone sang together, following the text of the song from a chart. Sometimes individuals composed songs during writers' workshop and then shared them with the class. And songs also encouraged children to play with language. For example, a popular song the class sang in first grade, "Willoughby, Wallaby, Woo" adapted by Raffi (1980) involves changing initial phonemes of names and can be personalized to fit the names of classmates. The children took delight in this song as they figured out whose name would be sung: "Willoughby Wallaby Wandrew, an elephant sat on Andrew, Willoughby Wallaby Waul, an elephant sat on Paul." They also discovered when they came to their classmate Winston, his names didn't change. Andrew was particularly involved in the class discussion as they tried varying the song to the following: "Billoughby Ballaby Bee, an elephant sat on me, Billoughby Ballaby Boo, an elephant sat on you." Then they discovered Brad's name didn't change in this version. The children's curiosity led them to investigate their language. Mrs. Manning did not have to address phonemic awareness through prescribed drills. Instead she relied on the natural, functional literacy experiences throughout the day (Yopp, 1995) to spark the children's interests.

Furthermore, Mrs. Manning's own knowledge of children's literature caused her to be very selective in her choice of books to read out loud. She knew that introducing the children to interesting books this way was a significant part of her literacy instruction. Children discovered wonderful books that fascinated them, and they wanted to read those books themselves. Her read-alouds demonstrated that books were to be enjoyed not only for their lovely illustrations and wonderful language, but also for the connections readers made with them. She encouraged students to respond to such books with personal transactions (Rosenblatt, 1983) and did not ask comprehension questions. Over time, the talk about books grew more and more sophisticated as the class had many genuine "grand conversations" (Peterson & Eeds, 1990).

From the first day of school, she also made it clear that she believed all her students could and would write. She accepted their approximations, engaged them in writing throughout the day (in math, science, and social studies as well as during writers' workshop). Here, too, she found legitimate ways to take advantage of public audiences for writing so there was authentic purpose in refining the conventions to make pieces ready for publication.

Likewise, Mrs. Manning provided many demonstrations of writing through shared writing. Many group and class science reports were created this way as well as numerous brainstormed lists. Talking about how print works, she would frequently serve as a scribe for a small group of students or for the whole class. Here was a time her phonics instruction was most apparent. She encouraged students to help her determine what letters to write, emphasizing words as she went along. When a student suggested an unconventional but logical spelling, she would tell them it was a good guess, but write the word explaining the conventional spelling. At times she would capitalize on the opportunity to talk about a spelling pattern, providing other examples for the children to see and talk about. Again, this is an example of how the functional use of literacy experiences offered her ample opportunity for instruction. She anticipated such instruction; she was alert for incidents when it would be appropriate.

In this context, she saw assessment as an ongoing event, one that allowed her to use students as her curricular informants (Short, Harste, & Burke, 1995) rather than rely on a published program written by authors who did not know her students. She nudged, facilitated, and coached children frequently on a one-to-one basis. Daily quiet reading and writing time allowed her the opportunity to meet with individuals and small groups. As she read with individual children, she made professional decisions about the kind of coaching she would do. Since she understood the reading process, as she noticed children's miscues she could determine appropriate response. She might suggest that a student skip a word in order to pick up clues further along in a text if the reader needed encouragement to develop an independent problem-solving strategy. She might ask, "Did that make sense?" if she noticed a student wasn't focusing on meaning. She would then encourage the student to reread, sometimes providing support by reading along herself. At times she would call a student's attention to the print, saying "I want you to point to each word as you read it." Andrew particularly needed that kind of nudge because he relied heavily on illustrations, sometimes nearly ignoring the written text. She would then read along with him, helping him to keep the reading going much the way a parent helps a child learning to ride a bicycle. Likewise, she was familiar with children's writing development and used this knowledge to frame her instruction. As she worked with individuals, she would support their efforts but also nudge them to think about the words they were writing, helping them to move closer and closer to conventional spelling. However, her instructional decisions were based on what she saw the child doing, not based on the next lesson in a teacher's manual. She also provided strategy lessons in reading and writing (Short et al.) as she saw them needed.

Readers and Writers Emerge with Time

Mrs. Manning moved with her students to second grade, although a few did not return to the school. A small number of new students entered her class. The class size remained at thirty-eight most of that second-grade year. At the end of second grade, a third-grade opening occurred at the school. Several parents urged Mrs. Manning to take their children on. The principal agreed, and again some of the students moved out of the school area. A few parents felt having the same teacher for more than two years was too much out of the ordinary and chose not to have their children stay in this classroom. A few new students joined the class, but the core of the group remained constant and the class size now held at around thirty-three. Brad, Paul, and Andrew were among those who stayed with Mrs. Manning.

Brad began second grade where he had left off in first. He depended on predictable books, and writing remained laborious for him. He listened to stories but made few comments. In the middle of the fall semester, he had a breakthrough in writing: his inventive spelling became readable, demonstrating his awareness of phonemes. He began including salient consonants and soon included vowels. His writing clearly demonstrated his careful attention to individual phonemes as he pronounced them. One day he wrote, "I LIK CaW BoWYs Tay r net CaW BoWYs Tac BaD GI Too ThE JaYoL ThE EnD." (I like cowboys. They are neat. Cowboys take bad guys to the jail. The End.) This was a time for celebration. Brad had figured out how print works, he was attending to graphophonemics as well as syntax and semantics. Mrs. Manning shared her excitement with Brad's parents.

Brad's writing appeared to level off for most of second grade. Although we could read his inventive spelling, writing was still a chore for him. As a reader he still depended on predictable books. At the end of the year, for a class performance, he and another boy read *Old Black Fly* by Jim Aylesworth, a rhyming alphabet book which they rehearsed and rehearsed. In third grade he latched on to *"Buzz" Said the Bee* by Wendy Cheyette Lewison, a cumulative text published as an "I Can Read" book. Mrs. Manning kept on encouraging and nudging, Brad kept on rereading favorite books, and his writing began to include closer approximations of conventional spelling. By the end of the year he was able to read early chapter books—the kind with three or four lines on a page and supported with ample pictures. The Henry and Mudge series by Cynthia Rylant were among his favorites.

Paul began second grade with Dr. Seuss books still high on his lists of favorites. He continued to have books he would choose over and over again, a pattern that would continue for two more years. Toward the end of the year he discovered Robert Munsch books and they carried him into third grade. He loved them. He would read them with much intensity and great gusto. He began asking questions when Mrs. Manning read aloud. He would ask, "What does that mean?" and began to make running commentaries as the oral reading continued. His comments about the books were still, however, overshadowed by classmates who were becoming literary critics (Peterson & Eeds, 1990), although by the end of third grade he was beginning to comment on character change and tension. When Mrs. Manning read *The Great Gilly Hopkins* by Katherine Paterson to the class, the discussions were lively, and Paul was entering into them more and more. His writing continued to grow in terms of quantity, but aside from a few conventionally spelled words like *to, is, the, he, you,* and *me,* he continued to use inventive spelling. He had particular trouble with the words *that* and *this,* which he spelled as *dat* and *dis* in spite of Mrs. Manning's repeated reminders of conventional spelling. Paul was still articulating "dat" and his spelling represented his speech. He wrote in manuscript, rarely leaving spaces between words, a characteristic that made it even harder for someone else to read his writing.

Like Paul, Andrew began second grade dependent on familiar texts for his independent reading and, like Paul, he began choosing Robert Munsch books during the year. Like the other students in the class, he had come to know these books because Mrs. Manning had read them to the class. Toward spring in second grade, it was very common for Andrew to choose *50 Below Zero*. He relied on familiarity with the story and use of illustrations to help him read, but, even with that, what he produced as he read did not approach a one-to-one correspondence with the book's text. During quiet reading time, Mrs. Manning often helped him track what he was reading. She nudged him to draw information from the print. She was careful not to overemphasize sounding out words because she did not want to send the message that reading is primarily decoding. She wanted him to know that the ultimate goal of reading is to construct meaning (K. Goodman, 1983). However, she knew he needed to learn to sample the print as well as use prior knowledge, syntax, and semantics. She encouraged him to predict what came next, drawing on what he knew about language and meaning and to check out his prediction by looking at the print. As he progressed into third grade, Mrs. Manning encouraged him and helped him read the very supportive "I Can Read" books. Even these simple texts with ample illustrations were a challenge for him.

Toward the end of third grade Andrew was able to read the Henry and Mudge books with assistance. Unlike Brad, he was not satisfied with such stories because his interests were far more sophisticated than his reading ability. He continued to be drawn to books about science. Andrew's writing remained a challenge to read without his help, and his reversals of letters and numbers continued. When writing with a friend, he always deferred to that person to be the writer. He found clever ways to conceal his lack of writing proficiency from his friends. Orally, however, he excelled. His contributions to class discussions continued to enlighten everyone, and for three years in a row he served as master of ceremonies for the class's end-of-the-year performance for parents. Even this opportunity was part of Mrs. Manning's thoughtful literacy instruction. She knew Andrew wanted to be the emcee. Andrew could stand before any audience, crack jokes, announce performers, and keep everyone laughing. He was clearly gifted in this arena. She also knew the role itself provided him with a genuine personal need to read. Although the side comments he would make to an audience could be ad-libbed, he did have to use the written program to check the titles of individual performances.

Taking Responsibility as Olders in a Multi-age Setting

When third grade came to an end, Mrs. Manning requested a multi-age classroom for the following year. She was to have a first- through third-grade group of students. As she reflected on the benefits of multi-age, she realized that having students who knew how the classroom operated would be of great benefit. She was also worried about her least proficient students, among them Brad, Paul, and Andrew. She approached their parents, asking if they would be comfortable putting them in her multi-age class as fourth-grade "olders." The parents agreed, and a new adventure began.

The multi-age setting put a lot of responsibility on the boys. They were in charge of the radio station, they had to set the examples for acceptable behavior in the classroom, and they had to serve as models for the rest of the students during quiet reading and writing time. Mrs. Manning also assigned each of the boys one "younger" (a first grader.) They were to read daily with their youngers, and they were to keep notes on the children's progress in literacy. The boys met with Mrs. Manning for breakfast early one morning each week to discuss the strategies they were using with their young friends and how they could all help out to make the class operate smoothly.

The boys rose to the occasion. Unlike the new students, they were used to extended periods of times to read and write. They had been treated as readers and writers for three years, and they knew how to encourage others. Brad seemed to mature almost overnight. He grew physically and academically. His comments about literature became more and more sophisticated as he, Paul, and Andrew often carried class discussions. It was as if Brad had found his "voice." His writing improved in quality and quantity. He took risks in spelling and began to write in cursive. Toward the end of the year he created the flyer for the class performance, spelling everything on the rough draft correctly except for the word "entertainment," which he spelled initially "entertainment." However, it was Brad's reading that most caught our attention. This child who had been reluctant to come to school in first grade because he could not read was now absorbed in chapter books. One day in June I tape-recorded him reading a chapter from *Summer of the Swans,* which he did with ease. His miscues were of high quality, and it was clear from his corrections that he was monitoring his reading. At the end of the chapter he was able to tell me about what he had read and predict what might happen next in the book. We knew Brad would be able to stand his ground in fifth grade.

Like Brad, Andrew grew physically and academically. Helping younger readers proved to be an important contribution to his self-esteem as a reader and writer. No longer did he hide his work from students, and as he began to write in cursive, his reversals diminished, and his spelling improved. As he became a stronger reader, at last he could tackle the text in books that interested him. As described in the beginning of these pages, *Zoo Book* magazine was a regular choice for him. He participated in numerous literature studies, and his foster mother provided support for him to get through books like *The Giver* by Lois Lowry and *Weasel* by Cynthia Defelice. At first, she read them to him, but by the end of the year they were alternating reading chapters to each other. In June I asked Andrew to read from his current chapter book for me, *Jeremy Thatcher, Dragon Catcher* by Bruce Coville. Although there were a few words he did not know or could not pronounce, he clearly had developed a keep-going strategy. Most of his miscues were of high quality, and his corrections showed he was comprehending as he was reading. In the end, he, like Brad, produced a good retelling, discussed the characters and tension in the story, and predicted what would happen next. Andrew had made it.

Paul also made great strides academically. He remained small in stature and several of the second graders were as big or bigger than he, but he could hold his own in any conversation. His comments about literature that had begun to emerge in third grade now blossomed. He always had something appropriate to say about books shared in the class. He was particularly astute at zeroing in on a book's message or theme. He also took keen interest in punctuation during a series of mini-lessons presented by a student teacher. In fact, it was Paul's questions and comments during these mini-lessons that drew other students into the conversation. One day as he puzzled over figuring out just where to put quotation marks in dialogue, it was clear he was figuring out how reading worked. He had to focus on the meaning while, at the same time, attend to the print. This fascination with text and how it worked continued on to the discussions on contractions and possessives. The mini-lessons originally intended to support the students' development as writers helped Paul as a reader.

For reading Paul continued to have favorite books which he read and reread. He still chose Robert Munsch books, as if he needed more time with such supportive texts, although he could read more complicated picture books. To participate in the literature studies described above, he read them with his mother. By the end of fourth grade, a book such as *Summer of the Swans* was still too complicated a text for him to read independently, but he had no trouble discussing the text.

He was comfortable reading easy chapter books, but even then Mrs. Manning had to insist that he spend some time each day reading in his chapter book. In June I tape-recorded him reading a chapter from Mary Pope Osborne's *Dinosaurs Before Dark,* an easy chapter book which contains a few illustrations. He read it with ease and expression, and he produced a solid retelling afterwards. He told me the best book he had ever heard was the one being read to the class at the time. He loved the author's way of leaving you wanting to read more an the end of each chapter.

While Paul's reading was not as advanced as the other boys', his writing was strong. He would write and write, and once he began to use cursive, his spelling improved and so did the legibility of his work. *Dis* became *this* as his articulation became more refined and as he had more experiences reading. Paul would need continued support in fifth grade, but Mrs. Manning was confident he would be able to succeed, largely because of his enthusiasm and his skill in discussions.

All three of the boys made a successful transition to fifth grade. Paul stayed at the same school and entered a self-contained class. His comment about the new experience was that his class didn't read but did lots of work. On his first report card he earned mostly B's with some A's. Brad and Andrew both transferred to a new magnet school for fifth to eighth grades. They had to adjust to having several different teachers during the day, and eventually Brad returned to Mrs. Manning's school where he could be placed in a self-contained class. On his first report card he earned all A's and B's except for a D in math. According to his teacher, this low grade was due strictly to his performance on timed tests. At last report, however, he had learned to do the tests well and was earning A's in math. Andrew has been successful in the middle school setting. His teachers are aware of his verbal ability but concerned about his penmanship. His first report card contained B's and C's. For three students who were among the least proficient in their class in first grade, they have succeeded quite well.

Lessons to Be Learned

All three boys had come a long way since first grade. Rarely do teachers have the opportunity to watch children learn and grow over time. When we do observe children over long periods, we realize that individuals grow in their own way and time, both in size and in academics. There are several lessons to be learned from the growth of Paul, Brad, and Andrew.

1. Children are individuals and need to be treated as such. No two children learn exactly alike, not in sequence, content, or skill. This means teachers need to look to individual children to determine appropriate instruction, not to "teacher proof" programs that dictate the curriculum.

2. Teachers need to make professional decisions based on children's needs and act on those needs. A teacher does not just sit by waiting for growth to happen. She arranges literacy experiences to enhance learning. She works with children individually and in groups, nudging, supporting, giving tips, helping, and encouraging. In reading, this means paying attention to how children are orchestrating the reading process. The teacher's role is to move children toward proficient use of cueing systems, including graphophonemics, as well as strategies such as predicting and confirming as they read. In writing, this includes an understanding of normal development toward conventional spelling, punctuation, and penmanship and helping children advance toward proficient writing. This is teaching.

3. It is unrealistic to believe that all children in a class will or should learn at the same pace or in an identical sequence. All too often teachers are pressured to have every student "on grade level," but what does that mean? In any one class children range in age as much as two years. Their experiences are different, their homes are different, and their personalities, interests, and talents are different. Stressing conformity causes schools to identify less advanced students as "learning disabled." Such a deficit model places blame on students' inherent capacities. In turn such students often get pulled out of classrooms and tend to experience meaningless drills instead of an enriched curriculum. This common practice does not solve literacy problems (Allington & Walmsey, 1995).

4. Teachers need to immerse all students in rich reading and writing experiences. Students who are less proficient need rich meaningful engagements in literacy as much as the more advanced students. Growing evidence suggests that when troubled students have lots of good reading material that interests them as well as time to read for enjoyment, they catch up easily (Fink, 1995/96; Krashen & McQuillan, 1996). Engaging students in reading and writing for real-world purposes enhances the opportunity for learning and encourages children to value what they are doing in school. All children need to see reading and writing as activities

that meet their needs as well as being meaningful in the world outside of school, not just in school.

The public has every right to hold schools and teachers accountable for their work. However, that accountability cannot be measured reasonably by comparing one child to another. Instead, teachers need to be accountable for providing rich, meaningful literacy experiences for each and every child. School libraries and classrooms need to be filled with books for children to read. Teachers *do* need to carefully observe children in order to meet their needs. Teaching is not technical. It is not the same as working on an assembly line building a series of look-alike automobiles. Teaching is a craft. It requires close attention to students' individual needs and interests. All children do learn, but not in the same way or sequence, nor do children develop according to identical time tables. Children would be better served if we used them as our curricular informants rather than depending on programs to direct the art of teaching.

References

Allington, R., & Walmsley, S. (Eds.). (1995). *No quick fix*. New York: Teachers College Press.

Church, S. (1996). *The Future of Whole Language*. Portsmouth, NH: Heinemann.

Edelsky, C., & Smith, K. (1984). Is that writing—or are those marks just a figment of your curriculum? *Language Arts, 61,* 24–32.

English-Language Arts Framework. (1987). Sacramento, CA: California State Department of Education.

Fink, R. (1995/96). Successful dyslexics: A constructivist study of passionate interest reading. *Journal of Adolescent and Adult Literacy, 39,* 268–80.

Goodman, K. (1983). Unity in reading. In A. Purves & O. Niles, (Eds.), *Becoming readers in a complex society*. Chicago: University of Chicago Press.

Goodman, Y. (1996). *Notes from a kidwatcher: Selected writings of Yetta Goodman*. S. Wilde, ed. Portsmouth, NH: Heinemann.

Krashen, S. (1993). *The power of reading*. Englewood, CO: Libraries Unlimited, Inc.

Krashen, S., & McQuillan, J. (1996). *The case for late intervention: Once a good reader, always a good reader*. Culver City, CA: Language Education Associates.

Manning, D., & Fennacy, J. (1993). Bringing children to literacy through shared reading. In B. Harp (Ed.), *Bringing children to literacy: Classrooms that work*. Norwood, MA: Christopher-Gordon Publishers, Inc.

Peterson R., & Eeds, M. (1990). *Grand conversations*. New York: Scholastic.

Rosenblatt, L. (1983). *Literature as exploration* (4th ed.). New York: Modern Language Association.

Short, K., Harste, J., & Burke, C. (1995). *Classrooms for authors and inquirers.* Portsmouth, NH: Heinemann.

Smith, F. (1981). Demonstrations, engagement, and sensitivity: A revised approach to language learning. *Language Arts, 58,* 103–112.

Smith, F. (1985). *Reading without nonsense.* New York: Teachers College Press.

Weaver, C. (1994). *Reading process and practice* (2nd ed.). Portsmouth, NH: Heinemann.

Yopp, H. (1995). A test for assessing phonemic awareness in young children. *The Reading Teacher, 49,* 20–29.

Children's Books Cited

Aylesworth J. (1992) *Old black fly.* New York: Holt.

Berenstain, S. & J. (1971). *Bears in the night.* New York: Random House.

Byars, B. (1970). *Summer of the swans.* New York: Viking Press.

Coville, B. (1991). *Jeremy Thatcher, dragon catcher.* San Diego: Harcourt Brace.

DeFelice, C. (1990). *Weasel.* New York: Macmillan.

Hoffman, M. (1991). *Amazing grace.* New York: Dial.

Lewison, W. (1992). *"Buzz" said the bee.* New York: Scholastic.

Lowry, L. (1993). *The giver.* Boston: Houghton Mifflin.

Martin, B. (1983). *Brown bear, brown bear, what do you see?* New York: Holt.

Munsch, R. (1993). *Fifty below zero.* Toronto: Annick Press.

Osborne, M. (1992). *Dinosaurs before dark.* New York: Random House.

Paterson, K. (1987). *The great Gilly Hopkins.* New York: Harper & Row.

Raffi (1980). *The Raffi singable songbook.* New York: Crown.

Scieszka, J. (1992). *The stinky cheese man and other fairly stupid tales.* New York: Viking Press.

Seuss, Dr. (1987). *Hop on Pop.* New York: Random House.

Shaw, Charles G. (1947). *It looked like spilt milk.* New York: Harper & Row.

30 Reading Recovery: Teaching Phonemic Awareness and Phonics in the Context of Strategies and Meaning

Grace Vento-Zogby
Sauquoit Valley Elementary, Sauquoit, New York

Vento-Zogby first explains that Reading Recovery is an early intervention reading program that teaches children to use effective reading strategies—a program wherein skills like phonemic awareness and phonics are reinforced and taught throughout various aspects of the Reading Recovery lesson. She describes in some detail how children's strengths and needs are assessed, to provide information on which to base Reading Recovery tutoring and instruction. As she explains components of the daily Reading Recovery lesson, Vento-Zogby notes the many ways that phonemic awareness and phonics are taught. Whenever possible, she illustrates with one particular child, Kaylie. In addition, Vento-Zogby discusses research on the effectiveness of the Reading Recovery program in helping at-risk first graders catch up with their peers in literacy development. Her conclusion: There is no "quick fix" for children who do not view themselves as readers and writers; they need rich opportunities to develop a love of literacy as they are guided in developing effective strategies and skills.

It appears that now more than ever, whole language teachers are subject to criticism from those advocating a "back-to-basics" (i.e., phonics) approach to the teaching of reading. Media ads, including infomercials, provide parents with the message that reading can easily be achieved through a systematic phonics program by assisting children in "breaking the code." In reality, helping a child who is experiencing difficulty with reading to make the connection between print and sounds is not an easy task. In the words of Ken Goodman (1996):

> [I]f reading and writing are to be learned easily and well, the learn-
> ers must have ownership over the process and its results. What they
> understand from their reading must be interesting and useful to
> them. It must bring pleasure, information, answers to their own
> questions. Learning is difficult if it has no present utility for the
> learners. (p. 128)

Reading Recovery is an early intervention reading program that is designed for first graders who are experiencing difficulty with the reading process. Once they are able to function comfortably within the average range of their class, the children are discontinued from the program. Children selected for the program receive thirty minutes of daily one-on-one instruction. The average length of time children receive individual tutoring is twelve to fifteen weeks; however, the program may last as long as twenty weeks for some students.

Instead of being taught isolated skills, children are taught strategies that help them to become independent readers, and they are taught how to become flexible in using these strategies while reading. Strategies include predicting (thinking ahead), monitoring comprehension, and correcting (or attempting to correct) miscues that don't make sense in context. Skills like phonemic awareness (awareness of the "separate" sounds in words) and phonics are taught in the process of teaching reading strategies and by helping the child write and spell. The Reading Recovery teacher focuses on each student's strengths, not deficits. Teachers directly and indirectly instruct the child in dealing with new or difficult tasks involving reading and writing while keeping the meaning of the text intact. They are taught how to predict, confirm, and understand what they read. It is important to note that this instruction does not replace quality classroom instruction, but is an extra support for the child.

Assessing the Child's Strengths and Needs

Children are initially selected for the program based on teacher recommendation. A Diagnostic Survey consisting of six measures is individually administered to each child.

Letter Identification

A letter identification test is given to determine if the child is able to identify fifty-four upper- and lowercase letters and the typed *a* and *g*. The child may identify a letter by stating the alphabetic name, an acceptable sound, or a word that begins with the letter. Incorrect responses are also noted. The teacher indicates the child's preferred method of identifying letters, any confusions she or he may have, and any unknown letters.

Word Test

The child is asked to read a list of twenty words in isolation. These words are drawn from a list of words frequently used in first-grade basal reading materials. The Reading Recovery program does not include drill on isolated words. This test is to help determine to what extent the child has accumulated a reading vocabulary of high-frequency words. This test also provides insight into the student's ability to look at print or use letter-sound relationships. Is the child attending to any part of the word while attempting to read? The analyzed information is more important than the score.

Concepts about Print

This test provides valuable information regarding the child's strengths and weaknesses in dealing with print. While reading a small book developed by Marie Clay, *Sand or Stones* (1979), the teacher elicits the child's help, for example, by asking the child to "Show me where I start reading. Which way do I go? Where do I go after that? Point to the words while I read." This provides information as to what the child knows about print at the letter, word, and text levels. It also reveals what the child knows about directional behavior in reading, book handling skills, and specific concepts regarding printed language.

Writing Vocabulary

The child is asked to write as many words as he or she can within a ten-minute time limit, beginning with his or her own name. The child may be prompted to write basic vocabulary and words personal to his or her experiences. Kaylie wrote her first name and the word *no*. She attempted to write *dog*, *cat*, *ball* and *see* (see Figure 1).

Dictation

A sentence that includes the basic thirty-seven sounds (phonemes) is dictated to the child, who is asked to attempt to write it. This is not a spelling test. The teacher is interested in learning to what extent the child is able to hear sounds in words and represent them with appropriate letters. This task assists the teacher in determining the child's phonemic awareness. A point is given for each sound he or she can

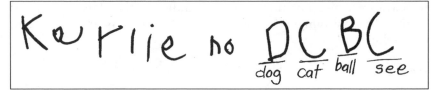

Figure 1. Writing vocabulary test.

correctly hear and record, even if the word itself may not be correct. For example Kaylie wrote *b s* and scored two points, indicating she could hear the *b* in *bus* and the *s* in *stop* (see Figure 2).

Running Record

The final assessment is a running record of text reading. The teacher determines the level of text difficulty that the child can read with 90 percent accuracy or higher. The purpose for later having the child read texts that he or she can read with substantial accuracy is to provide reading material that supports the reader in using and learning effective reading strategies. The teacher records reading behavior using coding similar to miscue analysis. This information is used to analyze the strategies the child is attempting as well as those that we are trying to develop. A running record becomes part of the child's daily instruction, since it provides ongoing assessment of the strategies being developed.

Once the child has been selected based on the results of the Diagnostic Survey and teacher collaboration, the Reading Recovery teacher writes a Diagnostic Summary. This allows the teacher to analyze the information obtained about the child based on the six tasks described. The summary assists in clarifying and solidifying the teacher's thinking about the child. The information is used during the initial phase of the child's program, known as "roaming around the known." During this time formal "teaching" does not occur; however, opportunities are provided for the child to become fluent with what he or she knows in reading and writing. During these ten sessions the teacher reads to and with the child and writes for and with the child.

Once lessons begin, time is spent ensuring that the child understands how the letters are used to represent sounds. This, of course, requires *hearing* the separate sounds and thereby develops phonemic awareness. However, the child is not required to sound out words letter by letter. The use of simple books allows the teacher to introduce the student to beginning reading strategies. The flow of the sentence

Figure 2. Dictation test.

and the first sound of a word often assist the child in reading phonetically irregular words such as *were, come,* or *was.* The illustrations help
the child to read longer words such as *hippopotamus, dinosaur,* or *elephant.*
Books are carefully selected for each student so the child will be able
to figure words out by checking the illustration, rereading the sentence
—to make sure meaning is preserved, using the beginning letter or
sound, recognizing a familiar spelling pattern within a word, or
attempting to articulate the word slowly, with teacher assistance in
using the recognizable "chunks" of letters (i.e., *sh, ch, ed, ing, ate, est*).
Instead of instructing a child to "sound it out," the teacher asks questions such as "Does that (or would that) make sense?", "Does that
sound right?" (Is the sentence syntactically correct?), "Does that look
right?" (Cues from the letters).

The Daily Lesson

The Reading Recovery lesson contains eight components. The teacher
integrates skills and strategies within a meaningful context. Each lesson begins with a fluent writing practice. Approximately one to two
minutes is devoted to this activity. The child is asked to write some
known words on a chalkboard as quickly as possible. The words may
come from the child's writing. This allows the student to practice and
eventually "over-learn" important basic words and therefore be able to
write them automatically while composing stories independently. At the
beginning of a child's program, these known words act as a vehicle for
connecting reading and writing. The teacher assists the child in developing an awareness that the words they have learned to write are the
same as those in the books they are reading.

Every lesson includes the rereading of familiar books. Some of the
books may be the child's familiar favorites, while others may be pre-
selected by the teacher because they offer the opportunity for teaching
and learning. This provides a chance for the child to use and practice

his or her developing control over the reading process and allows the child opportunities for developing fluency. Approximations are accepted and valued. The student is encouraged to make meaningful predictions. For example, positive explicit feedback is given when the student stops to employ a strategy. This is *not* guessing. For example, during the early stages of Kaylie's program, she independently read *Let's Have a Swim* (Cowley, 1993). When she attempted to read *The alligator jumped in,* Kaylie read *The,* paused, looked at the illustration, and correctly read, *The alligator jumped in.* After the reading, Kaylie's attention to meaning was reinforced: "Good job! I like the way you stopped to check the picture. Good readers do that." Later in Kaylie's program she selected *Just Like Daddy* (Ache, 1981), a predictable book with a repetitive pattern. At first Kaylie read, *I went my face, got dressed and ate a big breakfast.* She stopped and repeated the sentence. Then she reread the sentence, correcting the miscue: *I washed my face, got dressed and ate a big breakfast.* The response to Kaylie's ability to use several sources of information was intended to reinforce and encourage her strategic behaviors: "You got it right. I liked the way you fixed it when what you read didn't make sense. Going back really helped you."

The Reading Recovery teacher intentionally does not attempt to correct every miscue the child may make; often she or he refrains from interrupting the child's reading. Rather, the teacher focuses on one strategy the child needs to learn, ignoring behaviors that are unrelated to that focus. The effective Reading Recovery teacher is flexible and realizes that unexpected "teachable moments" may occur as a result of the child's responses.

Every day a running record is taken while a child independently reads a new book that was introduced and read once the previous day. The teacher's role is that of a neutral observer, recording the child's independent reading. The teacher uses this time to observe, noting processing problems and records appeals for help. The teacher encourages an attempt at the word but provides it if the student does not respond. The text is new and slightly difficult, offering the child some challenges and opportunities to employ reading strategies; therefore, he or she is not expected to read the book with 100 percent accuracy. During the reading, the teacher makes a notation on the running record form and notes those points which will be attended to after the reading. Substitutions, self-corrections, omissions, and insertions are watched for and noted. After this reading, the teacher points out to the child a powerful example of where the child employed a strategy effectively. This is followed by one or two powerful examples of effective strategy instruction such as directing the child to use the first letter of the word, or rereading to monitor his or her reading, thus helping the child learn to solve his or her own problems while reading. After the lesson, the teacher analyzes the running record, referring to the child's use of the cueing systems (meaning, syntax, or graphophonemic) and strategies (rereading, searching through a word) when making miscues, experiencing difficulty, or self-correcting.

For example, Kaylie independently read *The Hungry Giant* (Cowley, 1990) while a running record was being recorded. Although she was using graphophonemic awareness, the sentence did not make sense. At one point the text read, *The giant found a beehive.* Kaylie read, *The giant,* stopped and repeated the phrase, continued by reading *feeled a,* repeated this phrase, and continued by reading *bay.* After the reading, Kaylie received positive comments regarding her attempts at becoming an independent reader. Her previous self-corrections were brought to her attention. Then the miscued text was pointed out. "You worked hard on this page. I like the way you reread to try and help you. You said, 'The giant feeled a bay.' That word [pointing to *found*] starts and ends like *feeled.* Does that make sense? Try it again and think about what the giant did." This time Kaylie read the sentence accurately, correcting both miscues.

No more than three minutes per lesson are spent on letter/word work. During the early lessons it may be necessary for the child to learn letters and words through models and oral repetition. One to two minutes may be devoted to this. The child may trace, write on various surfaces, or manipulate plastic letters on a magnetic board at this time. Later in the student's program, work is done with initial and final consonant substitutions, and examining patterns in words. The teacher assists the child in discovering how words work. They begin with a known word, and the teacher draws the child's attention to details of words the child may overlook, assisting the learner in moving from the known to the unknown. This work promotes the development of phonemic awareness and phonics knowledge.

For example, Kaylie was able to read and write the word *like.* To help her think about how words work when the initial consonant changes, she was given the known word *look* and all the magnetic letters needed to form the word *book.* She was able to construct the word on the magnetic board. The word was removed from the board and Kaylie's attention was redirected to the word *look.* She was then asked if she could construct the word *took.* Again, she was able to do so. This activity promoted phonemic awareness and the ability to manipulate onsets and rimes, the beginning and ending chunks of syllables and one-syllable words.

The teacher needs to be aware that the intent of this activity is not to teach words in isolation. There are many inconsistencies in the English language, and the child needs to be aware that there are exceptions (i.e., *come, home*). Similar procedures are followed when working with simple analogies, predictable letter-sound sequences, less predictable sound sequences, etc., depending on the needs of the child. The purpose is to teach the child how words work and to have him or her use this knowledge when reading continuous text.

The child writes a story in a journal on a daily basis. While writing, the child is given the opportunity to slow down the reading process. "Auditory, visual, and motor systems are all at work when the child writes and all contribute to greater skill in reading" (M. Clay, 1982). The child generates a message that may come from personal experiences, or from a book read during the lesson. Using a journal comprised of unlined paper, opened and turned sideways, the student uses the upper portion to practice letters, words, and sound/letter analysis, as well as to make connections from known words to new words. Again phonemic awareness and phonics knowledge are being reinforced and taught.

The lower portion contains the child's message. Because this page is used for future reading experiences, everything is written in standard spelling. The words the child uses are those he or she really wants to use rather than words from a predetermined list of sight or vocabulary words. The message is written word by word. The child writes known words and attempts unknown words with the help of the teacher. The teacher encourages the child to say the word slowly and to predict the letters that represent the sounds in the word. With teacher support, children learn to analyze words and to make links between sounds and letters. In Reading Recovery lessons there is little focus on letter forms but much attention to learning to hear and record the sounds of words. The child is taught how to write words through sound analysis and to gain independence in writing new words he or she wants to use in stories. The focus is not on learning words or on writing words correctly but on how to analyze sound sequence in words, use letters to record sounds, and go from known words to get to new words. This is yet another opportunity for the child to use more phonemic awareness and phonics in an authentic context. Figure 3 shows Kaylie's writing journal. She composed the following sentence during her Reading Recovery lesson: *I lost my tooth 3 days ago.* After writing *I*, Kaylie did not know how to write the word *lost*, so four connected boxes were drawn on the practice page for her. Kaylie was asked to "say the word slowly," then asked, "What can you hear?" Kaylie wrote the *l* in the first box, said the word slowly again, wrote the *o* in the second box. She repeated the process again. Since she knew the *st* "chunk," she was able to complete the word. A similar process was used to write the word *tooth*. *My*, *days*, and *ago* were known words that she had learned to read and write as a result of prior instruction; therefore, Kaylie was able to write them with ease and fluency.

While composing the story, the child is encouraged to reread the sentence. This promotes self-monitoring and independence and also reinforces the purpose of standard forms, layout, and spacing. The rereading provides yet another opportunity to practice the strategies and skills of reading (directionality, monitoring, searching for visual cues, self-correcting, etc.)

After the message is written, the child rereads it while the teacher writes it on a sentence strip. The teacher cuts the sentence at word, letter, or phrase boundaries for the child to reassemble. The child uses his or her knowledge of language, letter-sound relationships, phonemic awareness, and reading strategies to check on the message when composing and reassembling the story. Many basic writing skills, such as left-to-right order within words, spacing between words, and directionality can be addressed during writing. Encouraging the child to write a daily message teaches the early reader that talking can be written, a central concept in the reading and writing process. The self-composed message may not be grammatically correct, but the teacher does not correct it because the intent is for the child to discover the relationship between oral language and the printed word. With time, the child's stories become more structurally correct.

The Reading Recovery teacher provides a new book introduction after carefully selecting a book that would be interesting to the child while at the same time appropriate for the child's needs. The stories contain vocabulary, language structures, and concepts that are within the child's control. The book must be easy enough to ensure success while offering the child challenges and opportunities to apply the strategies taught. The teacher introduces the book by providing a basic story line, explaining a concept. The teacher and child look at and discuss the illustrations in the book. Through oral language the child is given the opportunity to become familiar with the plot, major ideas, and the book's language. Each introduction varies according to the strengths and needs of the child. For example, when a child is nearing the completion of his or her program, the child may browse through the book and ask questions as needed. After the introduction, the child is asked to read the book for the first time. This provides critical teaching time. The teacher may prompt, support, and/or teach the child. As the reader experiences difficulty, the teacher chooses ways to make connections with the child's experiences, language, knowledge, and strategies to support the child in solving his or her own problem. The goal is to have the child read the story as independently as possible, using his or her developing strategies and skills for reading. This first reading provides yet another opportunity to observe and analyze in order to assist the teacher in making quality instructional decisions based on evidence of the child's reading behavior.

Success of Reading Recovery

Research studies conducted in Columbus, Ohio, have shown that overall, the children discontinued from the program continue to perform at a level appropriate for their grade level for three years following the Reading Recovery year (DeFord, Pinnell, Lyons, & Place, 1990).

Other studies, including those conducted by Gay Su Pinnell, who was among those who pioneered the implementation of Reading Recovery in the United States, reveal that the success of the program is due to a combination of factors. The thirty-minute individualized sessions

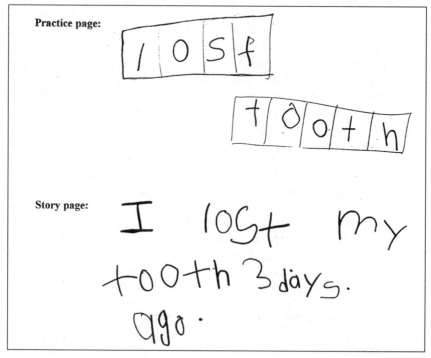

Figure 3. Kaylie's writing.

take place on a daily basis. The children read real books, not segmented texts or workbooks. They write self-composed stories. Teachers plan each student's lessons based on the child's strengths and assist the child in building upon what he or she knows to master new strategies and skills, including—but not limited to—phonemic awareness and phonics. Last, the teachers are trained in the program's techniques over the course of a school year, and not in a one-shot workshop. Teachers are able to practice and refine their teaching with the support of "teacher-leaders." These experienced Reading Recovery teachers assist the emergent Reading Recovery teachers in finding new ways of being effective in working with children.

There is no "quick fix" for those who do not view themselves as readers and writers. No glitzy programmed package, Madison Avenue video, or systematic phonics program can provide the answers. Instead, it is important to provide our children with the best conditions for literacy learning within school and home environments. Encouraging and teaching students to take control of their own learning while developing a love for literacy will help them to experience success.

References

Ache, F. (1981). *Just like Daddy*. Englewood Cliffs, NJ: Prentice-Hall.

Clay, M. M. (1979). *Sand or stones*. Auckland, New Zealand: Heinemann.

Clay, M. (1982). *Observing young readers*. Auckland, New Zealand and Portsmouth, NH: Heinemann.

Cowley, J. (1990). *The hungry giant*. Bothell, WA: The Wright Group.

Cowley, J. (1993). *Let's have a swim*. Bothell, WA: The Wright Group.

DeFord, D. E., Pinnell, G., Lyons, C., & Place, A. W. (1990). *The Reading Recovery follow-up study* (Technical Report, Vol. III). Columbus: Ohio State University.

Goodman, K. (1996). *On reading*. Portsmouth, NH: Heinemann.

31 From Reading Strategies to Strategies for Teaching in Tutorial and Small Group Situations

Constance Weaver
Western Michigan University
with a section by Suki Stone

Many of the reader support activities in this article can be handled by the regular classroom teacher, but some may need the support of someone who can spend more time with the reader individually: a classmate or older child, an aide, a parent volunteer, or a special services teacher.

The first section discusses and demonstrates how readers use syntactic and semantic cues as they predict, monitor comprehension, and confirm, correct, or try to correct what they have read. This sets the stage for the second section, on Retrospective Miscue Analysis, which deals here with helping readers develop strategies for dealing with texts and words (see also Chapter 17). The third and major section offers suggestions for working with students tutorially, beyond the primary years. It includes a section on writing Individual Education Plans (IEPs) and the fact that these do not have to be skills-oriented. Next is a chart matching reader characteristics with possible teaching strategies. These are followed by a description of Carol Chomsky's tutorial book/tape program; an account, by Suki Stone, of how a preservice teacher led a fifth grader to reading, through language experience stories that the child dictated; a discussion of secondary students learning to read through language experience; and an account from an article by Rigg and Taylor of a twenty-one-year-old learning to read with whole language experiences. The chapter ends with a discussion of the nature and success of a literacy program David Doake developed with and for some eleven- and twelve-year-old students who had not been doing well as readers.

This essay contains material taken from "Tutorial Situations Beyond the Primary Years" and "Small Groups . . .," from pages 526 to 537 of Weaver's *Reading Process and Practice* (Heinemann, 1994). The material includes a short section by Suki Stone.

The following discussion deals with reading strategies, how we can teach reading strategies through Retrospective Miscue Analysis, and other ways of helping readers beyond the primary years in tutorial and small group situations.

In "A Sociopsycholinguistic Model of the Reading Process and Reading Strategy Instruction" (this volume), Yetta Goodman and Dorothy Watson discuss strategies for sampling, inferring, predicting, confirming, and constructing meaning. These are all what we might think of as macro-level strategies: strategies for processing texts. When I discuss strategies, I typically focus just on predicting, monitoring comprehension, and confirming or correcting (using fix-it strategies). The latter set of strategies is appropriate for both the macro level and the micro level—that is, for processing the whole text and for dealing with individual words. Also, when dealing with the language cueing systems, I refer to the graphophonic (alternatively, graphophonemic), syntactic, and semantic. What Goodman and Watson call the pragmatic cueing system is roughly what I call context beyond the text and prior knowledge and experience, together. We are not really talking about different things: we're just cutting up the pie in different ways.

The following is an oversimplification, and therefore to some extent a distortion, of how the strategies of predicting, monitoring comprehension, and confirming/correcting make use of the language cueing systems (excluding the pragmatic, as explained). This discussion provides useful background for the subsequent treatment of how Retrospective Miscue Analysis can be used—in part, to help readers develop more effective strategies for processing words as well as texts.

Reading Strategies and Language Cues

When we analyze a reader's miscues to determine the strategies that the reader is or is not using effectively, we look at the reader's use of the language cueing systems to gain insight into the strategies of predicting, monitoring comprehension, and confirming or correcting. For example, most readers, even less proficient readers, will intuitively draw upon their grammatical knowledge to say something that fits with the preceding grammar:

expert
Every day except . . .

ramped
. . . the boys repeated . . .

This miscue *expert* fits with the preceding grammar (we can imagine the sentence continuing, for example, as "Every day expert witnesses testify"). Likewise, the nonword *ramped* seems to preserve the past tense ending of *repeated*, and thus to fit grammatically with what comes before—though not, of course, semantically. Often, such miscues will fit reasonably well with the preceding meaning too, even for readers who are not so obviously proficient:

> Day after day the sun beat down, and there was no shade from the ~~leaves~~ *leaves*
> leafless trees.

This particular miscue was not corrected, probably because the reader derived the essential meaning of the phrase even though *leaves* does not fit normally with the following grammar and meaning.

One of the major differences between more proficient and less proficient readers is that more proficient readers typically correct, or try to correct, miscues that don't go with the following context, while less proficient readers do so less often. That is, more proficient readers monitor comprehension and the grammatical flow of sentences, then either confirm the appropriateness of what they've read or at least try to correct or come up with something sensible to fit the context. Here are some examples:

> I first saw Claribel ©*saw* when I was working in my office.

> They simply saw a loose, lank ©*young* youth with tow-colored,
>
> sunburned hair . . .

The first miscue fits with the preceding grammar and meaning, but not with the following; it was corrected (the reader repeated the two preceding words also, in correcting). The second miscue adequately captures the basic meaning of the text word, but it doesn't fit grammatically with what comes afterward; it, too, was corrected.

From these examples, we see that the language cues that most obviously fit into strategies for processing words as well as texts are the syntactic and semantic cues (though *of course* we are also attending to the visual display and the graphophonemic cueing system inside our heads). Most readers' miscues fit with the preceding grammar most of the time, and many readers' miscues fit with the preceding meaning much of the time, suggesting that we intuitively use grammar and meaning to predict something that will fit with what came before. More proficient readers typically correct or try to correct those miscues that don't fit with the following grammar and/or meaning, while less proficient readers do so less often.

Retrospective Miscue Analysis

Originally developed in the 1970s by a Canadian secondary school reading specialist, Chris Worsnop, Retrospective Miscue Analysis has been popularized by Yetta Goodman and Ann Marek (1996; see also Chapter 17). In Retrospective Miscue Analysis, the reader is tape-recorded, the teacher usually selects miscues for discussion, and the reader and the teacher consider the miscues together, either by looking at the miscues marked on a copy of the selection, by listening to the tape, or both. That is, together they consider in retrospect the reader's miscues and the reading strategies they reflect.

The articles in Section III of this book on miscue analysis emphasize using RMA to help readers reconsider the nature of the reading process and revalue themselves as readers. The suggestions here also include helping readers develop the habit of monitoring comprehension and using fix-it strategies as needed. Often we may need to help readers use syntax and semantics along with graphophonemic cues so that their miscues are more likely to fit with the preceding context.

Below are some reader characteristics, with suggestions for the kinds of miscues a teacher might choose for discussion in each case.

The purpose of contrasting miscues that do exemplify a desirable strategy with those that don't is to demonstrate to the reader that he or she is capable of using the strategy and just needs to use it more consistently

Reader characteristics	*Kinds of miscues that could be examined*
Lacks self-confidence	Select miscues that fit the context appropriately.

Thinks reading means getting all the words	Select miscues that fit the context appropriately; might also consider the completely acceptable miscues of someone who is clearly a good reader—perhaps the teacher.
Seldom corrects miscues that don't go with following context	Compare miscues that didn't go with following context but were corrected with similar miscues that weren't corrected.
Makes miscues that don't go with the preceding context	Compare miscues that do go with the preceding context with those that don't.
Makes nonword substitutions that suggest underuse of syntactic and semantic cues and overuse of grapho/phonemic cues	Select miscues wherein all three kinds of cues were used effectively; contrast with miscues that reflect a sounding-out strategy with insufficient regard for meaning cues and/or grammatical cues.
Makes nonword substitutions for words in reader's oral vocabulary	Select miscues where persistence resulted in real words that fit the context; contrast these with nonword substitutions.
Makes miscues that suggest difficulty in sounding out long words that are in the reader's speaking vocabulary	Select miscues where sounding out has been successfully used in conjunction with prior knowledge and context; contrast with miscues where the reader seems not to have used an effective sounding-out strategy for multisyllabic words, or not to have used this strategy along with prior knowledge and context cues.
Consistently corrects high quality miscues that fit the context	Select fully acceptable miscues where correction is unnecessary.

These are a combination of my practices and those of Ann Marek (Marek, 1992), as described in Weaver (1994a pp. 274–76).

When listening to miscues that don't fit the context, teachers can ask "Does that make sense?" and/or "Does that sound like language?" Often, readers will quickly internalize these questions and comment spontaneously that "that doesn't sound right."

Variations on Retrospective Miscue Analysis

One advantage of retrospective miscue analysis is that the reader is not interrupted while reading. Another is that the reader can take more ownership over the reading process and the discussion of reading strategies. After the reading has been tape-recorded, for example, you can have the reader listen for certain kinds of miscues, if warranted by the reader's pattern of miscues. For instance:

1. While following along in the text, the reader can listen for miscues that fit the context appropriately and therefore don't need to be corrected. (This is for the reader who lacks self-confidence and/or the reader who thinks reading means accurate word identification; it is also for the reader who consistently corrects miscues that don't need to be corrected.)

2. The reader can listen for miscues that reflect good predicting, but that don't go with following context. This reinforces the predicting strategies and any strategies the reader sometimes uses to self-correct and demonstrates the need for correction in other cases. (This is for the reader who makes good predictions but seldom corrects miscues that don't fit with the following context.)

3. The reader can listen for miscues that don't sound like language. (This is for the reader who underuses syntactic as well as semantic cues and may overuse grapho/phonemic cues.)

Of course, similar instructional strategies can be used on the spot, with immediate playback of a paragraph just tape-recorded. And the discussion can be more open-ended. For example, the teacher can simply ask the reader to stop the tape at trouble spots as they listen to the tape together. The reader can explain why it was a problem and how he or she tried to deal with it; then together they can discuss any other strategies that might have been effective. Such instructional strategies as these can be developed as the teacher sees the need and opportunity.

Tutorial Situations beyond the Primary Years

Retrospective miscue analysis is, of course, a strategy that can be used both during and beyond the primary years. Many other strategies useful with young readers are also quite successful when employed with older readers, even adults. Most of the material in this section is taken from Weaver, 1994a, pp. 526–35, and these instructional suggestions often reflect practices of whole language teachers. Refer to Appendix I for a list of references that demonstrate the success of whole language with special learners, and to Appendix II for references with specific strategies for helping readers.

Writing Individual Educational Plans (IEPs)

More than a decade ago, Peter Hasselriis wrote a landmark article in which he argued that while Public Law 94–142, the Education of All Handicapped Children Act, requires the writing of Individual Educational Plans for all students labeled as handicapped, it does not require that these plans specify narrow behavioral goals or objectives. Though the achievement of intermediate objectives is supposed to be "measurable," this does not mean that standardized tests or so-called objective measures must be used. In short, IEPs can be written with the kinds of goals and objectives that teachers have for learners in whole language classrooms, and that learners have for themselves.

Progress can be measured by many of the same means used in whole language research studies: interviews and questionnaires, miscue analysis, writing samples, lists of books read, dialogue journals and literature logs, and so forth. In addition, records of daily and periodic observations can become an important part of assessment.

Given the diversity of assessment means and measures that can be used, almost any worthwhile goal can be set for, and with, students, giving rise to more concrete objectives that can be both specified and measured. One of three examples Hasselriis offers is the following, for a particular ten-and-a-half-year-old student (1982, p. 19):

- Present level of educational performance: Interviews, observations, and the Reading Miscue Inventory indicate that he is a reader but that he is word bound. When he reads aloud he tends to focus on letters and syllables. He does not sample from print but, rather, insists on making phonic matches with all graphic cues. He is proficient at retelling literal information but does not distinguish significant from insignificant details.

- Annual goal: Will read complete texts aloud in a way that shows he is making sense of what he is reading. His miscues will be characterized by meaningful substitutions, deletions, and insertions that indicate attention to language units as large as or larger than the sentence.

- Short-term objectives: Develop language experience stories on topics of interest. Dictate them to the teacher; write own stories. Read text with selected words deleted, filling in the blanks with appropriate words. Work on assisted reading with the teacher. Read text substituting appropriate words when necessary for unknown or unfamiliar language units.

Another useful article dealing with assessment and evaluation in the field of special education is Hilary Sumner's "Whole Language Assessment and Evaluation: A Special Education Perspective" (1991). One particularly useful aspect of Sumner's article is her discussion of classroom-based assessment rather than standardized tests as a means of determining which children have learning differences and difficulties that hamper them in actual reading and writing situations. Such measures are described in detail in Max Kemp's *Watching Children Read and Write: Observational Records for Children with Special Needs* (1989).

Matching Tutorial Instruction to Readers' Needs

Assessment is important in determining what kind of tutorial help to offer a student, but of course there is no magic formula for translating the perceived characteristics, strengths, and needs of a reader into instructional strategies. What may be valuable, though, is some suggestions based on experience. Below is a list of reader characteristics and possible teaching strategies that I have developed, an amalgamation from many sources over the years. Another useful chart is offered in an article by Rhondda Brill (1985). Teachers might compile a reference chart that complements Brill's and mine, or make a single comprehensive chart from these and other sources.

Reader Characteristics and Possible Teaching Strategies

READER CHARACTERISTIC: Reader doesn't seem to know that reading should make sense.

POSSIBLE EVIDENCE:

Seems to read word-by-word, in a monotone.

Miscues often do not fit with the following grammar or meaning —perhaps not even with the preceding grammar or meaning.

Reader expresses surprise when asked to tell what reading selection was about.

Reader makes nonword miscues (like *souts* for *shouts*).

POSSIBLE TEACHING STRATEGIES:

During a Shared Book Experience (group or one-on-one), preview the book about to be read. From the title and the cover, predict what the book might be about. Go through the book looking at the pictures and predicting.

Read books to the class, and discuss.

Do language experience; that is, write down what the reader wants to say about a topic or event, and have the reader read it back—again and again, until the reader is fluent. Perhaps the writing can be done, or redone, on a computer, with space on the pages for the reader/writer to illustrate.) NOTE: In various settings and situations, a language experience approach to reading has proved more effective than anything else with older readers who have little ability to read—even with secondary students and adults.

Do guided writing, which is similar to "language experience" except that the teacher helps shape the writing.

Provide tape recordings of books for the reader to listen to, along with copies of the books. Help the reader notice how the voice on the tape emphasizes meanings. Encourage the reader to reread the book while listening to the tape until the reader can read the book independently and fluently, with appropriate expression. (This may literally take weeks, but the next book will usually go faster, because the reader recognizes more words and has absorbed more letter/sound knowledge.)

Have the reader read with a buddy and stop after every page to discuss.

Use Retrospective Miscue Analysis. Tape-record the reader reading, and play back part of it. Stop the tape recorder when the reader has made a miscue that doesn't make sense. Ask, "Does that make sense?" Invite the reader to reread, offering help with reading strategies as necessary.

READER CHARACTERISTIC: Reader doesn't yet recognize many words or have much knowledge of letter-sound patterns.

POSSIBLE EVIDENCE:

Reader skips or misreads more than half of the words in a text.

Reader cannot pronounce even the first letter of very many words.

POSSIBLE TEACHING STRATEGIES:

Most of the strategies suggested for the reader who doesn't seem to know that reading should make sense. It's especially important for the reader to keep rereading favorite books until the reading is fluent, even if this takes weeks. Rereading develops letter/sound knowledge as well as word knowledge.

When using Shared Book Experience, be sure to point to words so the reader can begin to make connections between spoken words and written words.

Have emergent readers take turns pointing to the words as they read. This can be done with older readers whose shared reading is being projected onto a screen or wall.

Use Shared Book Experience as an opportunity to focus on selected and particularly relevant aspects of letter-sound patterns, such as onsets (initial consonants and consonant clusters) and rimes in words that end the same (vowel plus any consonants that may follow).

Have emergent readers come up to the Big Book or chart and "frame" a key word with two fingers, to focus on identifying words in context.

Do guided writing with whole class or group, being sure to focus on key letters and how they sound. Identify a sound and then invite emergent readers and writers to write the sound they hear. They can do this one at a time on large chart paper where the group composition is being written, or they can do this on individual chalk boards that they can readily hold up for the teacher to check.

Do this kind of guided writing with individual learners of all ages. Focusing on writing the sounds they hear will enhance their phonics knowledge. If desired, you can use Elkonin boxes for writing/spelling (as used in Reading Recovery, e.g., Clay, 1993, p. 33), having the individual write key sounds and supplying the other letters yourself.

READER CHARACTERISTIC: Reader doesn't read fluently.

POSSIBLE TEACHING STRATEGIES:

Provide tape recordings of books for the reader to listen to, along with copies of the books. Help the reader notice how the voice on the tape emphasizes meanings. Encourage the reader to reread the book while listening to the tape until the reader can read the book independently and fluently, with appropriate expression. (This may literally take weeks, but the next book will usually go faster, because the reader recognizes more words and has absorbed more letter/sound knowledge.)

READER CHARACTERISTIC: Reader doesn't seem to use prior knowledge and context to predict what's coming next.
Reader may not know that this is an important reading strategy.

POSSIBLE EVIDENCE:
Miscues often don't fit the preceding grammar or meaning.

POSSIBLE TEACHING STRATEGIES:
See suggestions for a reader who doesn't seem to know that reading is supposed to make sense.

Do and discuss relevant strategy mini-lessons, such as those in Goodman and Marek (1996) or some of the other sources in Appendix II. For example: Such readers may benefit from a lesson like that in Figure 9.8 of Weaver (1994), wherein a group

would discuss where they "get" the answers to carefully constructed questions regarding a text. (In this particular example, the
questions increasingly require use of prior knowledge.) Another
example: In a passage where one key word is repeated, you might
construct a strategy lesson by copying the passage and blocking
out the word with a dry marker, then having the student(s) try to
determine what the word is, using context and prior knowledge.
(See Chapter 13.)

**READER CHARACTERISTIC: Reader doesn't seem to monitor
comprehension.**

POSSIBLE EVIDENCE:

Miscues often do not fit with the following grammar or meaning—
perhaps not even with the preceding grammar or meaning.

Reader cannot tell what the selection is about—perhaps not
even after reading silently a selection that is appropriate to his or
her interests and background knowledge.

POSSIBLE TEACHING STRATEGIES:

Take turns reading with this reader. Stop after each page (and/or
after key paragraphs) to retell and discuss what was read.

For a story, create together (teacher-student, or peer-peer) a
semantic web of key information, such as characters, plot, etc.

For informational selection, develop and use together some
strategies for monitoring comprehension, such as:

Stopping after each paragraph or so and restating what it was
about.

Rereading or looking up key terms that are troublesome.

Preparing a visual organizer of some sort: semantic web, time-
line, graph, outline, chart, map, etc.

**READER CHARACTERISTIC: Reader lacks self-confidence and/or
reader thinks that reading means saying all the words correctly.**

POSSIBLE EVIDENCE:

Reader says that he or she can't read.

Reader says that he or she doesn't like to read. (May indicate
nonproficient reading and/orlack of confidence in reading.)

POSSIBLE TEACHING STRATEGIES:

Use Shared Book Experience with an emergent reader: the more
proficient readers will support the less proficient. With older readers who are relatively unproficient, an age-appropriate text can be
projected onto a screen or wall for shared reading.

Use Retrospective Miscue Analysis to point out good miscues
and good reading strategies, if possible.

Wean the reader from the idea that good readers know all the
words.

Help the reader develop a wider range of strategies for dealing with problem words independently, instead of always asking someone or giving up.

Invite the reader to listen to a book on tape and follow along, practicing reading the book until he or she can read it fluently.

Provide for echo reading, wherein a more proficient reader reads a text and the less proficient, less self-confident reader reads along, often a fraction of a second behind, echoing the more proficient reader.

Provide for buddy reading, wherein a peer can help when needed, but help with developing strategies or by discussing the reading, not just by telling the unconfident reader what some words are.

Provide for choral reading, wherein the unconfident reader can practice reading certain parts of a selection with other readers until they can all read it fluently. Perform.

Use reading strategy mini-lessons, as offered in many of the sources listed above. One idea is to demonstrate to the reader that he or she can get the essence of a passage without reading all the words. The "Kent State" passage on p. 145 of Weaver (1994) is one illustration of such a passage. Other variations on the cloze procedure may be suitable.

READER CHARACTERISTIC: Reader doesn't seem to be able to sound out words in pronounceable chunks.

POSSIBLE EVIDENCE:

Reader deals with problem words by saying a word that includes some of the letters, but that doesn't fit the context.

Reader makes non-word miscues that include some of the letters but that don't reflect an attempt to sound out the word in pronounceable chunks.

Reader gives other evidence that he or she doesn't know that reading should make sense (see the first of the reader characteristics listed here).

POSSIBLE TEACHING STRATEGIES:

First, be sure that the reader is reading to make sense of text, to predict, and to monitor comprehension.

Then, when the reader comes to a troublesome word, have the reader predict what might make sense. If the reader's predictions include the actual word, focus on the printed word to help the reader realize this; often, attention to just the initial letters will be sufficient to confirm the prediction. If the reader has not included the actual word among his or her predictions but the word is fairly predictable using prior knowledge, context, and the initial letters, try encouraging the reader to use all of this information to make a prediction. Guide as necessary.

If needed, help the reader sound out the word in pronounceable chunks and try to determine whether the word makes sense in the context. (It's not important to apply rules for determining syllables, but only to sound out words in chunks. You may need to help the reader try alternative ways of chunking, too—not only to get the particular word in question, but to realize that if at first one doesn't succeed, chunking the word differently may help. Again, help the reader use context to confirm or correct the sounded-out word.)

NOTE: If the word is not in the reader's listening vocabulary, the reader may find it difficult or impossible to sound out the word correctly, or to decide whether the word fits the context. This is typical of proficient as well as less effective readers.

Eight-Year-Olds in a Tutorial Book/Tape Program

In an early article titled "After Decoding: What?" Carol Chomsky reported on her work with five eight-year-olds. She described the children at the outset of the tutoring program as follows (1976, p. 288):

> These children were not nonreaders. They had received a great deal of phonics training and had acquired many phonetic skills. They met regularly with the remedial reading teacher with whom they had worked intensively since first grade. After much effort, they could "decode," albeit slowly and painfully. What was so frustrating was their inability to put any of this training to use, their failure to progress to even the beginnings of fluent reading. . . . In spite of their hard-won "decoding skills," they couldn't so much as read a page of simple material to me. The attempt to do so was almost painful, a word-by-word struggle, long silences, eyes eventually drifting around the room in an attempt to escape the humiliation and frustration of the all too familiar, hated situation.

What Chomsky succeeded in using with these children was essentially a whole language tutorial program, with skills and strategies taught in context as needed. She obtained for the children two dozen picture books, recorded on tape, from which the children were to make their own selections. The task was to listen to the tape while following along in the text, until the children had become familiar enough with the book to read it fluently. In effect, they would be first memorizing the book and then learning to read it: attending to the whole and then to parts as necessary.

Chomsky explained her rationale (1976, p. 289):

> When it comes to memorizing a book, these eight-year-olds are in a very different position from the pre-reader. They have already had two years of drill in word analysis, long and short vowels, word endings, blending, and so on. They can sound out words and have a fair sight vocabulary. They are beyond needing introduction to the alphabetic nature of the English writing system. What

they need is to shift their focus from the individual word to connected discourse and to integrate their fragmented knowledge. It is the larger picture that they need help with, in learning to attend to the semantics and syntax of a written passage, and in developing reliance on using contextual clues from the sentence or even longer passages as they read.

Using pages that the children could already "read" fluently in semirote fashion, Chomsky and her graduate assistant supplemented the reading with game-like activities involving mostly word recognition and analysis. In addition, the children did substantial writing connected with their reading: for example, they wrote stories, question-and-answer sequences, and sentences using words from the stories.

Progress at first was slow: it took four of the five children about a month to learn to read their first book fluently. After that slow beginning the pace increased, and subsequent books took less and less time, so that when the children were on their fourth or fifth book they were able to finish it in a week. Soon there seemed less and less need for the analytical work; after a while, the tutoring sessions became times for simply reading the books and discussing the story, doing some writing, or discussing some stories the children had written. Those children who progressed the most improved in both reading and writing—not a surprising outcome, given the holistic nature of the approach. In general, the children improved dramatically, not only in fluency but also in their attitude toward reading. They began reading TV commercials, cereal boxes, and magazines at home. They began picking up books to read instead of avoiding reading at all costs. In short, they began to feel and act like readers.

Repeated rereading of familiar, self-chosen texts seems to be critical in helping older readers develop proficiency, as the next section also demonstrates.

Sergio and Rudy: A Preservice Teacher and a Fifth Grader Learning Together

The following example indicates how an allegedly learning disabled fifth-grade Hispanic youngster, Rudy, learned to read with the help of Sergio Cordova, a preservice teacher and instructional aide who worked with him.

Doubtless Rudy's reading difficulties were caused, at least in part, by his educational history. Migrant workers, his family moved between Texas and California every year. Because his family speaks only Spanish, the only place Rudy uses English is in school. Results from his achievement tests in fourth grade showed him to be still functioning at a preprimer level: that is, his language arts/reading level was at a readiness stage, as measured on standardized tests. Before working with Sergio, he had never learned (or retained knowledge of) the alphabet. Although he had received special education services since fourth grade, Rudy was still, as a fifth grader, having difficulty reading. As an eleven-year-old nonreader, Rudy was easily frustrated and unsuccessful while learning to read using traditional basal materials and methods. He had also developed low self-esteem as a result of his academic difficulties.

As a student at the University of Texas at Brownsville, Sergio had been introduced to the idea of using whole language principles and practices with special education students like Rudy (Weaver, 1994a, 1994b; Rhodes & Dudley-Marling, 1996; Flores, Cousin, & Diaz, 1991). The whole language framework encompasses the basic assumptions of holism/constructivism, as articulated by Poplin (1988) and refined by Poplin and Stone (1992). One of these principles is that the learner learns best when he or she is passionately involved (Freire, 1970). Freire discussed the importance of passion as the impetus of transformational change, generating a love for learning whatever the learner is passionate about. So Sergio became acquainted with Rudy's greatest interests, his passions.

The first step was to interview Rudy about his interests outside the classroom. One of many things Sergio learned about Rudy was his willingness to help with cutting, pasting, and building projects in the classroom. Rudy also talked about his love for animals. Then Sergio approached him with a group of magazines containing pictures of things Rudy had talked about. Sergio told Rudy to cut out anything that interested him. Rudy chose animal pictures and wanted to write animal stories.

Sergio wrote the first couple of stories Rudy dictated. The first story was about a shark, and Rudy read it about 90 percent correctly. He reread the story three or four times, practicing until he could read it perfectly. After reading the shark story to the other resource room aide, he received much praise and encouragement from both that aide and Sergio. Then he read the shark story to a substitute teacher who had developed rapport with Rudy while teaching in his class.

After the initial story, Rudy wrote a different story every three days. He chose to put his stories into a photograph album. He began to build self-confidence as the teachers and aides complimented his ability to read. He was so proud of his book of stories that he brought a picture of himself as a three-year-old and put it in the beginning of the photograph album. Then he wrote an autobiographical piece for the front of the book, naming it his story book. As he became more self-confident, Rudy began to be comfortable with oral reading. While Rudy read his second story aloud to Sergio, students in the classroom stopped their work and listened attentively. He looked forward to reading the stories he created and shared with Sergio. At the end of six stories, Rudy remarked that he had to write only ninety-four more stories to complete his book!

During the time Sergio worked with him, Rudy was continuing in the class basal. In the fourth grade he hadn't gone past the third story in the basal, but through writing and reading his own stories he soon accumulated enough sight words and vocabulary to read fifteen of the stories in the basal reader. His progress and interest in reading helped him develop in other academic areas as well.

Sergio used another principle of whole language in having Rudy himself choose what words he wanted to learn to spell. Rudy chose ten words from each story, filing them in alphabetical order in a box. He had found a need and a reason for learning school-related skills, such as spelling and alphabetization. His interest in animals and his new-found reading ability have become the impetus for an excitement about learning. Having learned firsthand the power of teaching from whole language principles, Sergio hopes that by the end of the school year, Rudy will be reading library books in their entirety and will have written the remaining ninety-four stories for his book.

Secondary Students Learning Through Language Experience

Fortunately, many children just naturally read for meaning and predict and confirm/correct from context without being told to do so. Unfortunately, some do not; they read more to identify words than to construct meaning, because this is what their classroom instruction has emphasized. Such older readers benefit from the same kinds of assistance as young emergent readers. This conclusion is supported by observations from a three-year program in which British secondary-school English teachers worked intensively one-on-one, with secondary-level readers in difficulty. Margaret Meek explains (1983, p. 214):

> We confirmed our conviction that reading has to be taught as the thing that it is, holistically. To break it down into piecemeal activities for pseudosystematic instruction is to block the individual, idiosyncratic moves that pupils of this age make to interact with a text and to teach themselves how to make it mean. When we began, our pupils had one reading strategy. They held it in common because they had all been taught it when they first had reading

lessons in school. They were efficient sounders and blenders and
decipherers of initial consonants; so efficient, indeed, that words
they could have recognized "at sight" were subjected to the same
decoding as those they had never seen or heard before.

What they could not do effectively was use their grapho/phonemic
knowledge and sampling skills effectively in a coherent approach to
constructing meaning from a text.

The teachers working with these students tried focusing on the students' apparent needs, based in part on an analysis of their miscues.
What proved most effective, however, was adopting a language experience approach. The teachers became scribes for each student, writing
to the student's dictation, inviting the student to reread the evolving
text to see if he or she had said what was wanted, then writing and discussing some more, and finally providing opportunities for the student
to read the finished text to an appreciative audience. That approach did
more than anything else to affect the students' view of themselves as
readers and to increase their competence.

Assisting students in actually writing down parts of stories they
themselves are composing may also be one of the best ways to help those
who need to gain greater mastery of letter/sound correspondences. Just
as one might help a beginning writer in the phonemic stage, so one
might help an older writer/reader sound out words, teaching basic
letter/sound patterns in the process. The older writer/reader need not
write out the entire story this way, for that might become a laborious
process that would inhibit composition and the sense of satisfaction that
would otherwise come from having created a longer and more adult
story. However, guided assistance in hearing and writing the sounds in
words could greatly facilitate acquisition of the basic grapho/phonemic
knowledge needed for reading, just as it does for beginning readers. In
both cases, though, one must remember that a reasonable phonetic
spelling is the aim for a first or rough draft—not "correct" spelling.
Emphasis on perfect spelling would defeat the purpose for having the
writer sound out and write words for him- or herself.

Renée: A Twenty-One-Year-Old Begins to Read with Whole Language

Perhaps an even more remarkable success story is reported in Rigg and
Taylor's "A Twenty-One-Year-Old Begins to Read" (1979). The authors
worked with a young woman named Renée, who was diagnosed as
mentally retarded at the age of six due to the effects of cerebral palsy,
and who had been placed in a program for retarded children for the

next fourteen years. She had then been retested and was rediagnosed as having a normal IQ, after which she was placed in another program where the teacher taught her the alphabet and fifteen sight words. Little wonder that at the age of twenty-one she considered herself a nonreader—and not merely someone who did not read, but someone who could not learn to read.

Rigg and Taylor devised a whole language program designed to give Renée confidence in her ability to read. Into each hour of tutoring they tried to incorporate at least three of the following components, and ideally all five:

1. Sustained silent reading, with both Renée and the tutor silently reading materials of their own choice.

2. Language experience, with Renée dictating or writing stories and then reading and discussing them.

3. Retelling what was read, to focus on comprehension rather than on "wordcalling."

4. Rereading, to develop fluency and confidence.

5. Assisted reading, with the tutor reading and pointing at the words and Renée chiming in, which enabled and encouraged Renée to attempt stories that she might not have had the confidence to try on her own.

During the semester, Renée created twelve language experience stories, and read three short novels and eight stories—all in about twenty hours of instructional time. Like John's instructor (pp. 543–544), Renée's tutors didn't work at all on reading or writing "skills." Believing that she could and would read if given materials that interested her and that used "whole natural language," they structured their tutoring program accordingly. From the very first meeting, Renée was immediately able to read whole, connected text because she was reading stories that she herself had created. Because her attention was focused on getting meaning rather than on identifying words, she began to think of herself as a reader rather than a nonreader. Rigg and Taylor sum up the results of their whole language tutoring program (1979, p. 56):

> After fifteen years of formal instruction, Renée was convinced that she could not read, and she did not read. In twenty hours of tutoring, she became convinced that she could read, and she did read. We asked Renée to do what evidently she had seldom or never been asked to do in school: We asked her to read, and then we got out of her way and let her do it.

Such reports of success should again make us suspect that much of our skills instruction with beginning readers as well as "remedial" readers is not only unnecessary but actually detrimental to the goal of literacy.

Small Groups: Learners in a Literacy Recovery Program

In Nova Scotia, David Doake developed an exemplary literacy recovery program (he called it "reading recovery") for thirteen students aged eleven to twelve. Ten of the children had been retained a grade at some stage of their schooling, all were in the lowest reading group in their classroom, and most had had some "specialist," individually based tutoring. Though they had been classified on a variety of tests as being of average ability, they were making little or no progress in learning to read and write. On the Gates-McGinitie reading test, for example, their scores ranged from a grade level of 2.1 to 3.2. Doake characterizes their previous reading and writing instruction as follows (Doake, 1985, Appendix D; the program is explained more fully in Doake, 1992):

Highly structured:
- teacher controlled
- teacher the evaluating agent

Reading program (Basal type):
- controlled vocabulary
- heavy emphasis on learning word "attack" skills: phonics, little words in big words, syllabication
- more time spent on workbook exercises than on reading
- daily oral circle reading
- word accuracy emphasis rather than meaning emphasis
- seldom read to in school or at home

Writing program:
- accuracy oriented: spelling, grammar, punctuation
- little or no choice on what to write
- teacher the only audience

Handwriting:
- daily
- standard script drill aimed at perfection

In contrast, Doake's literacy program included the following activities, undertaken in the spirit of whole language (Doake, 1985, Appendix H):

- Shared reading (Big Books)
- Read-along with a listening post
- Story reading to students (extensive)
- Sustained silent reading
- Reading at home to and with parents
- Individualized reading (conferences and sharing books)
- Reading in the content areas related particularly to thematic studies
- Creating plays and dramatizing them
- Learning songs, rhymes, and poems from enlarged print
- Reading to younger children from predictable books
- Thematic reading and writing resulting from initial brainstorming sessions on a topic (began with whole class projects and moved to individual studies)
- Environmental written language (used initially)
- Language experience charts and individual books
- Board News composed daily and used
- Dialogue journals
- Story writing (initially modeled after stories read)
- Story writing, using wordless picture story books
- Writing directions
- Regular reading and writing conferences
- Books made from stories written (given library cards)
- Follow-up activities from reading (writing own ending to a story, constructing a game, rewriting the story as a play and acting it out, etc.)

During the two years they were enrolled in this literacy recovery program, the students' progress was dramatic. In the year prior to their enrolling in the program, the students' average (mean) scores on the Gates-McGinitie went from approximately grade 2.2 to 2.4, an increase of only two months. In the first year of the program, the scores rose from an average of 2.4 to 3.8, an increase of one year, four months. In the third year, the scores on the Gates-McGinitie rose from an average of 3.8 to over 5.2, again an average increase of approximately one year, four months. Yet convincing as such standardized scores must be to those who hold conventional notions of educational accountability, these scores tell only part of the story. The most significant gains were in the students' attitude toward reading and writing. As Doake says, "These students received no formal instruction in reading and writing, nor did they experience any correction in their efforts to learn to read and write—and yet they have become readers and writers. They now enjoy these activities and engage in them frequently of their own volition" (Doake 1985, pp. 5–6).

In Conclusion

Readers of this chapter will surely have noticed that the strategies suggested for readers who need extra help are essentially those that effectively enable most young children to learn to read. This is no accident. More isolated skills work is not the answer. More reading and writing is, with reading strategies and skills taught in the context of authentic, meaningful, and enjoyable texts.

References

Brill, R. (1985). The remedial reader. In G. Winch & V. Hoogstad (Eds.), *Teaching reading: A language experience* (pp. 142–59). South Melbourne, Australia: Macmillan.

Chomsky, C. (1976). After decoding: What? *Language Arts, 53,* 288–96, 314.

Clay, M. M. (1993). *Reading Recovery: A guidebook for teachers in training.* Portsmouth, NH: Heinemann.

Doake, D. (1985). *Whole language principles and practices in reading development with special emphasis on reading recovery.* Viewing guide accompanying videotape filmed at the 1985 "Reading for the Love of It" conference in Toronto. Richmond Hill, Ontario: Scholastic.

Doake, D. (1992). Literacy recovery, second language learning, and learning science through holistic practices. Chapter of unpublished book manuscript. Wolfville, Nova Scotia: Acadia University.

Flores, B., Cousin, P. T., & Diaz, E. (1991). Transforming deficit myths about learning, language, and culture. *Language Arts, 68,* 370–79.

Freire, P. (1970). *Pedagogy of the oppressed.* M. B. Ramos, Trans. New York: Herder and Herder.

Goodman, Y. M., & Marek, A. M. (1996). *Retrospective miscue analysis: Revaluing readers and reading.* Katonah, NY: Richard C. Owen.

Goodman, Y. M., & Watson, D. J. (1998). A sociolinguistic model of the reading process and reading strategy instruction. In Constance Weaver (Ed.), *Practicing what we know: Informed reading instruction.* Urbana, IL: National Council of Teachers of English.

Hasselriis, P. (1982). IEPs and a whole-language model of language arts. *Topics in Language and Learning Disabilities, 1* (4), 17–21.

Kemp, M. (1989). *Watching children read and write: Observational records for children with special needs.* Portsmouth, NH: Heinemann.

Meek, M. (1983). *Achieving literacy.* London: Routledge & Kegan Paul.

Poplin, M.S. (1988). Holistic/constructivist principles of the teaching/learning process. *Journal of Learning Disabilities, 21* 401–416.

Poplin, M. S., & Stone, S. (1992). Paradigm shifts in instructional strategies: From reductionism to holistic/constructivism. In W. Stainback & S. Stainback (Eds.), *Controversial issues confronting special education: Divergent perspectives* (pp. 153–79). Boston: Allyn & Bacon.

Rhodes, L. K., & Dudley-Marling, C. (1996). *Readers and writers with a difference: A holistic approach to teaching struggling readers and writers* (2nd ed.). Portsmouth, NH: Heinemann.

Rigg, P., & Taylor, L. (1979). A twenty-one-year-old begins to read. *English Journal, 68,* 52–56.

Sumner, H. (1991). Whole language assessment and evaluation in special education classrooms. In B. Harp (Ed.), *Assessment and evaluation in whole language programs* (pp. 137–57). Norwood, MA: Christopher-Gordon.

Weaver, C. (1994a). *Reading process and practice: From socio- psycholinguistics to whole language* (2nd ed.). Portsmouth, NH: Heinemann.

——— (1994b). *Success at last: Helping Attention Deficit (Hyperactivity) students achieve their potential.* Portsmouth, NH; Heinemann.

——— (1998). (Ed.) *Reconsidering a balanced approach to reading.* Urbana, IL: National Council of Teachers of English.

Appendix I: References on Whole Language with Special Learners

Allen, J. B., & J. M. Mason, (Eds.). (1989). *Risk makers, risk takers, risk breakers: Reducing the risks for young literacy learners.* Portsmouth, NH: Heinemann.

Allen, J. B., B. Shockley, & M. West. (1991). "I'm really worried about Joseph": Reducing the risks of literacy learning. *The Reading Teacher, 44,* 458–468.

Brill, Rhonda. (1985). The remedial reader. In G. Winch and V. Hoogstad (Eds.), *Teaching reading: A language experience* (pp. 142–159). South Melbourne, Australia: Macmillan.

Dudley-Marling, C. (1990). *When school is a struggle.* New York: Scholastic.

Five, C. L. (1992). *Special voices.* Portsmouth, NH: Heinemann.

Meek, M. (1983). *Achieving literacy.* Boston: Routledge & Kegan Paul.

Rhodes, L. K., & Dudley-Marling, C. (1996). *Readers and writers with a difference: A holistic approach to teaching struggling readers and writers.* (2nd ed.). Portsmouth, NH: Heinemann.

Rigg, P., & L. Taylor. (1979). A twenty-one-year-old begins to read. *English Journal, 68,* 52–56.

Routman, R. (1991). *Invitations: Changing as teachers and learners K–12.* Chapter 14, "The learning disabled student: A part of the at-risk population." Portsmouth, NH: Heinemann.

Stires, S. (Ed.). (1991). *With promise: Redefining reading and writing for "special" students.* Portsmouth, NH: Heinemann.

Weaver, C. (Ed.). (1994b). *Success at last! Helping students with Attention Deficit (Hyperactivity) Disorders achieve their potential.* Portsmouth, NH: Heinemann

Appendix II: More References with Ideas for Helping Readers with Special Needs

Gilles, C., et al. (Eds.). (1988). *Whole language strategies for secondary students.*Katonah, NY: Richard C. Owen.

Goodman, Y. M., & Marek, A. M. (1996). *Retrospective miscue analysis: Revaluing readers and reading.* Katonah, NY: Richard C. Owen.

Goodman, Y. M., Watson, D. J., & Burke. C. L. (1996). *Reading strategies: Focus on comprehension* (2nd ed.) Katonah, NY: Richard C. Owen.

Phinney, M. Y. (1988). *Reading with the troubled reader.* Portsmouth, NH: Heinemann.

Watson, D. J. (1987). *Ideas and insights: Languge arts in the elementary school.* Urbana, IL: National Council of Teachers of English.

Weaver, C. (1994a). *Reading process and practice: From socio-psycholinguistics to whole language* (2nd ed.). Portsmouth, NH: Heinemann.

32 "I Could Read If I Just Had a Little Help": Facilitating Reading in Whole Language Contexts

Janet Norris
Louisiana State University

This article by Norris focuses on a strategy that she developed, as a speech/language interventionist, for simultaneously enhancing children's language development and their ability to read. The strategy can be used either within the classroom or in another setting, with either an individual child or a very small group of children. Norris begins with examples of two children's reading: one child exhibits no obvious sign of difficulty when he reads aloud, but does not have a good understanding of what he has read; the other's miscues are often mere guesses based on beginning letters or are even non-words, but her comprehension is reasonably good. Norris notes that while these differing profiles might seem to call for very different instructional plans, this is not necessarily true when we view reading not as the result of separate processes, but rather as the simultaneous coordination of a constellation of interrelated processes—a whole language process, we might say. Thus both profiles can be viewed as calling for an instructional program designed to coordinate and integrate and coordinate the multiple language processes involved in reading. Norris discusses her more integrative model of reading in some detail, as a prelude to an in-depth illustration of strategies that adults may use to help children coordinate various aspects of the reading process.

Norris's tutorial strategy is actually a set of what she calls "Communicative Reading Strategies." In this procedure, or set of procedures, the facilitator interacts with the child and the text, providing information, asking questions, discussing illustrations and concepts, and having the child read selected sentences as he or she progress together through the text. Norris goes into detail as to how the facilitator can address disruptions in various processes within the overall reading process: establishing a preparatory set to activate the child's prior knowledge before the child begins reading a sentence or other meaningful unit of language; providing event structures that will help children organize and interpret information as it is read; pointing to a relevant word or phrase while

explaining or adding meaning to it (expatiations); presenting previously encountered information and then extending that idea to
include new, related information (extensions); clarifying concepts;
paraphrasing; and making associations with global ideas or concepts; chunking complex sentences into smaller idea units and
helping the reader see how the complex sentence works (parsing);
expanding the syntax of the text into grammatically more complete
or complex sentences; offering semantic cues to vocabulary; guiding the processing of letter/sound patterns (through various techniques); and generating phonemic spellings, an activity also
designed to reinforce the reader's understanding of letter/sound
relationships. Her final section discusses whole language as a constellation of instructional approaches.

Warm thanks to Connie Weaver for sharing her redundancy model, suggesting the
concept of the constellation of processes involved in reading, and for the insightful feedback on the original draft of this chapter. The collaboration is greatly appreciated.

When Christopher reads, there is no obvious sign of difficulty. His
reading rate is good, and more than 95 percent of the words are read
correctly and fluently. It is only when he is asked comprehension questions, particularly those that require inferential meaning, that his reading problems become apparent. When he is asked to retell what he read,
only a few facts are recalled, and even these may reflect misinterpretations of the actual meaning. Important information is left out or retold
in random order.

> "Well, there was this guy. And he was running some place. And
> I think someone else met him, but I'm not sure. And a man named
> Alex said 'Finish doing this, and you can leave with us on the bus.'
> And . . . I'm not really sure what happened next."
> Adult: "Why do you think he was running?"
> Christopher: "It didn't tell that."

In contrast, when Keisha reads, her difficulty is apparent to everyone. She struggles over nearly every word at a rate that is painfully slow.
Her attempts at word recognition or decoding often result in guesses
based on beginning letters or the substitution of nonwords for the actual
words. She reads past punctuation marks with no apparent notice, and
her reading expression is a monotone, with word-by-word phrasing.
Brief spurts of fluent reading across a series of four or five words are a
welcome reprieve from her struggle. Surprisingly, despite these severe
reading problems, Keisha does comprehend much of the story. An example of her reading, with the actual words in parentheses, follows.

> "One nit . . . nigit (night) in . . . lat—in late March, the boys
> went (were) walk . . . went walking . . . slow up (slowly up) that

(the)... trall (trail) tow .. towid (toward) home. His ... fes .. his face was stick (stiff) with cold even Bobby ... see ... seened (seemed) tried (tired).

Adult: "Why do you think Bobby seemed tired?"

Keisha: "Because its very cold and he's out walking in the bad weather."

These two readers appear to be opposite in their reading strengths and weaknesses. Christopher has adequate word recognition but poor comprehension, while Keisha can derive meaning despite severe word recognition problems. These apparently contrasting profiles may logically suggest very different instructional plans to assist each child to improve in their respective areas of reading difficulty. But perhaps these two readers are really not that different from each other. When reading is not viewed as the result of separate processes, but rather as the simultaneous coordination of an integrated constellation of processes, then both profiles are seen as symptoms of the same underlying problem. When reading is viewed from the perspective of a whole, integrated system, the outward problems with word recognition and comprehension are both manifestations of difficulty simultaneously coordinating and integrating the constellation of reading processes. Both profiles would therefore require an instructional program designed to integrate and coordinate the multiple processes.

The first goal of this article will be to describe the constellation of reading processes that must be coordinated and to explain how different outward symptoms may result from failure to integrate these processes during reading. The second goal is to describe how a reading instructional approach, termed Communicative Reading (Norris, 1988, 1991), may provide children the assistance they need while engaged in contextual reading to begin to successfully coordinate these processes. This whole language view of reading and reading difficulties provides alternative ways to think about and to assist readers to master the process of fluent, meaningful reading.

The model that we are imagining is an extrapolation of the principles of connectionist networks, or models that attempt to function similarly to the neural networks of the brain (Rumelhart & McClelland, 1986; Seidenberg & McClelland, 1989). The integrated model we propose, for purpose of our imaginings, will borrow the principles and take them beyond what these connectionist networks are currently capable of actually performing.

This integrated view is somewhat like the relationship between land, air, and water, where each is affected by and affects changes in the others. Evaporation from the water creates rising water vapor because of the direct connection to warm air, while water vapor in the air forms clouds that return the water to the earth, and so forth. One component (i.e., "air") is not held in suspension until the other completes its processing. Rather, at each moment in time, the land, air, and water are all in states of activity and all maintain a level of balance and coordination. The integration remains constant, while the dynamics within the system undergo continuous change. Thus, the smallest plant giving off the smallest amount of water through transpiration has an effect on the entire system. Different weather patterns, like the contrasting reading patterns of Christopher and Keisha, are symptoms or manifestations of the differences in the balance and coordination among the many different components and not the result of separate systems or discrete components.

A Constellation of Reading Processes

Often, theoretical models present reading as a step-by-step, part-to-whole process where first individual letters are recognized and then combined according to orthographic patterns, translated to corresponding sounds and syllables, recognized as words, associated with word meaning, and then interpreted within sentences to result in comprehension. When viewed as a step-by-step, part-to-whole process, instruction systematically focuses on each discrete skill until some level of mastery and automaticity is achieved. The majority of the focus is placed on more perceptually based skills, such as letter and orthographic pattern recognition, or establishing letter-sound correspondences in the belief that until these processes can occur rapidly and automatically, nothing higher up in the model can work efficiently. The belief is that skillful reading depends critically on the speed and completeness with which words can be identified from their visual forms (Adams, 1990), and efforts must be made to establish this through systematic instruction.

But alternative models of reading have been developed that work very differently. In such models, the many processes involved, from sensory input of letters through orthographic patterns, event structures, and representations of all available knowledge and prior experience can be thought of as existing within an integrated system. An example is the redundancy model of reading developed by Weaver (1994) and discussed in the introductory article of this volume. Within the integrated system, different units simultaneously organize information into patterns that are recognized as words, syntactic structures, orthographic units, event structures, and other elements. These units are interconnected and work in coordination to enable meaning to be derived from speech or from print.

An expanded version of the redundancy model (see Figure 1) will be used in this article to elaborate on the complexity of the reading process and to demonstrate how and why the strategies used within Communicative Reading work to facilitate fluent and meaningful reading. Within the elaborated redundancy model, all of the processing units form a constellation, with each unit connected directly and/or indirectly to all of the others. All of the units within the constellation function simultaneously in an unending stream of information exchange. Anything that happens at one point within the constellation has consequences at all other points (Rumelhart & McClelland, 1986; Seidenberg & McClelland, 1989; Weaver, 1994). As Weaver points out, such a system has the advantage of *redundancy*, or the accessibility of the same information through multiple sources. In a redundancy model, a single processor might be capable of a task such as recognizing a word, but if difficulty is encountered multiple other routes to meaning are available (Weaver, 1994). The resulting system manifests many different ways to achieve fluent reading, as well as many patterns of interaction that can generate miscues or misperceptions.

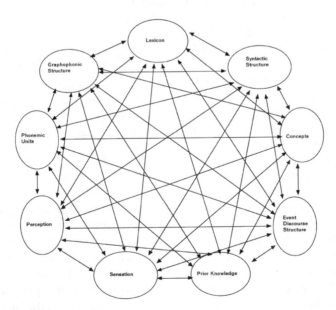

Figure 1. Constellation of perceptual and conceptual processes functioning interactively during reading.

The advantage of a model such as the expanded redundancy model is that it can accommodate findings from traditional reading research, and the findings of the psycholinguistic research of various kinds, especially miscue research into the nature of the reading process (see Pearson & Stephens, and Goodman & Goodman in the research section of this volume).

To facilitate talking about the interactions between the many different types of units working together, in the model they will be arbitrarily grouped into primarily perceptual processors and primarily conceptual processors. Perceptual processors include those units that receive sensory input, and form perceptual categories, phonemes, syllabic units, orthographic units, and word forms. Conceptual processors include units that work to express meaning through words, word order strategies, concepts, event and discourse structures, and prior knowledge. Because of the interconnectedness of the system, perceptual units are formed and function, in part, from input from conceptual units. Likewise, conceptual units are formed and function, in part, from input from perceptual units.

In such an integrated system, a disruption at one point within the constellation affects all other units. For example, suppose a child does not have the word "remote" in her vocabulary when reading, "Her gaze was remote and I began to feel frightened."

When the word "remote" is not in the child's vocabulary, or lexicon, then the entire constellation of processes is affected. For example, the graphophonic component would be left with no basis for choosing among the many possible word patterns. The word could follow the orthographic patterns re-mote (the actual pronunciation), but rem-ote is equally possible, or 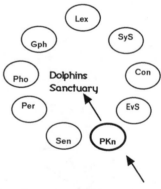 even re-mot-e (as in "coyote"). Thus the absence of information from the lexicon adds a degree of chaos or disruption within perceptual processors, such as orthographic structures or categorical perception. The symptoms of this might include slowed reading rate, repetition of words surrounding this word, or pronunciation of a nonword.

The disruption would also have an effect within conceptual processors. Meaning would have to be derived from surrounding context, so that the sentence could be interpreted to mean anything from a look of intense concentration to a look of distant distraction, or a look of focused anger to a look of unfocused disinterest. Comprehension would begin to become unclear, with a wrong interpretation potentially affecting the meaning imputed to preceding and successive sentences. Monotone reading and poor phrasing are among the possible symptoms of the difficulty.

To resolve the confusion or diminish the chaos, the entire system works together to find a solution (Rumelhart & McClelland, 1986; Seidenberg & McClelland, 1989). When no lexical item is found to correspond with the letters "r-e-m-o-t-e," then all units throughout the system focus on retrieving a word. The units related to syntactic structures activate potential adjectives to fit with the grammar of the sentence at the same time that the conceptual units call up the words that are semantically consistent with a look or gaze. Visual input from the letters provides simultaneous input, searching the lexicon for words that fit the letter and orthographic patterns that the eye actually perceives (Smith, 1988).Event structures use information provided earlier in the story to suggest what type of gaze to expect.

The word that the entire system retrieves is the best fit across all of the contributors in the constellation. For example, the word "removed" might be retrieved, as in "Her gaze was removed," in which case the contributions from the conceptual components reconstructed an interpretation of the perceptual input. It was not that the letters or orthographic patterns were not correctly seen, or not recognized, or not associated with appropriate sound patterns. Rather, the inputs from these units were merely among the many sources of information, and in this case the word retrieved was one that made sense in the context despite failure to fit all of the letter information. For the reader, the actual letter input was integrated into an interpretation made by the entire system, so that the mental representation was a transformation of the visual input.

This type of transformation is consistent with all other aspects of visual processing. For example, the principle of Pragnanz demonstrates that when a partially hidden figure is seen, the system converges on the most familiar and predictable perception that is consistent with the sensory information, thus interpreting something that is meaningful even though different from what is physically there. A circular shape partially covered by a square is perceived as a circle, and a human figure standing behind a table is perceived to have legs. Inputs from the conceptual units of processing are integrated with inputs at the sensory and perceptual units, resulting in interpretations that are different from what is actually seen. The interpretations are those that the system as a whole finds meaningful and predictable in the total context. The brain is quite willing to transform what it sees in the effort to make sense of the environment.

Such a system, where each point within the constellation of processing contributes to reading, can account for both the reading patterns of Christopher and Keisha. In Christopher's case, the inputs from written words are recognized by perceptual units of the constellation, but disruptions of the conceptual processors create only weak or partial interpretations of the information. The instructional solution would be to assist Christopher to add meaning at the lexical, syntactic, conceptual, event structure, and prior knowledge aspects of the constellation during reading in order to integrate this information into the reading process.

Keisha's frequent miscues indicate she struggles to make sense of the text as she reads, with disruptions such as failing to process the syntax correctly, or failure to group letters by the appropriate graphophonic units, creating interactive effects across the system. But when given any information that she can use to organize the fragmented pieces, such as the question, "Why do you think Bobby seemed tired?" she is able to integrate the information productively. The instructional solution would focus on making use of her ability to organize on the basis of meaning. Keisha should be helped to activate conceptual sources of information so that these units can guide word recognition and provide the redundancy of input (i.e., input simultaneously from all conceptual and perceptual sources) needed to recognize words more fluently.

Activating conceptual sources assists poor readers in the word-recognition process. Knowing what to expect the text to say relieves much of the processing load, enabling a guided, rather than a random focus on orthographic form. The multiple sources of conceptual information can integrate with and regulate the structuring of the orthographic patterns of the visual input. Strategies that adults may use to assist children to accomplish this will be described as Communicative Reading Strategies (Norris, 1989, 1991; Norris & Hoffman, 1993). With a little practice and understanding of why children produce errors (miscues) when reading, classroom teachers, special service providers, or parents can learn to effectively engage children in these interactions.

An example of the interactions that typically occur within Communicative Reading is provided in the appendix. The example summarizes the types of difficulties that may be encountered during reading to result in miscues, and then presents a plan and a corresponding script to demonstrate how to conduct scaffolded interactions that facilitate fluent and meaningful reading.

Disruptions and Strategies within the Reading Constellation

Fluent and meaningful reading implies that the reader is efficiently organizing information within and coordinating information between all units within the reading constellation. Conversely, disruptions in processing that can occur during reading result from ineffective organization and/or coordination of information within or between units. Fortunately, processing within such a system is never "all-or-none." The redundancy of the system will assure that when unknown information is encountered, at least partial word recognition and partial comprehension will be derived, although the resulting output may be slow, monotone, poorly phrased, and contain miscues. The more points of difficulty within the constellation, the less able the system is to compensate and the greater the loss in fluency and/or comprehension. An example of the complexities and problems that may be encountered at different points within the constellation during reading will be illustrated using a brief passage (see Passage 1).

Passage 1

Example of text written at a third grade readability level.

James stepped out of the sanctuary kitchen into the deep sand. In his arms he carried a huge bucket of fish. He pulled back the heavy gate of the dolphin's tank, and called "Dinner time!" Now, from the quiet waters arose a chorus of whistles and squeaks, accompanied by the sounds of splashing dorsal and tail fins. The dolphins knew that the one who put on the best show for him would receive the biggest fish as payment.

Reading as a Transactional Process

It is at first glance logical to think of reading as flowing in one direction, from the text to the reader. That is, the text contains information that is transmitted to the reader. But we now understand that reading is a bidirectional, transactional process, meaning the author presupposes that the reader brings a background of knowledge that can be used to interpret the text (Rosenblatt, 1982). Counting on the reader's knowledge, the author selects only those words needed to convey new information. The reader must use the words to invoke all of the appropriate background knowledge needed to read and interpret the author's meaning and intent. The more similar the reader's knowledge is to the author's intended meaning, the more successful the communication, and the easier the reading becomes (Bruce, 1981).

For example, none of the words in the two italicized sentences below are difficult to read or uncommon in their meaning. But the sentences are meaningful only to those readers with a background in neural networks. Readers making an honest effort to understand the following text may find that their reading fluency has decreased and that the rate at which they read is slowed down. *"The redundancy in population codes seems incompatible with the idea of constructing internal representations that minimize the code cost. A fairer measure of code cost is the cost of describing the center of the bump of activity plus the cost of describing how the actual activities of the units depart from the desired smooth bump of activity."* For most of us, the author presupposed far more background knowledge than the reader possesses, making reading and comprehension very difficult. If unfamiliar vocabulary is incorporated, as in *"The norepinephrine stimulates betareceptors, or adrenoceptors that mediate cyclic adenosine monophosphate inside nerve cells,"* the reading problems are compounded.

Prior Knowledge and Reading Challenges

For many children, the difficulties created by lack of sufficient background or prior knowledge are experienced every time they attempt to read. They either lack the appropriate prior knowledge, or are unable to rapidly retrieve relevant information as it is needed. For example, when reading the text profiled in Passage 1, a child lacking prior knowledge of dolphins would not fully understand the significance of stepping into the deep sand. To an informed reader, this suggests that the setting takes place near the ocean, in waters where dolphins are found. Similarly, those with knowledge of dolphins recognize that they eat fish, and that whistles and squeaks are used for dolphin communication. Prior knowledge also would provide the expectation that dolphins would perform playfully for the boy.

Similarly, lack of prior knowledge about a sanctuary would make it more difficult to comprehend that the dolphins were in a protected environment. Without this knowledge, the presence of a gate and a tank would be difficult to interpret. The kitchen would be likely to be thought of as one for humans rather than for dolphins. Because of the importance of background knowledge to all aspects of reading, children experiencing reading difficulty need to be assisted to develop and draw upon relevant background knowledge.

Communicative Reading

Fluent reading that focuses on the sense-making process can be facilitated if children are helped to coordinate the constellation of processes involved. To accomplish this, a communicative approach to reading can be used. Communicative Reading (Norris, 1988, 1991; Norris & Hoffman, 1993) is a method of providing assistance to readers that is consistent with whole language philosophy, but provides more intensive social mediation during reading than is typically provided to readers. Communicative Reading provides a scaffold to readers as they are engaged in reading meaningful, complex text. This scaffold helps the reader to coordinate and integrate the constellation of processes involved in reading so that reading always remains whole, and the reader remains focused on making sense of text.

The role of the teacher or adult reading with the child is to facilitate fluent reading and comprehension. The teacher is therefore called a "facilitator." The facilitator uses strategies to provide a scaffold that assures the child success in the meaning-making process while reading. To facilitate, decisions are made about the properties of the text that are likely to create difficulty for the reader, and then mediation is provided to minimize problems and maximize success. With mediation, the reader is enabled to reconstruct the text and refine knowledge of the reading process.

An explanation of the potential difficulties a child may encounter when reading a text that may result in miscues is presented in Appendix A. This explanation in the appendix continues with a script showing the Communicative Reading interactions that occur between a facilitator and a reader to make use of the redundacy properties of reading and consequently enhance fluent reading. After briefly examining the example in the appendix of the whole process of Communicative Reading, the remainder of this chapter will discuss the purpose and function of various strategies used in Communicative Reading.

Prior Knowledge

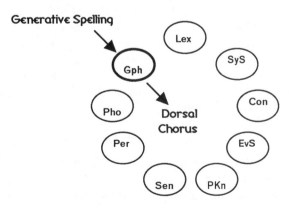

One strategy that a facilitator can use during Communicative Reading to activate prior knowledge is to provide a *Preparatory Set* immediately before a child begins to read a sentence or other meaningful unit of language. The preparatory set assists the child to activate appropriate prior knowledge and to form a tentative hypothesis about what is occurring (interpretations) and what is probably going to happen next (predictions). This type of processing is typical of what good readers do independently during reading (Afflerbach, 1987; Johnston & Afflerbach, 1985; Rumelhart, 1980). Examples of preparatory sets used with Passage 1 might include the following:

> Preparatory Set: James finished preparing the food, so find out where he went next.
> Text: James stepped out of the sanctuary kitchen into the deep sand.
> Preparatory Set: James was holding something for the dolphins.
> Text: In his arms he carried a huge bucket of fish.

Notice that the preparatory sets are conversational statements rather than confrontational questions, as in "Who left the kitchen? Where was the kitchen? What did James step into?" Also notice that the preparatory sets do not usually use the words of the text, as in "Find out where James stepped out of," but rather establish a background for understanding what is happening and predicting what might happen next. Preparatory sets vary in the amount and type of information they provide, depending on the needs of the reader. If the child's background knowledge is minimal, preparatory sets can be more elaborated, providing enough information to establish basic information. For example, the facilitator might say "James was inside the dolphin sanctuary, which is a place where they take care of or protect animals (pointing to beginning of the sentence). He was preparing special food for the dolphins. Find out where he went with the food (pointing to the end of the sentence)."

In Communicative Reading, the facilitator must judge what information is known to the reader, and how much information needs to be provided using a preparatory set. It is important that preparatory sets succinctly set the stage for what is to be read, and that the child then has the opportunity to use this prior knowledge to read and comprehend the sentence. Preparatory sets only enable reading of new information, while the act of reading provides the new information. Thus, preparatory sets are never more than a sentence or two in length and are very different in form and purpose from question/answer discussions.

Event and Discourse Structures

Event structures are general frames, such as knowing how to order food from a restaurant, or what activities take place at a birthday party, or how to wash clothes. Discourse structures are parallel structures of language, governing how to structure a story into a beginning, a middle, and an end, or how to organize a paragraph to start with the main topic and then to add supporting details or procedures. Both event and discourse structures help children organize and interpret information as it is read. These structures enable readers to follow the time sequence in which an event is told, or to understand how one action or event caused something new to happen (Mandler & Johnson, 1977; Nelson, 1991).

The importance of such structures for maintaining the coherence and meaning of an event, and for organizing new experiences according to familiar scripts, is one reason why children who can tell a complete story in the early grades are better readers. Complex, multidimensional events are easier to understand and mentally manipulate if they can be organized according to familiar patterns and symbolized in words (Bruner, 1983). Failure to organize into patterns results in the perception of a loose collection of isolated events that have no order, causality, plan, goal, or coherence. The lack of an organizational frame renders the event unpredictable and poorly remembered.

In our example story, many actions occurred, including leaving the sanctuary, carrying a bucket, pulling a gate, calling to the dolphins, whistling and squeaking, and splashing and swimming. Other actions are implied or anticipated, including watching the dolphins, choosing the best performer, and receiving the fish. Each of these actions must be organized in the correct relationship relative to the others for comprehension to occur and further text to be anticipated. Most of the actions occur in chronological order corresponding with the routine of feeding the dolphins. But causal connections also must be inferred. For example, calling "Dinner time!" caused the dolphins to surface, and anticipating receipt of the biggest fish caused the dolphins to perform.

Many words in the text signal these connections. For example, in the sentence beginning "Now, from the quiet waters . . . ," the word "now"

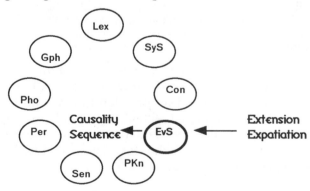

signals that some earlier event (i.e., now that he called "Dinner time!") caused a change in a current event (i.e., the dolphins became excited). Similarly, the time sequences marked by verb tense, and subordinate concepts (e.g., "dinner time" and "biggest fish") throughout the text all need to be interpreted correctly and coordinated during reading (Halliday & Hasan, 1985).

The facilitator can use strategies within Communicative Reading to assist the reader to become aware of the event structure and the words that signal connections and transitions from beginning to end.

Expatiations are one strategy that is useful for this purpose. Expatiation simply involves pointing to a relevant word or phrase while explaining or adding meaning to it (Carnine & Kinder, 1985). Temporal terms or other words that help to structure the story can be targeted for expatiation. The words also may be associated with ideas occurring earlier in the text that add definition or meaning to the word. Examples from Passage 1 include:

> Text: Now, from the quiet waters arose a chorus of whistles and squeaks
> Expatiation: (pointing to the word "now") *Now*, as soon as James called "Dinner time!", *now* that he is by their tank and calling to them, *now* the dolphins begin to get noisy and excited.

Extensions also are effective for helping the reader to link old events to new events. Extensions first present information from the last idea, and then extend that idea to include new, related information (McCormick & Hill, 1984). Extensions often are grammatical, linking the old and new information into a complex sentence using conjunctions (because, when, so, even though, despite, and so forth). They are often used as a type of preparatory set that establishes the new information to be read, while at the same time linking it to the old. The following demonstrates the use of an extension:

> Text: . . . accompanied by the sounds of splashing dorsal and tail fins. The dolphins knew that the one who put on the best show . . .
> Extension: The dolphins were splashing and making noise because ___ (indicating to the child to read to find out).

Expatiations and extensions provide opportunities during reading for the child to learn how words provide organization and order to an event. They both link old information to new information in the temporal, causal, intentional, plan-attempt relationships that are needed to understand the event and discourse structures that provide organization and coherence to the story. They provide a frame for the many concepts that the text presents.

Concepts

Concepts are different from words, but in reading, words combined with other aspects of context must be used to retrieve appropriate concepts. Some concepts are very concrete, such as a concept of a dolphin, including what it looks like, where it lives, and what it eats. Other concepts are more abstract or general, as in "intelligent animals." Some concepts maintain a close relationship to words, such as the word "dolphin" and the concept of a dolphin. Others maintain a more distanced relationship, such as the phrase "doing better," which relies on a context to retrieve the concept that could range from feeling better to getting better grades in school or making more money. Often, the concept has meanings that extend beyond the definitions of the words (Blank, Rose, & Berlin, 1978; Vygotsky, 1986).

In Passage 1, the intended concept of the word "chorus" is different from the word's definitional meaning. The concept is of several dolphins all simultaneously uttering sounds in a manner similar to an organized chorus of singers, rather than an actual chorus. Activation of the wrong concept could lead the reader to believe that a chorus was present and that the chorus and the dolphins were both part of a show or performance.

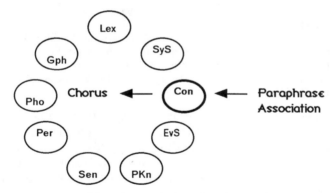

If the concept as retrieved did not make sense in context, the reader would be likely to substitute a word that not only made sense but also maintained some phonetic similarity to the actual word (Goodman, Watson & Burke, 1987). For example, a substitution of "crisis" for "chorus" might occur in this passage, resulting in the reading "Now, from the quiet waters arose a crisis of whistles and squeaks. . . ."

"In Communicative Reading, strategies such as *paraphrase* can be used by the facilitator to establish concepts. Paraphrase can explain the concept in different words or add information needed to understand the concept. Concepts often require recognizing the inferential or implicit meanings communicated by the text. Using paraphrase, the concepts can be put into different words, enabling these expanded meanings to be established (Brown & Palenscar, 1984). The example paraphrase demonstrates how information can be added to deepen the reader's understanding of the concept of "deep sand."

> Text: In his arms he carried a huge bucket of fish.
> Paraphrase: "He carried a huge bucket of fish in his arms. He didn't just hold onto the handle because that huge bucket was heavy, so he had to carry it in his arms."

Associations are a related strategy, but they focus on global ideas or concepts that must be understood relative to the "big picture." For example, the concept of the biggest fish really means the biggest one in the bucket prepared in the sanctuary kitchen. The facilitator uses associations to establish links between new information read, and ideas that had been given in previous pages, paragraphs, or episodes (McCormick & Hill, 1984). Associations help readers understand that meaning crosses the boundaries of sentences, and that earlier events are important to the interpretation of current actions or states. They also are useful for increasing awareness of the structure and order of the event.

> Text: . . . the one who put on the best show for him would receive the biggest fish as payment.
> Association: Yes, remember, James is carrying this huge bucket of fish that he had been preparing in the sanctuary kitchen. And so James knows which is the biggest and he can give it to the dolphin who puts on the best show (pointing to each passage in the text as it is summarized).

Paraphrases and Associations are strategies that enable the facilitator to model or demonstrate how to think during reading in a way that continuously updates understanding of the text. It helps readers to think beyond the most basic level concepts, such as the description of the fish as big, to develop critical or inferential thinking by combining multiple facts to derive an expanded concept. As children are exposed to this more complex way of conceptualizing an action or entity, they begin to contribute their own interpretations during these brief reflections on the passage. They also begin to pay more attention to the relationships between words, or the syntax of the sentences in which the concepts are expressed.

Syntax

Syntax is the use of word order and word endings (i.e., morphology) to communicate meaning. In languages such as English, word order is important, so that "sanctuary kitchen" (the kitchen inside the sanctuary) has a very different meaning than "kitchen sanctuary" (the refuge found in a kitchen). The order of each word in the sentence means something, so when, for example, the prepositional phrase is moved from its typical position at the end of a sentence to its beginning (*In his arms* he carried a huge bucket of fish), it is to place emphasis on the location of the action. Word order allows for very different things (i.e., James, a kitchen, and sand) to be related to each other for purposes of creating a specific image ("James stepped out of the sanctuary kitchen into the deep sand.") Without word order, expression of this type of meaning would be difficult to communicate (Brown, 1973).

The simplest word order strategies follow a noun phrase + verb phrase + noun phrase syntactic pattern (e.g., *James* [NP] *stepped* [VP] *out of the sanctuary kitchen* [NP]). (In transformational grammar, a NP must have a noun, but the noun may be preceded by determiners, such as pronouns or articles, adjectives, and postmodifiers, such as a prepositional phrase). But as more ideas are coordinated into one sentence, the word order strategies begin to become more complicated. Compound sentences link two simple sentences using connecting words such as "and," "but," "so," "because," or "when." The sentence, "He pulled back the heavy gate of the dolphin's tank, *and* called "Dinner time!" is of this sentence type.

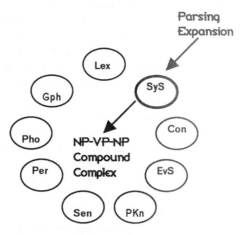

But most sentences are even more complicated, embedding one idea inside of another (e.g., "The one *who put on the best show* would receive the biggest fish"), or adding direct objects and adverbials (e.g., . . . who put on the best show *for him* . . . ; . . . would receive the biggest fish *as payment*.) This entire sentence can itself be embedded within another sentence, as in *"The dolphins knew* that the one who put on the best show for him would receive the biggest fish as payment." When the correct syntactic patterns are not recognized during reading, many word recognition and comprehension errors are likely to result. For example, if the sentence is interpreted according to simple sentence patterns, it could be read as follows: "The dolphins knew that. The one . . . (abandon).

Who put on the best show for him? Wou . . . Wold received the biggest fish as payment." The miscues that result are symptoms of difficulty recognizing and coordinating the many relationships of meaning communicated by syntax (Goodman, Watson, & Burke, 1987). The transformations in word order that occur are a result of the entire constellation organizing the text into alternative patterns that make the greatest amount of sense.

Loban (1979) showed that low-achieving readers enter school with less proficiency in the use of syntax, and that the difference between good and poor readers increases with each grade level through the high school years. Once again, these findings are undoubtedly reciprocal. Children with less syntactic proficiency have greater difficulty successfully reading text, and children who read less have fewer opportunities to learn the complexities of formal, written grammar. Instruction must assist children to process these complexities, to help them learn to understand how word order functions to communicate meaning as they are engaged in reading. The visual input provided by written words is ideal for this purpose, because children can be shown in print how the different parts of the sentence work together.

One strategy used within Communicative Reading to accomplish this goal is called *Parsing*. Parsing means chunking complex sentences into smaller idea units and then using preparatory sets and other strategies to help the reader see how the complex sentence works (Colwell, 1982). For example, the last sentence in Passage 1 might be parsed into the smaller units "The dolphins knew that / the one who put on the best show / for him / would receive the biggest fish / as payment." A facilitative interaction like the following would help to teach this complex sentence.

> Facilitator: (pointing to the clause "the one who put on the best show) [Preparatory Set] "Find out why the dolphins were whistling and splashing."
>
> Child reading: "The one who put on the best show . . ."
>
> Facilitator: [Expatiation] The best show, the most noise and the most exciting splashes and jumps. [Preparatory Set] "And this is who they are showing off for" (pointing to the prepositional phrase "for him")
>
> Child reading: "for him."
>
> Facilitator: [Paraphrase] "Oh, for him, for James, they are each trying to put on the best show for James." [Preparatory Set] "I wonder why? What would the dolphin with the best show get?"
>
> Child reading: "Would receive the biggest fish"
>
> Facilitator: [Preparatory Set] "Find out why that dolphin would get the biggest fish."
>
> Child reading: "As payment."
>
> Facilitator: (pointing to the respective sentences clauses) [Paraphrase] "As payment for putting on the best show for James, one

> dolphin would receive the biggest fish. And I bet they all wanted
> that big fish! [Preparatory Set] Do they know how to get that fish?
> (pointing to the first clause in the sentence.)
>   Child reading: "The dolphins knew that the one who put on the
> best show for him would receive the biggest fish as payment."

Using the visual input provided by the print, accompanied by the mediation provided by the facilitator, the child can begin to see how the word order works to combine many different actions and ideas together into one complex idea. This facilitation enables the child to begin to internalize these complex language patterns.

Expansions are another strategy that enable a child to learn about syntax while reading. Expansions are used to reword the text information into grammatically more complete or complex sentences (Bruner, 1978, 1983). Often these expansions put back into sentences information that has been deleted. English allows speakers to do this in the name of efficiency, but when children are not proficient at using these short cuts, they can easily lose the meaning of the sentence. An example of an expansion follows.

> Text: ... of the dolphin's tank, and called "Dinner time!"
> Expansion: *He* called "Dinner time!" *James* called "Dinner time!"

Word order and a small group of function words, such as articles, prepositions, conjunctions, or helping verbs, establish the relationships of meaning between the content words of a sentence. Omission of function words, poor phrasing, and incorrect interpretations of meaning are common when difficulties are encountered with syntax. The content words are those that we generally think of as vocabulary, and comprise the majority of the words in the language.

Lexicon

The lexicon within the system comprises vocabulary words, including root words and the derivations that result from adding prefixes and suffixes. Vocabulary is one of the best predictors of reading ability, both for comprehension (Nagy & Anderson, 1984) and for word recognition (Stahl & Fairbanks, 1986). Since words are a primary unit of reading, this finding is not surprising. First graders have been estimated to have a vocabulary of up to 26,000 words (Graves, 1986), and up to 3,000–5,000 new words are learned each year in school (White, Graves, & Slater, 1990). Approximately 88,500 different words are encountered in print by ninth grade, so by fifth grade, students reading only a moderate amount encounter up to 24,000 different unknown words per year. While not all of these words are learned from exposure to reading, up to 50 percent of the new vocabulary words acquired are through such incidental reading (Nagy & Herman, 1987).

Not all vocabulary words are equal in complexity. A word such as "sand" is relatively easy to learn through its association with the concrete concept of sand. The concept can be learned by seeing, touching, and walking through sand. The word maps onto the concept; once it has been learned, the word can refer to these perceptions. Other words, such as "accompanied," are more difficult to understand and learn. You cannot see, touch, or walk

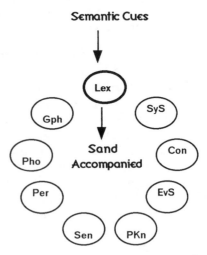

through an "accompanied," although you can be accompanied while walking through sand!

These more abstract words must be learned in a context, because they refer to specific relationships between other concepts. Only through understanding the relationship can the meaning of the word begin to form. Context is so important to learning vocabulary that it is considered one of the primary ways children acquire thousands of new words each year. Only a few of these words are learned through direct instruction, such as looking up the meaning of words in a dictionary, or vocabulary lessons on a worksheet. Most are learned through exposure to them during meaningful talking and reading (Clark, 1987; Nagy & Herman, 1987). In these whole, meaningful contexts, information related to syntax, concepts, event and discourse structures, and previous knowledge provide input regarding meanings that are compatible with the child's ongoing interpretation of the story or text. A single exposure to the word can only create a diffuse, imprecise understanding of the word's meaning, but with repeated exposures in a variety of contexts, the meaning begins to refine (McClelland & Rumelhart, 1986). This is one reason why repeated reading is beneficial when learning about a new topic or studying.

In Communicative Reading, strategies such as Preparatory Sets, Expatiation, and Association can help the child focus on these contextual cues to a word's meaning. Another strategy that can be used is called a *Semantic Cue*. Semantic Cues include the provision of synonyms, definitions, explanations, or related words as that word is encountered during reading (Beck, Perfetti, & McKeown, 1982). For example, the child might not know the word "dorsal" encountered in the sentence " ... accompanied by the sounds of splashing dorsal and tail fins." This may be indicated by a mispronunciation of the word, or by a long pause before reading it, or poor intonation as it is read. The facilitator can point to the word as soon as difficulty is indicated and begin to support the word with meaning.

> Facilitator: (pointing to the word "dorsal") It means the fin on the dolphin's back, the one that you see above the water as it swims. Not the flippers or the tail fin, but the dorsal or fin on the dolphin's back.

This meaning, provided not as an introductory activity before the reading is begun, but rather in context as the child is engaged in the meaning-making process, helps the child to learn how to use context to derive new word meanings. The meaning is supported not only by the explanation or definition, but also by the total context, including the syntax of the surrounding sentence, the concepts of the moving dolphin and the splashing water, the structure of the feeding event, and the prior knowledge about dolphins in general and specifically, the dolphins in the tank. Thus, the word and its meaning are incorporated into a rich, elaborated network of knowledge that will enhance remembering it and using it in new contexts in the future.

Graphophonic Structure

Prior knowledge, event structures, concepts, syntax, and vocabulary are all part of the system of representing information that occurs when we think. These things are internal aspects of processing that occur within the individual. But there has to be a method of exchanging information, or bringing in new input from the environment, and coding information for output so that ideas can be shared with others. In language processes such as listening, speaking, reading, and writing, the method of exchange is related to the sounds that we use to produce and listen to words. In English, the spelling of a word corresponds indirectly to the way that the word is pronounced. Goodman (1993) refers to the relationship between the pronunciation or sound system (phonology), the spelling or graphic system (orthography), and the system that relates the two (phonics) as "graphophonics." Within the reading constellation, the Graphophonic Structures are the necessary bridge between internal representations of meaning and external spoken or written words (Goodman, 1993; Smith, 1988).

Graphophonic structures function in much the same manner as syntactic structures. In syntax, words are combined according to word order strategies to communicate different meanings. Both the words and the word order are important to the message. Graphophonic structures have representations of sounds (phonemes in speech, letters in writing) that are combined according to sound order strategies to communicate different meanings. For example, changing the letter order from ON to NO changes the meaning (or the sound order from "no" to "own"). Thus, both the sounds and the sound order are important to the message.

Just as speakers organize the patterns of word order and speech patterns during development without conscious effort, the patterns of spelling, called orthographic patterns, also are organized. Orthographic patterns include letter combinations that occur together within many words. The more frequently these patterns are encountered, the more familiar and predictable they become, just as the structure of verb phrases or prepositional phrases become familiar and predictable word order patterns. The more integrated these patterns are within the whole system, the easier reading becomes and the more that it works in coordination (Rumelhart & McClelland, 1986; Seidenberg & McClelland, 1989). To the extent that the system is integrated and coordinated, then, word recognition and comprehension work simultaneously. When this integration is not present, then qualitative differences in reading will be manifested, such as those demonstrated by Christopher and Keisha.

When the system is exposed to whole, meaningful reading of stories or text, then all aspects of processing within the constellation contribute to and benefit from this organizational process. For example, research on vocabulary acquisition reveals that not only does context help to establish the patterns of meaning for the new word, but also the related orthographic patterns. The orthographic patterns merge with these aspects of meaning, forming a bond between them (McClelland & Rumelhart, 1986). Attending to the meaning of new words provides simultaneous attention to the spelling pattern of the word, thus helping to establish it as a consistent, recognizable pattern (Whittlesea & Cantwell, 1987). The orthographic pattern learned in this manner remains as recognizable even if its meaning cannot be remembered. Once established, the patterns enable a reader to recognize and pronounce new words that follow similar patterns even if meaning is unknown.

For example, the orthographic patterns in the word "dorsal" overlap with numerous familiar words, including *or, dorm, for, pal, sat, sally,* and so on. A child with a sufficient reading vocabulary to have established these patterns will recognize the word quickly and accurately despite the absence of this word in the lexicon. If context is available, meaning will be attached using cues from multiple aspects of processing. The meaning will in turn strengthen the orthographic patterns of the word as a whole.

The orthographic patterns in the word "chorus" also overlap with familiar words, such as *chore, chosen, us, rust,* and so forth. However, these patterns will result in an incorrect pronunciation of the word (i.e., chor-us or cho-rus). It is only through its integration with context and mean-

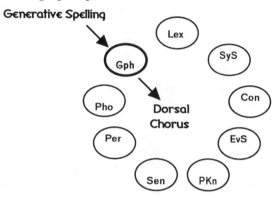

ing that the actual pronunciation can be derived. Thus, orthographic patterns, like all aspects of language, are acquired through their meaningful use. The patterns emerge because of their overlapping occurrence within the same word in different contexts, and within different words that share patterns. The entire system by design expects to find meaningful differences between words distinguished by contrasts between letters, such as "chorus" versus "chores." This is why, when a word as pronounced does not make sense in context, a second pronunciation is often attempted by the reader. Conversely, when an unfamiliar word is read, a meaning that fits the context is hypothesized (Goodman, 1993).

This natural, productive attempt to coordinate meaning and form frequently results in reading miscues as evidenced throughout Keisha's reading: she continuously revises her pronunciations when the words as recognized do not make sense relative to the lexical, syntactic, event, and prior knowledge sources of context. Similarly, Christopher's partial understanding of what was read reflects his continuous attempts to coordinate meaning and form as the words recognized by him do not make sense relative to the lexical, syntactic, event, and prior knowledge sources of context. Reading instruction for both of these children would require the same prescription: to help the reader coordinate and integrate all of the processes simultaneously.

In Communicative Reading, all of the facilitative strategies used by the adult are designed to enhance this integration and coordination. Preparatory Sets, Parsing, and Extensions are designed to activate appropriate conceptual processes, which in turn send activation to perceptual processes. The input from conceptual to perceptual units, occurring simultaneously with input from perceptual to conceptual units maximizes the probability that comprehension and word recognition will be coordinated before misinterpretations or miscues have a chance to occur. If the meaning of the word(s) can be activated before it is attempted, then a strong bond that mutually reinforces both the orthographic patterns and the lexical and conceptual meanings can be established as the actual word is encountered and read in print. The entire system under these circumstances is actively processing the word across multiple units, and all will contribute to and benefit from a coherent reading.

Other strategies, including Expansions, Expatiations, Paraphrase, Associations, and Semantic Cues maximize the probability that the word will be retrieved accurately, particularly when they are provided to address symptoms of difficulty, such as miscues, long pauses, or poor fluency and intonation occur. Facilitation that establishes the correct meaning will assist in retrieving the word and strengthening the bonds with the orthographic patterns. Similarly, supporting the word correctly pronounced but only partially interpreted in context will assist in establishing the bonds between the graphophonic patterns and the multiple other units, such as lexical, syntactic, conceptual, event, and prior knowledge (Afflerbach, 1987).

For those words that remain difficult to recognize even with the support of scaffolding during Communicative Reading, *Generative Spelling* can be used (Norris & Hoffman, 1993). In Generative Spelling, the reader is asked to spell the word so that insights can be gained into the graphophonic patterns that are known versus those that are not established for the word. Phonological and orthographic cues are then provided to enable the child to generate a positive change in the spelling. For example, if the child's generative spelling of the word "whistles" is WESOS, then the facilitator provides feedback, stating "As a reader you've told my mouth to pronounce 'wes-os.' There is a sound near the end of the word (pronounce the word, prolonging and emphasizing the /l/) that I'm expecting to read." With this feedback, the child makes another attempt at spelling the word.

The cycle of generative spelling and facilitative feedback continues until the child discovers the graphophonic patterns. Immediately after the child derives a correct spelling, the context in which it originally occurred is reread, thus integrating the constellation of processing units with the expanded and refined orthographic patterns for that word. Spellings that are phonetically accurate but conventionally incorrect, such as "w" for "wh", can similarly be facilitated. Feedback such as "I can read the word, wistle, but it doesn't look right to me. There is another way to spell the /w/ sound that a reader expects." The story currently being read can be searched for examples of possible alternative spellings if the child does not know the conventional representation. Generative spelling thus increases a reader's awareness of orthographic patterns, and also the phonemes that comprise the sounds of a language.

Phonemic Units

The phonemes in speech or letters in reading represent the minimal meaning-signaling units of sound in a language. Phonemes (in speech) and letters (in reading) occur together within syllables to produce meaningful words. In speech, some phonemes can be produced in isolation, such as the phoneme 's'. But most cannot be produced alone and minimally require a vowel to be pronounced (try to pronounce the sound associated with 'b'—it will always have a vowel attached, as in "ba" or "bi") (Pinker, 1995). Letters, because of their association with sounds, function in the same way. This makes sounding out words letter-by-letter a particularly challenging task, because the units do not match the pronounceable sounds. To be pronounceable, the phonemes must be integrated with the other aspects of processing such as phonological structures and lexical forms (Goodman, 1993).

Although many phonemic units do not have physical reality as isolated pronounceable units, they do have psychological reality. Readers can categorize the /b/ in "bat," "bait," "bet," "bit," and "tab" as the same, and thinking about phonemes in words according to these sound categories provides another bit of information that can be used when reading to figure out unknown or difficult words.

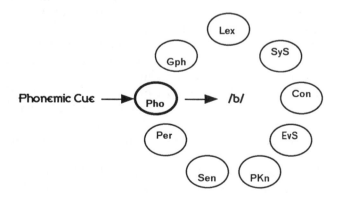

For example, the word "bucket" may be unknown to the child, but words that have many of the same orthographic patterns might exist. The words d*uck*, l*uck*, s*uck*, and t*uck* may be well established. Because the system is integrated across an entire constellation, the Graphophonic Structures would allow for the orthographic pattern to be recognized (e.g., *uck*) and combined with the unknown phoneme (e.g., "b") to create something new that is different from but consistent with the already established or known words (e.g., "buck"). Furthermore, this integration across the system would simultaneously result in activation of the lexicon, where a dictionary of meaningful words that fit this new orthographic pattern are activated, including "buck," "buckle," "buckeye," "buckboard," and "bucket."

The activated lexical entries would be integrating with information about the ending of the word, and with information from units related to concepts, syntactic structures, prior knowledge, and so forth, to find a "best fit" from the available choices. For example, the concept of some object that must be huge yet capable of being held, because of the syntactic and concept input (i.e., . . . *he carried a huge* bucket), eliminates most of the choices based on size, leaving only "buckle" and "bucket" as likely candidates. The context provided by prior knowledge further influences this choice, since buckboards and buckeyes are not generally found near the sandy ocean, and buckets are the most likely of the choices to be carried out of a kitchen. These sources of input all would be activating "bucket" as the best word choice. The choice of "buckets" would in turn activate expectations of which forthcoming letters and orthographic units to anticipate. This anticipatory input, combined with letters and orthographic units present in the print, are simultaneously merged to select the most appropriate word. This integrated contribution across all units enables print to be distorted or incomplete and still be read. Tops of letters, bottoms of letters, initial letters, middle letters, final letters, or all of the vowels may be missing or distorted with very little loss in reading rate or fluency (Weaver, 1994).

Thus, the psychological reality of isolated phonemes operating within the integrated system adds a valuable piece of information to the reading process, even though phonemes do not typically correspond to pronounceable units. They operate most effectively when they are within a context. The more sources of context that are available when they occur, the more they become an efficient part of the reading for meaning process. Conversely, the less integrated they are within the system, the more symptoms of a reading problem will be manifested.

These differences in integration are exemplified by Keisha's substitutions of "went" for "were" versus "trall" for "trail." The first substitution makes sense in context at the points within the constellation including the lexicon, syntactic structure, concepts, and prior knowledge, as well as being consistent with the first letter, or phonemic processing. The graphophonic structure is only partially maintained. In contrast, the substitution of "trall" is consistent only with phonemic and graphophonic processing. A high frequency of this type of error would reflect a more severe reading problem because of the lack of integration with conceptual units, compared with the more productive miscues that reflect greater coordination across the system.

The contribution of phonemic information is useful for reading but not sufficient. Dependence on this level as an entry into reading can lead to misperceptions because of the indirect and inexact relationship between letters and sounds and the unpronounceable nature of single phonemes. The indirect relationship is particularly evident in words such as "dolphin" where the 'p' is really part of a larger orthographic unit and is unrelated to the letter-sound association for the letter 'p'. Reliance on letter-sounds to decode words without interaction from other aspects of language makes the task nearly impossible because of the inability to produce single sounds. The word "stepped" would be sounded out as suh-tuh-e-puh-e-duh, which bears little relationship to the actual word. But inclusion of this aspect of language adds generativity to the system that would be not be present if words could only be processed as indivisible wholes, as in "sight-word" recognition. In Communicative Reading, strategies can be used to enhance this generativity.

In the context of meaningful reading, when words are not recognized they are focused on by pointing to the words while providing semantic cues. If the word still is not recognized, a *Phonemic Cue* can be given to focus attention on the initial sound or sounds. For example, "It's a pail. Something that fish and water can be carried in. It's a bu____." (while pointing to the initial letters of the word "bucket.") Other phonemes, such as final sounds or vowels, also can be focused on by covering up the rest of the word while producing the sound, and then immediately revealing the context of the entire word and sentence. However, various studies of how words are processed suggest it may be even more helpful to point to a vowel and any following (final) consonants as a unit (see Moustafa, this volume). Phonemic cues also are used with high frequency in the context of Generative Spelling.

For beginning readers, text that is easy to read at all points within the reading constellation and that is accompanied by pictures that overlap in meaning with the print is used. For example, a picture of a cow in a field might be accompanied by the text "Bess was a cow. She lived on a farm." Preparatory sets and other strategies can enable even nonreaders who do not know the alphabet, orthographic patterns, or phonemes to "read" the text. The reader can then be asked to find a word such as "cow," while the facilitator explains why the selected word is or is not the targeted word, based on first letters. The child is then encouraged to ask about or identify other letters seen in the text, followed by feedback such as "That word tells my mouth to say 'farm.' I know because this letter (pointing to 'f') tells my mouth to say "fffarm" (prolonging and emphasizing the 'f'). Norris and Hoffman (1994) demonstrated that kindergarten children introduced to the alphabet and letter-sound associations in this manner acquired as much alphabet knowledge as a comparison group that was taught each letter intensively. However, the group provided contextualized had the advantage of learning to perform significantly better in measures of reading for meaning.

Thus, attention to individual letters and corresponding phonemes during reading is an inherent and useful part of the reading process. Fortunately, phonemic knowledge appears to be as easily or more easily acquired when focused on within a context than it is when specifically isolated and taught directly. The advantage of facilitating learning of this information within a context is that it is, from the beginning, an integrated and coordinated part of the whole constellation, and doesn't have to be learned first and then generalized across many aspects of language processing. So learning phonemic information is interrelated with learning at all other components of the constellation. It also is closely associated with what is received and perceived by the sensory system.

Perception and Sensation

The sensory system, including vision for letters and audition for sound, enables the signals from the environment to function as input to the child during listening and reading. These highly refined sensory systems detect different frequencies and amplitudes of sound and visual waves, and transmit this information to our brains through auditory and optic nerves. The brain then categorizes this information at the level of perception.

Perceptions include categorization of information that is used to interpret sensory input. For example, sounds can be perceived as the same or different on the basis of features present in the input. The /s/ and /z/ sound are very similar to each other because both are produced with a continuous stream of airflow, and both are produced with the tongue near the front and top of the mouth. They differ only on the basis of voicing: /z/ is produced with vibration through the larynx while /s/

is absent of voicing. The brain uses these slight differences in the features of sounds to distinguish between them.

Letters function similarly. They, too, are perceived as the same or different on the basis of features. The letters C and O differ on the feature of an open versus a closed curve. In both the auditory and the visual system, newborn infants respond to differences in sensory input that are distinctive on the basis of a single feature.

But these perceptions are not just governed by sensory input. They become organized through development by meaning and function. Those sounds or shapes that are related to language form perceptual categories consistent with the language. For example, young infants distinguish among many of the sounds used in a variety of languages during the first six months of life. But as they near their first birthday, they increasingly begin to reorganize their phonetic categories to be consistent with the language they hear and produce. If no two words in a language differ from each other on the basis of a sound feature distinction, then those two variations of the sound are considered to be allophones of the same sound. In English, there are no two words that differ in meaning on the basis of a "t" produced with the tongue on the back of the teeth versus a "t" on the roof of the mouth. For English speakers, differences in the sound do not form different perceptual categories.

This means that perception is integrated and coordinated with all of the other components of language and meaning throughout the constellation. Perception is influenced by the phonemes of the language; what is considered a phoneme is based on meaningful word differences within the lexicon; understanding meaningful differences in words depends on syntactic, conceptual, event, discourse, and other aspects of context. Once again we see that the entire system functions as an integrated, coordinated whole.

In Communicative Reading, the strategy of *Modeling Fluent Reading* can help provide the reader with cues useful in perceiving these differences. Cues in intonation, stress, pause, and pitch provide the reader with a scaffold into making these meaningful distinctions. Looking at the print while a model of fluent reading is provided assists the reader to make parallel discriminations of meaningfully different letters. Especially for beginning readers or readers exhibiting great difficulty integrating the reading process, this modeling can provide important assistance. Many teachers of whole language have discovered the usefulness of this strategy in their work with readers at all ability levels.

> Text: James stepped out of the sanctuary kitchen . . .
> Child reading: "James stepped out of the san . . . sans . . . sanstery . . ."

Facilitator: (pointing to word "sanctuary") "The sanctuary, James stepped out of the sanctuary kitchen."

Whole Language: A Continuum of Instructional Approaches

The model that we are imagining is an extrapolation of the principles of connectionist networks, or models that attempt to function similarly to the neural networks of the brain (Rumelhart & McClelland, 1986; Seidenberg & McClelland, 1989). The integrated model we propose, for purpose of our imaginings, will borrow the principles and take them beyond what these connectionist networks are currently capable of actually performing.

This integrated view is somewhat like the relationship between land, air, and water, where each is affected by and affects changes in the others. Evaporation from the water creates rising water vapor because of the direct connection to warm air, while water vapor in the air forms clouds that return the water to the earth, and so forth. One component (i.e., "air") is not held in suspension until the other completes its processing. Rather, at each moment in time, the land, air, and water are all in states of activity and all maintain a level of balance and coordination. The integration remains constant, while the dynamics within the system undergo continuous change. Thus, the smallest plant giving off the smallest amount of water through transpiration has an effect on the entire system. Different weather patterns, like the contrasting reading patterns of Christopher and Keisha, are symptoms or manifestations of the differences in the balance and coordination among the many different components and not the result of separate systems or discrete components.

Whole Language is a philosophy, or a set of beliefs about language and how it is acquired in both oral and written modes. According to this philosophy, language learning is a process that occurs as children participate in the meaningful use of language. As the constellation model of reading in this article describes, all of the cueing systems of language are always simultaneously present and interacting in any instance of language use. Language use occurs in a situation, functioning as a tool to make sense of that situation. The situation is critical to meaning-making, and so real, purposeful learning situations that pursue the learner's interests and questions are the best context for learning (Goodman, 1986).

Clearly, whole language is not a methodology or instructional approach. Rather, a wide range of learning approaches are consistent with whole language philosophy. For example, reading stories or recountings of experiences using dictated writing is a common practice within whole language classrooms (Calkins, 1986). Shared book reading experiences that replicate many interactive characteristics of parent-child storybook reading for use with young, beginning readers also is consistent (Holdaway, 1979). Silent reading, reading aloud to children, literature study, and journals are other methods that adhere to whole language principles (Manning & Manning, 1989).

Each of these reading approaches differs in the type and degree of social mediation provided by the facilitator. Methods such as shared book reading or dictated writing are highly scaffolded, with the adult initially modeling fluent reading of the text, while children participate at the level of imitation and oral discussion. At the other end of the continuum, silent reading is conducted as an interaction between the reader and the author, without the support of a facilitator. Communicative Reading is another approach that adheres to whole language philosophy, providing social mediation at a level midway between. The scaffolding enables the reader to participate more independently when reading much more complex text than does shared book reading, but with greater assistance than is afforded by silent reading. The amount and type of scaffolding is reader-determined, in the sense that the teacher or facilitator judges at each moment why miscues or difficulty is encountered and how much assistance to provide. As children internalize and integrate the patterns of language at all points within the constellation, the amount of scaffolding is reduced.

In a series of dissertation and independent studies, Communicative Reading has been shown to result in significantly greater gains in word recognition and comprehension compared with other instructional methods for children at-risk because of low socioeconomic status (Badon, 1993); children with language and reading delays (Michaelson, 1995), low-achieving children in the regular classroom (Hernandez, 1989) or pull-out programs (Higgins, 1995), and for adult readers in basic adult education programs (Reichmuth, 1996). Gains in word recognition and comprehension have been obtained in as few as six weeks or thirty hours of instruction.

Communicative Reading enables children to successfully read, using their own abilities while refining and expanding their language and enriching their conceptual understanding. It immerses children in the process of constructing meaning from meaningful discourse. It enables children to engage in the meaning-making process, using text at a more complex and difficult reading level than the child could independently coordinate, working near the upper limits of the child's "zone of proximal development" (Vygotsky, 1986). These are all goals of whole language.

Whole language philosophy has provided us with guiding principles that enable us to understand how children learn. We are just
beginning to understand the implications and possibilities. Whole language provides us with an exciting future as we learn more about how
to apply the philosophy in different ways to meet the needs of different learners. Understanding the constellation of language abilities and
how to help children integrate and coordinate them during meaningful reading is one more step in this process. It provides a tool for
thinking about reading as an integrated whole and lends insights into
how to help children as they actively construct and integrate the constellation for themselves.

As all whole language teachers understand, children can learn from
a whole, meaningful context if they just have a little help. As we learn
more about the language learning process from beginning to advanced
stages of reading, we will learn better how to provide that help in a
way that meets the needs of all learners.

Appendix: Communicative Reading Strategies: Potential Difficulties and Script of Interactions

> Sentence 1:   James stepped out of the sanctuary kitchen into the deep sand.

Likely Miscues

- stepped out of the ["out of" is a two-word prepositional phrase,
  which is relatively uncommon. Since a noun phrase usually occurs
  after the first preposition, "of" is likely to be omitted or misread.]

- *sanctuary* [is an uncommon, low-frequency word, and has relatively uncommon orthographic and phonological patterns. Ordinarily it functions as a noun, but in this sentence it is an adjective.
  None of the cuing systems are likely to easily recognize this word
  and miscues are likely.]

- *kitchen* into the [by the time the word "kitchen" is reached, the
  meaning and sense of the sentence are likely to be lost. "Kitchen"
  may be easily recognized, but "kitchen into" doesn't make sense
  if the reader is trying to construct the meaning, starting with this
  word. Poor phrasing and odd intonation are possible.]

- prepositional phrase + prepositional phrase [the verb "stepped"
  is followed by two prepositional phrases, both addressing where

James stepped, requiring the coordination of two locations for one action. Poor phrasing and hesitations may result.]

Facilitation Plan

Parse the sentence by providing a *preparatory set* for the sentence up through the first prepositional phrase. Later point to the second phrase and provide a second preparatory set. If "sanctuary" is not recognized, begin by providing *semantic cues*, followed by *modeling* of the word in context if needed. Provide *expatiations* or *paraphrases* to clarify and reinforce difficult concepts after the sentence is read.

Facilitator: (pointing to the sentence) [Preparatory Set] "Find out what room James left."

Child reading: "James stepped out . . . of the san . . san

Facilitator: (pointing to "sanctuary") [Semantic Cues] "Its a place where it is safe, where animals are protected, a animal refuge or shelter."

Child reading: "the san-tur-y, san-tre-ry"

Facilitator: [Modeling] "The *sanctuary* (pointing to word in text and stressing it in speech), the safe place, this shelter called a *sanctuary*, the place where they were making food for the dolphins."

Child reading: "the sanctuary kitchen"

Facilitator: [Paraphrase] "So he was in the kitchen of the sanctuary making food, [Preparatory Set, Extension] and he stepped out of the kitchen and went outside ___"

Child reading: "into the deep sand."

Facilitator: [Expatiation] "His feet sank right into that deep sand, and that makes it hard to walk because he has to lift his feet through the sand."

Child: [association] "Yeah, cuz he's going outside to see the dolphins!"

Sentence 2: In his arms he carried a huge bucket of fish.

Likely Miscues

- *In his arms* [is a prepositional phrase, which typically occurs after the verb and ends a sentence. For emphasis, they can be moved to other sentence positions, but may be unexpected and result in miscues or inappropriate phrasing.]
- *he* ["he" is the actual subject of the sentence, but is juxtaposed next to the noun phrase from the prepositional phrase, creating

potential ambiguity. Both "he" and "his" are pronouns that function as cohesive ties, or words that obtain their meaning by referring to information outside of the sentence. The reader must
associate the pronouns with "James" to interpret the sentence.
Loss of comprehension, and word or phrase repetitions are likely.]

- *huge* [is a low-frequency word, with graphophonemic patterns in
  which the letter "g" takes on the same pronunciation as the letter
  "j." Consequently, typical "sounding out" strategies will result in
  an incorrect word derivation.]

Facilitation Plan

Parse the sentence to begin with the subject instead of the prepositional phrase. Later, extend the idea to include the prepositional
phrase. Build comprehension and associate the pronoun "he" with
its referent by including an *extension* in the *preparatory set*. Provide
semantic cues if difficulty is encountered on any word. Establish *associations* between events in the current and previous sentence to
increase comprehension.

Facilitator: (pointing to the sentence subject, indicating to begin reading with the word "he") [Preparatory Set-Extension] "I wonder what
James was taking out of the kitchen?"

Child reading: "he carried a hug . . hugge . . ."

Facilitator: (pointing to word "huge") [Semantic Cues] "It means
really big, enormous, something very large and heavy that he's trying
to carry."

Child reading: "he carried a huge . . . bucket of fish" (flat intonation).

Facilitator: [Association] "I see, he prepared a huge bucket of fish in
the kitchen, and now he is carrying it outside. It must be hard to carry
something that huge through the deep sand!" [Preparatory Set] "Find
out how he carried that huge bucket."

Child reading: "In his arms, James . . . he carried a huge bucket of fish."

Facilitator: (pointing to the word "he") [Association] "Right, *he*,
James, first *he* prepared the fish, and then *he*, James, he carried it outside in *his* arms."

Child: [Association] "And his feet are sinking in the sand because
the bucket is so heavy."

Facilitator: [Evaluation] "James sure is a hard worker, isn't he?"

> Sentence 3: He pulled back the heavy gate of the dolphin's tank,
> and called "Dinner time!"

Likely Miscues

- *He* ["He" functions as a cohesive tie, so the subject of the sentence must be identified from the referent given two sentences earlier.]
- pulled *back* ["back" is part of the verb phrase, called a particle, and functions differently from a preposition in this sentence (it can be reworded as "He pulled the heavy gate back" or even "He pulled the heavy gate of the dolphin's tank back.")]
- of the dolphin's tank [this prepositional phrase functions as an adverbial, describing where the heavy gate is located. The relationships between the verb, its object, and the adverbial must be maintained.]
- and (he) called "Dinner time!" [The noun phrase "he" is deleted from the surface structure of the sentence but must be understood by the reader. The roles of the narrator, telling who called the dolphins, and James actually speaking the words must be interpreted from punctuation cues.]

Facilitation Plan

Parse the sentence using a series of *preparatory sets*. Use *paraphrase* to clarify the meaning of the particle, and *expansion* to replace the subject of the final clause. *Expatiations* can be used to add explanation to the sequence of actions and relationships described within the sentence. *Associations* can establish the relationship between dinner time and the bucket of fish, if needed.

Facilitator: [Preparatory Set] "Find out where he went next with the bucket of fish."

Child reading: "He pulled . . . back the heavy gate" (incorrect phrasing)

Facilitator: [Paraphrase] "Right, he pulled back the gate, he pulled that heavy gate back to open it." [Extension] "Which gate was that?"

Child reading: "the heavy gate of the dolphin's tank."

Facilitator: [Association] "James must be strong to pull back a heavy gate while carrying that huge bucket!" [Preparatory Set] "As soon as he had the gate open, this is what he said."

Child reading: "and called dinner time." (incorrect phrasing, monotone)

Facilitator: [Expatiation] "Yes, he yelled, or called something to the dolphins. He wants them to know he is bringing them fish, so what did he yell or call to him?" (pointing to words "Dinner time!")

Child reading: "Dinner time!"

Facilitator: [Modeling fluent reading] "He called, 'Dinner time!'" [Expatiation] He's telling the dolphins to "Come and get it! Come get your dinner! Dinner time!"

Child reading: "and called, "Dinner time!" Child: [Expatiation] "Yum yum, fish!"

Sentence 4: Now, from the quiet waters arose a chorus of whistles and squeaks, accompanied by the sounds of splashing dorsal and tail fins.

Likely Miscues

- *Now,* ["Now" functions cohesively, referring to a time frame established by previous events (now that the gate is open and James called "Dinner time.") Furthermore, "now" is an adverb that is placed before the noun phrase of the sentence, resulting in syntactic complexity.]

- from the quiet waters [this prepositional phrase also occurs prior to the noun phrase. It actually is an adverbial modifying the verb "arose." (*the chorus arose from the quiet waters*)]

- (there) arose ["there" is a pronoun that operates as a function word in this context to provide the noun phrase of the sentence. It is deleted from the surface structure, and its absence can result in poor phrasing, or a nonsensical interpretation such as "waters arose a chorus."]

- (that were) accompanied [this represents an embedded clause that is usually signaled by the pronoun "that" to mark the subordination of ideas. Its deletion from the surface structure may result in rewording of the sentence to maintain grammatical and semantic sense, as in "whistles and squeaks accompanied (by) the sounds."]

- accompanied, dorsal [these vocabulary words may not be known, and the complexity of the context will make it difficult to infer a meaning.]

Facilitation Plan

Parse the sentence, using *Paraphrase* to reorder it and help the child see the subject-verb-object relationships present within the complex sentence. Use Extensions to establish the relationships of meaning between the clauses. Provide *Semantic_Cues* when needed, and *Model Fluent Reading* to provide multisensory cues to the meaning and structure of the complex sentence. For difficult words, engage the child in *Generative Spelling* to establish the graphophonemic patterns.

Facilitator: (pointing to first prepositional phrase) [Preparatory Set] "This describes the water in the tank as he opened the gate."

Child reading: "From the quiet waters . . ."

Facilitator: [Extension] "But it's not quiet anymore!"

Child reading: "arout . . . arrose a chor . . . chores of whistles and squeaks"

Facilitator: [Expatiation] (pointing to word "chorus") "Right, a chorus, like dolphins singing in a group, in a chorus, all of them were whistling and squeaking at the same time, like a chorus." [Expatiation] (pointing to word "arose") "And that chorus arose, it seemed to rise out of the quiet water, it was a surprise because it was quiet and then the whole chorus of noise arose almost out of nowhere."

Facilitator: [Preparatory Set] "But the dolphins weren't just making noise with their voices. Find out how else they were making noise."

Child reading: "accom . . . accom-panned by the sounds of . . . of sp . . . spash . . ."

Facilitator: "They are making sounds in the water by hitting the water with their fins, water is going everywhere because they are ____ [Phonemic Cue] "spl____"

Child reading: "splash . . . splashing dor-sale and tail fins."

Facilitator: [Model Fluent Reading] "Right, the sounds of splashing dorsal and tail fins." [Expatiation] "The dorsal fins on their backs, that they use for balance, the back dorsal fins and their tail fins." [Paraphrase] "The sounds made by splashing with their dorsal and tail fins are used to accompany the whistles and squeaks, so the water went from being quiet to sounding like a chorus!"

Facilitator: [Preparatory Set] (pointing to word "Now") "When did all of this noise begin?"

Child reading: "Now"

Facilitator: [Association] "Now, now that the boy has opened the gate, and now that he has called "Dinner time!" Now, from the quiet waters all of the dolphins arose and started to make all of this noise. Tell me what happened by reading this to me."

Child reading: "Now, from the quiet waters arose a chor . . . chorus of whistles and squeaks, accomplish, accumpo . . . by the sounds of splashing dorsal and tail fins."

Facilitator: [Generative Spelling] "If you were going to write a sentence with the word "accompanied" how would you spell it?"

Child: a c e m n e d

Facilitator: "First, let's figure out how many syllables we hear— ac/com/pa/nied." (repeated several times, slowly)

Child: "Four."

Facilitator: "What sounds do you hear in the first syllable" (Pronounce with overemphasis. Follow the procedure for each syllable.)

Child: a ka pe need

Facilitator: (focus on second syllable) "What sound do you hear at the end? [child writes /m/] Can you think of another letter that makes the /k/ sound?" [child writes /cam/] "Now you have spelled 'cam' but you need to get me to say 'com' when I read. What vowel could you use to change the word from 'cam' to 'com'?"

Child: a com pe need

Facilitator: "I can read this word—acompeneed—but it does not look like a reader expects it to look. In the third syllable can you think of another vowel that makes a sound that fits? [continue to help the child discover the graphophonemic patterns of the word.]

Facilitator: "That looks right to me. Tell me what accompanied the whistles and squeaks by reading the idea to me."

Child: "Now, from the quiet waters arose a chorus of whistles and squeaks, accompanied by the sounds of splashing dorsal and tail fins."

References

Adams, M.J. (1990). *Beginning to read: Thinking and learning about print.* Cambridge, MA: MIT Press.

Afflerbach, P. (1987). How are main idea statements constructed? Watch the experts. *Journal of Reading, 30* (6), 512–518.

Badon, L. (1993). *Comparison of word recognition and story retelling under conditions of contextualized versus decontextualized reading events in at-risk readers.*

Beck, I. L., Perfetti, C. A., & McKeown, M. G. (1982). Effects of long-term vocabulary instruction on lexical access and reading comprehension. *Journal of Educational Psychology, 74,* 506–521.

Blank, M., Rose, S., & Berlin, L. (1978). *The language of learning: The preschool years*. New York: Grune & Stratton.

Brown, R. (1973). A first language: The early stages. Cambridge, MA: Harvard University Press.

Brown, A. L. & Palinscar, A. S. (1984). Inducing strategic learning from texts by means of informed, self-control training. *Topics in Learning and Learning Disabilities, 2*, 1–17.

Bruce, B. (1981). A social interaction model of reading. *Discourse Processes, 4*, 273–309.

Bruner, J. S. (1983). *Child's talk*. New York: Norton.

Bruner, J. S. (1978). Learning how to do things with words. In J.A. Bruner & R.A. Garton (Eds.), *Human growth and development*. Oxford University Press.

Calkins, L. M. (1986). *The art of teaching writing*. Portsmouth, NH: Heinemann.

Carnine, D., and Kinder, D. (1985). Teaching low-performing students to apply generative and schema strategies to narrative and expository material. *Remediation and Special Education, 6*, 20–30.

Clark, E. V. (1987). The principle of contrast: A constraint on language acquisition. In B. MacWhinney (Ed.) *Mechanisms of language acquisition*. Hillsdale, NJ: Lawrence Erlbaum.

Colwell, C. G. (1982). Paragraph processing: A direct-functional-interactive model. *Reading Improvement, 19*, 13–24.

Goodman, K. S. (1985). Transactional psycholinguistic model: Unity in reading. In H. Singer & R. B. Ruddell (Eds.), *Theoretical models and processes of reading* (pp. 813–840). Newark, DE: International Reading Association.

Goodman, K. S. (1986). *What's whole in whole language?* Portsmouth, NH: Heinemann.

Goodman, K. S. (1993). *Phonics Phacts*. Portsmouth, NH: Heinemann.

Goodman, Y. M., Watson, D. J., and Burke, C. L. (1987). *Reading miscue inventory: Alternative procedures*. New York: Richard C. Owen.

Graves, M. F. (1986). Vocabulary learning and instruction. In E. Z. Rothkopf (Ed.) *Review of research in education, 13* (pp.49–89). Washington: American Educational Research Association.

Halliday, M. A. K., & Hasan, R. (1976). *Cohesion in English*. London: Longman Group.

Hernandez, S. N. (1989). *Effects of communicative reading strategies on the literacy behaviors of third grade poor readers*. Unpublished doctoral dissertation, Louisiana State University.

Higgins, K. (1995). Comparison of four scaffolding conditions for their effects on reading fluency and comprehension. Independent Study, Louisiana State University.

Holdaway, D. (1979). *Foundations of literacy*. Portsmouth, NH: Heinemann.

Hoffman, P. R., & Norris, J. A. (1994). Whole language and collaboration work: Evidence from an at-risk kindergarten. *Journal of Childhood Communication Disorders, 16*, 41–48.

Johnston, P., & Afflerbach, P. (1985). The process of constructing main ideas from text. *Cognition and Instruction, 2*, 207–232.

Loban, W. (1976). *Language development: Kindergarten through grade twelve.* Urbana, IL: National Council of Teachers of English.

Mandler, J. M., & Johnson, N. S. (1977). Rememberance of things parsed: Story structure and recall. *Cognitive Psychology, 9,* 111–151.

Manning, G., & Manning, M. (Eds). (1989). Whole language: *Beliefs and practices, K–8.* Washington, D.C.: National Education Association.

McCormick, S., & Hill, D. S. (1984). An analysis of the effects of two procedures for increasing disabled readers' inferencing skills. *Journal of Educational Research, 77,* 219–226.

Michaelson, M. (1995). The efficacy of communicative reading strategies with low achieving beginning readers. Doctoral Dissertation, Louisiana State University.

Nagy, W. E., & Anderson, R. C. (1984). How many words are there in printed school English? *Reading Research Quarterly, 19,* 303–330.

Nagy, W. E. (1988). *Teaching vocabulary to improve reading comprehension.* Newark, DE: International Reading Association.

Nagy, W. E. & Herman, P. A. (1987). Breadth and depth of vocabulary knowledge: Implications for acquisition and instruction. In M.G. McKeown & M.E. Curtiss (Eds.) *The nature of vocabulary acquisition.* Hillsdale, NJ: Lawrence Erlbaum.

Nelson, K. (1991). Event knowledge and the development of language functions. In J. Miller (Ed.), Research on child language disorders: A decade of progress (pp. 125–142). Austin, TX: ProEd.

Norris, J. A. (1988). Using communication strategies to enhance reading acquisition. *The Reading Teacher, 41,* 21–26.

Norris, J. (1989). Providing language remediation in the classroom: An integrated language-to-reading intervention method. *Language, Speech & Hearing Services in Schools, 20,* 205–219.

Norris, J. (1991). From frog to prince: Using written language as a context for language learning. *Topics in Language Disorders, 12*(1), 1–6.

Norris, J. A. & Hoffman, P. R. (1993). *Whole language intervention for school-age children.* San Diego, CA: Singular Publishing.

Pinker, S. (1995). *The language instinct: How the mind creates language.* New York: HarperPerennial.

Reichmuth, S. (1996). Efficacy of Communicative Reading Strategies as an instructional strategy for adult low-ability readers. Unpublished Dissertation, Louisiana State University.

Rosenblatt, L. M. (1982). The literary transaction: Evocation and response. *Theory Into Practice, 21,* 268–277.

Rumelhart, D. (1980). Schemata: The building blocks of cognition. *Theoretical issues in reading comprehension.* Hillsdale, NJ: Erlbaum.

Rumelhart, D. E., & McClelland, J. L. (1986). *Parallel distributed processing: Explorations in the microstructures of cognition.* Cambridge, MA: The MIT Press.

Seidenberg, M. S., & McClelland, J. L. (1989). A distributed, developmental model of word recognition and naming. *Psychological Review.*

Smith, F. (1988). *Understanding reading.* Hillsdale, NJ: Lawrence Erlbaum.

Stahl, S. A., & Fairbanks, M. M. (1986). The effects of vocabulary instruction: A model-based meta-analysis. *Review of Educational Research, 56*, 72–110.

Straw, S. B. (1990). Reading and response to literature: Transactionalizing instruction. In S. Hynds & D. L. Rubin (Eds.), *Perspectives on talk and learning* (pp. 129–148). Urbana, IL: National Council of Teachers of English.

Vygotsky, L. (1986). *Thought and language*. Cambridge, MA: MIT Press.

Weaver, C. (1994). *Reading process and practice: From socio-psycholinguistics to whole language* (2nd Ed.). Portsmouth, NH: Heinemann.

White, T. G., Graves, M. F., & Slater, W. H. (1989). Growth of reading vocabulary in diverse elementary schools. *Journal of Educational Psychology, 82*, 281–290.

Whittlesea, B. W. A., & Cantwell, A. L. (1987). Enduring influence of the purpose of experiences: Encoding-retrieval interactins in word and pseudoword perception. *Memory and Cognition, 15*, 465–472.

33 More on the Schools We Have versus the Schools We Need

Richard L. Allington
University at Albany

Allington begins by explaining that "The schools we have are better at sorting and labeling at-risk children than at accelerating their academic development." After discussing why this happens, Allington indicates what does *not* work: an extra year before or after kindergarten ("the gift of time"); retaining children; tracking children and giving them slow-it-down instruction; sorting them into "ability" groups and then giving them isolated skills instruction. Of particular concern is the kind of instruction typically given to "at risk" readers—instruction that too often perpetuates their continued use of ineffective reading strategies and continued low achievement, which prevents them from becoming fully literate. (See Strickland, this volume.) A steady diet of books too difficult for such children to read easily is another hampering factor, Allington explains.

The second and major part of this article, taken directly from Allington and Cunningham's *Schools That Work: Where All Children Read and Write* (1996)," focuses on some possible ways of creating "safe" blocks of classroom instructional time, plus "extended time plans," including before and after school programs (with individualized scheduling for support personnel), Saturday school, and summer school. They see instruction of at-risk children as first and foremost the responsibility of the classroom teacher, not of support personnel. The school should enable support personnel to support good classroom teaching, with alternative scheduling as needed. The bottom line is that at-risk and labeled students must engage in rich and enriched literacy experiences, not be kept busy with "basic skills" work; they must have accelerated instruction, more time, and more support—not a "slow-it-down" curriculum that maintains or increases the gap between them and their more fortunate peers.

(Drawn in part from Richard L. Allington and Patricia M. Cunningham, *Schools That Work: Where All Children Read and Write.* Harper Collins, 1996, pp. 110–115. Reprinted with permission)

Whether by accident or intention, our schools have been better at perpetuating than alleviating the inequalities that exist among children when they begin school. Or in other words, the schools we have are better at sorting and labeling at-risk children than at accelerating their academic development so they can catch up with their more fortunate peers (see Allington, 1994, reprinted in the research section of this volume).

Why is this? Why have we been better at perpetuating the low achievement of "at-risk" children than at educating them to take their place alongside those who come from mainstream middle class families? Most teachers and administrators sincerely want to provide an equal education for all children. However, teachers and administrators are simply hampered by the conventional wisdom and traditions of schooling that drive the design of programs, and often by a scarcity of resources.

In "The Schools We Have. The Schools We Need" (Chapter 18 in *Reconsidering a Balanced Approach to Reading*), I have discussed the conventional wisdom of schooling and noted several confusions and faulty assumptions that have blinded educators to the effects of their educational policies and practices. Probably the most pernicious of these is the belief that we must "slow it down and make it simple" for children of poverty and others labeled "at risk," learning disabled, and so forth. This assumption puts children at risk even more than their family's socioeconomic status or their being labeled as deficient in some way. Instead of a slow-it-down curriculum, these children need an accelerated and rich literacy program if they are to catch up with their peers.

What Doesn't Work

The evidence shows overwhelmingly that several things the educational system has been doing are not very successful: these pracitces do not really work. They include:

- Giving children the "gift of time" by holding them back from entering kindergarten, or by putting them in developmental kindergartens or in transitional-grade classes between kindergarten and first grade. The reason these have not worked very well is that the children have not usually been given what they need: the rich exposure to print and literacy that many other children experience in the home, and the opportunity to engage in many guided and independent reading and writing events. Or to put it another way, the special "gift of time" classes have often denied children involvement in the very literacy learning activities that they have not been getting at home, but need even more intensively in order to catch up with more advantaged peers.

- More and more children have been retained in recent years, partly as a result of state laws mandating minimum standards and assessment—yet retention in grade also increases the risk that children face in our schools (Allington & McGill-Franzen, 1995). While retained children commonly do better during the retention year, they again fall behind in the years to come. In fact, research suggests that retained children perform more poorly than they would if they had been promoted without repeating a grade (Shepard & Smith, 1989, 1990). Almost any alternative is more effective than retention. Even social promotion has fewer negative effects on children than retention, though it does little to address the problem of low achievement.

- Tracking does not get at-risk children back on track. In fact, tracking may actually increase the risk for children placed in the bottom tracks. Children in the bottom track achieve less than similar children placed in untracked classes (Gamoran, 1986). Why? Primarily because children placed in the low tracks are simply taught less: they are offered a slow-it-down curriculum. The problem with tracking is that it purposely fosters teaching that produces low achievement. Tracking programs assume that some children cannot learn and then create instructional programs that deliver that very result.

- "Ability" grouping has the same effect as tracking. In reading, for example, we have typically created groups—often as early as kindergarten—based on the prior literacy experiences children have had, which in turn often reflects their socioeconomic status. We have then called these groups "ability" groups, assumed that children in the lower groups cannot engage in real reading and writing, and so offered them steady diet of isolated skills activities—letters and sounds in isolation; repetition, drill, and games; copy, color, cut and paste—activities that have served to further increase the gap between them and those peers who have already had more extensive literacy experiences. In short, we have perpetuated the disparity instead of alleviating it (Allington, 1983).

- Other aspects of reading instruction for "at-risk" children has also served to keep them from becoming really competent or avid readers. Various studies (e.g. Stanovich, 1986) indicate that children placed in higher-achievement groups (misnamed higher "ability" groups) have more actual opportunities to read, especially to read silently; their instruction is more often focused on comprehension after reading than on the pronunciation of words

during reading; they are encouraged to use cross-checking strategies to identify and verify unknown words instead of just being
told "sound it out" or being given the word; they are asked more
thoughtful questions about what they read, rather than mostly literal recall questions, and so forth In contrast, children in the lower
groups are kept busy with more round-robin oral reading peppered with interruptions focused on sounding and matching, more
isolated skills and drills, fewer comprehension-stimulating activities, and more dependency-creating instruction; because of this
they also do less reading and writing (Allington, 1983). In short,
the differential instruction typically provided lower-achieving children too often works to perpetuate continued use of ineffective
reading strategies and continued low achievement.

- Finally, higher-achieving children are more likely to be provided
with an array of texts to read that are of a more appropriate complexity than lower-achieving children (Guice, et al, 1996). Too
often, the children who have difficulty in learning to read have
texts in their hands and in their desks that are simply too difficult
for them to learn to read from. All readers need much experience
reading texts that can be read smoothly, fluently, and with comprehension. When served a steady diet of texts that produce a halt-
ing, dysfluent reading with minimal comprehension, readers'
development is slowed, and they often become discouraged.
Ensuring that all children have three to four books in their desks
that they can read and want to read should become a primary goal
in planning instruction for all children but especially for lower-
achieving children.

The schools we created at the turn of the last century were designed to
sort children into three worker groups—laborers, craftspeople, and
professionals—with most children sorted into the laborers group.
Through most of the twentieth century, we have persisted in sorting
children—often by socioeconomic status—and then giving them differential instruction that perpetuates their initial status. Without debating the ethics of such practices, we must note that leaving many
children educationally behind is a luxury that the twenty-first century
cannot afford. We need schools that help children exceed their destiny—
schools where *all* children are successful, not just those lucky children
who came to school with rich literacy backgrounds or those who find
schooling easy.

To accomplish this will require considerable rethinking of our
assumptions about schooling, teaching, and learning, as well as creative

thinking about the options we might employ. It is important that the regular classroom provide the kinds of literacy experiences that all children need, but some especially need to receive *in school*. Support personnel must be viewed as just that: educators who support and enrich the effective literacy education provided by a classroom teacher, not as people who will provide rich literacy experiences in lieu of what is happening in the classroom. Or in other words, everyone concerned must first of all support the classroom teacher in providing numerous and varied reading and writing experiences that will support *all* children as emergent readers and writers and promote their success as independent learners.

Beyond that, there are more innovative alternatives that will require substantial rethinking of the school day, the curriculum, and the allocation of the educational resources available. Some of these alternatives are discussed below. These suggestions are reprinted from *Schools That Work: Where All Children Read and Write* (Allington & Cunningham, 1996).

Creating "Safe" Blocks of Classroom Instructional Time

As a first step in enhancing the time available for classroom teaching and learning, create "safe" periods or "safe" days in all classrooms. For instance, primary-grade classrooms might be offered the entire morning time block as a "safe" block when no special subjects would intrude nor would any children be scheduled for special-program participation. Primary-grade classes would have art, music, physical education, and library only in the afternoons. Children in those classes who receive speech and language therapy would only be scheduled for those services in the afternoon. Likewise for children who participate in Title 1, bilingual, or special education programs away from the classroom. Thus, primary-grade teachers could plan to have the whole morning for instructing all children. Upper-grade classes would have the afternoons protected from intrusions. The special subject classes and the special instructional programs would serve children in the upper grade rooms only during the morning time block.

Other schemes accomplish the goal of providing longer blocks of uninterrupted classroom teaching and learning time. For instance, you might schedule special subjects and special instructional programs on different days for different grade levels. Perhaps primary grade classrooms would have all special subjects and special-program participation scheduled for Tuesdays and Thursdays only. This would leave the classroom teacher with three whole uninterrupted days each week to teach! It is true that on Tuesdays and Thursdays, little time would be left perhaps, for classroom instruction—at least for instruction when all children were in the classroom. Nonetheless, there is little evidence to suggest that such a scheduling plan would result in less learning on the part of any children. As you have probably figured out, under this plan the upper-grade classes would have Tuesdays and Thursdays as "safe" days. More time, however, should be available for classroom instruction on the remaining days in these upper-grade classrooms since the specials are spread over three days instead of two.

Providing extended "safe" periods of time for classroom academic instruction requires little real restructuring of teachers' roles and responsibilities. In many cases it does require, however, that special-subject teachers' schedules and special-program teachers' schedules (and those of special-program paraprofessionals) are developed at the building level. This will require a shift in many school districts where these teachers have had their schedules set at the district level rather than the building level. Such shifts may also require a revision in special program applications to state and federal agencies. Nonetheless, creating "safe" time periods is a good idea that seems quite easily achieved in most schools. What is required, though, is a commitment to focus attention on the availability of classroom instructional time as a first priority in schedule making.

Extended Time Plans

Another restucturing of school schedules can complement providing "safe" instructional periods in the classroom. The basic notion involves extending the school day by a little or a lot for some or all of the children. We will begin by detailing a plan that extends the day a little for some of the children.

Students who participate in special instructional programs during the school day receive no increased instructional time. In fact, good evidence suggests that these students actually see a reduction in instructional time (Allington & McGill-Franzen, 1993). This happens because it takes time to leave the classroom, travel to a special program room, and settle in for instruction (and to depart that room, return to the classroom, and settle in). This lost time is called transition time, and it eats minutes away every day. Even if transition time loss is only ten minutes a day (and most studies indicate a twenty- to twenty-five-minute daily transition time loss), nearly an hour each week is lost for children who participate daily. A loss of ten minutes' time from a thirty-minute special-program period means the special teacher has to be at least 50 percent more effective than the classroom teacher just to keep the participating children even with the progress they would make if they did not participate.

In addition children who leave the classroom during the school day miss the instruction offered while they are absent. Currently, children who are finding learning to read difficult are most often scheduled for special instructional programs during some part of the classroom reading and language arts time. Thus, participation does not typically provide them with more instruction but with different instruction. Without real increases in instructional time or intensity, special programs cannot be expected to accelerate children's literacy learning. Without a collaboratively planned, coherent curriculum focus, we can expect more often to confuse children than to assist them.

The problems of interrupted classroom instruction and decreased instructional time for at-risk children can be addressed in several ways. First, special instructional program teachers might be shifted onto flextime schedules. Remedial, special education, bilingual, migrant, and gifted and talented teachers would not work the same hours as classroom teachers. Depending on the school and the community, these teachers might come to school an hour earlier than classroom teachers, or they might arrive an hour or more later. Some of the children who participate in the special instructional programs would then work with these teachers either before or after school.

In virtually all schools, for instance, some children walk to school and thus pose no transportation problems should their school day be extended. Even in schools where many children ride buses, bus transportation is often available after the regular school day as buses make several runs to transport children from different schools in the system. Even if special transportation must be arranged, the idea of working outside the regular school day has much to recommend it. Of course, flextime scheduling of special program teachers will not allow all participating children to be served in an extended day program, but moving even some of that instructional support into an extended day program expands the potential opportunity to learn for those children served.

One elementary school's faculty is scheduled in the building from 8:00 until 4:30 each day while children attend from 9:00 until 3:00. Each teacher and administrator (and librarian, nurse, secretary, and janitor) work with at least one child for a half-hour each day before or after school. Classroom teachers usually work with a child from their classroom while others work with whichever children seem particularly well matched to their strengths and interests. In addition, a few other adults, usually parents of children who attend the school, also work before or after school with children. These adults typically work with kindergarten and first-grade children and simply sit with them while they read and reread simple predictable books. The children read or reread four or five of these little books each day.

These before and after school efforts are so successful that only a few children participate in any remedial or special-education program beyond second grade (although a few upper-grade children do come to the extended day program when they need extra assistance). The children who participate vary as their need for extraordinary instructional support varies. Some children come regularly, while others are scheduled only after an illness or when a brief review or reteaching is necessary.

Saturday School

Another option to consider is developing a Saturday School instructional program for at-risk children. This effort might be staffed by special instructional program personnel who work a Tuesday through Saturday schedule instead of the normal Monday through Friday week. Alternatively, Saturday School could be a half-day program, and these teachers might work only a half-day on Friday, working instead the half-day on Saturday. Otherwise, Saturday School could be staffed with a combination of special teachers and classroom teachers, all earning extra pay for the extra service.

As long as the Saturday School instructional program offers a strong focus on teaching, this design expands children's opportunity to learn. A blend of tutorial, small-group, and large-group instructional activities could be organized to fill either a half-day or a full-day program. Children and their parents value Saturday School when real assistance is available.

Summer School

The availability of summer school instruction has decreased substantially from the late 1960s. This is unfortunate since summer programs offer the potential to expand children's opportunity to learn. Access to summer school seems especially important for at-risk children. Research suggests that disadvantaged children acquire literacy at approximately the same rate as their more advantaged peers during the school year. But advantaged children continue to develop literacy abilities during the summer (though not as rapidly as during the school year), while disadvantaged children actually lose literacy abilities during the summer months (Hayes & Grether, 1983). This "summer reading loss" is critical since these children begin school with fewer literacy experiences than their more advantaged peers and thus are "behind" them in literacy development from the start of school. While school experiences develop literacy in all children, it is the disadvantaged children who most often lose ground over the summer. Thus, even when the school is doing a good job, disadvantaged children often cannot match the rate of literacy development year after year because the lack of summer literacy experiences leads to an overall loss of some of the gains made in school.

Summer school could take several forms. In some Philadelphia elementary schools that serve many economically disadvantaged children, the faculty decided to use federal Title I program funds to extend the school year for a month. To this case, remedial services during the regular school year were substantially reduced to fund the summer school effort. However, these teachers were interested in shifting to this extended time model for another reason. Very simply, the number of children participating in one or more special instructional programs during the school year had grown so large that classroom teachers felt they had been rendered largely ineffective. So many children were coming from and going to special programs all day long that it was difficult to carry out effective classroom instruction. Moving to the summer school design not only worked to reduce the children's summer reading losses; it also resulted in enhanced classroom instructional efforts (Winfield, 1991).

Another school's summer program was redesigned so that all children participated in a daily half-hour tutorial focused on reading and writing strategy development, spent another hour and a half in independent and small-group literacy learning and practice, and spent a final hour in art, music, or creative dramatics linked to the children's books they were reading. In addition, the school opened its library for the summer, and funds were allocated to give each child a paperback book each week for their bedroom libraries.

A third school selected the Foxfire model for their summer school effort. Children engaged in authentic literacy activities that included collecting and illustrating (with artwork and Polaroid photos) oral histories of buildings, companies, and people in the neighborhood. The summer school took the shape of collaborative work teams and looked more like a newsroom, we suppose, than an elementary school. But children were almost constantly reading, writing, editing, summarizing, transcribing, discussing, and illustrating real stories of real places and people. Using desktop publishing software, the students created reports of their work that were then bound into books by paraprofessional staff in the fall and added to the school library collection.

A fourth option is the summer drop-in center. In this case, fewer staff are needed and most activities are group oriented, often as cooperative learning groups. Most activities are scheduled in a single large-group area or outdoors but the school library remains open. In some cases, bookstores, book fairs, and sleepy-time read-ins (where everyone sleeps over in the gym) are also scheduled. Story-hour sessions are a regular feature with older children also available to read selected books to small groups of preschoolers or primary students. Either morning hours or an evening schedule seem most popular with parents more often available in the evening for joint children and parent activities. This model emphasizes increasing the access children have to books with a much smaller focus on instructional intervention. Thus, enhanced achievement results from additional independent reading more than from additional instruction. But the need for only one or two staff members along with several volunteers (perhaps high school students or folks who are school-year volunteers) make this an inexpensive option.

A final option is quite different from traditional notions about summer schools but deserves consideration. The idea is to offer community-based access to books, stories, and print activities during the summer months. Many towns and cities offer a variety of summer recreational activities for children, many quite educational though rarely book oriented. We think schools need to become much better partners with other community agencies, especially for the summer months. The basic notion is to work with these agencies to develop ways to enhance children's opportunities to read and write during the summer. For instance, in one town an honor library of children's books, mostly paperbacks, was set up at the town recreational park where children came to swim, play in Little League and soccer games, and participate in assorted other forms of recreation. Children simply took home books they wanted to read, and everyone hoped they remembered to bring them back. The book collections were a bit ragtag to begin with and more so at the end of the summer, but hundreds of books were taken home each week and only a few were lost forever. Some of the recreation staff found that story-time activities were a wonderful way to occupy children during rest periods and waiting-for-parent periods at the end of the day. Such activities increased parental awareness of the honor library and increased the use of books by children.

This strategy is inexpensive because it involves no summer professional staff time. At the same time we must note that often children making the greatest use of the library were children who were not usually considered to be at-risk. Nonetheless, we offer this as our final model because of its simplicity and potential for increasing the time children spend reading. Such a plan could be easily expanded to other summer venues such as the YMCA/YWCA camps and centers or even to neighborhood commercial establishments such as grocery stores or ice cream shops. The basic goal is to put books into the community and stimulate community interest in reading to and with children.

Summer schools work when they expand children's opportunities to actually read and write and to receive instructional assistance and support. Nonetheless, it is possible to design summer school in the programs that do not work very well. In one program we studied, children attended summer school in the mornings for five weeks. But the only reading or writing instruction they received was during a daily half-hour instructional block. Even though instructional groups were small (two to four children), the daily half-hour resulted in only an additional 10 to 12 hours of reading instruction (or roughly equivalent to the reading time available during one and one-half weeks during the school year). No one should expect large gains from 10 to 12 hours of small-group instruction. In an attempt to make this summer program "fun," the planners included much playground time, much arts and craft time, and much breakfast, snack, and lunch time. Of course, not much time was left for teaching children to read and, predictably, participation generally fostered little reading or writing development.

Support for summer school and year-round programs is growing among parents as the number of work-outside-home mothers increases. America is no longer an agricultural society where children are needed to work in the fields during the summer months. It may be that all schools need to consider expanding the school year, not so much to catch up with our international competitors, but to catch up with the rest of American society.

Conclusion

We need to create schools that develop in all children the knowledge, skills, and attitudes that have historically been reserved for just a few children. We need elementary schools that break the gridlock of low achievement that stymies efforts to educate *all* children further along the schooling process. In short, we need schools where all personnel have examined how education has historically held some children back, have considered how to provide rich literacy experiences in the regular classroom, and have decided upon some creative options to provide additional literacy experiences for children considered at risk. We need schools that have reconsidered how best to meet the educational needs of these children and then have chosen to *act*.

References

Allington, R. L. (1983). The reading instruction provided readers of differing abilities. *Elementary School Journal, 83,* 548–559.

Allington, R. L. (1994). The schools we have. The schools we need. *The Reading Teacher, 48,* 14–29.

Allington, R. L., & Cunningham, P. M. (1996). *Schools that work: Where all children read and write.* New York: Harper Collins.

Allington, R. L., & McGill-Franzen, A. (1993). Placing children at risk: Schools respond to reading problems. In R. Donmeyer & R. Kos (Eds.), *At-risk students: Portraits, policies, programs, and practices* (pp. 197–218). Albany, NY: State University of New York. Press.

Allington, R. L., & McGill-Franzen, A. (1995). Flunking: Throwing good money after bad. In R. L. Allington & S. A. Walmsley (Eds.), *No quick fix: Rethinking literacy programs in America's elementary schools.* New York: Teachers College Press.

Gamoran, A. (1986). Instructional and institutional effect of ability grouping. *Sociology of Education, 59,* 185–198.

Guice, S. & Allington, R. L., & Michelson, N. (1996). Access? Books, children and literature-based curriculum in schools. *The New Advocate 9* (3), 197.

Hayes, D. P., & Grether, J. (1983). The school year and vacations: When do students learn? *Cornell Journal of Social Relations, 17,* 56–71.

Shepard, L. A., & Smith, M. L. (1989). *Flunking grades: Research and policies on retention.* Philadelphia: Falmer.

Shepard, L. A., & Smith, M. L. (1990). Synthesis of research on grade retention. *Educational Leadership, 47,* 84–88.

Stanovich, K. E. (1986). Matthew Effects in reading: Some consequences of individual differences in the acquisition of literacy. *Reading Research Quarterly, 21,* 360–407.

Winfield, L. F. (1991). Lessons from the field: Case studies of evolving schoolwide projects. *Educational Evaluation and Policy Analysis, 13,* 353–362.

Index

Editor

Constance (Connie) Weaver is professor of English at Western Michigan University, where she specializes in the teaching of language arts (reading, writing, and grammar). She is author and editor of numerous publications, including *Reconsidering a Balanced Approach to Reading* (1998), *Lessons to Share: On Teaching Grammar in Context* (1998), *Creating Support for Effective Literacy Education* (1996), *Teaching Grammar in Context* (1996), *Reading Process and Practice* (2nd ed., 1994), *Success at Last! Helping Students with Attention Deficit (Hyperactivity) Disorders Understand Their Potential* (1994), *Theme Exploration* (1993), *Understanding Whole Language* (1990), and *Grammar for Teachers* (1979). Dr. Weaver has also authored a videotape, *A Balanced Approach to Reading and Literacy*, and has co-authored another, *Reading Strategies and Skills: Research into Practice*. From 1987 to 1990, she served as director of the Commission on Reading of the National Council of Teachers of English. In 1996 she received the Charles C. Fries award for distinguished leadership in the profession from the Michigan Council of Teachers of English. Weaver is also co-founder of Michigan for Public Education, a nonprofit grassroots organization advocating equality and excellence in education.